A SHORT HISTORY OF GERMANY

THE MACMILLAN COMPANY
NEW YORK · BOSTON · CHICAGO · DALLAS
ATLANTA · SAN FRANCISCO

MACMILLAN AND CO., Limited
LONDON · BOMBAY · CALCUTTA · MADRAS
MELBOURNE

THE MACMILLAN COMPANY
OF CANADA, Limited
TORONTO

A SHORT

HISTORY OF GERMANY

BY

ERNEST F. HENDERSON

VOLUME I

9 A.D. TO 1648 A.D.

NEW EDITION WITH ADDITIONAL CHAPTERS

New York
THE MACMILLAN COMPANY
1940

Set up and electrotyped. Published February, 1902. Two
volumes printed in one, January, 1906; January, 1908;
January, 1910; January, 1911; March, 1913; June, 1914.
New edition with additional chapters, May, 1916; April,
1917.

DEDICATED

BY GRACIOUS PERMISSION

TO

His Royal Highness

PRINCE HENRY OF PRUSSIA

ON THE OCCASION OF

HIS VISIT TO AMERICA

PREFACE

GERMANY stands in the centre of Europe, and on her soil all the great international struggles have been fought, —the Thirty Years' War, the early campaigns of the Spanish Succession War, the Seven Years' War, the gigantic wars against Napoleon. It is the custom for modern educators to recommend the study of the history of France as a guiding thread through the intricacies of general European history; but is this choice justifiable? The two great, omnipresent factors of the whole mediæval period are the Papacy and the Empire; the Empire was German from the ninth to the nineteenth century, — from the days of Charlemagne until the days of Francis II., — and the Empire interfered in the affairs of the Papacy and of Italy far more than did France. When we come to the period of the Reformation, surely Luther and his kind were more prominent than the French reformers, and the Emperor Charles V. had more to do with the affairs of Europe than any of the French kings. In the Thirty Years' War, larger interests were at stake than in the Huguenot struggles, and the German Peace of Westphalia necessitated a recasting of the whole map of Europe. Louis XIV., it is true, gave the tone to the high society of his age, and French was almost universally spoken and written at the German courts; but this influence was neither very deep nor very beneficial. Nor can it be denied that the French Revolution produced great

vii

results for Europe. Yet its effects, as far as Germany
was concerned, have been overrated ; the liberation of the
serfs would probably have been accomplished without it,
while constitutional government, popular representation,
and trial by jury had still to wait for half a century.

If we look for striking personalities and events, the
reigns of Frederick the Great and of William I. were of
supreme importance to Europe, and, as was not the case
with Louis XIV. and Napoleon, their acquisitions were of
a permanent character. All in all, it has seemed to me
that I could engage in no more thankful occupation than
in writing the history of Germany ; the more so as German
treatments of the subject presuppose more knowledge
than is usually to be found in the American reader, and
as no other American writer has ever attempted the task.
The work of Lewis, founded on an antiquated German
text-book, does not fulfil the most modest demands.

My warm thanks are due to Professor Sumner, of the
Massachusetts Institute of Technology, for valuable suggestions; to my brother, Mr. H. G. Henderson, for stylistic
revision ; and to my wife for the detection of errors in the
proof. The tables in Lindner's *Deutsche Geschichte* have
made it easier for me to draw up my own chronological
view; while Putzger's valuable school atlas has been of
assistance in the matter of maps. For a complete bibliography of German history, the reader is referred to
Dahlmann-Waitz, *Quellenkunde*, and to the *Jahresbericht
der Geschichtswissenschaft.*

E. F. H.

WASHINGTON, D. C.,
February 13, 1902.

PREFACE TO THE NEW EDITION

IT is a source of gratification that the demand for my book has steadily increased and that, after seven separate printings, the publishers should feel warranted in bringing out a new edition with much additional matter. Behind the gratification is another feeling, one of wonder at being able in the new edition to describe a whole new era from its inception to its end. I had closed my narrative with the assumption of the imperial crown in the palace of Versailles on January 18, 1871 ; and although my book was completed thirty years later, I did not at that time feel that enough had transpired to warrant a single extra chapter. The *Kulturkampf*, to be sure, was ended, but everything else was in a state of transition. Now, on the other hand, we have seen the country advance to unheard-of power and prosperity ; we have seen it take its place as a world power and at the same time develop from a land unable to prevent its people from emigrating into one that attracted nearly a million foreigners yearly. And then, as though with the cut of a sharp knife, the old order ceased, the workers and traders turned into soldiers, the industrial plants into munition factories. Whatever may now happen, it will never be the same Germany again.

In order to avoid controversial matter I have closed the narrative with the murder at Sarajevo. Subsequent events are too numerous and too complicated, even were they not too much in dispute, to be treated of with any profit in a work of this kind. Besides, they belong to a new era, the end of which our children's children may not see.

MONADNOCK, N.H., March 26, 1916.

CONTENTS

CONTENTS

MAPS

A SHORT HISTORY OF GERMANY

CHAPTER I

THE EARLY GERMANS

LITERATURE : In Bruno Gebhardt, *Handbuch der deutschen Geschichte,*
there is a useful but dry treatment of the period covered by this chapter.
See Tacitus, *Germania,* and the extracts from the Salic Law translated
in Henderson, *Select Historical Documents of the Middle Ages,* a work
compiled with the idea of laying a foundation for the present history.
The most attractive treatment of these early times is that of Freytag,
Bilder aus der Deutschen Vergangenheit, as good from a historical as
from a literary standpoint. Kaufmann's *Deutsche Geschichte,* reaching
to the reign of Charlemagne, is excellent. Hauck's *Kirchengeschichte
Deutschlands* cannot be too highly praised, but only extends to 1125 A.D.

THE remains of lake-dwellings found beneath the sur- The lake
face of the water, the belongings of the dead rendered dwellers.
up by recently discovered tombs, a few comments of
Roman writers on a people with whom their armies had
come into hostile contact, a detailed description, finally,
by the hand of Tacitus, of Germany and the Germans as
they were in his day,—such are the sources from which
modern historians have reconstructed the first period in a
great nation's history.

No idle whim drove our forefathers out into the lakes
and caused them to erect their houses on posts driven
into the mud. Here alone in a wild age could they find
refuge from beasts of prey and from the greed of man ;

here they could readily supply themselves with fish, while not debarred from making hunting expeditions to the shore. None too restricted was the area of these watery homes, for in some of the settlements the superstructures rested on no less than from twenty to thirty thousand posts. One enemy, indeed, could not be avoided, for almost every one of the buildings of which the ruins remain ended by being burnt to the water's edge. Charred and broken the piles stand there to this day, while from the mud at their base have been extracted many a tool and weapon — chisels of bone, axes and saws of stone, daggers and arrowheads made from the stag's horn or the tooth of the wild boar.

Ancient graves.

The first traceable information concerning the Germans was brought to southern Europe by a Marseilles merchant named Pytheas, who, in the days of Alexander the Great, visited the shores of the Baltic and discovered great quantities of the useful product known as amber. From this period, the fourth century before Christ, seem to date many of the graves that have furnished such interesting relics. The age of stone and bone implements was passing into an age of bronze and iron. A certain striving for elegance and luxury becomes evident — we find necklaces of amber beads, of ivory, and of colored stones, while bits of yellow ochre lead to the inference that paint was not unknown as a means of personal adornment. Owing to the great number of graves laid open, and to the richness and variety of their contents, the museums of Germany are full to overflowing with these implements and trappings of prehistoric man. From the tomb discovered near Hallstatt in the Salzkammergut in 1846 there have been taken six thousand objects of various kinds, while with regard to the human remains themselves, the interesting fact is made apparent that about one-half of the bodies had been burned, one-half buried in their natural state. Strangely enough, in these old burial places, bodies laid to rest in oaken coffins have been found to be better preserved than those in stone chests. The tombs themselves are of every size and shape, the largest measuring some two hundred and fifty feet in length, by thirty-five to forty in height; some are regular chambers of stone covered each with an enormous slab; one such discovered near Luneburg measures some eighteen by fourteen feet.

These graves furnish information of more than antiquarian interest. The fact that the wives and servants of great personages were immolated with them is proved beyond dispute; one group has been found consisting of a single upright figure surrounded by eight others in a crouching position. Bones of animals mixed with those of human beings lead to the assumption that war-horses, also, followed their masters to Walhalla. The shape and material of the implements and utensils, the uses for which they were evidently intended, the character, finally, of the ornamentation, all throw light on the civilization of the time. Where razors and combs are found we can infer that attention was paid to personal appearance; while the curious urns with human face discovered in West Prussia point to an interesting attempt at symbolical and artistic expression. Eyes and nose are clearly marked, the cover of the urn is the top of the head, while in the ears hang bronze rings with drops of amber, and around the neck circlets of bronze and iron. Another class of inferences can be drawn from the fact that implements made from a certain kind of stone are found miles away from places where such stone abounds; an extensive trade in such objects must have been carried on, and, indeed, traces can be found of the very workshops in which they were doubtless manufactured.

Ancient customs.

Leaving the antiquarian's field for more solid ground, we find various items of interest in the works of Latin authors. Cæsar, Strabo, and Tacitus all mention the Germans as spreading out toward the south. To this they were driven by pressure from the rear, as also by insufficiency of territory resulting from superficial and extravagant methods of agriculture. Much that we hear is mere rumor, as when Pliny gravely asserts that the dwellers on the Baltic islands have horses' hoofs, and ears large enough to cover their bodies.

Of the clashes at arms with the Germans, Roman writers have more to say. In the days of the Consul Marius the flood-gates of the North seemed opened, and the Cimbrians and Teutons rushed in, making the Romans tremble for their very capital. A few details of the two great battles fought by Marius, one in southern France and one in northern Italy, have come down to us: how the barbarians were completely outwitted by superior tactics, allowing the Romans to fall upon them simultaneously in front and rear; how the burning sun of the South helped to weaken the power of resistance of the children of the North; and how, in both cases, defeat meant utter annihilation. On the field of Aquæ Sextiæ none were left but the faithful German dogs, who mounted guard over the bodies of the slain.

The first great organizer among the Germans was a certain Ariovistus with whom Cæsar came in contact; Roman discipline eventually prevailed, Ariovistus was worsted, and, after the flight of the formidable leader, a short era of friendliness and peace ensued. Germans entered the Roman service and even came to form the imperial body-guard, learning valuable lessons of strategy which they were afterward able to turn to telling account. Differences arose between Augustus and the tribe of the Sigambrians, who, joining with others, made an inroad into

Gaul, defeated the legate, and even secured a Roman eagle. Peace was eventually restored, but the emperor, determined that his provinces should never again be exposed to such danger, prepared for an invasion of Germany on a large scale. Year after year he sent his stepsons, Drusus and Tiberius, to tame this stubborn people. Fortresses were built, of which one, the Saalburg near Homburg, has remained to our own day, and is about to be reconstructed on the old lines; a canal was dug through which Roman fleets swept from the Rhine to the Yssel, passing thence through the Zuyder Zee, then an inland lake, into the North Sea.

A few years later, 9 A.D., came the crucial conflict for land and liberty. It was then that the Cheruscan leader, Hermann or Arminius, fell on the Roman proconsul, Varus, in the Teutoburg Forest, destroying his splendid army. "Varus, Varus, give me back my legions!" was the wail of the distracted emperor when he heard the disheartening news. He dismissed his body-guard and forbade the city to all German visitors. With a few unimportant expeditions the long series of Roman aggressions closed, and Tacitus does not hesitate to call Arminius " the undoubted liberator of Germany."

From now on, for several generations, there was peace, and the great Roman historian learns to love and honor the country about which he writes. Within the compass of a few pages he gives us a wonderful picture of the Germans of his day; he, the aristocrat, writhing under the imperial yoke, feels strangely drawn toward this simple and innocent people, this "special, unmixed race, like only to itself." The *Germania* of Tacitus.

Tacitus tells of a land full of "bristling" woods and "uncanny" marshes, but rich in cattle, which lacked, however, "a peculiar stately character" and the "proud adornment of its brows." To have a numerous herd was the "joy of the German, his favorite, his only, source of wealth." The settlements were made, not in towns as with the Romans, but in open spaces near fountains or groves; the houses stood by themselves — possibly, suggests the historian, through dread of fire, but probably because the people knew no better. Each village had its common pasturage and distributed its arable land in lots or parcels, prescribing rigidly to all its members what land should lie fallow, what crops should be raised, and when and how the seed should be sown.

The "marks," as they were called from the broad boundary line drawn around them, over which no stranger could come without blowing his horn, were populated by large groups of kinsmen or clans. Strong as in the old patriarchal days were the ties of family; the head of the clan commanded and watched over all the rest, and the Romans wondered at seeing chieftains as anxious to redeem their nephews from captivity as though they were their own sons. Justice was administered in the court of the "hundred," or district containing some hundred families with their slaves and dependants, and the " *centenarius* " or hundred-man, who opened and closed the "moot," remained for centuries the acknowledged mouthpiece of the old Germanic liberties.

The German warrior.

The German men as described by Tacitus were a strange mixture of high-mindedness and brutality. Loyalty and bravery were cardinal virtues. Each chieftain was surrounded by a war-band of chosen youths, who were to cover and defend him and to sacrifice their own heroic deeds to his glory; the chieftain fought for victory, the war-band for the chieftain. If, on the one hand, it was disgraceful for a leader to be outdone in bravery by any of his followers, it betokened, on the other, the ineffaceable shame of a lifetime to have deserted a leader or to have thrown away the shield in battle. To supplement these virtuous ideals it must be stated that reverence for old men and hospitality to strangers are mentioned among the characteristics of the ancient Germans. To refuse shelter to one asking it was considered a crime, and when a man's own stores were exhausted, he accompanied his guest to the house of a neighbor. For persons of distinction entertainments were inaugurated : naked youths would disport themselves in the sword dance among upturned blades and sharpened spear-heads; "pleasure it gave to the lookers-on, pleasure, too, to those who performed," which is more remarkable. When a chieftain died he was honored to the utmost in his burial, his body being burned amid the fumes of the richest and rarest of woods.

The reverse of the picture is highly unedifying. When not on the war-path the chieftains were wont to lie about like lazy dogs, leaving the care of the fields and all other peaceful labors to the women and slaves. For their own part they passed their time in gambling and in drinking a concoction which was new to the Roman historian, and of which he did not approve, but which we of wider experience have no difficulty in designating as a kind of beer brewed from barley. For successive days and nights these carouses would continue, to the accompaniment of the falling dice, the desire of winning amounting to a frenzy. On one casual throw the players would stake all their earthly possessions, yes, even the liberty of their own persons. Voluntarily the loser submitted to be bound and to be handed over to a neighboring tribe in exchange for merchandise. "Stubbornness in a wrong cause," is the verdict of Tacitus; but he adds that the Germans themselves consider it pride in keeping the word once pledged.

No less anomalous than the position of these sottish yet courageous chieftains was that of the German women.

The German in time of peace.

Legally considered they were chattels, like the slaves, and the very name "Weib" has come down in grammar as of the neuter gender. Their marriage contracts were regular sales, the union not being lawful unless the bridegroom could prove by witnesses that he had paid the required sum. It was a token of subjection when the free, waving hair was bound into a braid and knot.

The German women.

Yet Tacitus has much to say about the honor and respect shown to these same women, and about their helpfulness and strength of character They, with their children, stood by in the battles, exhorting or chiding as the case might demand. "In them," writes Tacitus, "each man sees his holiest witnesses — those best fitted to award him his meed of praise. To his wife or mother he brings his wounds, which they are not afraid to look upon and count. . . . History tells how, by their prayers, the tide of many a wavering and half-despaired-of battle has been turned." The marriage relation was respected, and polygamy only allowed among the princes, who for state reasons might make family alliances. Infidelity was punished by severe and public scourging: "there among the Germans," writes Tacitus, " vice is not laughed at, and to do evil with evil doers is not scoffingly called 'being up to date.' "

The Roman wall.

With the last page of the *Germania* the curtain falls for a long period of years, but we can trace developments from the final outcome. The Romans definitively abandoned an aggressive policy and built away at their protecting wall, a monumental fortification, second only in conception and execution to the great wall of China. There are sections of this *Limes* or *Pfahlbau* which must have been fifty feet broad at the base and as high as sixteen feet. The whole was some three hundred miles in length, flanked by hundreds of camps and towers, the latter near enough to each other to permit of communicating signals by lighting fires at night or by raising and lowering beams by day. Behind the wall was a moat, in front a waste stretch of land which Germans might only cross when escorted by Roman soldiers.

Meanwhile, within the precincts of the Roman Empire itself, numerous Germans had been allowed to settle; whole tribes at last were given tracts of land, receiving the official title of *fœderati*, or allies, and engaging to fight the battles of their adopted country. Their influence made itself felt in every direction; many individuals rose to honor and distinction in the state service, and allied themselves in marriage with the noblest families of the capital. The Romans, for their own part, found pleasure in the general appearance and cast of countenance of the foreigners; it became the fashion to imitate them, and the Roman ladies took to wearing blond wigs, or to smearing their own hair with the reddish oil which the German warriors used when they decked themselves for battle. Of such moment did the Emperor Honorius consider the matter, that he issued an edict against the practice. Even with the Germans who remained at home the Romans maintained a certain amount of intercourse and commerce. German traders, indeed, were subject to stern restrictions, and were only allowed to approach the *Limes* at stated points, but the Roman merchants penetrated into the very heart of Germany. Essentially Roman products, such as statues of Jupiter, not to speak of numberless imperial coins, have been found in Freienwalde and in the Lausitz — as far north, indeed, as modern Sweden. The Emperor Tiberius is known to have looked upon the German turnip as a delicacy, while the grain of which the *Schwarzbrod* is made is referred to in a decree of the year 301. About the same time, too, we hear of German smoked meats, beyond a doubt the famous Westphalian hams. Other staples were

Intercourse of Romans and Germans.

furs, goose feathers, sausages, antlers, human hair, and pomatum.

The Christianizing of the Goths.

Roman culture, to some extent at least, penetrated in the wake of the traders, while Roman Christianity, in the form of the Arianism just then in vogue in the Eastern Empire, found its way to the tribe of the Goths. Toward the end of the third century the latter had made an inroad into the empire and had carried away captive two Greeks from Cappadocia. To these exiles there was born in 311 A.D. a son named Ulfila or Wulfila, a gifted boy who made himself equally familiar with the Greek, the Gothic, and the Latin languages. As he grew up and regained his liberty he embraced that form of the Christian religion in favor at Constantinople, was consecrated bishop at Antioch, and returned as missionary to the scenes of his youth. Here, after making a number of converts, he incurred the enmity of Athanarich, king of the Visigoths, and was obliged to flee to Roman soil, where he founded a haven of rest in Mœsia. He labored and taught for many years, occasionally journeying to Constantinople, where we find his name in the records of a council in 360 A.D., as one of the subscribers to the Arian creed. When, twenty-one years later, he died, his loss was widely felt, and no less a person than the Emperor Theodosius walked in his funeral procession.

The Bible of Wulfila.

Of all Wulfila's services to his people and to posterity, one of the greatest was the translation of the Bible into the Gothic tongue, a large fragment of which work, including nearly the whole New Testament, is known as the Silver Codex and is preserved in the library of the university at Upsala, a treasure beyond price, the oldest existing monument of German learning and letters. To us, indeed, it has a value that is more than philological and literary, for from it we glean historically almost all that we know

of the culture of the Germans during the whole fourth century. There are native words for many a Biblical term that
show a fair degree of civilization: "smiths" are distinguished from "carpenters," "buildings" from "tents."
Jars and kettles, dishes, chests, and baskets seem to have
been in common use, as also threshing-flails and millstones.
Gardeners cultivated their gardens, deeds were drawn up
and sealed. Yet the written language of the Goths must
have been very imperfect, for we know that Wulfila was
obliged to extend the alphabet, supplying the deficiencies
from the Greek and Latin. Fondly and faithfully the old
bishop labored over his task; but in the midst of his work
the thought came to him that the warlike doings in the
Book of Kings might not edify his rude hearers, so he
quietly left it out.

All this time, while the Goths were being guided toward
Christianity and civilization, and while Roman armies and
Roman society were growing more and more Germanized,
a great and important change was coming over the face of
northern Europe. The marvellous prolificness of the Germans, added to their lack of intensive methods of culti-
vating the soil, precipitated the movement known as the
wandering of the nations. Already, in the third century,
the fifty or more tribes whose names are mentioned by
Tacitus had merged and coalesced into larger associations,
which had gradually pressed forward to the very borders
of Roman territory. The final impetus came from the rear,
when, about 375 A.D., the fierce Asiatic tribe of the Huns
crossed the Volga and entered on their career of conquest
and intimidation. With the Visigoths, whom they drove
before them, was that Alaric who was later to sack Rome.
There is no need here to follow in detail the different
migrations of the tribes, or to trace the rise and fall of
each small monarchy; of the eight Teutonic kingdoms

*The
wandering
of the
nations.*

founded on Roman soil in the fifth and sixth centuries, four, those of Odoacer and Theodoric, of the Burgundians, and of the Vandals, were quickly to wane and fall; two, those of the Visigoths in Spain and the Lombards in Italy, were to endure for a few centuries, while only two, that of the Anglo-Saxons in Britain and that of the Franks in Gaul, were to show real and lasting vitality.

Manner of settlement on Roman ground.

It must not be supposed of these wandering German conquerors that, wherever they came, they utterly stamped out the Roman civilization. On the contrary, the two peoples often settled down peacefully side by side, the new-comers merely claiming for themselves a certain fixed share, one-third or two-thirds of each estate. In this there was no great hardship to the Romans, for, according to the same principle, armies of so-called allies had often been quartered on them. For the student of institutions, nothing can be more instructive than to trace the gradual fusion of the two civilizations: the Romans gave language, literature, and law, as well as many of their time-honored customs, to their invaders ; the latter brought in new principles of government and a new conception of liberty and personal rights.

The question suggests itself, why Germany was not emptied, and rendered desolate by this constant pouring forth of peoples. In point of fact the migrators rarely constituted the whole of their tribe ; remnants, for instance, of Goths who remained behind on the Black Sea while their fellows invaded Italy could still be found in the seventeenth century. It was the surplus population, as a rule, that was anxious to be gone ; and their exodus, not infrequently, took place with the solemn sanction of a general assembly. Nor was the break with the parent stock considered final ; individuals might still hold land in their old settlements. Long after his conquest of the north coast of Africa, Genseric, the Vandal king, received a deputation from his former home in Silesia, urging that he and his followers should renounce their old possessions. The request was refused on the plea that no one could be secure against a change of fortune.

Far, then, from being depopulated, Germany's store of warriors seemed to the Romans fairly inexhaustible; "they increase, but we decrease," wrote Salvianus in the fifth century, while Paul, the son of Warnefried, who outlived the last invasions, contrasts his own desolate land with crowded Germany, and surmises that the ice and snow of the North are more favorable to propagation than the climate of poor, plague-ridden Italy.

The Franks, especially, never lost touch with their own and with kindred German peoples, — an important fact, when we consider the enervating effect of purely Roman influences on Goths and Visigoths, Burgundians and Vandals. These Franks were the founders of a new Germany; and with them our history will concern itself almost exclusively; they had begun their career of expansion about the year 400 A.D., at which time, unlike the Goths, they were still heathen. We hear of them, a little later, in northern Gaul, and in the present Holland and Belgium, roughly divided into two great groups, the Salians and Ripuarians, each group in turn consisting of many different tribes. It was Clovis, a Salian Frank of the family of Meroveus, who, by extensive conquests, and especially by the base murder of all possible rival princes, first consolidated these lands into a strong kingdom. He captured and put to death Syagrius, that enterprising Roman governor who, after the fall of the Western Empire, had continued to administer in his own name a large part of Gaul. He lopped off many of its provinces from the once powerful Visigothic kingdom of Toulouse, and carried off the treasures which Alaric had gathered together in Rome. He

The tribe of the Franks.

defeated the Allemanni in a memorable battle, and their former lands along the Main and the Neckar became known by the name of Franconia, with the principal city of Frankfort, or ford of the Franks. The Burgundians were partially, in the next generation wholly, subdued.

But Clovis was more than a conqueror, he was also a far-seeing statesman; no wiser political move was ever made than when, in 496 A.D., he determined to become a Christian, and to adhere to the form of religion authorized by Rome, as opposed to that spread by the Eastern church. Many writers have, with justice, attributed the fall of the other Germanic kingdoms to mutual hatred of the Arians and the orthodox. Clovis, on the contrary, rallied around him the entire clergy of Gaul, with all their wealth and influence. His biographer, the Bishop of Tours, lauds him to the skies as the champion of the true faith, and even when commenting on a treacherous murder, which the king himself had instigated, declares that thus the Lord laid low his enemies, as a reward for walking in His ways and doing what was pleasing in His sight.

The conversion took place publicly and with dramatic effect. The king had registered a vow that, should he prove successful in the battle of Tolbiacum against the Allemanni, he would yield to the entreaties of his Burgundian wife and accept her God. After the battle, with a number of his followers, he received baptism; and the proud Sigambrian knelt at the feet of Remigius of Rheims, and meekly bowed his head while the bishop bade him burn what he had adored and adore what he had burned. It must not, however, be supposed that this act was the result of any mere sudden impulse. Clovis was well prepared for it, and had well weighed its future consequences. He had always desired to win the support of the church, and had already allowed his infant sons to be baptized. The story

The conversion of Clovis.

has been often told of how at a distribution of booty he had interfered to save a sacred vessel for a Christian bishop; his design had been defeated, for his warriors were far from looking upon him as an absolute despot, but with his own hand he had afterward killed the man who thwarted him. The results of the conversion proved in the end more far-reaching than even Clovis could have foreseen; the way had been opened for a close alliance between the Roman Papacy and the Frankish kingdom. Had the Franks remained heretics in the eyes of Rome, the imperial crown could never have been placed on the head of Charlemagne. As for Clovis himself, he had found a watchword that legitimatized, as it were, his position: "I cannot endure it," he said of the Visigoths, "that these Arians should possess a part of Gaul. Let us, with God's help, set forth and conquer them and add their land to our kingdom!" *Results of the acceptance of Christianity.*

The Franks were able in a way to give their own stamp to the Christianity they adopted, and their Christ became the model of a warrior-leader. Clovis regretted that he and his followers had not been present to avenge the Crucifixion, and good Bishop Gregory praises the utterance. The miracles recorded in Merovingian times consist largely of saintly intervention in the midst of battle, and of similar godlike performances. Old heathen rites continued to be performed under the guise of Christian ceremonial; and saints' images, like idols, were carried round as a protection against fire, illness, and death. It was a change of name, but not of substance; Siegfried's dragon became the dragon of St. George, while the virtues of the old goddesses were transferred to the Virgin Mary.

For two and a half centuries after the death of Clovis the dynasty of the Merovingians continued to reign over the Franks; but only twice, and for brief spaces of time, were all the different lands united under one hand. The *The Merovingian kings.*

usual law of succession demanded that the father should provide equally for all of his sons ; the kingdom accordingly was riven, and sundered, and a premium set on fratricide and intrigue. Two more bloodthirsty women than those guardians of princes, Brunhilda and Fredegunda, would be hard to find in all history.

It is strange to note in these early times how the power of the kings was marked and estimated by purely external tokens, by wealth and display, or even by the length of the royal locks. The gold of the conquered Romans gave a chance for unaccustomed luxury, and monarchs vied with each other in reckless extravagance. King Chilperich had a dinner service of gold and precious stones, while one single dish of the many owned by King Gunthram weighed 470 pounds. Queen Fredegunda's son, at the age of two, possessed four wagon loads of silks and ornaments, while no less than fifty such accompanied the Princess Raguntha, who in 584 A.D. was sent to the Visigoths in Spain. The scale was often turned in favor of a candidate to the throne by the amount of his treasure, so that the relative who seized a dead king's belongings increased his chances of succeeding to the throne.

The long wavy hair was a distinguishing feature of this dynasty, and their particular pride and joy. We can see it still on all the coins and seals of the time, and we know from old chroniclers that he who lost his curls was debarred from the throne until they grew again. A distracted mother once chose death for her two sons rather than that they should suffer such indignity.

Decline of the Merovingian dynasty.

As time went on the Merovingian kings became more and more feeble and enervated ; we hear of vicious acts committed in earliest youth. The wonder is that the race did not sooner die out; its scions, at last, had not strength of mind even for the crimes and bloodshed that lend a shuddering interest to the reigns of their ancestors. They became the type for all future ages of *rois fainéants*, of shadowy, do-nothing kings. All the power had come into the hands of the chief officers of the household, the mayors of the palace, who for years and generations conducted the business of ruling. Einhard, the friend and biographer of Charles the Great, has preserved a most vivid picture of the weakness of the declining dynasty. He tells how the feeble king, content with the royal name, and with the waving hair and long beard, sat on the throne and played the part of ruler; how he received the envoys of foreign powers, and delivered to them, as if on his own authority, the answers which had been dictated to him, and which he might not dare to change.

No wonder that the practice of the Christian religion, which especially needed the fostering care of wise rulers, began to decline. So degenerate did the church become that Columbanus, the Irish missionary who sought these regions at the end of the sixth century, was forced to write home that "the love of mortification was scarcely to be found even in a few places." What man could do to stem the disorders Columbanus did. A member of that church of St. Patrick which had developed its own teachings in antagonism to Rome, he was a perfectly fearless, nay relentless, reformer. When still a youth he had determined to go forth into the world and preach the gospel, and had sprung over the prostrate form of his mother when she tried to bar his egress, declaring that he never wished to look upon her face again. With twelve comrades he had crossed over to the Continent, where his fiery enthusiasm won him many followers. Even bishops turned to him for guidance and powerful nobles placed their children under his care. His courage was unbending; he braved the heathen in the very act of sacrificing, and once poured on the

St. Colum banus.

ground the libation the Allemanni were about to offer to their god. He labored incessantly for fifty years, but at last was expelled from the land on the plea that his method of calculating Easter differed from that of the Gallic clergy!

St. Gall.

Columbanus founded three monasteries and drew up a rule for their guidance — so severe, indeed, that the pain of scourging was prescribed for an unguarded cough. More lasting than his own foundations was that of one of his disciples, St. Gall, who, at one of the loveliest points of the lake of Constance, established a settlement where, throughout the darkest of the Dark Ages, learning and art shone forth like a beacon light.

Administration of the Merovingian kingdom.

Meanwhile in other fields the spirit of order had been at work among the Frankish people. A form of local government had been established for all the different parts of the kingdom, and a code of laws drawn up, simple yet comprehensive, and readily sufficing for all the ordinary matters of daily life. Just as in modern times we see states divided into counties and townships, so the Merovingian land fell naturally into the canton (*civitas* or *gau*) and the hundred. In the latter the people still chose their *centenarius* or hundred-man, but the chief official in the district was now the king's count, who took for his maintenance one-third of the revenue drawn from fines and taxes. The count it was who now at regular stated intervals came to the spot on the village green where the hundred court was to be held, ascended the throne that was placed there for him, and hung up his shield on a post or tree to show that the solemn proceedings were about to begin. Those charged with crime and their accusers were brought before him, though very different were the proceedings from those of a modern trial. The merits of the case itself were not gone into ; the plaintiff brought the charge, the defendant furnished, not witnesses, but a number of kinsmen and neigh-

bors who were willing to swear that they did not consider
him guilty. Or, again, resort might be had to the judgment   The ordeal.
by ordeal or to trial by combat, the count, apparently assisted by priests, conducting the proceedings. Under the
Merovingian and Carolingian rulers a number of ordeals
were in vogue, but none was more common than that of
forcing the suspected person to seize with his bare hand a
stone suspended by a string in a caldron of boiling water.
If the water burnt his hand, the voice of God was believed
to have spoken against him, and he was handed over to the
law to suffer the penalty for his crime.

It is difficult to put one's self in the attitude of these
simple, superstitious people; it is all too evident that only
fraud on the part of the priest could save the victim from
injury. Yet in every case of ordeal the burden of proof
lay with the accused; in every case the commonest laws of
nature would have had to be reversed before he could be
declared innocent. Women as well as men were forced to
walk a certain distance with red-hot irons in their hands,
or to cross barefoot over glowing ploughshares. In the
ordeal by cold water the victim was bound and thrown into
a tank, where, if he sank, he was punished; if he floated,
he went free. Was the whole system a bit of priestly jug-
glery, to show their power of working miracles?

The ordeal or the combat over, the man who had suc-   The Salic
cumbed was obliged to submit to the penalty prescribed by   Law.
the law of his own tribe or province. These laws were
early committed to writing — in the Latin language — and
are among the most interesting records of the past. They
seem to have been drawn up originally in answer to a need
of regulating the relations of the conquerors to the subjected Romans. Most famous of all is the Salic Law, which
dates from the time of Clovis, and takes us down the whole
scale of punishments, from the fine required for the murder

of a bishop to that claimed for abusive epithets, like witch, perjurer, spy, fox, or hare.   Wounds were rated according to their length, depth, and relative position, and according to the amount of blood that flowed from them; and the sum was increased tenfold, with the fee of a doctor in addition, if the blow had been struck below the waist.   It is curious to note that crimes with the Franks were not offences against the state, but purely against the individual and his friends: " If any one shall have dug up and plundered a corpse already buried, and it shall have been proved on him, he shall be outlawed until the day when he comes to an agreement with the relatives of the dead man, and they ask for him that he be allowed to come among men." And again, " If any one's father have been killed, the sons shall have half the compounding money (*Wergeld*); and the other half, the nearest relatives . . . shall divide among themselves."

Poetic thoughts in old laws.

Through these old laws, as well as through the oldest legal formulas that have been preserved, there often runs a vein of poetry, while some situations are painted in the most dramatic language.   The guilty man, says an old curse, shall be outlawed so far as fire burns and earth grows green, so far as " the hawk flies through the long spring day with the wind resting under his two wings." According to the Salic Law the offender who has not wherewith to pay his fine is first to renounce all his property, "and he shall afterward go into his house, and shall collect in his hand dust from the four corners of it, and shall afterward stand upon the threshold, looking inward into the house.   And then, with his left hand, he shall throw over his shoulders some of that dust on the nearest relative that he has. . . .   And after that, in his shirt, without girdle and without shoes, a staff in his hand, he shall spring over the hedge."   A dismal picture of renunciation and ruin! But not more moving than the account in the Frisian Law of the three cases of necessity, in which the mother can lay hands on the heritage of her child: " when the child is captive and in chains in the north over the sea or in the south over the mountains;" "when years of scarcity come and fierce hunger stalks over the land and the child would die of starvation;" "when," finally, " the child is stark naked or homeless, and the misty dark night and the icy cold winter rise over the palings, and all men hasten to house and home, and the wild beast seeks the hollows of the trees and the caves of the mountains, there to eke out his existence; when the child, under age, weeps and bemoans its bare limbs and bewails that it has no roof, and that its father who should protect it against the cold winter and fierce hunger is lying so deep down in the darkness under earth and oaken planks, covered and held fast by four nails: then the mother may alienate and sell her child's inheritance ! "

The alliterative form in many of the old laws shows a joy in sweet sounds, and we know from other evidence that the Germans were already in the habit of singing popular melodies. Tacitus tells how they " filled the valleys and wooded heights with the echoes of gleeful song," though the Emperor Julian wonders how they can enjoy their own music, which seems to him " not unlike the croaking of violently shrieking birds." A later, still severer, critic was a certain Deacon John, who inveighs against the German rendering of the noble Gregorian chants : " when they try," he says, " to sing the mild melody with their own modulations and trills, the barbaric wildness of their thirsty throats emits harsh tones with a certain natural resonance, as if heavy wagons with confused noise of thunder were driving along over logs." Interesting animadversions, in the youth of their race, on the most musical people the world has known !

Popular melodies.

CHAPTER II

THE RISE AND FALL OF THE CAROLINGIANS

LITERATURE : *The Life of Charlemagne*, by Einhard, a contemporary, is of great interest. The Capitulary of 802, in Henderson's *Select Documents*, should be read in connection with the founding of the Holy Roman Empire. The most scholarly and complete work on the whole period is Mühlbacher, *Deutsche Geschichte unter den Karolingern*. Von Löher, *Kulturgeschichte der Deutschen im Mittelalter*, is valuable. Of lives of Charlemagne in English one of the best is that by Davis.

The mayors of the palace.

IN the seventh century we find three different divisions of the Frankish kingdom : Austrasia, Neustria, and Burgundy — each with its own petty Merovingian king and its own mayor of the palace. After frequent civil wars the mayor of Neustria, Pepin of Héristal, succeeded at Testry, in 687 A.D., in subduing the mayor of Austrasia, who happened at the time to be administering also the affairs of Burgundy. A significant date this 687, for by this battle unity was restored to the Franks, and the power concentrated in the hands of Pepin and his descendants. Pepin, we are told, "arranged all things and returned to Austrasia," leaving his own son as major-domus of Neustria.

Strong men were needed if the work of Clovis were not to be undone ; but the new rulers proved a warlike race for the next four generations, showing no weak member until after the days of Charles the Great. Each in turn — Pepin of Héristal, Charles Martel, Pepin the Short, and Charles the Great himself — put down with an iron hand revolts of the conquered tribes, finding in time new powers to reckon with, like the dukes of Bavaria, the Lombards and the

22

popes in Italy, the Avars in the present Austria, the Moors in Spain, or the untamed Saxons at home.

Most alarming of all because it threatened the downfall of the whole civilization of the West, was the war-cloud that approached from the South, where the devoted followers of Mohammed, ever since the Hegira, or flight to Mecca, in 622 A.D., had been steadily advancing and conquering everything in their way. Marvellous had been their progress from the sands of Arabia, along the whole northern coast of Africa, across the straits of Gibraltar, which were named after one of their generals, through Spain and Aquitaine, and well into Gaul. In one of the great battles of the world, fought near Poictiers in 732 A.D., Charles Martel — the dealer of heavy, hammer-like blows — drove them back, owing his victory largely to his own skill and bravery, but also to discords in the enemy's camp and to the ready response with which his call to arms was met in all the heterogeneous parts of the Frankish kingdom. Few details of the battle are known; but contemporaries place the enemy's losses at wild, extravagant figures, and the victory was in so far decisive that the Mohammedans ceased to assume the offensive and were soon driven out of Aquitaine.

Charles Martel and the Arabs.

From this war date the beginnings of the great feudal system that prevailed in Europe down into the 19th century, for in order to equip his nobles with horses Charles sequestered large estates of the church and granted out the usufruct. The recipients of these so-called benefices made certain agreements which placed them in the position of vassals. They took an oath of fidelity, and gradually acquired privileges and, especially, immunity from the interference of the royal justices. Their holdings came to be known by the name of *feuda*, or fiefs, whence the name feudal system.

Beginning of the feudal system.

A radical measure, this seizure of ecclesiastical lands, and one that has only been resorted to at great crises in the world's history. In spite of his great service to Christendom, the church could never forgive Charles's act of violence, and he died in bad repute, at least with his Gallic clergy. A pious bishop of Orleans, who was said to have descended into hell in the good company of an angel, declared that he had seen him there. The monks of St. Wandrille, in the monastery chronicle, bewail that their good lands have gone for the purchase of spurs and saddles; while a legend relates that once, when Charles's tomb was opened, diabolical fumes were seen to escape.

St. Boniface, the Romanizer of the German church.

Yet this same prince had been the constant friend and protector of the warmest advocate and most zealous servant the church of Rome had ever possessed, the English missionary Winfred, or Boniface, to whom he had given a letter of safe-conduct addressed to all the nobles of his land, and whom he had allowed to map out the whole Frankish territory into ecclesiastical provinces. Boniface founded the monastery of Fulda, became the first archbishop of Mainz, and completely Romanized the German church, so that it conformed in even the most petty observances. He once declared that without this support from Charles he could neither have governed his priests and monks, nor prevented the exercise of pagan and idolatrous rites.

This new and close union with Rome was of vast importance for the future. The eternal city had often been the goal of pious pilgrimages, a hunting ground for sacred relics. But never before had the popes attained to the exercise of any considerable influence within Frankish territory. Gregory the Great had adopted the humblest tones even to the murderess Brunhilda, whom he begged to protect his missionaries on their way to England. Now the German people were to be folded closely in Rome's embrace, not to be liberated until the time of the Reformation.

For the literary culture of Germany Boniface also did his part. Fulda became a home of letters, and many of the monks and nuns who at his bidding came from England were in turn the founders of new monasteries and thus of new intellectual centres. Boniface himself wrote a grammar and a number of poems, and could not refrain from interspersing verses even in his letters to the Pope. Not merely in spiritual matters was he applied to, but also in those relating to pure diction. The account of a vision that he has left us in one of his letters does as much credit to his poetic imagination and his powers of expression as to his sanctity.

All this while the position of the mayors of the palace, although they had assumed the rank and title of dukes, was, to say the least, anomalous; yet the people had sanctioned it and had wished for no change of dynasty. They still set store by their feeble kings, and once when Grimoald, Charles Martel's great-uncle, had tried to place his own son on the throne, he had forced a revolt that cost him his life. But by the time of Pepin, Charles's son, the complexion of affairs was altered, and nobles, clergy, and people alike were desirous of a change. Pepin, eager for a sanction that would command respect, sent to the Pope, in 752 A.D., and propounded the riddle on which the fate of nations rested, "With regard to the kings of the Frankish kingdom, who possessed no more royal power, was this right or no?" And Pope Zacharias answered in similar oracular terms, "Rather should he have the name of king who has the power than he to whom no royal power remains."

Then Pepin allowed himself to be chosen and done homage to by the people, and to be consecrated by the primate

Pepin as king of the Franks.

Pepin and the see of Rome.

Boniface. Mindful of this religious side to his elevation, he signed himself henceforth as "king by the grace of God," and when the next Pope, Stephen IV., announced his intention of coming over the Alps, he dutifully went to meet him at St. Maurice, taking with him his little boy of twelve, the future Charlemagne. Afterward, in St. Denis, Stephen solemnly anointed the new king and his two sons, and placed a diadem on the head of the queen. "What was done for none of your ancestors has been done for you," he later wrote, ". . . through our humility the Lord has anointed you king." By solemn papal fiat the crown was declared hereditary, and a curse pronounced on whoever should presume to choose a king from any other line. The two potentates then concluded an alliance which was to last "until the consummation of the ages."

Through his friendly union with the Roman pontiff, a great field of activity had been opened up for the newly made king. As champion of the church, he descended upon Italy, where the Lombards were threatening the power of the papal see. Wresting whole districts from their hands, notably the Pentapolis and the Ravenna exarchate, he handed them over to the Pope, and this gift, known as the "donation of Pepin," laid the foundation for the temporal greatness of the Roman see.

The conquests of Charles the Great.

Never have two men better supplemented each other's work than in the case of Pepin and Charlemagne. What the one began the other carried to completion, until, by perfectly natural steps, the crown of the Frankish kingdom merged into that of the Holy Roman Empire. For posterity, indeed, Pepin has remained far in the background, whereas Charlemagne has been the hero of all the ages. Whenever antiquity has been found desirable for a law or for an institution, it has been dated back to his reign; innumerable writings are spiced with anecdotes about him.

The image of his banner-bearer, Roland, became the accepted emblem of civic jurisdiction; the greatest emperors paid their reverence at his tomb. It was his coffin that Napoleon carried off to Paris, as the token of a whole dead empire; his crown, and his alone, that the Corsican coveted.

It is more as a lawgiver and administrator than as a conqueror that Charles has lived in the memory of the people, and it is with that side of his activity and with his dominating personality that we are here most concerned. We shall, therefore, follow him not too closely on his military career, as he rode along on his charger from one confine of his domains to the other, adding mile on mile until twelve thousand ultimately stood to his credit. In his forty-six years of rule he engaged in some sixty warlike expeditions, and the wonder is that he found time and inclination for his many works of peace. At the end of his reign he could look around on magnificent results. The Lombard kingdom in Italy, after a checkered life of two centuries, had been brought to an end, and the iron crown rested on his own head; the last free German tribes had been drawn within the limits of the Frankish kingdom; the last remnants of heathenism had gone down before the sword and the laws of the determined conqueror. A Bavarian duke had been brought to bay, had been shorn as a monk, and thrust in a cloister, while his land had been parcelled out as a Frankish province.

In the present Austria the fierce Avars had been put to rout; little had availed them their huge chain of "rings," or strong-walled fortresses; a death-blow had been struck to their pride as a people, while the booty they had stolen from the Eastern Empire had been carried off as a rich prize. Some of it came to England as a gift to the king of Wessex. A part of Spain, too, the land between the Pyrenees and the Ebro, had been won for the empire, while, in the North, the Danes and the Slavs had felt the weight of the imperial displeasure.

The subjugation of the Saxons.

In the broad plains between the Rhine and the Elbe had been waged the fiercest and longest of all the wars, and, after thirty-three years of heroic resistance, the heathen Saxons had been forced to bow their necks forever under the yoke of a Christian king. With unheard-of fury this contest had raged, and Charles had been reduced to the severest of all measures, to wholesale massacre; for the stern old Saxon race, with a native aristocracy so proud that to marry beneath one's rank meant death, was fighting for gods and for freedom.

But this king knew no half-measures. His will was to be law, and death and the cross of Christ were the only alternatives he offered. He felled the mighty Irmensäule, the sacred tree of Wotan, and carried off the treasure heaped up in the neighboring temple. He forced baptism on his captives at the point of the sword, and made them pay their tithes to the church and keep the Sabbath holy; so strict were the laws he passed that for converts to eat meat in Lent was a capital crime, unless the offender could gain the absolution of a Christian priest. To avenge two of his commanders, who had been defeated on the Weser, he caused forty-five hundred of the enemy who had fallen into his hands to be executed in a single day. At the end of the war whole districts, bereft of their inhabitants, lay waste or were left to the Slavs; tribe after tribe and clan after clan were transplanted to other parts of the kingdom; and to this day Sachsbach, Sachsenberg, and other places in Thuringia and Hesse preserve the name and the memory of these first unwilling colonists. Forever crushed was the spirit of opposition; and two generations later a Saxon poet could liken Charles to one of the old apostles, declaring that he had brought the Saxon people to the gates of heaven.

Charles's expeditions into Italy brought him into personal contact with various popes, and he continued for most part the close and friendly relations that had been inaugurated by his father. By his order, all the correspondence that Pepin had had with Rome was collected and copied, and is still preserved. It concerns of course the Lombards, their common enemy, but also those important questions upon which the Eastern and Western church differed so radically as never to be able to come to an agreement — the iconoclastic controversy, namely, and the dogma of the procession of the Holy Ghost from the Son as well as from the Father.

Charles had begun his reign by acceding to the wish of his mother, Bertrada, and taking to wife a daughter of the Lombard king, Desiderius. Pope Stephen IV. had been furious, and had written a most vehement letter, in which he spoke of the Lombards as propagators of leprosy and a horribly faithless and ill-odored people. Charles had afterward repudiated his wife, and become the warmest ally of Adrian I., at whose behest he had made war on Desiderius. In the midst of this conflict, at Easter, 773, he had made a pilgrimage to Rome, where he was received with pomp and rejoicing. The youth of the city had come out to meet him with palms and olive branches, and the Pope had received him in state at St. Peter's. Over the grave of the apostle they had sworn mutual fidelity, and Charles had solemnly ratified the donation once made by Pepin to the church. He had taken the title, " Patrician of Rome." In 781 the Pope had personally baptized Charles's eldest son, and when, in 795, Adrian died, tears of real sorrow were shed by the Frankish king. He caused to be prepared the memorial tablet that now stands embedded in the wall near the chief entrance of St. Peter's.

Adrian's successor, Leo III., had continued the friendly

Charles the Great and Pope Adrian I.

Charles
the Great
and Pope
Leo III.

intercourse, and had sent Charles the keys of St. Peter's tomb and the banner of the city of Rome. There stands to this day in the Lateran palace a picture of St. Peter laying his hands on the heads of the two chief potentates of Christendom, and granting to the one victory, to the other long life. Charles, for his part, considered himself the patron, protector, and censor of the papacy : " Admonish the Pope " — so he instructs his envoy — " to lead an honest life, and especially to observe the sacred decrees of the church." He himself makes rules for good order in the bishoprics and monasteries, and passes laws against the keeping of falcons, hawks, and conjurers by bishops, abbots, and abbesses, and the writing of sentimental ditties by nuns. Frequently he admonishes the clergy to read the service with due reverence, or to see that the children of their parishioners duly learn their letters ; he inveighs against the laying aside of shoes during the divine service, and insists on the use of altar-cloths. Choir practice was often held in his presence, and he took pains to have German singers trained in Rome, being shocked to find how superior in this respect the Italians were to his own people. The reed organ had recently been invented in Constantinople, and he ordered instruments to be sent to him in order that they might be copied by native workmen.

With such an interest in the affairs of the church and of the papacy, it is not surprising that when Leo came to Saxony as a fugitive with a tale of outrageous treatment at the hands of the Romans, Charles constituted himself judge and avenger. He received the Pope with great honor in the midst of his troops, and the court poet describes the occasion. We are in a perfect atmosphere of fluttering standards and sounding trumpets, while Charles, conspicuous for his height, rides round on a mighty war-horse resplendent in glittering armor. He leads the Pope to the church and afterward to a splendid feast, where the hall is adorned with rich carpets and with hangings of purple and gold.

In Rome the form of a trial was gone through. Leo ascended a pulpit, and, with the Bible in his hand, cleared himself of all charges against him. His enemies were then deported beyond the Alps. He himself showed his gratitude by the most important single act committed in the Middle Ages — the placing, namely, of an imperial crown on the head of the Frankish king. The scene took place in St. Peter's on Christmas morning, which, according to the then reckoning, was also the first day of the new year — 800 A.D. It all came on Charles in the nature of a surprise, and he declared to Einhard that, had he known of Leo's intention, he would have remained away. The Pope, whose interest in the matter was to establish a jurisdiction that could forever rid him of his enemies, had stepped forward as the king was rising from prayer at the tomb of St. Peter, and the people had greeted the act with warm acclamations, calling down long life and victory on the new Augustus, the crowned of God.

The imperial coronation.

Charles's reluctance was doubtless real, for his sudden coronation as king of the Romans gave rise to numerous difficulties that might better first have been removed. For the dignity he was called to enjoy was not merely a revival of the so-called empire of the West, but a distinct menace to the power of the emperor of the East. No single chronicler of the time speaks of him as the successor of Romulus Augustulus, but all regarded him as the direct heir of the last Byzantine prince. That throne was considered vacant, as an infamous woman occupied it at the time. Only after twelve years of acrid negotiation was a treaty concluded with Nicephorus, the successor of Irene.

It is not unlikely, too, that Charles objected to the prominent part assumed by the Pope. He may have foreseen the proud claims that were later to be put forth, although at the moment there was no cause to fear, for Leo was humility itself, being the first to fall down and "adore" the new emperor.

The programme of the new empire.

At all events, the emperor was well aware of the importance of his new position. The long capitulary, or series of laws, issued in 802 A.D., is his official programme, as it were — nothing less than the expression of his ideal of an empire. At the head of all things he stands himself, his chief duty being to provide for the welfare of his subjects. Every man in his realm has, in a new form of oath, to plight his troth to him. In his hands are justice, morality, and religion. His empire is to be a haven of rest where all discords are to cease, and no one to infringe on another's rights. In his personal care are all the churches of God, all widows, orphans, and strangers, "for the Emperor himself, after God and His saints, has been constituted their protector and defender."

Extent of the empire.

The territory over which Charles's rule extended embraced modern France and a part of Spain, as well as Holland and Belgium. Of what is now Germany but about one-half was included within his boundaries, the land beyond the Elbe being occupied by Slavic tribes; on the other hand are to be reckoned in modern Austria, Bohemia, and Moravia, and more than two-thirds of Italy. The distances were great and the roads and means of transport poor; yet often at the call of some distant province Charles travelled the length and breadth of his domains. He was frequently in Italy, frequently on the farthest confines of his Saxon lands.

Was it possible to make such varied elements, peoples of so many tongues and such opposite customs and ideals, submit to any one central form of government? Charles tried it, and for the term of his own life at least succeeded in his endeavors.   The newly conquered lands were divided into counties, each under its own count; regular courts were held, definite duties required of the people, and church tithes imposed.   The borders of the empire were protected by " marches," stretches of land studded with fortresses and garrisoned by Frankish troops, over whom was a " margrave," with extended powers.

Charles was determined to keep the threads of power firmly in his own hand, and to know just how his lands were administered; he despatched supervisors in all directions whose duty it was to report on the work and efficiency of all the different officials.   *The missi dominici.*

These *missi dominici,* or king's messengers, prototypes of the later justices itinerant in England, went forth two by two from the royal court, a clergyman and a layman being paired together.   Arrived in the special districts appointed for their activity, they called assemblies, inquired into the manner of administering affairs, listened to the representations of men chosen from the people, and heard the appeals of individuals who complained of denial of justice.   In addition to this it devolved on the *missi*, as the emperor's representatives, to receive the oath of fealty from all who had come to man's estate.   Over the relics of a saint the subject swore to be true to the monarch as a vassal to his lord, so far as God gave him intelligence. Another of the duties of the envoys was to see that military service was actually performed by those from whom it was due.   As a rule every able-bodied man was obliged to serve for a certain number of days, and to appear in camp equipped at his own expense.   This, in the case of poor men, was manifestly impossible, and a law was passed that several might join together in fitting out one common representative.   Even then, military service was the bane of this

otherwise mild rule.   Many, in despair, gave up their freedom and became the serfs of their more fortunate neighbors.   Thus the large landowners developed into petty
potentates, and a whole social revolution worked itself out.
The ultimate fall of the Carolingian dynasty is attributable in large part to the fact that the kings could no longer
rely directly on their subjects, but were often at the mercy
of powerful *seigneurs*.   The real lord of the peasant was
the man from whom he held his land.

The capitu-
laries.

At the end of their year of service the *missi dominici*
brought their reports to Charles, who made them the
basis of instructions for the next year's envoys.   Many
such instructions have been preserved, and afford some of
the best glimpses into the methods of administration.
They are called capitularies, because of their chapters or
headings.   They concern all branches of the service, the
management of the emperor's private estates, as well as of
the public lands.   Indeed, there was no distinction under
this greatest of autocrats.   Whatever revenues came in
from tolls and customs, from spoils of war, from tribute,
gifts, and payments for protection, from lordless lands, and
from his own farms, were disposed of according to his will.
Yet with regard to these same private estates, he kept the
most rigid reckoning, and is said even to have counted the
eggs as they arrived for use in the palace.

No one who has not read these capitularies can appreciate their attention to detail ; among thousands of directions for the welfare of the state they give the proper food
for hens, the plants, by name, that are to be in the kitchen
garden, the kinds of apples that must be grown.   The
juice is no longer to be pressed from the grapes, as
formerly, by treading them with the naked feet, while it
is decreed that the gardener's house can be made more
ornamental by trailing it over with green vines.   The

prices of food and clothing had been discussed in the Diet of 808 A.D., and a capitulary determines that a cloak of the best fur may be sold for thirty shillings, but that an ordinary one is not to cost more than ten. The value of the shilling had been previously fixed at the twentieth part of a pound; new coins had been issued — twelve pence to the shilling — and refusal to accept them, as far, at least, as Slavs were concerned, had been declared punishable with flogging. Against usury, " when one demands back more than one gave — when, for example, one lends ten shillings, and then claims more," strict penalties were decreed.

Many of Charles's capitularies concern the matter of education. He had learned in Italy to venerate the culture of his own and of past ages, and it became a fixed purpose with him to rouse in his own Franks an appreciation of art and of civilization. He gathered around him the great men of his time, often calling them, as in the case of Peter of Pisa and Alcuin of York, from distant countries. He took lessons himself, as did all his family, while a regular school was established in the palace for the sons of nobles. " We are seeking most zealously," he writes to his prelates, " to foster the sciences, which, through the carelessness of our forefathers, have almost fallen into oblivion, and we invite, through our own example, as far as in us lies, to the eager study of the free arts." Latin he himself spoke fluently, Greek not so well, and writing was an art or accomplishment to which, with all his efforts, he could personally not attain. He kept his tablets under his pillow, so Einhard tells us, and frequently rose in the night to practise forming his letters; but his stiffened fingers would lend themselves to no such petty work. We learn, nevertheless, that he was able to compose a grammar of his mother tongue, and that he gave German names to the four winds and the twelve months, besides ordering a collection to be

Charles the Great and the advancement of learning.

made of old German national songs.   Numerous were the
manuscripts, both of heathen and of Christian writers,
that he caused to be carefully copied, — a document badly
penned roused his anger to the utmost, — and, as grateful
scholars know, the utterly illegible scrawls of Merovingian
state documents gave place under his influence to the clear
and regular characters that are known as the Carolingian
minuscule.

The
clergy as
teachers.

Frequently did Charles enjoin upon his clergy the cultivation of a literary style, even criticising such of their
letters as came to his notice.   He bids them be not merely
chaste in their manner of living, but also to train themselves in the use of language; to edify the people, not
merely by their outward appearance, but also by proficiency
in reading.   "As a regular course of life," he writes,
"brings about purity of morals, so may constant teaching
and learning regulate and beautify the powers of speech."

The emperor ordered, and frequently repeated the charge,
that priests should consider it their duty to teach all people
the Lord's Prayer, and the Athanasian as well as the
Apostles' creed.   Whoever refuses to learn them "shall be
punished with blows and made to fast on bread and water
until he shall have thoroughly learned all," and "women
shall be made amenable through strokes of the whip or
through fasting."   Besides this religious instruction it was
evidently intended that the clergy should open schools in
the different villages; a law provides that "every one shall
send his son to learn his letters, and the child shall remain
at it with all industry until he shall have been instructed."

The learned
men at
court.

The chief teacher of the day was the learned Alcuin.
He it was who founded an academy, in the Athenian sense,
where the emperor himself and his chief courtiers discoursed
on learned subjects.   In order the better to keep up the
illusion they adopted the names of great men of old;

Charles himself was David, and Alcuin Horace, while Angilbert, the chief epic poet of his age, was hailed by the name of Homer. Alcuin was the head of the royal schools and main adviser in all points concerning the spread of learning. In such of his letters as have come down to us he shows a mental power and an independence of spirit that are worthy of all admiration. As friend to friend he writes to Charles, as likely as not opposing some intention of the latter; or, again, he rebukes the royal princes for some unseemly action. In old age, indeed, religious scruples assailed the brilliant scholar and made him question the morality of reading the heathen poets; he feels called upon to warn his pupils against the seductive charms of Virgil.

The poet Angilbert began an epic with Charles himself for a theme; passages have come down to us on the building of Aix; there is also a spirited picture of a royal hunt, and a lively description of the meeting of Pope and emperor at Paderborn.

We hear more of literary men at Charles's court than we do of designers and painters, yet decorative art had already reached a certain stage of development. Scratched on sword hilts and on other objects we can trace the first faint beginnings of an attempt at ornamentation, and see how in each succeeding epoch new motives or patterns come into vogue. The earliest of such decorations are interwoven bands with dots, then spiral lines, and finally the shapes of beasts and birds and the outline of the human form. Crude indeed were these early efforts; there existed a formal type for all beasts, and another for all birds. But already, in the time of the Carolingians, we can find new elements; the Italian influence is readily perceptible in the little scenes that illuminate the pages of breviaries and other books. Dainty lamps and candlesticks come in, and

The progress of art.

especially characteristic are the Italian ovules and acanthus
leaves. In the use of their colors the artists were little at
home ; all was still formal, with no thought of truth to
nature. The monk Gottschalk, who made a beautiful
Bible for Charles, employed various hues perfectly arbitrarily — rose-color when dealing with martyrs, gold to
signify virgin purity, and silver to betoken married life.
Other manuscripts of the time are full of green horses,
bright red rocks, and men and women with blue hair.

Death of
Charles and
coronation
of Louis.

All in all, however, this reign was a glorious renaissance.
But what was to become of the Holy Empire on the death
of the capable head ? A division document is known to
have been drawn up in 806, according to which the land is
to be divided into shares for the emperor's three sons; but,
strangely enough, of the imperial dignity itself there is
not so much as a word. Was the crown imposed against
Charles's will not to pass to his descendants ?

The death of two sons in succession altered the problem
and rendered division unnecessary. The old emperor himself, in the cathedral at Aix, placed the crown on the head
of the only survivor and soon afterward concluded his own
busy and useful life. All depended on the personality
of his successor. Was he brave and strong, or would he
yield to others ; if the latter, what were the influences
under which he was likely to fall ? How little men knew
Louis the Pious, the first regular bigot on the Frankish-
German throne !

Disintegra-
tion of the
empire.

The history of the century that followed on the death of
Charles the Great is one long study in the process of disintegration. Not a single great undertaking characterizes
the reign of Louis the Pious, nothing is added to the edifice already reared. For a few years the prosperity of the
empire continues from the impetus that Charles had given
it, but then the decline begins. The weak monarch falls

completely under the influence of the clergy, fasting and praying, and making lamentable confessions of his own worthlessness.   Numberless were his visits to churches and monasteries, constant his interrogating of his own conscience. He allows Pope Stephen IV. to cross the Alps and crown him, though Charlemagne with his own hands had already performed that act.   He had grown so superstitious that the falling in of a gallery over which he was accustomed to pass seemed a premonition of death, and with the help of his clerical friends he sets his house in order. The deed known as the division of 817 gives a share of the empire to each of his three sons, but constitutes one of them emperor, the other two merely kings.   Thus was preserved the unity that the church required; there was to be one pope and one emperor, as there was one sun and one moon, one spiritual and one secular sword.

A second marriage, with Judith, the proud daughter of the Guelphs, brought Louis into conflict with his former friends, and made the court a hotbed of deceit and intrigue. The fruit of the union was a boy known in history as Charles the Bald, and called, even by a contemporary, the " new Benjamin." His mother was determined that the shares of the older sons should be curtailed, and that her son should be appanaged with a kingdom. The clergy felt slighted that the document of division, drawn up so solemnly and with their aid, should so readily be laid aside. The older brothers refused to have their portions curtailed, and entered into open rebellion. Lothar, the future emperor, was declared already coregent. A reaction took place in favor of Louis, but the continued intrigues by the party of Charles the Bald precipitated a new revolt. And now for the first and last time in papal history, a vicar of St. Peter crosses the Alps and plays an active part on the field of battle — that

The advent of Charles the Bald.

particular field, indeed, owing to the Pope's conduct, has
gone down to posterity as the " Field of Lies."

The pen-
ance at
Soissons.

The army of the father lay opposed to that of the sons,
near Colmar, in Alsace. The Pope, Gregory IV., crossed
over and demanded to see the emperor. He was well
received and remained several days, being allowed to pass
freely to and fro among the soldiers. The night after his
return to the rebel camp, the greater part of the imperial
troops went over to the enemy. Louis himself, as well as
Judith and Charles the Bald, were made prisoners. For
the son of Charles the Great what deep humiliations!
Louis was compelled this time to drink the cup of bitterness to the very dregs, to regularly bow his neck beneath
the yoke. A Diet at Compiègne declared that through
this man's short-sightedness and neglect the empire had
sunk so low as to be regarded by its enemies with
mockery and derision. He is adjudged, therefore, to have
forfeited the temporal rule. Then openly, on the steps of
the church of St. Medard, at Soissons, the son of Charlemagne was obliged to confess, not once, but four times,
that he had offended God, given umbrage to the church
of Christ, and brought confusion upon the people. A list
of other sins was thrust into his hand, for which he was
told to ask forgiveness; among them were sacrilege and
murder and some public acts of which the clergy disapproved. Surely no monarch, not even Henry IV., ever
fell to quite such depths; Agobard of Lyon, writing at
this time, speaks of him tersely as "the emperor that
was!"

End of the
reign of
Louis the
Pious.

The severity with which Louis had been treated brought
about a revulsion of feeling; he lived to be restored to
power and to see a still grander assembly of bishops
reverse the proceedings at Soissons. Still, his reign ended
in a general atmosphere of family discord, civil war, and

social ruin. The once glorious Frankish kingdom was nearing the verge of destruction. All the contemporary writings that exist — reports of bishops, protocols of diets, visions declared to have been seen by saints, not to speak of chronicles, annals, and letters — give forth one continuous wail of complaint. " They love bribes and not justice," says one writer, referring to the leading personages of the time. The counts are accused of conniving at crime; the territorial lords, of falsifying measures; the clergy are charged with simony, extravagance, and neglect of duty. To add misery to demoralization, there came year after year of bad harvest and of plague. Einhard, in his description of the translation of a saint's relics, makes the devil gloat over all the harm he has done, and moralize about the prevalent injustice and iniquity. Then Einhard himself bursts forth: " Ah, how deep is our age sunken, when not good men, but evil demons, are our preceptors."

All this time, like moths fretting a garment, external enemies were rending and tearing at the confines of the empire. The Bulgarians oppressed its Slavic subjects; the Saracens from Africa and Spain harassed its southern coast; while the Northmen or Vikings had already begun those depredations which were to make them lords of the north coast of France, of the steppes of Russia, of southern Italy, and of all of England. *The coming of the Northmen*

Out from the stormy coasts of Norway, in those small, stanch boats, — one of which has been so miraculously preserved to us in the bowels of the earth, — they took their way, making for the mouths of the different rivers of the Frankish kingdom, and burning and slaying in all directions. They did not hesitate to attack even great cities like Hamburg and Paris, and to wring tribute from the grandsons and great-grandsons of Charles the Great.

Year after year, for the better half of a century, these depredations continued, until the Treaty of Clair-sur-Epte,
in the year 911, handed over to the troublesome guests
the present Normandy.

The wars of
the sons of
Louis the
Pious.
Of the four sons of Louis the Pious three survived him;
the death of one, Pepin of Aquitaine, had greatly simplified the situation.   Here was a real, existent kingdom that
could be bestowed on the landless Charles the Bald.   But
the war of the sons against the father had been but the
prelude to a bitter struggle among the brothers themselves.
The eldest, Lothar, claimed as emperor a supremacy that
Louis and Charles were not willing to grant.   At the battle of Fontenoy, in 841 A.D., the latter were victorious, and
in the following year they sealed by an oath at Strassburg
their intention to hold out together for their rights.   The
wording of this agreement has come down to us in the pages
of the historian Nithard, who took part in the battle of
Fontenoy, and whose vanity in ascribing the victory to his
own deeds of valor may be pardoned in view of his services
in preserving such valuable records.

Here in this document of Strassburg we have the first
great literary landmark to show that, from the fusion of
the Franks and the Romans, two new nationalities, the
French and the Germans, in the narrower sense of the
term, had resulted.   In order to be understood by the followers of his brother, Louis the German has to swear his
oath in a language that is not German and no longer Latin,
while Charles repeats the oath in the German tongue.

The Treaty
of Verdun.
Lothar eventually yielded to the strength of the alliance
against him, and on an island in the River Saone, not far
from Mâcon, the three brothers came together to make one
of the most momentous arrangements ever consummated
by three individuals.   It was decided to divide equally
among them all the lands that had belonged to the empire

of Charles the Great, and a body of one hundred and twenty men was appointed to map out and measure the territory, and to calculate the income from the different estates and bishoprics. The task was lightened by the fact that Bavaria as a whole already belonged to Louis, Aquitaine to Charles, and Italy to Lothar.

By August, 843, the survey was ended and the whole arrangement was ratified by the famous Treaty of Verdun. To Lothar, who retained the imperial name as a mere title of honor, was given the so-called middle kingdom, extending from the North Sea down through Italy. All to the west of him, in an almost straight line from Ghent to Arles, went to Charles; while Louis's possessions were, roughly speaking, bounded on the west by the Rhine. As an instance of the care with which the division was made we are told that a small district on the left bank of the river, including the town of Worms, was added to the German's share because of the abundance of wine, which doubtless served to balance other deficiencies.

It must not be supposed that even after the signing of the treaty an era of peace like the dew of heaven descended upon the land. One of Charles's vassals ran away with Lothar's daughter, and after this matter had been arranged a new dispute arose in which Charles and Lothar sided against Louis the German. It was difficult, indeed, to maintain law and order, the more so as the Treaty of Verdun had arbitrarily sundered existing divisions, such as church dioceses or even the lands of one and the same great noble. Quarrels and violence ruled the day; "innocent blood is shed unavenged, the fear of kings and of laws has departed from men, with closed eyes the people are approaching hell-fire," says a writer of the time.

The Treaty of Mersen.

All the same the Treaty of Verdun was for the Germans the birthday of their nation. He to whose lot it had fallen

to become its ruler was, fortunately, the strongest and most
capable of the grandsons of Charles the Great.   In numerous
battles Louis defeated the Bohemians, and a new enemy,
the Moravians.   When his brother Lothar's son, Lothar II.,
died childless in 869, he made a fight for a fair share of
Lorraine, and dispossessed Charles the Bald, who had
already taken possession.   By the Treaty of Mersen, 870
A.D., a line was drawn from north to south which coincided pretty nearly with natural race distinctions.   By his
energy and determination Louis had made the Rhine Germany's stream, not Germany's boundary.   Nor was he
content with merely increasing his territory, but did his
best to preserve law and order, calling upon the clergy
to aid his endeavors.   Acts of synods have been preserved
in which penalties were decreed for different crimes, and a
system of judicial procedure established; the nobles were
not to oppress the common people, while a serf accused of
the murder of a priest was to prove his innocence by the
ordeal of the red-hot ploughshares.

The deposi-
tion of
Charles the
Fat.

Owing to a succession of deaths the whole Frankish empire, as Charles the Great had possessed it, was reunited
under one of Louis the German's sons.   But the hand
of Charles the Fat was too feeble to hold the reins of government for more than a moment.   He was ill in body
as well as in mind, was frequently attacked by epilepsy, and
suffered tortures from an aching head.   He paid the Normans to leave him alone, closing with them a most unworthy treaty; but he incurred thereby the hatred of the
thousands of brave men who, for ten months, relying on his
coming, had been defending Paris against the fierce enemy.
The needs of the time demanded an able-bodied and a
whole-souled man; this the people came to realize, and they
fell away from their emperor, who crawled off to his estates
in Swabia to die.   Had the suffering and weak-spirited

monarch not gone willingly, he would have been compelled to go by force, for the bastard Arnulf of Carinthia, grandson of Louis the German, was already on the march with an army of Bavarians and Saxons, Thuringians, Franks, and Swabians.   Charles the Fat had sent an embassy to meet him, and to conjure him, by a bit of the true cross of Christ which they carried with them for the purpose, to be mindful of the oath of fealty once sworn.   At the sight of the holy token Arnulf had been moved to tears, but nothing could change his resolution.   He allowed himself now to be raised on the Frankish throne, his election denoting, as has been well said, the first independent action of the German secular world.   The nobles, eager for a warrior at their head, had brought it about.

Arnulf, too, was looked upon for a while as head of the whole Carolingian empire, and, though born out of wedlock, as a lawful descendant of Charles the Great.   But a reaction had set in against the whole idea of universal rule. In Italy and in France, in Upper and in Lower Burgundy, local kings, set up by the people, came to the fore, and Arnulf was wise enough to sanction the new development.   He took up zealously the practical duties of a ruler, and defeated the Normans in an important battle on the River Dyle.   He made, too, an expedition to Rome, and forced the imperial crown from the timid hand of Pope Formosus.

The end of the German Carolingian line.

With the death of Arnulf's son, Louis the Child, who barely attained to man's estate, the German branch of the Carolingian line came to an end.   It had waned and lost power after the manner of the Merovingians, and for a time it seemed likely that the heads of the different stem-duchies would follow the general trend, and set themselves up as independent rulers.   What civilization remained in these disordered times was kept alive in the monasteries. For that if for nothing else we owe the church a debt of gratitude.

Civilization in the monasteries. Throughout all the years of political anarchy the cloister was looked upon as a quiet refuge where the individual could give himself up, not only to pious contemplation and to learning, but also to the practice of many a useful art and accomplishment. By the ninth century the wise rule of St. Benedict had superseded all others, and according to its precepts the brethren were to busy themselves at certain hours with manual occupations. Unless a brother grew too proud of his skill and the idea happened to come into his head that he was conferring a favor on his monastery, his activity was to be unrestricted.

Many were the spheres within which the monks were called upon to labor. They made clearings in the forests and tilled the lands, so that wherever a monastery was founded the neighborhood began to assume a friendlier character. The cloister precincts contained many buildings and for various purposes. More than forty such are shown in the plan for St. Gall, which was drawn up under Abbot Gozbert in 820, and is still exhibited to interested visitors. Besides the abbot's stately house with its own kitchen and storeroom, there are schools for outsiders, hospices for travellers, infirmaries and dispensaries. The artisans and common workmen had their own abodes, hidden from the main edifices by hedges and walls, while a building was set apart for the letting of blood, which played so large a part in mediæval medicine. It is not impossible, in fact is known to have been the case in an English monastery, that the brothers were bled all round at stated intervals to tame their unruly passions.

Each such Benedictine monastery, in short, was a little world in itself, separated often from the outer life by palisades and intrenchments, moats and turreted wall

Masons and carpenters, tailors and shoemakers, weavers and brewers, dwelt therein, and the people from the surrounding districts far and near came to wonder and gape at the busy workers and to carry home the new ideas. If illness broke out in the vicinity, the monks were the great healers, and distributed their medicines free to those who sought them. If strangers came, they were the guests of the monks; and traders from a distance often journeyed to buy books or other products of monastic industry.

The monastery schools were always of two kinds, one for those who later expected to join the order and who were obliged to wear its frock, the other for the sons of neighboring nobles and freemen. Writing, reading, and arithmetic were the chief subjects taught; and very small children were made to imitate the letters of the alphabet by crossing and curving their fingers. The discipline was severe and consisted mainly in flogging; in St. Gall, in 937, a pupil, hoping to escape this punishment, set fire to the school, whereby the flames did great damage. *The monastery schools.*

A chief occupation of the monks of St. Benedict was the copying of old manuscripts, and it must not be forgotten, in estimating their services to the world, that to them, and to them only, we owe the preservation of the ancient classics. The greatest care was bestowed on making the letters and illuminating the initials, and many a tenth-century manuscript is still clear and legible. It is sad to note that some of the copyists found their task irksome; one occasionally comes upon expressions written on the margin, of relief that darkness has at last fallen, or of thankfulness that the whole is ended. Yet the joy of seeing the monastery library grow under their efforts must have atoned for much labor.

Various, as has been said, were the arts practised by the monks. Beautiful illustrations were made for breviaries, *The monks as artists.*

which were bound in leather, and sumptuously adorned.
Here, too, were wrought gold and silver chalices, shrines,
crucifixes, and candelabra. One and the same monk often
displayed a variety of talents. In the time of Charles the Fat,
St. Gall could count among its members a certain Totilo,
famous as a preacher and teacher, a writer of poems, and
composer of music, yet able to turn his hand at will to
painting, sculpture, or architecture. Charles cursed those
who had made a monk out of such a man, regretting that
his own court should have lost him as an ornament. Much
of Totilo's work has perished in the course of these last
thousand years, but a dypticum, or set of folding tablets,
has happily been preserved. Here, beautifully carved in
ivory, we have Christ surrounded by angels, while near him
are the four evangelists, and a series of allegorical figures
intended to represent the sun and the moon, the sea, and
the earth.

CHAPTER III

THE RELATIONS BETWEEN CHURCH AND STATE UNDER THE SAXON AND FRANCONIAN EMPERORS

LITERATURE : For a whole series of important documents on the struggle for the right of investiture see Henderson, *Select Documents*. Giesebrecht, in his *Deutsche Kaiserzeit*, gives a very extended and interesting treatment of the subject ; he is admirably supplemented by Hauck in the third volume of his *Kirchengeschichte*. The article *Investiturstreit* in Herzog's *Realencyclopedie* is excellent. See also Manitius, *Deutsche Geschichte*, 911-1125.

IN an age when there was practically no increase of territory, no war, excepting internal revolts, no foreign policy, it is difficult to find a thread through the mazes of German history. The development of the royal power forms an attractive theme, but our materials are too scant for its worthy treatment. We know that the election of Conrad I., in 911 A.D., saved the country from falling apart into five independent duchies ; but we know, too, that Conrad's dealings with the autocratic dukes ended in failure, and that at his death, in preference to keeping the royal dignity in his own family, he turned the choice of the princes on his chief rival, Henry of Saxony. The latter, by wise military reforms, by conciliating the dukes, by conquering the invading hordes of the wild Hungarians, brought things to such a pass that the coronation of his son Otto I., in 936, was a veritable triumph of concord. The three archbishops, of Mainz, of Treves, and of Cologne, placed on him the royal insignia — the sword, the mantle, the sceptre, the staff, and the diadem — and anointed him

The kings and the heads of the duchies

with the holy oil; while the heads of four duchies — Lorraine, Franconia, Swabia, and Bavaria — served as marshal, cup-bearer, seneschal, and chamberlain.   But, nevertheless, a great part of Otto's long reign was occupied in putting down revolts.   In vain he changed the persons of the heads of the duchies — they all refused to become mere tools of his will.   As a last resort he turned to the bishops and abbots for support, and formed with them an alliance that was greatly to influence the future course of history.

The kings and the bishops.

In the reign of Charlemagne the clergy had been humble and dutiful; no forged donation of Constantine, no false Isidorian decretals, had as yet furnished a basis for extravagant claims.   In the reign of Louis the Pious Gregory II. had interfered in favor of Lothar I., but he had acted more as an adviser than as one with authority.   It was reserved for Nicholas I., in the matter of the divorce of Lothar II., to promulgate the all-might of Rome, to threaten Germans with ban and excommunication, and to summon foreigners before his judgment seat.

Between Conrad I. and the church there had been a firm alliance ; it was by the efforts of an archbishop that he had been raised to the throne ; a bishop, Salamo of Constance, was his chief adviser.   A synod, held at Hohenaltheim in 916, at which a papal legate was present, had spoken a threefold curse against those who should break their oath of fealty, and had declared treasonable undertakings against the king to be punishable with lifelong imprisonment in a monastery.

Otto the Great and the bishops.

But these same ecclesiastical influences had widened the breach between Conrad and the dukes, and Henry I., whose policy was one of conciliation, had begun his reign by repulsing the Archbishop of Mainz.   Conrad had not been able, Henry did not care, to go to Rome and negotiate with the Pope for the restoration of the imperial dignity. Church and state had little in common.·

Under Otto I. there was again a change. The failure of his attempt to bring the duchies into the hands of men who would do his will led once more to a favoring of the clergy, while holding them, indeed, with a strict hand. Otto allowed the different cathedral chapters to choose their own bishops, but subject always to his own final approval. He was sure thus of having about him men whom he could trust, and he drew them still closer by obliging them to come to him for the sign of their office, the shepherd's crook or staff. In the matter of endowment he was generous in the extreme, as were all of his successors down to the time of the great struggle in the following century. It was thus that mere church dignitaries became powerful princes and pillars of the throne — the immense advantage being that, with sacerdotal celibacy a rule of the church, these holdings could never become hereditary, but could always be regranted at the pleasure of the crown. In the meantime great services were required and performed; as holders of fiefs the bishops and abbots sent their regular contingents of vassals to the army, as members of the royal chancery much of the business of the court was in their hands. Even in their own sphere they were not unrestricted ; Otto drew them before his own tribunals and disposed arbitrarily of church funds.

Otto's interference in the politics of Italy brought him into closer contact with the Papacy. He had been called in by a helpless woman, Adelaide, heiress to part of the land, who was being oppressed by Margrave Berengar of Ivrea, and whom he not only freed from her persecutor but also made his own wife. Later still a new call came against this same Margrave Berengar, this time from the Pope. Such was the chain of circumstances by which Rome came within

Otto the Great and the popes.

the circle of interest of the German kings and a new direction was given to their policy.

The condition of the Papacy during the middle years of
the tenth century was such as to cry aloud to heaven for
betterment. An infamous but powerful woman, Marozia,
had been the paramour of one Pope, had caused the fall and
death of another, and had finally placed her illegitimate
son, a boy of twenty, on the chair of Peter, whence he was
cast out by his own brother, Alberich, who became the
head and ruler of Rome. Alberich's mantle descended on
Octavian, a mere boy, who, however, was soon chosen Pope,
under the name of John XII., thus combining in his own
person the secular and spiritual headship of the eternal
city. He it was who, when his lands were threatened
with invasion by Berengar, sent an appeal to the powerful
ruler of Germany, offering to revive, in his honor, the old
custom of the imperial coronation, which had been in
abeyance for more than a generation. In February, 962
A.D., Otto received the crown in St. Peter's, from the
young Pope's hand; — not altogether trusting his host and
benefactor, for he had given orders to his sword-bearer to
watch with weapon drawn, even while he knelt by the
grave of the apostle. John was furthermore obliged to
swear by St. Peter's holy bones that he would not make
common cause with the enemies against whom he had
applied for aid.

Deposition
of Pope
John XII.

The precaution proved not unnecessary; the young Pope
felt crushed and oppressed by the greatness of his visitor.
He sent propitiatory envoys, not only to Berengar's son
Adalbert, whom he welcomed in Rome, but even to the
heretical Greek emperor. The letters to the latter were
intercepted; it remained to be seen how the Northern hero
would take such perfidy. His first step was to march into
Rome and make the people swear to submit all future papal

elections to the confirmation of himself and of his son. At a synod which was called in St. Peter's, and over which the emperor presided, the most damning charges were brought against the head of the church. He was proved to be sacrilegious, unchaste, a brigand: he had drunk the devil's health, — at least, so the charges ran, — and had invoked heathen gods while playing dice; he had chosen a ten-year-old boy to be bishop of Todi, and had given a deacon his consecration in a horse's stall. Otto himself accused him of being a perjured traitor, and of conspiring with the enemies of the empire.

The matter did not end here. John was declared deposed, and soon died, but the Romans refused to accept the Pope whom Otto chose, and elected a cardinal-deacon, Benedict. It was only after a siege of the city, which ended in famine and capitulation, that Benedict was induced to appear in an assembly and beg for mercy. He came clad in the papal robes and holding the bishop's staff; he was led out, stripped of his pallium; his staff was broken in pieces, and he was carried off to Hamburg to die in captivity. These measures had been drastic, but they proved efficacious; some of the following popes were sober, honest Germans, and the end of Otto's reign marks a complete imperial supremacy over the church.

Otto II. died too young, and Otto III. was too unaffect- Otto III. edly pious to enter into new conflicts. The latter was a man possessed of two strong but absolutely contradictory passions, the one for imperial magnificence, the other for abject asceticism. Throned on the Aventine, surrounded by a host of obsequious officials, he went so far as to sign himself "emperor of all emperors," and to deck himself in wondrous garments; but again, as a pilgrim, barefoot in the coarsest of sackcloth, he approached holy places, or retired for a fortnight at a time to a cave or a cloister, and humbly called himself "servant of the apostles." He descended into the tomb of Charles the Great, to pay his reverence to the illustrious dead. To his bishops he was more than generous, deeding to them whole counties, involving them deeper and deeper in secular cares and interests, teaching them to serve two masters, God and mammon, Pope and emperor.

Henry II. and Conrad II.

With the popes there was no further interference until the reign of Henry III. Henry II. had been most churchly minded, and, after his death, was regularly canonized as a saint. He had treated his own clergy with great generosity, with some severity, and at times with a sort of playfulness. He was in despair, he said, at the rich gifts Bishop Meinwerk of Paderborn induced him to make to that bishopric; a charter or deed is extant which begins by asserting that there are two sides to man's nature, a manly commanding and a womanly obedient: outwardly seeming to slumber but inwardly awake, and following out this thought he, the Emperor, has made these gifts to Paderborn! Just what he meant would be difficult to say.

Conrad II. had enjoyed a magnificent coronation in Rome at the hands of Pope John XIX., the occasion being graced by the presence of King Rudolph of Burgundy, Abbot Odilo of Cluny, and King Canute of England. But under .this same Pope, a mere layman who had been chosen for political reasons by the counts of Tusculum, the papacy begins to sink back into the slough from which Otto the Great had raised it. Europe was scandalized by a proposition said to have emanated from John himself to abandon the papal rights in the East to the Patriarch of Constantinople for a round sum of money.

The character of Henry III.

Unfortunately for pleasure-loving popes there was developing at this very moment, in the important monastery of Cluny, a decided tendency toward asceticism and a determination to reform the government of the church. Its most triumphant product was to be Pope Gregory VII., but its influence was already widely felt when the young Henry III., in 1037 A.D., succeeded to the German crown. He was a pious, God-fearing man, a warm opponent, even to his own detriment, of the besetting sin of simony, or selling of church preferments to the highest bidder; so strong an advocate of peace and good-will among his nobles that he frequently at the celebration of mass rose up before the high altar and uttered eloquent exhortations. On the field of battle he had often been seen to kneel and pray; like Otto III., he went on pilgrimages, and even allowed his royal back to be scourged by fanatic priests.

Such was the man who was called upon to confront a situation of affairs hitherto unheard of even in Rome. There had been cases of rival popes, but here were three at a time; while into the whole complication there entered the most trivial and unworthy of motives: The crime of Simon, the selling of the gift of the Holy Spirit, had reached the worst stage of its development. Three claimants of the papacy.

Through the gold of the Tusculan counts, Benedict IX., a mere boy, but the best representative the family could muster, was raised upon the papal chair. He proved a monster of vice, but the Romans bore with him for years, hoping for amendment. At last, in 1045 A.D., a portion of the citizens rose against him, drove him out, and, in the following year, John, bishop of the Sabine district, was recognized as his successor. Silvester III., as he called himself, was little better than Benedict, for he too had bought his election. A conflict ensued in which Benedict carried off the victory.

Benedict was not averse to resigning the Papacy, — it was said, indeed, that he was most anxious to settle down and lead a respectable married life, —- but he and his friends had risked too much capital for him to retire empty-handed. Doubtless, no one would have cared for the papal dignity as a mere matter of speculation, but a purchaser was found in the person of an honest man filled with ambition to cleanse and reform the church. John Gratian, who took the name of Gregory VI., paid a thousand pounds of silver for the opportunity to carry out his philanthropic ideas.

Henry III. and the three popes.

All this was an abomination in the nostrils of right-thinking men, and Henry III. was called upon to raise his hand and sweep away the vast web of defilement. Even on purely political grounds the state of affairs cried aloud for interference. Henry with an army marched to Italy, and in synods held at Sutri and at Rome procured the deposition of all three popes. Silvester was relegated to a monastery, Benedict was publicly stripped of the tokens of his dignities, while Gregory VI., forced to decree his own fall, was exiled to Germany. With the latter there went as companion the monk Hildebrand, the man beyond all others who was to build up a strong, pure Papacy, and to resent all royal interference in church matters. In the terrible wrestling of papal and imperial claims, he was to bring his rival to the most abject penance.

For the moment the triumph of Henry III. was absolute; the great ascetic and reformer, Damiani, proclaimed that next to God it was this emperor who had snatched Rome from the maw of the insatiable dragon and driven out the money-changers from the temple. Like King Josias of old, he had cast down the false altars and destroyed the idols. The vacant pontifical throne was bestowed by Henry on a German, the bishop of Bamberg, who took the name of Clement; while the Romans agreed, as in the days of Otto, to submit to the emperors the confirmation of future popes-elect. On Clement followed quickly Poppo of Brixen as

Damasus II., and Bruno of Toul as Leo IX., both directly appointed by the emperor — the latter, indeed, his near relative and a German by birth.

In Leo IX. the church had found a head who almost for the first time in its history convinced the world that he really meant to exercise a wide rule. A determined reformer, he held his synods as kings had held their diets: compelled bishops, Germans as well as Italians, either to cleanse themselves of charges or to renounce their sees ; and proclaimed war to the death on simony and sacerdotal marriage. He was a pope well able to awaken popular sympathy, handsome and with pleasing voice. Indefatigable in the exercise of his duties, he would travel hundreds of miles to hold a synod; his journeys occupied a great part of his time, one visit to Germany lasting as long as six months.

The re-
forms of
Pope
Leo IX.

By efforts such as these the people gained a new conception of the high priest of Christendom, and the German bishoprics were bound closer to the Papacy than ever before. Leo demanded that each of the archbishops should appear personally in Rome at least every third year, and regular reports were required from the monasteries. Yet even now some of the clergy resented the papal interference. In Leo's very presence the Archbishop of Mainz refused to end the mass because the Pope had criticised the singing and ordered the removal of one of his deacons. The Bishop of Frisingen had a grievance so serious that he would rather, he said, have his own throat cut than that Leo should remain in office.

This Pope inquired too closely into the matter of episcopal elections, although no one could as yet have been conscious whither such interference was to lead, for with the autocratic Henry III. he remained on the best of terms. The emperor was so completely master of the situation that when Leo died, in 1054, he kept the matter of a successor open for months, and then appointed another of his own relatives, Victor II.

Emancipation of the Papacy from German influence.
It seemed, indeed, as though the imperial supremacy were safely and lastingly established; yet soon a shadow fell over the house of Franconia that changed all things, gave the clergy and nobles a chance for independence, and allowed the Papacy not only to emancipate itself, but to claim jurisdiction over wide stretches of German land. Henry III. died suddenly in the prime of life, leaving a child as heir, with no strong member of the family, but only a weak woman, to act as guardian.

The very next Pope was chosen hastily without regard to German interests; the election was not even announced to the Empress Agnes until months had passed. At the Roman court there began to be mutterings against all interference of laymen in ecclesiastical affairs. Humbert, one of Pope Stephen's cardinals, ventured to say plainly that lay investiture was a species of simony, that the ring and the staff were spiritual, not secular symbols, and that no one appointed by a king was a real bishop, while the idea of a woman interfering in such matters was simply preposterous.

On the death of Stephen, in 1058, the right of the German regent to nominate a pope was acknowledged again, but only because the reform party was in desperate straits, the Roman nobles having revolted and set up a pope of their own. The whole was a clever move on the part of the monk Hildebrand, who now makes his entry on the stage on which he is so long to be the principal figure, and who succeeded in gaining the acceptance of his own candidate. That the tendency of his party was toward emancipation from the German yoke is shown by the famous decree concerning papal elections that was passed in a synod at Rome in 1059. The cardinals and clergy of the city were to form the whole conclave; laymen were to play no part. Matters were not yet ripe for an absolute denial of the rights so recently accorded to the emperor, but the wording was so ambiguous, the recognition so half-hearted, that the clause was capable of almost any interpretation. Moreover, scant as the concessions were, they were only incorporated in that version of the document that was intended for German eyes; we have a papal rendering, the one designed for Europe at large, in which they are absolutely lacking.

As yet the Papacy had the strength of its convictions; it had prestige, but it had no great resources, no powerful ally in arms. In Hildebrand's mind, however, there was forming the idea of a bold alliance. A generation earlier, brave Norman knights returning from the Holy Land had taken service with the Lombard princes against the Greeks and Saracens in Apulia. On the strength of their representations as to the wealth and agreeableness of the land, Norman settlers had come to Italy in great numbers, and a career of conquest had been inaugurated which reached its climax when the blue-eyed, fair-haired giant, Robert Guiscard, became master of Calabria. It is true these Normans had been the bitterest enemies of the Papacy, and had even taken prisoner in battle the august person of Leo IX. But Hildebrand, in 1058 A.D., journeyed to meet and make friends with Count Richard of Aversa, who lent him three hundred fighters to help him batter down the castles of recalcitrant Roman nobles. In the following year Pope Nicholas II. himself, in the presence of Hildebrand and Cardinal Humbert, interviewed Richard and Robert, and solemnly invested the former with Aversa, the latter with Apulia, Calabria, and Sicily. These were lands that by no stretch of the imagination could be held to belong to the Papacy; yet, in return for his inexpensive

The Normans as allies of the Papacy

gift, Nicholas was allowed to dispose of the whole military force of the Normans, they taking oath to uphold his honor and the rights and possessions of St. Peter.

In Milan at this time a revolutionary party had come to the fore, desirous of civic power, but wise enough to write upon their shields the watchword of reform, and to choose for their special objects of attack the married priests and simonistic clergy. The allies of the Papacy were increasing in number. Hildebrand went to Milan as papal legate and gave his hearty support to this "Pataria," or rag-mob; they, in turn, proved a counterpoise to the power of the archbishop, who, as his appointment came from the German court, adhered to the imperial party.

Capture of the young king, Henry IV.

In Germany, during all this time, there was discord instead of the much needed unity. Early in 1061 a party among the bishops met in a synod, renounced the Roman decree of 1059 concerning papal elections, condemned the person of the Pope, cancelled all his acts, and ordered that his name be wiped off the records of the church. On the death of Nicholas there resulted a schism; the Hildebrandine party chose Alexander II., the party of the empress, Honorius II. In the neighborhood of Rome there was fighting between the adherents of the two men; the cause of Honorius was in the ascendant, when events in Germany bereft him of nearly all his followers. The most radical, although the most bloodless, of revolutions had taken place. The heads of the discontented party, Archbishop Anno of Cologne, Bishop Gunther of Bamberg, the Margrave of Meissen, and others, having formed a plan to seize the young king's person, prepared a gayly decorated vessel and enticed him on board at Kaiserswerth. As the boat receded from the shore a deep gulf opened up between the old policy and the new; the young king, indeed, panic-stricken, leaped into the quick stream and was rescued with great difficulty, but in no other direction was there any resistance. The empress retired to a monastery; Henry himself came under the tutelage, first of Anno of Cologne, whose severity made him moody and morose, then under that of Adalbert of Bremen, who by ill-judged complaisance weakened his moral fibre.

To judge by his actions as a whole, Henry was a passionate and somewhat unsteady character, though able to arouse devotion in the lower classes. Probably never in the whole course of history have more opposing statements been made about one man. That he was the monster his enemies depict him is now no longer believed; still less can we trust the panegyrics that flowed from the pen of his devoted friends. Yet our sympathies may well go out to him, for never did ill-luck and failure more persistently dog a man's path; far out over the grave did the curse of the church pursue him, and for years even his dead bones could find no rest.

Character of Henry IV.

A dispute regarding the incumbent of the Milan archbishopric precipitated this most bitter of all conflicts, Hildebrand, of course, supporting the candidate of the Pataria. The matter was doubly important from the fact that the latter league now embraced many other of the north Italian cities. In the very year that this matter reached its climax the all-powerful monk ascended the pontifical throne, taking the name of Gregory in memory of the sixth pope of that name, whom he had once accompanied to Germany. One of the last acts of the dying pope, Alexander, had been to hurl the ban of the church against five of Henry's councillors. From the latter's point of view, no more ill-timed moment for a quarrel could possibly have been found, a revolt having broken out among his own Saxon nobles that threatened his liberty if not his life.

Beginning of the conflict with Gregory VII.

It was an old feud, this with the Saxons, due, it would seem, in the final instance, to a jealousy of the ruling house of Franconia. These proud people could never forget that during more than a century the rulers of Germany had been men of their own tribe. And this young Franconian came among them, they said, like a master among his slaves, refused to regrant their duchy to the old and popular line of Billung, and built mighty fortresses in the Harz Mountains the better to crush them down. Indeed, everywhere there had arisen walls, ramparts, and towers, ostensibly against the savage Wends. In one of these castles, the Harzburg, Henry was surrounded, and only escaped by letting himself down with a rope from the window and fleeing through the winter night. The struggle went through various stages, and the king's attitude to the Pope fluctuated accordingly. When at the lowest depths, with not an ally, Henry wrote a submissive letter, promising obedience in the Milan affair and the avoidance of intercourse with his excommunicated followers. " We have sinned against heaven and against thee," he tells Gregory, " and are no more worthy to be called thy son." His situation was indeed desperate ; the princes at large had been horrified at the disclosure of a pretended plot in which the king was concerned, to murder one of their number, Rudolf of Swabia. But the accuser, who was to have proved his case by the ordeal of battle, became a maniac before the day appointed. The Saxons, too, ruined their cause by the unhallowed vindictiveness with which they pillaged the royal tombs on the Harzburg, wantonly desecrating the bones of Henry's brother and of his infant son. The tide of feeling changed, many princes came back to their allegiance, the battle of Homburg on the Unstrut quelling the whole revolt.

This was the time that Gregory chose for one of his

most autocratic letters to the king, charging him with having failed to keep his promises of submission, and with continuing to practice simony and lay investiture in spite of the papal command — a command which, if obeyed, would have withdrawn the bishops from the royal obedience and made them independent heads of principalities within the confines of the empire. Exalted claims of Gregory VII.

It has been noted by one of Gregory's biographers that he knew no bounds where " justice " was concerned, and that his idea of justice often consisted in overthrowing the precedents of ages.   This was the Pope: a little pale man of fifty, but so eloquent that he caused his listeners to think that a heavenly spirit was speaking to them, who made St. Peter what he has since become for the whole Roman Catholic world — a lord and emperor second only to God Himself.   And he, Gregory, as St. Peter's vicar, claimed all the honor and obedience that was due to the apostle, claimed that the bishops of Christendom should obey his will without questioning, and that in the moment of disobedience all allegiance of their flocks should cease.   And if the clergy, how much more the laity !   He, the Pope, is the ultimate ruler; a king who acts counter to his decrees is no longer king.   Compared to apostolic prerogatives, he declares, all royal power is but ashes and spray.   The founders of kingship were tyrants who, driven on by the devil in blind lust and insupportable presumption, strove to raise themselves above their equals.   The foundation of the priesthood, on the other hand, rests on the providence of Almighty God; for His own glory he has created it; in His mercy He has given it to the world; its head is Christ, and the least of its members is greater than the mightiest ruler.

Gregory's letter of December, 1075, has been designated as the ultimatum of the Papacy; on the manner of its re- Deposition of Gregory VII.

ception depended war or peace. Henry chose the former.
He hastily summoned a council of bishops to Worms,
where, amid feverish excitement, judgment was passed on
the head of the church. "Since thou hast defiled thy life
and conversation with such manifold infamy," they wrote
to Gregory, "we renounce the obedience which we never
promised to thee, and which we shall not in future at all
observe." Henry's language was even more violent; he
calls himself "king not through usurpation, but through
the holy ordination of God," and speaks of Gregory as
"Hildebrand, at present not pope but false monk." "As
if we," he cries, "had received our kingdom from thee; as
if the kingdom and the empire were in thine and not in
God's hand!" He traces the steps by which the Pope has
ascended the throne of peace, by perfidy, bribery, favor,
and the sword, and bids him descend and relinquish his
usurped eminence: "I, Henry, king by the grace of God,
together with all our bishops, do say to thee, Descend,
descend, unto everlasting damnation!" The king's fatal
mistake was that he did not emphasize his words by
appearing with an army in Italy.

Anathema-
tizing of
Henry IV.
Gregory for his part could find no more fitting form in
which to express his horror and abomination than a vehement address to the apostle Peter himself: "Hear thy
servant," he prays, "whom thou hast nourished from
infancy"; "the wicked hate me," he continues, "for my
faithfulness to thee." He is sure that by St. Peter's own
wish and favor the power has been bestowed upon him of
binding and loosing in heaven and on earth": "through
thy power and authority, in the name of Almighty God,
Father, Son, and Holy Ghost, I withdraw from Henry the
king, son of Henry the emperor, who has risen against
thy church with unheard-of insolence, the rule over the
whole kingdom of the Germans, and over Italy!" He

absolves all Christians from their oath of fealty and forbids any one to serve Henry as king. By the token of this anathema the world is to know beyond the shadow of a doubt that " thou art Peter, and upon this rock the Son of the living God hath built His church, and the gates of Hell shall not prevail against it!"

For the first time the regenerated Papacy had rallied its full forces; for the first time its vaunted absolutism was pitted against the sovereignty of a great throne. Nor did Gregory rely on the power of the ban alone; he cast out his nets among the discontented bishops and princes of which Germany was full, and drew in a rich haul. He sent an open letter to all the upholders of the faith, reviewing the course of the quarrel from the beginning, justifying his own acts and appealing for aid. When Henry attempted to call a national council at Worms, he found that the general defection was becoming alarming, and that many of those who had been most violent against the Pope were now listening to his overtures.

The Saxon rebellion was fanned into new flame; a number of South German princes began to form a threatening alliance and to talk of electing a rival king; the bishops, having to choose between the power which had raised them to what they were and the princes whose equals they had become, declared for the latter. Henry had taken up his position at Oppenheim, separated by the Rhine from the arbiters of his fate. He was ready for any humiliation, and daily sent envoys begging his enemies to name their conditions, but to leave him the royal title and insignia. He would better his mode of life, he would answer to the princes, if need be, for every act of government. Not a manly attitude, but the needs of the moment were great.

The ultimatum of the princes was severe enough, but

Ultimatum of the German princes to Henry.

stopped short of deposition. They declared that the throne would be forfeit in case within a year and a day Henry should have failed to obtain the papal absolution. The Pope was to be invited to come to Augsburg and discuss affairs with the princes — in other words, in the heart of his own dominions to sit in judgment on the king! Henry in the meantime was to take up his abode in Spires, to refrain from all public acts, and to abandon the citizens of Worms, who had furnished his chief support.

Henry's determination to seek the Pope's pardon.

Like a criminal under pledge of good conduct, Henry lived in Spires, avoiding all intercourse with the world and deprived of all the consolations of religion. But in quiet he had taken his measures : above all it was necessary to sunder the union of the Pope and the princes ; this meeting in Augsburg meant lasting degradation for German kingship. It must not, it should not, take place. The first step was for Henry to obtain for himself, at any cost, the papal absolution. This could be done by appealing, as it were, from the Pope as ally of the princes to the Pope as high priest of the Christian religion. The whole teaching of the church required that a sinner who turned and repented should have pardon, and the outward form of repentance was sufficient for the simple and literal mind of that day. An age that insisted upon the actual shedding of tears and on actual corporal prostration when humility was in order, or on refusal and modest flight behind the altar in the case of elevation to a church office, was not going to be too severe on a king ready to kneel in sackcloth and ashes, or to stand barefoot in the winter snows.

Henry sent an envoy to Rome to announce that he was coming as a penitent. Gregory pretended to doubt his sincerity, and started on his journey to Augsburg. In Mantua, however, he was met by the news that the king had

already crossed the Alps. The Pope retraced his steps
and took refuge in the castle of Countess Matilda of Tuscany — that pillar of the church who signed herself in life
" Matilda, if anything, then so by the grace of God," but
whose tomb stands in St. Peter's, among those of the
popes, with the proud inscription, " Champion of the
Apostolic See."

The scene that now took place in Canossa is one that
must appeal strongly to the imagination even at a distance of centuries : the high precipitous hill guarded by
its triple wall and surmounted by a palace, a church, and
a monastery ; the blue peaks of the Apennines in the distance ; the snow-covered landscape ; the king in penitential
garb and bare feet standing before the rigidly closed door.
The mental struggle that went on, indeed, was rather in
the mind of Gregory than of Henry. The Countess Matilda
and also the Abbot of Cluny beset him with tearful entreaties and implored him to relent. He attempted at
first to make the condition that Henry should renounce
the royal crown and name ; he remained obdurate for three
long days, on each of which the king presented himself
with woful mien. At last the demands even of inexorable
justice seemed to have been fulfilled, and the head of Christendom gave way. Beyond a doubt his political triumph
would have been greater could he have sat in the midst
of the princes at Augsburg and taken his revenge for the
day of Sutri ; but this Henry had forestalled. Through
the mediation of the Countess Matilda, Henry signed certain general agreements relative to the German princes ;
then the gate of Canossa was thrown open, and the king
entered, accompanied by his excommunicated councillors,
who were included in the amnesty. All the penitents
threw themselves weeping on the ground ; the spectators
too were melted to tears and Gregory's own eyes moist-

The days at
Canossa.

ened. The absolution was administered in due form, the Eucharist partaken of, and the apostolic blessing crowned the work of peace. Henry rode away a humble victor, but none the less victorious because of his humility.

Renewal of the ban. The cause of the church had now been separated from that of the rebellious princes, but the latter were more fiercely hostile than before. They raised up a rival king in the person of Rudolph of Swabia, who expressly renounced the right of investing bishops for which Henry had always fought. But even this did not at once win Gregory; for three years he maintained neutrality, summoning both kings to appear before him. He seems really to have longed for peace, for the German church was coming into sore straits. Only when he found that he could not be arbiter, that his whole influence, indeed, rested on his being a partisan, did he once more take sides. There was no doubt as to how to choose; Henry had paid no attention to his measures against lay investiture, but had calmly annulled elections and publicly invested whom he pleased. Rudolph had been more pliant; his army, too, had just won a victory over that of Henry at Flarcheim. A renewal of the decree against investiture, in 1080, was followed by a second hurling of the ban. Once more St. Peter is bidden to incline his ears to a whole list of the enormities of this " Henry whom they call king," who " did raise his heel against thy church and strive, by casting me down, to subjugate it." His crime is disobedience, " which is the crime of idolatry." In the apostle's name the power and dignity of kingship is granted to Rudolph for his humility, obedience, and truthfulness. More clearly than ever does Gregory in this prayer show that his aim is universal rule. The world is to know that if ye (Peter and Paul) can bind and loose in heaven, " so ye can on earth take away empires, kingdoms, principalities, duchies, margravates, counties, and all possessions of men, and grant them to any man ye please according to his merits."

But Gregory was claiming too much; even among good, pious, and churchly men there were many who would not follow him in this theory of St. Peter's omnipotence. The second ban harmed nobody but its promulgator; few could see that the king had in any way deserved such severity. "Nobody," writes the papal-minded Gebhard of Salzburg, "considers us worth listening to." Nineteen bishops, assembled at Mainz, threw all the blame of the civil war on Gregory. A synod at Brixen not only declared him deposed, but even appointed his successor, Clement III.

Gregory's straits.

All Gregory's efforts to raise up allies were in vain. William the Conqueror of England, once strongly under papal influence, would not interfere. Robert Guiscard was hastily loosed from the ban that his depredations upon holy property had brought down upon him, but even then could give no assistance. Rudolph of Swabia was slain in battle. Henry, unmolested, could lead his Pope in triumph to the very gates of Rome. Entry was, indeed, a different matter; not for three years was it successfully accomplished. Gregory then took refuge in the castle of St. Angelo, and when Henry demanded the imperial crown he refused to give it until the king should do penance and be loosed from the ban. When the nobles urged the Pope to the contrary he is said to have offered to let down the crown by a string from the castle wall if Henry would dispense with the consecration! He was completely at bay. "Help!" he wrote in an encyclic letter, "lend support to your father and mother, as you hope through them to achieve forgiveness of sins, blessing, and grace in this world and the world to come!"

The Roman nobles, at last worn out by Gregory's obdurateness, and experiencing more harm than good from his

Death of Gregory VII.

ally, Robert Guiscard, determined to abandon him and allow Henry to enter the city. The proud judge of Canossa, the man who had considered himself second in rank to none but St. Peter, was now deposed by a Roman synod: Clement III. was acknowledged pope, and on Easter Day, 1084 A.D., crowned Henry and his queen with the imperial crown. Gregory fled to Salerno, but his race was run. For the fifth time he reiterated the ban against Henry: with the hand of death already upon him he refused him absolution — that, he said, should only be granted to those who believed that in him, Gregory, as rightful Pope, was vested the power of the apostles, Peter and Paul. "I have loved justice and hated iniquity, therefore I die in exile," were his last recorded words.

The death of Gregory did not bring peace either in Italy or in Germany. His party chose first Victor III., who shortly died, and then Urban II., the inspirer of the crusades. The polemical writings of the next few years outnumber and outvie in bitterness those that had gone before: the old antagonism of view seemed only to have deepened and broadened. Is the Pope really above the emperor even in secular matters? Are the bishops more subject to their temporal or to their spiritual head? In many, if not the majority, of German sees there were rival incumbents: many refused intercourse with those anathematized by Gregory.

The Countess Matilda.

The rallying-point for all the discordant elements in Italy was the Countess Matilda of Tuscany. From purely political motives, and at the instigation of Pope Urban, she now married the son of Guelph of Bavaria, Henry's bitter enemy. The countess was forty, the bridegroom seventeen, and the union was never consummated; the only bond was the common determination to drive Henry from his throne. They corrupted the young Prince Conrad, caused him to rise against his father and to receive independently the crown of Italy. There was nothing this woman would have left undone to further the interests of the Papacy. When she died she left to it all her lands, though many of them were fiefs of the empire, thus starting a new conflict that went on for a century.

Henry's chief foes henceforward were they of his own household. At that council of Piacenza that first broached the subject of a crusade his wife appeared, instigated it is said by Matilda, and made most loathsome charges. Soon after, the second son, Henry, who had been declared heir to the throne after Conrad's defection, left the camp by night and joined his father's enemies. The climax was reached when this same prince, pretending to seek a reconciliation and offering to escort the emperor to a diet, decoyed him instead to a castle near Bingen and kept him like a common prisoner. Discouragement and discomfort did their work; utterly broken, Henry agreed to abdicate and to surrender the insignia of empire. He asked for absolution from the ban and confessed to a papal legate that from first to last he had sinned against the Roman church. The comfort he received was but cold; only in Rome, the legate said, could the sentence be reversed.

Wretched ending of Henry IV.

The young Henry V. was now recognized as king by the Diet of Mainz, and an embassy was despatched to Rome to invite the Pope to Germany. Henry IV. made a last attempt to regain his throne, but died in the endeavor; twice his body was dug up by order of the church before it found rest in an unconsecrated chapel near Spires; not for five years did Rome remove her curse. To such extremities had the struggle for the investiture reduced the head of the empire.

As for Henry V. it remained to be seen how he would act when confronted with the problems that had troubled

Henry V. and Paschal II.

his father. He had been called to the throne by that
father's enemies, and with the understanding that he
should reverse the former policy. Yet this question of
investiture could not be thrust aside; like the trail of
a serpent, it poisoned everything. It was as impossible
for Henry V. to give up inalienable rights as it had been
for Henry IV.; he too became involved in a long struggle
with the Papacy, which had once more vehemently proclaimed that the clergy disgraced their calling when as
vassals they laid their consecrated hands in the blood-
stained hand of a layman.

In the year 1111 Henry crossed the Alps and approached Rome with an immense army. He had sent
envoys to tell of his willingness to treat on the old subject
and to demand the imperial crown. They arrived at a
time when Pope Paschal II. was almost friendless; he
had looked around for the traditional allies of the Papacy,
but the Normans were enjoying the excitement of the
crusades, and could not respond to his call. It was under
these circumstances that Paschal proposed the most
remarkable, the most startling, solution of the difficulty
that had ever yet been evolved. The church was to
return to the Arcadian simplicity of its early days; the
bishops were to give up their principalities, fiefs, and
jurisdictions, and the empire to take back all the lands
and rights which, since the time of Charlemagne, had
come into the hands of the clergy. The latter were to
content themselves with tithes and pious offerings; but, on
the other hand, their nomination, election, and investiture
were to be entirely free. To give splendor and emphasis
to the occasion, both acts, the renunciation and the imperial coronation, were to take place on one and the same
day.

Once more this struggle for the investiture gave rise

to a never-to-be-forgotten scene — a scene that wiped out, indeed, that shameful humiliation at Canossa. On the day appointed, Henry entered St. Peter's magnificently escorted. He was determined that the odium of what was about to happen should fall on the Pope, and declared that for his own part he had no wish to rob either bishops or abbots. Then Paschal read the church's renunciation, and a tumult arose, fiery, unquenchable. The Pope, in the very citadel of the apostle, was loudly accused of heresy and other crimes. Not one of the clergy, it seemed, was willing to give up his imperial fiefs. The king grew impatient at the long delay, declared that the Pope had broken his compact, and demanded back the full and free right of investiture as enjoyed by his forefathers. The penalty of refusal was a bitter one for the successor of a Gregory VII. — nothing short, indeed, of the arrest and carrying off of Paschal and his cardinals. They were taken for safety to a neighboring hospice, and, in the midst of heavy fighting, were finally removed from the city.

Capture of the Pope and cardinals.

For weeks this captivity lasted, and the poor pontiff's soul was racked by news of anarchy in Rome and by fears of a fresh schism. When flesh and blood could no longer stand it, he at last gave way, renouncing, without equivalent, everything the king demanded, especially that right in defence of which Gregory VII. and Urban II. had filled all Europe with war and tumult. In the camp before Rome, on April 12, 1111 A.D., a document to this effect was placed in Henry's hands, and on the day following the coronation ceremony was performed. With hostages in his train the emperor withdrew triumphant.

Was this the solution of the long war? Could any one for a moment have believed that the Papacy would continue grovelling in the dust? The wonder is, not that the Pope and the Gallic clergy should have repudiated

Paschal repudiates his concessions.

these forced concessions, but that a year should have elapsed before they did so; then, indeed, the anathema was hurled with all force at this Henry, this second Judas, who, by treachery, perjury, and desecration had forced Paschal to sign the deed.

Thus again the question of the investiture became the centre of a fierce conflict; again, too, Germany was ravaged by enemies who tried to dethrone the emperor. A chronicler assures us that men raged against each other with bestial delight, that the clergy could scarcely count on their bare lives, that fields lay waste and villages in ruins, that churches had ceased to celebrate the service of the mass.

It was indeed high time for a settlement; a new anti-pope had been elected under Henry's auspices and new schism introduced into all the bishoprics. For a moment it seemed as if peace might be achieved at the Council of Rheims in 1119, but the new Gregorian pope, Calixtus II., was seized with a panic after the treaty of peace had actually been drawn up, and the council ended with a more formal promulgation than ever of the ban against Henry and his Pope. Hundreds of candles were lighted and simultaneously extinguished, symbolic of the thrusting into perpetual darkness of the wretch who was burdened with the awful curse of Rome.

The Concordat of Worms, 1122 A.D. In Germany the war dragged slowly on, but ever since that eventful proposition of Paschal II. there had been germinating an idea that was now at last to bear fruit. Was it not possible, after all, to render unto Cæsar the things which were Cæsar's and unto God the things that were God's? The cloud lifted on the eve of what promised to be a bloody battle, and after much negotiation there resulted what is known as the famous Concordat of Worms.

There were to be two investitures : one on the part of the emperor with the sceptre as the symbol of temporal power, the other on the part of the Pope with the pastoral staff and ring.   Elections were to be held in the presence of the emperor, and in Germany proper the function in which he was especially interested was to precede the ecclesiastical act.   In Italy and Burgundy the order was to be reversed.

Where lay the victory?   It would be hard to say. Calixtus indeed was proud of his work, and caused the text of the document to be placed as an inscription in one of the apartments of the Vatican.   The world at large gave way to unbounded rejoicing that the long and desperate struggle was over.

In the Rhine meadows near Worms, in the presence of a crowd so great that the city had been found incapable of containing it, the reconciliation of state and church after their war of fifty years was concluded in all form.   The papal legate publicly extended to the emperor the kiss of peace, the ban was loosed, and the body and blood of Christ partaken of in common.   The old contentions were laid aside, but the future was to show whether or not there was room in Europe for two claimants to world rule.

CHAPTER IV

THE POPES AND THE HOHENSTAUFENS

LITERATURE : For the relations of Frederick Barbarossa with Popes Adrian IV. and Alexander III., see Henderson, *Select Documents.* For treatment of whole period, see Henderson, *History of Germany in the Middle Ages,* — founded mainly on the Jahrbücher, — which contains also a bibliography. Prutz, Toeche, Winkelmann, and Schirrmacher are the main authorities.

Lothar and Innocent II. " THE king comes before the gates, first swearing due honor to the city. He then is made the vassal of the Pope, and takes the crown which he bestows." Such was the inscription under a painting in the audience hall of the Lateran in which King Lothar, Henry V.'s successor, was represented as kneeling before Pope Innocent II. The special occasion was doubtless the investiture with the estates of the Countess Matilda, which this Saxon king was weak enough to accept as a fief, after claiming them in full ownership. He was to pay for their use a hundred pounds of silver.

Lothar could never have gone so far as this motto implies ; but he was too yielding, too fond of a compromise. He and the Pope were vastly afraid of offending each other and thus reopening the old conflict, an attitude for which the German nation on the whole was grateful. "He left behind him such a memory of his time," writes the annalist of *Pöhlde*, " as will be blest until the end of the world," while we know from another source that " quiet and abundance prevailed, and peace between church and state." So far did this complaisant spirit go, that Lothar at Liège

76

performed the service of marshal for Innocent, leading his horse by the bridle after holding the stirrup for him to mount. When a question arose as to the feudal ownership of Apulia, which was to be conferred on Rainulf of Alife, — the Pope held the point, the emperor the shaft, of the banner of investiture!

Lothar's title at home was disputed by one of that house of Hohenstaufen that was to play such a brilliant and tragic rôle for more than a century; for his own part he formed an alliance by marriage with the Guelphs of Bavaria, thus inaugurating the unhallowed struggle of Guelph and Ghibelline — just why the Hohenstaufen were so called is not known — which in a different form was to be fought out in the cities of Italy. As a rule Ghibelline came to mean imperial and Guelph papal, though there were times when the two terms denoted little more than blind, malignant opposition. At Lothar's death in 1137, the Guelph, Henry the Proud of Bavaria, was pitted against Conrad of Hohenstaufen, and, though the latter was the choice of the princes, a bitter struggle ensued, which did not end on the death of the rival candidate, but was continued with various fortunes for nearly ten years.

Guelph and Ghibelline.

In the midst of these dissensions and mishaps the news came that Edessa, the stronghold of the Christians in Syria, had fallen. St. Bernard of Clairvaux appeared in person before Conrad, and, after several attempts to make the king take the cross, was at last successful. On the feast of St. John, 1146 A.D., the monk rose up in the cathedral at Spires and gave vent to a burst of overwhelming eloquence. Conrad was moved to tears and declared that the Lord Himself had spoken. Delighted with his success, Bernard seized the standard from the altar and bestowed it on the king as leader of the crusading hosts. But of all the great expeditions none ended more wretchedly than this second

The second crusade.

crusade. Jealousy, treachery, and disaster dogged Conrad's steps, and when, sick at heart, he returned to Germany, it was only to become involved in new struggles with the Guelphs.

The *Decretum Gratiani*.

The Papacy, too, had suffered greatly in prestige by the failure of the crusade it had inaugurated, but it did not cease to put forward new claims and pretensions. Toward the end of Conrad's reign these claims found a lasting form in a collection of canon law, the *Decretum Gratiani*, which was to control the life of the church for centuries. It is full of sentences from that famous forgery of the ninth century attributed to Isidore of Seville; it rings with assumptions of papal omnipotence. And more and more the popes were striving to become the first princes as well as the first bishops of Christendom. They commenced to surround themselves with retinues of nobles as well as of clergy, and the imperial diadem with which Hildebrand had crowned Nicholas II. was now regularly worn with the mitre. It professed to be the crown of Constantine.

Accession of Frederick Barbarossa.

It was well for Germany that a brilliant and determined man now came to the throne. The empire was to succumb in the end to the Papacy, but it would have succumbed miserably and weakly had it not been for Frederick Barbarossa. To him it is due that the war of the popes and Hohenstaufens became a war of gods and Titans. Around his name cluster some of the most glorious traditions of German history.

Inextricably interwoven with Frederick's struggles with the Papacy are his dealings with the cities of northern Italy. Ever since Charlemagne conquered and Otto the Great recovered Lombardy, the Germans had maintained their claims to sovereignty. Those claims were now to be enforced and legalized, but the free communes that had grown up since then were to prove very different antagonists from the

Berengars and Lamberts of earlier times. The citizens, whose houses were actual castles, had drawn into their own hands all the jurisdictions, tolls, and revenues, had conquered stretches of surrounding territory, and were on the alert for further conquests at the expense of smaller towns.

Frederick, at the time of his election, was thirty years of age, small, fair-complexioned, with reddish hair and beard. Endowed by nature with great capacities, he was likewise extremely ambitious. On the very day after the election he informed Pope Eugene III. of his intention to restore to its pristine glory the empire " bestowed upon him by God." By God, not by man. He promised love and respect for the Pope's person, but, unlike his predecessors, demanded neither sanction nor confirmation. Difficulties began almost at once with the important city of Milan. Frederick had sent a letter ordering the inhabitants to cease their persecution of the little towns of Lodi and Como, but the missive had been received with scorn and the royal seal trampled under foot. In the autumn of 1154 the king crossed the Alps and mustered his army in the Roncaglian fields near Piacenza. All of the Lombard cities, Milan included, seem to have taken the oath of allegiance, and gifts were sent from all quarters — ostriches, parrots, lions, and rare silks. But treacherous conduct was discovered on the part of the Milanese consuls, and the ban of the empire was spoken over the devoted city.

Frederick Barbarossa and Milan.

The first duty, however, seemed to be to march to Rome and secure the imperial coronation, which had been promised by Pope Adrian IV. On the way the disobedient city of Tortona was levelled to the ground. Adrian advanced to Sutri, but a disagreement at once arose because of the king's refusal to hold the stirrup for the Pope, who had ridden up to the royal tent. Either this holding of the stirrup, or else no kiss of peace! Adrian withdrew in

Adrian and Frederick

anger. The question was hotly discussed, and several car
dinals followed their master; but, finding that the papal
claim was grounded in precedent, Frederick yielded. On
reaching Rome he showed his devotion to the Pope by
seizing his enemy, Arnold of Brescia. The coronation
day ended, indeed, in a bloody tumult, and eight hundred
Romans are said to have fallen.

Submission
of Milan.

The negotiations with Milan went on for some years,
but at last, in 1158, Frederick recrossed the Alps with one
of the largest armies that ever a head of the Holy Roman
Empire had led into Italy. Now came a sad time of reckoning for the valiant commune. The conditions of pardon
were hard: the rebuilding of Como and Lodi, an oath of
allegiance, a fine, the right of the emperor to maintain a
castle within the city walls and to appoint the consuls or
rulers, finally the delivery of three hundred hostages, fifty of
whom were to be taken to Germany. The submission was
made with all the dramatic formalities customary in the
Middle Ages. The twelve consuls of the city humbled themselves before the emperor, who awaited them in his camp,
seated on his throne. They approached barefoot, with
ropes around their necks, through two long lines of German
soldiery, and delivered up their swords to symbolize the
surrender of all the weapons in Milan. The humiliating
ordeal ended with the unfurling of the imperial banner
from the top of the cathedral.

The Italian
com-
munes.

This war with the Italian cities was a conflict of two
utterly incongruous principles : the liberalism of communities which, long left to themselves, had wrought out their
own prosperity, and an imperialism that had begun to claim
its root in the old traditions of Rome. On the one hand
the golden lion of Durazzo, on the other the code of Justinian. The Archbishop of Milan himself, after the submission of the city, addressed Frederick as follows : " Know

that all the right of the people to make laws has been vested
in thee. Thy will is law, according to the saying. 'What
pleases the prince has the vigor of law.'" Yet how little,
in reality, did the precepts of the sixth suit the needs of
the twelfth century!

Frederick had clearly recognized the value to himself The *regalia*
of the renaissance in Roman Law that was taking place at or royal
Bologna; he now enlisted the services of a number of rights.
doctors of the new university and set them to formulating
the imperial rights, or *regalia*, in Italy. He began with the
communes, but he intended afterward, in a similar manner,
to adjust his relations to the Normans and the Papacy. His
commission reported that the throne might justly claim the
tolls and taxes from public roads, rivers, and harbors; the
product of mines, salt works, and the like; the estates of
felons, and the half of treasure trove. The emperor might
call in an emergency for horses, transport wagons, or ships,
and even levy an extraordinary war tax. He was to have
the right of building his own palaces in cities where such
had formerly stood, and, finally, of appointing the chief
civic magistrates.

Thus armed with the majesty of the law, Frederick set Annihila-
about his task of making northern Italy submit to leading tion of
strings; his officials collected revenue to the amount of Milan.
some million marks; everywhere he set up his own *podestàs*
in opposition to the local authorities. Disaffection at once
became rife; Genoa maintained that she had grown rich
from her shipping and not from her imperial fiefs, and,
although the claim was moderated, took care to strengthen
her fortifications. Crema had to submit to one of the most
terrible sieges in history, a single incident of which will
here suffice. Frederick caused a movable tower, the advance of which had been checked, to be literally festooned
with the persons of hostages and captives, who were let

down in baskets and thus exposed to the missiles of their own friends. There was no faltering; almost all were killed, and the city itself was eventually given over to pillage and flame.

But the fate of Milan was hardest of all. The people refused to accept the emperor's new officials because the treaty of 1158 had expressly permitted the Milanese to have their own consuls. Frederick maintained that the new Roncaglian decrees had abrogated all old agreements. He laid waste the fields and vineyards and cut off every avenue of supply; the crowded city could at last hold out no longer and sent eight of its consuls to surrender the keys and the tokens of their own dignity. Never were people more thoroughly humbled and abased; hundreds of the proudest nobles were made to approach in the pouring rain, barefooted, with ashes strewn upon their heads, and to kiss the emperor's feet and cry for mercy. The mast of the sacred *caroccio*, the last rallying point in all battles, was lowered before him, and the city's banner removed. All the standards of the army were given over. Frederick and his princes decreed that the city should be blotted from the face of the earth, that within a week the inhabitants must withdraw to four appointed spots in the vicinity, there to make new settlements. In the ruins, Lodi, Como, and Cremona, bitter enemies of old, were allowed to riot at will. "A second Troy has perished," writes Godfrey of Viterbo; while Frederick in his triumph signs his public documents, "Roman Emperor, crowned of God, great and peace-bringing; glorious Triumpher and continual Increaser of the Empire."

Frederick
Barbarossa
and
Adrian IV.

From a German point of view the question of the Lombard cities seemed happily and finally settled; the emperor's officials ruled absolutely, showing themselves, indeed, tyrannical and oppressive, and, above all, extortionate. Frederick himself was too busy, during these years, in asserting his position regarding the Papacy, to look too closely into administrative matters.

With Adrian IV., the only Englishman who ever sat on the throne of Peter, a trivial incident had reopened the old quarrels. In a letter regarding the capture of a bishop by a highwayman, whom Frederick had taken no steps to punish, Adrian casually spoke of the empire as a "benefice" which he had seen fit to "confer" on the emperor. In his answering manifesto the latter tells how the papal envoys, "as if inflated with the mammon of unrighteousness, out of the height of their pride, from the summit of their arrogance, in the execrable elation of their swelling hearts, did present to us a message in the form of an apostolic letter, the tenor of which was that we should always keep it before our mind's eye how the lord Pope had *conferred* upon us the distinction of the imperial crown, and that he would not regret it if our Highness were to receive from him even greater *benefices*." After some more mockery and invective against this "message of paternal sweetness," Frederick goes on to give an eloquent assertion of his own theory of the imperial power. It is his by election of the princes and from God alone; it is one of the two necessary swords to which Christ subjected the world; did not St. Peter himself say, "Fear God, honor the king"? The Pope's assumption is a lie; the honor of the empire has remained glorious and undiminished *since the founding of Rome and the establishment of the Christian religion*, and this emperor wishes it known beyond the shadow of a doubt that he would rather incur danger of death than submit to shame and disaster. In his letter to the Pope the incident of the picture in which the Emperor Lothar figured as a vassal was not forgotten. The Pope was fain in the end to explain away his objectionable utterance by means of a convenient sophistry. By *beneficium* he had not meant the technical feudal term for *benefice*, but simply a benefit — and surely a pope was conferring a benefit on an emperor by crowning him !

It may be that, after all, Adrian's breaches of etiquette were due to his being a blunt Briton ; for he soon committed another offence that was taken almost equally ill, by addressing the emperor in the second person singular and putting his own name before that of Frederick. Still again he roused the imperial ire by sending a personal letter through the hand of a minor official. Relations were decidedly strained at the time of the Pope's death in 1159.

Alexander III. and the rival popes.

The choice of a successor seemed to be a challenge of the most outspoken kind. Alexander III. was not only a man known as a political opponent of the emperor, but as Chancellor Roland he had been the bearer of that very letter about *benefices* that had so angered Frederick. His whole manner on that occasion had been haughty and insolent. No wonder that Frederick almost hanged the envoys sent by Alexander to announce his accession, and that he took advantage of a schism among the cardinals to recognize another as pope. The synod of Pavia, of 1160 A.D., which was indeed nothing but an assembly of German and Lombard bishops, pretended to review the whole question of the election from the beginning, and declared for Victor IV. In his opening address, the emperor had vindicated his right to hold the council by appealing to the examples of Constantine, Theodosius, and Justinian, of Charlemagne and Otto the Great. After the fateful decision, he received Victor at the door of the cathedral, held the stirrup for him to dismount, and led him to the altar. The anathema was hurled at " Chancellor Roland " and the bishops who had consecrated him, and was naturally returned in kind.

Little could Frederick have known that this enemy

whom he thought to annihilate was a man of the stamp The oath of Würzburg.
of Gregory VII.; it was this same Alexander who later
humbled Henry II. of England in the matter of the murder of Thomas Becket. And the emperor's cause was
weakened still more by the death in 1164 of his own pope;
many who had supported Victor were not willing to acknowledge Paschal III. Yet Frederick and many of his
clergy and nobles took a solemn oath at Würzburg to fight
the fight to the bitter end, never to acknowledge Roland or
a pope chosen by his party. All that oaths can do this
oath was meant to accomplish: the Diet of Würzburg engaged in case of Frederick's death to elect no one who
would not renew it; the temporal and spiritual lords
promised to impose it on their vassals and to consider all
recusants as enemies of the empire.

This new Justinian was very sure of his cause. He took Conquest of Rome.
this occasion to glorify the empire by the canonization of
its founder, Charlemagne; the bones were raised from the
tomb and placed in a golden shrine. He might well have
occupied himself, as he was frequently implored to do, by
redressing the wrongs of the Lombard cities; but his main
idea was to reach Rome and strike at the heart of the
opposition. In July, 1167, he seemed at the goal of his
desires; after much fighting the Leonine city fell into his
hands, St. Angelo was besieged, Santa Maria in Torre set
fire to, and an entrance thus forced into the interior of St.
Peter's. After a skirmish in those holy halls themselves
the opposition ceased and the church of the chief of the
apostles was in the emperor's hands. Pope Paschal was
solemnly enthroned; Alexander escaped from the city.
The inhabitants agreed to abandon him, and the senate
took the oath of fealty.

Here was a triumph without equal, but it was followed Pestilence breaks out.
like a flash by the hardest blow of fate the emperor had

ever experienced — a blow that marks a turning-point in
his career. On the first day of August, amid general
rejoicing, he and his empress had worn their crowns in a
grand assembly at St. Peter's. On the day following the
weather changed; a violent thunderstorm was succeeded
by a deadly heat; the mists of the Campagna rose to battle
for Alexander. A pestilence broke out in the camp and
also in the city; death was wafted on every current of
air. The emperor hastened to reach the Tusculan hills, but
many of his soldiers were too ill to move; his losses were
simply enormous — a contemporary places them at twenty-
five thousand in a single week. High and low sank alike
beneath the scourge.

The people of the twelfth century saw in Frederick's
mishap nothing less than a judgment of God. Thomas
Becket, in one of his letters, breaks forth into a perfect
hymn of praise. He likens the emperor to Sennacherib,
who was struck down while opposing Hezekiah: "The
Lord has crushed the hammer of the godless, and, if they
do not come to their senses will shortly crush the rest"
(meaning his own king); John of Salisbury implies that
Frederick had better consider Italy a lost land.

The victory
of the
Lombard
League.

The time had at last come for the Lombard cities to
avenge the wrongs inflicted by the imperial officials.
During the five years that succeeded the terrible vengeance
of 1162, the sufferings of the banished Milanese had been
intense; a horrible burden of taxation had pressed the life
blood out of the wretched people. Every rod of land,
every hearth, every span of oxen, had to pay its inexorable
tribute; swine and poultry were requisitioned for the private tables of the officials. No wonder the annals of the
city name the record of taxable objects the "book of pain
and mourning"!

Already before Frederick reached Rome the bow had

stretched to breaking, and in quiet the beginnings had been made of the famous Lombard League. From the first it took sides with Alexander, but its most daring act of insubordination was the leading back of the Milanese to the scene of their former glory. All the cities lent a hand, and like magic the walls arose from their ruins; a bas-relief of the time, representing the happy return, is still to be seen.

As for the former conqueror, his position became desperate. An appeal was sent to Germany for reënforcements, but they were too late in coming. Attacks on Milan and on Piacenza failed, and at last, with few followers, he prepared to fly from Italy. At Susa he was shut in, and would have been taken, had not a faithful chamberlain counterfeited his person.

Frederick's desperate straits.

The Pope and the Lombard League continued to prepare for the final struggle that was sure to come; a new city was founded and strongly fortified. It was to be a common rallying place for all the forces, and was named Alessandria in honor of the Pope.

In the long interval that elapsed before Frederick's return strong efforts were made to bring about a reconciliation with the church. Frederick was bound by the Würzburg decrees, but he went so far as to send an envoy to Italy with the astounding proposition that he for his own person should recognize no Pope at all, "save Peter and the others in heaven," but that his son Henry, the young king of the Romans, should acknowledge Alexander and receive the imperial coronation.

Frederick's first act on entering Italy in 1174 was to wreak vengeance on Susa, which was soon a heap of ashes. But Alessandria, situated in a swampy plain and surrounded by massive earthen walls, proved an effectual stumbling-block. Heavy rains came to the rescue of the

The return to Italy and the battle of Legnano

city, and the imperial tents and huts were all but sub-merged. The besieger at last burnt his own battering rams and movable towers, and retreated to Pavian territory. On the failure of long negotiations he prepared for a decisive battle, and sent a strong appeal for aid to his most powerful vassal, Henry called the Lion, Duke of Saxony and Bavaria and brother-in-law of Richard Plantagenet. On the refusal of this mighty prince hung the fate of the campaign; no threats could move him, no entreaties availed. Frederick went into the battle of Legnano fore-doomed to defeat. He was wounded and thrown from his horse; his army mourned him as dead, but he finally reached Pavia after days of adventurous flight. Legnano was thoroughly decisive; by the advice of his nobles Frederick determined to abandon the policy he had pursued for so many years and to make his peace. This could be done to the greater advantage, inasmuch as the cities believed that reënforcements were surely on the way from Germany, and were, moreover, disunited among themselves. The treaty of Venice was far from being the dictate of a conquering power.

The peace of Venice. Many of its clauses were in the form of a compromise: a truce of six years with the Lombard cities, during which time a peace was to be arranged; a continuance on the emperor's part in the enjoyment of the revenues from the estates of Matilda for fifteen years, when it was hoped the differences would have been adjusted by commissioners; a truce with other allies of the Pope, such as the emperor of Constantinople and the king of Sicily. There were to be mutual recognitions of each other's dignities on the part of Pope and emperor.

The pageant at Venice. Now that the peace was to become an accomplished fact, all concerned united in arranging a worthy pageant; Venice and the emperor seem to have shared the expense.

When on Sunday, July 24, 1177, Frederick landed on the Lido, he was met by cardinals whom Alexander had sent to release him from the ban. The Doge, the patriarch of Grado, and a crowd of lesser dignitaries furnished a brilliant escort with their gondolas and barks. On the piazzetta the emblem of the lion of St. Mark's floated from tall masts, and a platform with a throne for the Pope had been erected at the door of the church. A dense crowd of all nationalities and of all ranks filled the square, to witness the outward and visible sign of an imperial surrender at discretion. No fitter setting for such a scene could have been found the whole world over, and Frederick, in spite of his small stature, must have played his part with becoming dignity. When he landed, his mantle of royal purple was still around him ; he threw it off as he advanced to the foot of the papal throne, then knelt on the ground before his old enemy and kissed his feet. The world looks to-day on the exact spot where this occurred, and three marble slabs have been placed to commemorate it. On the following day a friendly meeting was held and the conversation was amicable and gay.

The peace with the Lombard cities was duly arranged, and was signed at Constance in 1183. The emperor retained some show of sovereignty, but the real advantage was on the other side; the League was recognized as a lawful power, the consuls were to be chosen by the cities but invested by the crown; the ordinary revenues, jurisdictions, and right of fortification and defence were to remain with the towns. One characteristic episode ended the struggle of so many years: Frederick was determined that the city of Alessandria, so long from its very name a thorn in the flesh, should technically cease to exist. The demand was granted, and it was agreed that the name should be changed to Cæsarea in honor of the emperor himself. We

Settlement of difficulties.

still have the treaty which binds all the inhabitants to quit
the city and remain away until led back by an imperial
envoy.   Then all the males were to swear fidelity to Frederick and his son.

Crusade of
Frederick
Barbarossa.
Frederick's further relations with the popes were not
altogether smooth; and once his son, Henry VI., as king of
the Romans, led a regular plundering expedition through
the domains of Urban III., who in turn incited a small
rebellion in Germany.   But on the whole it may be said
that the questions at issue were unimportant, and Frederick finally showed his zeal for the church in the most convincing way.   At the Diet of Mainz, in 1188, in the midst
of wild excitement, he and his younger son took the cross,
while thousands of knights, following the example of their
gray-haired sovereign, also assumed the votive emblem.
On May 11, 1189, the crusading army started on its way;
on that day the crowds assembled at Ratisbon looked for
the last time on their beloved emperor.   In the river Sa-
leph, not far from Seleucia, he found his death while seeking refreshment in the cool waters after a hot day's march.
According to the legend so beloved in the fatherland, he
sits in the heart of the Kyffhäuser Mountain, waiting for
the time when his country shall need him.   Then, like a
second Messiah, he will come again.

Henry VI.
and Sicily.
With the marriage and accession of Henry VI., a new
and fatal element comes into the struggle for supremacy
between empire and Papacy.   His bride was Constance,
last descendent and heiress of the Norman kings.   Not
only did this marriage and the successful assertion of the
claim to Sicily greatly increase the resources of the Hohenstaufens, but the Papacy awoke to the fact that its own
possessions were now threatened as much from the South
as from the North, held fast, as it were, in a strong vise.
Whatever the special occasions of the quarrels that ensued,

this one never healing grievance must be kept in view.
We shall soon see the shadows deepen all along the line;
we shall see an almost comedy-like trifling of the heads of
Christendom give place to the dark episodes of the greatest of mediæval tragedies, as a climax to which royal blood
is shed on the scaffold, and the whole original structure of
the mediæval empire falls to the ground in a heap of ruins.

Henry VI. inherited his father's stature and cast of
countenance, his iron will, his power of forming grand
conceptions, and also his cruel severity; we hear of rebels
being skinned alive, crowned with redhot crowns, or
covered with pitch and ignited. Fortune more than once
stood him in good stead, as when the lion-hearted Richard
of England fell into his hands, and, by the magnitude of
his ransom, enabled him to carry out his plans for the
conquest of Sicily; yet in general his successes were due
to his own courage and perseverance. His scope of conquest was all-embracing; for the first time a German
emperor came forward in the Orient — to quote a Byzantine chronicler — as "lord of lords and king of kings."
The Emperor Alexius was reduced to such straits that he
had to impose the so-called "German tax" on all his
provinces — a measure so odious that it was repealed, and
an attempt made to raise money by confiscating the holy
utensils of the churches. As a last resort the tombs of
the Greek emperors were plundered and the bodies
stripped of their ornaments.

With the popes there were differences but, as yet, no
open break; indeed, at his imperial coronation in 1191,
Henry went so far as to kiss, as though making a cross, the
brow, mouth, chin, breast, and two cheeks of the aged
Celestine III. He had, indeed, to withstand a league of
the Pope, the Lombard cities, the Sicilians, and his own
empress Constance, and also, because of Celestine's opposi-

Character and achievements of Henry VI

tion, to renounce the projected coronation of his infant son. Henry died on the point of embarking on a great crusade, for which he had brought together some sixty thousand men ; but Celestine declared that, for taking captive a crusader, in the person of Richard of England, he had *ipso facto* incurred the ban, and long refused to have him buried in consecrated ground.

Philip, Otto IV., and Innocent III.   Frederick II., Henry's son, grew up in Palermo more of a Sicilian than a German. His uncle, Philip of Hohenstaufen, had intended to temporarily assume the German crown as his guardian ; but, in view of the troubled times, accepted it in his own right, becoming involved in a long war with a rival king, Otto IV., the son of the now humiliated Henry the Lion. To the papal throne there had come, in 1198, Innocent III., the worthy peer of Alexander III. He it was who later forced King John of England to pay a yearly tribute for his crown. For years he fed the flame of civil war in Germany, first turning the scale in favor of Otto, then promising to crown Philip, and finally, after Philip's murder by Otto of Wittelsbach, taking Otto IV. once more completely under his wing and teaching him, like a pedagogue, the art of ruling. "Do not be backward in making concessions," he writes, "do not be sparing of promises, but also keep them faithfully. . . . Thou must educate thyself to the dignity and the bearing of a king." The news of Otto's unanimous acceptance by the princes, he wrote, had cured him of an illness ; then he casually mentioned a number of concessions "which thou altogether must grant without making difficulty." Among them were the imperial privileges sanctioned, after fifty years of warfare, by the Concordat of Worms, and the suzerainty over Sicily.

Innocent crowned Otto emperor in 1209, but soon found him making common cause with Sicilian rebels, and accused him of stretching out his hand for that crown. "If thou dost continue in thine obstinacy, we cannot help but punish thee with the anathema," he wrote a year later, and on hearing that Otto had actually crossed the boundary of Sicilian territory, carried his threat into execution. He wrote to the German princes that he had been deceived in this man as God Himself had once been deceived in Saul, and worked upon their feelings by declaring that Otto, brought up in England, would try to reduce them to the miserable state of the English barons. God had reproved Saul, he wrote again, and had substituted "one younger than he," who had obtained and held the kingdom.

As the "one younger than he" who was to succeed this modern Saul, Innocent had fixed upon Frederick of Sicily, of whom his mother at her death had appointed him guardian ; it was true the dreaded union of Germany and Sicily would thus be accomplished, but Innocent considered that he held this youth completely under his thumb. It would be possible to bind him by all sorts of promises and agreements. Without fear for the future he therefore enlisted the services of Philip Augustus of France, who placed large sums at the young prince's disposal. The English court was equally zealous in sustaining Otto IV., and thus was brought about the first great international complication in the history of Europe. It culminated in the battle of Bouvines, fought in 1214 A.D., where Philip Augustus thoroughly routed Otto's English and German forces, sending to Frederick as a promising token one of the imperial eagles. It was a death blow to the house of Brunswick, and Frederick was soon formally acknowledged as head of the German nation.

In person, like his immediate ancestors, Frederick was not imposing. According to one account he was "red,

The battle of Bouvines.

Personality
of Fred-
erick II.

bald, and short-sighted," while a Mohammedan historian opines that as a slave he would not have brought a hundred drachmæ. He had grown up among Saracens and had imbibed many of their tastes, to the detriment of his morals as well as his orthodoxy. He kept a harem like any Oriental potentate, and the popes succeeded first and last in citing a goodly number of his heretical acts and utterances. But in his love of art, science, and literature, in his views on philosophy and on the duties of a monarch, he was far in advance of the Christians of his age; he tells us himself that he spent his spare moments in reading; we have a work on falcons from his hand; and we know that with clear common sense he ridiculed the belief in ordeals or judgments of God. The laws that he passed for Sicily were far in advance of the age and contain the germs of modern legislation.

Frederick
II., crusad-
ing vow.

The outbreak of Frederick's great quarrel with the Papacy is usually ascribed to his failure to perform a crusading vow, which in the excitement of the moment he had taken on the day of his coronation. But will this account for the inordinate hatred of one pope after another? Doubtless they wished him to undertake the crusade, but rather to get rid of him than from unadulterated zeal for the cause. This young man was making his Sicilian kingdom too powerful, he was interfering too much with the Lombard communes. Year after year he postponed his promised journey, though in 1225 A.D. he married Iolanthe, daughter of John of Brienne and heiress of Jerusalem. By the Treaty of San Germano, drawn up in July, 1225, Frederick bound himself to the Pope by promises more definite than any he had yet given. He agreed to cross to the Holy Land in August, 1227, with a thousand knights, a hundred transport ships, and fifty galleys, and to maintain these forces for a period of two years. He was also to furnish sums amounting to about eleven million francs of modern coin. Should he fail to cross, or to provide the knights and the money, he was to be *ipso facto* under the ban, and his kingdom of Sicily was to pay the forfeit. Already before the day appointed there had been a falling-out with the Pope because of Frederick's renewed interference with the affairs of the Lombard League. " Take care," the Pope wrote, in a long letter of reprehension, " that God do not annihilate thee and wipe out thy race." Already the conception was forming that this was a " viper brood," to be relentlessly pursued from one generation to another.

Honorius died before the term agreed upon, but his successor, Gregory IX., was peremptory in requiring the fulfilment of the promise. The ships came together at Brindisi, where thousands of pilgrims awaited them. But the heat of a southern summer, joined to poor accommodations, brought about a pestilence of which many died. Frederick himself was taken with fever, and resigned his enterprise at the eleventh hour, though whether he was quite sincere is open to doubt. Gregory maintained that the illness was feigned, and would listen to no excuse, but declared the emperor under the ban, and forbade the Sicilians to pay him further taxes. In fact, his hatred went to the most incredible lengths; for when Frederick, though still under the ban, nevertheless undertook the crusade, he, the Vicar of God, sent monks to preach against him, and *wrote to the head of the infidels asking him not to surrender!* Frederick maintained, ten years later, that he still had this intercepted letter in his hands.

Frederick II. and Gregory IX

This crusade of Frederick II., though bloodless, had greater results to show than any but one of its predecessors. By the Treaty of 1229, arranged by negotiation, the sultan of Egypt agreed to surrender Jerusalem and an

The crusade accomplished.

important strip of seacoast. Before a crowd of pilgrims, in the church of the Holy Sepulchre, Frederick placed the crown of Jerusalem on his own head. But on that very day the *clavegeri*, or papal troops, had wrested from him his mainland provinces in southern Italy; he hastened home, routed his enemy, and reduced the Pope to terms. In August, 1230 A.D., he was loosed from the ban, and a year later Gregory acknowledged him as king of Jerusalem and confirmed the treaty with the Saracens.

Further hostilities with Gregory IX.

All this was but prelude to a fiercer struggle that broke out nine years later with this same Pope. The causes were Frederick's bestowal of Sardinia on his son Enzio, and a new Lombard war which had resulted for the Emperor in the victory of Cortenuova. By papal decree all his subjects were released from allegiance and his body given over to Satan. Both parties issued manifestoes to the world at large which leave nothing to be desired in point of vehemence. "Princes, take heed," writes Frederick, "people, listen to your own cause! . . . Run for water for the protection of your own houses when that of your neighbor is on fire!"

Gregory's letter, especially, is a model of invective. A furious beast, it declares, has come up from the sea with feet like a bear, teeth like a lion, and limbs like a leopard. She only opens her mouth to blaspheme the name of the Lord. The old story is repeated, which we meet in so many papal letters, of Frederick being an ungrateful son to Mother Church; all the old grievances pass in review: the vow so often deferred, the plague in Brindisi, which is ascribed to the emperor's bad management, the favoring of Saracens in Jerusalem. Then comes the most damning, and possibly the most true, of all the charges. This king, says Gregory, maintains from the throne of pestilence "that the whole world has been deceived by three impostors —

Moses, Mohammed, and Christ; of whom two died honorably, the third on a cross." A most serious charge in an age when burnings for heresy were already becoming popular.

As the struggle went on Gregory stooped to conspire for the election of an anti-king, but, failing in this, decided to call a general council of the church for Easter Day, 1241. Frederick was asked to suspend hostilities, and to grant the prelates a safe-conduct, but refused on the ground that the Pope was only seeking time to strengthen his forces. It was altogether a time of strain and excitement, for the Tartars or Mongols, under the grandson of the great Timour, were ravaging the Eastern dependencies of the empire, and had defeated Duke Henry of Silesia at Liegnitz. Frederick ordered every one of his German male subjects with an income of over three marks of silver to take to arms. Gregory maintained that the danger had been purposely exaggerated, and that the army was destined for use against the Papacy. Wits of the time said that the khan meant to destroy the empire, but had asked Frederick what office the latter could fill at his, the khan's, court. The emperor had answered that he knew something about birds, and would take the position of falconer. The great Oriental leader, it was further asserted, in despair at the discords of Christians, had in reality come to make peace between Pope and emperor.

The capture of the prelates.

The conflict of church and state had indeed reached a stage where no blow was too ponderous, no means too unprecedented. The Pope repeatedly preached crusades against Frederick, offering the same remission of sins to those who would take up arms as to those who went as pilgrims to Jerusalem. Gregory is even charged with having used the funds which the faithful had already subscribed for the liberation of Palestine in crushing this personal enemy. Frederick's measures were no less radical:

a Genoese fleet had been chartered to carry prelates to the Pope's great council at Rome; the emperor had issued a warning that all who attended would do so at the risk of their lives. These shiploads of cardinals, bishops, abbots, and Lombard deputies he considered fair prey. Enzio, the emperor's natural son, assisted by Pisan ships, fell in with the Genoese fleet off the island of Monte Cristo in April, 1241, gave them battle with such effect that two thousand men, among them an archbishop, found their deaths in the waves of the Mediterranean, and carried off as prizes some hundred high ecclesiastics. They were incarcerated at Melfi and Naples, and held as hostages, the last of them not being liberated until after some years had elapsed.

Death of Gregory IX.

This blow was followed up by the taking of Tivoli and by an advance on Rome. But death at this juncture most inopportunely snatched Gregory away. Frederick was warring against the person of the Pope, not the institution of the Papacy, and he waited to see what effect the new election would have on his affairs. He waited long and vainly, for the cardinals could come to no agreement. He wrote to remind them of their duty in the style in which his correspondence with the late Pope had given him facility, calling them sons of Belial, troop of perdition, the laughing-stock of nations: "Like serpents you cling to earth instead of rising to heaven. You each want the tiara, and no one will leave it to the other." He is said to have advocated, in a pamphlet written by his chancellor, that the Papacy should be done away with altogether, or that he himself should be made Pope.

Innocent IV.

When, after two years, Sinobaldo Fiesco ascended the papal throne, as Innocent IV., it seemed as though the struggle had at last reached its end. A peace treaty was drawn up and signed by which Frederick was to be loosed from the ban, and, in certain questions, notably regarding the Lombard cities, the Pope and cardinals were to be arbiters. But difficulties and misunderstandings arose; Innocent felt that the Papacy was not receiving its due, and took a sudden determination to fly beyond the emperor's reach. At Lyons he issued a summons to a general council, and received a deputation from Germany, with whom he agreed to put through the election of a new king.

At the third session of the council that was opened at Lyons, in 1245 A.D., and at which a hundred and fifty prelates were present, sentence was passed on Frederick and he was declared forever deposed from the throne of the empire. In his boundless self-partiality Innocent asserted later that he could remember no case that had ever been more carefully and deliberately tried by experienced and holy men. Their sessions had been secret, it is true, but some had undertaken the rôle of plaintiff, others that of defendant. The formal act of accusation calls Frederick the prince of tyranny and destroyer of the universe, and recommends that he, drunken with the blood of so many saints, be given over to everlasting ignominy; the name of this Babylonian, *and of his offspring*, is to be wiped out eternally, inasmuch as he is boundlessly merciless and cruel!

Final anathematizing of Frederick II. by Innocent IV.

When the act was read, Thaddeus of Suessa, Frederick's legal representative, rose in solemn protest; he had already declared that the council was not universal, and had been told that it was as much so as the ambushes of the emperor would allow. He now proclaimed that this was the day of wrath, of misery, and of anguish. And, indeed, the end of all things seemed at hand. The empire that had been so glorious was crushed to earth. To gain means to carry on his struggle, Frederick had been obliged to deed away its most cherished privileges, which there was no hope of

A struggle to the death.

ever regaining. Its crown was now to be bandied about and despised and rejected by German princes; unworthy foreigners were to wear it, one of whom, Alfonso of Castile, never dared to show his face within his own domains. And the last scions of the proud Hohenstaufen dynasty, so great in peace if not in war, were to be pursued like vermin, to be preached against and prayed against as worse than infidels, and, finally, to be literally extirpated by the Sicilian henchman of the papacy. Ably did Innocent follow up his declaration to the council of Lyons, "Until our last breath we and our cardinals will maintain the struggle for the cause of God and of the church."

End of the reign of Frederick II. Frederick's last years were spent like a lion at bay. The rival kings in Germany, first Henry Raspe, who fattened on the papal generosity, and then William of Holland, occupied the full attention of his son Conrad; the emperor himself was constantly in the field against the papal adherents in Italy. He returned one day from a hunting expedition to find his camp near Parma a heap of ashes, and many of his soldiers captive. Constant attempts were made against his life, and the Pope rewarded those would-be assassins who were fortunate enough to escape alive. Frederick's own chancellor and most cherished friend, Peter de Vigne, is believed to have offered him a poisoned cup; the betrayed monarch ordered his eyes to be pierced with glowing irons, and the blinded wretch beat out his own brains against the pillar of a church.

Death and burial. The final blow was the capture by the Bolognese of the capable and beloved Enzio, who was to remain incarcerated for the next score of years. Frederick himself fell a victim to dysentery while still in the field. In his tomb in Palermo he was able at last to rest long and well, for when the grave was opened in the eighteenth century the body was in a perfect state of preservation, save that the nose had been crushed by the weight of a superimposed coffin.

Conrad IV. abandoned Germany in 1252, and fought with his brother Manfred for their common Sicilian heritage until his death, two years later. Manfred, for a time, became reconciled to the Pope, accepted the lieutenancy of Sicily, and held the bridle of Innocent's palfrey at Naples. But the proud spirit of his race again asserted itself; he fled to Lucera, where the Saracens received him with open arms, aiding him to gain a victory over the papal troops and to have himself crowned king at Palermo.

The last of the Hohen-staufens.

But Clement IV. signed a treaty in 1265 with Charles of Anjou, brother of the king of France, transferring to him all rights over the Sicilian kingdom, and the great reckoning with Manfred took place at Benevento in the following year. Manfred was slain after deeds of such valor that the French knights themselves carried stones to mark his place of burial; but a papal legate ordered the body exhumed and thrown into the waters of the Volturno.

Charles of Anjou.

Thus had the race of Barbarossa dwindled, until no one was left but Conradin's son, the young Conradin, a boy of fifteen, who had been brought up by his uncles in Bavaria. Fugitives from Benevento came to offer him the crown of Sicily; six thousand knights rallied round him, and he crossed the Alps as liberator of Italy. Yet Clement IV. likened him more justly to a lamb going to the slaughter. At Tagliacozzo he was defeated; after a week's flight he was betrayed by a Frangipani, a former Ghibelline, to Charles of Anjou. On the latter rests the direct responsibility of that cruel execution in the market-place of Naples; but the real murderer was the claimant to the crown of Constantine and to the chair of Peter, who stirred no finger in his behalf.

Execution of Con-radin.

CHAPTER V

THE AGE OF CHIVALRY

LITERATURE: Prutz, *Kulturgeschichte der Kreuzzüge*, contains much information. In August Sach, *Deutsches Leben in der Vergangenheit*, are many chapters on this period. See also Freytag and von Löher. Richter, *Deutsche Kulturgeschichte*, is a similar work to Sach. Alwin Schultz, *Das höfische Leben*, describes the material side of knighthood. Scherer's *German Literature* should also be consulted.

Character of the period.

FOR the greater part of a century and a quarter the House of Hohenstaufen, like an eagle returning to the charge, had been bruising its wings against an enemy with supernatural resources. But there is another aspect to the whole period that we cannot afford to pass over; in many ways it was the brightest time that Germany was to know for five hundred years. The court was brilliant and magnificent; the festival that Frederick Barbarossa gave at Mainz in 1184, in honor of the knighting of the heir to the throne, outdid anything the chroniclers had ever seen. The princes were growing powerful within settled boundaries knights jousted and tourneyed, practised leaping full-armed upon their chargers, or busied themselves in acquiring the latest French accomplishments; burghers worked away at their counters, gradually developing commercial greatness and civic liberty; monks and missionaries increased in numbers and activity, and found congenial fields for enterprise in reclaiming and colonizing Slavic lands; in law and medicine there was a general awakening, and also in learning and art. Castles and churches were built that have lasted to this day, while the literature furnished two

undying epics ; lyric poets sang as they were not to sing
again until the days of Goethe.   Material prosperity kept
pace with the intellectual growth ; the rich began to
clothe themselves in velvets, silks, and satins, to sit on
divans, sleep on mattresses, pour their wine from carafes,
and flourish coats of arms with fields of azure, gules, and
rampant beasts.   The poor, too, found the ordinary articles
of diet cheaper and far more varied.   Rice and Indian
meal were introduced.

If we seek for the cause of all this movement and activity, Influence
we shall find that the chief impulse was given by the cru- of the
sades, a term which is here used to denote, not merely the crusades.
eight well-known invasions of the Holy Land, but also the
countless minor expeditions that filled two whole centuries.
Twice a year fleets went out from Marseilles, Genoa, and
Venice, and we hear of single ships carrying as many as a
thousand passengers.

What must it have been for a narrow-minded, poverty-
stricken German to come suddenly out into this chaos of
races, languages, and religions !   From the Italians he
could learn naval tactics and many secrets of trade ; from
the French, who predominated in Syria, the more polite
arts ; and from the infidel himself many a good, sturdy
virtue.

We are too apt thoughtlessly to acquiesce in the ecclesi-   Culture of
astical view of the bloodthirsty Oriental who stood in the   the Moham
way to prevent innocent Christians from proceeding bare-   medans.
foot to the tomb of Christ.   Were these Mohammedans so
wicked and were our pilgrims so utterly without guile?
We know positively that many of the latter, up to the
moment of taking the cross, had been robbers and cut-
throats, that others had gone merely to escape poverty and
a burden of debt.   The kind of excitement that drew them
was the excitement of newly discovered gold-fields.   Re-

cently deciphered historical sources of the Mohammedans have changed the conventional picture. These heathen, whom the church proclaimed to be raging so furiously, found time to be shocked beyond measure at the gambling, drinking, and worse excesses that went on in the Christian army. The taverns along the road were dens of vice; the frivolous way in which oaths and compacts were made and broken is held up to execration, not only by the Arabs, but by the better-minded crusaders themselves. And, as to cruelties exercised on helpless prisoners, we hear of nothing more absolutely wanton than the crucifixion of the captives in Edessa or the sending to the Greek emperor by Bohemund of Antioch of a whole cargo of sliced-off noses and thumbs. It was one thing for Christian knights to band together to obtain toleration for their new religion; but to send an expedition to the holy city of Mecca for the express purpose of seizing the bones of the dead prophet was blind and heartless desecration. What a broadening effect it must have had on these invaders later to find that men could lead moral, useful, and generous lives without ever having heard of the Church of Rome!

Broadening of the mental horizon.

What Europe in general and Germany in especial gained from these Oriental wars cannot be overestimated. The geographical horizon was widened in all directions; guidebooks that showed the different stopping-places on the route were eagerly devoured; pilgrims from different localities interchanged views and experiences. And as new needs arose efforts were made to meet and overcome them. On the first crusade, coins of all sorts were carried along and sold for what they would bring; later, drafts and letters of credit were invented and a general coin adopted, the Saracen besant, that could be used for all occasions. For nearly a hundred years no offence was taken at the fact that these coins were dated from the Hegira and adorned with mottoes of praise to Allah and Mohammed. When the church at last forbade such emblems, the merchants contented themselves with keeping the same appearance and the same Arabic letters, but making them spell Christian texts!

It must not be supposed that trade was confined to lands conquered by the Christians, or that it went on only in the intervals of peace. On the contrary, the seaports of Syria were an outlet for the commerce of the whole East, and so brisk was the interchange of commodities that the church frequently interfered, and even found it necessary to issue fiery edicts against the sale of weapons and supplies to the enemy in time of war. It was in these days that many of our most common articles of daily use first found their way to the West, — drugs and spices, dyes, incense, sandalwood, Tyrian silks, camels'-hair garments, not to speak of fruits and oil. It is natural that many of the new words that at this time came to be common to the European languages should refer to commercial products; tariff, bazaar, muslin from Mosul, damasks from Damascus. The "arabesque" becomes a well-known form of ornamentation, while amulets, talismans, elixirs, grow to be familiar terms. " Rosaries " are taken over from Buddhism and applied to Christian use, while heraldry is the gainer, not only of new terms, but also of the Byzantine cross. Mohammedry becomes "mummery," while "assassin" is one of the deadly tribe of hasheesh eaters. It is to these times that the use of Arab numerals — nine digits and a cipher — dates; it matters little whether they came in by way of Spain or Palestine. Commercial activity called for quicker methods of reckoning, and the more convenient system, long in vogue with the Saracens, was rapidly adopted, after the middle of the twelfth century, in all parts of Europe.

Commercial activity.

The increase in the volume of commerce was enormous; not only were the religious orders of knighthood great traders and bankers, but the merchants of
Genoa, Pisa, and Venice had quarters in all the Syrian
towns, where they lived under their own laws and were
accorded every possible trading privilege. The liveliest
intercourse was kept up with the neighboring centres of
industry, especially with Damascus, itself a terminus for
the caravan trade with the Persian Gulf; Christian ship-
pers did not hesitate even to sell other Christians as slaves
in return for the much-prized Oriental products. Germany,
of course, her seaports being so distant, took little direct
part in this trade; but the castles of her nobles were decked
out with every Oriental comfort, and their gardens filled
with new plants and trees.

Fostering of
a national
sentiment.
For Germany one important result of the spirit of criticism and comparison aroused by the crusades, was the fostering of a feeling of nationality. It is now that in the
literature we find the first expression of love for the fatherland, and joy at returning to it after long wanderings.
Walter of the Vogelweide doubtless voiced the sentiments
of thousands when he praised the virtue, the true love, and
the plenteous delight to be found in his own country: " Oh,
that I may dwell long therein!" is his sudden and hearty
outburst. It is always a sign, too, of national self-appre-
ciation when the heroes of the past are drawn from the
mists of oblivion and made the objects of reverence and
devotion. Charles the Great is now brought into prominence both as a lawgiver and a man. The *Chanson de Roland*, which dealt with the unfortunate Spanish expedition,
was translated into German and eagerly and widely read;
while Frederick Barbarossa, well knowing how popular
such an act would be, caused the bones of the founder of
the empire to be exhumed and enshrined and himself canon-

ized. The gifts that were made on this occasion still adorn the wonderful chapel that Charles had built at Aix.

For the church in general, and the German church as well, the crusades, so long as they were in any way successful, denoted an increase in power, prosperity, and prestige. The Papacy had been allowed to assume the headship of the whole movement; there were times when the response of Christendom to its appeals for men and money was more than enthusiastic. But also in another way there was an actual increase in material wealth. Many a knight and noble, in order to secure ready money for his expedition, sold or pledged his estates to a neighboring bishopric or monastery. Too often, instead of returning, he died on the way, or disappeared for years from view. A favorite theme in the literature of the time is this Christian warrior, who spends a good part of his life as a captive among the infidels, undergoes most thrilling experiences, and is at last set free by the loving daughter of his Saracen captor. In the meantime the church will have been enjoying his revenues.

Increase in the power of the church.

It may safely be said, then, that never were the ecclesiastical coffers so full as in the earlier days of the crusades, never were her general commands more implicitly obeyed, never were more love and reverence shown for her buildings, her emblems, and her ritual. Those who had taken the cross wore it on the front of their garments while accomplishing their vow, on their backs when returning home, and once again on their breasts when consigned to their last rest. Even Frederick II., when his coffin was opened, was found to have the sacred emblem conspicuously attached to his imperial robe.

This idea of the Bible or the sword, this belief that the blood of a heretic was pleasing in the sight of God, had seized on high and low. Crusades were preached, not only against the Turks and Saracens of Palestine, but also against the Jews, the Moors of Spain, the Waldensians of Italy, the Albigensians of southern France, the Wends and Stedingers of Germany. Such skill with the sword as should enable a man worthily to smite God's enemies, wherever they might be found, became as much a Christian virtue as unselfishness or humility.

Divergent religious opinions.

But, as has been intimated, familiar intercourse with those holding alien beliefs, and the growing perception that the dreaded infidels might, after all, have brave and noble qualities, gave rise to a great deal of independent thought. Men began to reason about the supremacy of the Papacy, and the justification for its claims. The circumstance is significant, that, in his greatest of all mediæval poems, Wolfram von Eschenbach introduces us to a Christian brotherhood, entirely outside of the accepted priestly hierarchy, and makes his knights of the Holy Grail answerable only to Heaven. What would Gregory VII. or Innocent III. have said to such an association, claiming as it did that the highest of all earthly honors was to become the Grail's king! As the thirteenth century progresses it shows more and more enlightenment, and at the same time an ever increasing divergence of religious opinion. The poet Freidank doubts if, after all, heretics and heathen are to end in hell-fire. Walter of the Vogelweide thinks Christians, Jews, and Mohammedans serve all the same God, while Frederick II., as we have seen, is openly accused of declaring the head of the Christian religion an impostor.

The early Inquisition.

But in proportion as its enemies increased, so too did the church gird itself for the conflict, and the age of chivalry is, likewise, one of inquisitions and of burnings at the stake. Pope Innocent III. was a mighty heretic hunter. The Lateran Council of 1215 passed new and stricter rules, and crimes which a generation before were dismissed with a simple "let him go to the devil," were now punished by a horrible death. Committees were appointed to inquire into men's inmost beliefs. In some districts the people were obliged, at stated intervals, to prove their orthodoxy ; houses were searched for hidden heretics, and trials held over dead bodies.   In Strassburg, in 1212 A.D., eighty men and women were subjected to the ordeal of glowing iron, and all but a few found guilty, and executed.   In Verona sixty persons were burned at one time. The laws of Innocent IV. provided that even those who recanted should be imprisoned for life, and their children and grandchildren be legally dead, unless they could prove that they had aided in bringing to justice these same progenitors.   The very dwellings of heretics were to be torn down, and Innocent's successor, Alexander IV., decreed the same fate for the houses of those who had harbored heretics, or even of neighbors who could not prove that they *had not* so done.

In Germany the fortunes of the Inquisition are mainly connected with the name of one man, Conrad of Marburg, to whom the popes intrusted unheard-of powers for the rooting out of pestilential opinions. Priests and monks were placed under his jurisdiction, inasmuch as his tribunal was declared competent in all cases where heresy was concerned ; he might preach crusades against the recalcitrant, and offer absolution from sins to all who would join the hunt — a privilege expressly extended to murderers who might enlist in the good cause. This same Conrad of Marburg was father confessor to that Landgravine of Thuringia who is known in history as St. Elizabeth, and with whose name are connected such a host of pretty miracles. The landgrave disapproved of her charities, it was said, and found her once with a basket of bread under her arm ; but when

Conrad of Marburg.

the lid was removed nothing was to be seen but a pile of sweet-smelling roses. In connection with Conrad she appears in another light: as a conscientious disciple who, do what she would, could never satisfy her stern mentor. He could scarcely be brought to forgive her, we are credibly told, for having missed one of his sermons; while for another offence, of no greater magnitude, he caused her to be soundly scourged. When the landgrave died, Elizabeth left the Wartburg and settled in the vicinity of Marburg, so as to be near Conrad; the latter made her dismiss her favorite serving-maids and keep repulsive creatures around her person.

Pursuit of heretics.

In his pursuit of heretics Conrad was aided by a certain John, the one-eyed and one-handed, and also by a monk, Dorso, one of that order of *Domini canes*, or sleuth-hounds of the Lord, which had just been founded and given extensive privileges at Rome, with the understanding that they were to act as guardians of the faith. These two particular men had themselves been heretics, but had returned to the fold with a rabid hatred of their former associates. They professed to be able to tell from a man's exterior to what pernicious sect he belonged, and they laid it down as a fixed principle that better a hundred innocent persons should perish than one guilty one escape. The assurance and zeal of the inquisitors imposed at first upon the common people and induced them to permit the persecutions and burnings; still other friends were made by a judicious distribution of the lands of the victims; while the cause of the Emperor Frederick II. was itself in too great jeopardy to admit of his interfering on the side of mercy.

End of the Inquisition.

Under these favoring circumstances, Conrad of Marburg and his friends became so courageous that they dared to accuse even venerable prelates and persons of the highest rank. Even Frederick's elder son, that unfortunate Henry who was later denied the succession, became an object of their suspicion, while against a Count of Sayn the accusation was soberly brought that he had been seen in the act of riding upon a crab. This very Count of Sayn forced matters to a climax by appealing to a Diet of the empire and by sending directly to Rome to Pope Gregory IX. himself. The latter expressed surprise at the lengths to which his representative had gone, but before he could interfere the Germans had found a way of their own for freeing themselves from the thraldom of the Inquisition. An uprising had taken place against the whole spirit of the institution, and Conrad and his subordinates had been murdered, though not in time to prevent the slaughter of thousands of Frisians, against whom a crusade had been preached. The final blow to the Inquisition was given by the Diet of Frankfort of 1234, which decreed that henceforth offences against the faith should be tried in the regular courts, with the ordinary means of defence. Four extra sessions were to be held monthly, over which the young king was to preside in person.

This rise of heretical sects and the church's intolerance toward them is one dark shadow on the history of the time. A brighter side is the new impulse given to chivalry by the crusades, and the rise of a general order of knighthood, with its code of virtues and observances, and its new and fascinating literature. There had been a time when any man whose trade was war, and who fought on horseback, with one or more followers, could call himself a *miles*, or knight, and hold his *feudum*, or fief. That was now to change. Closer contact with other countries, and especially with France, where the institution was more fully developed, had led to a different determination of rank, and to the adoption of the *ordo militaris*, or rule of knightly conduct. "Polite society," as we should call it to-day,

A general order of knighthood.

became narrowed to those of good birth, who had undergone
the ceremony of " knighting," or initiation.   Doubtless the
religious orders in Palestine served largely as a model, for
this order, too, prided itself on its Christianity and on its
ability to fight.   Certain courtly graces were indispensable,
and also a reverence for woman — like that due to a patron
saint.

German chivalry never emancipated itself from French
influence; the names that refer to the tourney and other
knightly sports are all taken from that language.   French,
too, are the dishes on the well-ordered table, the materials
for the courtly garments, the more elegant of the dances.
French formalism, even, passed over to Germany, and men
troubled themselves about their manners and about points
of etiquette as they did about their sins.   Great stress was
laid on how to meet and greet, or how to enter and leave a
room.   Godfrey of Strassburg, in order to be edifying,
weaves into his poem of *Tristan* a long dissertation as to
whether it is better to speak, or simply to make a silent bow.

Duties of
a knight.

There was much that was admirable even in this conventional knighthood, for the whole system rested on a
basis of sincerity and fidelity.   To his liege lord the knight
was to be a true vassal, to aid him in the administration of
justice, to take part in his wars and in his feuds, to repair
to his court whenever summoned — even if to some mere
festivity.   On receiving his fief he swore to be " faithful,
devoted, and willing," laid his hands in the hands of his
lord, or sealed his vow with a kiss.   He might bring no
charges in court that affected his master's life, limb, or
honor; he was bound to furnish pecuniary aid, if needed,
for ransom, for the marriage of the eldest daughter, or for
knighting of the eldest son.   Altogether his conduct was
to be courtly : — *höfisch* is the German term, and *höflich*
is still the word for all that is pretty and polite.

There were duties toward others besides the lord. For God, for his country, for justice, or for honor, the knight was to be ready to sacrifice his life without so much as a moment's hesitation; he was to protect the helpless with his heart's blood and be true to the death to his friend or to his lady. That he should have such a lady was one of the rules of the game; he became her vassal and knelt to her as he knelt to his lord. In her service all his jousts were fought, at her feet he laid all his prizes. Her banner, veil, or garland, or even her linen undergarment, would be fastened to his helm or spear, a constant token of his devotion.

The requisite as to good birth grew more and more severe with time; descent from three generations of knights or from three generations of men who might have been knights had they so chosen — for many never were initiated — became a *sine qua non;* indeed, the rule was later extended to sixteen quarterings of the shield. The tournament regulations of the time provide that he who attempts to enter the lists with imperfect lineage shall atone by public disgrace — as a hedge-knight be made to ride the barrier. Similar was the punishment for those found to be tainted with heresy, to have committed treason, deserted from the army, broken their oath, or borne false witness. *(margin: Perfect lineage.)*

One priceless mirror of these times we have in the splendid poem of *Parsifal,* a study not only in the externals, but also in the ideals of knighthood. A purer, more beautiful character than that of the hero has never been conceived, and the reader is allowed to assist, as it were, at its development toward perfection. A boy of ancient lineage, with a face like an angel and the tenderest of hearts, is brought up in seclusion, away from the clang of arms, by a mother who fears she may lose him as she has already lost her husband. But knights whom he chances to meet in the forest, and *(margin: Parsifal the ideal knight.)*

whom he takes for gods, fire his imagination; he must and will away to the court of King Arthur, and he forces his mother to give him a horse. Hoping, however, that ridicule will dishearten him with the project, she decks him out in the garments of a fool, herself falling dead with grief after he has left her. The youth, raw and untutored, does mean and unchivalrous acts, but learns from Gurnemanz, one of Arthur's followers, the rules of the order of knighthood. The wonderful skill of the poet, Wolfram von Eschenbach, of whom his own contemporaries said "never did mouth of layman speak better," is shown by the way in which, all through the long poem, what is conventional is contrasted with what is spiritual. Gawain is the exponent of the one type of knight, brave and correct in all his doings; Parsifal, of the other. But the latter has first to free himself from the shackles of this same conventionality: Gurnemanz has told him that a well-behaved knight never asks troublesome questions; so when in the mysterious mountain of Monsalvat he sees the terrible pain of Amfortas, the bloody lance, the mystic power of the Holy Grail, he omits to show the interest of ordinary human sympathy. Though received the day before with the honors of a king, he is now ignominiously dismissed, and a mocking laugh rings out from one of the receding towers. To Arthur's court Kundry, the messenger of the Grail, follows him, denouncing him as false and dishonored; for the first time he learns that one word of sympathy would have freed Amfortas from his pain.

The purification of Parsifal.

Now begins the long process of atonement and purification; Parsifal wanders forth in absolute despair, no longer believing in a God, but determined to the last to be true to his wife, Condwiramur, and to be strong in battle. His one thought is to reach the mountain of Monsalvat and make good his fault; a pious hermit whom he meets in the magic calm of a Good Friday, tells him that only through faith in

God, through pity and humility, can the Grail be found. With hope in his heart he continues his wanderings, performing generous and brave deeds, and being received back with honor at the court of Arthur. Here Kundry reappears, and, worshipping at his feet, tells him the Grail has appointed him lord and king. Constancy and fidelity are the virtues which have brought about his salvation; these are the ideals of a true knight.

Not only the poems, romances, and chronicles of these times, but even the dry legal documents, bear witness to the spirit of chivalry. In the charters of privileges, in the deeds of gift, where people signed according to their rank, the title of knight assumes a leading importance; those who have a right to bear it, seldom, if ever, omit it, and its owner has the place of honor next to the king's count and banner-bearer. Even princes, if the ceremony of knighting have not been performed, are on a lower plane; while, strangely enough, doctors of law are, *ipso facto*, knights.

Importance of title of knight.

The ceremony of knighting was considered such an epoch in the life of a layman as the consecration by the bishop in that of an ecclesiastic; it usually took place at some festival or on the eve or morrow of a battle. The knighting of the young King Henry VI., in 1184, was made the occasion of the grandest rejoicings in the history of the Middle Ages, seventy thousand knights being entertained by Frederick Barbarossa in his own great camp. Not for a hundred years, declares a poet, will the occasion be forgotten. The actual ceremony itself consisted of a blow struck with the flat of a sword across the shoulders of the kneeling candidate, in token that this was the last insult of man he might ever bear in silence. At the same time there was taken the vow of obedience to the laws of chivalry, a step so important that the record of it was placed on the tombstones of the dead.

Ceremony of knighting.

Preparation
for knight-
hood.

As with every other calling in the Middle Ages, the preparation for knighthood was very long and very thorough, and the youth who was destined to become a "courtly man" went through various stages of apprenticeship. In his seventh year he was sent to the castle of some great noble, where for seven years he performed the duties of a page, and learned the elements of good manners. Some of the rules of conduct to be observed at such a lord's table have been handed down, and serve, although trivial matter in themselves, to illustrate the spirit of the times. As forks had not yet been invented, it was not forbidden to take the food from the plates with the fingers, which, however, were not to be put into the mustard-pot or other general dishes. When helping one's self from the latter, a spoon was to be used or a crust of bread, but one that had not already been in the mouth. No leaning of the elbows on the table was allowed, no blowing into the food to cool it, no using of the tablecloth for other than the regular purposes, no picking of the teeth with the points of the knives.

The squire.

As the page grew older he became a squire, often leaving the home of his first master to seek other service. He was now instructed in the use of weapons, in the art of hunting with falcons and greyhounds, in singing, dancing, and polite intercourse with women. After being dubbed a knight his daily occupation was the necessary training for the joust and tournament. As endurance was the chief object, this training consisted in running, jumping, and taking long walks; leaping into the saddle was a feat much affected and extremely difficult, on account of the heavy armor.

The joust.

The joust was a simple encounter between two knights armed with spears, and was entered into by any two strangers who felt inclined for adventures. Redoubtable champions would travel from land to land, fighting every one who came in their way. The man of quality was recognized at once by the finer points and special polite observances of the sport. The chief object was to thrust the spear at the adversary when in full gallop, so as either to unhorse him, or, more usually, to shiver the weapon; a good jouster could break some fifty lances in the course of a day. The blows were good or bad according to what part of the shield they struck; and to wound the horse, or to let one's own steed trample on a fallen foe, was unpardonable awkwardness. The conflict was to cease the moment one of the antagonists raised the visor of his helm.

The chief and climax of all knightly encounters was the tourney or tournament, in which hundreds and even thousands took part at a time, and which closely resembled a battle; these encounters, indeed, formed a regular part of military training, just as do the manœuvres, reviews, and sham battles of to-day, and they gave the only opportunity to the prince or lord of judging the valor of his knights and promoting the deserving. It would be difficult to understand, otherwise, how violent was the opposition when the church took upon itself to forbid tourneys.

The giver or arranger of a tournament would divide the participants into two sides, each under its own leader. The day began with certain conventional evolutions, after which the knights singled out their special antagonists. The roughest form of the pastime was the so-called sword-war, in which, with mighty thrusts and slashes, the adversaries sought to cut off each other's helm-plumes, to split their wooden shields, or to strike their swords from their hands and thus render them defenceless. The ultimate aim of such encounters was to take as many prisoners as possible, and afterward demand a heavy ransom. Even in

The tournament.

an ordinary joust the steed and armor of him who was un-horsed fell to his conqueror. Besides such general booty there were often special prizes consisting of horses, dogs, or falcons. The Margrave of Meissen, for one of his tournaments at Nordhausen, had a tree erected with leaves of gold and silver, which were distributed among the knights according to their deeds of valor.

Features of the tourna-ment.

A favorite feature of the tournament was the disguised or masquerading knight, who with visor down and clad in some remarkable garment — snow-white or pea-green — would enter the lists at a critical moment. Or a dozen horsemen, garbed exactly alike, would sweep over the crest of a neighboring hill and turn the tide of victory. Such incidents added to the interest, and doubtless were often pre-arranged. Some of the disguises were expressly designed to raise a laugh, as when knights of tried valor fought in the skirts of women. Ulrich von Lichtenstein rode through the land as Frau Venus, challenging all comers.

The church and the tourna-ment.

There was a very serious side to these encounters, that justified the church in its attitude toward them. We hear of sixty and even a hundred knights falling dead in a day from wounds, heat, and exhaustion; Ulrich von Lichten-stein tells of a tournament, in which he himself took part, that lasted for twelve hours; on this arena bitter enemies fought out their old quarrels. Not once, but a hundred times, papal bulls were issued regarding the matter; it was made a law of the church that those who fell in such a contest might not be buried in consecrated ground, and many a woman went as a pilgrim to Rome to gain a dis-pensation for her dead husband. Occasionally, indeed, as when Innocent III. tried to win all Europe for his last crusade, general concessions were made to the knights, and permission accorded to hold the much-desired meetings.

Besides his jousts and tourneys, the knight had to be

ready at any time, either on his own account or on behalf Trial by
combat. of the helpless and oppressed, to take part in the judicial duel or trial by combat. All through the age of chivalry, all through the twelfth and thirteenth centuries, recourse was had to this means of proving guilt or innocence; it was the usage of the ordinary county courts. A favorite artifice, not only of the author of *Lohengrin*, but also of other poets of the time, is to present a disconsolate heroine with no one to fight in her defence, until at last some unknown champion makes his appearance, just as the allotted term of grace is about to expire.

If this ordeal of battle went against the accuser, he was subject to the same punishment that would have been inflicted on the defendant. The duels were held in enclosed spaces from which the combatants could not escape; before the conflict, both parties heard mass, and over the sacred relics each swore to the justice of his cause. The struggle was begun on horseback, but, so soon as one of the participants lost his saddle, was continued on foot and with the sword. At the last moment, when one had the other at his mercy, it was customary to remit the death-stroke if the vanquished man would confess his guilt, or, as the case might be, withdraw his charge.

Should a woman prefer, she might fight in her own Women
as com-
batants. defence, and not the least curious of ancient legal remains are the provisions for such a combat. The man is to stand waist deep in a circular pit, with a club in his right hand with which he may hit his antagonist; but he may not chase her nor even support himself against the edge. She for her part has a heavy stone tied in the end of a veil; she is further allowed, if she can seize his head from behind, to bend it back and throttle him. Should her veil become entwined about his free arm, he may draw her down into the pit.

It may be that such regulations date already from a time when the devotion to woman was waning. At the beginning of the thirteenth century the poet Reinmar of Zweter had still been able to compare a beautiful lady to the Holy Grail on which only the pure in heart might gaze. But soon into this *Minnedienst*, or love service, there began to creep exaggerations and extravagances. Ulrich von Lichtenstein tells us in his memoirs how, although the disease was considered contagious, he mingled with lepers to gain his lady's sympathy; how he drank of the water in which she had bathed her hands; how he had his lip cut because it projected too far for her taste; how, finally, he sent her his finger in a rich receptacle because she had mocked at the trifling nature of a wound he had gained in her honor. And all this Ulrich does simply and solely because he wishes to be in the fashion; he has a wife at home with whom he is on the best of terms and who has presented him with a numerous progeny.

Occasionally such extravagances met with deserved ridicule, as when the friends of a Reinmar von Hagenau twitted him with having sung the praises of one lady so long that she must have grown quite ancient. A certain Tannhuser, who died about 1270, complains of having been asked to capture salamanders, moon-reflections, and the like, and to stop the Rhine from flowing by Coblenz; he declares that his whole fortune has gone in serving ladies and in baths twice a week.

It is a wonder that knights could joust and play, and make love so merrily, when we consider how, after all, the greater part of their lives were spent. Behind their thick bare walls, throughout the cold winter months, they played their games of chess, drank their cups of wine, and listened to tales of the crusades sung by the wandering minstrel. For the woman it was still worse. Is it mere chance that in the poems of the time the maiden is always looking out of the window as the knight comes winding up the glen? Then there was constant danger from the assaults of enemies. In every one of the castles of the time there is the donjon tower, the last despairing resort in case of need; in many there is the "pitch-nose" through which boiling tar can be poured on the heads of the besiegers; while below is the dark, damp dungeon, in which captives were literally left to rot.

With the interregnum, as the period that followed on the fall of the Hohenstaufen dynasty is called, the demoralization of poverty began to set in. The age of chivalry is over, the age of the robber-knight has begun. Commerce and industry work a social revolution; the burgher becomes the important man in the state; military tactics change, and there is no longer room for a set of men whose chief merit was bearing the burden of a now useless armor.

Decline of knighthood.

CHAPTER VI

THE KINGS FROM DIFFERENT HOUSES

AUTHORITIES: The chief authority is Lindner's *Deutsche Geschichte unter den Hapsburgern und Luxemburgern.* Prutz, *Staatengeschichte des Abendlandes im Mittelalter*, is a useful résumé. Riezler, *Die literarischen Widersacher der Päpste*, tells at length about the *Defensor Pacis.* See also Creighton's *History of the Papacy.*

The election of Rudolph of Hapsburg.

AT the time of the execution of Conradin the uppermost thought in many minds was that vengeance must be taken for the cruel deed — vengeance against the Papacy, or at least against its henchman, Charles of Sicily. Legends had arisen as to how, from the scaffold, the brave young prince had thrown his gauntlet far out into the crowd, and how an eagle had wetted its wings in the blood of the last Hohenstaufen. The troubadours had taken up the theme; one of them wonders that he still has power to depict the calamity, that the mere thought of it does not strike him dead. "How can the Germans continue to live," he cries, "bearing in their hearts the memory of this loss. The best has been taken and only disgrace harvested!"

But the pressing problems of the moment occupied too much attention. How to get rid of this anarchy, of these petty foreign kings! At last, in 1272, Pope Gregory X., who found himself in danger of worse thraldom under the Anjevins than ever under the Hohenstaufens, took matters into his own hands. On the death of Richard of Cornwall, the rival of Alfonso of Castile, he wrote to the German electors that if they did not speedily choose a head of the empire, he and his cardinals would impose one upon them.

Obeying his behest, they gave their votes for Rudolph, Count of Hapsburg. The most striking phenomenon of the period which this reign inaugurated is the frequent change of rulers and of dynasties; but connected with this are two features of great interest: the growth and assumption of power of the seven electors, and the rise of a popular and literary, as well as of an imperial, opposition to the Papacy. We shall first sketch the incidents in the reigns of the rulers from Rudolph to Louis of Bavaria, and then take up in detail these main lines of development.

Of the six different kings, from four different houses, that ruled in the seventy years between 1273 and 1346, the one that has left the chief impression on German history was Rudolph of Hapsburg. We even know how he looked, which cannot be said of the others, for the marble image on his tombstone is one of the most carefully executed of monuments. Begun long before the king died, the sculptor is said to have visited him at frequent intervals to note and change the wrinkles that appeared in his face. He was tall and gaunt, with a Roman nose, and with curls that covered his ears. In character he was renowned for cleverness, astuteness, and firmness, but also for zeal in increasing his boundaries. "Sit still on Thy throne, O Lord," once prayed the Bishop of Basel, "or the Count of Hapsburg will shove Thee off!" There was a gravity about this pale face that was supposed to denote great virtue, which gravity and which pallor were handed down to a long line of descendants. *Personality of Rudolph of Hapsburg*

It has often been supposed that Rudolph was chosen "king of the Romans" rather for his insignificance than for any other qualities, but such is not the case. He could boast, indeed, of no compact principality, like Saxony, Brandenburg, Bavaria, Bohemia, or the Palatinate; but in other respects he was reputed one of the richest men of his

time, and his lands stretched from the Alpine passes well
into Alsace.   He was a relative of the Hohenstaufens and
had supported them to the best of his ability, accompanying
Conradin at least as far as Verona on his last fatal march.
All this spoke greatly in his favor; still more so the fact
that he had many eligible daughters, and that three of the
electors were in search of wives.   Six of these women
were advantageously married, the seventh entering a nunnery; and when in his old age Rudolph wished to make an
alliance with Burgundy, he had no one left to sacrifice on
the altar of Hymen but himself.   At the age of sixty-six
he wedded a princess of fourteen!

The strug-
gle with
Ottocar of
Bohemia.

Rudolph's great achievement, the overthrow of King
Ottocar of Bohemia and the confiscation of Austria, proved
of private more than of public benefit, enabling him, as it
did, to provide an appanage for his family, which they have
held down to the present day.   The struggle had been one
for supremacy, inasmuch as Ottocar denied the validity of
Rudolph's election; it had been long and fierce, for the
Bohemian had a strong following and the revenues of
many lands.   Ottocar had once been reduced to submission
and had agreed to do homage; but his friends declared that,
during the performance of this act, which was to be in private, Rudolph had purposely let fall the walls of his tent
and displayed his enemy upon his knees.   The tables
turned, indeed, and there came a time when, to use the
words of a contemporary chronicle, "all the family of
King Rudolph ran to confessors, arranged their affairs,
forgave their enemies, and received the communion; for a
mortal danger seemed to hang over them."   But these
troubles ended with that scene on the Marchfeld near
Dornkrut, where Ottocar, defeated and deserted, still refused to submit, but rather fought on with the strength
and spirit of a giant until unhorsed and mortally wounded.

To the disgrace of the Germans, his seventeenth wound was inflicted after he was already captive. Dante, writing his immortal poem a few years later, gives this hero a prominent place in purgatory.

On the whole, Rudolph's reign may be considered distinctly beneficial to Germany, and he left a memory that was revered for centuries. Much that he attempted remained unaccomplished, but he was firm in his endeavors to put down crime, and is known to have included as many as twenty-nine robbers in one sweeping sentence of death. He did his best, also, to stop private feuds, but with no great success. What could one expect of an age in which there was absolutely no conception of such a thing as "breach of the peace"? Not for two whole centuries was any general law passed making it a crime to take private vengeance for the infliction of wrongs.

False Fredericks and false Conradins.

Quiet and peace did not return at once; whole classes of men found their cherished hopes not fulfilled. There was no lack of minor revolts, while strange delusions seized upon the people. False Fredericks and false Conradins cropped up on all sides, the exposure of the one seeming not to deter the rest. A certain Dietrich Holzschuh, the most famous of all, was from the first recognized in Cologne as an arrant impostor. He was imprisoned for a while, then brought into the market-place, crowned with tinsel, and seated on a ladder in lieu of a throne. But this was the beginning, not the end, of his experiences. With half of his hair torn out, and with mud-spattered garments, but stoutly maintaining that he was Frederick II., Dietrich was finally driven from the city, but took refuge in the neighboring Neuss. Here he gave, it was said, convincing proofs of his identity to Frederick's old soldiers, and was encouraged to set up his court, which was visited from far and near. Such rumors were spread of his power and wealth that the Marquis of Este sent a special envoy to inquire into the matter. Princes were summoned before the new mercy-seat, and Rudolph was ordered to come and do homage for his royal office. Dietrich later moved to Wetzlar, before which town the king appeared in force, demanding his surrender. He was finally brought into camp chained to the stirrup of Marshal Pappenheim's horse, was tortured, then burnt at the stake.

Adolphus of Nassau and Albert of Austria.

Rudolph's successor, Adolphus of Nassau, was a young, almost poverty-stricken nobleman, who was noted chiefly for his fighting qualities, and who had more than once consented to act as a paid *condottiere*. Once on the throne, which he achieved by bribery, his chief idea seemed to be to gain for himself a dynastic appanage like that of the Hapsburgs — a step to which he was driven, indeed, by the fact that the crown, as such, was almost without revenues. But this endeavor led him into shifty ways and into acts of downright violence.

In the background was always the stern figure of Albert of Austria, the son of Rudolph, who regarded as his by right the crown from which the electors had excluded him because of his autocratic ways. He had even gone so far as to possess himself of the imperial insignia, but had been obliged to surrender them to Adolphus. Now all the enemies of the latter rallied to the Austrian's banner. With an army of Rhenish knights Albert marched to Göllheim and flung down the gauntlet to his rival. The two flaunted the same imperial banner — a white cross on a red ground. Albert's men, armed with poniards, were told to strike for the horses and not for the heavily armored knights. One exciting moment has made the battle memorable: the two kings suddenly found themselves face to face; Albert's blow struck his enemy full in the bared face and the blood streamed down to the ground.

His horse fell under him, and the daggers of the Austrians
put an end to his reign and to his life.

Albert was a stern, strong man — "hard as a diamond"
one chronicler calls him.   In one of his illnesses he had
submitted to being held upside down by his physicians
until the blood gushed forth from eyes, nose, and mouth,
in consequence of which he was half blind.   He was
rigidly zealous in upholding the empire's rights, and he
came, as we shall see, in another connection, into bitter
war with the electors.   On the whole, he was successful,
but in the midst of his triumph occurred the horrible
crime that gained for its perpetrator the name of John the
Parricide.   Albert's own nephew, a moody, discontented
youth who claimed that a part of his inheritance had been
withheld, formed a plot to lure the king to a lonely spot
on the bank of the Reuss; here they fell upon him and
stabbed him to the heart.   The principal culprit fled to
Italy, where, seven years later, the new king came suddenly upon him in a monastery and imprisoned him for
life.

Character of Albert of Austria.

Henry of Luxemburg, known as Henry VII., is described
by a contemporary as forty years of age, half French by
education, graceful of figure, not tall, but "just about tall
enough," with prominent eyebrows, bright cheeks, and fair
hair.   He had a very high sense of his own importance and
earned the name of a second Barbarossa.   He spoke of
himself as head of the world, and of his crown as the crown
of crowns, and had the code of Justinian amended to read
that every human creature must obey the Roman emperor.
He went to Italy in all the pride of a heaven-ordained
restorer of law and liberty: we have his own description
of how in the long interregnum the communes had possessed themselves of all the imperial prerogatives; how
the citizens, divided into factions, were warring to the

Personality of Henry VII.

death with one another or driving the vanquished into exile. In every city the powerful Guelph nobles were opposed by equally powerful Ghibellines.

Henry VII. in Italy.

The coming of a new emperor, the first since Frederick II., was hailed with unmixed delight. Even the Pope in Avignon grew eloquent over the prospect; he calls Henry the peace-bringer, the glorified of God, the cynosure of all eyes, the gentle one who is to sit upon the throne of majesty, and with his nod dispel all evil. Another voice we hear, too, — that of a banished Florentine, who thought to see the day dawning after a night of perpetual woe. Full of joyous excitement, Dante wrote a circular letter to the princes and cities of Italy: justice, he tells them, weak as heliotrope without the sun, will now revive again; the strong lion of Judah has pricked up his ears; a second Moses will snatch his people from the torments of the Egyptians. He is coming — he the bridegroom hasting to the wedding, the compassionate Henry, glory of his people, the godlike Cæsar and Augustus.

Dante's disappointment.

Henry came, but he came as a partisan rather than as the mild, compassionate one. It is true he told exiles who came to him at Turin that he was completely unprejudiced, but the new stadtholders he imposed on the communes were invariably Ghibellines; in Milan he declared for the Visconti; in Cremona he threw down the golden lion and imprisoned three hundred citizens. Dante and his party grew weary of waiting for the deliverer's appearance; there in Tuscany, the poet had declared, was the sink of iniquity, there the heart of the hydra. In a letter to the emperor he still speaks of him as the Lamb that is to take away the sins of the world, but cannot conceal that many are asking, "Art thou he that shall come or must we look for another?"

Henry died in Italy in August, 1313, among the rever-

berations of papal thunder. There were rumors of foul
play. Into the cup of the Eucharist, which the emperor
alone of laymen might enjoy, a priest was said to have
infused poison concealed under his finger-nails. Men
declared that the pious Kaiser had refused to take an
emetic for fear of profaning the body of Christ.

At each successive election the Hapsburgs had come
forward as pretenders to the throne. Just as Albert had
hoped to succeed Rudolph, so Frederick the Fair had hoped
to succeed Albert; he had failed then, but now on the
decease of Henry VII. he was able to play an important
part. He was the least gifted of three brothers; but the
youngest and most warlike, Leopold, was willing to draw
sword in his behalf. Their rival now was Louis of Bavaria,
who had drawn down on him, by his bravery at the fierce
battle of Gammelsdorf, the eyes of all Germany. Louis had
secured four out of the seven electoral votes, but the Hapsburgs maintained that an adherent of their own, Henry of
Carinthia, as true king of Bohemia, should have replaced
the actual king, John. There were two royal coronations:
the one (that of Frederick) in the wrong place but by the
right person; the other in the right place (Aix-la-Chapelle)
but by the wrong person (the Archbishop of Mainz).

There followed another of those long, wasting wars that
Germany had known so well. The private resources of
the Hapsburgs were greater, but Louis's followers more
numerous. In physique, too, the Bavarian had the advantage; he was tall, slender, muscular, and fitted by nature
to rule, says a chronicler, *as sometimes happens among the
bees!* Men praised his eye like that of a stag, his elastic
step, his healthy, bright coloring, his finely pencilled eyebrows, his hearty, merry nature. There was a trace of
timorousness about him, indeed, for he daily took an anti-
dote for fear of being poisoned.

Capture of
Frederick
the Fair.

For years the struggle went on between Frederick and Louis in a desultory fashion; but at last, at Mühldorf on the river Inn, the three Hapsburg brothers, aided by tribes so wild that they fed on cats and dogs, came upon Louis and King John of Bohemia, whose forces outnumbered their own. It was the day of St. Wenceslaus, the Bohemian patron saint. Frederick was urged not to fight, but declared that he had already made too many widows and orphans to desist now. He headed his troops, and a chronicler awards him the praise that "straight through the fight there was no better knight than he." But Bavarian reserves won the day; fourteen hundred Austrian nobles were taken prisoner, among them Frederick himself. "I was never so glad to see you," Louis is said to have remarked; "And I never so unwilling to see you," was the rejoinder. Louis's later conduct toward Frederick was influenced by each twist and turn of his quarrel with the Pope: he released him after two years and a half of captivity, and afterward asked him to share his throne; a document was signed at Munich in which he was formally accepted as coregent. "In the church, in the street," it ran, "and everywhere, we are to have similar honors; each shall sign and call himself King of the Romans and Augmenter of the Empire; we shall speak of each other as brothers and write to each other."

The events that conclude the reign of Louis are so intertwined with his relations to the electors and to the Papacy that it now becomes necessary to retrace our steps for more than half a century, and follow the developments that led to such complications, taking up the events once more reign by reign.

The electoral college, consisting of the three archbishops, — Mainz, Cologne, and Treves, — of the king of Bohemia, the Margrave of Brandenburg, the Duke of Saxony, and the

Count Palatine, first came into prominence at the election of Rudolph, though just on that occasion Bohemia's vote was usurped by Bavaria.   From that time on, until the end of the empire, in 1806, these seven, and eventually nine men, played a part in German history scarcely second to that of the emperors; they claimed themselves to be the seven pillars on which the empire rested.   They imposed what conditions they pleased upon their candidate, and forced him to sign an instrument called the *Wahlcapitulation*, which may well be translated an "election surrender."   When the monarch began to grow restive and to walk in other paths, they often warred with, and occasionally deposed him. Their insatiable greed brought things to a most wretched pass; never in all history have there been worse scandals connected with elections than at the time of Rudolph's death.   Adolphus of Nassau was called upon to reward his electors with incredible grants, — hand-ointment, a poet of the time calls it, — and was threatened with debtor's arrest and attachment of his private property until he should have paid.   His final inability to keep these promises was one of the chief causes of their pronouncing the throne vacant and calling in Albert of Austria.   Their act of accusation was full of the most bitter reproaches and the most partisan and unfounded charges, such as breaking into churches, slaying priests at the altar, and scattering the bread and wine of the Eucharist about the floor.

The rise of the electoral college.

If the electors had hoped to find Albert a more subservient tool than Adolphus, they soon found that they had reckoned without their host.   In order to make sure of his election he did, it is true, make promises as ruinous as those of his predecessor; but no sooner was he on the throne than he took the offensive against those who had placed him there.   Indeed, he seemed fairly to court the conflict, to such extremes had these men carried their pre-

Albert of Austria and the seven electors.

sumption and insolence; "In there I still have many kings," the Archbishop of Mainz is said to have remarked to the monarch himself, proudly tapping his own hunting-pouch. One of Albert's upholders wrote to the Pope that such rapacity made it fairly impossible for any king to rule with dignity; "Hence come wars and tumults, and there is nothing to look forward to but desolation and ruin for our land and danger for our souls."

The unlawful imposition of exorbitant tolls on Rhine shipping, at a point where there was no passing round by land, gave Albert his opportunity. This matter he declared had been settled by law and precedent in the reign of his father. In a war manifesto issued in May, 1301, he accused the electors of every kind of avarice.

Albert of Austria and Pope Boniface VIII.

The ally upon whom the archbishops would naturally most rely was Boniface VIII., Pope of Rome, and a lineal descendant, in a spiritual sense, of Gregory VII. At his jubilee, in the year 1300 A.D., the most successful demonstration over which the Papacy had ever presided, he is reported to have appeared in costly robes and to have declared, "I, I am the emperor!" He now summoned Albert to come to Rome within six weeks, assuming as a matter of course that his voice was final in the matter of elections to the German throne. Among the charges for which the king was to answer was the killing of Adolphus of Nassau; should he fail to cleanse himself, his subjects were to be freed from their allegiance.

The news of Albert's military successes, joined to the Pope's own critical situation with regard to France, soon caused him to change his tone. The king had brought the Count Palatine to his knees in a single expedition and held the Archbishop of Mainz besieged in Bingen; Boniface's conflict, moreover, with Philip IV. of France was fast nearing its ignominious and fatal conclusion. Loftier than ever, indeed, were his assumptions; "It is altogether necessary to salvation that every human being be subject to the Roman pontiff," was the ending of one of his decrees. But Albert he now formally acknowledged as rightful ruler, explaining his change of front on sufficiently remarkable grounds; the German people, he declared, were corrupt and diseased in every fibre of their being, and their ruler must be left free to heal their wounds with "soothing oil and sharp vinegar." The emperor has been placed above kings and kingdoms to the end that, sitting on the throne of justice, he should dispel all evil with his glance.

On the murder of Albert, King Philip of France tried hard to seat his own brother, Charles of Valois, upon the German throne, and to this end a French writer of renown had the audacity to propose that a papal decree should once for all do away with the whole electoral college. But the latter body was far from moribund, and returned to its policy of choosing a weak instrument of its will. Henry of Luxemburg, acceding to all their demands, had abandoned the field to them for the sake of pursuing his ambitious, but unsuccessful, policy in Italy.

Babylonian captivity of the Papacy.

By this time the popes had altogether fallen from their high pedestal. Boniface VIII. had been bearded in his own palace at Anagni by the envoys of Philip the Fair, and grief and indignation had put an end to his life. Figuratively, if not literally, the iron glove of the Colonna had smitten him in the face. The Papacy had gone into its captivity at Avignon, to last, like that of the Jews by the Babylonians, for seventy years. When Henry VII. demanded the imperial coronation in Rome, it had to be performed by cardinals deputed for the purpose. St. Peter's was held by Robert of Anjou, king of Naples and son of the murderer of Conradin, who was the mainstay of the Guelph party; accordingly, after some fierce fighting, the ceremony was held in the church of the Lateran, and Henry revenged himself by swinging his sword toward all four quarters of the heavens in token that the whole world belonged to him.

Death of Henry VII. in Italy.

Henry issued a manifesto against Robert, in which he charged him with growing fat on the spoils of the empire, kicking up the heels of rebellion, and spewing out the poison of injustice. He is declared to have forfeited his titles and dignities and is sentenced to death on the block. Robert replied with similar vituperations: Henry was a garrulous old woman, he said, who talked instead of fighting; he was following in the footsteps of those Fredericks, Manfreds, and Conradins who "had sown the bitter pest of sedition and hate" against the zealous upholders of the church.

Pope Clement's friendship for Henry had grown cold as ice the moment he found that there was a chance of his invading Naples. The memory of the Hohenstaufens rushed back upon him when he found the emperor allying himself with Frederick of Sicily, who, on the female side, was one of that "viper brood." The shades of the past seemed, indeed, to have risen when the Germans adopted as their ensign the head of Conradin. Clement sent to remind Henry of the oath of fealty taken at his coronation, but received answer that oath of fealty the emperor owed to no man, nor was he aware that his predecessors, the Roman emperors, had ever sworn such oath. Then came threats of instant excommunication against any one, "be he of priestly, imperial, or kingly rank," who should attack Robert of Naples or his lands. The attack was made, but this was the juncture at which Henry was seized at Buonconvento by the fever of which he died.

The struggle between Pope and emperor, the last but not the least bitter of a long series, broke out almost immediately, but on other grounds. John XXII., who ascended the pontifical throne in 1316, at the age of seventy-two, was tiny in stature, bald, lean, and of sallow countenance. He went around with his little body bent forward and muttering all sorts of things to himself; he spent his time in hearing reports, in discovering new ways by which to tax his clergy, and in issuing countless bulls and briefs. Although needing little for his personal wants, he loved to amass gold for its own sake; and the Florentine historian, Villani, whose brother was papal banker, is authority for the statement that, at John's death, his fortune amounted to the enormous sum of twenty-five million guldens.

Pope John XXII.

Strange that a Pope who lived at Avignon almost as a minion of the French king should have continued to hold so lofty a conception of his own prerogative! There is no reason to doubt but that John shared the views of the popular theologian, Augustino Trionfo, who dedicated to him a writing in which he declares that secular laws have no force, except in so far as the Pope confirms and approves them, and that, should the welfare of the church demand it, he can withdraw the power of choice from the electors and set up an emperor of his own.

In the beginning John had held aloof from the dispute between Louis of Bavaria and Frederick of Hapsburg concerning the possession of the German crown. In the same non-committal terms he had announced his own accession to each of the rival kings; his hope seems to have been that they would hold each other in check at home and allow to him full sway in Italy. Had not one of his predecessors, Clement V., formally declared that so long as the imperial power was in abeyance the administration of the imperial lands in Italy rested *ipso facto* in the papal hands? John appointed Robert of Anjou, the old enemy of the

Conflict of John XXII. and Louis of Bavaria.

Germans, his vicar general, and Robert's subordinates were sent all over northern Italy. Here they came in contact with similar emissaries of Louis of Bavaria, and it was on this matter of disputed jurisdiction that the conflict broke forth.

John took the ground that the struggle of two kings for the German, and consequently the imperial, throne constituted a state of affairs with regard to which the Pope was, by the nature of the case, the arbiter. Louis should have applied to him, he claimed, and have bowed to his decision in the first place before exercising the royal functions. It was necessary for him, now, to lay down his crown within three months under penalty of the church's ban. In March, 1324, the Pope actually did resort to this weapon, which had done the church such good service against the Hohenstaufens. The times of Barbarossa seemed, indeed, returning when Louis, having heard of John's intention, issued furious manifestoes, declaring that the election of a German king needed no confirmation from the Pope of Rome, and that the person chosen, even without receiving the crown of the empire, might exercise all imperial rights; that between rival claimants not the papal fiat, but the sword alone, was to decide; that this Pope was wallowing in crime and endeavoring to subvert the empire; that he had openly said that the peace of the church meant Germany's discord; that he would use all his power, he had declared in the consistory of cardinals, to crush that brazen serpent; that he was himself a heretic for not believing in the doctrine of the poverty of Christ.

The Minorites against the Pope. This last allusion was to a violent dispute that was going on within the fold of the church, and that had split the Franciscan friars into two hostile factions. Whereas the rule of its founder prescribed absolute poverty, that order had in reality, through gifts of pious persons and in other ways, acquired great riches. In order to quiet rising scruples, the nominal ownership of this property had been vested in the Papacy, and the Franciscans retained simply the usufruct of their estates. The discussion was revived with great spirit in the time at which we have arrived, and it was debated at endless length whether or not Christ and His apostles had held possessions in common. The Minorite friars, without consulting the Pope, promulgated Christ's poverty as a dogma, to which John retaliated by pronouncing them heretics and making them take back their own property. They were thus forced over to the side of the Pope's political antagonists, and did Louis good service by gaining the ear of men of high position — princes, and even electors.

John for his part drew closer to the Hapsburgs, though not willing to commit himself to the extent of acknowledging Frederick the Fair as king. Yet this fear of closer union of his two chief antagonists seems to have greatly influenced the policy of Louis. We find him liberating his rival after two and a half years of arrest; we find him soon after not merely making a treaty of peace, but also arranging a marriage alliance between his own son and Frederick's daughter. Should the peace fail to be sanctioned, however, by the Pope and by Leopold of Austria, the Hapsburg was voluntarily to return to his prison.

Alliance of the Pope with the Hapsburgs.

As a matter of fact this sanction proved impossible to gain. John insisted on Frederick's breaking his oath to Louis — he would absolve him from it, he said — and roundly forbade him to return to captivity. Leopold in the meanwhile had had dealings with France, promising in return for the aid of Charles IV. to procure him the throne of the empire. These foreign complications explain in part Louis's treatment of Frederick; in part we have to reckon with the king's own fickleness and caprice.

Was it really merely to propitiate Leopold of Austria that Frederick was appointed successor to the throne, with right to exercise the royal prerogatives in case of the absence of Louis?

When the plan of the anomalous double rule was placed before the electors, they seem to have rejected it absolutely; but Louis soon afterward came out with a scheme still more radical, and offered to resign altogether if the Pope would confirm Frederick in his stead. The grounds for such a proposition are not altogether clear; but Louis seems to have known, for a certainty, beforehand, that the Pope would refuse to enter into the project.

Literary assailants of the Papacy.

The time had now come when the German king was less under the necessity of making concessions. The death of Leopold rendered Frederick less formidable; as a matter of fact, he plays no further rôle to the time of his death, in 1330. And against Pope John, Louis was now able to marshal the force of literary assailants that have made his reign so memorable. It is the dawn of a new age, the first sign of mediæval assumptions bowing their head beneath the crushing blows of a popular literature. In a manner unprecedentedly free the whole relation of church to state was beginning to be ventilated.

The *Defensor Pacis*.

Marsilius of Padua, the body physician of Louis, developed a new political system, differing in many respects from the teaching of the long-revered Aristotle, yet rational and thorough. His great book, the *Defensor Pacis*, in which he defines the position of the church within the state, contained the deadliest single assault ever aimed at the Papacy. No wonder Pope John dubbed its author and his assistants "monsters from the deeps of Satan and the sulphur-pools of hell!" Clement VI. maintained that he had extracted from the work no less than 240 heretical utterances.

Marsilius started with the assumption that the legislative power, in the final instance, rests with the people themselves; the head or ruler, who should be chosen for his merits, not for his parentage, simply carries out their will. Every citizen has rights to enjoy and duties to perform; a priest is in no wise exempt and in no way superior to others. Within the hierarchy itself the last resort is not the Pope, but a general council of the whole church; such a body and none other may rightfully impose the ban or interdict; all priests are equal among themselves, and equally subject to conciliar decrees. Did Peter ever assume authority over his fellow-apostles? Or, granted that he did, was there any real proof that the popes were his successors, could any one state positively that he had ever been in Rome? Why was the Gospel of St. Luke, why were the Acts of the Apostles, silent on the matter? As for heresy, it was not a crime, but possibly a disease to which the priest might minister. A man's opinions and convictions were his own; he was not to be punished for them unless they led him into acts contrary to the law.

The claim to jurisdiction over the affairs of the empire, continues the *Defensor Pacis*, and to the right of controlling elections, was laughable — nothing more; if the Pope could calmly set aside the results of their deliberations, any seven blear-eyed barbers could fill the offices of the electors. The Pope's assertion that he will not interfere with the rights of the latter, strikes Marsilius like the assurance upon the part of a man who knocks out another's eye, that no harm is intended; the claim that the head of the church must watch over elections to the headship of the empire, lest some heretic be chosen, is baseless when one considers that three out of the electoral college are high church dignitaries.

The success of the *Defensor Pacis* was phenomenal;

Imperial coronation of Louis the Bavarian.

it spread all over Europe, and very old manuscripts of it have been found in Germany and England, as well as in Italy.   When the Reformation came and the art of printing was pressed into its service, this writing was among the first to be published with great care and magnificence. Marsilius was, indeed, the direct precursor of Luther. The ideals of the *Defensor Pacis* seemed about to achieve their realization when, in 1328, Louis entered Rome and was proclaimed emperor, not by a Pope, but by the Roman people, who had assembled for the purpose on the Capitoline Hill. The two Italian bishops who anointed him were under the church's ban; the city itself was declared under the interdict, and orders given that that most precious of all relics, the handkerchief of St. Veronica, should be hidden away in the Pantheon from the desecrating gaze of heretics.   The duty of actually placing the crown on the emperor's head was performed by a Colonna, in all probability the very one who is reputed to have flung his iron gauntlet into the face of Pope Boniface VIII.

Judgment passed on John XXII.

Louis's next step was to hold such judgment over John XXII. as Otto the Great had once held over John XII. News had meanwhile come that the Pope had declared a holy war against the emperor, and was offering to those who took part in it such absolution as was otherwise given only to crusaders.   Collection boxes were to be placed in all the churches, that funds might be forthcoming for the enterprise.   Louis, for his part, caused to be publicly read in the Square of St. Peter a list of the Pope's misdoings, — Marsilius had helped to draw it up, — his miserliness, his promulgation of heretical dogmas, his attacks on the rights of the empire.   He is the mystical anti-Christ, the rider on the red horse who is mentioned in the Apocalypse. In absenting himself from Rome, in preaching the cross against innocent people, he is scorning the express com-

mands of Christ.   He is declared deposed from the Papacy
and is ordered to be handed over to the secular arm.   The
election of a new Pope is promised, who shall take up his
permanent residence in Rome, and not absent himself for
more than a two days' journey without permission from
the clergy and people.   An acceptable candidate was found
in the person of Pietro Rainalducci, who took the name
of Nicholas V.   For a short time the new emperor and he
who was thus declared to be the spiritual head of Christendom basked together in a flood of glory, but the rays were
the rays of the setting sun.   Not ten weeks later the failure to repulse Robert of Anjou, the defection of the Minorites, the demand of a subsidy from the Romans, had so
lessened the reverence of the people that Pope and emperor
alike had to flee the city for fear of being stoned.   After
two years Nicholas repaired to Avignon, craved and
obtained forgiveness of John XXII., and remained in
honorable durance to the end of his life.

The later years of Louis the Bavarian's reign are as
unedifying as those of the worst of Germany's rulers; his
impetuosity, his vacillation, his utter want of true statesmanship, brought it about, to use the drastic figure of a
contemporary, that "his good odor began to stink in the
nostrils of the princes."   The most impracticable plans
rushed through his head: he would restore the imperial
prestige in Italy; by humbling himself to the ground, if
need be, he would force the Pope to grant him absolution
from the ban; no matter at what cost to others, he would
increase his own family possessions.   Then came an astounding project, which undoubtedly originated in the
councils of the Papacy and France, for abdicating wholly
in favor of a cousin, Henry of Lower Bavaria, a prince
who, by a secret compact, which may still be read, had
agreed to give a large portion of his gains — the whole of

Growing
unpopu-
larity of
Louis.

Burgundy and the bishopric of Cambray — to the French king should his efforts in his behalf meet with success.

The mere idea of this arrangement, of which, naturally, the half was not known, raised such an outcry that Louis was forced to deny all concern in the matter, to request that such "fables" be not believed, and to declare that nothing would induce him just then to lay down the responsibilities of his position.   Soon afterward we find him ready to make peace on the most unfavorable terms with Pope Benedict XII., successor of John XXII.   He will give up all communication with Marsilius of Padua and his like, he will openly condemn the *Defensor Pacis*, he will submit to a new imperial coronation at the hand of the Pope, thus acknowledging the invalidity of that pompous ceremony in Rome.   He will do any penance that may be imposed.

The meeting of the electors at Rense.

Benedict insisted that Louis should go one step deeper in his humiliation, and actually lay down his royal and imperial dignities until his title should have been more thoroughly investigated by the church; but this was too much for the emperor — too much even for the self-centred electors; and now we see a demonstration against the Papacy which marks an era in German history.   Indignation meetings were held at Rense and in Frankfort, and at the latter place, in 1338, a manifesto was drawn up by the electors, which vindicated in powerful language the rights of the empire.   That empire's head, so the writing declares, is head by election of the seven; his legislative power has descended to him directly through the Son of God; unto Cæsar must be rendered the things that are Cæsar's; there is absolutely no need of the approbation, authority, or consent of the apostolic see or of any person whatever; to doubt this assertion is high treason.

These were utterances such as many a better king than

Louis had never heard from his subjects.   They are to be explained in part by the fact that the emperor had for once made a popular move in espousing the cause of Edward III. of England against the king of France.   It was the beginning of the great struggle that was afterward to be known in history as the Hundred Years' War.   King Edward, who had promised large subsidies in return for two thousand men, came in person to Coblenz and placed himself at the feet of Louis, who sat on a throne in the crowded market-place in full imperial splendor.   Philip of Valois was declared deposed from the throne of France, and Edward was named imperial vicar for the German provinces on the lower Rhine.

Well might a contemporary call Louis of Bavaria the "foolish wise man, the dallying eager one, the lazy zealot." On a mere pretext and apparently only in the hope that the French king might speak a good word for him with the Pope, he broke the English treaty by stopping the supplies for the German contingents.   A storm of abusive pamphlets greeted the step.   A complication with regard to the Tyrol brought matters to a climax, and brought forward the House of Luxemburg as a rallying point for all the long pent-up discontent.   The Tyrol, through a marriage with its sole heiress, Margaret Maultasch, had come into the hands of John Henry, son of King John of Bohemia, and therefore grandson of the Emperor Henry VII. When, now, a party of the Tyrolese drove out John Henry after declaring that his marriage with Margaret had never been consummated, and offered her hand to Louis's son, Louis of Brandenburg, the emperor was foolish and grasping enough to accept the offer.   The discarded husband, the worst charge against whom was a bodily infirmity, was held up to the general derision of Europe, the pride of the Luxemburgers being cut to the quick by the shame

Opposition to Louis of Bavaria.

and injustice of the whole proceeding. Fiery King John, who had all the more influence from the astounding number of political intrigues he had carried on in all parts of Europe, and his eldest son, Charles, who was now openly brought forward as a candidate for the throne of the empire, became the centre of a strong opposition.

Charles of
Luxemburg
as anti-
king.
The Pope, now Clement VI., who had inherited the hostility of his predecessors and who had a new, tangible grievance from the fact that the marriage of Margaret and Louis was bigamy according to canon law, roused himself to deal a last crushing blow. Receiving the young Charles of Bohemia at Avignon, he agreed, in return for base concessions, to support him as candidate for the German throne. Then he issued a new bull of deposition against Louis, which, taken all in all, is the best example extant of a withering papal curse. With blindness, idiocy, and madness the Lord was to afflict the so-called emperor. Lightning was to strike him, flame to envelop him in this world and the next; the earth was to open and swallow him up. Nor was he to be alone in his hideous sufferings, for his sons were to be homeless and share in his fate.

In summoning the electors to proceed to a new election, the Pope renewed once more the old threat of Gregory X., of himself imposing a king on the land. At Rense, in July 11, 1346, the vote was cast, the three archbishops, the Duke of Saxony, and the king of Bohemia voting for Charles; the Palatinate and Brandenburg, being in Wittelsbach hands, were not represented.

It soon became evident that the German nation, as a whole, were not in sympathy with this revolutionary proceeding; a diet held at Spires declared roundly that they would never recognize this Luxemburg usurper; the cities of Cologne and Aix refused to admit him within their walls. Charles and his father retired to Luxemburg, and

when next we hear of them they are both in the heat of
the world-famous battle of Crécy, on the side of their
friend the French king.   King John reached here the end
of a checkered and adventurous career; by this time
utterly blind, he was led into the battle by two knights,
and fell desperately fighting.   It is said that the English princes, doubtless in memory of his bravery, adopted
from him the emblem of the three feathers and the motto
" Ich dien."   His son, too, was wounded, but was able to
return to Luxemburg, and thence, but only in disguise,
to Bohemia.   He found adherents in the Tyrol, and was
about to inaugurate a fierce struggle for the crown when
the news came that the old emperor had died while bear-
hunting, from a stroke of apoplexy.

CHAPTER VI.

THE RULERS OF THE HOUSE OF LUXEMBURG

AUTHORITIES : Lindner covers this period as well as the preceding, as does also Prutz. We are fortunate in having a detailed biography of the Emperor Charles IV. by Werunsky, in which separate chapters are devoted to the persecution of the Jews, the Flagellants, and the Black Death. The Golden Bull is translated in full in Henderson's *Select Documents.* See also Lamprecht, *Deutsche Geschichte,* and Sach, *Das deutsche Leben.*

Personality of Charles IV.

By the sudden death of Louis of Bavaria Charles IV. was left master of the situation. Here was a successor all ready to hand; he had been chosen with some show of legality ; he belonged to one of the great houses from which the selection must necessarily have been made; his lands, including Bohemia, were nearly as extensive as those of the Hapsburgs themselves. Charles was too little known in Germany to be personally popular; he had spent the greater part of his time in Paris, where he had been educated after the manner of a French prince, and in Bohemia and Italy. He had shown bravery and received a wound on the field of battle, he was not backward in the joust or tourney, but his strongest talent was for settling matters by diplomacy. For this, from Petrarch down, he has been generally decried by all, — accused of lack of heroism and of having the soul of a petty merchant.

When the Germans came to know Charles better, they found that he had a habit of never looking one straight in the face ; that, while listening to reports, he seemed to be bending all his energies to whittling wood; that he was

hypochondriacal, superstitious, and far too subservient to
the Papacy, through which, indeed, he had been elevated
to the throne. He was simple in his dress and his personal
wants were few. Ready and eager to administer justice, he
requested that complaints should be made directly to himself. For Bohemia he caused to be drawn up an elaborate
code of laws — the *Majestas Carolina* — which his nobles,
however, refused to adopt. He was zealous in his religious
observances — not from ulterior motives, but from a decided
bent in that direction. On his frequent journeyings, the
most eager of relic hunters, he caused many a tomb to be
opened that he might kiss the holy remains ; the skulls and
bones of which he acquired possession were splendidly
housed and richly adorned with gems ; when not in use, his
new Bohemian crown habitually rested on the hallowed
pate of good St. Wenceslaus. In memory of visions that
had once appeared to him he founded monasteries ; and in
his famous autobiography, which he carried down to the
time of his accession, he has much to say of mystic influences.

Not altogether unnaturally, this monarch's heart turned
more fondly to his own hereditary lands than to his German kingdom. The Emperor Maximilian once spoke of
his predecessor as the arch-father of Bohemia and arch-
stepfather of the empire; indeed, Charles is quoted as
having said himself that, could he have been sure of being
left in peace within his own dominions, he never would
have stretched out his hand for the German crown. The
city of Prague was his idol, and he devoted much time
and money to beautifying it. Here, as a lasting memorial
to his name, he founded the world-famous Carolina — the
great Prague University, the earliest of all such institutions in German-speaking lands and the destined scene of
the labors and sorrows of John Huss.

Hapsburg
against
Wittels-
bach.

With the dukes of Bavaria, the sons of the former

emperor, it was only natural that Charles should remain in hostility. They refused to concur in their fate, and were able to procure the calling of an assembly at Lahnstein, at which four men, claiming to be electors, were present. Here the forms of a new election were gone through with, and, to the surprise of no one more than the person most concerned, the vote for head of the Holy Roman Empire fell on Edward III. of England. That Edward never for a moment seriously thought of accepting the proffered honor is shown by the gracious reception he accorded to Duke William of Julier, Charles's own special envoy.

The false Waldemar of Brandenburg.

The latter monarch, for his part, found a means of annoying the Wittelsbachs beyond measure by encouraging a rival claimant to the margravate of Brandenburg, to which office also was attached the electoral vote. Down to 1320 A.D., Brandenburg had been ruled by the descendants of Albert the Bear, a contemporary of Frederick Barbarossa; but in 1319 had died the spendthrift Waldemar, and in the following year, his son, the last scion of the line. Waldemar had been given a sumptuous funeral, pompous and impressive, as a last tribute to his extravagant tastes. After four years of contention between various claimants, Louis of Bavaria had pronounced Brandenburg a lapsed fief of the crown, and had bestowed it upon his own son. Now, after twenty-eight years, the story was diligently circulated that the old Margrave Waldemar was not dead at all; that, conscience-stricken at having offended the church by his marriage with too near a relative, he had determined on a crusade of expiation, and had caused the corpse of another, a wandering conjurer, to be laid in the tomb prepared for himself. Then, taking the pilgrim's staff, he had trudged to Palestine, had for years remained a captive in the hands of the infidels, and, at last escaping, had heard of the woes that had fallen upon the Mark under the Wittelsbach rule, and had determined for the sake of his people to return and resume his sceptre.

Few knew at the time what is well known now, that the real Waldemar had long since obtained a dispensation for his marriage from Pope Clement VI., so that conscientious scruples could scarcely have driven him to such renunciation and penance. In the story itself there was nothing inherently improbable; Count Henry of Schwerin, long given up for dead, had returned after a similar captivity for a similar length of time. To romantic tales in connection with crusades there was no end. The people of the Mark, finally, were not likely to prove over-incredulous when it came to be a question of ridding themselves of a hated ruler. The Wittelsbachs' one idea of ruling had seemed to be to squeeze money out of the nobles and cities of this northern possession, and to spend it for the advantage of Bavaria and the Tyrol.

For the weak and the wavering the decision was made as easy as possible. The elector of Saxony and the counts of Anhalt vouched for the genuineness of this man's claim. According to common report, the Archbishop of Magdeburg had heard the whole story in the confessional, and given his word of honor that this was the real Waldemar. A signet ring played a prominent part in the matter of identification, while facts were repeated which could only have been known to the margrave and his intimates. The pretender must indeed have borne a strong likeness to the person he was counterfeiting, for men of all classes — priests, knights, and squires, declared that this was the prince they had known in their youth.

Charles IV. reaped more advantage than any one else from this conspiracy to oust the Wittelsbachs from Brandenburg, though there is not the slightest evidence to show

Acceptance of Waldemar by Charles IV.

that he was in any way directly concerned with the original imposture. A commission, made up apparently of fair-minded men, was appointed to look into the matter; on the strength of their report that persons who had seen and known the margrave were sure of his identity, Charles invested the false Waldemar with the Mark, having first, however, stipulated that his own share of the spoils should be the Lower Lausitz. The chief conspirators seem to have been Saxony, Anhalt, and Magdeburg, who hoped for the realization of claims of their own. The ceremony of investiture took place in a public assembly held on the heights of Heinersdorf near the road to Frankfort-on-the-Oder. The false Waldemar approached Charles's throne, which was erected on a richly decked platform, and took the oath of homage; the king then bestowed upon him the Mark and the electoral dignity, promising protection against all comers and exhorting the people to accept him as margrave. A number of cities had already handed in their allegiance.

Election of Gunther of Schwarz-burg as anti-king.

As a counter move to these doings in Brandenburg, the Wittelsbachs hastened once more to obtain the election of an anti-king — this time at Frankfort-on-the-Main. They could reckon on the votes of Mainz and of their own relative, the Count Palatine. The head of their house, that Louis who had been ousted from Brandenburg, they naturally considered as still an elector, while the requisite additional vote was gained by recognizing the Duke of Lauenburg as claimant to Saxony. By these four, Count Gunther of Schwarzburg, brave as a knight, but possessed neither of wealth nor of following, was invited to Frank-fort, and, after some demurring, done homage to by the citizens. They proved, indeed, his only adherents. Charles IV. soon made one of his master-strokes of diplomacy by offering his own hand in marriage to the daughter of the

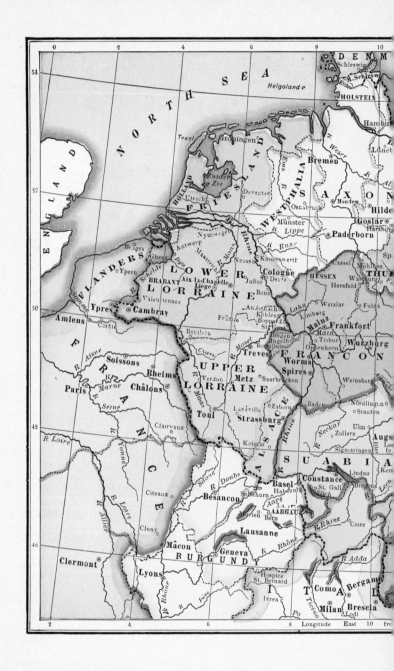

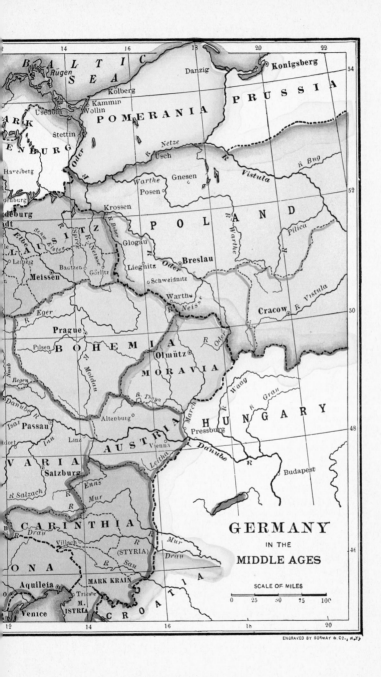

GERMANY
IN THE
MIDDLE AGES

SCALE OF MILES

0   25   50   75   100

ENGRAVED BY BORWAY & CO., N.Y.

Count Palatine, who, in consequence, weakly abandoned Gunther's cause. A short, fortunate campaign rendered the other Wittelsbachs more pliable; concessions did the rest. The dukes agreed to make peace; Charles to let fall the false Waldemar. Gunther had already been overtaken by what proved to be a mortal disease. Having agreed to abdicate, he was borne on a litter to Frankfort, where, before he died, he solemnly released the citizens from their oath.

The Brandenburg matter was not so easily settled; in 1350 A.D. Waldemar was declared an impostor by the Diet of Nuremberg, but not until five years later did he formally abandon his claims. By a treaty with the Wittelsbachs, by half compelling and half bribing, Charles procured the reversion of Brandenburg for his own family. We shall see how one of his sons finally conferred it on the line that has now held it for nearly five centuries. *Settlement of Brandenburg affair.*

If from the larger political events of the reign of Charles IV. we turn to the social developments and striking occurrences, we find this period more remarkable than any of its predecessors. An unheard-of calamity half depopulates Germany, and gives rise to superstitious excesses and wholesale persecution. On the other hand, in these days a document is drawn up, deliberated upon, sealed, and signed, which for the next 550 years is to be the criterion for imperial elections and for the rights and privileges of the electors. *The Black Death.*

Epidemics and even plagues were not infrequent in the Middle Ages, but the most deadly of all such visitations was the Black Death of 1348 – 49 A.D., the same great wave of destruction of which Boccaccio wrote, and which swept England as well as the Continent. Lasting for six or seven months, there were few German towns that escaped its ravages. The rate of mortality was incredibly high, and

Bremen alone, according to statistics drawn up at the time by the *Rath*, or city council, lost seven thousand of her citizens. The sickness was a loathsome one, where even in the most favorable cases the body of the patient was covered with great sores, and where death usually intervened on the third day.

The Flagellants.

In the wake of this plague, and in many cases undoubtedly spreading the infection, came the Flagellants, or flying penitents, calling upon men to repent and to rend their hearts in the face of so evident a judgment of God. There were scenes of indescribable excitement, and whole populations of towns would march out to meet the fanatics, who would approach in long procession, with flags flying, candles burning, and crosses borne on before, chanting the while the dreariest of hymns and dirges. Bound by their vow not to stop more than one night in any one city, the Flagellants moved like fleeting spirits from place to place. In the course of their religious exercises, which were publicly held in the streets, they roused themselves to frenzied pitches of enthusiasm, scourging themselves with flails bound with iron spikes which entered so deeply into the flesh that, as an eye-witness assures us, great strength was required to remove them. It was easy for the Flagellants to gain recruits : we are told that in Strassburg alone they were joined by a thousand citizens, although their rule was by no means to accept every one who presented himself ; husbands had to bring express permission from their wives before their cases would be considered at all. Distinctive of the sect was their hatred of the clergy, and in so far they were precursors of the Reformation ; indeed, they openly attacked the dogmas of the church and denied to the priesthood its spiritual supremacy. Like all such associations or brotherhoods, the Flagellants degenerated in consequence of too much success. Vagabonds joined them, in order to gain the nimbus of martyrdom and to be well cared for by generous admirers. But the clergy girded itself for the attack; the Pope banned and proscribed the whole organization as a danger to the state and an insult to the Divine Majesty. The civic authorities and the territorial lords took such stringent measures that before long the whole agitation had entirely subsided.

Not so the general spirit of alarm and unrest among the people. In so far as they had ceaselessly recommended the wholesale massacre of the Jews — who, they declared, had polluted the wells and caused the Black Death — the leaven of the Flagellants continued to work. No darker blot upon mediæval civilization can be found than the relentless persecution of one whole, defenceless part of the population by another, of Jews by Christians. The fanatical attacks upon the Jews had begun at the time of the crusades; until then they had been allowed to live quietly in the towns and to engage in trade like the rest of the inhabitants. In certain towns, like Spires, they had even been given special commercial privileges; they were allowed, too, to hold real estate, to have their own special burial place, to sell meat to Christians, and to have Christian servants. But with the crusades had come in the wild desire to avenge the blood of Christ on all who might be classed among His enemies. Countless stories were invented of sacrilege and murder committed by the Jews; the chronicles tell frequently of children sacrificed or of the bread of the Eucharist stolen and dishonored.

Fanatical attacks on the Jews.

The Hohenstaufen emperors interfered in favor of the Jews, but with the unfortunate result that their legal status came to be that of special dependants on imperial protection, for which protection they were compelled to pay a high tax; *Kammerknechte*, or slaves of the exchequer, was their official title. But one step further, and the theory was formulated that, whenever the specific time for which

Legal status of the Jews.

the protection was granted had elapsed, the emperor might do as he pleased with the belongings of this outcast race. Each new lease of protection meant a new heavy payment; Charles IV. went so far as to farm out these revenues to the cities, which then, in turn, extorted all they could from the luckless victims. Louis the Bavarian had already invented the shameful "golden sacrificial penny" which was retained by his successors. Every individual Jew or Jewess over the age of twelve, and owning more than twenty guldens, was to pay a tribute of one gulden, the collection of which was likewise eventually placed in the hands of revenue farmers. And added to the regular taxes were the still more galling special ones — a policy of oppression that was to reach its climax in the next century, when the Emperor Sigismund demanded that the Jews should pay the expenses of the Council of Constance!

Insults
heaped on
Jews.

It is useless to dwell on the frequent slights and indignities that were put upon this people; no amount of details could open up a darker vista than the decrees of the Lateran Council of 1215 A.D. Jews are not to show themselves upon the streets from Maundy Thursday until Easter. Christians are never to eat with them under pain of excommunication. Jews are to dress in such a manner as to be easily distinguishable; they are to buy no fish in Lent lest the prices be increased for fasters.

The Jews
driven
to usury.

Is it any wonder that the victims of such a policy became as despicable as even their tormenters could wish? Forbidden to hold office over Christians, forbidden to look on while honorable knights were disporting themselves in the tournament, forbidden even to carry on the commercial enterprises in which they had hitherto been leaders, they sank lower and lower in the social scale. Only one resource was left them, the loaning of money; for centuries the church had pronounced the taking of interest to be usury and had forbidden all Christians thus to soil their hands.   Yet borrowing money was an essential part of economic and mercantile advance, and all classes of men, from the emperor down to the knights and students, were at all times heavily in debt to the Jews.   Among the objects pawned as security we find state revenues and even church tithes.   Efforts were made to restrict the rate of interest, but we find it rarely, if ever, below $21\frac{2}{3}$ per cent, and rising from that to $96\frac{2}{3}$.   Strangers, indeed, might be cheated to any extent; a contemporary bond has been preserved that calls for 166 per cent.

If hatred and jealousy had existed before, we can imagine how those feelings increased as the Christians saw these usurers fattening on the sweat of Christian brows, the handsomest dwellings coming into their hands, honorable men absolutely at their mercy.   It was all directly opposed to the spirit of the trade guilds, that stood for honest manufactures and for equal profits; and communistic and revolutionary thoughts were already rife in all directions.   The legend revived with full force as to how Frederick Barbarossa was to awake from his slumbers in the Kyffhäuser Mountain, and bring salvation to the oppressed, how rich men were to marry poor maidens, and how the clergy were to be made to cover their tonsures, with filth if need be, and go to work as common laborers.

The Jewish massacres of the years 1348 to 1351 A.D. were, then, one phase in what would to-day be termed a socialistic uprising.   And barbarous enough were the details of the movement.   In Basel the guilds with floating banners marched to the Rathhaus, and wrung a promise from the councillors that they would murder the Jews, and forbid any of the sect to enter the town for the next two hundred years.   All the Jews within reach were then locked up in a building on a little island in the

Jewish massacres.

Rhine; fire was set to the base of the structure and all the inmates perished. In Spires a regular funeral pyre was erected in the cemetery, and a crowd of victims driven into the flames. In fifty different towns similar scenes were enacted; in some cases the Jews were buried alive; more frequently they ignited their own houses and perished in the ruins rather than fall into the hands of their pursuers.

The crown and the massacres.

It shocks the sensibilities to see the attitude taken by the crown in the matter of all this persecution and violence. There was no attempt to punish the heathenish excesses; in fact, formal charters of amnesty were issued to various towns. The proof, indeed, seems indisputable that Charles IV., even before any uprising had taken place, promised the citizens of Frankfort the ownership of all property that might accrue, should there be a general massacre. After all was over, on the strength of the Jews having belonged to his own exchequer, he claimed all ownerless lands, and even took over the lists of uncollected debts due to the victims. Many of these debts he forgave, but the rest he gave to the cities in return for a fixed sum.

In the end king, princes, and people alike found they could not subsist without these same Jews; their high taxes were too important for the public treasury, no one could be found to replace them in the matter of making loans. Almost immediately the reaction came: a large number of the extant deeds and charters of Charles IV. consist of permissions issued to various nobles, to receive back and tax Jews. Nor did the condition of the latter improve with time; indeed, the regulations concerning the wearing of the "Jew token," or mark of their outcast condition, became more frequent and more severe. In Nuremberg they were obliged to wear a red cap, in Augsburg yellow circles on their clothes. Ever pointed at with the finger of scorn, it is only in the most recent times that they have been able to vindicate their racial abilities.

In the midst of pestilence and of the disturbances caused by the fanatic persecution of the Jews, Charles IV. had not altogether lost sight of the usual goal of German kings, the imperial crown. But whatever steps he took toward acquiring it were marked by his usual caution and clever reckoning. In the spring of 1350 there appeared before Charles IV. him a fugitive, but one who for many months had centred and Rienzi. upon himself the eyes of the world, and who to-day is far more widely known and remembered than Charles himself. Cola di Rienzi, driven from that Rome where, as tribune of the people, he had displayed so much power and magnificence, came to Prague with the story that a holy hermit had pronounced it the will of God that a divinely chosen saint, aided by the emperor-elect, should divest the clergy of all their influence. He, Rienzi, would lead Charles to Rome, where both might be sure of a hearty welcome.

But Rienzi had made his reckoning without his host. Louis of Bavaria, indeed, had been willing to accept the crown from the hands of the populace; not so this devoted son of the church. After several interviews Charles placed Rienzi under arrest; for a year and a half he kept him near him, and then allowed him to return to Rome by way of Avignon and in company of the papal legate, Cardinal Albornez. The Roman populace received their former demagogue with great rejoicings, but soon after, in October, 1354, stormed his dwelling on the Capitol, and drove him to his tragic death.

Before this, already, while Rienzi was still chafing in Charles captivity, a second demand had come to Charles to hasten IV. and to Rome and assume the crown. The poet Petrarch, as Petrarch. Dante in the case of Henry VII., sent a passionate appeal depicting the wretched condition of the city, and urging him to come and complete the work begun by his grand-father. Charles returned answer that the old Roman Empire was a thing of the past, and could never be resus-citated.

Just how far this attitude was due to a desire to emanci-pate himself from the sponsorship of a patriot like Petrarch will never be known. Certain it is that Charles was very far from despising the title of Emperor of the Romans; for in 1355, when he found that he could have it in an or-thodox way and that Innocent VI. would send legates from Avignon to perform the ceremony, he prepared in earnest for the expedition. Indeed, in return for the glory of the one day in Rome, he consented to recognize all those old pretensions of the popes against which his predecessors had struggled so furiously; his agreement that, in his official capacity, he would not remain over night in the Eternal City, amounted to a renunciation of every claim to jurisdiction. An emperor of the old stamp would never have condescended to steal in, garbed as a pilgrim, that he might enjoy a few days of sight-seeing previous to his cor-onation. No wonder Petrarch exclaimed that a title thus achieved would prove an empty honor, and in a reproachful letter asked Charles what his father and grandfather would have said could they have met him on the crest of the Alps. Bravery, he declared, was no hereditary quality.

Italian ex-pedition of Charles IV.

At sunrise of Easter Sunday, 1355, the king in purple robes of state prepared to make his entry into Rome. His queen at his side and followed by a brilliantly accoutred escort, he rode in at the gate of Crescentius, conferring knighthood right and left as the procession passed along. Descending from his horse, he mounted the steps of St. Peter's accompanied by prelates and notables. In the vestibule he was received by the Cardinal Bishop of Ostia, the Pope's representative, and by all the clergy of Rome.

Before them he swore the coronation oath, and renewed a number of special agreements; then followed the confirmation of all the possessions, rights, and privileges of the church, the consecration with the holy oil, the celebration of mass, and the placing of the crown on the heads of the new emperor and empress. Mounted on white chargers which awaited them at the foot of the steps, and sheltered by a magnificent baldachin of silk and gold brocade, they then rode through the densely lined streets of Rome to the sound of the city bells and escorted by all the chief dignitaries. Gold coins were scattered in profusion among the crowd. There followed a feast in the Lateran palace, in the midst of which, just as the sun was setting, the emperor rose from table, mindful of his oath to leave the city.

Little glory did the whole course of this Italian expedition bring to Charles; the party-torn cities had looked to him as they once looked to Henry VII., but they were equally disappointed. Everywhere his policy had been to avoid danger, to side with the strongest in the civic disputes, to temporize and to make treaties which he would not or could not keep. He had been right from a practical point of view when he declared to Petrarch that the old Roman Empire was not capable of being revived; he for his part did not intend to try. We soon find him abandoning Italy and deep in the internal affairs of Germany. He called a Diet of the Empire to meet at Nuremberg with a view to settling various questions — the duties and privileges of the electoral college, the peace of the land, the Rhenish tolls, the general finances of the empire.

The outcome of this Diet was the elaborate document known, from its peculiar seal, as the Golden Bull of the Emperor Charles IV., which, after careful deliberations, was promulgated in the year 1356. In point of importance it can be compared only to the Magna Charta of England, *The Golden Bull.*

for its provisions were followed in part down to the end of
the Holy Roman Empire in 1806. Starting out with a
prayer to God, that the Emperor Charles may lead His
people through the pleasant glades of flowering forests
into the holy shades, where the heavenly waters will
quicken the seeds that were sown in the life, and where
the ripe crops will be " cleansed in supernal founts from
all of the thorns they have gathered," the Golden Bull
goes on to point out the evils of discord in a state, declaring that, had it not reigned between Helen and her husband, Troy would never have fallen, nor, but for the
quarrels of Pompey and Cæsar, would the Roman republic have come to an end. And now against the empire,
and, more specifically against its seven columns, the
electors, Envy is "spewing with the ancient poison." In
order, then, to eradicate all occasion of discord, the Bull
goes on to settle definitely certain cardinal matters: the
exact proceedings at elections, the functions of each of the
seven, the order of succession to an electorate, the indi-
visibility of the holdings, the amount of escort to be furnished by those princes through whose lands the electors
may pass on their way to Frankfort. One sees what
sovereigns these men have become; tolls, coinage, and
treasure-trove are to be absolutely theirs; from the judgments of their courts no one can appeal even to the emperor. A crime against their persons, and even a refusal
to provide them with the required escort, is to be punished
as high treason to the empire. Their electorates are to
be hereditary, and now for the first time the laws of reversion are firmly fixed — exactly in what manner, in default
of male progeny, they are to pass to collateral relatives.
Carefully and thoroughly the heirs apparent are to be
educated for their office; with minute precision the languages are enumerated which it will be necessary for them

to learn, and the exact age at which such instruction shall begin.

On the death of an emperor, or king, of the Romans, the Archbishop of Mainz was to summon the electors to Frankfort, but no one of the seven was to enter the city with more than two hundred mounted followers. While the election was going on no other persons, of whatever dignity, condition, or standing were to be allowed admittance, and the citizens were to see to it that the peace was kept and objectionable persons removed. Following the example of the Roman conclaves, the seven were to carry their deliberations to the bitter end; if thirty days should have passed without their having come to an agreement, their sumptuous fare was to be changed to bread and water.

Method of election.

Gladly would Charles have made use of the electoral college as an advisory body in the affairs of the empire. He inserted a clause providing for regular yearly meetings; it was not his fault, but that of the electors themselves, that this remained a dead letter. For the occasional functions in which they would be likely to take part,— imperial courts or assemblies,— the most rigid ceremonial was established; each elector was to have his permanent place in every procession, his regular seat, so much higher than that of an ordinary prince, at every feast. The four secular electors, being at the same time arch-officials of the empire, were on grand occasions to perform their functions, the marshal to ride his horse to the flanks into a heap of oats and distribute them to the first comer, the chamberlain to hold the silver ewers and the fine towel, the seneschal and the cup-bearer to bring dishes of food and a goblet of wine. Doubtless, in arranging such pageants, the effect on the popular mind was fully taken into consideration. When a newly chosen monarch and his seven electors

Ceremonial.

passed through the streets of Frankfort and took their seats in the hall, with all its various platforms and tables, it must have seemed to the onlooker as if all the majesty of the empire were actually and visibly unfolding itself before his gaze. The imperial insignia lent their splendor to such occasions — the crowns of Aix and of Milan, the orb, the staff, the sceptre, and the sword. The seat of the emperor in the hall of assembly was always three feet higher than that of any one else in the room; on the level immediately below him sat the empress by herself, lower still the seven electors, and below them the generality of the princes.

The chief aim of the Golden Bull was to prevent double or disputed elections; it seemed as though there could be no longer the slightest doubt just to whom the votes belonged and how they were to be cast. Yet in the next half-century came every kind of schism and disagreement.

Charles IV. and Gregory XI.

If the various regulations of the Golden Bull were of great importance, still more so was one striking omission. There is no mention of the Pope, no acknowledgment that his assent or coöperation was necessary, either in the matter of electing a king of the Romans or of raising him to the imperial dignity. In spite of the fact that Louis of Bavaria had been ready to grant almost every claim the church put forward, the Papacy, in reality, was completely losing its grip on Germany. When, in 1376, Charles determined to revive the old Hohenstaufen custom of having his successor crowned in his own life-time, Pope Gregory XI attempted to assert what he considered his time-honored rights; he made the peremptory condition that the emperor and his son in person should come to Avignon and swear the same submissive oath that Charles had sworn at his own election in 1346. They were then to formally petition the Pope to permit the electors to proceed to the election, and, finally, to promise that at no time in future should a son be elected during his father's lifetime without such express permission.

Charles's conduct during this whole affair was most characteristic, and quite of the kind that roused the ire of Petrarch in earlier days. He temporized with Gregory, and held him off until the preparations for the coronation were completed; to the very last he could, with a good conscience, stand up before the electors and tell them that the Pope's consent had neither been asked nor given. But the votes once fairly cast, he determined to stand as well as possible with the Papacy. He sent polite messages to Avignon; he even went so far, now that nothing could be lost, as to compose a writing dated back before the day of the election, in which he asked for the papal sanction. Indeed, a whole correspondence in falsely dated letters took place, the election always being alluded to as about to be held in the future. One is surprised at the lengths to which in his subserviency the emperor was willing to go. He asked for the Pope's "assent, grace, favor, consolation, and benevolence," and, when Gregory insisted on his adding the words " good pleasure," that also he did without scruple. In the midst of these hollow negotiations the Pope died, and soon afterward, in 1378, the great schism broke out in the church, laming its resources and effectually preventing either the Pope at Rome or the Pope at Avignon from interfering in the affairs of the empire.

Whatever one's verdict as to Charles IV.'s character, it must be acknowledged that almost all of his ventures met with success. He had regulated the footing of the crown with the electors; he had not only secured the imperial dignity for himself, but had practically made sure that it would be handed on to his eldest son; he had, finally, brought into his hands larger territorial possessions than

Charles IV and Brandenburg.

any monarch since Henry VI. Starting with Luxemburg in the west, and Bohemia and Silesia in the east, he had made it one object of his life to form, as it were, a bridge across Europe by purchasing numberless estates — the "Bohemian Islands" they have well been called. In order to provide for a great heritage in the future, he had wedded his son, Sigismund, to the heiress of Poland and Hungary. But his master stroke was the acquisition of Brandenburg, of which we have already spoken. Discords had broken out among the Wittelsbachs, and Charles took the side of the Princes Louis and Otto against a third brother, Stephen.   The emperor had made the stipulation that, in case both of his allies should die without heirs, the electorate should pass to his own sons.   Louis did die, and without heirs, whereupon Otto refused to be bound by that former compact, and Charles determined to go to war.   In the end the matter was peaceably settled; once more untying his purse-strings Charles bought the right of succession for some half-million of guldens.   Here was a dynastic appanage such as few of the earlier emperors had ever enjoyed, but it profited little either to Charles or to his house.   On the emperor's death, in 1378, Brandenburg fell to the share of his second son, Sigismund, who, bent on making good his claim to Hungary, and wofully in debt, pawned it ten years later to his cousin, Iodocus of Moravia, and finally, in 1415, bestowed it on Frederick of Hohenzollern.

Charles succeeded by Wenceslaus.

To Charles's eldest son, Wenceslaus, there passed the rule over Bohemia and Silesia, as well as the throne of the empire ; but never did prince fail more signally to rise to the height of his responsibilities. At the time of his father's death he was only in his eighteenth year. As he grew older dissipation claimed all his thoughts and caused him to neglect the weightiest affairs of the empire.

Whatever business he transacted had to be done in the morning before he was entirely overcome with drink.   At decisive moments he was simply not to be found, and no one knew where to look for him.   He was once taken prisoner by his cousin, Iodocus of Moravia, and the Germans knew nothing about it for a considerable period of time.   The administration of Bohemia, and plans for family alliances, kept him from visiting Germany save at very rare intervals.   From 1387 to 1395 he never came at all.   Again and again the electors sent to remind him of his duties, and urged him, if need be, to appoint a regent, or to allow them to form a council or directory.   Their complaints became louder and louder, their accusations more and more violent; it was common talk that this wretched rule must end.   A league was formed among the electors, and joined by all but Brandenburg; conferences and assemblies were held, to which the princes and cities were invited to send delegates.   No attention was paid to a message from Wenceslaus forbidding important deliberations in the king's absence ; instead he was warned that, if he did not mend his ways, the electors would consider themselves loosed from their oath of allegiance.   Nevertheless, because his brother Sigismund would not accompany him he remained in Prague, to quote a contemporary, "like a pig in his pen."

At last the crisis came.   In August, 1400, a majority of the electors came together at Lahnstein, whither they had called as witnesses a large assembly of nobles and people. Then sentence of deposition was read against Wenceslaus, on the ground that he was lazy and useless, and that, far from being fit to govern the Holy Empire, he had attempted to dismember it for his own advantage. He had done nothing to end the great schism in the church, nor had he established peace and order in Germany ; he was

Deposition of Wenceslaus.

guilty of murder of both laymen and churchmen; he had issued signed blanks to his favorites allowing them to enrich themselves with grants and privileges at the empire's cost.

The best-founded of the charges against Wenceslaus, that of dismembering the empire, was based on the fact that he had sold to Gian Galeazzo Visconti — that Milanese tyrant who had annexed Verona, Vicenza, Padua, and Siena, and was intriguing against Florence — the right to the titles of Duke of Milan and Duke of Lombardy, and permission to bear in his coat of arms the imperial eagle. The price paid had been a hundred thousand guldens ; the princes had not been consulted or advised with in any way. On the whole the action of the electors in deposing this worthless king, though technically indefensible, must be considered patriotic and necessary; indeed, in all these trying times, bereft for decades at a time of a proper head, the electoral college showed strength and firmness. The lasting harm of the whole episode was that the first attempt in centuries to have the son elected in the father's lifetime, as in the days of the empire's greatest prosperity, had produced such miserable results.

Rupert of the Palatinate. The choice of the electors fell now upon Count Rupert of the Palatinate — Rupert the mild, he was called ; but a little ferocity would have stood him in better stead. Wenceslaus, indeed, proved but a feeble antagonist, uttering terrible threats which he never carried into execution. A descent upon Italy, however, undertaken by Rupert, harvested him such mockery as to ruin his chances of gaining the respect of the Germans. He, the head of secular Christendom, was defeated by plain Gian Galeazzo Visconti in the first insignificant encounter; his funds ran so low that he had to send his crown to Venice and have it pawned. At home Baden, Würtemberg, and eighteen cities formed the league of Marbach against him and forced him into galling concessions. The Council of Pisa, which had undertaken the reform of the church, laughed at his protest against its proceedings and declared for Wenceslaus.

The year of Rupert's death, 1410 A.D., saw the unique spectacle of three rival emperors over against three rival popes: the Council of Pisa, in setting up a new head of the church, failed, as we shall see, to secure the abdication of the two already in the field; in Germany Wenceslaus returned to the charge, while one party of the electors chose Iodocus of Moravia, another, Sigismund of Hungary, Charles IV.'s younger son. The death of Iodocus, by poison or otherwise, soon cleared the atmosphere, and Wenceslaus compromised with his brother for the consideration of an empty title.

Three emperors and three popes.

The reign of Sigismund was another long record of disappointment and failure; the best that was in him came out, as we shall see, at the time of the Council of Constance, but even then his achievements were small and his treatment of Huss left a dark blot on his character. He was in the bloom of manhood in those days, brave and handsome. A contemporary has left a description of how, at the time of the great assembly, he one day rode in disguise into the lists, overthrew two antagonists in turn, and then, raising his helm, was greeted by the spectators with rapturous applause. We have descriptions of his kingly presence, his striking, slender, graceful figure, his rich coloring, curly hair, and long beard parted in the middle. He possessed the gift of oratory as few kings before or after, could be denunciatory or persuasive by turns, could unfold a wealth of imagery or draw on a vast store of wit. At least seven languages stood at his disposal, and if, occasionally, he sinned in his Latin quantities, he had more right than

Personality of Sigismund.

most men to boast that he was *supra grammaticam* — superior to grammar.

But there were shadier sides to this pleasant character
Sigismund, as many people learned to their disadvantage,
proved also superior to the ordinarily accepted moral considerations. His officials at home in Hungary had already made
up their minds how much they could exact in chancery
fees from these rich Germans; throughout his long reign
this emperor had a habit of borrowing and not returning
that drew down upon him general contempt. A Frenchman who knew him personally avers that men of all
nationalities suffered equally at his hands, and that "this
man who wants to set the universe on fire and who
threatens even the antipodes" is in reality the meanest
beggar, ready to accept the smallest favor. We hear of
the strangest alternations at court between extreme luxury and extreme shabbiness; we are seriously told how
the head of the empire would sometimes go about with
patched shoes and with rents in his clothes that showed
the skin. We hear, too, alas, of nights spent in carou-
sal and of escapades shocking even to those easy-going
times.

Neglect of
duty.

Perhaps the most fatal for Germany of Sigismund's
characteristics was a propensity to neglect even the most
important business. Incredible as it may sound, it was
four years after his election before he made his appearance
at all in his new empire; then, indeed, he attempted to reform some of the crying evils, but was soon disheartened
by opposition. After a similar failure in 1429 A.D., he retired in a rage to Hungary, intimated to the Germans that
if they wished him to hold a Diet they must come to him at
Pressburg, and told the Estates, when they protested at his
absence, that he had never, as a matter of fact, set much
store by the German crown, and had only retained it at the

request of the Pope; bread and wine sufficient for his wants
he could find at home.   Of the twenty years of his reign
that followed on the Council of Constance but two and a
half were spent in Germany.

How far the general administration of justice suffered
from this absence may be imagined when one considers the
fact that the supreme court of justice was attached to the
king's person.   Only the most desperate state of affairs
could account for the success of a secret organization like
that of the Westphalian peasant court, the Holy Veme.
In other parts of the empire the jurisdiction of the territorial lords replaced that of the emperor; for the electorates,
indeed, the clause of the Golden Bull *de non evocando* had
expressly forbidden all kinds of appeals.   The Holy Veme
could never have achieved its great fame, both in and outside of Westphalia, had not its methods at first been admirable, its judgments swift and sure.   It was a local survival of the old free courts of Carolingian times, where
judgment was passed by *Schöffen*, or bailiffs, whose president, or *Freigraf*, was accountable only to the emperor.
The Veme concerned itself exclusively with a certain class
of crimes, those against "God, law, and honor," and only
with cases where a hearing had been denied by other courts.
Death by hanging was the usual penalty.   It accepted appeals from all parts of Germany.

The Holy Veme.

Sigismund eagerly seized upon the Veme as a means of
upholding law and order; he himself became one of the
Wissende, or initiated.   Under him the institution may be
said to have reached its most flourishing development; its
members were counted by thousands, and many of them
were nobles.   The most striking peculiarity of the whole was
the inviolable secrecy that was demanded and maintained.
The *Wissende* formed a great brotherhood, with strict rules
and observances, with an elaborate initiation, mystic signs

Procedure of the Veme.

and tokens, and a special grip. Strangely enough, a number of formulas for procedure and other acts of the organization have been preserved: the candidate for membership was obliged to swear " to hold and conceal the Holy Veme from wife and child, from father and mother, from sister and brother, from fire and wind, from everything upon which the sun shines or the rain falls, from everything between earth and heaven." The penalty for betrayal was hanging "seven feet higher than a corrupted, outlawed, ill-doing thief." The traitor was to be killed at once whenever and wherever found.

Tradition and romance have represented the courts of the Veme as much more terrible than they really were. We know now that, for ordinary cases, the *Schöffen* came together publicly in the open air, and not, like the terrible Venetian council, behind closed doors, with mummery and masking. Only on rare occasions, when the most serious matters were in hand, did they go into secret session. Sentences of death were accompanied by impressive ceremonies, the uttering of a most terrible curse, the throwing out from the assembly of a twisted rope, the spewing from the mouth of every member.

Decline of the Veme.

When the Veme grew bolder in its attacks, when it began to coerce whole cities and to make war against them, when it dared even to summon before its tribunal the Emperor Frederick III. and all his councillors, it was already well on toward its decline. It degenerated as the Flagellants had done before it, and doubtless from the same causes. Its judgments could be bought for pay, and towns regularly hired *Freistühle*, or chapters, to look out for their special interests.

Death of Sigismund.

But by this time the Emperor Sigismund had long since passed away. For all his indifference, he had possessed a certain pride in his rank; "See what a king of the Ger-

mans can do!" he is said to have exclaimed, as Frederick
of Austria, the friend of Pope John XXIII., knelt before
him at Constance to renounce all his worldly possessions.
When now, at last, in 1437, he realized that death was upon
him, he elected to meet his great enemy sitting upright on
his throne. As the cold chill began to pervade his body, he
directed that a shroud should be cast over his rich vest-
ments. He had already given directions that his corpse
should remain long upon view; men were to know beyond
a doubt that the "lord of all the world" had passed away.

CHAPTER VIII

THE TEUTONIC ORDER AND THE HANSEATIC LEAGUE

LITERATURE : Lamprecht gives a good account of the rise and fall of the Hansa and a less good one of the Teutonic Order. See also Prutz. The best monographs on the Hansa are Schäfer, *Die Hansastädte und König Waldemar von Dänemark*, and especially Lindner, *Die deutsche Hanse*. For the Teutonic Order good literature is scarce. I have culled many facts from Voigt, *Geschichte der Marienburg*, and from articles in Sybel's *Zeitschrift*.

Independent development of parts of the empire.

THE absence of central predominance in Germany was productive of certain results that were not altogether evil. In the different states that had become almost independent — like Saxony, Brandenburg, and Bavaria — much was being done toward organizing a stable government ; indeed, in those very three the ruling families of the fifteenth century have remained the ruling families ever since. Moreover, room and opportunity were given for certain quite abnormal political formations, like the Swabian League, the Swiss Confederation, the curious theocracy of the Teutonic Order in Prussia, and the great commercial organization known as the Hansa. The needs of the emperors, too, fostered civic independence; for, in return for pecuniary gifts, there were few privileges that the crown did not renounce. Last but not least, the tide of colonization flowed slowly but steadily on into the Slavic east, until the territory thus acquired more than equalled the rest of Germany. Much of this colonization, which had already made great progress under the Hohenstaufens, was peaceful in its nature; the Germans, Dutch, and Flemings knew infinitely more about agriculture than did the Slavs, and especially about reclaiming marshy or waste lands, and were simply called in by the native owners and became their tenants. But much of it also was due to fierce wars, undertaken usually in the name of religion and often supported by the funds of crusaders.

Of all civilizing and Germanizing agents none worked greater wonders than did the Teutonic Order in the swamps and wilds of Prussia. Unlike the Knights of St. John and the Templars, from whom they had borrowed their organization and dress, the Teutons, or "Servants of St. Mary of the German House," unfolded the greater and better part of their activity after leaving the Holy Land. Banished from Transylvania by King Andreas II. of Hungary, they had taken part in wars against the heathen Prussians, and, through the efforts of Herman von Salza, the friend of the Emperor Frederick II., had been regularly intrusted with the mission in those lands and endowed with the province of Culm. The knights had made the important condition that they should be responsible directly to the emperor and the Pope, and subject to no intermediate power.

The first object was to subjugate numerous wild tribes that were scattered over a vast area; in civilization they were centuries behind the Germans, still worshipping in sacred groves and tending a never dying flame. The discipline and determination of the Teutons were at this time magnificent; their vows of chastity, poverty, and obedience were well kept, the slightest infringement being visited by the dreadful "year-penance," by which for the space of a year the culprit was condemned to the life of a slave, allowed no chair, but the hard ground to sit upon, fed for the most part on bread and water, and once a week publicly scourged. At best the life was one of extreme

The Teutonic Knights in Prussia.

hardship, for the cells in which the brothers dwelt were bare and unheated.

Subjuga-
tion of the
Prussians.

By the year 1231 the knights had crossed the Vistula and founded the town of Thorn; soon the whole bank of the river as far north as Culm was in their possession; by 1237 A.D. they had reached its mouth and begun spreading along the Baltic; in 1251 Memel was founded, in 1254 the important town of Königsberg. The manner of proceeding was the same that had been practised in Palestine; armies of crusaders sent out by the popes were drilled and led to victory. So soon as a strong point was captured, a fortress was built and a garrison left behind, while the main army pressed ahead, each such little centre in turn enlarging its sphere of power. Some of the conquests were made by water; as early as 1233 the order possessed two ships, the *Pilger* and the *Friedeland* — the oldest German war vessels of which we know the names. The progress was often checked by bloody uprisings and attempts to massacre all Christians, and more than once the whole enterprise was on the verge of failure. But perseverance and enthusiasm at last won the day, and within little more than half a century from the time of their first coming, the rule of the knights was practically undisputed. Such Prussians as were left after all the cruel warfare settled down as a subject people. Colonists from Holland and elsewhere streamed into the land, and by the year 1410 there were ninety-three new cities and fourteen hundred villages.

Adminis-
tration of
the order's
lands.

More marvellous even than this triumphal progress was the perfection of the administration that was imposed upon the whole land. Here was an ideal republic, untrammelled by the traditions of neighboring states, or by any of the fetters of feudalism. Where in history can such a proceeding be paralleled? Where elsewhere can we find an established hierarchy settling down, just as they were, upon a conquered land ?   The organization of the old order simply expanded into the organization of the new state.   The grand master became the head of the whole ; the *tressler*, or treasurer, the minister of finance; the marshal, the minister of war.   Each knight became commander of a small district, and was bound, as before, to give frequent account of himself to the heads of the order.   According to the original statutes, the marshal was to purchase the horses and mules, the armor and weapons, the mantles, undergarments, and leather hose for all the brothers; this he continued to do even as minister of state.   But in addition to this a great commerce grew up in the products of the newly acquired lands, which far exceeded the needs of the order.   In the year 1263 A.D. Pope Urban IV. issued a bull permitting the knights to exchange or even sell commodities, provided always this were not done for the sake of gain, but merely to get rid of a normal surplus.   As the resources increased, and the demand for grain, wax, and amber required larger and larger exports, the clause in Urban's bull became more and more onerous, until at last the brothers helped themselves, as many a mediæval saint and abbot had already done before them, by forging a new bull which omitted the objectionable passage.   The revenues became considerable, for in addition to the commercial gains there were imposts and duties ; old ledgers and exchequer accounts show that these alone amounted yearly to some five million marks of modern German money. Works of considerable magnitude, extending over many years and requiring the services of skilled engineers, were undertaken, and immense tracts of land reclaimed.

The building of the castle of Marienburg, on the delta of the Vistula, was of great importance for the future of the order, forming as it did a centre for all the different

The Marienburg.

commanderies. Striking enough it was, with its lofty walls and its great statue of the Virgin, twenty-six feet high, which to this day looks out protectingly upon the landscape. Here, in September, 1309, the grand master held his solemn entry, abandoning the beauties of Venice for the rigors of the North. Here, too, an active, bustling life began to unfold itself, potentates and knights journeying thither, partly out of curiosity, partly to help in those wars against the heathen Lithuanians which now became the order's holiest object. So much dreaded was this enemy that, on the lands adjacent, belts of impenetrable forest were left standing, and every avenue of approach was fortified and guarded. But the missionary zeal of the Teutons was not to be daunted; Lithuanian captives were very serviceable as drawers of water and hewers of stone, and thousands of them were set to work on fortresses and city walls.

Winrich
von
Kniprode.

The golden age for the Teutonic Order fell in the time of the Grand Master Winrich von Kniprode, who, from 1351 to 1382, wielded a firm sceptre; those were days when agriculture and trade were flourishing at home and armies were successful in the field. Winrich had ceased to depend on crusaders and mercenaries, and had raised a force of native Prussians. The brethren themselves were particularly trained in all the arts pertaining to defence; regular archery practice was introduced, wooden birds being set up on poles as targets. But more than all this, Winrich made the Marienburg a centre for science and learning. "Many people of distinction," says a chronicler of the time, "declared that in no other land had they seen such wise, sensible, learned people, and so skilled in the law." Winrich had founded a Latin school which he maintained at his own cost. Altogether the knights had reason to be thankful for having obeyed the supernatural voice that is said to have spoken out at the election and turned the votes on this candidate.

Soon after Winrich's death we find the order famous for its gun foundry and also for its falcon training. These birds were sent all over Europe as tokens of regard from the grand masters, while orders for artillery came from great distances. Gunpowder, too, was manufactured in quantities, and the tressler's accounts show large sums expended on saltpetre.

All through the fourteenth century the order flourished and grew in strength, but the old singleness of aim, the old simplicity, was gradually vanishing. Step by step we can trace the descent to Avernus. The entertainments at the Marienburg become more magnificent; we hear of princes and knights from the ends of the world being received and feasted in royal style; we hear of banquets that lasted two days and two nights, of fiddlers and trumpeters, rope-dancers and conjurers, leaders of tame bears and stags. At the beginning of the fifteenth century we find the good Grand Master Conrad of Jungingen contending against this too great luxuriousness of his knights, against the number and price of their horses, their inability to practise self-denial. They, for their part, began to mock at his preachings and to write satiric verses on the wall, telling him that he had better become a monk or nun. The license became broader and broader; the court jester dubbed Grand Master Conrad "Madam Abbess," and on one occasion threw into a ditch the image of the Virgin Mary, because, as he said, she had not graced with her presence a certain frivolous assembly. *The order degenerates.*

By this time the expeditions into Lithuania had ceased, after having degenerated into the merest hunting parties arranged to give pleasure to some distinguished guest. The order kept its scouts or pathfinders to track the *Lithuanian heathen hunts.*

enemy like bloodhounds. Under their guidance the forest would be crossed and a descent made upon some quiet settlement; the men would be slain and the women and children dragged into captivity. Such raids always ended in feasting and self-glorification and in wholesale dubbing of knights. Yet shameful as was this border warfare against a weak, defenceless enemy, its sudden forced termination proved an insupportable blow to the Teutonic Order. So long as the Lithuanians remained heathen there was a pretext at least for the order's activity, an excuse for its continued existence and for the maintenance of its many and great privileges. But the rational occupation of the knights vanished forever when, in 1386 A.D., Prince Jagiello of Lithuania married the heiress of Poland, united the two countries under his own sceptre, and imposed Christianity as the state religion. The weak neighbors had become part of a strong nation, and the wars with Poland fill the greater part of the order's remaining history.

The battle of Tannenberg, against the Poles.

Conrad of Jungingen had done his best to stave off these conflicts, though constantly opposed by his thoughtless knights, who little dreamt what disaster and servitude would be the outcome. As long as he lived, indeed, Conrad managed to withstand these influences; but he could not provide for what might happen after his death. "Do not choose my brother," he said on his death-bed, " though he is a fearless, brave warrior and bold hero; for I fear his wild thirst for war will plunge the whole order into irreparable woe." But a time of panic came, the warning was forgotten, and when the army of the order marched out Ulrich of Jungingen was in command. The largest cannon ever yet seen in Germany had been forged for this war; but the battle fought on the Polish frontier, near the village of Tannenberg, in 1410 A.D., was the most disastrous the order had ever yet fought. Grand Master Ulrich himself fell in the fight; the contemporary estimate of the numbers of the slain is too enormous for belief. The Prussian lands lay open to the Polish hordes, and fortress after fortress surrendered, until at last the invading army came under the walls of the Marienburg itself. By taking this, King Vladislas, as his own chroniclers tell us, hoped to put an end to the whole Teutonic Order.

But this time the Virgin Mary showed herself the best of patron saints, for there sprang into the breach one of the bravest knights of whom the order ever boasted. Hastening from the field of Tannenberg, Count Henry of Plauen had ridden into the castle ahead of the Poles, and had taken command. Determined to save what could still be saved he levelled all the surrounding buildings, offering the shelter of the Marienburg to all fugitives. So successful were his efforts that the Poles charged in vain from all sides; their shot recoiled against the heavy walls, but not without inflicting serious damage. Through the window of the Grand Master's hall crashed a great ball of stone, and lodged in the wall over the mantel, where it has remained embedded to this day.

Grand Master Henry of Plauen.

The force and cunning of the enemy alike failed of their effect, the frequent sorties of the garrison wrought havoc and dismay; starvation and sickness of man and beast did the rest. One by one the Polish contingents melted away, and after two months the siege was raised. Amid loud rejoicings Henry of Plauen was elected grand master, but his rule was destined to be short. The order was terribly impoverished, yet money was needed for everything, for repairs, for the payment of mercenaries, for the ransom of prisoners. As the iron hand of taxation descended upon them many of the knights became bitter and dissatisfied; a conspiracy was even formed to take the life of this stern taskmaster, although no one could ever have said that he in any way spared himself. In the end his enemies succeeded in having him called to account by a conclave of the chapter. Declared deposed and banished to a lesser command-ery, he was then accused of secret dealings with the Polish king and was placed in a strong prison. For years the rescuer of the Marienburg lived in a lonely castle on the seashore, reduced to abject misery. A letter of his is extant in which he begs a later grand master for mercy, or at least for sufficient food and drink.

Poverty of the order.

The order was indeed by this time very far downward on its way to the condition in which Martin Luther found it, "a thing serviceable not to God and not to man." Poverty was the worst curse of the once wealthy brotherhood; indeed, future generations could not believe that so much treasure had simply vanished, and frequent excavations have been made to find where it was buried. The granaries were nearly empty, and all appeals to the princes of Europe proved in vain. There came a time when a grand master had to literally beg for "a jewel, a relic, or anything at all that is decent and honorable" with which to requite the Danish king for a load of herring. In spite of small fluctuations of improvement, the flourishing days were gone forever; the Veme Gericht began to encroach on the order's jurisdiction, and its only resource was to have the burgomaster and one of the councillors of the town of Marienburg initiated into the dreaded court.

Ruin of the order.

Disputes with its Prussian subjects sealed the order's ruin. It became clear that its yoke, however light, had always been regarded as a foreign one; there had been little murmuring so long as the knights had been true to their mission, but they were looked upon now as mere dissolute idlers. There was defiant murmuring at the heavy grants that were asked for in order to pay the

indemnities to Poland, and wild revolt when resort was
had to trickery and violence. Two of the burgomasters
of recalcitrant Danzig were lured into one of the order's
castles and put to death. The result was a formal league
of the Prussians, an appeal to the emperor's court, and a
regular trial before Frederick III. When the latter declared the league unlawful, the last fatal step was taken:
the insurgents called in the aid of the Poles, who eventually
occupied every castle in the land. Never did a once flourishing state so completely compass its own destruction.
The war lasted for thirteen years, and the country was
devastated from end to end. Danzig, Thorn, Elbing, and
finally the Marienburg itself fell into Polish hands; by the
Treaty of Thorn in 1466 half the land was annexed absolutely; the other half became a vassal dependency, the
first duty of each new grand master being to swear the
oath of allegiance to the order's old enemy.

At one point and one only did the Teutonic Order come
into very close touch with the rest of Germany, and that
was in the development of its cities; those along the Baltic
became particularly important, and formed one whole group
or quarter of the Hanseatic League. Danzig was one of
the busiest ports on the whole continent of Europe.

From rural to civic life.

The great change from rural to civic life took place in
Germany in the thirteenth century; the question has been
raised whether the revolution of ideas was not greater at
that time than even in the fifteenth century, with its
compass, its gunpowder, and its printing-press, or in the
nineteenth, with its steam and railroads. As Schmoller has
pointed out, the transition was certainly a startling one
from peasant communities to towns of fifty thousand inhabitants, from rural huts to the Strassburg cathedral,
from country bartering and payments in kind to the use of

money and bills of exchange, from exclusively ecclesiastical culture to the reading and writing of the masses,
from monastic workers to civic artisans.

Burgher *vs.*
knight.

Among the German cities, particularly in the south and
west, some sixty of the most flourishing grew to be free or
imperial, owing allegiance to no one but the head of the
empire, and securing his protection and the management
of their own affairs by the payment of fixed sums. Such
were Nuremberg, Augsburg, and Ratisbon, Ulm, Strassburg, and Frankfort-on-the-Main.   Here centred eventually all industry, all wealth, and all refinement ; the
decisive rôle in history passes over from the knight to
the burgher.   The former finds it hard to acquiesce in his
fate, and with a grim sense of being wronged takes to
robbery and plunder.   The *Raubritter*, the man who
depends on fist-right for a living, becomes as distinct a
type as ever the knight-errant or professional jouster.
From behind his strong walls he descends on the cattle of
the farmer or the goods-train of the merchant, or carries
off their persons and demands a large ransom, leaving
them in damp vaults until occasionally their very legs rot
off — indeed, to " rot a peasant " becomes a well-known
proverb in the language.   The knights themselves only
saw the humorous side of the matter, and gloried in such
names as " hedge-rider," " highwayman," " bush-clapper,"
" pocket-beater," and " snap-cock."

Unsanitary
condition of
the cities.

The proportions of the cities were generous compared to
their population ; the walls often enclosed gardens, vineyards, and pastures, and even miniature forests.   Many of
the old laws concern themselves with the pigs that were
kept by private families.   Frankfort in 1387 decreed that
sties might not be built in the public streets, while Ulm in
1410 required its swine to be locked up except between
the hours of eleven and twelve.   The want of cleanliness

was universal, and to this cause is attributable much of the sickness that was prevalent. There was no paving, no drainage, until nearly the end of the Middle Ages. The foulest matter, including dead animals, was allowed to collect, and was only removed on grand occasions. When the Emperor Frederick III. entered Reutlingen, in 1485, horse and rider all but disappeared in the bottomless filth. The state of the roads was a valid excuse for not attending the sessions of cathedral chapters, and wooden overshoes were such a part of every man's daily equipment that in the pictures by the old masters even the saints are made to wear them.

Even had we no other means of knowledge, we could form our opinion of the cities of the fourteenth and fifteenth centuries from the churches, city halls, and private dwellings, the bridges, fountains, and stone Rolands that still exist. The high walls were flanked with numerous towers — Munich had a hundred, Frankfort nearly seventy — and pierced by handsome gates. Within those carefully guarded confines was passed a busy, joyous life that was not thought of elsewhere ; old feudal distinctions were battered down, and even runaway bondsmen became free if they could prove that they had breathed the air of a town for a full year. *Fine buildings.*

The rule of the civic authorities, indeed, was strict, and their right of interference with men's private affairs practically unlimited. Every article bought or sold was subject to their inspection, and bakers whose bread was not up to the mark were ducked under water. For certain cases of fraud the penalty was death ; for other offences men were flogged, publicly mutilated, or exposed to the general view in iron cages. Blasphemers were tweaked with red-hot tongs, forgers boiled in oil, with cold water now and then poured in to prolong the agony. *Vigilant administration of the cities.*

The city watched over its inhabitants to see that they were not too extravagant, that they did not live beyond their means; it provided that at weddings only so many guests might be invited — in Frankfort, in 1350 A.D., the number was fixed at twenty, while a hundred years later it was extended to fifty, exclusive of spinsters, foreigners, and servants. But also the cost of wedding presents was restricted, even totally forbidden at times in Rothenburg, Ulm, and Nuremberg. In the duchy of Würtemberg, in 1400, it was enacted that parents, brothers and sisters, and brothers-in-law and sisters-in-law might give whatever they pleased, but that, with regard to others, the limit for married couples should be seven shillings, and for widowers, three. In Frankfort, in 1489, we find a rich patrician obtaining the formal consent of the city council before making as large a present as he would have done had his wife been still alive. Still more common was the interference of the authorities in the matter of dress; one of the first symptoms of civic prosperity had been a love of display, and the natural bad taste of the people had led them into curious excesses. Not content with wearing garments which did not accord with each other, they took to dividing the colors on their cloaks, their hose, and their shoes. One leg would be pink, another green. On festal occasions men wore silks and satins embroidered with gold and silver and adorned with pearls and other jewels. The borders were hung with little bells, an ornament much in vogue. The city councillors saw to it especially that in this matter of dress no one class of the population infringed on the rights of another; servants and apprentices in Frankfort, in 1453, might not wear " colored shoes with points or beaks "; while in Ratisbon, in 1485, none but the authorities themselves might appear in silks, in satin, or in damask. The different garments a person might own were often enu-

Dress regulations.

merated, while women were stopped in the street on the charge of wearing longer trains than were legally allowed — matters with which not only the local laws, but even the imperial edicts, concern themselves.

Of all civic institutions none affected the life of the people more closely than the guilds, great organizations embracing all the artisans of a given trade, with a rigid division into masters, apprentices, and servants. The guilds enjoyed, not only a commercial monopoly, but a political power so great that the old native patricians who held all the places in the *Rath*, or council, were almost everywhere obliged to give away before them. " The labor leagues and associations," writes an old chronicler, " are formed to the end that the whole life of the members may be ordered according to Christian discipline and love, and the work itself be consecrated." Brotherly love and fidelity were required by the statutes; mutual support was assured, and the more unfortunate were assisted from the general treasury. " Who does not help to bury his deceased brother," runs one of the articles, " and does not pray for the salvation of his soul, has broken the word he plighted at his entry into the guild." *The guilds.*

In Lübeck in the middle of the fifteenth century there were seventy different guilds, in Cologne eighty, and in Hamburg more than a hundred. In Nuremberg the weavers had their own quarter; in Augsburg, in 1466, they could boast of no less than 743 members. No one might ply his craft who had not joined one of these leagues, for their power was absolute. The guild provided all raw material; it determined the rate of wages and the amount of production, and tested the finished work. It prescribed what agreements the master should make with his apprentice, and directed that he should stand to him in the place of a parent; " he shall lodge, feed, and care for him day *Purpose and province of the guild.*

and night, and shut him in with lock and key." He must see that the apprentice is honorably brought up and that he goes to church; should he be "wanting in the fear of God and in obedience, he shall punish him severely; that does the soul good; the body must suffer pain that the soul may prosper." If, through negligence of the master, on the other hand, the apprentice shall have failed to learn his trade, he shall be handed over to a more worthy instructor at the cost of the first one, who, in addition, must pay a fine.

All-embrac-
ing activity
of the
guilds.
To enter into the spirit of these most characteristic of mediæval organizations one must see them from all sides; work, religion, mysticism, and pure joviality all form part in their composition. Each guild had its patron saint, its private altar in the cathedral, or often its own chapel, where masses were said for the living and the dead. The members had their grip and their signs and their lodges in different towns, where by making themselves known they would be sure of free entertainment. The feeling of solidarity was very strong; the brothers were bound by their vows *in Lieb und in Leid*, in love and in sorrow; the authority exercised, too, was very real. Regular courts were held that could inflict pecuniary penalties, and the legislation went so far as to punish even a matrimonial *mésalliance*. The wife of a master, says a decree of 1459 A.D., must be of honest and lawful birth and of German origin. Just as it had its hospital, so the guild had its own prison. Its festivals, too, were of frequent occurrence and lasted for several days. When war broke out, and the great bell called the people to the city walls, the members marched out together and formed a separate division in the army.

In time, as intimated, bitter conflicts arose between these democratic organizations and the old predominant aristo-

cratic elements, and they ended usually in the fall of the
latter.   These struggles took place all over Germany, but
were not always bloody; it often happened that for a sum
of money the guilds could obtain the privileges they coveted
of representation on the *Rath*, and a voice in the disposal of
the public funds.   At times, however, actual war was waged
with brutal ferocity; in Magdeburg, in 1302 A.D., ten guild
aldermen were burnt at the stake.

All through the time of these internal troubles the cities
were obliged to wage war against the knights and princes,
and, occasionally, against the emperors.   Their ever recur-
ring demand was for an acknowledgment of their claim to
be considered an estate of the empire, and to be given a
vote equal to that of the ecclesiastical and secular princes.
The latter, for their part, complained that the towns were
attracting a number of their subjects, who nominally became citizens, — *Pfahlbürger* or "stockade citizens," they
were called, — but in reality retained their old possessions.
As a means of putting through their demands, many of
the towns joined the Swabian League, but the victory
of the princes at Doffingen, in 1388, gave the death-blow
to the whole movement so far as South Germany was
concerned.

The most legitimate and the most successful of all these
civic leagues was one formed, not for political purposes, but
for the better carrying on of commerce with foreign lands.
The early trader who went beyond the confines of his own
town had almost inconceivable difficulties with which to
contend.   He was fair prey for almost any one he might
chance to meet.   On land he was subject to highway robbery, and, worse still, to the barbarous custom that allowed
the ruler of a district to appropriate any vehicle, with its
contents, that came to grief within his boundaries.   This
claim extended to any article that might chance to have

fallen off. Still worse was the condition of things at sea,
for piracy was carried on, not merely by the offscourings
of society, but by men of rank in organized bands. And
the so-called strand law was fully as burdensome as the
evil customs on land. Not only did a ship that was
wrecked upon the shore, together with its cargo, fall to
the owner of the coast, but the persons and belongings of
all the crew were his to do with exactly as he pleased.
They were his perquisite, as much a part of his revenue as
treasure-trove or any other unexpected yieldings of his
land. Even scows that temporarily ran aground were subject to the same rule, while in Höchstädt, in 1396 A.D., a
claim was entered for a whole ship's cargo because of one
single cask that had floated away.

That these evils were not sporadic is proved by the
many local laws on the subject; the town of Lübeck, up to
the year 1312, had already signed twenty-one strand-law
treaties. The shores of the North Sea were particularly
dreaded because of the constant changes being worked by
the water in the friable banks; new islands rose up unexpectedly, and in 1277 a whole immense bay, known as the
Dollart, was formed by the washing away of an interven-
ing strip. And, to make these natural dangers still worse,
it was not unusual for avaricious coast dwellers, by false
lights and signals, to entice vessels on to the rocks, or to
purposely refrain from offering help to those in distress.
At best, lighthouses were rare, charts unknown, and com-
passes of very imperfect construction.

Necessity
of coöpera-
tion.
There were other reasons, too, which rendered it natural, nay, imperative, that traders should unite for mutual
protection. The owner of a single ship, if he stopped at a
foreign port, was apt to be subjected to the most unjust
and oppressive taxes. There would be thrown in his way
impediments to further trade like the so-called staple law,

which forbade his passing through a given town, — say to a larger and better market, — without first offering his goods to the local burghers. The home traders, who only admitted him at all because he brought products they could not obtain in any other way, were apt to receive him with envy and hatred.

Everything tended to consolidation. These merchants, for the most part, were God-fearing men. They needed common churches where they could register their vows at setting out, or return thanks for blessings received; they needed courts of justice to decide quarrels and legalize transactions, and to regulate weights and measures. It was necessary to have treaties with foreign countries to prevent the hurtful custom of reprisals, as well as to secure the property of men dying abroad for their rightful heirs at home. Out of all these various needs arose the great organization known as the Hanseatic League, the members of which could be either individuals or whole cities. It was a very gradual growth — a development, indeed, from earlier associations. For centuries a brisk trade had been kept up with England, and the city of Cologne, especially, had possessed important privileges in that country. The Osterlings, too, merchants from the cities along the Baltic, had been welcome visitors, their credit standing so high that the pound Osterling, or sterling, and Osterling silver, became the model unit of full weight.

Hansa was the common term used for a commercial union of cities, and many such unions had already been formed, the earliest of which we have record being one between Hamburg and Lübeck, in 1241. The crisis with Denmark, of which we shall speak later, brought about the general and more famous confederation. At no time, indeed, did the league in any way resemble a political

The first Hansas.

organization ; it possessed no central fleet or army, no common treasury, seal, standard, or flag. Nor did it ever attempt to punish secession otherwise than by pronouncing the Hansa ban ; a sort of ostracism for a long period which was only terrible if it happened to maim the trade of the city concerned. Individual citizens, indeed, who broke rules or treaties were subject to fines which might be so large as to utterly impoverish them, and even to arrest.

Membership of the league.

The membership of the league varied from year to year, cities often being allowed to withdraw and afterward to return. Indeed, there existed certain smaller organizations within the large one, each with an important city at its head. We find three, and later four, divisions, known as quarters : the Wend quarter under Lübeck, the Saxon under Brunswick, the Cologne under Cologne and the Prussian-Livonian, which included the prosperous cities of the Teutonic Order, under Danzig.

Extent of the league.

The Hanseatic League soon gained for itself a practical monopoly of all the commerce of the Baltic and of the North Sea, and numbered at its greatest some seventy-seven cities. It made treaties with all the more important commercial powers, and must be credited with the performance of a great civilizing task, abating many of the inconveniences, nay, horrors, that had hitherto hampered foreign trade, and opening up communication in every direction. Its vessels sailed out in fleets some thirty or forty strong and regularly accompanied by a man-of-war.

Pirates.

The pirates, indeed, seemed rather to increase in boldness as the years went on ; we hear of a considerable band of them who, from 1390 onward for nearly fifty years, were a terror to the European coasts from Reval to the Bay of Biscay. As late as 1491 we hear of a wicked escapade of a Duke of Holstein, who fitted out a ship and sailed in all directions, taking whatever booty came in his way. The

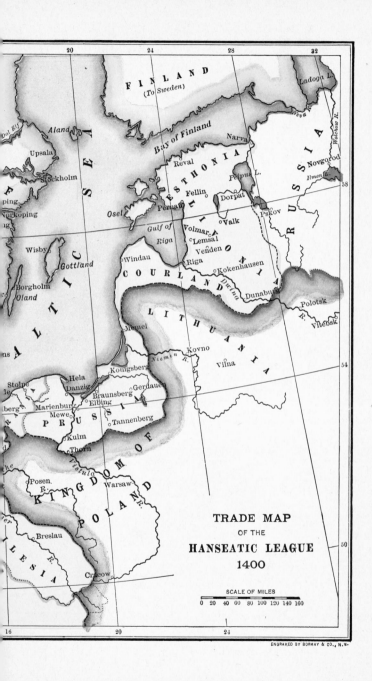

TRADE MAP
OF THE
HANSEATIC LEAGUE
1400

SCALE OF MILES

0 20 40 60 80 100 120 140 160

ENGRAVED BY BORMAY & CO., N.Y.

league kept regular police-boats in certain neighborhoods, and at times, when this did not suffice, sent out really warlike expeditions. The culprits once caught, their punishment was such as might well have deterred others from following their example. In 1401 the Hamburg fleet, one of the ships of which is known to have rejoiced in the name of the "gay-colored cow," took captive Hans Störtebeker and his crew after a sharp fight, and brought them to Hamburg to be executed. The story runs that Störtebeker offered to ransom himself with a gold chain, to be made from hidden treasure, which should reach around the city walls. This being refused, his last request was that so many of his companions might be pardoned as his body might run past after the head was cut off. He had reached the fifth, when the executioner, ill pleased at losing so many victims, threw an obstacle in his way that tripped him up.

Numerous indeed must have been the ships that plied in the name of the Hansa, even though we discard the estimate of an unusually sober modern historian, according to which from four to five hundred sail passed daily in and out of Danzig harbor. The vessels were often of considerable size — built broad and solid, and with high bows and sterns. The *Peter of Danzig*, in 1474, possessed a crew of four hundred men, and many others outrivalled her in this regard. These ships were never mere common carriers; their owners often sailed along with them, having purchased their cargo in one port with a view to selling it in another. The discipline on board was strict; some regulations that have come down to us for one special ship of the sixteenth century provide that there shall be no swearing by God's name, no mentioning of the devil. It was a serious offence to sleep through prayer-time or to play at dice or cards after sundown. The sailors were not to be hin-

Number and style of ships.

dered in the performance of their duty, and care was to be taken not to annoy the cook.

Products traded in.

It is not uninteresting from the point of view of the civilization of the time to look at the sort of products the Hansa ships carried in their holds. In general these consisted of raw materials. Furs were in great demand, not merely for their serviceableness, but because, in a way, they were tokens of rank. To this day, we associate ermine with princely magnificence. Then, as now, the best skins came from Russia, with which there had long been a brisk trade. " Furs are as thick as manure there," — writes an old chronicler, Adam of Bremen, — "to our damnation, I fear, for by fair means or foul we try to get at a garment of martin skin as if it were our eternal salvation." Adam is sure that from all this comes the "deadly poison of sumptuousness and pride."

Some of the products then popular have since lost their importance; enormous quantities of wax went for seals to parchment deeds, and for candles to be used in churches. With Protestantism, too, amber rosaries, which once fairly glutted the market, have gone out of use. The trade in beer was very large, for it took the place of tea and coffee, and was consumed by rich and poor. We find fourteen casks a year set aside for the use of each of the nuns in one of the convents. The Hanseatic League paid great attention to correctness of measure, weight, and quality, and strange enough was the test which in some neighborhoods was applied to beer. It was smeared over a bench on which a man with leather breeches was made to seat himself; only in case, on rising, the bench adhered to him, would the specimen pass muster.

Trade with England.

To England the Hansa ships carried woods for many purposes, but especially for the crossbows that did such excellent service against the French; furthermore, grain, of which it is calculated there were sent yearly six or seven hundred cargoes. The ships brought back woollen manufactures, silver, and tin from the mines of Cornwall. In London, as at Novgorod, Wisby, and on Schonen, the league had one of its famous permanent settlements — "courts" or "factories," as they were commonly called. The right to establish them was purchased from the various governments, and the high yearly taxes that the merchants paid made them welcome to those in authority, if not always to the native traders. To Edward III. these foreigners within his gates became almost indispensable. During the war with France they furnished immense loans, on one occasion redeeming the crown jewels, which had been placed in pawn. In return they obtained valuable privileges, as, for instance, the almost exclusive right to export English wool.

The "courts" consisted of enclosed spaces of considerable size in which were buildings of different kinds — warehouses, salesrooms, lodgings for the merchants, hospitals, breweries, and the like. The settlement, which was owned by the Hansa as a whole, in perpetuity, and was practically independent of the laws of the land in which it happened to lie, possessed its own docks, and usually its own churches. These latter, being solidly built, served occasionally as repositories for the more valuable goods. The Steelyard, as the court in London was called, was situated on the Thames, above London Bridge, and was strongly fortified — a necessary precaution against popular tumults, which more than once occurred. Contrary to the usual rule of the Hansa, the alderman or chief official of the Steelyard was always a London citizen. Occasionally, as we shall see, the Hansa merchants were altogether banished from England, and the Steelyard was taken from them, but they always regained it in time. Even when, in

The courts or yards. The Steelyard.

1666, the great fire of London swept away all of their buildings, they clung to the land on which they had stood, and hastily erected shops which, as their own trade was by this time ruined and their league was reduced to the cities of Hamburg, Bremen, and Lübeck, they rented to others. In 1853 they sold their site for £72500 sterling, and where their settlement once stood, one now alights from the Cannon Street railway station.

Discipline of the " courts." These Hanseatic courts, as far as their internal organization was concerned, present one of the most curious and interesting phenomena of the later Middle Ages. Monasticism and practical commercialism seem here to have met and agreed upon a compromise. The religious element is never wanting; in some of the courts clergymen were regularly installed, while large expeditions carried their own pastors. All of the settlements were under aldermen who, in some of the courts at least, had jurisdiction over life and limb — power to execute murderers or to mutilate those guilty of assault and battery. Ordinary disobedience was punished by expulsion. The *esprit de corps* was carefully guarded; there was at one period, at least, to be no associating with the people of the country, although in London we find the members of the Steelyard as a body taking part in public functions and occupying places next in rank and honor to the civic officials themselves. During his period of service the merchant might not marry, nor might women enter the confines of the court. We even hear of vows of celibacy administered for as long a period as ten years.

The members were divided into three classes: masters, apprentices, and servants or "children," each class sitting by itself at table. The occupations of the day were prescribed with monastic regularity — so many hours for work, so much time for pleasure. At an early hour the gates were closed, and all were obliged to betake themselves to bed. Heavy fines were placed on drunkenness, dice-playing, and immorality. In other ways more license was allowed; the entrance of new members into a court was accompanied by initiatory rites of incredible severity and cruelty; we hear of men half suffocated in noxious smoke and then thrown suddenly into ice-cold water. In vain the Hansa diets passed laws upon the subject.

Aside from the London Steelyard the principal Hanseatic courts were in Wisby, Novgorod, Bergen, and on Schonen; in Bruges and Antwerp the league had rights and privileges and even separate buildings, but no monopoly of trade as in other places. Indeed, the Germans met here with entirely different problems, with a rich set of merchants who lived in almost royal magnificence, with methods of trade better than their own, with cosmopolitan interests of every kind. These Flemish towns were the mediums through which the goods of the South were exchanged for the goods of the North; here Genoese and Florentines, Spaniards and Portuguese, met with the Germans on common ground. The latter learned to appreciate the artistic side of life, and we soon find their guild halls at home adorned with the rarest works of Flemish and German masters. Cologne had two Holbeins; Danzig, Hans Memling's *Last Judgment*, which the town still possesses. The latter picture, indeed, was one of the prizes secured by the good ship *Peter of Danzig*, which during the English War of the Roses went out with letters of marque and captured a Florentine galley on its way from Sluys to England, whence it had doubtless intended to carry the treasure to the rich gallery of the Medicis.

From 1568 onward the league possessed in Antwerp a rich palace of its own, with two great halls and a hundred

Various "courts."

Antwerp

and fifty smaller apartments. But the town lost its trade during the terrible wars with the Spaniards, and in 1593 all the valuable books and documents of the Hansa were removed to Cologne. The remnants of the league clung to their possessions in Antwerp, however, and in 1862 sold the *domus Hansæ Teutonicæ* to the Belgian government for a million francs. In 1893 the venerable building was totally destroyed by fire.

Wisby.

Interesting monuments of the Hansa are still to be seen in Wisby, on the island of Gotland. The city walls are still standing, 11,200 feet in length. They were flanked by forty-eight towers, the great majority of which were from 60 to 70 feet high. The town had always a reputation for immense riches; the very hogs ate out of silver troughs, at least so King Waldemar of Denmark told his soldiers when urging them, in 1361 A.D., to descend upon the island. According to an old tradition, such fiery carbuncles were set in the rosette-shaped ornaments on the church of St. Nicholas that sailors at night steered their ships by their gleam. St. Nicholas was but one of eighteen churches built by the Hansa merchants; all of them now lie in ruins save two, which are still used for their original purpose.

The fisheries of Schonen.

A Hansa court of great interest, yet differing from all others in character, was that on the peninsula of Schonen; here the one object of trade was the herring, and the season of activity was very short. The fish ran in to spawn in such quantities that the schools covered miles of area, yet so closely were they pressed together that they could raise a small boat out of the water. Hither in late summer and early autumn came men and women to the number of twenty thousand, eager to engage in what, all in all, was the Hansa's chief industry. It is difficult to realize now, when half of Europe no longer observes the church's fasts, what those cheap, salted fish meant to the Roman Catholic

of the Middle Ages. For forty days they were his chief
staple of diet, and doubtless the law forbidding Jews to
purchase them during that time was salutary and necessary.
A monopoly of the trade might otherwise have resulted.

Suddenly, in 1560 A.D., from no known cause, the supply
of herrings off Schonen practically ceased ; the useful little
fish changed the habits of centuries and sought other shores.
With them went the glory of Schonen, and the peninsula
sank into utter insignificance.

The outwardly most flourishing period of the Hansa,
the period when it played its part in the world as a great
political power, falls in the second half of the fourteenth
century. This is the time, indeed, of highest prosperity
for all of the German cities ; their architecture achieved
triumphs which are still reckoned among the greatest of
their kind ; their master singers worthily took the place
once held by the troubadours ; learning had abandoned the
monasteries for the public schools and for the universities,
of which Heidelberg, founded in 1386, was the first to be
established on German ground ; the German language had
superseded the Latin as the language of public affairs.
These civic leagues, moreover, represented all that was
left of German unity.   What other powers than the Hansa
could at this time have gone to war with Denmark, and
achieved victories which actually gave them a voice in the
disposal of the Danish crown?

Flourishing period.

These victories followed on a long period of dejection
and almost of discouragement. The rule of the Baltic,
always the goal of their desires, seemed slipping away
from the grasp of the allied cities; a Count of Holstein,
Gerard the Great, sat on the Danish throne and showed
himself a most redoubtable and inconvenient neighbor.
He it was who first temporarily united Schleswig and
Holstein under one rule.   On the violent death of Gerard,

The Hansa aids Waldemar of Denmark.

in 1340, it was but natural that the Hansa should help the exiled Waldemar, who had been brought up at the court of Brandenburg and always signed himself "true heir to the crown of Denmark," to regain his lost inheritance and throne. The attempt succeeded, though only by slow degrees; the Holstein counts, who had taken up their brother's cause, were finally banished from Denmark and restricted once more to their German principality.

War with Waldemar.

For all the gratitude that the new king showed, the cities might have spared their efforts. This slim youth, who goes in history by the name of Waldemar Atterdag, or Waldemar Some-other-day, had no intention of remaining the mere ward of foreigners; indeed, for twenty years the key-note of his policy was to purge his country of that same foreign influence. During that time he succeeded so well that, at the end of his reign, he could fairly call the greater part of Denmark his own, and was feared at home as well as abroad. Sweden and Norway, formidable only so long as they remained under one ruler, he managed to separate, causing a Duke of Mecklenburg to be made king over the former land. A severe blow to the Hansa was the reconquest of Schonen, which for thirty years had been in Swedish hands, and which, during that time, the German merchants had practically governed according to their will. To be sure, Waldemar at first seemed amenable enough to reason and ratified the Hansa's privileges, though only in return for a goodly sum of money. But when, soon afterward, Waldemar attacked the Swedish Wisby, a commercial centre of the league, and a strategic point of great importance; when, in July, 1361, he defeated a Gotland army before the city, and, disdaining to enter by the gates, marched his army through a breach in the wall to show that he was conqueror, it was felt that a vital question had been brought to issue. Four days later an embargo was laid on Danish trade by the Wendish and Prussian cities; a common tax, or pound-toll was levied, an agreement was made with other enemies of Denmark, with Sweden and Norway, and with the Counts of Holstein. Mercenaries were employed, nor did knights of renown hesitate to enter into the service of the cities.

None the less this first venture met with disaster and defeat. The fleets encountered each other off the coast of Schonen; of the Hanseatic ships, which numbered fifty-two, one-fourth were destroyed. The preparations had been hasty, there was nothing in reserve, and it only remained to be seen what could be gained by negotiation. Purposely Waldemar dragged along the matter for several years, and at last, in 1365, signed the Peace of Wordin-borg, which could not have been more unsatisfactory had it been concluded in the greatest haste. Everything was shifting, everything temporary. Nor did Waldemar seem inclined to observe even these unsatisfactory terms. Not six weeks had passed, when, according to his enemies at least, he had broken his agreements, restricting the commerce and interfering with the fisheries of the Hansa. "Tyrant" and "pirate" are the terms that were applied to him.

Peace of Wordin-borg.

The cities, one and all, were now fully alive to the dangers that threatened them, fully aware that they must make a desperate struggle, if they were to keep their supremacy in the Baltic. Bitterly they had felt the disgrace of the recent impotent struggle. Lübeck had condemned its burgomaster, Hans Wittenborg, who had shown incapacity in leading the city's forces, to death in the market-place by the hand of the common executioner.

Renewal of the war.

Very different was to be this expedition from the former one, for the cities were unfolding their whole power and might. In November, 1367, a firm defensive and offensive league was formed, and was joined by fifty-seven towns; those refusing their assistance were to be boycotted for ten years, their havens to be avoided by all loyal ships. The most memorable Diet in the whole history of the league took place in Cologne in that hall of the Rathhaus which has ever since, in honor of this one occasion, gone by the name of the Hansa Hall.

Expedition against Copen- hagen.

Never before had so firm a front been shown to an enemy, never had there been such general unity of aim. There was help from without, too, for Mecklenburg and Holstein on the one hand, and King Albert of Sweden on the other, joined in the war against the common foe. Even from Jutland itself twelve nobles joined the expedition. Waldemar was surrounded as by an iron ring. He could count only on Norway, of which the new king, Hakon, was his son-in-law.

The great fleet of the Hanseatic League sailed forth to a whole succession of victories. Waldemar did not even await its coming, but fled to the mainland to seek help from different foreign princes. He left, indeed, a competent council of state, and it is not improbable that he hoped for better terms for his land in the absence of his own hated personality. At all events, resistance seemed hopeless. Copenhagen was taken, twice plundered, and finally razed to the ground; its harbor was rendered impassable by ships sunk midway in the channel; the great fortress or castle was kept for a while as a base of operations, and then, after the capture of Helsingborg, dismantled. The coasts of Norway, too, were plundered, the royal residence at Bergen destroyed; the whole land lay at the mercy of the indignant cities, and their ships could now venture unmolested on all the high seas.

Peace of Stralsund.

It was with the war council, not with Waldemar, that the Peace of Stralsund was signed in 1370, the unfortunate king being obliged to ratify it in the following year. The most glorious treaty it was to which the cities had ever affixed their names; it marks the culminating point, the climax of their greatness. All their old valued privileges on the coast of Schonen were renewed to them, and as a pledge of good faith, the fortresses in the settlement were placed in their keeping; a war indemnity was granted and pledges given for its payment. In Denmark itself the Hansa received concessions that amounted to a monopoly of trade. Most humiliating of all, however, was the clause that no successor to the Danish throne, either now or at Waldemar's death, might be chosen without the sanction and approval of the league.

But no sooner had the latter reached the culmination of its glory than there began for it a long period of decline. The causes were varied and numerous: chief among them were the civil dissensions arising from the usual struggle between aristocratic Raths and plebeian guilds; the fact that the former were here unusually successful only served to keep the old wounds open. Then, too, Denmark rallied from its fall; under Margaret, the Semiramis of the North, all Scandinavia became united, and under her successor, Eric, Dutch and English ships were allowed to pass through the "Sound" into the Baltic and enter into competition with the Hansa trade. In spite of the strongest opposition a mercantile bureau or exchange for English merchants was opened in Danzig. *Decline of the Hansa.*

Worst of all, violent dissensions, fomented by England, arose between the Westerlings and Osterlings — between Cologne and her satellites on the one hand, and the Baltic ports on the other. Her cold reception by the Osterlings had caused England to retaliate on the Westerlings and to curtail their trading privileges. A great crisis came in 1468 A.D. King Edward IV., claiming that English ships *Internal dissensions* had been plundered in the "Sound," seized upon the persons of all the German merchants in his lands. Cologne, more seriously crippled than the other cities, made her own separate peace, but by doing so called down upon herself the whole wrath of the Osterlings. She was formally placed under the Hansa ban, which meant expulsion from the league. The remaining cities were still strong enough, and still had the courage and fire, to declare war against the whole mighty realm of England. It was the last heroic struggle of a waning power. A dauntless little fleet sailed against the English, and succeeded so well that the Peace of Utrecht, signed in 1474, ratified all the Hansa's privileges and accorded damages to the extent of ten thousand pounds.

Antiquated methods.

Cologne was taken back into the league after a long banishment, but the old solidarity of interests could never be restored; in the fourteen years from 1476 to 1490 A.D. but one general Diet of the cities was held. To add to all this, by the end of the fifteenth century the Hansa's methods of commerce had grown antiquated. The discovery of new lands and of new routes opened up far-reaching opportunities, of which, however, the German cities were the last to take advantage. The tide of traffic receded and left them stranded, while the dominion even of the Baltic passed over to Sweden. No longer dreaded either commercially or politically, the cities had to stand by inactive while their privileges were annulled by Gustavus Vasa and Queen Elizabeth in their respective kingdoms. Lübeck and Danzig continued to enjoy some measure of prosperity until even to them the death-blow was struck by the Thirty Years' War. An attempt of ten cities to renew the league in 1641 A.D. failed completely, and Danzig, which had exported a hundred thousand tons of grain in 1619, sent out in 1659 but little over five hundred.

CHAPTER IX

THE ERA OF THE CHURCH COUNCILS

LITERATURE : Lindner is good authority for German affairs at the time of the councils. See also Prutz. For the transactions of the councils themselves, no better accounts can be found than those of Creighton in his history of the Papacy during the Reformation.

MORE, even than the other nations of Europe, — because political weakness kept pace with religious disunion, — did Germany suffer from the discords and scandals that throughout the fourteenth and fifteenth centuries disgraced the Roman church. For more than seventy years, the term of the so-called Babylonian captivity, the popes at Avignon intrigued constantly in the interests of France. Then followed the great schism, during which one pope sat at Rome and another at Avignon, each drawing heavily on those lands which remained in his obedience, and too often spending the money for secular and political purposes. It is known that the Avignon court made loans to the amount of more than three and a half million guldens to the French king. The burden of taxation, thus doubled by the schism, grew fairly intolerable; no church office or church benefice, no exemption or dispensation, no hope of future preferment, not even forgiveness of sins, could be gained without cash payment. There seemed no limit to the number of ecclesiastical holdings that one man, were he sufficiently rich, could bring into his own hand. We have the record of these transactions under the first Avignon Pope; for the sixteen years of his pontificate, they fill no

Extortionate demands of the Papacy.

less than ninety-one volumes. The matter was open, notorious. Æneas Sylvius Piccolomini, who later himself
became Pope as Pius II., declared frankly at the time
of the Council of Constance, "Nothing does the court of
Rome give without payment, inasmuch as the very laying
on of hands, and the gifts of the Holy Ghost, are for sale."
That simony, against which the Gregorian popes had
fought so bitterly, was everywhere rampant; each slightest
opportunity was exploited to the utmost. Boniface IX., —
a better man than his predecessor, who had inflicted physical torture on his cardinals, — yet brooded, like a perfect
vulture, over his clergy when they lay dying, ready to swoop
down upon their belongings the moment life was extinct.
Their benefices he disposed of several times over, selling
to one candidate a promise of "preference," and to another
one of "prepreference," whereby it might happen after all
that a third party carried off the prize. Even the institution of the Jubilee, which was lucrative because of the
offerings the pilgrims brought to Rome, was distorted more
and more into a purely money-making scheme. Boniface
VIII. had started it in the year 1300, intending that it
should be held at the beginning of every century. But the
temptation of presiding over such a remunerative function
proved too great; succeeding popes quickly reduced the
term to fifty, to thirty-three, and eventually to twenty-five
years, while the full absolution, which was to reward the
pious journey, could finally be bought for the sum that
journey would have cost.

The great
schism in
the church.
We have here in this general system of extortion one of
the prime evils that was driving the church toward the
great catastrophe of its history. It was Germany's place
to enter in and administer a cure, a task which, under
stronger rulers, she undoubtedly would have attempted.
How many of her former emperors had descended upon

Rome to cleanse those Augean stables! By its very position, as well as by its traditions the empire was called upon
to be the arbiter in the matter of the schism, for the reason
that, unlike Italy and France, no pope was in its midst. It
was to the emperor that men were looking with longing
eyes; one of the avowed grounds for deposing Wenceslaus
was his failure to restore the peace of Christendom.

On the death, in 1394 A.D., of the Avignon Pope,
Clement VII., the university of Paris wrote to his cardinals that the golden opportunity had now come; it was as
though the Holy Ghost were standing and knocking at the
door. But fearful that their own power and prerogative
might become extinguished if not used, they proceeded,
nevertheless, to a new election, salving their consciences
by agreeing to bind their candidate to resign the Papacy,
should the interests of the church so demand. Benedict
XIII., at the time of being chosen, declared that he would
abdicate as readily as he would take off his hat; but even
when Wenceslaus of Germany and Charles VI. of France
combined together to depose both existing popes and elect
a new one, he clung to his position with great tenacity.
Boniface IX. died in Rome in 1404, and his successors,
first Innocent VII., then Gregory XII., acted much as
Benedict had done.

Gregory was known as a good, quiet old man at the time *The Council*
of his election, in 1406 ; but he was possessed of a host of *of Pisa.*
ambitious relatives, who descended on the Vatican like a
swarm of bees; it was soon reckoned that the sums expended for sugar alone equalled what previous popes had
paid for their food and clothing. And all attempts at
settling the schism in personal interviews with Benedict
XIII. failed utterly: to use the simile of a contemporary,
one pope, like a land animal, refused to approach the
shore ; the other, like a water animal, would not leave the

sea.   But such obstinacy gradually defeated its own ends;
adherents and resources melted away from both, and
Gregory XII. was reduced to such straits that he sold the
papal states and even Rome itself to his ally, Ladislaus of
Hungary, for a paltry twenty-five thousand florins.   By the
Council of Pisa, in 1409, both Gregory and Benedict were
declared in contumacy and a new pope elected, who took
the name of Alexander V.   He, dying soon afterward, was
succeeded by the pugnacious John XXIII., a man whose
past had been open to the gravest reproach.

Three
popes at
once.

It has been necessary to dwell upon these matters in
order to appreciate the highly dramatic yet wretchedly
unfortunate condition of imperial-papal affairs.   In one
and the same year, 1410 A.D., three emperors — Wenceslaus,
Sigismund, and Iodocus of Moravia — claimed the secular
headship of the world; while three popes — Benedict, Gregory, and John — pulled and tore at the seamless coat of
Christ.   The Council of Pisa had acted too hastily; before
deposing two and electing a third pope it should have made
more sure of the general allegiance of Europe; now it had
engendered new evils instead of doing away with the old
ones.   It is true, the sentence which was read at the door
of the Pisan cathedral had been formulated by one hundred
and twenty doctors of theology; it had been proclaimed
by the magistrates with bells and trumpets, and signalled
on from village to village.   But Benedict merely retired
to his rocky fortress of Peniscola, while Gregory called an
opposition council at Cividale and declared the proceedings
of Pisa void.

Calling of
the Council
of Con-
stance.

Fortunately at Pisa it had been voted that a new council
should soon be called, and this command John XXIII.,
as the council's pope, did not dare to disregard.   In the
struggle for the imperial crown, Sigismund, as we have
seen, had come forth triumphant, and he, while acknowl-

edging John as pope, soon showed that he was determined
to bring about a radical reform.   John had first fixed upon
Rome as the place for holding his council; but, failing to
procure attendance, and beset by Gregory XII.'s patron,
Ladislaus of Hungary, he was fairly driven to join forces
with Sigismund and accede to his conditions.

The result was the holding on German ground of the
Council of Constance, the greatest assembly of its kind that
had come together in a thousand years.   A summons had
been sent to Gregory XII. and to Benedict XIII., as well
as to all the nations of Europe.   It was evident that the
whole matter of the schism was to be probed to the bottom,
and also that a man of such evil record as John XXIII.
had everything to fear.   " This is a trap for foxes," he is
said to have cried as he stood at the top of the pass and
looked down on the town of Constance.   A short time
before, his sleigh had broken down and he had invoked the
devil in no orthodox terms.

This council was in reality an international congress;
the sovereigns were represented by envoys, while princes
with splendid retinues took their places among the cardinals and bishops.   John had created fifty new bishops as a
sort of body-guard, but the council frustrated his schemes
by deciding to vote by nations and not by absolute majorities.

John
XXIII.
promises to
abdicate.

The pomp with which Sigismund, accompanied by his
queen and a host of high-born personages, entered Constance on Christmas Day, 1414, must have shown John
XXIII. the insignificance of the rôle that was apportioned
to himself.   In the wake of the royal party came pleasure-
seekers, mountebanks, and musicians, until the number of
strangers in the little town, which ordinarily contained but
seven thousand inhabitants, rose to more than ten times
that number.   It was a giddy, adventurous throng, and it
is worthy of note that during the sessions of the council

there were some five hundred deaths from accidental drowning in the lake.

John XXIII. received a severe blow when the council decreed that the envoys of Gregory and of Benedict were to be received with respect and allowed to wear their cardinals' hats; a severer one still when his own cardinals joined in recommending that all three popes should be made to resign as a preliminary to further proceedings. Under dread of an inquiry into the whole sullied history of his own past life, he was at last brought to promise to abdicate if his rivals would do the same. *Te Deums*, tears, shouts of joy, and clanging of bells greeted the news of his decision. When, publicly in the cathedral, he had read the formula prescribed, Sigismund knelt before him and kissed his feet, in sign of gratitude. Ten days later the emperor accepted from him the consecrated golden rose, the highest mark of papal approval.

Flight of
John
XXIII.
from Con-
stance.

But all these outward signs of amity only masked a determination on John's part to escape at any and every cost; his absence from Constance, he thought, would invalidate all the proceedings of the council. He won over to his side Frederick, Duke of Austria, who had his own private and particular grievances against Sigismund. Frederick arranged a tournament outside of the city walls, in which he himself was to break a lance with the brother-in-law of the emperor; in the midst of the excited throng few noticed a man looking like a servant, in a gray cloak and slouched hat, mounted on a poor steed, with his bow dangling from the saddle. It was the fox escaping from his trap.

Although seven of John's cardinals left Constance the next day, although such disturbances arose that many really thought the council had come to an end, the Pope's flight on the whole did more good than harm to the cause of unity. It gave Sigismund an opportunity to assert himself more boldly than was his wont; he showed himself everywhere, and his speeches and proclamations did much to restore quiet. But beyond and above this there was brought fairly and squarely to an issue the question: Just what authority was wielded by a general council of the church, — did it or did it not stand above the elect of the cardinals, the acknowledged head of Christendom? The council answered this question in its own favor; it decreed that a synod lawfully assembled in the Holy Ghost held its power directly from Christ, and that all men, irrespective of rank, were bound to obey it in matters of faith, and to aid in extirpating schism. A terrible indictment was then brought against John, charging him with the commission of fifty-four crimes ; he was a liar, a robber, a poisoner, and a pagan, and not the least of his offences had been an offer to sell to the Florentines the holy skull of John the Baptist. He was pronounced " unworthy, useless, and noxious," was declared deposed, arrested, and sent off to the castle of Heidelberg, where he was kept confined during the three years that the council still continued in session.

Decree that councils are above popes.

Meanwhile the council had long been busied about another matter that was arousing intense excitement, and that was to plunge Bohemia and parts of Germany into civil war, — the trial for heresy, namely, of John Huss. The latter represented in his own person the ideas not only of the famous university of Prague, which up to the secession of the German element in 1409 had been the largest in Europe, but also of the extreme patriotic Bohemian party. His love for his countrymen extended to their language, from which he strove to banish foreign expressions ; the orthography that he introduced has ever since held its own. From the point of view of the church there is no doubt that he was a dangerous man — a

John Huss

violent political agitator, a heroic reformer.   He preached
doctrines that had been formally condemned—mainly those
of the English reformer Wyclif—and he preached them
with a flaming eloquence that carried all before it.   Not
content with holding up to scorn the vices of the clergy,
he struck at the whole pretension of the Papacy to absolve from sin through the granting of indulgences, John
XXIII. having promised the rewards usually offered for a
pilgrimage to Palestine to those who would undertake a
crusade against the ever active Ladislaus of Hungary.

Huss and
the Arch-
bishop of
Prague.
It was with the Archbishop of Prague, Sbynek, that Huss
had first come in conflict.   Armed with a bull from Pope
Alexander V., the archbishop had summoned the reformer
to answer before his inquisitor for defamation of the clergy,
upholding of Wyclif, and political intriguing; and had
finally excommunicated him, and ordered that two hundred
volumes of Wyclif's writings should be burned.   But Huss
was supported by King Wenceslaus and a large portion of
the population of Prague.   As Sbynek appeared at the door
of the cathedral to make public the act of excommunication, he was driven back with contumely, and his revenues
were seized until he should have paid back the price of the
books he had burned.   Huss's affair had become a political
matter and also played its part in the struggles of the rival
popes.   When John XXIII. excommunicated him for opposing the sale of his indulgences, the students of the university,
headed by Jerome of Prague, dragged through the streets a
car on which stood one of their number dressed as a cour-
tesan, with the Bull fastened around his neck.   The Bull
was then formally consigned to the flames.   Three students,
for calling out in church that the indulgences were a lie,
were publicly executed by the magistrates.   Their comrades
took possession of their bodies and buried them to the
sound of the martyr's chant "*Isti sunt sancti.*"   Thus was

ushered in one of the bloodiest periods in Bohemia's history. Prague was declared under the interdict, and the papal excommunication was repeated against Huss, who, indeed, at the request of Wenceslaus, went into temporary exile. This did not prevent him from writing controversial treatises, or from keeping up a brisk correspondence with his followers. He had declared his intention of appealing from the Pope to Jesus Christ, the true head of the church.

The Emperor Sigismund, full of enthusiasm for his council and anxious to purge from the taint of heresy that kingdom of Bohemia which he hoped soon to inherit from his childless brother Wenceslaus, had urged Huss to go to Constance and submit to an inquiry into the whole question of his belief. Totally, as the event showed, did he misconceive the reformer's character and the strength of his convictions. Huss might have bearded a pope, he thought, but surely he would submit without murmuring to the decrees of a body representing the whole Christian church. He willingly furnished a safe-conduct to cover the journey to and from the council and the time of sojourn there. Huss expected to be able publicly to defend his doctrines, and hoped to sway and electrify his hearers as he had done to his Bohemian congregations.

Huss goes to Constance at Sigismund's invitation.

How different was the reality! Huss arrived at Constance before the advent of the emperor, and therefore before the flight of John XXIII. By order of the latter, who sought to make a scapegoat of him, he was placed under arrest, a short hearing having been given him before the cardinals, but not before the council at large. The charges against him were: teaching that laymen as well as priests should be granted the cup of the Eucharist, attacking transubstantiation, and insisting that the moral character of the priest affected the validity of the sacrament, and that the discipline and organization of the church ought to be reformed.

As a result of the hearing, Huss was soon thrown into a dark, damp dungeon, close, we are told, to the mouth of a sewer.

Sigismund and Huss.
Sigismund, on his arrival, stormed and raged at the violation of his safe-conduct, and threatened to leave the city at once if the captive were not liberated. The council took the attitude that a heretic was outside the limits of even a king's protection, and formally declared that no promise was binding to the prejudice of the Catholic faith. It was impossible, wrote King Ferdinand of Aragon, to break faith with one who had already broken faith with God.

As for Sigismund, on learning more and more the perniciousness of Huss's doctrines, a real horror of such heresies seems to have grown up within him; there was no longer any question, even after John's flight, of allowing Huss to ventilate his teachings, but at each of the four hearings that were now held before the council he was treated as guilty and was urged to retract. At the second audience Sigismund publicly abandoned him. " If you persist in your errors," he said, "it is for the council to take its measures. I have said that I will not defend a heretic; nay, if any one remained obstinate in heresy, I would burn him with my own hands." Huss thanked him for his safe-conduct and went back to prison. Sigismund had become the reformer's worst persecutor; the evidence was more than sufficient, he declared, let this heretic be burned.

The burning of Huss.
The final hearing, July 6, 1415, was marked by the bringing forward, without witnesses, of the monstrous charge that Huss had declared himself the fourth person of the Trinity, and by the blush that was distinctly seen to mantle Sigismund's face when Huss looked fixedly at him, and mentioned his own coming to Constance, trusting in the imperial safe-conduct. That very same day, with all the cruel symbolic acts that outraged orthodoxy could invent,

the victim was degraded from the priesthood, expelled from
the church, handed over to the secular arm, and, wearing
a paper cap, — that was painted with fiends and adorned
with the unchristian motto, "We commit your soul to the
devil," — was led out to the stake, where he sang from the
Liturgy till the flames swept up and choked him.

We have dwelt so long upon the story of Huss, partly
because of his influence on the later reformation, partly
because this funeral pyre was the signal for the fierce war
that spread over into Germany, lasted for half a generation, and left behind it ineffaceable memories of ruin
and misery.   The remaining history of the Council of
Constance may be disposed of in a few words.   Two
days before the execution of Huss, Pope Gregory XII. had
formally handed in his resignation and agreed to content
himself with the title of Cardinal of Porto.   Benedict
XIII. remained obdurate, but agreed to have a conference
with Ferdinand of Aragon and Sigismund.   In order to
fulfil this engagement, thus ending the schism, and then to
pacify Christendom by making peace between France and
England on the one hand and between Poland and the Teutonic order on the other, Sigismund peregrinated Europe
for a year and a half.   Everywhere his efforts wrought
harm instead of good, except that Ferdinand of Aragon was
induced to send a deputation of Spaniards to the council.
Far from healing the discords of England and France,
and making France forget Agincourt, Sigismund openly
espoused the cause of England, and reappeared at Constance wearing the Order of the Garter; thus calling
down upon himself the unbending hostility of the whole
French contingent.   By the alliance of the Latin nations
the German-English project of reforming the church
before choosing a new head was thoroughly frustrated,
though the schism at last was brought to an end.   Benedict

End of the
schism and
frustration
of reform.

was formally summoned to appear at Constance, and, on his refusal, was sentenced to degradation and expulsion from the church. With incredible stubbornness he held out until his death in 1424, one of his last acts being to create four new cardinals, who promptly proceeded to inaugurate a new schism of their own, which troubled no one but themselves.

Martin V.   The council had meantime proceeded to the new election, and the votes had fallen upon Odo Colonna, who took the name of Martin V. The folly of merely changing the men and not correcting the abuses now became apparent. So unhampered was Martin by restrictions, that on the very day after his accession he issued rules for the papal chancery which upheld the whole former iniquitous scale of taxation and extortion. Yet so happy were men to be free from the long weary sessions, that the general sentiment was one of rejoicing. Even Sigismund prostrated himself with fervor before Martin, kissing his feet and afterward holding his bridle. Then the emperor of the Western world prepared to leave the scene of his labors, but was prevented by his clamorous creditors. Calling them together, he persuaded them by his eloquence first to consent to take his gold and silver plate in pledge, and then to accept instead his fine linen and hangings, which he never took the trouble to redeem.

Excitement over death of Huss.   Indescribable was the excitement which had ensued in Bohemia when the news of the death of Huss became known. The clergy, nobles, and cities sent a stirring protest to Constance against the " eternal, shameful wrong." To their last breath they agreed to uphold religious freedom. Stung to madness by the derision and taunts of the Catholics of Prague, a number of Hussites rushed into the Rathhaus, seized some seven of the councillors, dragged them to the windows, and hurled them to the crowd below, who, with the fury of wild beasts, tore them limb from limb. It was the irrevocable signal for a bloody revolution, and one of the first victims was the much-tried King Wenceslaus, who, in the midst of the tumult and excitement, died in a fit brought on by rage at what had happened. He passed away, to quote a contemporary, "with great clamor and with a roar as of a lion." The rôle he had played had contented no one, and his body had to be secretly buried in order to escape the wrath of the Hussites. To the other difficulties there was thus added the question of choosing a successor to the throne of Bohemia. Sigismund, the natural heir, had ruined his prospects by his treatment of Huss ; it was all too evident that nothing would induce the people to recognize as king the man who had put to death their saint and hero. He tried to fight for his rights, but could not prevent the election of Withold, the Lithuanian prince.

This Hussite rebellion that fills the years between 1415 and 1433 A.D. was peculiar in its character; it was no mere act of revenge nor yet solely an outbreak of religious fanaticism; it was a revolt against the whole narrow spirit of the Middle Ages, much as the military tactics adopted were a protest against the old heavy armor, the unwieldiness of the forces and, in general, the worn-out methods, of mediæval knighthood. It was a national, anti-German uprising, and at the same time a peasants' war or communistic outburst. According to the proclamations, all class distinctions were to fall away, all goods to be held in common, all wrongs to be righted. For it had come at last—the year of retribution and the day of vengeance.

Character of the Hussite war.

A grim, desolating war was thus started, and cruel and stern were the efforts made for its suppression. The Pope decreed that a crusade against the Hussites should be

Ziscka's methods of warfare.

preached all over Europe, and, in 1421 at least, the German contingent were instructed to kill right and left, sparing none but children. In the eyes of the church, these utraquistic heretics who demanded the equality before God's altar of priests and laymen were a thousand times worse than the rankest infidels. One after the other, immense armies were sent against Prague, but only to recoil before a power that seemed invincible. The soul and inspirer of the movement was the one-eyed, and later wholly blind, leader, John Ziscka of Trocknaw, who has been called the Cromwell of Bohemian history. A man of great natural ability, he had gained experience on many battlefields, had fought with the Poles at Tannenberg, with the English at Agincourt, and with Sigismund in Hungary against the Turks. And he admirably understood the training, and disciplining of the enthusiastic crowds that flocked to his banner. Armed with their threshing flails, which they bound round with iron, his peasants were a match for heavy cavalry in any hand-to-hand conflict. A chief feature of their tactics was the use they made of the *Wagenburg*, a moving fortress of heavy wagons, which protected the soldiers as they marched, or which could at will be drawn up into a square or circle, roofed over with boards, and firmly held together by huge iron chains. From behind these refuges, which served as a perpetual vantage-ground, the cannoneers could take deliberate aim, and the cavalry and infantry could form anew after making their sallies. Occasionally, the camps would be formed in the shape of different letters of the alphabet, so that while an enemy would find himself in a mere labyrinth, those who were initiated could readily trace their way. When the lay of the land permitted, the wagons could be filled with heavy stones and rolled down upon the enemy. But the boldest of the manœuvres of these improvised war-chariots was to drive in a line into the midst of the enemy, then, separating right and left, to enclose a considerable number, who were thus cut off from the rest and could be hewn down at will. Altogether Ziscka relied a great deal on feints and quick evolutions, which were a new experience for the heavily armed Germans.

As has been already intimated, the Hussite war was by no means confined to Bohemia; these brown, sinewy, wild-eyed fanatics made terrible inroads into Saxony, and indeed into nearly every part of the empire. In 1430 they penetrated as far as Meissen, invaded Franconia, and threatened to besiege Nuremberg. The spread of their socialistic ideas, too, filled Sigismund with alarm. He tried his best, though in vain, to gain means for equipping a really powerful army by imposing a small tax on every inhabitant of the empire. *Inroads into Germany.*

The battle of Tauss, fought in 1431, proved one of the bloodiest of the whole war. The stateliest army that Sigismund had yet been able to raise went down, almost without a struggle, before the grim, determined Bohemians. The whole empire was in an uproar, and the general feeling was one of shame and dread: these heretics were growing too presumptuous for endurance. To the door of Martin V.'s own palace at Rome a protest was affixed, by one of their number, against the whole attitude of the church; a new council was necessary, it said, and every Christian who refused to strive for it was guilty of mortal sin, while a pope who put obstacles in the way must himself be condemned as a heretic. *The battle of Tauss.*

The Council of Basel, which opened in this same year, was the result of all this agitation, although the settlement of the Bohemian troubles was not the only one of its objects: reformation of the church, the reconciliation of the schismatic Greek church, also a crusade against the Turks, were in- *Opening of the Council of Basel.*

cluded in the programme. It was the bane of Christendom
that the Pope would not unreservedly concur in such worthy
objects. The narrow-minded and self-satisfied Eugenius
IV. had jealous fears regarding the council's activity, and
scarcely had it assembled before he declared it dissolved.
In vain Cardinal Cesarini urged upon him that the Bohemians had been formally and regularly summoned, and
that a shrinking from the conflict on the part of the church
would be as disgraceful as the flight of the German army
at Tauss. The position of Eugenius was much stronger
than that once occupied by John XXIII., for he was the one
legitimate and universally recognized head of the church;
nevertheless, he only called down upon himself a reissue of
the famous Constance decree affirming the absolute supremacy of a council.

Sigismund
and the
council.

The Emperor Sigismund was far from holding the commanding position at Basel that he had once held at
Constance. He felt, to use his own expression, like the
fifth wheel to a cart. More than ten years of unsuccessful
warfare had greatly damaged his prestige. Nor were his
motives as unselfish as of yore. He wished to pacify
Bohemia that he might himself rule it; he dreaded
to offend the Pope, with whom he was negotiating for the
imperial coronation at Rome. To him and to the Pope's
own straitened circumstances in Italy was due a temporary
truce between Eugenius and the council, during which the
coronation ceremonies were performed with great pomp.
The Pope went so far in his gratitude toward his imperial
supporter as to pay the expenses of the coronation banquet,
and thus rid Sigismund of the necessity of pawning more of
his belongings. So low were the latter's finances at this
time that on his arrival at Basel in October, 1433, he had to
send to the magistrates for a pair of shoes, on the plea that
his baggage had been detained. The emperor's advocacy

of the Pope had the effect of staving off severe measures
that the council was debating against him, in the midst of
which deliberations Eugenius, driven to bay by the attacks
of his political enemies in Italy, sent in a full and free
withdrawal of all his animadversions against the assembly.

At this juncture it was that envoys sent by the Hussites
in answer to an invitation from the council arrived at
Basel. As early as 1421 the demands of the Bohemians
had been formulated into four articles, known as the "Four
Articles of Prague," and accepted by the clergy, nobles,
cities, and peasants. They called for freedom of preaching,
for the communion under both kinds, for poverty of the
clergy, and the repression of open sins. Here at Basel,
after endless discussions on each point, after envoys of the
council had twice travelled to Bohemia to negotiate on the
spot, and a new embassy had been despatched from Prague,
a compromise, remarkable for its fairness, was agreed upon.
For the first time in its history the church treated on equal
terms with heretics. Into its fold the Bohemians were
now to be called back; but the so-called Prague Compactates, signed in 1436, allowed them communion with the use
of the cup, the free preaching and reading of the gospel, and
the right to draw the clergy before the secular tribunals.

*The Bo-
hemians
and the
council.*

It was the bane of the Hussite movement that from the
first its promoters were divided into factions, between
which, even before the signing of the compactates, a war of
annihilation had broken out.   There were on the one hand,
the Calixtines or utraquists, and on the other, the more
fierce and radical Taborites who had rallied around Ziscka,
not to speak of minor sects and subdivisions. The terrible
earnestness with which men clung to their special tenets
is shown by the joy with which some fifty of the so-called
adamites accepted the sentence pronounced by Ziscka that
they should be burnt to death at the stake.   " To-day we

*Civil war in
Bohemia.*

shall reign with Christ," they declared, as they entered the
flames with a smile on their lips.   Yet Ziscka's party, which
after the death of its adored leader took the name of the
" Orphans," was less extreme than the fanatical Taborites.
Over the question of what concessions to make to the
council, bitter disputes had arisen which ended in civil war.
The weapons that had done such good service against the
outer world were now turned inward, and the battle of
Lipan or Böhmisch Brod witnessed a bloody holocaust of
the Taborites.   The exhausted land soon after made peace
with Sigismund, and allowed him in 1436 to enter Prague
Schism in   as king; but he died in the following year.   At Basel,
the Council   meanwhile, the reforms that should have rendered un-
of Basel.   necessary the great struggles of the next century were far
from making progress.   Incredible it seems that this great
assembly, which lasted for eighteen long, weary years,
should have found it possible to accomplish so little.   The
secret lay in the renewed antagonism between the council
and the Pope, and this, strangely enough, was fomented by
the application of the Greeks for such a conference as might
lead to an ending of the old schism of centuries.   It came
to be a burning question whether the splendid embassy that
was projected should appear before the council at Basel or
before Eugenius IV. at Ferrara or Florence.   A number of
severe decrees that cut every possible revenue from under
the Pope's feet were directly owing to a desire to render
it impossible for him to receive the Greeks with honor.
One blow after another was dealt to his authority.   The
annates, or first-fruits of benefices, were sweepingly
abolished, as were also the dues for the pallium, the mark
of the archiepiscopal dignity.   The number of cardinals was
reduced, the methods of election changed, and popes were
not to be recognized until they had sworn to observe the
Basel decrees.

This council was growing democratic and revolutionary; it assumed the right itself to bestow the pallium, and to grant indulgences from sin. There was some truth in the accusation that the vote of a cook was as good as that of a legate or an archbishop. The undignified proceedings that went on in its sessions lost for it, gradually, the respect of Europe; there were scenes of outrageous violence between the rival parties, — thundering protests and hubbubs, we are told, as on a field of battle. Thoroughly wearied with the course events were taking, Eugenius called together a council of his own, first at Ferrara and then at Florence, and scored a great triumph by inducing the Greeks to attend. Thus a new kind of schism had broken out in the church. Of popes and antipopes the world had seen enough; new and strange, it was to have a council and an anti-council. The assembly at Basel summoned Eugenius before its tribunal, and declared him contumacious for not coming. He retaliated by pronouncing the council dissolved, or, rather, transferred to Ferrara. In January, 1438, he was suspended from office by the council, and in June, 1439, formally deposed. In his stead Amadeus of Savoy was made pope, and the ban hurled at all those who should refuse to obey him. Thus once more was the seamless coat of Christ rent in twain. To this point had things come after so many years of common deliberation.

To the new emperor of the Romans, Frederick III., who had followed Albert of Austria, Sigismund's short-lived successor, it was no hardship to have to pursue a waiting policy. For a time he advocated the closing of both councils and the summoning of a new one; but as the cause of Eugenius slowly gained the ascendant, it became evident that it was for Germany's advantage to do as France had already done, and, by means either of a concordat or a pragmatic sanction, to secure the benefit of such salutary decrees as

The Emperor Frederick III. and the schism at Basel.

the council had already passed, even while making peace with that council's enemy. Many of the oppressive exactions of the Papacy would thus be done away with, and the valuable principle upheld, that councils were above popes. Such was the course advocated by a large party, to which many princes of the empire belonged, and the mouthpieces of which were John of Lysura and Gregory of Heimburg. Unfortunately these two men, who were sent to Italy as delegates in the matter, were far inferior to such antagonists as a Cardinal Cesarini or an Æneas Sylvius Piccolomini. Gregory is mockingly described by Æneas himself as totally lacking in self-command — as stalking around Rome in the sweltering heat, with dishevelled hair and disordered garments, cursing loudly against the Papacy.

Æneas Sylvius. Æneas, himself, on the contrary, was circumspect and full of cunning, and not choice in the selection of his means. From serving many masters and sojourning in many lands, he had become an adept in all diplomatic arts. As secretary of Frederick III. and poet-laureate at his court, he had learned thoroughly to know both the emperor's character and the ways of looking at things at Vienna. Æneas, at first, had been a warm adherent of the Council of Basel and of its pope, Felix V.; but, ever on the watch for his own advantage, he had found means of being reconciled to Eugenius IV., and had become his henchman. To this man is due the credit, if credit it be, of drawing over Frederick III. to the cause of papal reaction.

Character of Frederick III. The reign of Frederick III., which lasted for the unusually long space of fifty-three years, was, all in all, an infliction upon the land. There was, during all of that time, no great public calamity, no important war; but, from beginning to end, there was a certain stagnancy and want of progress. The House of Hapsburg was everything, the empire nothing. It was Frederick's unalterable conviction that Austria was destined to rule the whole world. His favorite motto or device, which he even stamped on his clothing, consisted of the five vowels (a, e, i, o, u), signifying in German "alles Erdreich ist Oesterreich unterthan," or, in Latin, "Austriæ est imperare omni universo." In daily life Frederick must have been a most exasperating personage; conservative to the last degree, phlegmatic, seemingly possessed of no human passions whatever, whether good or bad, he had always a trite remark with which to settle every emergency. "Time avenges all things," he would say to his Portuguese wife, when she urged him to right some wrong; when told of confusion in the courts of justice, he would answer that such things were nowhere perfectly managed; and once, when grossly insulted to his face, he simply remarked that thunderbolts usually made for high towers.

Frederick had been brought up in the narrow atmosphere of the Styrian court, and was anything but princely in his tastes and habits. His favorite way of opening a door was to kick it, through which propensity he is said to have become lame. His mother, a Polish princess, was noted less for her intellect than for her intense piety, and for a physical strength that enabled her to crack nuts with her fingers, or to press nails into a wall. The emperor himself delighted in trivialities, and a memorandum book that he has left behind is full of feeble plays upon words and of household recipes, estimates, and inventories. An ardent collector of jewels, he would sit and play with them by the hour; he dabbled in astrology, astronomy, palmistry, and transfusion of metals. Especially fond of fruit, he is said to have fixed his residence near Vienna, simply because the pears were plentiful.

Under Frederick, the zenith of indifference on the part of the rulers toward the affairs of the empire was reached.

Again and again he summoned diets at which he himself
failed to appear. Once, leaving Germany in disgust at the
failure of his plans, he remained beyond its boundaries, or
at all events away from its diets, for twenty-seven years.
Even when, in 1453, Constantinople, the very bulwark of
Christianity, fell into the hands of the Turks, he could not
be roused to action. "He sat idly at home," writes one
of his chroniclers, "planting his garden and catching
birds."

The Con-
cordat of
Vienna.

One can readily understand how a weak character like
this could be completely turned round the fingers of the wily
Æneas Sylvius. Frederick was induced to play traitor to
conciliar reform by an elaborate series of bribes conducing
to his own private advantage and not to that of Germany
at large. The benefits were assured to him in two treaties:
the one with Eugenius in 1446; the other in the form of a
concordat, two years later, with Nicholas V. By the first
instrument he was granted the right to nominate the incumbents of six great Austrian bishoprics and the overseers
or visitors of the Austrian monasteries. He could dispose
at will of one hundred ecclesiastical benefices. Should he
succeed in winning over the German nation to the papal
side, he was to have the imperial crown, a hundred thousand
guldens for his coronation expenses, and certain revenues
from church lands.

The Concordat of Vienna, which did not even mention
the Council of Basel or its decrees, consisted mainly of
concessions to the Papacy, over and above those granted at
Constance, and of petty favors conferred for his lifetime on
the emperor. Nicholas V. was to grant him a magnificent
coronation at Rome, and a tenth of the clerical revenues of
the empire. Frederick and a hundred others whom he
was at liberty to name were empowered to choose their
own father confessors, and the emperor was to have the

special privilege of carrying around an altar at which, even in places that were under the interdict, mass might be said at any time.   At seasons when other people were obliged to fast, he and his guests might indulge in milk and eggs; he might impose certain moderate taxes upon the clergy of Austria in order to provide a dowry for his daughters; where it would be greatly to his advantage, he might employ the services in war of men who were not Christians.

It was a paltry price for which to betray one's country; a miserable ending to conciliar deliberations that had been going on for nearly a score of years.

It is interesting to glance for a moment at the attitude of the seven electors during all these happenings, for it must not be supposed that they, in general so much more active than the emperor, remained absolutely quiescent where it was a question of such important reforms.   In the year after Sigismund's death, in 1438, they had taken a very decided stand.   They had publicly announced in a formal document that they would pay no heed to measures passed either by the Pope or by the council, until such time as the unity of the church should have been restored.   They had induced the short-reigned Albert of Hapsburg to join them in their policy of neutrality — a policy which was maintained for nine years, during the whole of which time the only ecclesiastical jurisdiction allowed in Germany was that of individual bishops.   When in 1446 A.D., secure finally of Frederick III.'s assent and obedience, Pope Eugenius had taken the bold step of deposing as heretics and rebels the archbishops of Cologne and Treves, the whole electoral college had arisen in its might, had renewed the old agreement made at Rense in 1338, had demanded the reinstatement of the two deposed electors, and insisted that the reform decrees passed at Basel should be clinched and ratified.   Eugenius was to acknowledge

the supremacy of councils over popes, and a new assembly
was speedily to be called.

Negotiations were still pending on these matters, and
some slight concessions had already been made, when
Eugenius died in 1447. But bribery and dissension had
meanwhile done their work among the seven, who now
receded from one position after another. The Margrave
of Brandenburg, one of the most stubborn champions of
church reform, and the last to withdraw his opposition to
the papal-imperial alliance, finally did so on receiving permission to nominate for the three bishoprics in the Mark,
and to turn the cathedral chapters of Havelberg and
Brandenburg into secular institutions. As to the Archbishop of Mainz, Æneas Sylvius acknowledged to having
spent two thousand florins in bribing his advisors.

Frustration
of the re-
forms of
Basel.

The result of the whole agitation was that Pope Nicholas
V., successor of Eugenius, was able in April, 1449, to declare the Council of Basel at an end.   Frederick III. had
already withdrawn his safe-conduct from it, and forbidden
the city of Basel any longer to harbor it within its walls.
The remnants of the great assembly then removed to Lau-
sanne, where, finally, its pope, Amadeus, came to an
amicable understanding with his rival, renouncing the
Papacy, but receiving the rank of cardinal, and being
granted in all things the place of honor next to Nicholas
himself.

Had Frederick III. acted a different part in this matter
of the council, the whole course of German history would
have been altered. The decrees that he failed to ratify had
struck deep down into the roots of papal absolutism, had
declared that bishoprics and abbacies were to be filled by
free election, that the use of the interdict and the competency of the papal tribunals were to be restricted, that
the annates, the pallium dues, and other burdensome taxes,

which were to cause such an outcry a few years later, should be done away with altogether. Now, as things had turned out, nothing whatever was gained. Even the principle insisted upon both at Constance and at Basel, that councils were above popes, was annulled and obliterated by Æneas Sylvius himself, who ascended the papal chair in 1458, and, in memory of pious Æneas, took the name of Pius II. By his bull, *Execrabilis*, issued in January, 1460, he pronounces it an " execrable abuse, unheard of in former times," that any one should appeal to a future council. The last trace of the conciliar movement was thus wiped out of the ecclesiastical law, and all the old abuses allowed re-entry — soon, indeed, to become so glaring that nothing short of secession could remedy them.

CHAPTER X

GERMAN LIFE ON THE EVE OF THE REFORMATION

LITERATURE: Brant, *Ship of Fools*, and Erasmus, *Praise of Folly*, give brilliant satirical pictures of the times. Bezold, *Geschichte der deutschen Reformation*, devotes considerable space to the causes that led to the Reformation. See also Lamprecht, *Deutsche Geschichte*, and Sach, *Deutsches Leben.* Jansen's *Geschichte des deutschen Volkes*, written from a Roman Catholic standpoint and endeavoring to prove too much, is nevertheless an invaluable storehouse of facts for our period. It has been translated into English. For Maximilian, see Ulman, *Kaiser Maximilian*, and Huber, *Geschichte Oesterreichs.*

Condition
of the
empire.

FROM the middle of the fifteenth century on, Germany progresses rapidly towards a crisis that can only be compared, in its world-wide importance, with the crusades and the French Revolution. It becomes necessary, therefore, in order to have a fitting background for stirring national events, to picture in small compass the general condition of affairs: the weakness of the state, the peculiarities of the ruler, the material and intellectual, the social and religious, position of the people, and the spread and effect of new ideas.

The Holy Roman Empire, as it still was officially called, although it embraced little territory that was not German, had come to be scarcely more than a lofty conception. Its revenues were those of an ordinary well-to-do private individual; its hold on its outlying districts was so slight, that one hardly knows whether the land of the Teutonic Order belonged to it or not. We do know that the Hanseatic League could make war on foreign powers and close treaties

without consulting it at all; that Switzerland, rather than contribute to a common tax, went to war with Maximilian, the son and successor of Frederick III., defeated him in 1499, and wrested itself entirely free. Italy had been practically lost ever since Hohenstaufen times; but Maximilian still clung to his claims and spent much of his time in warring on Italian ground — first as ally of Spain, the Pope, and Venice to drive out the French king, Charles VIII.; then as ally of France, Spain, and England, to dismember Venice; then as enemy of the Pope, to dismember the papal states and perhaps ascend the chair of Peter himself; finally as ally of Venice, the Pope, and the Swiss, to dismember France. In all of these wars he was unsuccessful, and they cost him much treasure as well as the confidence, though not the love, of his subjects; but in another direction, from the point of view at least of the House of Hapsburg, he was more fortunate, thoroughly exemplifying the old adage, *Bella gerant alii ; tu felix Austria nube.*

While his father was still alive, he had wedded Mary of Burgundy, daughter of that Charles the Bold who, in his effort to form a middle state equal to France or Germany, had become involved in war with the Swiss, had been defeated in the great battles of Granson, Murten, and Nancy, and had fallen on the last-named field. The effort to secure his wife's inheritance led Maximilian into a war with France, in which he won the battle of Guinegate, and, by the Treaty of Arras in 1479, secured the Netherlands for his house. Later, he changed the history of Europe for better or for worse by affiancing his son Philip to the princess known as Joanna the Insane, daughter of Ferdinand and Isabella of Spain, and mother of the great uniter of kingdoms, the Emperor Charles V. *The marriage alliances of Maximilian.*

Even within the acknowledged confines of the empire the process of disintegration could not be prevented.

Sub-
divisions.

Saxony, in 1485, divided its territory between two branches of the House of Wettin — the Ernestine, or electoral line, and the Albertine, or ducal, with its capital city of Dresden. Their respective heads were the two princes whose abduction in their youth forms such a dramatic page in Saxon history. It mattered little that this subdivision was counter to the provisions of the Golden Bull, in disregarding which the Palatinate also had done its part.

Weakness
of the
administra-
tion.

If, on the whole, the political organization of the empire was weak, still more was this true of the internal administration. We have seen that the Emperor Frederick III. was present at no Diet for 27 years. The chief court of justice followed the monarch's person, and the course of justice was halting and slow. Quarrels between individuals were settled by private feud — too often by burning of house or barn. The system of recruiting the army was so cumbersome that without the troops of the Hapsburg dependencies Maximilian could have accomplished nothing, and, at the first suggestion of taxation, there were revolts in all directions. Some of these evils were remedied at the famous Diet of Worms of 1495, where an *ewige Land-frieden*, or perpetual peace of the land, was decreed for the whole empire, a *Kammergericht*, or standing court of justice, established; and also, much against Maximilian's will, a *Reichsregiment*, or virtual council of regency.

Personality
of Maxi-
milian.

As regards his personality, Maximilian, known as the "last of the knights," is one of the most attractive figures in German history — a really popular ruler. His deeds and doings were in every one's mouth, whether it was a matter of the latest eloquent speech, of a dangerous hunting adventure, of a daring deed in battle, or of some purely mythical happening, as when a stone is said to have fallen from heaven to give him special warning, or two stags and a pheasant to have done him homage. People had that enthusiastic love and sympathy for him that stopped at no extravagant utterance; since Christ, it was declared, no man's sufferings had equalled his. The dream of his life was to lead a crusade against the Turks, an object which he might have accomplished but for the enmity of France.

Yet there was another side to Maximilian's character that made his reign a failure; he was too little of a statesman, too violent, too unreliable. His contemporary, Machiavelli, speaks of him as in a state of constant excitement, both bodily and mentally; as often taking back in the evening what he had determined upon in the morning. He was all indignation, all petulance, all vehemence. Through his head chased too many different projects. He could not make up his mind at a given moment whether troops were to be sent to France, to Italy, or to the Netherlands. He could brook no opposition from his Diet, but would declare that he had no intention of being bound hand and foot and tied to a nail ; or, again, that he would soon be driven to throw down the crown of the empire and snatch at the pieces. He even threatened to renounce his idea of taming the Turks, and to join with them against his other enemies. Some of his political plans are almost too wild for credence, as when he aimed to do away with the Papacy altogether and unite the two highest offices in Christendom in his own person ; or when he took up the cause of the pretender, Perkin Warbeck, and allowed himself to be designated as eventual heir to the English throne. He was always combining, always making projects; yet the prospect of a good hunt would chase even the most important political plans from his head, and while in the midst of a campaign he would endanger his person and his cause for the sake of a chamois or a stag. A bad husbander of resources, he was always in debt; we

Wild projects of Maximilian.

have a notice of a payment to come to him from the banking house of Fugger, of which a thousand guldens are imperatively demanded in advance, "or his majesty will have nothing to eat." Machiavelli declared he would never have enough, "though the trees bore ducats instead of leaves."

Inventions and reforms of Maximilian.

Nevertheless, in some respects, — chiefly in the fields of military science and of humanistic learning, — Maximilian's reign was of great benefit. Strangely enough, this "last of the knights" did more than any other man to kill knighthood, for he it was who replaced the old, useless, heavy-armed and undrilled cavalry by artillerymen and by nimble foot-soldiers, organized on the plan of the Swiss mercenaries, and known as the *Landsknechts*, or "country knaves." The artillery itself he greatly improved, inventing new kinds of cannon and transport wagons, and giving pet names, such as *Weckauf*, or Wake-up, and *Purlepus*, to individual guns. He rearranged his troops so that one category seconded the other, the riflemen the cannoneers, and the *Landsknechts* the riflemen.

The *Landsknechts*.

The *Landsknechts* made war their trade, not caring greatly on which side they fought; the yellow gold was their god, and they would desert the most renowned leader were it not forthcoming; many a campaign was thus frustrated. In time of peace noisy and swaggering, they were a perfect infliction on the land; but once in the midst of fighting they displayed magnificent courage, and their bristling squares did even more than gunpowder to destroy the remnants of chivalry.

The *Landsknechts* were for the most part burghers; but many knights also joined the regiments, receiving double pay and being allowed to fight in the front ranks. Uniforms were as yet unknown, and the ordinary costume was as gay and varied as the plumage of birds. If the "pious" *Landsknechts* sacked a town their first care was to masquerade in all the rich attire they could lay their hands on. The ordinary covering of their lower limbs was the so-called "*Pludderhose*," or bag-trouser, consisting of yards and yards of rich material drawn together at the waist and knees. The *Landsknechts* were called pious because of their habit of kneeling in prayer or singing a hymn before a battle; on rising they brushed the dust from their doublets and threw earth behind them, in token that they were casting off everything common or vile. Then, to the sound of drums and with lowered spears, they would rush to the attack.

In the reign of Maximilian, and greatly fostered by him, falls the height of the period known as the German Renaissance. It came later than in Italy, had its home rather in the universities than at the petty courts, and had to contend with a scholasticism that was not worn out but distinctly aggressive. The aim and object of the Renaissance may be designated as the search for the naked truth, — the truth brought forth from the concealment where authority had placed it, the truth in life itself, in literature, in philosophy, in art. But one step farther and it merged into the search for truth in religion, where the movement known as the Reformation took up the work.

The German Renaissance.

As in Italy, so in Germany, there was immense activity in studying languages, in unearthing old manuscripts, and in publishing the classics in the original texts. John Reuchlin of Pforzheim even went back to the Hebrew, and published the first grammar and lexicon of that tongue. Erasmus of Rotterdam edited numberless Latin authors. He could not read Cicero's ethical writings without kissing them, and thought Cicero and Horace worthy of eternal salvation. He tells us that he felt like praying: *Sancte Socrates, ora pro nobis*. The study of Greek was fostered by the flight of Greeks from Constantinople, which fell into the hands of the Turks in 1453. Men like Ulrich von Hutten welcomed the new language in the most extravagant terms. "The spirits have awakened, it is a delight to live," Hutten wrote. But narrower minds felt aggrieved and injured. "A new rebellious language has been invented," cried a Dominican from the pulpit; "it is called Greek; in it has been written a book full of dangerous passages, the New Testament by name!"

The new-found enjoyment of life.

A distinguishing feature of the Renaissance was the enjoyment of life that it inculcated; the monastic theory of the vileness of the body was thrown aside, humanity and nature became the subjects of literature and of art, and the appeal to the senses was no longer a sin. One might even be amusing, might talk philosophy without technical terms, and sing the praises of wine and conviviality. We find the most learned men drinking in the fresh air of life, we meet them supping together, we hear them warning against too close an application to study and recommending a little joking and hilarity. "I have left you," writes Celtes, in an ode to the people of Ingolstadt, "because I cannot stand your bad beer; because no wine grows on high mountains, no hill rises above your city, no shady river flows by you except the huge Danube." He will go to the Rhine, where delicious wine grows, and where "merriment accompanies drinking."

Invention of printing.

Of immense importance in disseminating learning, as well as in fostering new ideas, was the invention of printing with movable type, for which the credit is to be given to John Gutenberg, who was active in Mainz in 1450, and whose productions are still preserved. Books of importance, hitherto existing in very few copies, could now be in the hands of every student. There was some truth in the mocking words of Conrad Celtes, that priests could no longer keep their holy science to themselves, and that heaven and hell must give up their secrets.   The rapidity with which the art was taken up shows what a need was felt; there are known at the present day the names of some thousand printers who carried on business before the year 1500, and there still exist some thirty thousand books published before that date.   Anthony Coburger of Nuremberg, in 1470, worked with twenty-four presses and one hundred apprentices.   In connection with printing, wood engraving was brought to its highest perfection, and the works of Albrecht Dürer and others in this line have rarely been surpassed.   The influence of woodcuts in moulding public opinion cannot be overestimated; it was greater, as regards the lower classes, than printing itself, and the productions ran the whole scale from inspired illustrations of sacred themes to the most scurrilous caricatures.

If we take the trouble to inquire into the relative popularity of the more important publications of the presses of the fifteenth century, we shall find that, while the interests of the students ran to classical learning and science, the burning questions with the masses were socialism and hierarchical reform.   From the point of view of the printer, the Bible was already the most important book; up to the year 1500 no less than ninety-eight editions of the Latin Vulgata had appeared, some of them printed in a type that has never been surpassed for clearness, and with exquisite woodcuts.   The *Imitation of Christ* was also widely read and went through many editions, while school-books and texts of classic authors found a wide circulation.   Strangely enough, the most popular form of general literature of the day was the almanac or calendar: the belief in astrology was widespread, and it was taken for granted that the " knowing " could lift the veil of the future.   Horoscopes and weather prophecies were taken

Relative popularity of publications.

with absolute seriousness; and the poor man searched eagerly to see under what constellation he had better be bled or what was the meaning of the new comet. Strange effects of light or massing of clouds portended blood, famine, pestilence, or drought.

**Erasmus's
Praise of
Folly.**

In the matter of inflaming the masses against the priests and the nobles, and in driving them on to the great outbreaks that were so soon to take place, the pamphlet, the satire, and the news-leaf played as prominent a part as did the spoken words of the political or religious agitator. Erasmus, in his *Praise of Folly*, which ran through twenty-seven editions, and for which Holbein the Younger supplied illustrations, attacked the evils of the church in the wittiest terms, though sparing that church's doctrines. He scourged the *fictæ scelerum condonationes*, or imaginary forgiveness of sins; the reckoning of time in purgatory by hours, days, months, years, and centuries; the running to this saint for toothache, to that one for the pains of childbirth; the ridiculous subjects that theologians were wont to discuss, — whether God if he wished could have taken on the form of a woman, an ass, a pumpkin, or the devil; how the pumpkin would have spoken and what miracles it would have performed. The monks come in for their share of blows; we are told how little piety they display, how they roar out their psalms with the bray of donkeys, how they appear before the throne of heaven and are refused admittance. Even the popes are not spared, but are accused of having persons of doubtful reputation at their court, and of leaving their work to Peter and Paul, while claiming for themselves the splendor and enjoyment.

**Inflammatory
writings.**

Sebastian Brant in his *Ship of Fools* had written in a similar strain, as did dozens of lesser lights. Geiler von Kaisersberg says of the bishops, that their chief occupation is " to ride many horses, fill their money-bags, eat good pullets, and run after the girls," while an unknown writer declares of the nobles, that they no longer need either senses or limbs since their letters are read for them, their bread cut, and their clothes put on by others. Woodcuts represented the peasants with pitchforks and threshing-flails, and driving before them the Pope and the emperor. Thousands of sheets were sent abroad representing Rome as a hideous monster, the ship of St. Peter going to pieces on a rock, the clergy being maltreated by the common man, the peasant conducting the service before the altar, or the priest guiding the plough.

For success in attaining a definite object, no satire can compare with the *Letters of Obscure Men*, in the composition of which Ulrich von Hutten had a share. The greatest of the actual clashes between the old theology and the new learning of the Renaissance had been the conflict of the great Hebrew scholar, John Reuchlin, with the Dominican monks of Cologne, whose mouthpiece was Ortuin Gratius, a lecturer in the university, and who were egged on by one Pfefferkorn, a renegade Jew. The latter had celebrated his conversion to Christianity by writing venomous articles against his former brethren, and was so successful in his propaganda that he obtained a decree ordering that all Jewish books should be brought to the town hall and carefully searched for insults against the Christian religion. As the greatest Hebrew scholar, Reuchlin was invited by the Archbishop of Mainz, in the name of the emperor, to report on a plan for burning all Jewish books with the exception of the Old Testament. In a formal writing the humanist gave his judgment in the negative; the Jews, whose religion was allowed by law, could not, he said, be reproached for explaining and defending their faith; only where there were direct attacks on holy persons or institutions should the books be con-

The Letters of Obscure Men.

demned — otherwise it would do Christians good to study
them; indeed, he would warmly recommend that chairs of
Hebrew be established in each university.

The Reuch-
lin feud.

The feud that was now carried on was of the bitterest
description, Pfefferkorn even accusing Reuchlin of having
been bribed by the Jews.   Pamphlets rained thick and
fast on either side.   Hochstraten, the censor and inquisitor
for the diocese, summoned Reuchlin to declare his horror
of the Talmud and to prove his allegiance to the Christian
faith.   Gradually the old humanist lost his temper, and
attacked Ortuin Gratius in particular with bitter insults —
calling him a perverter, not a professor of good arts; a
versifex, metrifex, imo fex omnis sceleris et perfidiæ.   Hochstraten caused Reuchlin's chief pamphlet, the *Augenspiegel*,
to be burnt as heretical, but in turn was made to do penance for his act by the Pope.   A suit at law was begun at
the papal court, but before it was decided Leo X., although
a humanist himself, although he was having an edition of
the Talmud printed for his own use, and had established
a chair of Hebrew at Rome, pronounced against Reuchlin
merely for the reason that he could not afford at that
moment to break with the Dominicans.

Contents
of the
*Letters of
Obscure
Men.*

The *Epistolæ obscurorum Virorum* are a collection of 118
letters purporting to have been written, during the course
of this struggle, by Dominicans themselves.   Out of their
own mouths they are to be made to condemn themselves,
for their expressions, their manner of thinking, their pet-
tinesses, are shown forth with such veiled ridicule that
members of their own order were deceived.   The letters
are addressed to Ortuin Gratius, and present problems
that are supposed to be troubling the "obscure" men.
Is a person about to receive his degree at the university to be called *magister nostrandus* or *noster magis-
trandus?*   Can you say a "member of ten universities,"

when a member can only form part of one body? If you eat a hatching egg on Friday, have you broken your fast? Will it not make the Jews too proud if everybody learns their language? Some derivations of words are discussed: magister is from *magis*, more, and *ter*, thrice, because a master should know three times as much as other people; or is it from *magis* and *terreo*, I frighten, seeing that he should inspire his pupils with fear? It crops out in the course of the correspondence that the monks have many weaknesses, that Ortuin himself is in love with a *bellula mulier*, who turns out to be none other than Pfefferkorn's wife. He defends himself by saying that friends should have all things in common. The satire grows more and more pungent and more and more comical, the language being turned and twisted in every way, rendering it impossible to translate. Its effect was to convulse the literary world, and to rouse its victims to fury.

But satire apart, the evils in church and state alike were crying to heaven for redress. The popes of the last half of the fifteenth century, whose deeds were soon to be trumpeted throughout Germany, were making for themselves a record for shamelessness that has never been surpassed. Their names have become a byword for hideous depths of crime. Paul II., successor of Pius II., was so inordinately vain that he would have preferred to call himself Formosus, and so fond of jewels that he would appropriate them if he could obtain them in no other way. Sixtus IV. was renowned for his worldliness and for his nepotism, and his nephew, Cardinal Riario, who gave Lucullan festivals, brought forward a plan for secularizing the Papacy and for making it hereditary. Innocent VIII. filled the Vatican with his sons and daughters, and became the jailer of the Turkish Djem, whose throne the latter's brother Bajazet had usurped. There was money to be

Evil character of the popes of the period.

earned, and, lest Bajazet might secretly poison Djem, his envoys to the Vatican were rubbed down, told to kiss the towel they had used, and also to lick the letters they presented. Innocent's death involved that of three young boys, whose blood the doctors were transfusing into his own veins. If a climax were possible, it was reached under Alexander Borgia. He did, indeed, refuse an offer of three hundred thousand florins for Djem's dead body, but sold him living to the king of France. Of the innumerable murders laid to his charge, two at least are conceded, even by his defenders, to rest on strong evidence. The last scene in his career was a supper at the house of a rich cardinal, where he and his son Cæsar partook by mistake of poison they had prepared for their host. Julius II. chose his name in memory of Julius Cæsar, and took the field in person ; while Leo X. openly expressed an intention of enjoying the Papacy while he had it, and is quoted as saying that the "fable of Christ" had been very lucrative. The triumphal arch erected in honor of his inauguration was adorned with heathen gods, and the inscription upon it ran that the reign of Minerva was about to follow on that of Venus and of Mars!

Character of the German clergy.

If the German people as a whole troubled themselves little about the orgies that went on at Rome, there were plenty of examples at home of wicked and worldly priests and members of religious orders; — we hear of cardinals who went to masked balls and joined the dances; of bishops making war and using the ban and interdict for their own personal advantage. Archbishop Gunther of Magdeburg read his first mass in the thirty-fifth year of his pontificate, while Robert of Strassburg never read one at all. The lower clergy paid blackmail to the higher for liberty to evade the law of celibacy, and, in turn, took their share of the profits of wine-shops and gambling resorts. The monks of Leubus refused to hold masses for the dead unless

the abbot would give them daily a measure of beer as good
as that which he drank himself; an abbot of Volkesrode,
in 1484, restricted the usual quantity of wine so that his
monks might at least be sober when entering the choir.
We hear of cathedral chapters so aristocratic that candidates for membership had to show at least thirty-two noble
ancestors; we hear of men who held as many as twenty-
four ecclesiastical livings without occupying or performing
the duties of any.   The nunneries were too often mere
temples of frivolity.   " I never saw so many pretty women
in one convent in my life," writes a Nuremburg citizen, in
1466, and tells as a matter of course of the pleasurable
dances, the number of men-servants, and the pretty dresses.

What affected the Germans more than the personal
character of the popes, or even of their own clergy, was
the fact that much of their money found its way to Rome,
which had become the great central trading house of
Europe. A perfect army of notaries and copyists, of jurists
and accountants, was employed, and church livings and
indulgences for sin were dealt in like any other wares. A
brisk trade was carried on in expectancies, or the right to
succeed after the death of the first and even the second
incumbent. Some bought them on speculation and re-
sold them at a profit, and even laymen, like the bankers
Fugger in Augsburg, are known to have been mixed up
in transactions of the kind.   Enraged at the extortionate
prices paid at every turn, an envoy of the Teutonic Order,
whose report we have, bursts forth indignantly, " We
poor Germans continue to look on him [the Pope] as an
earthly God; better if we could look on him as the earthly
devil he really is ! "   The number of the taxes and the
amounts required were appalling : bishops-elect had to pay
thousands of guldens to be confirmed in their positions,
thousands more for the pallium, the narrow neck-band that

The mercenary spirit at Rome.

was the badge of their office. The lower clergy had to pay
the annates, which amounted regularly to half the income
of the first year. Add to these the extra payments for
special occasions, the gifts that had to be distributed right
and left, and the continual levies for crusades which never
came to pass.

The theory of the indulgences.

When Pope Leo X., the patron of Raphael and Michael
Angelo, set his heart on rebuilding St. Peter's, and
determined to raise the money by selling indulgences
throughout the whole of Christendom, there was nothing
in the measure itself to shock the public sentiment of the
time. The institution dated back some three hundred years,
and toward the end of the crusades it had been a common
proceeding to remit the vows of pilgrimage for sums of
money, which would procure the same absolution as the
burdensome journey itself. Even at that time the scho-
lastic philosophers had begun to teach that the church
possessed, in the works of supererogation, or surplus good
works of Christ, Mary, and the saints, an inexhaustible
supply of wealth. Of this St. Peter held the keys, and
from him the right of administration descended to the
popes. The indulgences were drafts on these treasures,
which were to be sold now at a fixed price. Why should
not the church's possessions, it was argued, conduce to her
own emolument, the more so as people were only too willing to commute their severer penitential duties for money
payments? The Pope for a time seems really to have been
considered as conferring a great boon on heavily laden
sinners. It was, after all, but an application to religious
offences of the method followed for centuries by the old Germanic law of labelling each crime with its appropriate fine.

It is true that remission of sins had been obtainable
for centuries at a much less price than was now asked.
Pope Boniface VIII. was once quoted as saying that if the

people only knew what absolutions were heaped up in St. John Lateran they would sin a great deal more. By merely looking at the handkerchief of St. Veronica one could gain remission of sins for fourteen thousand years; by listening to a mass in St. John's on Saturday one could free one's mother from purgatory; one could do the same by kneeling before a certain altar in St. Peter's, putting one's finger in a hole in the stone, and saying five pater-nosters. One Pope granted as many years "as it rains drops of water in a single day."

All this would be incomprehensible should we fail to recognize that this whole age, before science had unlocked her mysteries, was one of the grossest and most widespread superstition. No one, for instance, in all Christendom seems to have doubted the existence of magic or supernatural powers. Pope Sixtus IV., in a bull of 1471, expressly reserved for himself the manufacture of certain little figures representing lambs, which were efficacious against witches, and the touching of which would insure against fire, shipwreck, lightning, and hail-storms. The *Hexenhammer*, or *malleus maleficarum*, published in 1489, reduced the hunting of witches to a system, and the most distinguished men, even among the humanists, egged on the persecutors and were present when the victims were burnt at the stake. Men spoke seriously of giants with heads higher than the roofs, who brought plague in their course; of dances of death; of battles between spirits in the air. Alchemy, and particularly the transmutation of metals, was experimented in at various courts.

One phase of this belief in the supernatural, was that constant running to saints for the cure of evils, which called forth the ridicule of Erasmus. St. Anthony was especially good for inflammation of the limbs; St. Erasmus for stomach-ache; St. Martin for sick cattle; St. Gumprecht

Superstition of the age.

for hydrophobia; St. Blasius for stiff neck. There were even fashions in saints, many having their day of glory only to be afterward neglected. At the very end of the fifteenth century there arose a new star of the first magnitude in the person of St. Anna, whose glory almost outshone that of her daughter, the Virgin Mary. Alexander VI., of poison fame, decreed that whoever should say an *Ave Maria* before her image, and acknowledge the immaculate conception, should have remission for 10,000 years from deadly and 20,000 from ordinary sins.

Collections of sacred relics.

In these dying days of a church universal all this was taken very seriously : because of a notorious swindle with regard to the Virgin Mary four monks were put to death in Berne in 1509. Pilgrimages to holy shrines seem to have been undertaken in greater numbers and with greater fervor than at any time since the crusades. Arrived at their destination, men would fall in ecstasy, stretch out their arms so as to form a cross, and adore the sacred object. At no other period do we hear of such zeal in making enormous collections of relics : Nicholas Muffel brought together enough to procure him remission for 246,400 days ; he was eventually hanged by the city of Nuremberg for stealing public funds, a part of which had doubtless gone toward increasing his hoard. The collection of the Saxon elector, Frederick the Wise, could boast of more than 5000 numbers, consisting of the skulls, the bones, the hair of saints, the different objects with which Christ came in contact at the time of His passion, the skin of the face of St. Bartholomew, drops of the milk of Mary, bits of the rod of Aaron, of the burning bush, of the hay and straw on which the Christ child lay — enough in all to give absolution for half a million years. Yet even these did not equal the treasures of Archbishop Albert of Mainz, who possessed eight entire bodies and 9000 particles, not to speak of wine from the wedding of Cana, manna from the wilderness, a sample of the earth from which man was created, and a pair of nether garments once worn by Thomas Becket.

A peculiar feature of the period we are considering, was the formation of numerous brotherhoods for the heaping up of good works, which could be drawn on in time of need. Membership in the association of the 11,000 Virgins at Cologne could be gained by repeating 11,000 prayers. Regular ledgers were kept, and this particular brotherhood could show at one time a balance of 6000 masses, 3500 whole psalters, 200,000 tellings of rosaries, the same number of *Te Deums* and 10,000 times 63,000 Lord's Prayers and *Ave Marias*. When the Counts Palatine, in 1501, joined the Dominican order, they were assured by charter a share in all " masses, prayers, divine services, vigils, meditations, tears, sighs, penances, disciplines, fasts, abstinences, pilgrimages, studies, and other good works that are performed by the brothers and sisters."

Prayer brotherhoods.

All this was the straining of a bow that was soon to break. While the timid were clinging blindly to the old church, and trying to prop themselves up with the good deeds of others, bolder men were already coming forward with sentiments that a few years earlier would have cost them their lives. Church usages and even fundamental doctrines were being held up to ridicule. Conrad Celtes declared that he wished to practise his devotions in the woods and fields, and not within musty church walls which echoed with the babble of priestlets. He mocked at fasts and remission of sins, at hell and devils, and was not even sure of the existence of God or of the soul's immortality. In the *Letters of Obscure Men* the holy coat of Treves is called a lousy old doublet. Reuchlin, in translating the Old Testament, departs from the authoritative renderings of St. Jerome ; " Although I venerate Jerome as an angel,"

Rise of scepticism.

he wrote, " I adore truth as a God ! " We find other humanists comparing the Christian with the Mohammedan religion, the birth of Christ with that of Hercules, the Virgin Mary with the true Diana and Lucina who " brought for us the threefold giant into the world."

Condition of the German peasant. The class in which hatred of the priesthood and of ecclesiastical authority in general took deepest root, was the great body of the peasants ; but no less deep was their hatred of the noble. Indeed it is a question if the old Hussite ideas concerning personal liberty and community of goods had not much to do with their feeling against both. Nor can it be denied that there were many real and crying grievances, or that at the beginning of the revolt they acted with dignity and moderation.

Of the German peasants some few were completely free, some few were absolutely slaves, but between these two extremes lay the whole body of the rural population, bound by every gradation of servitude. The undoubted tendency, however, at the end of the fifteenth and beginning of the sixteenth centuries, was in a downward direction. Old liberties were taken away, new hardships imposed, while more and more disregard was shown for all the smaller distinctions. The blame for this state of affairs is to be thrown chiefly upon two great causes : the increase in luxury of the upper classes, consequent in part at least on the improved facility for intercourse with other nations; and, secondly, the introduction of the old Roman system of legal procedure into the law courts of Germany.

Luxury and gluttony. That luxury, or in other words extravagance in dress and the tendency to excess in eating and drinking, was felt by the better minds of the day to be the canker-worm eating at the heart of the national prosperity, is shown by the frequency with which the matter was brought up, both in the imperial and in the local diets. At Nuremberg, in 1524, it was seriously proposed that, as the current modes of apparel were out of all proportion to the demands of rank and station, and as drunkenness and revelling were becoming far too common, there should, on the one hand, be stringent dress regulations, according to which he who procured the conviction of any one on a charge of wearing a forbidden article might be given the article in question; and, on the other, that crimes committed while in a state of intoxication should be much more seriously punished than ordinary offences. The committee to which this motion was referred reported the reform impracticable, unless it were to be made applicable first of all to the princes themselves. The city of Nuremberg had its own particular wagon to bring in the drunkards from the streets.

We have the memoirs of a tailor's apprentice, who tells how he was obliged to adorn the most ordinary garments of the nobles : "Like painters we had to embroider upon them clouds, stars, blue skies, lightning, hail, clasped hands — not to speak of dice, lilies, roses, trees, twigs, stems, crosses, eye-glasses, and countless other foolish things." "The lords and knights," says another contemporary, "think of nothing save of making their long hair curly and blond; they try to imitate women in clothing, voice, and gait, put on jewelry, and tear out the hairs of their beards." We know from other sources that men occasionally laced, wore long hair, bared their neck and shoulders, and displayed necklaces and bracelets. While their upper garments, of the richest and gayest materials, were ridiculously short, their legs would be encased in tight-fitting hose of the most startling colors and with the two sides differing completely. The length of the points on their shoes was often so great that an ordinance of Ratisbon, in 1485, restricts it to two inches.

Nor were women far behindhand in the matter of

Extrava-
gance in
dress.

extravagance; they wore strange head-dresses and immensely long trains of costly material. "There are a thousand different inventions as to costume," writes Geiler von Kaisersberg, "at one time wide sleeves as in monks' frocks, at another so narrow that one can scarcely get into them." A law of Ratisbon for the suppression of luxury sets as maximum for each woman eighteen dresses and eighteen cloaks or outer garments.

The grinding down of the peasant.

All this is not unimportant, for inability to keep pace with such expenditure completed the moral and material ruin of the knights; while the burden too often fell upon the poor peasants, whose labor was their masters' only source of income. The most hated impositions were the *Frohndienste*, or menial services, and the *Todfall*, or inheritance tax, that took from each property so often as it changed hands the best head of cattle or the best piece of raiment. Among the services required were some of the most trivial and galling character — to frighten off the wild beasts from the garden by continuous shouting, or to quiet the frogs in the pool while the master slept. Small was the chance for redress, for the introduction toward the end of the fifteenth century of a system of law that had originated in an imperial slave state furnished timely aid in this process of grinding and oppression. What did Roman law know of the old Germanic liberties, what sympathy did it have with the old custom by which the villagers enjoyed their woods and pastures in common? The code of Justinian had no words for the different relations between master and man; the term *servus*, or slave, was a convenient one under which to group all peasants. Many who had considered themselves mere tenants came to see that they had been bitterly mistaken. At the same time they were goaded to madness by numberless petty oppressions. Their children were required to do service in the master's household ; they themselves were called upon for extra labor without payment; water was withdrawn from their mills, their fields were hunted over, and their crops ruined with no possibility of obtaining compensation. Their general condition at the beginning of the sixteenth century was one of extreme wretchedness; their farms were mortgaged at a high rate of interest, and it was a common thing to pledge the coming harvest in return for an immediate loan.

All the while just enough enlightenment was spreading among the masses to enable them to perceive the degradation of their position.   Exactly how many of them were able to profit directly by the art of printing, is a question that cannot be answered, but certain it is that long before the Reformation inflammatory pamphlets circulated widely among them.   Many editions were struck off between the years 1476 and 1497 of a curious writing, entitled *Emperor Sigismund's Reform*, which recommended an entirely new order of things, in which the "lowly were to be exalted, and the mighty cast down."   In the country, water, wood, and pasture were to be free ; in the cities, monopolies and guilds were to cease.   The clergy were to be deprived of their estates and to live on a small yearly salary.   An even more dangerous form of literature was that furnished by the astrological pamphlets and woodcuts, which are said to have actually outnumbered the theological writings of the reformers.   With their silly prophecies they kept the people in a fever of excitement: for the year 1524 they had announced that all the signs had united in foretelling a general deluge, which was especially to drown the mighty.   Nor were there wanting direct appeals to the worst of human passions.   One such writing, issued anonymously, called for the annihilation of all lords, and pointed out that, of seventy-six Roman emperors, thirty-four, on

Inflammatory writings.

account of their tyranny, had met with a violent death. The day of slaughter, it declared, was now at hand for the fattened herds which had so long pastured their lusting hearts on the poverty of the common man.

Peasant
revolts.No wonder, in the face of such agitation, that various attempts at open revolt should have taken place from time to time. The conventional emblem of such an uprising had come to be the *Bundschuh*, or common laced boot of the peasant, as opposed to the buckskin of the knight ; it was depicted on a banner or raised aloft on a pole.   For years a certain Jost Fritz had been active in different parts of Franconia in rallying followers to his standard, and in trying to effect the downfall of all princes and prelates.   He is said to have "spoken such honeyed words as to make all who heard him believe that from that time on they would be happy and rich." In Würtemberg, in 1514, it had been found necessary to put a bloody end to the activity of a league known as the Poor Conrad, and more than a dozen ringleaders had been seized and beheaded. So the *Bundschuh* had not been idle, and its very name struck a certain terror into the hearts of the upper classes.

Into religious and social agitation such as has been described fell the first manifestations of the Reformation; it was like sparks igniting gunpowder.   In the rock on which Peter had built his church clefts were riven that never again could be bridged over.

CHAPTER XI

MARTIN LUTHER AND THE EMPEROR CHARLES V

LITERATURE : An English translation of Luther's three great addresses to the German people has been made by Wace and Buchheim. Beard's *Martin Luther* is excellent for the first four great years. Köstlin is exhaustive. Baumgarten's *Karl V.* is a monumental work. Freytag's *Dr. Luther* is a charming sketch. Bezold has written the best history of the whole German Reformation, more full, even, than the work of Ranke. Egelhaaf's *Reformation* has its own merits ; his smaller work, *Deutsche Geschichte im Zeitalter der Reformation*, is convenient and well written.

THE age being fully ripe for revolution, all that was needed was a leader fearless, overbearing it might be, but strong enough to win the respect of friend and foe alike. Such a one was the monk Martin Luther, a man who had fought such struggles with his own conscience that at times in the monastery at Erfurt he would fall on the ground and remain in a swoon for hours. To use his own language, he had "suffered such great and hellish pain as no tongue could tell and no pen describe"; he had reached a condition of such utter despair as to make him recoil before every image of Christ, seeing in it the devil in person. The strength of such a nature lay in its conservatism ; it would take much to destroy its creeds and ideals, but the process once begun had to go on at any cost, even to the bitter end.

An experience of great moment for the future had been a journey to Rome in the interest of his order, a journey which he made on foot, relying on the hospitality of monasteries. He had long been anxious to go, expecting to

Mental struggles of Martin Luther.

The journey to Rome.

find there more holiness than in other places. He intended to make a grand confession of all the sins he had ever committed in his whole life. He once said himself, later, that he was in those days a "most mad papist, so drunken, so drowned in the papal dogmas" as to be willing to slay the Pope's detractors. The consecrated priest, so he thought, was to the ordinary Christian as the morning star to the flame of a candle. On reaching the city which was the home of his beloved saints, he fell on his knees with a "hail, holy Rome!" He ran round among the churches like a "mad saint"; he was sorry his father and mother were still alive, so simple a matter would it have been to release them from purgatory. He began to mount the *scala santa* on his knees with prayers and contrition; but there kept ringing in his ears the words "the just shall live by faith," and he desisted before he reached the top. His was indeed a rude awakening! He heard priests at the altar make blasphemous witticisms in Latin; he was himself once told when performing mass to hurry and send back her son to the mother of God!

Tetzel the indulgence-hawker.

The sale of papal indulgences in the neighborhood of Wittenberg brought about the crisis of Martin Luther's life. It was not the institution itself that aroused his wrath so much as the particular attendant circumstances. The Archbishop of Mainz, that same Albert of Brandenburg who possessed such a quantity of relics, had borrowed a large sum of money from the banking house of Fugger, to pay for his pallium; but was allowed to set aside for repayment of this debt a portion of the indulgence money collected in his diocese. That the sum might be as large as possible, the conduct of the affair was handed over to one Tetzel, a Dominican and a man of great experience. Tetzel had sold papal privileges for the benefit of the Teutonic knights, for a copper roof on the church at Görlitz, for a bridge across the Elbe at Torgau, and had also been agent for the so-called butter-charters, or permits to eat butter when otherwise forbidden. On the present occasion he offered various kinds of privileges, for which men were to pay on a sliding scale, according to their rank and wealth: plenary remission for the moment, the release of souls from purgatory, the right to choose a confessor, and to be absolved in the last agony. Accompanied by an agent of the Fuggers, who was provided with a duplicate key to the strong box, Tetzel, with a noisy train bearing banners and tapers, and holding the papal bull aloft on a golden or velvet cushion, would enter a city and march to the church to the clanging of bells. There in the nave would be erected a great crucifix displaying the crown of thorns and the nail holes, as well as the papal arms and standards; on particularly solemn occasions the red blood of the Crucified One was seen to run down the wood. In front of the cross was an iron-bound coffer; to one side a pulpit, to the other a table at which the actual business was transacted. It was a royal road to salvation that was here presented; for a paltry sum of money an instant escape was offered from all the weary pilgrimages, all the fastings, and all the abject creepings to the foot of the cross.

If Tetzel's methods were shocking to sensitive souls, it must be said in his defence that he preached exactly as he had been told to preach by the archbishop of the diocese. One of his well-known sayings, that as the money rattled in the box the soul flew out of purgatory, was later defended by a churchman of high standing as a justifiable spice for an indulgence sermon. Another that Luther mentions, to the effect that absolution could be bought even if one had offered violence to the mother of God, was formally denied by Tetzel. Luther was most directly

Defence of Tetzel.

affected by the permission to choose a confessor; for members of his own flock, on whom he had imposed penance, left him and sought remission elsewhere.

The ninety-five theses.

In a hesitating way, not entirely denying their value, or the right of the Pope to issue them, Luther began to preach against the indulgences; finally, on the eve of All Saints' Day, 1517, he formulated his objections into ninety-five theses and nailed them on the door of the Wittenberg church. There was nothing defiant in his attitude; the same door had often done service as a university bulletin board, and the academic nature of the theses was shown by the fact that they were written in Latin. Luther took the ground that the church had never formulated its doctrines regarding indulgences, and that the matter was open to discussion. No one was more surprised than he at the sensation caused by his act. We are told that within four weeks his theses flew, as though borne by angels, sheer throughout Christendom.

Luther maintained that he was not attacking the Pope, but merely the excesses of the pardoners; that could Leo know the truth, he would let St. Peter's burn to ashes, rather than build it up with the skin and flesh and bones of his sheep; that Christians must seek Christ through pains, deaths, and hells, not by royal roads. "Away with all those prophets who say to the people of Christ, peace, peace, and there is no peace!" Yet he could not refrain from asking a few plain questions:—if Leo could release souls for money, why does he not empty purgatory, "for the sake of most holy charity"? or, seeing that he is richer than Crœsus, why not build St. Peter's himself?

Effect of theses.

In the Roman camp the effect of the theses was tremendous. Archbishop Albert, though he rebuked Tetzel for "injuring the holy business," instituted a formal trial, and Luther was summoned to appear before the Pope, in

Rome, within sixty days. Orders were sent to arrest him, to bind him hand and foot, while ban and interdict were to be hurled at his defenders. The elector of Saxony, whose subject he was, was asked to hand over this child of iniquity. Tetzel, now Doctor of Theology, wrote counter theses, in which he answered Luther's appeal to the authority of the Bible with the naïve remark, that many of the Catholic truths were contained neither in the Scriptures nor in the church Fathers. Prierias, " Master of the Holy Palace," argued so ably, to his own mind, that Luther, he said, " must have an iron nose and a brazen face" if he refused to be convinced. Yet, in rough terms, his argument was simply that the Pope, as highest sovereign in the world, might do as he pleased in all things, and was to be thanked for not demanding, as a direct tax, the sums he deigned to accept in return for the indulgences.

Luther's own humility at this crisis was almost excessive; he begged that his theses be not accepted as an irrevocable expression of his opinions; he was doubtful on some points, ignorant on others, some he would even deny. In a letter to Albert he speaks of himself as the " dregs of humanity," of the archbishop as " at the height of sublimity." He says later that he felt " more like a corpse than a man"; he writes to Leo, asking him passionately for comfort and advice, " I cannot revoke, though I see the multitude inflamed against me! " He is only a plain, narrow, not finely educated man, in an age that might displace even a Cicero; " but necessity drives me on; the goose must cackle among the swans. At thy Holiness's feet I prostrate myself with all that I am and all that I possess. . . . In thy voice I will recognize the voice of Christ dwelling and speaking in thee. If I have deserved death, I am not unwilling to die."

Leo X. was no persecutor; his chief delight was the dis-

Luther's humility.

covery of a new manuscript or a new work of art; provided there were no interference with his own extravagances, he was willing that all should be happy around him. When he first heard that Luther, an Augustinian, was in conflict with a Dominican, he attached little importance to the matter. "This Brother Martin is a clever fellow," he said, "and it is only a case of jealous monks." Yet all the same Leo was dangerous because not master of his own actions, and a journey to Rome would have exposed Luther to the fate of a Savonarola or a Huss. The reformer was not minded to submit to useless peril before his work was half begun; he even suggested, through his friend Spalatin, that the Saxon elector refuse him a safe-conduct. As a result of correspondence between Frederick the Wise and the Pope, permission was gained for the " son of iniquity " to remain on German ground, but he was to appear at Augsburg before the Cardinal de Vio, known as Cajetanus.

Luther and Cajetanus.

A greater contrast than the two men who now confronted each other could scarcely be imagined: the one humble, yet alert and honestly seeking for truth; the other haughty, magnificent, and overbearing, fast bound in the chains of scholasticism ; — so ardent an admirer of Aquinas, indeed, that he had changed his own name to Thomas. Hutten declared sarcastically that the cardinal slept in his purple robes and drank out of goblets of gold ; that the wines of Germany fairly made him weep, and that he considered it, therefore, a barbarous country. A firm upholder of papal infallibility, Cajetanus had been known to intimate that the church only existed for the sake of the Pope. He had come now to Augsburg, where the Diet of the Empire was in session, to preach a crusade against the Turks ; to make Bohemia conform to the mother church ; and to bring the red hat to the Archbishop of Mainz.

Arrived in the city after parting with friends who feared

greatly for his safety, Luther was visited by various persons who gave him sympathy if not encouragement. "Do you wish," said Serralonga, a good-natured Italian diplomatist, "to play at running the ring with the cardinal? Do you think that the elector will take up arms on your account?" — "I do not think it," was the reply, "nor is it my wish." — "And where will you be then?" — "Under the heavens."

At the first interview with Cajetanus, which was held in the presence of three of Luther's friends, of a papal legate and of this same Serralonga, the monk showed to the cardinal all the respect that was due from a subordinate to one so vastly above him in rank. He threw himself on the ground the whole length of his body, and only rose when bidden. The churchman had evidently thought that the mere magic of his presence was causing this heretic to quail; but Luther now asked him to point out in detail his particular errors. Cajetanus mentioned two, — the denial that the merits of the saints formed a treasure of the church, and the doctrine that faith was necessary to make the sacrament effectual. Papal bulls were brought out in favor of the church's position, and Luther found himself declaring that the papal bulls were of no account if contradicted by the plain sense of Scripture. The issue had been fairly joined, papal omnipotence had been denied, and the old conservative, stubborn theology stood over against the new spirit of criticism. Cajetanus kept repeating incessantly, "Recant and see thine error; thus the Pope wills it and not otherwise, whether thou like it or no." The interrogation was continued a second and a third day; Luther's request to have his teachings submitted to the great universities was denied, and the interviews grew more and more stormy. Upon Cajetanus imputing to one of the bulls a meaning which was manifestly false, Luther lost all

The hearing at Augsburg.

patience. " Do not let your Reverend Paternity think that the Germans are wholly ignorant of grammar," he cried in anger. " Go," said the cardinal, " and come back to me no more till you are willing to recant." He afterward said to Staupitz, " I will speak no more with this monster, for he has deep eyes and wonderful fancies in his head."

The flight from Augsburg.

The next that we hear of Luther, he is flying for his life from Augsburg, at night, through a postern gate, on a hard-trotting nag, and clad only in his monk's cowl, without trousers. He had heard that an attempt was to be made to hold him fast and deliver him up, and we know now that Cajetanus was actually provided with a papal brief designating Brother Martin as a stubborn heretic and ordering his arrest. Ban and interdict stood at the disposal of the cardinal; in whatever locality refuge might be offered to Luther no bell could be rung, no sacrament performed, no corpse even receive Christian burial. The fugitive had left behind him a letter for Cajetanus, in which he said that he had done everything as became an obedient son of the church. Notwithstanding the distance, his poverty, the infirmity of his health, he had come to Augsburg to be called to account. The legate had bid him begone unless he were willing to recant; now he could stay no longer. His last resource was to make an appeal, not only from the cardinal, but from the Pope himself, so long as the latter should continue to be misinformed concerning him. This appeal, which called for a fair and impartial hearing before learned and just men and in a safe place, was attached by a friendly notary to the door of the Augsburg cathedral soon after the escape. Luther carried with him one comfort in his flight: he had seen that there were other complaints against Rome than those which he himself had formulated; he had learned that his cause was in a fair way to become the cause of the country at large. The imperial diet at Augsburg had refused to contribute to the crusade on the express grounds of the evils inflicted by Rome on the German nation.

Nothing shows more clearly Luther's growing importance and influence in Germany, than the timid and cautious manner in which he was next approached. The case was intrusted now to a very different man from the haughty Cajetanus — to the papal chamberlain Miltitz, who was to begin the attack by bribing the elector Frederick with the golden rose. Miltitz, a German who had gone to Rome to seek his fortune, because he was hampered at home by being one of twenty-four children, was excellently fitted for his mission. He could rise to any occasion, could be serious and dignified, or could hold his own at the wildest drinking bout. The conduct of the present campaign was to be left to his discretion ; he was to be affable or severe, to strike or conciliate as the case might demand. Should he need them, anathemas of various kinds were supplied against the " son of perdition, yea of Satan." " Miltitz has brought the rose," wrote a friend of Luther's, " and with it briefs by no means rosy."

But when the legate found how widespread was the movement, and how warm the supporters of the reformer, he determined that severity would be of no avail, and called upon Tetzel, not Luther, to appear before his judgment seat. Tetzel refused ; it was as much as his life was worth, he wrote, to leave Leipzig, " for Martin Luther, the Augustinian has so roused and moved the mighty against me, that I am nowhere safe." Miltitz went to Leipzig, interviewed the indulgence-hawker, heard all that he had to say, and then pronounced him a rogue. The poor Dominican, accused among other things of embezzling part of the money he had collected, was terribly hurt at the outcome of the interview, and never raised his head again.

Miltitz and Luther.

Miltitz and Tetzel.

Six months later, hearing that he was on his death-bed, Luther had the generosity to write him a letter bidding him "be comforted; that the affair had not been begun on his account, but that the child had quite a different father."

Luther was little affected by a hint of one of Miltitz's followers that a bishopric awaited him if he would only recant; but the legate did persuade him to enter into a truce in the course of which the matter was to be referred to some erudite bishop; in the meanwhile a conciliatory and submissive letter was to be despatched by the reformer to Rome. Outwardly on the best of terms, the two men took their evening meal together, and at parting Miltitz gave the kiss of peace; "The kiss of Judas," Luther called it later, and the legate's tears he described as "crocodile's tears."

John Eck.

The little period of rest did not last long. Unaware of the agreement of Miltitz, other champions of the church were preparing to come forward, notably the great disputant of the age, the theologian John Eck. As knights of old, seeking a joust, went round from court to court, so this literary gladiator of imposing presence and loud voice was ready for any fray. It was said that it mattered little to him which side he espoused: he had once been employed by the banking house of Fugger to controvert the teachings of the church with regard to lending at interest.

Eck had written a commentary, called the *Obelisks*, upon eighteen of Luther's theses; the latter had answered by *The Asterisks of Luther against the Obelisks of Eck*, and his erratic, flighty friend, Andrew Bodenstein, called Carlstadt, had written no less than four hundred and six theses attacking Eck and Tetzel. Eck, who posed as a warm upholder of the old philosophy, and who was peculiarly annoyed at this time by the appearance of a satirical woodcut representing scholasticism in a coach and four driving

rapidly to hell, while another coach surmounted by a crucifix was mounting heavenward, challenged Carlstadt to
a public disputation at some university, and at the same
time sent word to Luther, "You will see by the schedule
of dispute that I have laid down propositions not so much
against Bodenstein as against your writings."

Duke George of Saxony, liberal to a certain extent, Disputation
though holding fast to the fundamental doctrines of the of Leipzig.
church, was pleased that his university should be honored
by the presence of such great men, and offered his city of
Leipzig, and even the hall of his own castle, as the scene of
the dispute. The greatest preparations were made for the
event, and Luther, in the interim, plunged into studies in
church history that were to yield him remarkable results.
Gradually his horizon was broadening in all directions; he
had already begun to have his doubts about the fundamental pretensions of the Papacy. "I do not know," he wrote,
"whether the Christian faith can bear having any other
head of the universal church on earth than Christ himself;" and again, "I am looking through papal decrees
for my disputation, and must whisper in your ear that I
find it hard to decide whether the Pope is Antichrist or
merely his apostle." He was going to Leipzig "to strike
out straight at the Roman snakes, at papal tyranny and
deceit"; he was climbing a very different kind of *scala
santa* from the one he had found in Rome!

The proceedings at Leipzig were opened with great
form and ceremony, Leipzig students being detailed to
walk with the Wittenberg masters in the grand procession,
and Duke George himself attending the sessions. The
combat began by a discussion between Carlstadt and Eck
on divine grace and free-will, — a discussion that unfortunately proved so wearisome as to send many of the hearers
to sleep. The professional disputant proved superior to

his antagonist at every point, the more so as the latter desired and needed aid from books which he was not allowed to produce; nor was the dignity of the occasion enhanced by Carlstadt's willingness, when at a loss for words, to be helped by whispers and by notes from the lookers-on.

Luther a
Hussite.

But after a few days the real combat began, and Luther and Eck locked arms on the question of the divine right of the Papacy. The views that were now brought forward differed as totally as did the outward appearance and manner of the two antagonists. Eck, tall, solid, square, with the voice of a tragedian or of a town crier, insisted that, in the bishopric of Rome and in the power of the keys alike, the Pope was, and had always been, recognized to be the direct successor of St. Peter. Luther, at this time spare of frame, spent with care and study, though always with a cheerful countenance, pointed out that the church had flourished elsewhere before the see of Rome could possibly have been founded, that the proofs of Rome's precedence and antiquity were only the "very frigid" decrees of the pontiffs of the last four centuries, as opposed to the proven history of eleven hundred years. Had not the Greeks for centuries belonged to the Christian church and acknowledged nobody save their own patriarchs? Had the Council of Nicæa or the church fathers looked upon the Pope as head of Christendom?

But Eck had his quiver full of poisoned arrows, and he suddenly forced his antagonist into admissions that terrified his hearers, and evoked an oath from Duke George, which was heard in every corner of the hall. Eck answered the argument about the Greek church by saying calmly that the Greeks were heretics beyond reach of salvation, and showed triumphantly that among the errors for which John Huss had gone to the stake in Constance were the assertions that faith in the headship of the Roman church was not necessary to salvation, and that the church on earth needed no head at all.   Luther was fairly caught in the toils of his adversaries; it was a part of the gospel of every Saxon to believe in Huss as the incarnation of sedition and heresy.   Up to this time Luther himself had had the same feeling; he had once come upon a writing of the Bohemian preacher and had slammed the book to, and thrust it away as a thing of evil.   Now, driven to bay, he was forced to acknowledge before friends and foes that many of these teachings were right Christian and evangelical, thus sealing his breach with Rome.   He had asserted that a council of holy church could be in error; that the Council of Constance had been in error when it tried John Huss and condemned him to a cruel death: what need of further inquiries or disputations? " We are all Hussites without knowing it," he wrote to his friend Spalatin, the secretary of Frederick the Wise, "yea, St. Paul and St. Augustine were actual Hussites."   He was amazed, he declared, that the pure evangelical truth should have been accursed for more than a century.

Meanwhile, of great importance for the future of the Reformation was the fact, that in January of this same year, 1519, the Emperor Maximilian had succumbed to an attack of illness, brought on, it is said, by rage at the attitude of the tavern-keepers of his own Tyrolese city of Innsbruck, who refused to harbor his retinue without better prospect of remuneration.   It was June before the question as to who should succeed to the " Holy Roman Empire of the German Nation " was finally brought to a settlement.   Within the limits of those five months falls one of the most active and exciting electoral campaigns ever waged in Germany.   The rank and prestige of the different candidates, the sacrifices made by all parties to attain

The
imperial
election.

their ends, the interested concern of the chief European powers, the importance of the outcome for the rising tide of Protestantism, — everything combined to make this imperial election different from any that had gone before.

It is difficult to understand just why the imperial office should have been such an object of desire; neither Maximilian nor Frederick III. had seemed to greatly prize it; pecuniary benefit there was none. Yet in a way there was great respect for the time-honored institution; it was the fourth of the great monarchies mentioned in Daniel's vision, the one that was to endure until the end of time; a certain tacit precedence was accorded its head by all other European sovereigns. Moreover, the title was a convenient stepping-stone for men of large ambition — he who held it was, as a matter of course, considered the proper leader in a war against the Turks.

From the beginning of the sixteenth century, on through the next two hundred years, complications with the Ottoman Empire form the key-note to European politics. It is the reversal of the crusades — under the sign of the cimeter as many expeditions are hurled against Christian Europe as ever troubled the repose of Islam. The dream of Maximilian's life had been to lead a host against this enemy; ever since they took Constantinople, in 1453, they had harassed the borders of Hungary. Now, more than ever, there was need of stemming the swelling tide. No Adolphus of Nassau, chosen for his mediocrity, but a strong and resolute and warlike emperor was needed, with great resources at his command.

The early years of Charles V. Although Maximilian, in fits of impecuniousness, had more than once bartered for the sale of his influence as regarded the succession, — notably with England and with Hungary, — he had, in his heart of hearts, always intended that the imperial mantle should fall upon the shoulders of his own grandson, the young King Charles of Spain. With Hungary, Bohemia, Naples, the Netherlands, Mexico, Peru, Jerusalem, and other realms, some real, some visionary, there would thus be united on one head no less than twenty-five crowns.

Naturally enough, a youth with such splendid prospects had been the object of solicitude in many directions. From the time when he was a year old, the question of his marriage had agitated all the courts of Europe; no less than ten times had he been affianced before wedding his Portuguese bride; for his guardians and councillors, chiefly leading statesmen in the Netherlands, like Chièvres and Adrian of Utrecht, had not scrupled to break one projected union after another, according to the weather-vane of policy. Nor had there been wanting other intrigues. The regent Margaret had been regularly paid by old Ferdinand of Aragon to keep the boy from appearing in Castile and attempting to gain popularity.

In such an attitude of calculation, with all natural family life rendered impossible by the insanity of his mother, who spent her time in brooding over the grave of her faithless husband, the boy had grown up cold, selfish, and taciturn. "He is as unapproachable as an idol," so an English ambassador described him when he had reached the age of seventeen. His development had been singularly slow; although before his tenth year he had shown a strong love for hunting, much to the delight of Maximilian, who was sure, now, he said, that the boy was a Hapsburg. A portrait of Charles, painted after he had already, at the age of sixteen, become king of Spain, shows the features of a much younger lad; nor had he up to this time succeeded in mastering either the Spanish or the German languages. His health often gave rise to anxiety; we hear of fainting fits, of something like epilepsy, of

attacks so severe that recovery was doubtful. Was it con·
sciousness of his own deficiencies, or was it the sense of a
certain dormant power, that made him appear in a Spanish
tourney with a snow-white shield on which was emblazoned
the word *nondum*, or "not yet"? The regular motto that
he later adopted was *plus ultra*, or "more beyond."

Maximil-
ian's efforts
to secure
Charles's
election.

By the time Charles, born with the century, was eighteen, Maximilian had determined to have him appointed
"king of the Romans and future emperor" during his own
lifetime. With this end in view, and supplied with funds
from Spain, the emperor approached different members of
the electoral college, and persuaded four out of the seven
to promise him in writing that they would vote in favor of
the plan. It was hoped that within a month the coronation might take place. The chief opposition came from
the court of Rome, and one at least of Leo X.'s objections
was entitled to consideration. How could there be chosen
a new king of the Romans when Maximilian himself could
boast of no other title, having never been crowned at
Rome with the imperial crown? It is true he had commonly been called emperor, but that was by courtesy of
the Pope! Never in the history of the empire had there
been two kings of the Romans at the same time.

Leo's real cause for dread was lest a man who was
already king of Naples should come to wear the imperial
crown: it was the old fatal combination of Hohenstaufen
times, the combination that made the Papacy feel as though
its dominions were enclosed in a vice. "Do you know,"
Leo once said to the Venetian ambassador, who has
recorded the remark, "how far it is from here to the borders of the Neapolitan territory?"—"Forty miles." "The
Catholic king must not become king of the Romans." So
bulls and decisions of former days were brought forward
to support the contention, and it was evident that if a rival

could be found for Charles, he would be sure of the Pope's favor.

Before his schemes had ripened into fulfilment, Maximilian was gathered to his fathers. In spite of the sums expended, in spite of the compacts made, the agreement as to the succession was pronounced null and void. It was a far different matter, said the electors, to choose a king of the Romans who might not be called upon to rule for many years, and to elect the actual head of the nation. The lists were thus thrown open and the great contest began. In answer to a letter of the young Spanish king announcing his hopes and expectations, Francis I. of France wrote back that he and Charles were " two friends who were suing for the favor of one and the same dame." Nor could a more redoubtable antagonist have well been found. Since the battle of Marignano, won over the Swiss in 1515, Francis had been known as a brave warrior and skilful general. Young, ambitious, unscrupulous, he was at the head of a strong, well-consolidated monarchy and with vast resources in his hands. Charles, on the other hand, lord though he was of many scattered lands, was already hard pressed for money; his Spanish cities, on the verge of revolution, turned a deaf ear to all his demands, while his old device *nondum* would as yet have fitly applied to his experience in war.

The rivalry of Charles and Francis I.

Pope Leo espoused the cause of Francis as though it had been his own ; his legates were instructed to instil into the mind of the French king that he was about to acquire the imperial dignity through the " favor and grace of his Holiness," for which favor and grace he was expected to make some substantial return. Nor was Leo's boast so utterly vain, — three of the seven electors were dignitaries of the church, and each was now promised advancement in rank in return for his vote. Treves and Cologne were to

Pope Leo and the German election.

receive cardinals' hats, while the Archbishop of Mainz was to become perpetual legate of the Roman see for the whole of Germany. Had the Pope been actuated by the least regard for the larger interests of the church, he would, indeed, have thrown himself into the arms of Charles and moved heaven and earth to procure his election; for he, far better than his rival, was in a position to ward off the two great dangers that threatened Catholic Christendom. The rapacious Turks, who but recently had been ravaging the shores of the Mediterranean and had all but succeeded in capturing his Holiness himself, were actually quartered on the lands of the house of Hapsburg, and Charles's every personal interest would impel him to head an army that should drive them back. The bigoted character, on the other hand, and the early training of the grandson of Ferdinand and Isabella made it just as certain that he would wage war to the knife with the rising power of Lutheranism. It is true, with regard to both of these matters, Francis made great professions. His hand in the hand of the English ambassador, he swore on his honor that in the event of his election he would be in Constantinople within three years or die in the attempt. Already he had laid plans for restoring the empire of the East with the Pope's aid, and placing its crown on his own head. But all this was the mere selfish dream of ambition; Francis had no real reason for hating either Turks or German Lutherans, and the future was to show that, when it served his ends, he could condescend to an alliance with both.

Rival efforts.

The sums formerly squandered by Maximilian in the matter of Charles's election were the merest trifle in comparison with the outlays that now were needed. The French king had expressed his willingness to spend one-half of his yearly revenue for the attainment of his object; his agents travelled like princes, and eight hundred horses at one time were provided for the retinues of three of them. Their set plan was to dazzle by reports of their master's power, of his riches, of his great deeds. "As the sun out-shines the stars," they proclaimed, "so far does he surpass all other princes." The young king of Spain, with his finances already considerably involved, could not begin to compete with Francis in the single matter of bribing the electors, although it was computed afterward that he had spent in all nearly a million ducats.

The supporters of the Spanish aspirant were for a while in the depths of despair; the one and only escape from disastrous defeat seemed to be for Charles to renounce his pretensions in favor of his brother Ferdinand. The latter, although only sixteen years of age, had shown qualities that were likely to endear him to the German nation. He passed for clever and thoughtful; Pope Leo considered that he had *piu spirito* than Charles, while Erasmus wrote of him *in Ferdinando mayna spes est*. But when the plan of withdrawing his own claim in favor of another member of his family was broached to the young king of Spain, it met with a downright refusal. The choice of Ferdinand, Charles declared, was not to be thought of for a moment, it meant loss and dishonor to himself, it meant the complete and perpetual ruin of the house of Hapsburg. Was he not the elder, had not his grandfather nominated him his successor, and the electors given their promise in his favor? It was absolutely necessary that he and no other should become emperor of the Romans, "for the good of the holy faith and the hurt and destruction of infidels."

In the rush and strain of the electoral contest a third and even a fourth candidate came to the fore. A hint from the Pope put it into the head of Cardinal Wolsey that there was a chance of success for the English king. An envoy was sent from England with directions to make

Other candidates for the imperial throne.

cautious proposals and see how they would be received; but unfortunately for the result of his mission, he was supplied with no funds for purposes of bribery. He was well treated on his arrival, but politely told that he had come too late. Far different was the candidacy of Frederick of Saxony, the patron of Martin Luther. This prince could easily have obtained the crown had he so desired; three of the electors, unable to unite on either Charles or Francis, were willing to compromise on him, while his own vote, which, according to the sentiment of the time, might well have been cast for himself, would have given him an absolute majority. But fear of responsibility and consciousness of the limited nature of his own resources caused this excellent prince to refuse the proffered honor.

Charles wins the election.

In the end the French king overreached himself by his very zeal. The autocratic electors came to the conclusion that a man so powerful as his envoys pictured Francis would not be at all to their liking; he had crushed all independence in France, he would, it was feared, do his utmost to be absolute in Germany. The emissaries from Spain had used far more tact and judgment; they had lauded the electors as the powerful allies whom their master needed and longed for in his approaching conflict with the Turks. A great tide of public sentiment set in in Charles's favor, and public sentiment was beginning to be a power with which it was absolutely necessary to reckon. Was not this a Hapsburg prince? Was he not the grandson of that brilliant Maximilian whom all had loved in spite of his faults? As for Francis, he was wholly of foreign blood; he was the natural ally, too, of the Pope, and even the hearts of good Catholics were filled at this time with anger on account of the abuses practised by the Roman court. The majority, indeed, would still have preferred Ferdinand, not only for his personal good qualities, but also because, unhampered by the possession of foreign crowns, he was likely to pass the greater part of his time in Germany. But this, as we have seen, was not to be; and at the final election, held at Frankfort, the vote in Charles's favor was unanimous. At the eleventh hour Pope Leo withdrew his opposition, and, in the face of the inevitable, tried to make friends with the Mammon of Unrighteousness.

The electors before finally committing themselves had seen fit to bind their new lord by making him sign a capitulation or electoral compromise in which he not only agreed to respect their own liberties and prerogatives, but promised to bring neither foreign soldiers nor foreign officials into the land, to hold all intercourse in the German or Latin languages, and to hold no courts of justice and summon no imperial subjects outside the boundaries of the empire. No one might be placed under the ban unless formal proceedings should have first taken place. In all the affairs which it covered the Golden Bull was to be carefully observed; vast monopolies like those in the hands of the banking-house of Fugger were to be restrained, and a halt was to be called to the aggressions of the court of Rome. *The electoral compromise.*

So undoubted a triumph as the election had been, the rejoicing in many quarters was forced and hollow. The new emperor himself was on the verge of bankruptcy; the discontent in the Spanish cities had blazed into open warfare. All the gold that Cortez could offer from the newly discovered mines of Mexico could furnish little relief, and at the different courts of Europe outward signs of good-will, such as public *Te Deums* and fulsome writings of congratulation, could not effectually conceal the most hostile intrigues. The Pope was arranging for a coalition of which the French king was to be the head; Francis was moving heaven and earth to secure the friendship of

England, and had already appointed that meeting near Calais which was to be known in history as the Field of the Cloth of Gold.

Charles's coronation. In spite, however, of his poverty and his political cares, Charles's coronation at Aix was a magnificent pageant; the splendor of his apparel, the number of his mounted attendants, the skill with which he managed his splendid white steed, — all excited the utmost enthusiasm. In accordance with the tastes and desires of the person most concerned, the religious character of the ceremony was brought into special prominence. At the door of Charlemagne's cathedral the new emperor was met by the archbishops of Cologne, Treves, and Mainz, who gave him their blessing "as though he had been a bride." Before the high altar he prostrated himself in the form of the cross; he swore to uphold the Catholic faith, to protect the holy church with due subjection and fidelity, — vows which he never forgot and the maintenance of which became the ruling passion of his life.

Luther to the Christian nobility. The most formidable antagonist the church had ever had was meanwhile keeping several printing-presses busy with ringing addresses to the German people, and with defences of his position. One to the "Christian Nobility" presented with the directness of a bombardment the most damning array of charges against the Papacy; "the time for silence is past, the time for speech has come," were the opening words, and one by one the walls of straw and paper set up around the church were undermined and demolished. It is not true that no one may judge a Pope, that he alone may interpret Scripture, he alone call a council. He is full of worldly pomp and pride, he is "carried by men like an idol," he is attended by three thousand secretaries — a "crowd of crawling vermin" — and rides out with from three to four thousand mule-riders. For his traffic in Ger-

man benefices, for his "cheating and lying, robbing and
stealing, debauchery and villany, and all kinds of contempt
of God" he must needs have a special counting-house at
Rome.   All the grievances of the ages are mustered up:
the Constantine Donation, the forged deeds of gift of Charlemagne, the claim to having founded the Holy Roman
Empire, the question of investiture, the demand that the
emperors should kiss the Pope's foot, should do him homage, should hold his bridle and stirrup, the spurning of the
Hohenstaufens, and the assumption of temporal rule over
Naples and Sicily.

In another writing, *On the Babylonian Captivity of the*   The *Baby-*
Church, Luther attacked the fundamental doctrines of   *lonian*
the church, and declared that four of the seven sacraments   *Captivity.*
were of no binding force whatever.   He thereby aroused a
fiercer storm than by any possible attack on open and apparent abuses.   Glapion, the father confessor of Charles V.,
who up to this point had been in favor of conciliation,
declared that he felt now as though he had been scourged
and pummelled from head to foot.   Erasmus of Rotterdam,
too, anxious as he was to reform certain abuses, turned
coldly away and definitely declared for the old doctrines;
while no less a person than Henry VIII. of England took
up his royal pen against the bold iconoclast, and wielded
it with such effect that he gained from the church the title
of "Defender of the Faith."

Luther's third great writing of this year, 1520, *On the*   The *Free-*
Freedom of a Christian Man, was not polemical in char-   *dom of a*
acter, but rather gave a positive system of religion and   *Christian*
showed the relation of faith and works.   It was prefaced,   *Man.*
however, by the letter he had once promised Miltitz to
write to Leo X.   This begins respectfully, though it warns
the Pope against thinking he can do what he will in heaven,
hell, and purgatory.   The Roman court, on the other hand,

is compared to Sodom, Gomorrah, and Babylon, and Leo is represented as sitting like a sheep among wolves, like Daniel with the lions, or Ezekiel with the scorpions. Luther is sorry for Leo; it is a pity he could not have been Pope in better days, and that he cannot now support life on a simple benefice or on his private income. But there is no help now for the pestilential state of affairs: "All is over with the papal see; God's unceasing wrath hath fallen upon it; it opposes general councils and will neither be instructed nor reformed; . . . the malady scoffs at the cure; neither horse nor chariot heeds the driver."

Papal bull of condemnation.

The *Babylonian Captivity* and the *Freedom of a Christian Man*, as well as the dedicatory letter to Leo X., were written with the knowledge that Rome had at last done her worst and issued a decisive bull of condemnation; the letter, indeed, was dated back so as not to seem a direct retaliation. This bull, *Exsurge Domine*, was to be the righteous retribution for the whole catalogue of the reformer's past misdeeds; in its composition all of his old enemies, Prierias, Cajetanus, and Eck, had a hand, and many a session was necessary to its completion. The former Leipzig disputant was intrusted with its publication in Germany. Beginning with an appeal to God, the saints, and the whole church, against the foxes, boars, and other wild beasts that are devastating the Lord's vineyard, the document goes on to vaunt the fatherly long-suffering of the Pope, — even now his heart is so oppressed that he can scarcely speak out, — and to declare that various errors condemned by church councils are being sown among the German nation by godless babblers incited by the devil. Forty-one passages are then quoted from Luther's writings and pronounced heretical, among them the denial that to burn heretics is in accordance with the Holy Spirit. The most prominent place is given to reflections upon the sanctity of the priesthood and upon the power assumed by the Pope. All of Luther's books, wherever found, are at once to be burnt; he himself and all his favorers, if they do not retract within sixty days, are to suffer the punishment of notorious, stubborn, and condemned heretics. Princes and potentates, all in short who do not help to carry out the sentence and eventually to bind and deliver over the chief offender, are freely threatened with ban and interdict.

Slowly the papal legates made their way northward with this dire instrument of destruction. Eck was given the privilege of inserting as many as twenty-four names of those who were to share in Luther's punishment; Carraciolo and Aleander were to appear at the Diet of the Empire, and rouse that body to a sense of its bounden duty. The reception accorded the bull differed greatly in different places: in some towns it was obeyed and the Lutheran books were committed to the flames; in others it met with scorn and derision. In Magdeburg it was affixed to the pillory; in Mainz, when the executioner from the scaffold asked the people whether he whose books were to be burned had been lawfully condemned, there was a universal shout that he had not been condemned at all; the ceremony was interrupted and Aleander almost stoned to death. At the very time when Luther was engaged on his *Babylonian Captivity of the Church*, it had appeared in Leipzig and been received with honor. "I hear," he says, in his peroration to that work, "that bulls and papal threats have again been published against me, in which I am urged to recant or be declared a heretic. If that be so, may this book form part of my future recantation." When the bull at last reached Wittenberg, his first thoughts turned to the emperor, the "noble young scion" who was just making his first appear-

The publication of the bull.

ance in Germany. "Oh, that Charles were a man," he cried, "and in Christ's cause would attack these Satans." But failing such help, he had long since made up his mind what steps to take in his own defence. He had written some months before, "I despise alike the favor and the fury of Rome; . . . let her condemn and burn my books; I, in my turn, unless I can find no fire, will condemn and publicly burn the whole pontifical law, that swamp of heresies."

The burning of the bull.

The moment for this demonstration had now come. It was announced to the students of Wittenberg that they were invited to the pious and religious spectacle of a judgment by fire. By the hour appointed a vast crowd had assembled in the square before the Elster gate, where a quantity of wood was heaped together and ignited. There was thrown into the flames not only a copy of the obnoxious bull, but a collection as well of the decretals and of the canon law. The fire was meant to symbolize the consignment to destruction and oblivion of the whole papal see. The students outdid their master in zeal for his cause; they sang dirges and *Te Deums* as the decretals vanished into smoke, and with a papal bull two yards long fluttering from a pole, they drove round the town and collected the books of Luther's enemies with which to feed the flames. Such a demonstration as this was of the kind that leads to revolution and bloodshed. "Hitherto," wrote Luther to Spalatin, "the matter has been mere play, now it becomes earnest." And again soon after, "The tumult rages gloriously; it seems to me as if it never can be calmed until the day of judgment!"

The Diet of Worms.

Up to this point the ways of Charles V. and of Martin Luther had not directly crossed, but the emperor's first general Diet, held in Worms in 1521, was to prove an epoch in the lives of both. Never before had an imperial

Diet been graced by the presence of so many distinguished princes; the city could scarcely harbor their splendid retinues. Young Philip ot Hesse brought six hundred horses; while even before the sessions began, Elector Frederick the Wise had paid out some four thousand guldens in food for his followers. Games and pageants filled the intervals not occupied by serious business. The main question before the Diet, apart from the affair of Luther, was the reëstablishment of the council of regency, or *Reichsregiment*, which Maximilian had allowed to fall into abeyance. The matter resolved itself into a trial of strength between Charles and his princes, which ended in a compromise: there was to be a council, but with a *Stadtholder*, not a president, and the first *Stadtholder* was to be the emperor's brother Ferdinand. The council was to be permanent, but could only unfold its full powers in the absence of Charles from Germany. The import of all this for the Reformation was, that at the critical moment the emperor's actions were hampered by others, he could not proceed, as he would have proceeded in the Netherlands, and stamp out this heresy with fire and sword. Nor could he, without breaking his electoral compact, place Martin Luther, unheard, under the ban of the empire. He would gladly have done so; the papal legate, Aleander, who was constantly at his side, urged him to the step; but the princes had first to be consulted, and the princes decided to grant the reformer a hearing.

It was a strange position for Charles, who in this very same year defended the severity of the Spanish Inquisition against the Pope himself, to have to despatch a summons to the worst of heretics and to use the conventional form of address, " Honorable, beloved, and pious " ! Luther was asked to place himself under the charge of the messenger and to come to Worms and render an account of his

The summoning of Luther to Worms.

books and of his teachings. In the interval the Diet discussed the reform of the chamber court, and actually brought to pass a new military schedule or *Reichsmatrikel*, based on the "Roman month," or simplest levy of twelve thousand men with funds to support them for six weeks — the minimum term for an expedition to Rome. An artificial arrangement, but each prince knew henceforth what was his proportion of the general levy, and the whole number of Roman months could be indefinitely increased.

Charles's attitude toward Luther.

Luther's appearance at the Diet had been awaited with the greatest eagerness. Many believed that, could he be made to recant his errors of doctrine, he might prove a chosen instrument to correct the flagrant abuses in the church. Soon after the election of Charles V. the latter's ambassador in Rome had urged him to show favor to a certain Brother Martin, as the Pope was extraordinarily afraid of him and might through this fear be gained as an ally. Charles had been pleased with Luther's early writings; neither he nor his father confessor was blind to the need of reform. Glapion had even threatened him with divine punishment unless he should rid the church of scandal. But the heresies uttered at the Leipzig Disputation, the writing against the holy sacraments, and the burning of the papal bull were too much for the man whose one thought, as he wrote himself, was "the exaltation and the increase of our Holy Catholic faith." At this very Diet he angrily threw on the ground a letter from Luther appealing to him, as Athanasius had done to the emperors of old, and imploring that, true or false, his doctrines be not condemned unheard. The legate Aleander could write confidently to the Pope: "Cæsar has the best inclination of any man born this thousand years; . . . if he persevere as he has begun, he will carry everything according to our wishes."

Whatever the attitude of the emperor, Aleander could

not blind himself to the general sentiment at the Diet of
Worms. For his own satisfaction he calls Luther thief,
assassin, monster, Arius, and Mohammed, but he has to
acknowledge that a legion of poor nobles as well as the
" race of grammarians and poets of whom Germany is full "
are all on the reformer's side. " All Germany," he writes,
" is at present in commotion, nine out of ten cry ' Luther,'
and the tenth, even if he cares nothing for what Luther
says, cries ' Down with the court of Rome ! ' Every one
shrieks and calls ' Council, council,' and will have it on
German ground." At the very door of the hall of assembly the legate was treated to a humiliating poke in the
ribs by a zealous Lutheran.

Public
sentiment
with regard
to Luther.

The man who had caused all this commotion was now
hurrying rapidly to Worms. Never for a moment had he
thought of disregarding the summons ; well or ill, he would
set out, he wrote to Spalatin, " for it is not permitted to me
to doubt that if Cæsar call me I am called of the Lord."
He hoped for Charles's own sake that the latter would not
stain his hands with his, Luther's, blood ; no good had come
to the Emperor Sigismund after the murder of Huss, seeing
that his queen, Barbara, had eloped with another man, while
he himself had died without offspring. When Spalatin
warned him against trusting to the safe-conduct, Luther
answered that he would go to Worms though the devils
there were as thick as the tiles on the roofs. John Huss
had been burned, but the truth had not been burned with
him. The journey to Worms proved a veritable triumphal
progress. The town of Wittenberg had placed a covered
carriage at the reformer's disposal, and with him rode
Amsdorf, a young Pomeranian noble, and a monk of his
own order — two other friends, Schurf and Jonas, having
gone on before. From every city crowds streamed out to
see and welcome the man of the hour ; at Erfurt, the home

Luther's
journey to
Worms.

of humanism, he was met by a mounted deputation from the university, with the rector, Eoban Hess, at its head; the walls, the streets, and even the roofs of the houses were thronged with excited people. He preached in the Erfurt church, and Hess records that when he showed the long-closed way to Heaven's blessings, the force of his words melted the hearts of his hearers as snow melts before the breath of spring.

<small>Luther's reception in Worms.</small> Arrived in Worms, a crowd of some two thousand persons, men and women, accompanied Luther to his lodging in the house of the Knights of St. John. One of Aleander's servants reported to his master that a priest had taken the monk in his arms, "and having touched his coat three times had gone away glorying as though he had touched a relic of the greatest saint in the world." Each day of his sojourn in Worms was marked by some such incident. The young Landgrave of Hesse came to talk with him in his lodging, and cried out, " Dear doctor, if thou art in the right, so may our Lord God help thee." "Blessed be the womb that bare thee!" cried a voice in the street as he passed on his way. As he entered the hall of assembly to face the grand ordeal of his life, the old *Landsknecht* leader, Frundsberg, clapped him on the shoulder, — " Little monk, little monk, now goest thou thy way to take such a stand as I and many a commander even in our sharpest battles have never taken; art thou of good intent and certain of thy affair, so go in God's name and be comforted; God will not forsake thee."

<small>The first hearing.</small> On the afternoon of Luther's first hearing, the crowd in the streets was so dense that the herald had to lead his charge to the hall of audience, in the episcopal palace, through gardens and by back ways. Within the building was gathered one of the most august assemblies of electors, princes, prelates, nobles, and delegates that had ever met

together in Germany. The reformer was told not to speak
unless in answer to a question, and was then shown a heap
of books which he was ordered to acknowledge and retract.
To the surprise of all, the man whose message had rung
like a clarion note through the length and breadth of the
land seemed now, with the eyes of all upon him, actually
to quail and tremble. In a low voice, in words that were
hardly comprehensible, he declared that if he spoke without due consideration he might be overbold and run into
grievous peril; would not his Imperial Majesty grant him
more time for deliberation? The answer was that he well
knew the grounds on which he had been summoned, and
had had sufficient time for preparation; in the end, however, there was granted a delay of twenty-four hours.

The general impression among Luther's friends was one
of disappointment; even the Saxon elector was not quite
satisfied with his protégé. As for Charles, he could hardly
believe that he had seen before him the author of such
aggressive books; "That man would never make a heretic
of me," was his final opinion. Aleander was jubilant, and
even waxed witty at the expense of "the fool who had
come into the assembly laughing, and had left it in a sadder
frame of mind."

On the second day, with studied words and at some
length, Luther gave his reasons for not denying his works
so long as they could not be refuted from Holy Writ. His
voice was steady now, and every trace of shyness had vanished. He asked for evidence against himself and for a
fair trial, and then, suddenly striking a warning note, he
turned to the young emperor and held him a fiery discourse, excusing his own boldness on the plea that it was
a duty he owed to his country. He exhorted "this most
excellent youth, Prince Charles, on whom after God many
hopes are fixed," to walk in the fear of the Lord; not to

The second hearing.

make an evil beginning of his reign, and thus come to a shameful end, like the old kings of Egypt, of Babylon, and of Israel. Called to order and asked to give a plain yes or no to the questions that had been asked him, Luther answered in stirring words: "Since your most Serene Majesty and your lordships ask for a simple answer, I will give it 'neither horned nor toothed,' after this fashion: unless I shall be convinced by witness of Scripture or by plain reason (for I do not believe in the Pope or in councils alone, since it is agreed that they have often erred and contradicted themselves), I am overcome by the Scriptures which I have adduced and my conscience is caught in the word of God. I neither can nor will recant anything, for it is neither safe nor right to act against one's conscience. God help me. Amen." One of the contemporary reports, of which there are several, inserts before "God help me," the words, " Here I stand. I can no more."

By this time it was evening and the candles had already been lighted in the hall. Charles hastily dismissed the assembly. One who followed Luther reports that he seemed to feel an immense joy, and that on entering his inn he waved his arms and fairly shouted, " I am through! I am through!" He was through, indeed, though his worst dangers and perils had but just begun. Frederick the Wise said that night to Spalatin: " Well did Dr. Martin speak before the lord emperor and all the princes of the empire. He is far too daring."

Charles's
dictum.

If at this hearing Luther had impressed and astonished the members of the Diet, no less a surprise was in store for them the following day, when their emperor and head presented to them his written opinion on the case in point. It was the first public deliverance of this boy of twenty-one ; yet so incisive was it, so imperious, so utterly charac-teristic of the bigoted Spanish tyrant, that many of the

princes, as Aleander tells us in his report to the Pope,
"turned paler than if they had died." He, the descendant
of kings, archdukes, and dukes who had ever made it
their care to defend the Catholic faith, was not going to
be moved by this single monk, who, led astray by his own
imaginings, was opposing the truths that had prevailed
for a thousand years. "We have determined in this
matter rather to stake all our kingdoms and dominions,
our friends, our own body, blood, life, and soul." The
very suspicion of heresy must be wiped away as an everlasting shame from the noble and most distinguished
German nation. Luther is to be denied a further hearing;
he is to be told to withdraw and his safe-conduct to be
respected, but thenceforward he is to be proceeded against
as an actual and convicted heretic.

In spite of the vehemence of this utterance, the princes
demanded and obtained further hearings for the reformer,
lest he should say that he had not been given a fair
chance. These hearings were of a more private nature,
two of them being before the Archbishop of Treves, who,
if Aleander can here be believed, offered Luther a high
church office if only he would recant at the eleventh
hour. Charles was anxious to hasten the affair; he was
alarmed at the various signs of sympathy and of revolt.
A paper was found on the door of his own apartment with
"Woe to the land whose king is a child": a placard on
the town hall announced that four hundred knights had
thrown down the gauntlet to the Romanists and intended
to uphold Luther. The sign of the *Bundschuh* appeared
on the wall, with a warning that the peasants "meant a
great damage." The deliberations of the princes were
hastened, and ended in the pronouncement that this man
was incorrigible, that he must leave Worms, and that,
after the twenty-one days reserved in his safe-conduct, he

Alarming
demonstra
tions.

must be declared under the ban. To Aleander was intrusted the congenial task of drawing up the instrument
of condemnation. Luther's own comment, addressed to
the painter, Lucas Kranach, was that absolutely nothing
had been accomplished by the hearing, and that it had
not been fairly conducted. " Oh, we blind Germans," he
wrote, " how childishly we act and how wretchedly we let
the Romanists make fools and apes of us ! "

The edict
of Worms.

By the edict of Worms, which branded him as the evil
one in human form, as the instigator of schism, murder,
and arson, as the subverter of all laws, Luther was declared under the empire's ban; no one might shelter or
nourish him, but he was at once to be seized and handed
over to the emperor. This decree was signed in irregular
fashion by Charles and by a number of the princes, after
the last session of the Diet and after the elector of Saxony
and other possible favorers of Luther had already taken
their departure. The petty subterfuge was adopted of
dating the document back some three weeks, in order to
give color to the introductory statement that it had been
passed " by the unanimous advice and with the good will
of all the estates." " Now you will be content with me,"
said Charles to Aleander, as he handed him the parchment with his seal and signature. " Surely, sire;" was the
answer, " but much more will be contented his Holiness,
the Holy See, and all Christendom, and will thank God
for giving them so holy and religious an emperor."

CHAPTER XII

FRIENDS AND ALLIES OF THE REFORMATION

LITERATURE : Spalatin's *Life of Frederick the Wise* is a contemporary account by that prince's secretary. For Hutten we have the excellent biography of Strauss, for Sickingen the equally good work of Ullman. See also Bezold, Egelhaaf, and Ranke, as before.

THE account given by Aleander of the religious ferment into which Germany had been thrown was by no means overdrawn ; there was no class of the population that was not touched by the movement, and no form of expression in which men's feelings did not find vent. Between the years 1513 and 1523 the number of yearly publications rose from ninety to nine hundred, and by far the greater part of them were polemical. Luther's own individual writings up to the latter date numbered more than one hundred. Hans Sachs, the cobbler of Nuremberg, wrote a poem on the *Wittenberg Nightingale,* and announced that the false shimmer of the moon that had lured so many to the wilderness was now to be put to flight by the red love-light of the morning. Albrecht Dürer painted his famous Four Apostles with Peter standing behind " John whom Jesus loved." Lucas Kranach drew a series of twenty-six wood-cuts of the church as it was, and the church as it should be, — on the one hand, the Pope with his triple diadem and with princes kissing his toe ; on the other, Christ with the crown of thorns washing the feet of His disciples.

Not that all who railed at the abuses of the church were in favor of Martin Luther. Erasmus had come out in an

Religious ferment.

285

open attack upon some of his doctrines; Reuchlin repudiated him, and sent a weak letter of justification to the Catholic dukes of Bavaria. But even within the camp of Lutheranism there were fatal differences as to ways and means; what the scholar expected to gain by arguments and persuasion, the knight thought he could achieve more rapidly by force of arms, and the peasant by revolt and violence. Each of these elements .was to try its turn singly in the course of this long struggle, with what success we shall see as our narrative proceeds.

The youth of Melanch- thon.   The chief representative of the peaceful party, and Luther's most devoted personal friend, was a certain Philip Schwarzerd, of Bretten, son of an armorer who was so skilful in forging a suit of armor for Maximilian that the latter gave him as coat of arms a lion with one paw on a hammer, the other on an anvil. Young Philip had always had a strong religious bent, a keen sense of beauty, and an independent, critical spirit. The ceremonies of the old church, indeed, had so attracted him that he had erected an altar at which, in private, he imitated the forms of the mass; yet, even at this early age, he doubted a preacher who declared that the wooden shoes of the Franciscans had been cut from the original apple tree of paradise.

Reuchlin, who was Schwarzerd's granduncle, had taken the warmest interest in the training of the boy, selecting his tutors and his schools, and providing him with rare books. Out of love and gratitude Philip had induced some comrades to learn and perform one of the old humanist's own Latin comedies, which so delighted Reuchlin that he would not rest till he had changed the barbarous name of this learned youth into its Greek equivalent — Melanchthon. At every stage in his career the young scholar was looked upon as a prodigy; once at Heidelberg, when the professor was at a loss for a translation and won

dered who could help him, there was a general cry of Melanchthon, Melanchthon, though the latter had not reached
the age of fifteen, and was denied his master's degree on
the ground of his childlike appearance. Before he was
nineteen Erasmus was in raptures over him, and called
immortal God to witness the promise in this youth; whose
complete command of Greek and Latin, whose penetration,
and whose purity of diction, whose extraordinary memory
— in short, the "noble, even royal grace of whose gifts" —
made a profound impression on the first scholar in Europe.

Called at the age of twenty-one to preside over the
Greek studies in the university of Wittenberg, Melanchthon
by his very first discourse on improved methods of study
made a conquest of all his hearers. Short of stature,
slender and weak-looking, with a bad habit of holding
one shoulder lower than the other, he had none of the
natural advantages on which orators are wont to depend.
He knitted his brows in an ugly manner, made awkward
and violent gesticulations, and occasionally stuttered. But
on those who observed him closely, his beautiful eyes and
fine features did not fail of their effect, and all followed him
with breathless interest when in masterly sequence he
showed the evils in the prevalent methods, and went on to
unfold his plans for improvement. A return to original
sources, the concernment with things themselves and not
with their shadows, the reading of Greek and Latin classics
in the tongues in which they were written, the study of theology from the Scriptures and not from bad text-books: —
these were his earnest injunctions. "Who makes a beginning
has won half the battle — go bravely forward. It may seem
difficult, but let not that deter you; industry and zeal
conquer hardships. I will help you to the extent of my
powers!" "One marvels," a listener declares, "how in such
a little body there can be concealed so enormous a mountain

*Melanch-
thon in
Wittenberg*

of cleverness and wisdom," and indeed the fame of the new
lecturer soon raised the number of students from the hundreds to the thousands! Luther's relation to Melanchthon

was from the very first warm and confidential. "Whoever"
he writes, "does not recognize and treasure our Philip
as just the right teacher, must be a perfect ass and eaten
up with self-esteem. There is no one on earth, no one
on whom the sun shines, who has such gifts as Philip,"
and again: "He is a perfect Greek, learned to the core,
friendly and of cheery disposition. He has a perfectly
crowded classroom, and has brought it about that especially all theologians — high, middle, and low — have
taken to Greek. . . . His devotion and industry pass all
bounds."

Nor was Melanchthon behind hand in his appreciation of
the great pioneer of the reform movement. He speaks of
him as the " God-inspired messenger of eternal wisdom and
justice," as the " blessed dispenser of the life-giving word,"
as the " faithful, never sleeping Shepherd who with the rod
of Moses casts down the superstitious priests and the foolish
hair-splitting sophists." He accompanied Luther to Leipzig at the time of the disputation with Eck, and incurred
the latter's mortal enmity by occasionally prompting both
Carlstadt and Luther. Eck declared that though Melanchthon might know Latin and Greek, it was not worth while
for any theologian to dispute with him, and thus called forth
the remark from Luther that he cared more for his Philip's
judgment than for a thousand dirty Ecks. " I will not
praise Philip," he said on this occasion ; " he is a creature of
God, nothing more ; but in him I honor the word of God !
Perhaps I am Philip's forerunner, destined like Elias to
prepare the way." The influence that Melanchthon was to
have on the future of the Reformation cannot be overestimated. It is an old simile that makes him the coiner of

the gold which Luther brought to light; he it is who first reduced to a theological system the teachings of the new religion. Luther once excuses his own violence by the constant necessity of fighting against mobs and devils; he it is who must dig up the stumps and stones, level the thickets and hedges and break a path like the woodsman through the forest; "but Master Philip drives cleanly and quietly along, sows and waters to his heart's content according to the rich gifts that God has given him." When Melanchthon wrote his *Loci Communes*, or "common truths of religion," Luther ranked the book as second only, in point of excellence, to the Bible itself.

Melanchthon's great aim was to give a scientific form and scholarly basis to the theology of the Reformation. His was not a nature that would try to storm the fortresses of the Romanists, he sought rather by reasoning to show how antiquated and useless they were. His chief fault was a desire to please in all directions, and the future was to show how his efforts in the matter of conciliation were to weaken his party and to draw down upon him the disapproval, if not the contempt, of his own friends.

In complete contrast to the life of this quiet scholar was that of another man who, for a short season, concentrated upon himself the gaze of all Germany as, rushing and storming on, he wildly endeavored to rouse his nation to that pitch where, once for all, it would irrevocably break with the tyranny of Rome. It is a singular part that which Ulrich von Hutten plays in the history of the Reformation. Knight of the pen as well as of the sword, he is, above all, the ardent patriot smarting and writhing under his country's wrongs. Independently of Luther, he had begun his attacks on indulgences and papal extortions. Long after the posting of the theses he had looked on the Wittenberg reformer as a mere squabbling monk, and more than once had been

Melanchthon as conciliator.

Hutten and Luther.

known to pray that Eck and Luther might annihilate each
other. "My desire is," he wrote, "that our enemies should
live as much in discord as possible. . . .   God grant that
all who hinder the ripening of the new culture shall be
destroyed!" However, the Leipzig disputation and the
great writings that quickly followed it had awakened
Hutten to glowing enthusiasm, and he had unreservedly
placed himself on Luther's side. "Day and night," he
wrote to him, "will I serve thee without wage; many a
brave hero will I rouse up for thee. Thou shalt be the
captain, thou the beginner and ender; all that is needed is
thy command."

For a time the two names were constantly linked together; their portraits appeared side by side on the cover
of one of Hutten's works; they were likened to Orestes
and Pylades, and the litany was paraphrased into a prayer
for their safety. Men watched with breathless interest to
see how they would extricate themselves from the meshes
cast round them by the agents and friends of Rome. But
soon a cleft became apparent, their paths divided, and Hutten, having failed in his own great designs, died ruined,
heart-broken, and in exile.

Hutten's
early years.

Hutten's family was of the old Franconian nobility. His
immediate ancestors had been no better than their neighbors, and there were times when their castle of the Steckel-
berg was nothing less than a den of robbers and had to be
raided as such by the emperor's commands. The young
Ulrich's father, harsh and tyrannical, had destined his son
for the church, had sent him to the monastery of Fulda
to be trained for this vocation, and would hear of no argument in favor of any other career. In the very days when
Luther, braving the wrath of his own father, was entering
the Augustinian order at Erfurt, Hutten too cast off the
parental yoke, burst these irksome monastic bonds, and fled

from Fulda to worship the rising sun of humanism. To the full he experienced the hardships of the vagabond scholar's life, begged and worked his way from one university to another, endured shipwreck and plague, and ruined his health forever.

The knowledge of his peculiar powers came to him in a curious way and in the midst of his worst misfortunes. At Greifswald a certain Henning Lotz, professor of law and son of the burgomaster of the town, had received him into his house, had clothed and fed him, and supplied him with funds; then, for what reason we know not, a bitter quarrel had ensued, and the young scholar set out for Rostock without being able to reimburse his benefactor. The burgomaster and his son sent their retainers after him. He was seized and stripped of all he had, down to his own poetic compositions, and was forced half naked to continue on his way. Boiling with rage, he soon after wrote a satire on the two Lotzes, which revealed to the world of humanism its greatest master of invective.

Hutten as a writer.

Not many years had passed before the power of Hutten's pen was felt by the highest in the land: a poem addressed to the Emperor Maximilian exhorted him in stirring words to march against the Venetians who had obstructed his way to Rome; a number of epigrams were launched against that warlike pope who had taken the name and wished to emulate the deeds of the great Julius; a panegyric on Albert of Mainz gained for its author two hundred gold guldens and a position at the archbishop's court. There came a time when, in the presence of his whole court, Maximilian placed a laurel wreath on Hutten's head, proclaimed him orator and poet with all the advantages that officially pertained to those titles, and freed him from all jurisdiction save his own. The emperor hailed this scion of a noble knightly house as one whose writings were in every one's hands and whom the most learned men in Germany and Italy called their friend.

Hutten
against
Duke
Ulrich of
Würtem-
berg.

Nothing spurred on the genius of this man like some injury to himself, to his family, or to his country. When Duke Ulrich of Würtemberg, the most profligate and reckless of the German princes, struck down with his own hand a relative of Hutten's who had scorned the suggestion of a dishonorable compact, the poet pursued him in a series of orations that roused all Germany. Every chord was struck that could move to pity and to indignation : the advantages to which the murdered man was bidding farewell, the sorrows of disconsolate relatives, the iniquity of the princely offender. Ever and anon a perfect volley of abuse was let loose against this " blot on the Swabian name," this " Eternal shame of his people," no longer a prince, no longer a German, no Christian, not even a man. Although the Duke of Würtemberg had married the emperor's own niece, Maximilian was forced to place him under the ban of the empire. He soon forgave him, it is true; but Hutten's day of vengeance came quickly enough, and he himself was able to play a part in the overthrow of his enemy. Duke Ulrich permitted himself in a moment of anger to commit acts of terrible violence against the city of Reutlingen which belonged to the famous Swabian league. The league raised an army and occupied his lands, and Hutten accompanied the expedition, being allowed the satisfaction of exhuming the remains of his relative and transporting them to Franconia. Duke Ulrich went into exile, his lands were handed over to the mercies of Charles V. in return for payment to the league of the costs of the war. It was thus the Würtemberg staghorns found their way into the coat of arms of the house of Hapsburg.

In the Reformation, Hutten finally found a cause well adapted to call out to the full his magnificent powers of rhetoric.   The dialogues that he now wrote contained utterances that never were, and never could be pardoned him: anathemas and excommunications, and the whole assemblage of papal weapons, were exposed to withering mockery; the abuses and the claims of the Roman court were scourged with a force and a realism beyond conception.   The past, too, was made to give its relentless testimony: a writing of the time of the bitter quarrel between Henry IV. and the church was drawn forth from its long resting-place and given to print; a new edition was made, with a preface dedicated to the Pope, of the masterly writing in which Laurentius Valla exposed the utter falsity of the document known as the Donation of Constantine.

The writing in which Hutten may be said to have first thrown down the gauntlet to the Papacy is known as the Vadiscus, or Roman Trinity, in which, three at a time, the prevalent scandals and abuses are dragged to light.   It is a terrible arraignment of the whole papal system, and here, as ever, Hutten's chief grievance is Rome's contempt for the credulity and generosity of the Germans.   "Look there," he cries, "see the great central barnyard, where is heaped together the plunder of all lands.   In the midst sits that insatiate weevil, which, with its followers, swallows unheard-of amounts.   They have sucked our blood, they have gnawed our flesh, they are coming to our marrow; they will break and crush our every bone!   Will the Germans never take to arms, will they never rush in with fire and sword?   Those are plunderers of our fatherland, reeking with the blood and sweat of the German people; they are robbing us like hungry wolves, and we, forsooth, must continue to caress them, may not stab, or smite, or lay hands upon, or touch them!   When will we finally grow wiser, and avenge our shame, which is the common shame of all!"

Hutten as
champion
of Luther.

Every step in Luther's progress is followed by some new publication on the part of his literary champion, who now throws off the trammels even of humanism, and, disdaining the more elegant and scholarly Latin, writes directly for the people in the German tongue. A poem on the burning of Luther's works in some of the German towns, was followed by a republication of the papal bull, with ironical comments and glosses. We shall see presently how, at the Diet of Worms, each of the persons most concerned on the Catholic side felt the weight and the sting of this avenging pen.

Sickingen
as robber
knight.

Hutten's course, meteor-like as it actually was, would have been checked still earlier had it not been for the powerful protection of a man who was feared from end to end of Germany, and who now, for a brief moment, became intimately concerned with the fate of the Reformation. This was Franz von Sickingen, who was soon to perish in the double attempt to " open the gates for the gospel," and satisfy his own overweening ambition. Sickingen was a robber knight, but with certain noble traits, and with such a conception of his calling, that one wonders if he ought not rather to be put on the level of a belligerent prince. In carrying on feuds he seldom aimed lower than a duke, or a free city of the empire; and there are persons who insist to this day that his weapons were only drawn in favor of the oppressed, and of those to whom justice had been denied. Be that as it may, he was not above exacting enormous fines; and being an excellent manager, he greatly increased his family possessions. He was lord of many castles, the chief of which were the Ebernburg, near Kreuznach, and Landstuhl, near Kaiserslautern, which he furnished with splendid defences.

The feud which first brought Sickingen into prominence, was that against the town of Worms. With seven thousand men he laid waste its fields and vineyards, stopped its

commerce, and cut off all communication with the outer
world. Nothing daunted by the ban of the empire, which
no one dared to carry out, he continued his hostilities until,
after years had passed, his demands had all been granted.
In the end, the ever needy Maximilian, instead of punishing the peace breaker, freed him from the ban, took him
into his service, and sent him off to fight against Hutten's
old enemy, Duke Ulrich of Würtemberg. His position as
the emperor's commander did not hinder him from falling
upon the young landgrave of Hesse, and wresting from him
an agreement in favor of some neighboring knights, nor
from compelling the magistrates of Frankfort to make him
a large payment of money. At the time of Maximilian's
death, his position at the head of an army made him such
an important personage that his favor was regularly sued
for by Spain and France alike. He declared for Charles V.,
who rewarded him with the title of imperial chamberlain,
and even deigned to accept from him a loan of twenty
thousand gulden.

Hutten and Sickingen first came together in the days
just preceding the Würtemberg campaign; the poet visited
the *condottiere*, probably in connection with that affair,
and afterward sent him a translation for which Sickingen
had expressed a wish. From that time on, through the
three stirring years that followed, the two men were bound
together by a friendship that knew no slackening. It was
under Sickingen's standard that Hutten served in the
bloodless campaign, even sleeping with him in the same
tent. Himself without learning, Franz well knew how to
appreciate it in others, while Hutten conceived a great
admiration for his friend's natural abilities. In a letter to
Erasmus he speaks of him as "a man such as Germany has
long been without and who doubtless will bring the nation
fame and glory."

Sickingen
won for the
Reforma-
tion.

Far as theological matters had hitherto been removed from Sickingen's horizon, he was not without respect and feeling for religion. He had founded a nunnery near the Ebernburg, and Hutten was able to ridicule him roundly for a plan he had long cherished of "building the wooden-shoed Franciscans a new nest." Tolerant by nature, he had offered his support to Reuchlin when the latter's interminable difference with the Dominicans seemed to bring him once more in danger, and did him good service by declaring a formal feud against his tormenters. Hutten now talked to Franz of Luther, and little by little the knight became thoroughly interested in the man whom the Romanists so hated and pursued. He at last sent word to Wittenberg that, should Luther through his teachings come into difficulty and have no other resource, his castles were at his disposal. It was about this time that another knight, Sylvester von Schaumburg, offered to come to the reformer's aid with a hundred followers. Luther was pleased, if only for the moment, and he wrote to Spalatin, "Schaumburg and Sickingen have made me secure from the fear of men."

Hutten in danger from the Pope.

In the meantime Hutten's affairs had taken a new turn. The matter is somewhat obscure, but it seems clear that, about the time of Charles V.'s arrival in Germany, the poet had the definite prospect of a position at the court of the archduke Ferdinand and set out for Brussels, rejoicing profoundly that a new field for his activity had thus been opened. "Hutten goes to Ferdinand," writes Melanchthon, "to prepare a path for liberty with the aid of the great princes. What hopes may we not justly cherish!" On the eve of departure Hutten wrote to Luther, renewing his protestations of absolute and entire devotion, and urging him to fight for the common cause of liberty and to free the oppressed fatherland : "We have God on our side, if he be with us who can be against us? . . . To-day I start on my way to Ferdinand, to work for our cause as best I can." Hutten reached Brussels; but what happened to him there is clouded in obscurity, and the next that we hear he is hurrying back as a fugitive to the refuge offered by the castle of his knightly friend. The Pope meanwhile had awakened to a sense of this man's importance, and roundly rating the Archbishop of Mainz for having had him in his service, had sent word to a number of princes that Hutten must be seized and sent to Rome. Warnings of intended violence were sent him by his friends and caused him, in terror for his life, to write an appeal to the German nation. Was he, who had worked for the common good, to be torn with impunity from the land of his birth? Was he to be forced to leave altar and hearth, and to be dragged not even to a miserable life in exile, but to cruel tortures and to shameful death? "Help, help, my countrymen! Let not him who has undertaken to loose your chains himself lie in bondage!"

For many months, now, Hutten remained in hiding in the Ebernburg, still full of his plans of rousing the German nation to warlike endeavors. In the long winter evenings he began reading Luther's writings to his host, at first only in extracts and with copious explanations. That is an episode to be long remembered in German history as one of the famous conversions to a new cause. It was a slow process, but gradually the robber knight began to wonder and to comprehend, and soon the words carried entire conviction. He could not see, Sickingen declared, how any one could hope to overthrow such proofs, and soon it was the custom at every meal to have readings from Luther's or from Hutten's own works. The Ebernburg became, as Hutten expressed it, a "refuge for righteousness"; religious services were instituted under a regular

The Ebernburg.

chaplain, and numerous Lutheran leaders, among them
Aquila, Bucer, and Œcolampadius, found shelter under
these friendly walls. Sickingen himself tried to convert
some of his great friends, and we have letters from him on
such subjects as communion in both kinds, the evils of celibacy, and the futility of adoring the saints.

Hutten's
estrange-
ment from
Luther.

Deeply did Hutten grieve at this time over the signs of
a growing coldness on the part of Martin Luther. We hear
complaints from him that the great reformer seldom answers his letters; that he does not send him his new writings. The fact was, that a radical difference of opinion had
arisen between the two men. If Martin Luther had ever
seriously thought of war,— and some of his violent utterances rather point to that conclusion,— on further consideration he had changed his mind. "What Hutten desires
is known to thee," he wrote to Spalatin; "I, for my part,
am not willing that the gospel be fought for with violence
and bloodshed. I have written to the man to that effect."
On the whole, if we take the verdict of history, Hutten was
right and Luther wrong; the future showed that wars and
revolutions could not be avoided. The poet-knight had
the surer gaze; he knew what he was doing when he veered
round from the traditional standpoint of his class, and tried,
in one of his most thoughtful dialogues, to point out to the
burghers, whom his kind had so often wronged, the identity
of his and their interests. More than a century of misery
and retrogression might have been spared to Germany had
the knights, cities, and peasants, as a unit, instead of each
separately, come forward at once in a fierce assertion of their
religious freedom.

Hutten and
the Diet of
Worms.

The culmination of Hutten's career came in the days of
the Diet of Worms. Never did his chosen motto, the Cæsa-
rian *alea jacta est*, have a truer meaning;—and he lost
the throw. He had plans for a great uprising, plans which

included the capture of the papal legates. The time had come, he declared, when Germany's rulers must show whether they were real men or whether they were dressed-up statues. From the Ebernburg, which was only a few miles from Worms, and whither secret messengers brought instant tidings of all important happenings, a perfect flood of small pamphlets was let loose upon those present at the Diet. The two legates, Aleander and Carracioli, came in for the chief share of abuse, and Hutten next turned the torrent of his eloquence against the assembled Catholic prelates. They were pronounced unworthy and immoral, unfit to be trusted with money or with woman's honor: "The measure is full. Away from the pure springs, ye filthy swine. Out from the sanctuary, ye cursed money-lenders, no longer touch the altars with oft-desecrated hands. . . . The measure is full. Can ye not see that the breeze of freedom is blowing; that men are wearied of the present state of things and would fain bring about a change?" It is his own vocation, Hutten declares, to "sting, spur, goad, and shove to freedom."

With unexampled audacity, Hutten, in a special writing, took the emperor himself to task. Has Charles nothing better to do than to please these priests, who can help him neither in the field nor in the council chamber? He can never gain Germany's favor unless he dismiss such men. He should sternly have repudiated Aleander's demands. "What has Germany done that with thee, not for thee, it should go to destruction? Lead us into danger; lead us against swords or through flames . . . but bid us not succumb like weak women." Then, in a sarcastic vein, "So great an emperor, king of so many peoples — yet so ready for servitude that he does not wait to be subjugated! . . . How will men speak of Charles, who has as many masters as there are around him cardinals' hats and bishops' mitres?"

Hutten accomplishes nothing.

All that Hutten had yet done was but child's play to challenges such as these. He who used such language must, it was universally thought, have an armed force at his back and be ready for revolution. When, on the contrary, nothing happened, reproaches came in from every side. " Men say of Hutten," wrote a friend, "that he barks but cannot bite." He was urged to rise and show what he could do, and above all not to let the papal legates withdraw with whole hides. He did indeed, if his own words can be trusted, lay an ambush for the latter which was unsuccessful.

In point of fact, Hutten had relied too much on Franz von Sickingen. There was no quarrel now ; but the master of the Ebernburg, who was in the pay of Charles and had just accepted the command of fifteen thousand men against France, was not ready for the kind of uprising that his friend wanted, and was determined not to have his castle made the centre of such intrigues. He had even formed a plan of converting the emperor to Protestantism, or in some way, by an interchange of ideas, of healing the religious differences. Just before the Diet of Worms he had persuaded Glapion to come to the Ebernburg, and Luther was asked to stop and confer with him ; but the reformer feared some trick, friendly or otherwise, to prevent his appearing at the Diet, and hurried on his way.

After the Diet of Worms, which had stirred him up to such violent denunciations, Hutten rapidly degenerated. Bereft of his strong protector, who had started on his French campaign, tortured by a dreadful disease, hiding in out-of-the-way places from real and imaginary enemies, he took to venting his spleen in discreditable feuds. We hear of an abbot robbed upon the highway and subjected to shameful indignity — a crime for which one of Hutten's servants atones with his life. Erasmus tells of two friars who lost their ears at the instigation of the embittered poet-knight. The revolutionary intrigues still went on, and Hutten is supposed to have been the author of a stirring appeal to the masses entitled the *Neu Karsthans*.

The fortunes of Sickingen, too, had undergone a change for the worse. The French expedition proved a failure, and the army was forced to disband. We know now that the fault rested, not with Sickingen but with a higher commander, yet at the time the knight's prestige was greatly impaired, and he suffered material losses. With his heart full of rancor, he fell back into his old ways and determined, by one brilliant feud, to restore the tarnished splendor of his name. Yet his own glory was not his only aim; he would help the whole order of knighthood to assert its dignity against the power of the princes and also carry out his cherished plan of blazing a way for the gospel; he would "honor God by fighting against the bishops and priests." A number of knights formally chose him as their leader at Landau, and he raised an army of seven thousand men with reënforcements in prospect.

Sickingen's last feud.

Never had the adventurous man aimed higher than in this, his last undertaking; his mark was the Archbishop of Treves, an elector of the empire and a tower of strength for the Romanist party. Sickingen hoped that the archbishop's recent attitude in the French war would have rendered him unpopular, also that the great body of the Lutherans might be drawn into the struggle. But he reckoned without his host; the archbishop hastily fortified the town of Treves, while the count palatine and the landgrave of Hesse hurried to his rescue; and Sickingen, beating a retreat, took refuge behind the mighty walls of his castle of Landstuhl, where for a time he was unmolested though abandoned by all and declared an outlaw by the imperial council.

Sickingen's
end.

A few months later the enemy appeared in full force, demolished in a single day an outer tower with walls the thickness of twenty feet, and made a breach in the actual ramparts. Hurrying to the spot the grim commander was hurled back by a falling beam, and a bit of projecting wood tore a frightful wound in his side. He was carried to a deep, dark vault of the castle, where it was thought he would be safe from the cannon balls of his pursuers : such an unchristian shooting, he declared to an attendant, he had never heard in all his days. He was still of good courage, and by his commands Landstuhl was held until it was a mere heap of ruins which the enemy could easily storm. Then he surrendered, remarking to those near him that he would not be a prisoner for more than three days. His principal enemies, Treves, Hesse, and the count palatine, descended into his dark dungeon; the two latter seem to have addressed him kindly and gently, but the archbishop could not refrain from reproaches to which the dying man made a proud reply. He had now to do, he said, with a greater lord, and a few hours later he closed his eyes. The three princes knelt at his side and prayed God for the peace of his soul. Then hastily and unceremoniously he was buried at the foot of his castle.

Results of
Sickingen's
death.

Sickingen's death had far-reaching consequences. On the one hand, the Catholic faith escaped a great disaster ; Pope Adrian rejoiced heartily and sent a special letter of congratulation to the Archbishop of Treves. On the other hand, the cause of the knights had received a fatal blow ; the Swabian league united with the three avenging princes and razed to the ground some fifty three castles of those whom they considered favorers of Sickingen or thought to be dangerous in other ways. The day of glory for the free knights of the empire had passed away ; never again do they unite in any common undertaking. But some of them

have retained their rank and their possessions almost down
to our own day; and one of them, the Baron Stein, was
destined to do alone for his country what hundreds of his
like had failed in union to accomplish.

Among the indirect results of Sickingen's fall was the
failure of the most earnest attempt at representative government made in many generations. The fate of the council
of regency which had been revived at the Diet of Worms,
and which had placed Sickingen in the ban, became so
strangely linked with that of the robber knight that it
would willingly have seen him defeat his enemies. Anxious to proceed against him by the ordinary means of
justice, it had seen its authority defied by the three powerful princes who practically renounced their allegiance.
Bitter disputes concerning the disposal of the captured
property ensued, and the council completely lost its influence and its prestige.

Even before Landstuhl fell, Ulrich von Hutten, pursued
by Sickingen's enemies as well as by his own, had left Germany. The king of France offered him an honorable post
at his court; but he refused to serve his country's enemy,
and sought rest and refuge in Basel. He had looked forward eagerly to meeting here with his learned friend
Erasmus, and even cherished hopes of converting the noted
humanist to the teachings of the Reformation. But a blow
was in store for him which, in his wretched condition,
doubtless hastened his death. Erasmus, not wishing to
offend high patrons who were Hutten's enemies, afraid,
too, as he later said himself, that he might be forced to take
this demoralized knight into his own house, that he might
catch his disease, that he might have to lend him money,—in
short, in a nervous tremor for his own reputation,—sent word
to his former friend not to compromise him by a visit unless he had matters of great importance to tell him; even

*Hutten and
Erasmus.*

then, he said, he doubted extremely if Hutten would be able to bear the cold of his rooms; he, Erasmus, could never endure the heat of a stove!

The poor dying poet threw all the venom of his nature into one last invective against the former friend in whom he had placed such hopes; pusillanimity, envy of Luther, were cast up to his account, and above all, outrageous vanity. "One sees how it delights and tickles thee when great men greet thee and talk to thee on familiar terms!" The wonder of Europe, for his part, threw all self-restraint to the winds, and answered in terms that, for meanness and for downright cruelty, could hardly be surpassed. He named his writing the *Sponge;* it was to wipe out the little spatterings or aspersions with which Hutten had polluted him. He taunted him with his poverty, even with his sickness; and it was doubtless his doing that the poet was banished from Basel. He went so far as to write to Zwingli and to the city council of Zurich to beware of giving the fugitive an asylum, lest he should reward their good offices by some poisoned writing.

Hutten's death.

But Zwingli was not the man to be influenced by such advice. He nursed Hutten and was with him to the end, thus throwing a gleam of sunshine over the unutterable gloom of his last days. He had become absolutely indigent; even a collection of some two thousand letters written to himself by great men of all nations had in some way been lost. "He left behind him positively nothing of value," writes Zwingli, "no books, no household effects — nothing but a pen."

The personality of Frederick the Wise.

Among the friends and allies of the Reformation must be reckoned one who persevered in the observances of the Catholic religion to the day of his death, and who never spoke to Luther face to face, but who yet stood over him like a guardian angel, and more than once warded off harm.

A more attractive personality than that of Frederick the Wise of Saxony would be difficult to name in this whole age. He was so beloved by the old emperor Maximilian that if, at a diet, he stood too far away from him, there took place, to quote Spalatin, "such a waving, such a tugging of the hand, such an uproar altogether," as never before. His popularity would have gained him the imperial election, had he been willing to come forward as a candidate. His tastes ran altogether to the quiet pursuits of peace; he would suffer injustice rather than go to war; he forgave his enemies, spoiled his servants and retainers, and was never known, says Spalatin, "to utter a whole curse." Frederick had been on a pilgrimage to Jerusalem in his youth, had received the honor of knighthood, and had brought home the nucleus of his great collection of relics. He was punctilious, almost ostentatious, in the performance of his religious duties. Spalatin notes with regret that at a critical juncture in the affairs of the Reformation his master was attending mass as often as three times a day.

Frederick's attitude in the matter of Luther was more firm than might have been expected from so gentle a prince. He discussed the case with papal legates, he wrote letters about him to German princes, but always in the same strain: — The man had not been given a hearing before "just, learned, pious, and unsuspected judges"; his doctrine had "not been refuted by true and solid arguments and clear witness of Scripture." The elector feared that if Luther were "put down by the mere terror of the church's power, the inevitable result would be to excite in Germany the sharpest offence and horrible and deadly tumults." It is probable that this enlightened ruler had already accepted in his heart some of his protégé's teachings; probable even that he refrained from openly adopting them because of a plot, in which the legate Aleander was

Frederick's attitude to Luther.

concerned, to oust him from the electorate and confer it on
the Albertine line.   Luther himself well knew the dangers
that threatened his lord on his own account.   "I leave
your territory," he wrote, after the hearing at Augsburg
before Cajetanus ; " I will go whithersoever a merciful God
may lead me, trusting myself in any event to His divine
pleasure.   For there is nothing I desire less than that any
man, and your illustrious Lordship least of all, should on
my account be led into any odium or peril."   The reformer
had already assembled his friends for a farewell meal, when
a letter of Spalatin's changed his purpose.

Luther
carried to
the Wart-
burg.

After the decided attitude taken against Luther at the
Diet of Worms, the partisanship of the elector became a
more serious matter ; had he openly refused to allow
the ban of the empire to be carried out, that ban might
have been turned against himself.   One way and one only
led out of the difficulty : the reformer must disappear,
must be put out of harm's way.   A few days after the
great scene in the Diet, on the road from Worms to Wittenberg, Luther's carriage was attacked by five wildly
gesticulating horsemen.   To the accompaniment of loud
curses which were supposed to be characteristic of fierce
bandits, the victim, who had been warned of what might
take place, was seized and carried past Eisenach up the
slope that leads to the glorious old castle of the Wartburg.
Here he was kept under gentle compulsion for nearly a
year, unable to venture out save in the disguise of " Squire
George."   To be true to that character, he tried to hunt ;
but the sight of a hare he had killed made him think of
himself and his followers pursued by the fury of the papists.
Many hours of each day he occupied in writing, and here
he began that translation of the Bible which was to exercise
such a powerful influence on German literature.   Trans-
lations there had been before, but none directly from the

original tongues, and none in the terse, clear style that
appealed so strongly to north and south, to uplanders and
lowlanders, as to make them forget their differences of
dialect, and accept this as their highest model of literary
excellence.

At Worms and elsewhere, Luther's fate at first remained
a mystery. Many feared the worst for him. "O God
in heaven have mercy upon us," wrote Albrecht Dürer,
"Luther is dead . . . would that with my own life I could
purchase the life of this man, the most godly on earth in
these days!" Who, he wondered, would now be able to
reunite the holy church? Aleander came in for a great
wave of popular indignation; he was thought to have
connived at Luther's destruction, and he narrowly escaped
being stoned to death.

But soon the reformer's intimate friends found cause for
comfort; letters arrived for them dated " from my Patmos,"
" from the region of the birds," and they knew that their
hero was in safety.

CHAPTER XIII

ANABAPTISM AND CIVIL WAR

LITERATURE: Bezold, Ranke, Egelhaaf, and Lamprecht give good accounts of the Peasants' War. See also Zimmermann, *Geschichte des Bauernkrieges*, and especially for the anabaptists in Münster, L. Keller, *Geschichte der Wiedertäufer und ihres Reichs zu Münster*.

Deviations of doctrine.

A SUCCESSFUL attack having once been made on the authority of the established religion, numerous sects and individuals found courage to come forward with their own peculiar views, and many who had broken with the Pope soon found themselves in no less bitter hostility to Martin Luther. Their ideas seemed to the Wittenberg reformers no less poisonous than the doctrines of Roman Catholicism: there were those who presumed to deny the existence of the devil — a being so real to Luther that he is popularly supposed to have flung an inkstand at him; there were those who could not and would not believe that there is any original sin in new-born babes; others doubted the Trinity, and others still maintained that the body and blood of Christ could not be actually present during the administration of the Lord's Supper. Luther himself says, at the beginning of the year 1525, "There are absolutely as many sects and beliefs as there are persons; the very lowest or coarsest fellow, if he dream or imagine anything, gives it out as an inspiration of God, and wishes to be thought a prophet."

There was common ground on which many of these dissenters could meet, and thousands of them were soon herding together under the general name of anabaptists. It is easy to account for the spread of a sect, the basis of which was rejection — rejection of all theological subtleties whatever and a clinging to the literal text of Scripture. The point which their enemies seized upon, the necessity of rebaptism in later years, was with them an external and minor matter, one phase in their endeavor to shape their lives according to the simplicity and truth of the apostolic age as described in the Scriptures. The Bible said, "Believe and be baptized," which must apply to adults, as babes could not believe. This aim, a literal interpretation under all circumstances, was just enough like Luther's own insistence on the actual wording of Scriptural texts, as, for instance, in the matter of transubstantiation, to fairly infuriate the reformer. It was the *reductio ad absurdum* of his own methods. If told to preach from the housetops, the anabaptists would swarm upon the roofs; in order to be as little children, they would run about without clothes. There was once an exodus from all the gates of St. Gall in obedience to the command, "Go ye out into all the world and preach the gospel"; at Appenzell twelve hundred persons waited in vain for the food their heavenly Father was to send them if they "took no heed to what they should eat."

These extreme radicals of the reformation movement, whom Luther accused of "devilish stubbornness," came into conflict with all the institutions of daily life; they would not serve in the army, and, as their "yeas were to be yeas and their nays nays," they refused to bind themselves by any oath. What was still more unpardonable in the eyes of the reformers, they seized on texts that struck at such cardinal truths as eternal damnation, the existence of the Trinity, and the divinity of Christ. There was no possible length to which these deductions did not go:

Biblical phrases were adduced to show that there was a higher authority than even the Bible itself; the words "where two or three are gathered together in my name, there am I in the midst of them" were taken to mean that Christ held actual communication with the faithful; and, for many, dreams, visions, and inspirations gave the ultimate sanction to strange conduct, and led, as we shall see, to the wildest conceivable excesses. And with these religious theories went others of a socialistic nature — an aversion to secular authority and a strong desire to abolish property distinctions; crimes were committed on the plea that they were the will of God, and the magistrates of St. Gall were obliged to decree that divine inspiration was no valid defence in a court of law.

The Zwickau prophets.

Switzerland was the real home of the anabaptists, but the little Saxon town of Zwickau soon came to be a hotbed for such sentiments. Here Nicholas Storch, the weaver, Marcus Stübner, a former student of Wittenberg, and Thomas Münzer, a wandering preacher, became the leaders of a band of "prophets," who declared themselves inspired of God, and set to work to overturn the existing state of affairs. Münzer we shall meet with again in the midst of flame and battle; his one aim in life was to create a sensation, to which end he had been known to sound a false alarm of fire and to run madly about the streets as though pursued. In the programme of the Zwickau prophets there gradually developed a plan to annihilate the "godless," by whom were meant all who were not anabaptists, but more especially the priests and pastors; Münzer adopted the hammer as an emblem of his prowess in smiting. But the day of triumph for the agitators had not yet come; the magistrates of the town interfered, the ringleaders were banished, and some fifty anabaptists placed in prison.

Surrounded with a halo of martyrdom, the prophets
turned their steps to Wittenberg, arriving there at the
time when Luther was half guest and half prisoner in the
castle of the Wartburg. Eloquent these men were, if
nothing else, and they soon won followers in the citadel
of their enemy; even Melanchthon was moved by their
appearance and showed them kindness and hospitality,
while in Carlstadt, Luther's old supporter in the Leipzig
disputation, they found a man after their own hearts.
Strongly attracted by the idea of a higher personal inspiration, Carlstadt conceived a contempt for all learning and for
all social forms. He dismissed his class from the university, telling them that learning was a vain thing, and then,
donning the garb of a peasant, went to carry beer for his
inferiors, and to sit at the feet of the lowly and learn from
them. Others there were who, to emphasize their contempt
for conventions, walked into their neighbors' houses and
sat with their legs cocked up on the benches or tables.

The
"prophets"
in Witten-
berg.

The dreams so rudely interrupted in Zwickau seemed
likely to be realized in Wittenberg. The agitation against
the clergy met with signal success; monks were induced
to marry, and Carlstadt himself publicly plighted his troth.
Communion in both forms was freely administered; students and burghers broke into those churches where Catholic rites were still retained, and, with knives which they
had concealed in the folds of their gowns, drove the priests
from the steps of the altar. War was declared on crucifixes and confessionals; better, cried Carlstadt, that they
should be in hell or in a fiery furnace than in the houses of
God. Were they not the graven images of which the Lord
had spoken in the Decalogue? Nor was the confusion and
uproar confined to the precincts of the city; in one neighboring village an ass was marched through the centre of
the church, in another contempt was shown for most

sacred religious rites by allowing an unconsecrated butcher to administer the Lord's Supper.

The elector of Saxony was not a man to put down by force even such excesses as these; he was the friend of the lower classes and had immense charity for their weaknesses and aberrations. And who could tell just in how far these teachings were to be condemned? The authorities of the university met together to discuss the matter, but showed such lamentable disagreements among themselves that their only common action was to discuss a resolution for the total abolishment of mass. In the midst of the general confusion the thoughts of all lovers of order turned to Martin Luther; now, if ever, was he absolutely needed by his flock. The magistrates of Wittenberg finally sent an informal, but urgent, request that he might come among them and quell the uproar — and Luther decided to come.

The return of Luther from the Wartburg.

It was in vain that Frederick the Wise warned his protégé not to leave his sure refuge, and expose himself to the dangers that lay in wait for a proscribed man. He declared that he, the elector, would be powerless to defend him, and that Duke George of Saxony, through a part of whose domains led Luther's path, would surely take him prisoner. To such representations as these the reformer answered in the firmest and manliest tone: he had done enough, he said, in consenting to be taken to the Wartburg eleven months before; the devil knew well that fear had not brought him there. As for Duke George, were he, Luther, needed in Leipzig as he was now needed in Wittenberg, he would ride there though it rained Duke Georges for nine consecutive days. As for protection, Frederick must know that he was under the care of One higher even than his electoral highness; that his electoral highness, in fact, might be more in need of protection than himself. The letter ends with an exhortation to turn and believe and see the glory of God.

So Luther returned to Wittenberg and ascended the pulpit of his old church, whence, day after day, with untiring energy, he poured forth warnings and exhortations with regard to the new spirit that had crept into his fold. Warmly he urged his hearers not to imitate the fierce intolerance of the Roman Catholics, who saw in every one who differed from them a blasphemer tearing at the seamless coat of Christ, a heretic worthy to be put to death. It was a hard task the reformer had set himself, for a mighty breach had been made in the edifice so carefully reared. "All my enemies," he declared, "and all devils, nearly as they have touched me, have not wounded me to the quick as I have now been wounded by our own adherents. I must confess that the smoke bites deep into my eyes and stings and smarts almost to my very heart."

The line of argument adopted by Luther was that many of the abuses so recently attacked were *adiaphora* or indifferent things that might continue without hurt; crucifixes, it is true, might have led some men to make fools of themselves, but so, for that matter, had wine and women. Should the latter, too, be swept away? What was needed most was Christian charity; even where innovations were requisite they were not to be attained by violence and blasphemy, but by quiet coöperation with those in authority.

While thus inveighing against force, Luther pointed to his own example: he had done nothing but to speak, preach, and write, yet that, "even while I slumbered or drank Wittenberg beer with my Philip (Melanchthon) or with Amsdorf, has done more to weaken the Papacy than was ever accomplished by prince or emperor!" And, indeed, so conservative up to this time had Luther been

Luther restores order in Wittenberg.

that, save when employing his disguise of knight, he still retained his monastic dress.

In the end such language and such an example could not fail of their effect, and quiet was restored in Wittenberg. Priests in their robes were once more allowed to perform their ministrations at the altars, and whoever desired the communion in both forms was obliged to take it in a separate place and at a special time. In recognition of his services, the magistracy of the town donated to Luther a present of wine and furnished him with cloth for a new frock. Carlstadt, for the moment at least, made his submission, and Stübner and his fellow-prophets from Zwickau left the city. For the second time they had failed in their plan of moulding men of common clay into fit denizens of an earthly Zion; but they did not give up the attempt, though few of them were to live to see the realization of their dazzling dream.

Religious agitation partly responsible for Peasants' War.

The next that we hear of the Wittenberg agitators they are playing a smaller part on an infinitely larger stage. Within two years of Luther's return from the Wartburg the whole of southern and central Germany was given over to scenes of violence that have never since been equalled in the civilized world, save at the time of the French Revolution. The Peasants' War, beyond a doubt, would have taken place without the efforts of the anabaptists; but their communistic ideas, falling on ground that was already thoroughly prepared, bore abundant fruit, and their unceasing activity in spreading those ideas would have entitled men like Carlstadt and Münzer to the doubtful glory of having been leaders in the disastrous movement, even had they not been prominent as actual combatants.

Nor is it possible to say that Luther's own teachings had nothing to do with causing the uprising; it is true that, as he said, he had only "spoken, written, and taught," but with him language was a weapon equal to many hundred peasants' flails. He had urged the people to wash their hands in the blood of "these popes, these cardinals, and all the rabble of this Roman Sodom"; his usual epithets for Roman Catholic bishops had been "wolves," "murderers," "tyrants," "apostles of anti-Christ," "thieves," and "usurers." The princes were "the greatest fools or the greatest rogues on earth"; "God deliver us from them," he once said, "and give us other rulers;" and he several times preached on the text, "He shall put down the mighty from their seats." The emperor was a "maggot-bag," who presumed to think himself the true protector of the Christian faith; the monasteries were dens of murderers and *ought to be reduced to ashes.* Whatever Luther's intentions in delivering such utterances, they were nothing more nor less than an invitation to iconoclasm, and as such they were understood by the peasants; Luther's name was foremost among those on whom they pinned their faith.

The actual incentive to the Peasants' War was the petty oppression of the Count of Lutphen, whose domains were down on the Swiss border near the Lake of Constance. The count drove his subjects to desperation by requiring them to abandon their fields in harvest time, in order to perform such trivial service as to catch fleas in the castle beds, to gather snail shells, on which the countess might wind her yarn, and to hush the croaking of the frogs in the neighboring pond. The movement, once begun, gathered force like a rushing flame. Superstitious fears helped to spread the excitement, for the astrologers had foretold for this very year, under the sign of the fish, a terrible revolution, in which the mighty were to fall and the lowly to be exalted. A leader was found in Hans Müller of Bulgenbach, of whom a chronicler tells us that he had a

Outbreak of Peasants' War.

ready wit joined to a singular power of oratory; that he was "good-looking, the right size for a man, and had previously taken part in the French war." At the head of his little army, and waving a black, red, and white banner, he rode into the town of Waldshut and formed a league with the citizens for mutual safety and protection. The next step was the founding of the "Christian Brotherhood in the Black Forest," which acknowledged no master save the emperor, and vowed destruction to castles and monasteries. Each member paid a small subscription, and a vigorous propaganda was begun. Clad in a red cloak and a red cap with plumes, Hans Müller made a dignified progress from place to place. He was preceded by a herald, who pronounced the "worldly ban," a form of ostracism, with threats of vengeance, on all who would not join the brotherhood. There followed him a wagon decorated with boughs and with ribbons, on which was erected a great standard, as a token of the liberation of the people. In some sections a stake was driven into the ground before the house of any one who refused to join the revolt, by which sign all should know him for a public enemy.

The movement once fairly under way, other bands and other leaders started up, and the numbers of the insurgents were swelled by contingents from the Swiss cantons. Jost Fritz, now an old greybeard, appeared in Hegau and declared that he would not and could not die until the *Bundschuh* had proved triumphant. Thomas Münzer, the Zwickau prophet, made a flying visit to South Germany, and is said to have furnished Hans Müller with many of his ideas. He returned to Thuringia, where he raised and equipped an army.

Duke Ulrich of Würtemberg, the old enemy of Ulrich von Hutten, thought that now the time had come for him to regain the duchy from which, six years before, he had been so ignominiously driven. He had curried favor with the peasants around his new home on the Lake of Constance by turning Lutheran, and he now gained their substantial help by promising, should he ever regain his power, to tax his rich subjects "till the blood burst from their eyes." He went so far in his affability toward his new allies as to sign letters with "Peasant Utz" (diminutive for Ulrich). The French king provided gold for this bold *coup* against the House of Hapsburg, into whose possession, it will be remembered, Würtemberg had come. With a band of Swiss mercenaries for the nucleus of his army, Ulrich came as an invader into his own lands, and settled down before the walls of his capital of Stuttgart. But the battle of Pavia, which, as we shall see later, ended so disastrously for the king of France, dashed all the hopes of the Würtemberg duke. The French subsidies ceased, the Swiss mercenaries were called home, and Ulrich himself, having taken to flight, was glad enough to find refuge at last in his Swabian castle of Hohentwiel.

Considering that within a short time the peasant revolt had spread over Swabia, Würtemberg, Franconia, and Thuringia, it is surprising to find what moderation was at first exercised on the part of the insurgents. Almost the only forces in the field against them were those of the Swabian League, an organization to which belonged a number of princes and cities, but which needed time to raise and equip its army. With this end in view it began to temporize and enter into fruitless negotiations. Ten months had passed since the beginning of the revolt before it dawned on the simple peasants that nothing could be gained by further parleying; that the lords, indeed, were determined to make no concessions unless they asked them barefoot and on bended knee.

Duke Ulrich invades Würtemberg.

The "twelve articles" of the peasants.

In the meantime, in various parliaments held in the free city of Memmingen, the peasants had drawn up a regular formulation of their demands in the so-called "twelve articles," which were adopted, with local changes, in all parts of Germany. They seem mild and harmless in view of the awful ferocity of the attempt to carry them through. First and foremost is freedom of choice and election, in each community, of a spiritual pastor, who shall preach the pure faith; then relief in the matter of tithes, the abolition of serfdom, the free enjoyment in common of water, woods, and pasture, a truce to the cruel death tax that took from widows and children the best portion of their inheritance. The ultimate sanction for their demands the peasants drew from the words of Scripture, and countless Biblical texts were inserted in the document; names were mentioned of those competent to expound the true meaning of the holy words, and among them were Luther, Melanchthon, and Zwingli.

The sack of monasteries and castles. At last, on March 30, 1525, the long pent-up fury of the masses burst with all its violence, and an assembly at Memmingen voted nothing less than death to all nobles and destruction to all monasteries. There resulted a carnival of violence, in the course of which numerous castles were destroyed and numerous religious houses devastated; in which the wine stored up in the cloister vaults flowed in torrents, and indescribable scenes of drunkenness added to the general disorder. The holy vessels of the church were used at riotous banquets; priests' robes and knights' plumes figured at ghastly masquerades. A horrible levity took the place of that grim seriousness which alone could have achieved a favorable result. Although three hundred thousand men were in arms, no attempt was made to regularly train and discipline them, no *Landsknechts* appointed to teach them the new tactics. The league, it is true, could oppose scarcely more than one-tenth of that number, but these were commanded by men like Philip of Hesse and the dukes of Bavaria and Brunswick, while reënforcements were rapidly mustering.

One and one only of the princes of distinction, Frederick the Wise of Saxony, seems to have felt sympathy for the rebels, and he at this moment lay dying — only the faint mutterings of the great revolt penetrated to his darkened chamber. He turned to his household servants at the last and confessed to them that the people had cause for discontent, seeing that the masters imposed upon them all sorts of hardships and useless things. On the very verge of the grave he came out in his true light; with trembling fingers he seized the cup and broke the bread, for the first time in his life taking the holy communion under the Lutheran form. Luther himself, with whom he had steadily refused to have personal relations, was hastily sent for, but arrived too late. The electorship fell to his son and soon after to his grandson, who was to prove a warm and heroic, though not fortunate, advocate of the Reformation's cause.

Death of Frederick the Wise.

Many were the different phases that the Peasants' War assumed, according to locality, to the particular form of the grievances, and to the personal peculiarities of the leaders. In general the Swabians would have been contented with the simple righting of their wrongs, while the Franconians unfolded a plan for the reorganization of the empire that should do away with all intermediate powers between the masses and the emperor. They established a parliament and chancery at Heilbronn, in Würtemberg, and debated the plan of establishing a standing army and dismissing the rest of the peasants to their homes. That in Thuringia the movement was more fanatical than elsewhere was due to the influence of the anabaptist, Thomas Münzer. In the town of Mülhausen he vituperated Luther

Thomas Münzer in Thuringia

and preached his own kingdom of God on earth, while choruses of youths and maidens chanted the promises of Jehovah to the sons of Judah. The goods of the clergy and the lands of religious houses were declared confiscate, and Münzer ensconced himself in a comfortable dwelling that had belonged to the Knights of St. John. After gaining for himself a prominent place in the government of the city, he set to work to raise an army and to procure weapons, openly preaching the annihilation of the godless, and especially of monks and priests. "How merrily," he cried, "will God strike among the old pots with His rod of iron!" With pen as well as tongue he scourged the nobles and inflamed the masses; "You miserable maggot-bag," he wrote to the Catholic Count of Mansfeld, "who made you prince over that people whom God redeemed with His precious blood?" and he signed himself "Thomas Münzer with the sword of Gideon." To the Mansfeld miners he wrote to have no mercy even though Esau should give them smooth words: "Be ye not moved by the misery of the godless; upon your swords the blood must not grow cold. Strike a cling-clang on Nimrod's anvil!" The immediate response to such exhortations was the sack of some fifty monasteries and castles.

Horrors in Würtemberg.
Probably no single episode of the war aroused such a bitter desire for vengeance against the peasants as the events which took place at Weinsberg in Würtemberg. The peasants of the Odenwald, led by George Metzler, the tavern keeper of Ballenberg, had surrounded the town, in which was a small Austrian garrison commanded by Count Louis of Helfenstein. As so often happened in this war, the body of citizens sided with the peasants, and the count and his followers, many of whom were noblemen, fell into the hands of the insurgents. With the deliberate purpose of striking terror into the neighborhood, it was decided

to make the prisoners run the gauntlet between two lines of spears. The poor countess, a natural daughter of the Emperor Maximilian, was obliged to stand by while, with hideous mockery, her husband, together with several nobles, was led to his doom. His former piper, Melchior Nonnenmacher, declaring that now he would play him the right kind of a dance, preceded him down the terrible avenue, wearing a hat with a waving plume which he had snatched from his master's head. Another of the ringleaders, Jacquelin Rohrbach, dressed in the count's damask doublet, stepped boldly before the countess as she clung to her infant son, who had been wounded in the confusion. She herself was afterward placed in a common manure cart and driven off to Heilbronn. Such scenes as this, it must be acknowledged, were rare in the history of the war. Valuable property was destroyed, nearly one thousand castles and monasteries were laid in ashes, and no heed was paid to the priceless treasures of the libraries and art collections. We hear on one occasion of the peasants wading knee-deep in the torn manuscripts of a monastery. But, on the whole, life seems not often to have been wantonly sacrificed. Nevertheless, enough had been done to rouse to furious opposition, not only the princes and lords of Germany, but also the very man on whose moral support the peasants had most counted, and who might, could he have adopted a different tone, have guided the movement into gentler courses.

The attitude of Martin Luther, himself a peasant's son, to the great movement which his own teachings had undoubtedly helped to further, can scarcely be defended or condoned with any show of fairness. The most that can be said in his favor is that he was, in a way, true to himself. He saw in the war the logical outcome of the doctrines of Münzer and Carlstadt; his whole theory, based

Martin Luther's view of peasants.

on texts of the Bible as to the humble place in society that the serf should hold was undermined and outraged. The man who could look at men and maid-servants as mere possessions "to be sold at will like other animals," or who could call God to witness that the "ass must have blows and the rabble must be ruled by force," must indeed have trembled at seeing Germany actually on the point of succumbing to the power of the masses. Nor was he alone in such feelings; the gentle Melanchthon quotes Scripture *ad libitum* to prove that it is a presumption and an act of sedition on the part of the peasants not to wish to be serfs. Did not St. Paul say, "Let each man abide in that calling wherein he was called"? "They are so obstinate, so bloodthirsty, the Germans, that they ought to have their liberties still more curtailed: for Solomon says the horse needs a bit, the ass a bridle, the fool's back a rod; and Ecclesiasticus xxxiii: 'Fodder, a wand, and burdens are for the ass; and bread, correction, and work for a servant.'"

Violence of Luther against the peasants.

In the beginning, as might have been expected from him, Luther had tried to mediate. He had written an "exhortation to peace," in which he addresses first the lords and then the peasants. The former, and more especially the "blind bishops and mad priests and monks," with their fleecing and extortion, their pride and love of display, are charged with having caused the whole disorder; the peasants, on the other hand, grievous as are many of the wrongs that they have suffered, are not to be excused for rebellion and rioting. But after the perpetration of some of the excesses already chronicled, Luther flung himself into the struggle, on the side of the lords, with a violence that knew no bounds. His next writing bore the title "Against the murderous and rapacious hordes of the peasants," who are called "brands of hell" and "limbs of Satan." Every man who can is urged to "strike

them down, throttle and stab them in secret or in public."
They are like mad dogs, who must be killed in self-
defence; they have deserved death in body and soul, and
a "prince can now deserve mercy better by shedding blood,
than others by prayer."

These are not words written in a moment of excitement
and repented of at leisure.   Luther was as sure that God
was speaking through him as when he stood under the
flare of the candles in that august assembly at Worms.
Nor were the consequences of such language hidden from
his view.   "All that God has done through me is now
forgotten," he wrote a few days later; "lords, priests,
peasants, and all others are now against me, and threaten
me with death."   And Melanchthon exclaims, "We see
how the rabble hates us."   Years afterward Luther wrote
as follows: "All their blood is on my head, for I bade
that they be struck down; but I put it all on to our Lord
God, who commanded me thus to speak!"

It was, indeed, to quote a Protestant writer of our own
day,[1] "a sad rôle for the greatest son of the then Germany
to serve as the herald and path-breaker of a reaction that
can find no equal for inhumanity."   The intolerance of
this man against all who thought differently from himself
is shown here in its ugliest possible aspect, and his undaunted courage and indisputable greatness of intellect
should not blind the impartial observer to this other side
of his character.   His own words are his most terrible
accusers; "I am very angry," he wrote in 1529, "at the
peasants, who cannot see how well off they are, sitting in
peace through the help and protection of the princes.
You impudent, coarse asses, can you not understand this?
May thunder strike you dead!"

Meanwhile the princes and lords were very far indeed

[1] Bezold.

The down-
fall of
Münzer.

from needing such inflammatory remarks to lead them on,
in the very days when Luther's most violent writing appeared the hammer of fate had already fallen in Franconia,
and had crushed the sword of Gideon. Bitterly the peasants had now to atone for not allowing themselves to be
regularly drilled. By the middle of that month of May,
1525, of which the beginning had seen the absolute
supremacy of the peasants in whole provinces of Germany, the dukes of Saxony and Brunswick and the Landgrave of Hesse had come up with a small but disciplined
army, and had met with the forces of Thomas Münzer
near the town of Frankenhausen. On the day of the
engagement Münzer did all that he could to animate his
followers and inflame them to great deeds. While, drawn
up on a hillside and surrounded by an improvised fortress
of wagons, they awaited the enemy, he held them a fiery
discourse. His appearance gave emphasis to his words;
clad in long robes and with flowing beard, he pointed to a
rainbow in the heavens and declared, in prophetic tones,
that God by this same token would surely help his people.
The peasants raised their voices in the hymn of "Come,
Holy Spirit, heavenly Dove," and advanced to the attack,
but a moment later they were all in mad flight. According to the Landgrave of Hesse's own report of the battle,
three-fourths of them were mercilessly cut down, while
three hundred prisoners were afterward beheaded. Münzer
himself was able to escape for the moment, but was soon
found and put to the torture. As the thumb-screws slowly
tightened on him, Duke George of Saxony is said to have
called out, "That hurts, Thomas, but still more have you
hurt those poor souls whom you led into such misery and
caused to be cut down."   "They would not have it otherwise," was Münzer's reply; but his defiant spirit soon
left him, and before he died he revoked his heresies,

making his confession and taking the Eucharist in the regular Catholic form. The town of Mülhausen, where he had been so active, was forced to make bitter atonement for its wrong-doings. Its inhabitants appeared in camp, with bare heads and bare feet, bearing the keys of the city. A yearly tribute was imposed, the goods of the clergy were restored, and, in order to take away the last chance of renewed resistance, the walls, towers, and fortifications were levelled with the ground.

Once the current had begun to turn, the peasants learned how feeble were the ties by which they had bound to themselves many a supposed ally among the cities and among the nobles. Heilbronn, where their parliament had already begun to assemble, declared against them, while the famous Götz von Berlichingen — who had taken command of the Odenwald forces, ostensibly to check violence, but in reality from love of war and a desire to strike a blow at the Swabian League — stole away like a thief in the night, and his little army of eight thousand men disbanded without a blow. In all, some seven battles were fought, but the majority of these were the merest massacres. At Zabern, in Alsace, where seventeen or eighteen thousand were cut down after they had surrendered, the ditch where the corpses were buried is called to this day the *Ketzergrube* or heretic ditch. Another encounter, near Königshofen, was likened by a contemporary to a wild boar hunt; while of a third battle, near Ingolstadt, one of the participants relates in his autobiography, "Such a slaying and strangling there was, and with no attempt at resistance, as when a pack of wolves falls upon a flock of geese or a herd of sheep." *Subjugation of the peasants.*

One hundred thousand peasants are estimated to have fallen before the swords of the victors; but more terrible even than the fortunes of war was the vengeance that was *Vengeance on the peasants.*

afterward taken upon the survivors. The Margrave of
Ansbach caused the eyes to be bored out of sixty persons,
while of many others the fingers were cut off. The Swabian League gave orders for wholesale executions, and the
official list, which a year later was laid before its federal
council, numbered ten thousand victims. In the duchy of
Saxony a formal report of the privy councillors declared
that the peasants showed too little dread of ordinary death,
and pronounced it a matter of imperative necessity to proceed against them with fire. Special tortures were meted
out to those who had participated in the scene at Weinsberg, in which the Count of Helfenstein had been forced
to play such a ghastly part; Melchior Nonnenmacher, the
piper, and that Jacquelein Rohrbach who had insulted the
unfortunate countess, were fastened by chains to trees and
slowly roasted to death. Galling in the extreme were
some of the punishments inflicted on those who had been
less guilty; men were forced to shave half of their beards
or to wear women's veils, so that every one might recognize them; others were forbidden to enter taverns or to go
beyond certain fixed bounds. Some fifty thousand, who
had fled, lost all their goods, while the Swabian League
offered immunity to those who should strike them down.

Never did any great movement have a more utterly hopeless ending. The condition of the survivors became worse
even than it had been before. The peasants in their fervor
had torn up all agreements concerning tithes, rents, and
services; in the most favorable cases, now, these were replaced by more burdensome ones, while many of the lords
refused to be bound by any writing. A spirit of dumb
submission settled down upon the masses; their condition
became utterly wretched even in districts where they had
not rebelled. No wonder that their faith in the newly
revealed God was rudely shaken, and that Luther from

this time forward had to look elsewhere for friends and supporters.

Of the anabaptists we hear little in the next few years, yet their tireless propaganda continued, and paved the way for the most extraordinary episode in the history of any country. The death of Thomas Münzer and of many others, in 1525, had been the beginning rather than the end of the movement. It was in that year that, when driven out of Nuremberg, Hans Denk, one of the chief apostles of the sect, began his ministrations. Two years later the anabaptists had grown so formidable to Protestants and Catholics alike, that in every part of Germany fearful punishments were decreed against them. The Swabian League sent out four thousand knights to hunt for delinquents, and to slay them without mercy; at Ensisheim, in Lower Austria, some six hundred, in Tyrol and Gorz, one thousand, were put to death in accordance with the Archduke Ferdinand's orders. In Vienna, Balthasar Hubmaier, once a Lutheran preacher of renown, was burnt at the stake, while his wife was drowned in the waters of the Danube. Duke William of Bavaria gave the merciless command that anabaptists who recanted should be beheaded, and those who did not should be burned. A Diet of the empire, in 1529, decreed death without form of trial to all members of the sect!

Persecution of the anabaptists.

In spite of all this persecution, or possibly because of it, the anabaptists were able, after various failures in other places, to carry out their ideal of a separate community, of a "kingdom of God on earth," in the Westphalian town of Münster. Here Bernard Rothmann, a young, handsome, and eloquent preacher, had begun, in 1531, to thunder away at Catholic usages quite in the spirit of Luther, and had succeeded in winning for the Reformation the merchant guilds and the city magistrates.

Bernard Rothmann in Münster.

When the bishop of the diocese, Franz von Waldeck, seeing his authority disregarded, tried to beleaguer and starve out the town, the citizens rose in a body and took prisoner the members of the cathedral chapter, as well as a number of knights. His resources at an end, the bishop was forced to make a treaty of peace and give over six churches to the Lutheran form of worship.

The victory of ana-baptism in Münster. But Münster lay in a district where anabaptist doctrines were rapidly gaining ground, and better soil for extravagant theories could nowhere have been found than in this home of the mystics, of Lollardry and of Hussitism. Rothmann himself and his faithful adherent, Cnipperdolling, were drawn first under the influence of Zwinglianism and then of the more dangerous sect, and joined hands with noted anabaptists of the neighboring Netherlands, with John Matthias, the baker of Haarlem, with John Bock-ellson, the tailor of Leyden. The city councillors were horrified at the words that now fell from Rothmann's lips; they enjoined silence, they declared him deposed from his pastorate, they even drove him from the city, but his friends escorted him back through another gate. It came to violent encounters between the two parties, to a regular battle in the market-place, in which artillery played a part on both sides. "God" and "Christ" were the opposing battle cries. The anabaptists conquered, the magistrates were overthrown, and in the new appointment of offices Cnipperdolling became burgomaster, while John Matthias was recognized as head prophet of the whole sect. John of Leyden, a man of attractive personality and really remarkable abilities, married the daughter of Cnipperdolling, and thus secured an influential voice in the management of affairs.

When it became known among the brotherhood at large that here in Münster the old dream of a separate kingdom was at last to come true, a double process of purging and renewal went on; the more moderate minded persons being obliged to leave the town, while into it flowed a steady stream of those who had been exiled from other places or were otherwise ready for change and adventure. The most pressing invitations had been issued on all sides; letters are still extant written by persons within the town and painting in most glowing colors the advantage of coming to Münster. The last judgment was declared to be at hand; here in the new kingdom alone could salvation be found. Books and pamphlets of the most inflammatory nature were spread far and wide throughout Westphalia.

Expulsion of the "godless" from Münster.

At last came a day, it was the 27th of February, 1534, when the anabaptists in Münster felt strong enough to complete the process of purifying their city and ridding it finally of all the "godless." John Matthias had voted to strike them dead, but the more moderate counsels of Cnipperdolling prevailed, and it was decided that those who would consent to receive the second baptism might remain, while the rest were to be driven into exile. On the day appointed preachers were stationed in the market-place with buckets of water; those who would not accept their ministrations were mercilessly driven out, although a fierce snowstorm was raging at the time. No regard was paid to sickness, weakness, or old age. The newly baptized were then called together, and, after humbling themselves in the dust, were given a warning and placed under supervision.

Now at last the anabaptists were able to proceed to the realization of all their dreams. The municipal council was disbanded, and an assembly of twelve elders, with the Bible as their law book, took its place. The head of the community was John Matthias, who terrorized his subjects and suppressed a revolt with a hand of iron. Community

The realization of the anabaptists' dream.

of goods was established; willingly or unwillingly, the people were obliged to deliver up their valuables, which were taken in charge by deacons. In accord with the Scriptural command, "Be ye fruitful and multiply," polygamy was declared not only lawful, but necessary; and the women, who greatly preponderated, were divided among the men. In order that "everything that is exalted" might "be humbled," church towers were cut down, while on other pretences Christian names were abolished and all distinction between the Sabbath and ordinary days declared at an end.

War with the Bishop of Münster.

The events going on in Münster soon attracted the attention of all Germany. Bishop Franz von Waldeck raised an army and settled down to besiege the town; but his forces were not strong, there were constant defections to the enemy, and such infringements of discipline that the bishop was obliged to order the erection of "gallows, wheels, and other barriers to wickedness" for the coercion of his own men. Various princes, Protestants as well as Catholics, had offered to help him, but misunderstandings arose which greatly delayed these reënforcements.

The garrison of Münster, for their part, fought with the utmost daring and desperation: there were many among them who had served as *Landsknechts* in the imperial armies. Once the city was all but taken; the moat was filled up with sunken wagons and with bales of straw, banner-bearers had mounted to the top of the walls and were waving to their fellows to come on. But the defence was as heroic as the attack; men stood with clubs and beat back the invaders, women and boys poured quicklime and burning pitch upon them; others were allowed to enter the city that they might the better be overthrown.

There is no doubt that behind all the extravagances of the anabaptists there was an immense strength of conviction. John Matthias suddenly left a meal, declaring that a vision called him to meet the enemy. With only forty men he marched out to inevitable death. He was succeeded in office by John of Leyden, more cruel, more unyielding, and more fanatical than himself. More than once he struck men down with his own hand for disobedience to his commands.

On the strength of a vision announced by one Dusentschur of Warendorf, the new prophet took the name and rank of king, with the title of "John the Just, on the throne of David." He began to claim the rule, not only over Münster, but over the world at large, and caused a second crown to be made in token of his increased dignity. He established his throne in the market-place, surrounded himself with a body-guard, and dressed in splendid garments. The widow of John Matthias became his queen, and together they administered the sacrament to the "brothers and sisters" in the Lord. He despatched twenty-eight apostles to announce to the world the coming of the "King of Sion"; and it is a significant fact that nearly all went to certain death without a murmur.

For a whole year this anomalous community at Münster, although forced to rely entirely on its own resources, continued to hold the enemy at bay. An expedition with thirty ships had, indeed, been despatched by the faithful of Amsterdam, but it was intercepted and overcome. A certain Hille Feiken, burning to emulate Judith, had gone forth from the beleaguered city meaning to bring back the bishop's head; she met instead with torture and death. The heroism with which the garrison endured starvation and every other hardship was in keeping with the usual fortitude displayed by the adherents of this strange sect. The town fell at last, but not until a diet of the whole empire had met to take action in the matter, and decreed

John of Leyden.

Overthrow of the "kingdom of God on earth."

that each estate should provide the equivalent of a "Roman month." By treachery one of the chief gates was won, then lost, then won again; a desperate struggle was kept up to the last, no mercy nor quarter being shown on either side. Rothmann was cut down by the blow of an axe; the king, queen, and Cnipperdolling were taken prisoners. John of Leyden acknowledged that as a rebel he had deserved death, but insisted to the last on the truth of his religious system. He was tortured on the spot where he had once erected his proud throne; his tongue was torn out, and an eye-witness tells us that red-hot pincers were applied to "all fleshy and veinous parts of his body." The same punishment was meted out to Cnipperdolling and to Krechting, another faithful follower. The bones of these three were then placed, as a perpetual warning, in the famous iron cages that still hang from the tower of St. Lambert's church in Münster. The anabaptists chose a new king, who remained concealed in Utrecht, where he was discovered and burned in 1546. About this same time Menno Simons began to exert his great influence on the sect, causing it to relinquish its most pernicious doctrines.

CHAPTER XIV

THE EMPEROR'S WARS AND THE PROTESTANT PARTY IN GERMANY

LITERATURE : See the lives of Luther by Köstlin, Lenz, Kolde, and Ledderhose, all excellent. Baumgarten's *Karl V.* extends to 1540. See also Bezold, Ranke, Egelhaaf, and Lamprecht.

THE ultimate success of the Reformation is largely due to the fact that Martin Luther was no political agitator. Had he seized the proffered leadership of the peasants, he would have estranged the upper classes; had his teachings threatened the thrones instead of the pulpits of the princes, the latter would not have been willing to remain so blind to his whereabouts as after the Diet of Worms. Yet if Luther's movements were unhampered by political considerations, such was not the case with Charles the Fifth. The latter had declared, it is true, that he would give his body, blood, life, and soul to extinguishing this heresy; but in point of fact he was forced by external circumstances to adopt a most tortuous policy, now sternly repressing, now actually making advances to the new party. This incarnation of bigotry, this true descendant of Ferdinand and Isabella, was once carried so far by irritation at papal intrigues as to declare that Martin Luther might after all prove a useful man.

Charles V. hampered by political considerations.

If we look closely into the matter, we shall find that there was another object to which Charles was equally determined to devote his entire being, — that was the restoration of imperial preponderance in Italy. In the way stood the claims and pretensions of Francis I., the French king, and until this rival should be removed from his path the emperor could pay little heed to German affairs. These wars with the French were to fill the best part of his life; not for nine years after the Diet of Worms was he again to set foot on German soil; not for a quarter of a century was he to be in a situation to oppose the progress of the Reformation by force of arms.   It is true there were other tasks to perform in the meantime, such as the holding in check of recalcitrant Spaniards and the leading of expeditions against Turkish pirates; but none of these enemies could compare in pertinacity to the old rival for the imperial throne.

The wars for the possession of Milan.

In Milan the French had maintained a garrison since the battle of Marignano in 1515, which had brought about the expulsion of the dukes of Sforza.   But the recovery of this territory had occupied Charles's thoughts ever since his accession, and to that end, on the very day on which he issued the Edict of Worms against Martin Luther, he had also signed a treaty of alliance with Leo X.   There is reason indeed to think that his severity to the reformer was partly out of complaisance to the Pope.   Into the details of the campaigns, fought as they were with mercenaries and on Italian soil, it is not our province here to enter.   The utter hollowness and corruption of the French administration is shown by the fact that the sums needed by Lautrec, the stadtholder of Milan, and despatched to him by Francis, were intercepted by the queen mother and appropriated to her own private uses.   It is interesting to note that Swiss mercenaries fought on both sides, and that those in the pay of Lautrec, for quailing before the idea of shooting their own countrymen, were punished by their home government.

Charles captured Milan, Pavia, and Lodi; but at the news of the victories Leo X. died of joy.   The loss of this ally and the recall of his Swiss troops crippled the emperor for a moment, but the victory of Bicocca made all good again. Pious old Frundsberg, the same who had bidden Luther Godspeed at the door of the assembly hall at Worms, bent the knee as he saw the French coming, then, with a "forward in the name of God!" plunged into the thick of battle.

For a time the scene shifts to France, against which country, in alliance with England, Charles made a futile invasion; he was aided by Bourbon, the former constable of France, who had turned traitor to Francis; and when in 1524 the latter sent Bonnivet to attempt the recovery of Milan, Bourbon led the opposing army.

Bourbon had, indeed, gone over heart and soul to his new master; on the eve of heading an expedition into southern France in this same year, he wrote to Charles: "Your affairs will prosper, sire. Should we fight and win our hoped-for battle against the king of France, you will be the greatest man that ever lived, and can dictate laws to the whole world." But the promised battle was not won. A few not unimportant towns in Provence fell into the renegade's hands, who fought *con amore* for the conquest of his own territories. But the protracted siege of Marseilles, and the feeling that they were needed in Italy, proved too much for the patience of his soldiers. The news of their retreat gave courage to Francis, and he determined to risk all on a personal expedition for the recovery of Milan. On the sleeves of his body-guard was embroidered the motto, "Once more and for the last time." So rapid was his march, that he crossed the river Tessino, farther up the stream, on the very day that the army which had been invading France traversed it near Pavia; as he entered Milan by one gate, Pescara passed out by the other. To Pavia with its garrison of imperialists, Francis now

Expedition of Francis I. into Italy.

laid siege. He hoped for an easy victory; he had reason to believe that there were traitors within the enemy's camp. But all his efforts recoiled against the high spirit of the Germans and Italians; even aristocratic ladies took part in the throwing up of earthworks for defence. Every moment was of importance; for Bourbon, Pescara, and Lannoy, the viceroy of Naples, were eagerly recruiting in different quarters. Of natural objects in the way, the river Tessino proved the most serious; in vain Francis tried the adventurous experiment of turning aside the waters into another channel. Violent autumn rains made the undertaking impossible. The days rolled on; imperial reënforcements arrived and concentrated at Lodi. The French were between two fires.

The capture of Francis I.

Francis sought the strongest position he could find, which happened to be the park where stands the beautiful Certosa di Pavia. Pescara's soldiers tore a breach in the park wall. A hand-to-hand conflict followed, in which the French king took part with desperate courage. He was still confident of victory: "To-day," he said to one of his suite, "I shall be able to call myself lord of Milan." But his Swiss mercenaries trembled as the Spanish musketeers, advancing with glowing fuses, their mouths full of bullets, sent volley after volley at regular intervals. They held their ground reluctantly, until they saw the Duke d'Alençon take to flight, when many of them followed suit. At this moment the long-penned-up garrison of Pavia made its appearance on the scene. Although Francis saw that all was lost, he still fought on. Before leaving France he had promised the lady he loved best — not his wife; she lay at the moment at the point of death — never to turn his back to the enemy; through all his fighting he wore her token upon his sleeve. But when at last his horse was stabbed under him and fell to the ground, he consented to yield up his sword. The richest prize that a monarch could desire fell to the lot of Charles the Fifth. An envoy of the Duke of Mantua was present when the splendid news was brought to Madrid, and relates what occurred : " Your Majesty has won the victory," said the messenger, " the French army is annihilated, the king himself was taken, and is in your Majesty's power." Slowly the emperor repeated the words, as if scarcely comprehending ; then silently re- tired to his bedchamber and knelt down before a crucifix.

" To-day," wrote one of Charles's generals from the scene of battle, " is the feast of the apostle, St. Matthew ; on this day, twenty-five years ago, your Majesty is said to have been born. God be praised and thanked for his mercy twenty-five thousand times. From this day on, your Majesty is in a condition to dictate laws at will to Christians and Turks." It seemed, indeed, as though all his enemies, Lutherans included, would have to bow before the all-powerful emperor ; but it was Charles's misfortune never to reap a full harvest from his various victories. He was apt to misuse his triumphs ; in the present case he pulled the bow so tightly that the string broke. He ignored the fact that the French nation might be willing to abandon their king, and that even the queen mother herself would rather have seen her son a prisoner all his days, than submit to such humiliations. Charles began by demand- ing terms of peace from his captive which would have ruined France. All of Burgundy was to be given up to the emperor, all of Provence was to go to Bourbon, and a number of small claims of imperial adherents were to be gratified from other parts of France. Had Charles restricted his demands to Italy, had he merely demanded a ransom, however large, the results of the battle of Pavia might have been more lasting. As it was, the French king, after passing miserable months in captivity in Spain ; after

Captivity of Francis.

being brought to death's door by the climate, by vexation, and by the studied neglect of Charles; after having made a fruitless attempt at flight, which brought upon him further severities; after having actually caused to be drawn up the deed of his own abdication: agreed to sign a treaty which he never meant to keep. Italy, Burgundy, — the Netherland border-districts were formally renounced; the king was to marry the emperor's widowed sister, while his two sons were to remain as hostages in Charles's hand.

The treaty of Madrid.

Such was the famous treaty of Madrid of 1526 A.D. When the day came for signing it, an altar was erected in the prison chamber of the king, an archbishop celebrated mass, and the captive, who was thus to regain his liberty, swore on the gospel to keep his promises. Nor was this all. The emperor's representative, Lannoy, asked the king on the honor of a knight if he meant to fulfil his agreement, and Francis bared his head, laid his hand in the hand of Lannoy, and promised as a nobleman to return to his captivity if within six weeks the terms of the peace should not be carried out.   Yet on the very day before this solemn asseveration, Francis had formally declared to his suite that the emperor's demands were exorbitant, that he regarded these promises he was about to make as null and void, and that nothing should force him to sacrifice the rights of the crown of France. The miserable farce of exchanging the king for his sons was gone through: ships set out from the French and Spanish coasts and met at the Bidassoa, the transfer taking place on a pontoon that was anchored in the middle of the stream.   The king embraced his sons and took his place in their bark.   On reaching Bayonne, he could not wait to land, but sprang through the water and mounted his horse, with a shout of, "Now I am King, I am still King!"

The league of Cognac against Charles V.

Francis might not have dared to break his word had he

not been sure of the moral support of England and of the
Papacy. Henry VIII., as fickle in his alliances as in his
love affairs, was willing to desert Charles when he found
that the latter could not procure him the crown of France.
Wolsey, the great cardinal, who wanted to be pope, had
also lost faith in an emperor who gave him only fair
words. Clement VII., the Medici who sat upon the throne
of Peter, was a time-server of the worst kind. It is said
of him that he always took the side of him who had
slightly the advantage. An ascendency, such as that
gained by Charles at the battle of Pavia, frightened him
and caused him to veer back to his first predilection. His
one idea now was to drive the emperor and his German
landsknechts from the soil of Italy; he found sympathizers
in Venice, Milan, and Florence. In order to make matters
easier for Francis, he freed him by apostolic authority
from the fetters of his promises to Charles.

For Clement VII. no treachery was too base. He connived with the Milanese chancellor, Morone, in an attempt
to bribe the imperial commander, Pescara; the glittering
bait was the crown of Naples. But Pescara, while apparently taking the matter under serious consideration, kept
the emperor informed of the progress of the intrigue.

The league that was now entered into at Cognac between
the Pope, the king of France, and the representatives of
Florence, Venice, and Milan, is known in history as the
"most holy league," because of the part played in it by the
head of the Roman church. Its outspoken object was to rid
Italy of all strangers and to recover the persons of the sons of
Francis I. It has well been described as a union of all Western
Europe against the consequences of the battle of Pavia.
With England ready to join his enemies at any moment,
with his pecuniary resources, which from the day of his
accession had never been satisfactory, now in a really des-

perate condition, Charles's whole plight was pitiable in the extreme. Blow upon blow continued to fall upon him. His mainstay, Pescara, was taken ill and died; petty revolts took place in different parts of Italy against the German troops, who, unpaid and starving, had been forced to make cruel requisitions on the lands around them.

No time to attend to Luther.

We have reached a point where we are able to pause and inquire more closely how these political happenings and the results of the war in Italy reacted on the fate of the Lutheran party. It was fortunate for the new sect that the two men who had the strongest interest in combating it — the most holy Pope and the most Christian emperor — had found a common concern in questions of a different character. Already early in 1525 Clement, pressed with the necessity of declaring for or against France, had written to the emperor's envoy, " There is no time now to discuss this matter of Luther "; a few weeks later Charles had uttered his astonishing remark as to the possible usefulness of the reformer. We can now see why it was that the Edict of Worms, pronounced with such emphasis in 1521, had remained to all intents and purposes a dead letter. It was never formally revoked; nine years later, because of it, Luther was not allowed to be present at the diet that heard the first regular profession of the Protestant faith; but, on the other hand, reiterated efforts at different diets to have it rigidly enforced had been of no avail.

The governing council.

When Charles V. left Germany in 1521, the conduct of affairs had fallen into the hands of that governing council which had been created or rather resuscitated at the time of the great diet. The establishment of this council was the most liberal measure that had ever been tried in the history of the Holy Roman Empire. Its members were made up of delegates chosen by the electors and the circles, as well as by the emperor. At the first session of the new body, which took place simultaneously with the meeting of a general diet at Nuremberg, really excellent plans for taxation, and for the establishment of a common customs tariff for all Germany, were brought forward. But the council never succeeded in putting through a single salutary measure; it never was able even to raise money enough to pay for its own expenses. It aroused the enmity of the free cities by wishing to tax them too highly; of the Landgrave of Hesse, the Count Palatine, and the Archbishop of Mainz, by not proceeding as they wished in the matter of Franz von Sickingen; of many other Catholic princes by its lenity toward the Reformation. After a checkered existence of ten years, it died a natural death in 1531, at the time of the election of Charles's brother Ferdinand as king of the Romans.

One reason why the council had not in the beginning been more severe against Luther is to be found in the fact that one of its influential members was the elector Frederick the Wise. Another ground for its inaction was because it feared a popular outbreak should it use too great severity against Luther. Besides, Luther's conduct in putting down the revolt at Wittenberg, and in showing up abuses which the then Pope, Adrian, Leo's short-reigned successor, frankly admitted to have existed at Rome, had won for him considerable sympathy. It was in vain that Duke George of Saxony, Luther's fiercest enemy among the princes, tried to insist on the carrying out of the edict, sparing no effort to this end. The duke sent to the diet the violent writing composed by Luther against King Henry VIII. of England as a proof of the manner in which this heretic treated the allies of the emperor. The papal legate Campeggi did finally succeed in wresting from a diet the

No enforcement of the Edict of Worms.

acknowledgment that it was bound to carry out the edict. But the restraining clause, " so far as possible," robbed the concession of all its force.

Confused
beginnings
of Luther-
anism.

Thus practically left to itself, Lutheranism made rapid progress, and struck deep, strong roots. When the legate Campeggi came to Germany in 1524, he found it a changed land from that which he had known a few years before. At his entry into Augsburg, when he raised his hand to give the church's customary blessing, he was so derided that on going to Nuremberg he thought best to leave his cardinal's hat behind him, to give no blessing, and to make no sign of the cross. Among the thousands who flocked before his very eyes to take the twofold communion were members of the governing council itself. When he began his plea in the diet for carrying out the edict, some of the members grew angry and others fell to laughing. Yet there is no denying the fact that in many ways the condition of things was deplorable : the old order of things had been destroyed, and the result was temporary anarchy. At the time when he nailed his theses to the door of the Wittenberg church, Luther had no programme ready for the unanticipated revolution ; he had thought out no form of ecclesiastical government; had arranged no liturgy; had made no plans for distributing the spoils from the Catholic bishoprics and monasteries.

Luther's
organizing
activity.

Yet manfully in the years that ensued did Luther take up the burden thus cast on him, frequently changing his views, but gaining experience as he proceeded, and learning to control the whole vast field of reform. No man ever more completely accepted the consequences of his own acts. He wrote catechisms to unify the faith, liturgies for the use of preachers, forms of prayer for every occasion ; he introduced the custom of congregational singing, wrote hymns that are known and loved to this day, and, indeed, composed the first serviceable hymn-book in German. Eras-

mus had drawn attention to the fact that the love of pure
literature was altogether vanishing; that men bought nothing at all save the writings for or against the new doctrines.
Luther, too, grieved at the decline of secular learning, and
wrote a stirring exhortation "to the burgomasters and
councillors of all German cities" to found schools for the
study of languages. He recommended the establishment
of libraries which should contain not merely sacred books,
but works on oratory, poetry, and the liberal arts, "be their
authors heathen or Christian." At his instigation, doubtless, Melanchthon composed a Latin grammar, which continued in use in Germany until the beginning of the
eighteenth century.

When the monasteries began to throw open their doors, Luther's
and helpless nuns returned to the world with no knowledge marriage.
of life and without means of support, Luther made it his
especial care to find shelter for them and to arrange the
difficult matter of their future subsistence. One especially,
a person of high station named Catherine von Bora, gave
him considerable trouble; he found a husband for her, but
the man broke his word and left her in the lurch. To the
scandal of his friends and the jubilation of his enemies, he
decided to make her his own wife. He himself has admitted frankly that love had little to do with the match, but
his Käthe, as he called her, proved a solace and a comfort.

The outbreak of the peasant war had greatly altered The princes
Luther's views and policy. His first idea had been to have as supreme
the main authority in religious matters reside with the bishops.
different congregations themselves. In his great address to
the Christian nobility he had laid stress on the common priesthood of all believers, and he had been particularly averse
to state interference of any kind. But a closer experience
showed that neither the peasants nor the lesser nobility
could be trusted with the choice of pastors, still less with the

administration of the rich revenues sequestered from
Catholic monasteries. Partly, therefore, at Luther's instigation and partly by the natural trend of events, the
political rulers of reformed districts became the spiritual
heads, the *summi episcopi* or "supreme bishops." As a rule
they devoted the income of the lands that had formerly
belonged to the church to maintaining poorhouses, hospitals,
and educational institutions. Visiting boards were established in the different states, with a view to procuring
uniformity in the religious services, and to seeing that
preachers did their duty.

At the head of the princes who took up the cause of the
Reformation stood John, the new elector of Saxony, and
Philip, landgrave of Hesse. By their efforts was formed the
Torgau or Gotha League, which was joined by Luneburg,
Mecklenburg, Anhalt, and others, and the object of which
was to form a compact party at the next diet of the empire. When that diet came together in 1526, the world
saw for the first time the spectacle of princes of the Holy
Roman Empire flouting the usages of the holy Roman
church; the Lutheran preacher of Philip of Hesse held
public services, while on one of the regular fast days the
landgrave caused an ox to be roasted whole in front of his
lodging. As a device on his coat of arms he had placed
the words, *verbum Dei manet in aeterno*.

The con-
ciliatory
Diet of
Spires.

The progress of this Diet of Spires showed plainly the
intimate connection between the foreign wars of Charles V.
and the fate of the new religious party. To the astonishment of all who knew the emperor's actual straits, Charles's
commissioners at first came out with a stern demand that
the Edict of Worms be immediately enforced; it seemed a
strange moment, when voluntary contributions of men and
money were most needed, to press an almost obsolete claim,
sure to be repellent to a number of the princes and still

more so to the cities, which were counted upon to furnish the main pecuniary supplies. But it soon developed that the envoys had received their instructions before the breach of the treaty of Madrid, and before the forming of the holy league of Cognac. It was out of the question that now, while practically at war with the Pope, Charles should make great sacrifices to uphold the authority of the Roman See over his own German subjects. It was a time for compromise and for concentration of all national interests, and the Catholics at the diet came to the conclusion that some concessions must be made. By unanimous vote, therefore, an embassy was despatched to the emperor to acquaint him with the impossibility of carrying out the edict, and to ask him to call a general German council for the settlement of religious affairs. Until it could convene, there was to be a truce to hostilities; and one of those ambiguous formulas was invented, of which the Reformation was to furnish still other specimens, and which either party might interpret as it pleased. Each estate of the empire was to shape its conduct with regard to carrying out the Worms edict, "according as it might hope and trust to be held answerable before God and his imperial Majesty." If this meant anything, it meant that the Lutheran princes, without fear of interruption, might conduct the religious affairs of their lands as pleased themselves. But they did not take into account how completely the emperor's attitude would change so soon as the fortunes of war might turn; they could not know that the archduke Ferdinand wrote to his brother that matters with regard to the "accursed Lutheran sect" were going too badly for words; that Charles must hasten home or all would be completely lost.

But Charles at the moment was in Spain, celebrating his nuptials with Isabella of Portugal, and the moment he could move Italy claimed his serious attention, his affairs Charles's straits.

there continuing for some time in a desperate condition. The Milanese were in open revolt, the allied forces of the Pope and the French king had captured Lodi and Cremona. At the same time the Turkish sultan, taking advantage of the discord between the heads of Christendom, was threatening Hungary, the latest acquisition of the house of Hapsburg. Thus attacked on all sides, and with England threatening in the background, the emperor had written to his brother Ferdinand at all hazards to raise an army, which should come down to Italy and coöperate with Bourbon, who was still holding Milan as best he could. Ostensibly, the new forces were to be directed against the Turks: "What Turks are meant, every one will know."

Frundsberg raises an army.

Unable himself to leave Hungary, Ferdinand gave the commission to George von Frundsberg, the brilliant leader of landsknechts; — how completely religious matters had been, for the moment, thrust into the background, may be judged from the fact that Frundsberg was known to be at heart a Lutheran. But what of that? No other commander of the age could instil such devotion into his troops. When, at Pavia, he had called upon his landsknechts to help free his captive son, they had declared with one voice that he was their father and they would follow him to the very death.

The chief difficulty at present was to raise the necessary funds. Ferdinand gave full powers to his representatives to mortgage lands, cities, or castles. Frundsberg himself sold his own estates, and even pawned the jewels of his wife. He was filled with bitter hate against the Papacy. Its methods had been made clear to him in his last Italian campaign. His private secretary, too, James Ziegler, had lived long at the Roman court, and was eventually to write a life of Clement VII. that shows to the full the contempt and scorn felt for the Pope by honest Germans.

In great haste, and by a narrow, dangerous, and almost unknown path, Frundsberg crossed the Alps on what was to be his last undertaking. A body-guard of landsknechts protected the aged commander and lent him the support of their spears at all troublesome places. His intention had been to join the rest of the imperial forces in Milan, but the enemy blocked the road; Bourbon, however, with half of his forces, cut his way through to Frundsberg's camp. The mercenaries by this time were clamorous for their pay, loud, too, in their denunciations of the Pope, on whom the blame of the whole war was laid. The notion had been formed, and received with enthusiasm, of marching on Rome and extorting a subsidy from Clement, when news came that the latter had made peace with the emperor through Lannoy, the stadtholder of Naples. The result was a mutiny of the Spanish and German soldiers, who saw no hope of obtaining their pay. Bourbon fled for his life to Frundsberg's tent; his own quarters were plundered, and his richest garments were later found in a neighboring ditch. Frundsberg himself, ordering the drums to beat and a circle to be formed, would have held a discourse to the mutineers; but to his bitter mortification his own landsknechts levelled their spears against his breast, and the old hero of twenty battles fell in a convulsion to the ground and never recovered from the shock.

Frundsberg and Bourbon in Italy.

But the episode had, at least, the one good result of calming the passions of the soldiers, and, under Bourbon's leadership, they continued on their way to Rome, which they reached without further incident. Here they found that, although Clement had in truth closed a treaty with Lannoy, the terms had not proved acceptable to the emperor, and it had not been ratified. Disregarding the command of the Pope to begone under pain of hanging, they laid siege to the city, and though unprovided with cannon or

Steps that led to the sack of Rome.

battering rams, they managed to scale the walls by the aid of ladders formed from the trellises of neighboring vineyards. A great misfortune overtook them in the death of Bourbon, who fell at the first onslaught; Benvenuto Cellini, the inimitable worker in metals, claims to have fired the shot that killed him. Bourbon lived long enough to see his troops in possession of the city, and his body was buried, it is said, in the Sistine chapel.

Such were the steps that led to the horrible and ever memorable sack of Rome of the year 1527, an event that had great consequences for the power of Charles V. and for the fate of the Reformation. The Pope was preparing to say mass in St. Peter's when he was attacked by the Germans, and two hundred of his body-guard were hewn down before his eyes; he himself had barely time to escape through a secret door — in such haste, says an eye-witness, that he "sweated as though soused in water." But the sheltering walls of St. Angelo once gained, he remained obdurate to the demands for a subsidy.

The sack of Rome.
Outside in the streets there began meanwhile the wildest carnival that Rome had seen since the days of the Goths and Vandals. With Bourbon's death the last lawful restraint had been removed, and the soldiers rioted and plundered with inexpressible greed and wantonness. Catholics and Lutherans joined hands in one great outburst of iconoclasm; the skulls of martyrs and saints were kicked about the streets; horses were stabled in the chapels of St. Peter's, and their beds were made of bulls and indulgences; an effigy of Luther was paraded about clad in the Pope's own garments; a priest was ordered to administer the sacrament to a dumb beast and was killed for refusing.

For ten days the starved adventurers from the north revelled in the richest city of the world. All the horrors of the Spanish inquisition were practised on those who were suspected of concealing their valuable property. Clement VII. held out in St. Angelo for more than a month: on his head fell the blame and the retribution for much of what had taken place. " I have been in Italy twenty-eight years," wrote the emperor's envoy in Genoa, " and have noted that of all the wars and misfortunes during this time the popes alone have been guilty." Charles is exhorted, now that he is lord of the whole earth, to eliminate the cause of so much evil. It became a question whether such a worn-out institution as the Papacy should continue to exist at all, and the young Gattinara wrote seriously to Charles for information on this point. The Pope was, at last, forced to surrender, with twelve of his cardinals. Schärtlin, the landsknecht captain, described the entry of his own troops into St. Angelo with all the terseness of a modern telegrapher, " Great grief among them and much weeping: we all became rich."

The march on Rome and the subsequent acts of violence had taken place without the command and without the knowledge of Charles the Fifth. His attitude in the matter is curious and interesting. He professed to be horrified at all that had happened, and caused prayers and masses to be held for the deliverance of the Pope. Yet far from giving orders for Clement's release, he prepared to make capital out of the Pope's misfortunes. He first planned to carry his Holiness off to Spain, but desisted for fear that the prisoner might be rescued under way. He then demanded possession of all the important strategic points in the papal states, intending to leave to Clement nothing but his spiritual power.

Charles V and the sack of Rome.

But the exigencies of the European situation at last forced Charles to be less severe than he had originally intended. The crushing blow was averted from the head of the Pope, as it had been the year before from the Lutheran party. Charles learned to his dismay that France and England, alarmed at the course of recent events, were drawing closer together. Henry VIII. declared that this matter of the Holy See, this infliction of the greatest injury the Papacy had ever suffered, was the common concern of all princes. In August, 1527, Cardinal Wolsey, in the name of his master, brought to Francis England's renunciation of her claim of centuries to the French crown. France in requital offered to pay England a yearly sum of money, regularly and unremittingly, " until the end of the term which Divine Providence has set for the human race." The peace of Amiens was drawn up on these lines, and France, aided by English gold, was free to concentrate her forces upon Italy. Various towns in northern Italy were taken, Genoa joined her fleet to the French forces, and Lautrec marched off to the south to strike a decisive blow against the kingdom of Naples. Henry VIII. meanwhile put the seal on his enmity to Charles by attempting to divorce Catherine of Aragon, the emperor's own aunt and the trusted representative of Charles's policy in England.

The peace of Barcelona.
In the great struggle for supremacy that seemed approaching, Charles could hope for no assistance from his brother. Ferdinand, so often his stanch supporter, was now engaged in the struggle that was to confirm the house of Hapsburg in the possession of the crowns of Bohemia and Hungary. In his early youth, Ferdinand had contracted a marriage with the daughter of Vladislav of Hungary. Her brother, the last king, who was childless, was killed by the Turks at Mohacs in 1526. A party of the Hungarians attempted to put up John Zapolya as their own king, and a civil war resulted, in which Ferdinand with difficulty held his own.

With France and England actively opposing him; conscious of the fact that his treatment of the Pope was awakening marked displeasure in Spain; eager, too, to employ for the defence of Naples the troops stationed in Rome, Charles determined to grant to Clement better terms than the latter could possibly have expected. He gave him back his liberty and the main part of his possessions, only requiring him to pay an indemnity, to remain neutral, and, it is said, to refuse his consent to the divorce of Henry VIII. The negotiations culminated two years later in the peace of Barcelona, whereby Charles was to have Naples, Clement was to be securely reëstablished in the papal states, and Florence to be given back to the Medicis. The two heads of Christendom became once more the closest friends, — an evil token for the cause of Lutheranism, — and in February, 1530, the last coronation of an emperor by a pope took place in the cathedral of Bologna.

Meanwhile in Europe at large the heavily charged atmosphere had cleared itself. One by one the restraints fell away that had hitherto forced Charles V. to deal so charily with his Lutheran subjects. Cardinal Wolsey's fall was followed by a change of policy which drew England away from the French alliance; while upon France there fell at this time a series of heavy misfortunes. The fondest hopes had been placed upon the expedition against Naples, in which Lautrec was assisted by a Genoese fleet; but Andrea Doria for some petty reason became offended with Francis and recalled his ships. Then the plague broke out in Lautrec's army, the ranks were decimated, and the commander himself was among the victims. And at the same time, within the confines of the French monarchy, the continued warfare was engendering famine and riot.

Charles V. also, unable to arouse much interest in Germany for these Italian wars, had well-nigh exhausted his resources, and welcomed any chance for a favorable

The "ladies' peace."

peace. He had already thought out one way of settling his difficulties, and that was to summon the king of France to fight a duel. After all, the questions at issue were largely of a personal nature; the mutual jealousy between the two rulers had been the cause of most of the bloodshed. Charles sent a message to the French king that was sure to provoke a challenge; he was told in return that he lied in his throat and had better prepare for single combat. But matters were not allowed to come to such extremities. After the last French army in Italy had been defeated, Louise, the queen mother of France, and Margaret of Austria, the aunt of Charles, were able to bring about that peace of Cambray which is known in history as "the ladies' peace." The negotiations were conducted entirely by the two women themselves, who inhabited adjoining houses at Cambray, and had a door cut through to better insure privacy of communication. The basis of the new treaty was the peace of Madrid; but great concessions were made to Francis, who gave a large ransom for his sons, and renounced his Italian possessions, being allowed to retain Burgundy until the emperor should have made good his claim by legal procedure.

Charles free to act against the Lutherans.

The conclusion of the treaties of Cambray and of Barcelona had paved the way for what was to be the crowning work of Charles's policy, — the suppression of the hated heretics in Germany. With the repulse of a Turkish invasion the last obstacle was removed. The infidels had besieged Vienna, but had been gloriously beaten back; not only the arms of the Germans, but also the cold of the northern winter had, to quote the words of a Mohammedan chronicler, "saddened the mood of Islam's warlike champions."

Meanwhile, events had been happening in northern Germany which rendered the solution of the religious

difficulties, in a Catholic sense, more and more problemati- Progress
cal. Deeper and deeper the Reformation had been striking of the
its roots; the time-honored institution of the Teutonic Reforma-
Order had been abolished in 1525, save for a few scattered tion.
chapters, and on its ruins had risen a secular duchy, which,
although a fief of Catholic Poland, had formally accepted
the new teachings. In Bavaria, the Lutherans were already
clothed with the nimbus of persecution, and between the
years 1527 and 1529 a not inconsiderable number of martyrs
had gone to the stake. In Brandenburg, the elector had
given his own consort a term within which to recant her
heretical opinions, and had seriously thought of putting her
to death for having caused the new form of communion to
be celebrated in her apartment. The electress had fled
to Saxony, where she had been entertained at court, but
where she had also spent three months under the humble
roof of Martin Luther and his wife.

Among the Lutheran princes there had already been The Pack
signs of a willingness to fight to the death. Philip of affair.
Hesse had held a notable interview with Otto von Pack,
chancellor of the savagely orthodox Duke George of
Saxony. Pack had agreed, in return for a sum of money,
to furnish conclusive evidence of the existence of a great
league for the instant and violent suppression of all religious innovations, and had laid before the landgrave what
seemed to be an authentic copy of the hostile agreement.
It was sealed with the seal of the Saxon chancery, as well
as with the private signet of Duke George, which bore the
well-known crown of rue and the two lions. It declared
that Mainz, Saxony, Brandenburg, and Bavaria, as well
as the archduke Ferdinand and a number of bishops,
had united for the purpose of dispossessing all princess who
should continue to favor Martin Luther. Philip of Hesse
hastily raised an army of eighteen thousand men and

2 A

invited Charles V.'s enemy, the king of France, and Ferdinand's rival in Hungary, John Zapolya, to join his standards. He issued a war manifesto, calling the Catholic princes servants of the devil, and extorted money from the Archbishop of Mainz. To Luther and to his patron, Elector John of Saxony, belongs the credit of having averted a horrible catastrophe. An investigation was begun, the document was published, and was found to be an arrant forgery. Pack was arrested, and atoned for his villany with his life; but the rancor kindled in Catholic hearts by Philip's attitude did not abate.

The Diet of Spires of 1529.

Meanwhile the future course of Charles V. became of more and more moment to the people; the emperor would soon be coming to Germany, his sentiments were not in doubt, and certain advance measures foreboded little good. The citizens of Augsburg were told that, because of their changes in ritual, they no longer enjoyed the emperor's favor; the councillors of Strassburg were threatened with loss of their fiefs for not opposing the abolition of mass. A diet had been called to meet at Spires in 1529, and it was generally understood that it would mainly concern itself with religious affairs. When this memorable assembly met, the favorers of the Reformation found themselves in the presence of an overwhelming Catholic majority; every single adherent of the old church who had a right to sit in the diet was present in person or was represented by delegates. Those who were known to have Lutheran sympathies were not treated with the ordinary forms of politeness. No one visited the Elector of Saxony, who, for his part, made a point of publicly running counter to the old ecclesiastical usages. The emperor had sent his brother Ferdinand and several commissioners, and, at the instigation of these envoys, a most radical measure was proposed, discussed, and carried. This was nothing less than the repeal of that article passed in the diet of 1526, which had been interpreted as granting to the different estates the liberty of choosing their form of faith until such time as a general council should definitely settle the matter.

In the form in which the vote of repeal was passed, the Lutherans were not boldly ordered to return to the lap of the old church; but the new measure, if rigidly enforced, would inevitably have brought about this end. No one was to interfere with a bishop's jurisdiction, no one to hinder the performance of mass. Such toleration would, at that time, have meant the crushing out of the new religious party.

On the 19th of April, 1529, when the protocol embodying the hateful clause was drawn up, the Lutheran princes asked for a moment's delay and withdrew for consultation to an adjoining room. Archduke Ferdinand, acting in the emperor's name, refused to await their return, and, declaring the motion for repeal passed, withdrew from the building. Greatly angered on their return, the princes, in the presence of those of the assembly who still remained, read the famous protest that has ever since given its name to their whole party. It was not couched in vague or general terms ; its authors took the firm attitude that this diet of 1529 had no legal right, without the consent of all parties concerned, to undo such an arrangement as had been entered into three years before. For their own parts, in matters that pertained to the honor of God and to the salvation of individuals, they proposed to continue to conduct themselves according as they should be answerable before God and their emperor. They requested that this their declaration be appended to the protocol, and placed with it among the archives. On Ferdinand's refusing this, the document was read in the presence of a notary and then made public. It bore the signatures of six princes, at the head of

The Protestants.

whom were Hesse and electoral Saxony, and of fourteen cities.

The die had been cast, the declaration of independence made. Henceforward there were to be the two parties, the Protestants and Catholics, and no efforts of rulers or governments were to be able to heal the breach. And the process of disintegration was to go still deeper; for within the Protestant party itself new disagreements and ultimately new secessions were to take place.

The very year that witnessed the great protest at Spires saw also the disputation at Marburg, and the thrusting away, on the part of Luther, of the hand offered by the Swiss reformers; it was a foretaste of the still more relentless struggle between the orthodox Lutherans and the Calvinists — a struggle that was to result in the loss of many districts for the Reformation.

Independently of Luther, Ulrich Zwingli, the Swiss patriot, had in 1516 begun his preachings. Called to Zurich three years later by a city council which was thoroughly in sympathy with his advanced views, he had begun a crusade against all the enemies of Swiss progress. He saw in the hiring out of citizens as mercenary troops the evil that was most harming his country; but his attempt at reform in this direction brought Zurich and its ally Berne into a war with the other cantons, in the course of which the reformer himself was to perish on the field of battle. In all his sentiments, as well as in the outward circumstances under which he labored, Zwingli differed widely from Luther: Luther was a born peasant, Zwingli a nobleman; Zwingli was a disciple of Erasmus, Luther, as far as humanism was concerned, was merely "a goose cackling among the swans"; Zwingli from the first had at his beck and call a body of magistrates ready to banish, imprison, or slay those refusing to accept the new doctrines. Zurich became a veritable theocracy, where the inhabitants were shadowed in their homes lest they should relapse into Romanist usages.

There was something political, something socialistic, something warlike about the Swiss Reformation that never could appeal to Luther; but the greatest difference between himself and Zwingli lay in the field of doctrine. The theories of the two men regarding sin and salvation were diametrically opposed, and on one point at least the difference was one that could never be reconciled. Luther believed in the actual presence of the body of Christ at every true celebration of the Eucharist: the Swiss Reformer, on the contrary, considered it a debasement of the Most High, who was in heaven at the right hand of God, to think that at the bidding of men He must so often descend to earth. To the one theologian the words of Scripture, "this is my body," meant "this is a token or reminder of my body," while the other never could and never did abandon the literal meaning of the phrase; as Luther afterward expressed it, in order to remove every chance of misconception, the actual body of Christ was "bitten with the teeth" at every proper celebration of the solemn rite.

Differences between Luther and Zwingli.

The darling wish of Philip of Hesse had been to reconcile the differences within the fold, and to form an alliance with the Zwinglian towns of South Germany, and for that purpose he had arranged a formal disputation that was to take place in his own town of Marburg. Luther joined in the disputation most unwillingly; he seems to have feared for his personal liberty, and sought and obtained a formal safe-conduct before crossing the Landgrave's frontier. Luther's mood was intolerant to the last degree; he was determined to crush and not to conciliate; he had come, he declared, not to change his beliefs, but to bear witness to them. He had laid down for himself the unbending alternative, "The one side or the other, they or we, must be servants of

The disputation of Marburg.

Satan." As he sat facing Zwingli, he wrote in chalk on the table before him, "this is my body," and maintained to the end that these were words which he "truly could not disregard." After various efforts to effect a settlement, the meeting broke up; the attempt had only served to foster rancor and bitterness on both sides. Philip of Hesse declared the schism to be "madness and raving," and indeed, for the time being, it utterly prevented Protestantism from becoming a decisive factor in the history of the empire. The spirit of passive acquiescence, the unwillingness of Luther to believe for a moment in the fallibility of his own judgment, had gained the victory over the progressive anti-imperial policy of the landgrave and the Swiss. As for Luther's personal feeling toward the Zwinglians, he regarded them exactly as he did the anabaptists. In his new system only two sacraments, baptism and the Lord's supper, had been retained: Thomas Münzer and his like had attacked the one, this new antagonist was endeavoring to undermine the other. No papal anathema could have been stronger than the terms of his condemnation of the Swiss: We cannot, he said, look on them as members in Christ; "they may claim our charity, nothing more."

Charles
obliged to
conciliate.

Surely at this time there was every need of a united effort; Charles V. was returning to Germany, and the Protestants had good reason to fear his coming. They knew that he was very angry; he had treated the envoys who announced to him the protest made at the Diet of Spires like so many convicts. The papal legate, Campeggi, was urging him to proceed with fire and sword, and, if need be, to introduce the Spanish inquisition; his new father confessor, Loyasa, advised conciliating the heretics of high rank by flattery and bribes, but applying to those of lower degree the "true balsam for their wounds." If Charles did not at once proceed with the utmost severity, it was not from lack of the will to do so, but because of new constellations in his political firmament, and because of the knowledge that he could not trust too much to the good conduct of France and of the Pope. The emperor favored the project, which now took form, of having his brother Ferdinand chosen king of the Romans; the elector of Saxony had grounds for denying the legality of the whole endeavor, and it eventually became necessary to propitiate him by kinder treatment of the Protestants. Loyasa's very practical advice to Charles was to make the heretics serve his own purposes, "even though toward God they are worse than devils." "If they will be dogs," he wrote, "let them have their way. Do thou, then, close thine eyes since thou hast not the power to give them their merited punishment." So the emperor sent a friendly summons to the Protestant princes, for a diet to be held at Augsburg, promising to give due consideration to every man's opinions. The invitation was received with joy; it was felt that to some extent this assembly would take the place of that general council for which men had been clamoring for so many years, and many of the estates brought with them skilled theologians and disputants.

The emperor was received with honor at Augsburg, where he displayed great magnificence; a single garment that he wore is said to have cost some two hundred thousand guldens. But it was evident, from the beginning, how frail were the hopes of achieving anything like lasting agreement. On the feast of Corpus Christi, Charles took part in the procession with bared head and with a burning taper in his hand. He had invited the Protestant princes to join him, but they deliberately stayed away. He forbade their preachers to hold public services in Augsburg, and in this they had to obey; for even by the decree of 1526 Charles had a right to say what form of religion should prevail during his presence in one of his own imperial cities.

Charles V. at Augsburg.

The Protestants had been invited to draw up a confession of faith which they were to be given an opportunity to publicly read. Melanchthon had undertaken the task, and with infinite labor had composed what was to be the accepted creed of his party for many generations. It described all the accepted doctrines with great exactness, drawing the line, not only against Catholicism, but also against the Zwinglians and the anabaptists. One single paragraph, that which defined that "in the communion the true body and blood of Christ are actually present under the form of bread and wine," was later to be slightly changed by Melanchthon's own hand, and to give rise to a long and unhallowed strife. In its original wording it served as a conclusive rebuff to the South German cities which had adopted the doctrine of the symbolic nature of the Lord's Supper. Four of them, accordingly, — Strassburg, Constance, Lindau, and Memmingen, — drew up their own "apology," which goes by the name of the Tetrapolitana.

Melanchthon's "confession" was read as agreed, but the emperor had appointed a chapel so small that only some two hundred persons could be present. However, a reader was chosen with voice so stentorian that those below in the courtyard could catch every word. The reading lasted some two hours: Charles was present, but his ignorance of German prevented his following what was said. A Latin copy was given him for his own perusal.

The confession was most conciliatory in tone, Melanchthon's one object being apparently to secure at any cost a reunion with the church of Rome. The document carefully avoided all offensive questions; papal infallibility, the sacredness of the priesthood, the proper number of sacraments, were not brought under discussion at all. Some matters that needed reform were mentioned at the end. In the negotiations, too, that followed the reading, Melanch-

thon showed himself so servile, so ready to make concessions, that he lost the respect of both parties.   The Catholics concluded that he would do anything for a bribe; the
Protestants lamented his lack of firmness.   He would even
at one time have gone so far as to allow the restoration of
private mass.   Luther, who, still under the ban, was not
allowed to come to the diet, but who, from a neighboring
fortress, had followed its proceedings with bated breath,
grew weary of the whole discussion, and wrote to urge its
discontinuance.   A reconciliation between himself and the
Pope he declared to be as feasible as a union between
Christ and Belial.

The Catholics, for their part, had drawn up a confutation
of the arguments used by the Protestants.   Their writing
displayed no logic and showed little merit of any kind;
abuse took the place of discussion and proof.   Not one
concession was made, and all the old teachings of the
Papacy with regard to the sacraments, to transubstantiation, to celibacy of priests, were maintained with the utmost
tenacity.   Yet to the bitter disappointment of the Protestants, Charles simply adopted the confutation and forbade
further discussion.   When some of the princes tried to
leave, they found the doors guarded, although to the
emperor's great anger Philip of Hesse managed to escape.
When the protocol of the diet was drawn up, it merely
stated that the Protestants had been proved in the wrong,
and must make their submission within a term of six
months; should they fail to comply with this demand, the
emperor "would do his duty."   As to the hostility of
Charles's attitude, there was no longer room for doubt.
He intended, as he had told the Pope, to "avenge the
shame inflicted on the Lord Christ."   Luther had already
written to a friend: "If war must come of it, then let it
come; we have prayed and done enough."   After the diet

The con-
futation of
the con-
fession.

had closed he wrote to Elector John and congratulated him on having escaped from that " hell at Augsburg." In a published " warning to his beloved Germans " he promised not to resume the attitude he had adopted during the Peasants' War, and not to brand as seditious men those who should take arms against these " murderous and blood-thirsty papists."

CHAPTER XV

CHARLES V AT WAR WITH THE PROTESTANT PRINCES

LITERATURE : As for previous chapter.

IT must have been extremely difficult for Charles V. to determine just what sort of measures to inaugurate against the Protestants. He could not well cause a crusade to be preached against them, as the Emperor Sigismund had done against the Hussites ; while a declaration of war against any individual prince would have simply meant adding one more to a long list of dangerous enemies, with many of whom religion was only a side issue. Charles finally took the most rational course open to him, and appealed to the Chamber Court, that body of judges which had been established in 1521, and which was reorganized in the very year of drawing up the Confession of Augsburg. One suit at law after another was now brought, for the recovery of church lands that had come into possession of the Protestants through the change of faith of their holders. — *Charles V, appeals to the Chamber Court.*

It was mainly for the purpose of resisting the decrees of this court, which was overwhelmingly Roman Catholic in its sympathies, that a number of princes and civic delegates came together in the Hessian town of Smalkald, in 1531, and laid the foundation of a Protestant league. The first signers were the elector of Saxony, the fiery landgrave of Hesse, the dukes of Anhalt and Luneburg, and the counts of Mansfeld. As the months went on more than a dozen cities handed in their allegiance, among them several of those South German towns which, on account of their — *Formation of the Smalkald League.*

Zwinglian sympathies, had been debarred from a share in the Augsburg Confession. But recent events had made Luther more ready to make friends; he had come to the conclusion that " the world, the flesh, and the devil, the Papacy and the Turks combined," had not injured the cause of the gospel so much as this schism. He was ready now to waive at least one disputed question, whether godless men partook of the actual flesh of the Saviour when they ate the consecrated bread. Melanchthon, on the one side, and Martin Bucer, on the other, drew up a formula with regard to the Eucharist, on which both parties, in Germany at least, declared that they could agree: Christ's body was " actually present," but as " food for the soul." The Swiss Zwinglians, indeed, filled with bitterness at the outcome of the Marburg disputation, refused to reopen the subject: unaided they fought out their own fight, and succumbed to superior numbers on the field of Cappel.

Agreements of the Smalkald League.

The formation of the League of Smalkald was a very decided step in the direction of armed resistance. The league was for six years, and provided that, if any member should be attacked, either by arms or in the courts, the rest should render him assistance. A rigid line was drawn against the anabaptists, and the severe punishments decreed against them by the government were expressly affirmed. A much-discussed question, and one that was finally decided most unfortunately for the cause, was that concerning the headship of the league. For the first time the fatal import of a certain jealousy between the elector of Saxony and Philip of Hesse became apparent. The young landgrave, warlike and fond of bold combinations, would have been the natural head of the new organization and the leader of its forces. This, Saxony could never brook, and the unnatural subterfuge was resorted to of dividing the presidency of the organization as well as the command of the armies: Philip and John were to wield the chief power in turn for six months at a time, while the military headship was to be exercised by the one or the other, according as the tide of war should flow near to his domains.

What made the Smalkald League especially dangerous to Charles V. was the fact that a rallying point was thus given for all his enemies, Protestant and Catholic, domestic and foreign. The powerful dukes of Bavaria, rigid Catholics though they were, did not hesitate to make a formal alliance with Hesse and Saxony in order to oppose the choice of Archduke Ferdinand as king of the Romans. Another avowed object of this union was to reinstate Duke Ulrich of Würtemberg, who had been obliged in 1519 to relinquish his lands to the Hapsburgs. To add to Charles's perplexities the Sultan of Turkey was preparing to invade Germany with an army like that of Xerxes. He refused to address Charles as emperor, — that title, he declared, belonged to the ruler of Constantinople, — but wrote to him merely as "king of Spain." *Enemies of Charles V.*

This danger from the Turks soon assumed such alarming proportions that all other conflicts were dwarfed for the moment, and Catholics and Protestants alike eagerly sought a basis for reconciliation. Even the Pope was roused to a sense of the perils that threatened Christendom, and interfered, as no Pope had yet done, to straighten out the religious affairs of Germany. He laid the Augsburg Confession before Roman theologians, who gave their verdict that some clauses were actually Catholic, others capable of a Catholic interpretation, and that, as to others still, a compromise was possible. He was willing, if need be, to grant communion in both kinds and the marriage of priests. Charles V., however, finally determined to make no specific concessions, but rather to declare a general truce. *The religious peace of Nuremberg.*

Of such nature was the so-called first religious peace, signed at Nuremberg in July, 1532. Until the meeting of that *fata morgana*, a general council, there was to be a cessation to all hostile measures, including the suits at law in the Chamber Court. Only actual members of the Smalkald League were to be included in the peace, Charles refusing to consider the possibility of new accessions to the cause.

The
Turkish
war.
All barriers being thus removed, Catholics and Protestants prepared with a will to march out against the Turks. A stately army of eighty thousand men was speedily brought together, but the greater part of it never saw active service; a slight skirmish near Vienna with Suleiman's light cavalry was the extent of the fighting that fell to its lot. Once more the " warlike champions of Islam " had had their mood saddened; a garrison of seven hundred men in the little Hungarian town of Güns had withstood their attack for three weeks. The Turks had withdrawn at the very moment when they might have triumphed, frightened, it is said, by the yells of the inhabitants.

No less incomprehensible than the retreat of the Turks was Charles V.'s neglect in not pursuing them: sharp-tongued Schärtlin was probably right when he compared the emperor's usual method of making war with the slow progress of a ruminating ox from field to field. King Ferdinand declared the unmolested retreat of this enemy to be the most painful experience of his life. But Charles thought otherwise. Leaving his army, he hurried off to Italy to talk with Clement VII. about the general council. He naturally found the Pope averse to the idea; one of the first effects of such a council as the emperor wished would have been to curtail the papal prerogatives, and of this Clement VII. was fully aware.

After the Peace of Nuremberg and the retreat of Suleiman, the Protestants entered on an era of prosperity.

They soon felt strong enough to repudiate the Chamber Court, which, under one pretext or another, had continued its objectionable suits at law. Before the period for which their league was formed had run out, they renewed it for another ten years. Elector John of Saxony had died in the year of the Nuremberg Peace, but his son and successor, John Frederick, proved an equally zealous upholder of the Reformation. As for Philip of Hesse, he was at last able to indulge his warlike propensities, and, as champion of Ulrich of Würtemberg, to bring that long-banished prince back to his own. The armed opposition of Ferdinand's viceregent in the duchy was of no avail; the great mass of the people were tired of the Hapsburg rule, and the revolution was accomplished with little difficulty, and in a short time. Charles V. just then was away, taking part in his first really successful campaign — chasing Chaireddin Barbarossa and his Turkish corsairs from their newly founded settlement at Tunis. Ferdinand, isolated in his brother's absence, and fearing a popular uprising which might have cost him not merely Würtemberg, but also his crown as king of the Romans, signed the Treaty of Kadan (June, 1534), the terms of which included Ulrich's reinstatement, although the duchy was to revert to the Hapsburgs should there ever fail to be male heirs.[1]

Ferdinand had fought hard to obtain a promise, that Würtemberg should retain the shallow Catholicism he had succeeded in imposing upon the land. In this he failed, and the duchy became a new stronghold for the Protestant teachings, drawing in its wake, too, the neighboring principalities of Baden, Hanau, Falkenstein, and Fürstenberg. It even joined the Smalkald League in

[1] This latter clause was formally abrogated at the Treaty of Pressburg in 1805.

common with Pomerania, Anhalt, and four free cities. When an imperial envoy protested that violence was being done to the Peace of Nuremberg, he was answered that the first to break that peace had been the imperial Chamber Court.

In every way the Protestant princes were rising in importance. We find Ferdinand inviting them to his court and treating them with marked respect. The king of France, although sternly repressing religious freedom in his own lands, sought the alliance of the league, as did also Henry VIII., once official defender of the Catholic faith, now "Supreme Head" of the English church. Pope Paul III., too, successor of Clement VII., sent his legate, Vergerio, to try and win back the lost adherents of the church, and to soften their hearts to the idea of having the looked-for council held on Italian instead of on German ground. Vergerio went so far as to invite Martin Luther to table, on which occasion, in order to do proper honor to the rank of his host, the former monk donned a fine garment with satin sleeves, bright jewels, and fur trimmings. He felt uncomfortable in his finery, but did not lose the opportunity of talking to the legate in very plain language. He soon after drew up the Smalkald Articles, which were to be the programme of the Protestants should they appear before a council. Here, more than ever, does he emphasize the utter hopelessness of a reconciliation with the Papacy.

The death of Duke George of Saxony, who, from the time when he had uttered his curse at the Disputation of Leipzig, had been a steadfast enemy of the Reformation, immeasurably strengthened the Protestant cause. George had taken every precaution to keep his duchy from falling into the hands of his brother Henry, even deeding in his will the whole land to the emperor. But all in vain.

There was no power that could change the lawful order of succession firmly established by the Golden Bull. Henry succeeded quietly in 1539, and Luther was soon preaching from the chief pulpit in Leipzig. In this same year, too, Joachim II., elector of Brandenburg, having inherited the faith of his fugitive mother, publicly took the utraquistic communion. Two more powerful states were thus won, and North Germany assumed the exclusively Protestant form that it bears to this day.

No doubt the spread of the Reformation might have been greatly checked, had Charles been able to remain in Germany; but now as ever he was forced to pay regard to other interests, and to fight for the possession of his outlying territories. No sooner had he ended his Tunis campaign, fought under the heat of a tropical sun, than the death of his ward, Sforza, reopened the dispute with the French king as to the succession in Milan. To the astonishment and scandal of Europe, Francis went so far as to ally himself with Mohammedans, and in 1536 Turkish and French ships joined in a descent on the coast of Italy. All France was just then in a state of bitterness and wrath against the emperor, believing that he had hired an Italian to murder their dauphin, who had died under suspicious circumstances; the Parliament of Paris declared him guilty of felony and rebellion, and withdrew his Burgundian fiefs. After a campaign in France, in which the French devastated their own fertile plains of Provence so as to cut off the enemy's supplies, an unsatisfactory truce was patched up by the Pope. Threatened as he was with a renewal of the war, in dread of a new invasion on the part of the Turks, and having found a new enemy in the person of Duke William of Cleves-Julier, whose possessions extended like a wedge into the Netherlands, and who was on the verge of changing his faith, Charles could not think of resuming

Charles hampered by new enemies.

2 B

hostilities with the Protestants. On the contrary, he now made sincere efforts to bring about a peaceful settlement of the religious differences. Disputations were instituted to which the Pope, too, sent delegates. At Ratisbon, in 1541, great concessions were offered, but this very assembly brought more clearly than ever to light the fundamental antagonism of the two creeds. The Protestants could not and would not yield; they stood as yet upon a vantage ground from which neither storm nor siege nor gentle wiles could dislodge them; it remained to be seen if the task could be accomplished by internal dissensions and jealousies.

Religious
scruples of
Philip of
Hesse.

An incident relating to the private life of Landgrave Philip of Hesse proved in the end the cause of the downfall of the league armies. When the commander-in-chief goes over to the enemy, no matter what reservations he may chance to make, all hope of ultimate victory may safely be abandoned.

Philip's morals were not much worse than those of his contemporaries. But in his case dissoluteness was tempered by an excessive tenderness of conscience. It troubled him greatly that the class of evil-doers to which he belonged was included among those shut out by St. Paul's words from the enjoyment of the kingdom of heaven; only once in a period of several years had he, one of the official heads of the Protestant party, ventured to partake of the Holy Communion. He was anxious to reform, but in the way stood his antipathy to his wife, Christine of Saxony, who, to use his own words, he found "unfriendly, ugly, and ill-odored," which was probably a calumny; at all events, Christine proved most faithful to him in his worst adversities.

It had come to Philip's notice that nowhere in the Bible, neither in the Old nor in the New Testament, is bigamy declared a sin; no prophet had ever chidden a king or prince for the number of his wives; St. Paul had not included bigamists among those debarred from entering the kingdom of heaven. Moreover, the Wittenberg theologians themselves, in the case of Henry VIII. of England, had declared the taking of two wives to be preferable to divorce, on the express ground that it was not prohibited by divine law. Moved by these considerations, the landgrave determined to marry Margarete von der Sale, with whom he had already been all too intimate. The lady's mother gave her consent, but only on condition that the wedding should take place in the presence of noted theologians, and of an envoy of the Saxon elector. Luther and Melanchthon, when approached by Philip, were placed in a position of great perplexity: fatal as it would have been to alienate the powerful landgrave from their cause, they were powerless to argue with him on his own ground since Scripture gave no solution of the difficulty. They recognized what confusion was likely to ensue were bigamy to be generally allowed in the Christian church, yet were finally brought to acknowledge that Philip's was a case for a special dispensation, and to give their consent to the wedding with Margarete. Lest evil should come of it, they insisted that the whole matter be kept a profound secret, and that in the eyes of the world the new wife should be nothing but a concubine. On these terms the strange wedding, to which even Christine was brought by specious arguments and by various guarantees to give her sanction, took place in due form at Rothenburg-on-the-Fulda. Among those present were Bucer, Melanchthon, and a councillor of John Frederick, the Saxon elector. The ceremony was performed by Philip's court preacher, Melander, who is himself said to have been the husband of three wives. In the marriage instrument it was expressly stated that the landgrave took this step for the purpose of saving his body and soul. A few days later Philip wrote to Luther that " with a joyous conscience " he had again gone to Communion. He thanked the reformer for his kindly offices and sent him a cask of wine.

Evil results of Philip's marriage.

This marriage was, taken all in all, one of the most unhallowed incidents in the history of the Reformation. Where so many persons were concerned the facts could not be concealed, even though Luther, unswerving as he was in other matters pertaining to the truth, counselled a downright denial of everything. He urged that the " private yes remain a public no," compared this secret to a secret of the confessional, and said openly in a conference with Philip's councillors at Eisenach, " What is the harm of a good plump lie for the sake of the Christian church?" Well might the gentle Melanchthon fall ill from having this ill-odored matter thus dragged to the light. And the consequences of the marriage, and especially of its disclosure, were worse than even he could easily have foreseen. The Elector John Frederick refused to uphold Philip before the world, and stung him by his reproaches into fierce counter accusations. The landgrave, finally, at odds with his own party and fearing the severe punishment for bigamy which the law allowed, and which the emperor would otherwise have gladly inflicted, accepted Charles's overtures and became his friend and ally. All this at a time when swift and united action on the part of the Protestants was their only hope, — with France pressing for an alliance against the emperor, and Cleves-Julier only waiting for an invitation to join the Smalkald League ! Philip promised to prevent, and did prevent, all overtures to France, England, or Cleves ; he declared, indeed, that in case Charles directly attacked the league he should still consider him his enemy. The future was to show

what he could do and what he could suffer for the cause
he now abandoned; but the fact remains that he was a
traitor, — he kept secret his relations to Charles, — and
that he seriously injured the prospects of the league.

The elector of Saxony was unable, in spite of all his
efforts, to organize the proper sort of union or to make
proper preparations for common defence. Charles proceeded, without let or hindrance, to lead an army against
William of Cleves, whom he utterly vanquished, depriving
him of two provinces, Zutphen and Guelders, and forcing
him to put down Protestantism throughout his domains.
This Cleves expedition harmed the league in more ways
than one, for it opened the emperor's eyes to the disunion
and want of preparation of his enemies. For the moment,
indeed, a new war with France forced him into further concessions, but the time was not distant when he was to profit
by his knowledge. The Peace of Crespy (September 15,
1544) promised to be more lasting than any other of these
French treaties. By its terms Francis was to renounce his
Burgundian and Italian claims and not to join the Protestants; the Duke of Orleans, his son, was to marry a daughter
either of Charles or of Ferdinand, in the one case her dowry
to be the Netherlands, in the other Milan. In the following
year a long truce was entered into with the Turks, who
were meditating an attack on Persia. All was now quiet
on the borders of the empire; the field was clear, and
Charles could make final preparations for hunting down
his prey. He felt now that his honor was at stake,
that with the German Protestants so active he could no
longer maintain himself in Flanders, Spain, or Italy. As
his minister, Granvella remarked, it was time to show signs
of life; and Charles himself wrote that, dead or alive, he
wished to remain emperor in Germany. Luther's death,
September 18, 1546, coincided with the fading of the lucky

*Charles
rids himself
of his
enemies.*

star that had so long watched over the Protestants. Clouds
of every kind were gathering round them. The great
Catholic council, proclaimed as the fulfilment of the promise given so long before, met at Trent in 1545; but the
very wording of the summons was such that no friend of
Luther could think of responding. The Papacy had
begun to fortify itself by the aid of the Jesuits and the
Inquisition. The success of Calvin in France and Geneva
had roused the church to greater efforts than ever before.
" Hardly is it possible," wrote an Italian, " to be a Christian and to die in bed." It is true, the numbers of the
German Protestants were increased at this time by the
accession of the Palatinate, but that made Charles only
the more eager for war. Four out of the seven electors
were now in the ranks of his enemies, and endless opposition was foreboded in the diets.

Maurice
of Saxony
goes over to
Charles.

It was unfortunate for the Protestants that their period
of prosperity had lasted so long; Charles's policy of pro-
crastination had for once proved eminently successful. It
had lulled the league into a false security; it had worn
off the first great enthusiasm, and had given opportunity
for a new generation of princes to grow up who were
lukewarm in the cause. The emperor was quick to see
his opportunity, and, on one pretext or another, but especially by playing upon their greed and avarice, he drew
over to his own side the two Hohenzollern princes,
Albrecht Alcibiades of Culmbach and Hans of Küstrin,
and also Maurice, the son and successor of Henry, Duke
of Saxony. This latter prince, who was to play such a
part in the future of the Reformation, was a man in whom
splendid qualities were mixed with much weakness and
pettiness of character. He was selfish to the core, so
prone to excess in drinking as to excite comment and
blame even in that lax age, and so jealous of John Fred-

erick's power that the latter's acquisition of the bishopric of Magdeburg, on which Maurice had cast longing eyes, finally caused an irreconcilable quarrel. This drove Maurice into the emperor's arms; the immediate reward of his neutrality was to be the possession of Magdeburg and Halberstadt. But in a personal interview Charles intrusted to him, in addition, the duty of carrying out the imperial ban against the elector of Saxony, with the right to keep what lands he might conquer. He was not to be called upon in any way to oppress or injure the cause of Protestantism; in fact, Charles did his utmost to represent this war as having nothing to do with matters of faith. "These deserters will know well enough that it concerns their religion," he wrote to his sister, "but it will none the less be advantageous to assign to it another cause." So he seized on a quarrel which had occurred between the Smalkaldians and the Duke of Brunswick; declared that the former had broken the peace, and caused the eagles of the empire to be carried at the head of his troops, to show that the struggle concerned the welfare of the whole land. At the same time, in the interests of the Catholic religion, he gained the alliance of Pope Paul III.; who proclaimed a year of jubilee, agreed to send an army of 12,500 men to be used against "Protestants and Smalkaldians and every other kind of German heretic," and turned over to the imperial treasury one-half of the year's revenues of the church of Spain.

A prime condition for a successful campaign is that advantage be taken of the enemy's straits, and that no hesitation be shown when the chance offers of striking a decisive blow. If ever a war was lost through the blundering of leaders and advisers, it was this of the Smalkald League. The pacifically minded Protestant princes, who were thus thrown into a struggle for life and death, had had

Shortcomings of the Protestant leaders.

little experience with real war. The terrible Duke of Alva, whom Charles appointed general-in-chief of his forces, far outmatched them, one and all, in coolness and patience as well as in skill. Poor John Frederick of Saxony, with his burden of superfluous flesh and his slowness of decision and quickness of temper, was fitted for anything rather than a military command. Philip of Hesse had once written to his chancellor, "You know the elector; if he has not been asked to have a hand in a matter he is apt to throw chairs and benches into the mess so as to spoil it all." John Frederick proved now a very millstone around the landgrave's neck, while whatever harm was left undone was fully achieved and consummated by a timid and short-sighted war council that directed operations from Ulm.

Failure to capture Charles V. Charles V. was at this time at Ratisbon with a mere handful of men; the forces that he awaited were to come from the four quarters of Europe, — from Italy, the Netherlands, from Spain, and from Austria. The Protestants, on the other hand, had almost immediately a large army in the field. Ulrich of Würtemberg commanded 10,000 infantry and 700 horse; the imperial cities of South Germany, which in addition controlled the powder-mills and cannon foundries, placed in the field 12,000 men; Saxony and Hesse could be counted on for 21,000 more. Charles himself, in his own accounts, designates the failure of the Smalkaldians to attack him in Ratisbon as one of their fatal mistakes. Their general, Schärtlin von Burtenbach, was sent, instead, to try and intercept the papal troops; he was hampered by contradictory orders and was soon called home by the panic-stricken war council, which feared for the safety of Ulm. Even then, had Ratisbon been chosen as the rallying point for all the Protestant forces, the small imperial army might have been surrounded and captured; but the different

contingents united instead at Wörth, and Charles escaped
to Ingolstadt, which was far more capable of defence.   This
town was at last bombarded on four consecutive days, but
in a thoroughly unskilful manner, nine-tenths of the shots
failing to take effect.   The emperor moved quietly about
without fear for his personal safety, and is said to have
remarked sneeringly, "The Hessian shoots like a friend,
not like an enemy."   After exhausting their ammunition,
the Protestants withdrew.   From this time on Charles
himself took the initiative, and Count Buren, with reënforcements to the number of 22,000, managed to join him
without molestation.   By Alva's advice the imperialists
avoided pitched battles, while the Protestants made marches
and counter marches without fixed plan.

The two armies at last found themselves face to face a
little to the north of Ulm.   The power of resistance of the
league was fast wavering; the South German cities had
already expressed their unwillingness to make further pecuniary sacrifices, beginning, as they did, to realize what it
meant to lose their trade with Spain and Portugal.   At this
juncture the long-prepared blow fell on the electorate of
Saxony.   Maurice, with an army of his own subjects, aided
by Ferdinand and his Bohemians, had invaded John Frederick's territories.   The electoral dignity was formally transferred by the emperor from the old Ernestine house, which
for so long had been his enemy, to the Albertine or Dresden
branch of the Wettin family.   This gave the *coup de grâce*
to the Smalkald League.   John Frederick hastened home
to fight for his hereditary rights, though intending to return in the following spring.   Philip of Hesse, too, fore-
seeing an attack on his own lands, and hopeless as to the
general outlook, withdrew in turn with all his forces.

One by one the towns and minor princes then made
their submission, which the emperor accepted in the

*Maurice
invades
electoral
Saxony.*

haughtiest spirit. The envoys of Ulm were received in the little town of Hall, and in obedience to Charles's command, fell on their faces before him. "In Philip Buschler's back room," writes a simple chronicler, "he let them lie a quarter of an hour before he granted them his pardon." The terms of surrender for the members of the league were hard, though not crushing: large fines were imposed, and the money that their own side had failed to secure, now found its way into the coffers of the emperor.

The latter intended to taste to the full the sweets of victory, and remitted none of the tokens of subjection that he thought his due. Before this worn-out man, whose hair had grown gray in the struggle, whose face was ashen pale, and whose limbs refused him their obedience, envoys and princes were forced to kneel in a long line, and sue for mercy.

The last act of the Smalkald War remained to be played in Saxony. Here John Frederick showed himself in a new and more favorable light. All hesitation was gone for the moment, and he won the hearts, not only of his subjects, but of many of his enemies, by his energy and tact. The Bohemians who came from Prague refused to fight longer against a prince who partook of the body and blood of Christ with the same ceremonies as themselves. Maurice's own subjects came to the conclusion that, while on general principles the emperor's commands were to be obeyed, the latter had no right to say to his subjects, "Thou shalt call on dead saints," or "Thou shalt not believe in forgiveness of sins." John Frederick not merely recovered his own lands, but also occupied Magdeburg and Halle, and carried the war into the heart of the enemy's country by besieging Leipzig.

But already Charles, the Duke of Alva, and Maurice were on the march. No amount of personal courage could atone for the elector's real incapacity in military matters. He made no preparations for intrenching himself or for meeting the advancing force : he believed an idle tale according to which the emperor was dead and the Spaniards were marching behind his corpse. One misty Sunday at Mühlberg, after he had quietly listened to the usual sermon and then taken his morning meal, he suddenly found himself involved in the great disaster of his life. The sun broke through the fog and showed him the imperial army, five times the size of his own, on the opposite bank of the Elbe. His one thought was to reach the fortress of Torgau in his rear, although, according to the simplest rules of war, he should have left a detachment of his soldiers to dispute the passage of the river, until night could cover his retreat. He hoped instead to outdistance his pursuers in a fair chase. But some of the Spaniards swam the stream, seized his own boats, and hastily formed a bridge, while others found a ford by which seven horsemen abreast could pass over at a time. Charles V. crossed by this latter way. He was arrayed that day in the armor in which Titian afterward painted him. Don Luis d'Avila, grand master of the Knights of Alcantara, was with him at the time, and describes him on his brown Spanish courser, with " dark red, golden-fringed saddle-cloth, and a broad red gold-edged sash over his burnished breastplate ; on his head a German helmet, in his hand a short spear."

As twilight was coming on the vanguard of the imperial army overtook the Saxons. The latter made no attempt at serious resistance ; the infantry, trampled upon by their own horsemen, took to mad flight, and even such artillery as was ready to hand was not employed. Every man looked to his own safety, and John Frederick, less agile than the rest, was taken prisoner and handed over to the

The capture of John Frederick.

Duke of Alva. Blood poured down his face from the sabre-cut of a Hungarian hussar. Charles met him in this plight. "Most gracious lord and master," the elector began; but the emperor cut him short with, "Am I *now* your imperial master?" John Frederick hastily replaced the hat that he had doffed. "I am in your power; do with me as you will." Even the Spaniards and Italians were impressed by his dignity in the midst of ruin. Charles caused a court-martial to be held over his captive, who was at once condemned to death; but no one, least of all the unfortunate elector himself, thought it likely that the emperor would venture to carry out the sentence. In point of fact, after the surrender of Wittenberg, the last Saxon position of importance, Charles began to show John Frederick some consideration, feeling perhaps that he might need a counterpoise against the pride and presumption of Maurice. The prisoner was treated with some regard to his princely rank, and on the occasion of a visit which the emperor allowed him to pay to his wife, Spanish noblemen held the baldachin which protected him from the sun's rays. Charles himself went so far as to go to Wittenberg to pay his respects to the Saxon electress. It is on this occasion that the younger Granvella is said to have urged the emperor to have Luther's bones cast out of their grave. But Charles answered, "I war with the living, not with the dead."

By the terms of an agreement known as the "Wittenberg Capitulation," John Frederick renounced the electoral dignity and relinquished the greater part of all his lands, reserving for his sons only the districts west of the Saale, including Weimar, Jena, Eisenach, and Gotha. The demand had been made, that in religious matters he should submit to the emperor or to the Council of Trent, but this John Frederick stubbornly refused. Though he might never regain that liberty for which his wife Sybilla had so urgently pleaded on bended knee, he would hold fast to the Protestant faith as laid down in the Augsburg Confession. He had to agree, under watch and ward, to remain at the emperor's court.

The fate of Philip of Hesse was even harder than that of the elector; these princes were atoning bitterly for their long attitude of passive opposition. Charles demanded nothing short of unconditional surrender; he had every reason to mistrust the landgrave and meant to secure his person. He did concede to Joachim of Brandenburg and to Maurice of Saxony, who had undertaken the office of mediators, that Philip's imprisonment should not be perpetual. Maurice was Philip's son-in-law, and seems to have felt that, out of regard for himself, Charles would exact only nominal submission. Philip shared this impression, and came to the appointed place of meeting at Halle in an unduly hopeful frame of mind. His cheerful smile angered Charles V.; "All right, I will teach you to laugh," he said threateningly as the landgrave knelt before him. Philip was decoyed to a dinner at the quarters of the Duke of Alva, where Joachim and Maurice were also present. In spite of all that the latter could say and do, the landgrave was forced to remain a prisoner when the feast was over. Charles spared him no humiliations; he was kept in close confinement under the most irksome surveillance — even by night he was not left alone, and at every change of guard the heavy steps and clanking arms disturbed his rest. An attempt at flight drew down upon him further severities; the man who had been the head of a league of princes, as well as the hope of the Protestant party, was actually threatened with torture.

Charles V. stood at the zenith of his power; the year which was marked by the victory of Mühlberg witnessed

The arrest of Philip of Hesse.

Charles V.
triumphant
in all
directions.

also the closing of a long truce with the Turks, as well as
the death of two monarchs, Francis I. and Henry VIII.,
who had given the emperor much trouble. Two German
electorates, Saxony and Cologne, had just been filled
according to his wish; to a third, the Palatinate, the
Catholic Duke of Bavaria laid claim, — Charles needed
but to speak the word, and the Protestant incumbent
could be driven from his lands. The emperor's breast
swelled with the pride of success; he had risen in
his own estimation as well as in that of the world. At
the "armored Diet" of Augsburg, so called, perhaps, because of the imperial guard of ten thousand Spanish soldiers, he had but to dictate his terms. It was noticed
that when he dismissed the princes, he omitted his usual
custom of accompanying them to the head of the stairs.

The Diet in question arranged more than one matter to
Charles's liking. The rich province of the Netherlands was
recognized as a Hapsburg possession and as practically independent of the empire.   Money was granted for various
purposes ; while, with unheard-of foresight, a fund or treasure was levied to be used in case of emergency. Last, but
not least, all promised, through their mouthpiece, the elector of Mainz, to conform to the so-called "interim," — an
elaborate *modus vivendi*, or provisional settlement, of religious matters — which was to remain in force until all
questions at issue should be definitely settled by the long-
looked for council.

The "in-
terim."

The "interim" had been drawn up, with ostensible fairness, by a commission consisting of Catholics and Protestants alike; but prominent among the latter were men
who were renegades to their cause.   John Agricola, court
preacher to the elector of Brandenburg, had long been at
enmity with the Wittenberg faction. He was inordinately
vain, and boasted of having by his own efforts reformed

the Pope and converted the emperor. He had held a service of praise and thanksgiving in honor of the outcome of the battle of Mühlberg. He rejoiced, he said, that the sons of the fallen elector, at whose court there had been such immoderate feasting, should now have to eat out of tin dishes and drink out of tin cups.

It may be imagined to what sort of a document a man like this would set his hand. The "interim" has been well described as a "strait-jacket for German Protestantism." Communion in both kinds and the marriage of priests were allowed, and a few differences of doctrine condoned; but this was all. The people who for a quarter of a century had enjoyed religious freedom, were to be driven back under the care of Catholic bishops, while all the hated observances — the seven sacraments, the daily mass, the stated feasts, the adoration of saints — were to be revived. Yet only one of the Protestant princes, the comparatively insignificant Hans of Küstrin, had the courage to set his face resolutely against the introduction of the measure into his lands. Joachim of Brandenburg seems to have forged an interim of his own, and passed it off upon his subjects as the real one; Maurice of Saxony made an equally weak attempt to soften the imperial measures, and employed Melanchthon to draw up what is known as the Interim of Leipzig.

It is incomprehensible that a man once so fine, so loyal, and so brave as the Wittenberg theologian, could work in the interests of a time-server like Maurice; and perfectly gratuitous seem the insults which he saw fit at this juncture to heap on his dead friend and companion, Luther. He declared to a councillor of his new master that he would not oppose Maurice, whatever measures the latter might see fit to introduce; he would be silent and bear the inevitable. He had suffered, he said, an "almost impossible ser-

Melanchthon's disloyalty

vitude" under the violence of Luther. He denied having
helped to form a separate or schismatic church, and pointed
out how much, in his youth, he had loved the Catholic
ceremonies. It was the case of Peter denying his Lord:
when the letter was read to Charles V. in Augsburg, he
exclaimed, " You have him fast; see that you keep him!"

John
Frederick
in captivity.

Very different from the attitude of Melanchthon was that
of the imprisoned Elector, John Frederick. When ordered
to accept the "interim," or suffer the consequences, he
replied, that to subscribe to doctrines which ran counter to
the word of God, would be to commit the one unpardonable sin against the Holy Ghost. He bowed his head
meekly under the storm of the emperor's wrath. When all
his Lutheran books were taken away from him he said
with a smile " *Omnia mea mecum porto*," "I carry with
me all my belongings." That which he retained in his
memory no one could seize. His attendants were ordered
to give him no meat on fast days; his preacher was
driven from him. No friendly intercourse would have
been his whatever, had it not been for the faithfulness
of the painter, Lucas Cranach, who would willingly have
shared his captivity, and who constantly visited him.

Failure
of the
"interim."

If, in spite of the pusillanimity of the princes and the
dubious attitude of Melanchthon, the "interim" of Charles
V. never really gained acceptance, the reason lay, on the
one hand, in the attitude of the Pope, — who for political
reasons, as he frankly acknowledged, and mad with rage at
the murder of his son, Ferrante Gonzaga, for which he held
Charles responsible, refused his dispensation for even the
slight concessions that had been made to the Protestants, —
but primarily in the stand taken by the common people.
A new force, public opinion, had come to the front, and
had developed mightily in the course of a single generation. The masses greeted the "devilish interim" with

scorn and derision : after twenty years of pregnancy, wrote
a journalist of the time, the emperor has given birth to a
horrible monster — a three-headed dragon with a snake's
tail, a scorpion's sting, and the foot of an eagle or a frog.
The "Judas," Maurice, and Agricola and Melanchthon as
well, came in for perfect storms of abuse, while the Virgin
Mary was made to utter a fervid prayer for the downfall
of the house of Ahab and the death of its royal head.
The emissaries of "Pharaoh" or of "Herod," as the emperor was variously called, were glad enough as they passed
through the land to hide their eagles in order to escape
with their lives. Never had Charles V.'s inability to
make a rational use of his triumphs and successes been
more clearly marked than now. His insistence on the
acceptance of the interim, his severity to John Frederick
and the Hessian landgrave, and the tyrannical manner in
which he trod with his Spanish heel on the susceptibilities
of all his German subjects, brought about the catastrophe
that marks the last act in the long drama of his reign.
The crisis came when the emperor tried to secure the ultimate succession to the throne of the empire to his son,
Philip. One dreads to think what might have been the
fate of Germany had the husband of "Bloody Mary," the
future grim lord of Spain and the Netherlands, actually
achieved the imperial crown. Unfortunately for Philip,
however, he had as rival candidate the knightly and popular Maximilian, King Ferdinand's son. Even those
German princes who had but lately supported Charles, had
now had more than enough of his foreign and oppressive
ways. Already complaints had been made, that the presence of Spanish troops in Germany was contrary to law
and to the solemn promise made by the emperor in his
electoral compromise. Charles's stern reply had provoked
the remark from a Brandenburg envoy that the Germans

Revolt of the younger princes.

2 c

were being treated as actual slaves.   Early in 1552 a revolt
broke out, headed by Maurice of Saxony and by several of
the younger princes of the Hohenzollern family, among
them that Albert Alcibiades of Culmbach-Baireuth whom a
councillor of Ferdinand not unjustly called a "monstrous,
senseless wild beast."

Maurice's
grounds of
complaint.

Maurice's two private grounds of complaint were, first,
that, in spite of his constant intervention, his father-in-law,
Philip, had been kept in captivity for five long years, with
no immediate prospect of being set at liberty ; second,
that the reward for his own services to the emperor had
not come up to his anticipations.   He had contemplated
completely crushing the family of his cousin by taking away
all trace of sovereignty, and granting the sons of the former
elector a mere annuity ; but to this Charles had objected, requiring lands and offices for the young men.   Moreover,
Charles had reserved for himself the disposal of Magdeburg
and Halberstadt, the very bishoprics which had first caused
the quarrel between the two branches of the Saxon house.
Magdeburg, indeed, had held out against the emperor
himself ; it had stubbornly refused to follow the "interim,"
and Maurice had been empowered to raise an army and
carry out the imperial ban.   It was this that gave him his
opportunity against Charles.   Magdeburg submitted in
November, 1551 ; but the real terms were not the ones that
were made public.   Many of the garrison enrolled themselves under Maurice's own banner instead of under that
of the emperor, raising the numbers in the rebel army to a
total of thirty thousand.

Charles
in great
straits.

In danger of being penned up in Innsbruck by Maurice's
army, the emperor made the attempt to escape to the
Netherlands in a closed carriage, which ostensibly contained
a "lady going to Wildbad."   Finding the way beset, he
was obliged to return, but later succeeded in crossing the

Brenner to Villach. The Saxon soldiers entered Innsbruck
to find that their bird had flown. No particular deeds of
violence are recorded against them, save that they seized
the effects of the Spaniards, strutted round in their rich
garments, and amused themselves immoderately by addressing each other as " Don."

All the old phantoms of his past were now rising up to
terrify the sick and weary emperor, and to punish him for
all his pride. King Henry II. of France issued a pompous
manifesto in which he dubbed himself " vindicator of the
liberties of Germany and avenger of the captive princes."
The cover of the document bore the device of the old
Roman freedmen — a hat between two swords; the murderers of Cæsar had adopted it to show the purity of their
designs. Henry had signed an alliance at Chambord with
the rebel princes of Germany at the price, everlastingly
disgraceful to the latter, of a surrender of the towns of
Metz, Toul, and Verdun. The French king was to hold
them as " vicar of the Holy Empire," but Toul and Verdun
were never disgorged ; Metz only in our own day. At the
same time the Turks declared their truce with the empire
at an end, and the Pope recommenced those Italian intrigues which had for their purpose the aggrandizement of
his own relatives.

But Charles had, at last, learned how to yield to
the inevitable. Before leaving Innsbruck he had
sent his forgiveness to the former Saxon elector, setting
him free, but requesting that he remain in his vicinity,
to negotiate concerning the carrying out of the ban that
the emperor now intended to hurl at Maurice. Three
days after the latter's entry into Innsbruck a truce was
declared, and Ferdinand went as his brother's representative to a meeting of the princes held in Passau. The chief
demands here formulated were : the liberation of the land-

The Treaty
of Passau.

grave; the restoration of a "free empire of the German nation," within the limits prescribed by the Golden Bull; security against Spanish influence; and, finally, a perpetual peace between Protestants and Catholics. On the subject of this latter clause all real agreement was found to be impossible; Charles would not and could not accept it as it stood. He insisted that the peace should be merely temporary, to last until a Diet should take the matter in hand. He had not yet given up the hope of bringing the Protestants back to the fold; he considered that when he should do so, it would be time for him to retire forever from public life.

But even the temporary peace, as finally agreed upon at Passau, was a great gain for the cause of the gospel. For the first time an equal protection was to be granted to the adherents of the two faiths; neither party was to use violence against the other, and the "interim" was to be tacitly let fall. Assurance was given that the other reforms would be taken in hand at the coming Diet. The chief sufferer by the peace was John Frederick of Saxony. There was no longer any talk of dislodging Maurice, and although the former elector was allowed to return to Saxony, he was obliged to promise to keep the peace. He assumed the title of "elector born," and was received like a martyr and a saint. The magistrates, the clergy, the citizens, and the common people in "their armor or their best clothes" came out to meet him and to do him honor.

The release of Philip of Hesse.

Similar ovations awaited Philip of Hesse, whose case had come to be considered typical of imperial oppression and severity by nearly the whole nation. The poor landgrave, indeed, bowed and broken, was no longer in a condition to enjoy such scenes. He had been through the bitterest experiences of his life, and had even fallen so low as to offer by his own example to induce his subjects to accept the mass, if Charles would sign his release. His wronged wife, Christine, had repeatedly begged pardon for him on her knees in the presence of the emperor and his court. She had died before her prayer was answered, and the efforts of his friends had only served to increase the weight of Philip's misfortunes. We still have a letter of the emperor, written shortly after the attempt at flight, in which instructions are given for terrifying the captive into a confession: " Some one must whisper in the ear of the captain of the guard, without, however, directly threatening the landgrave with the rack." Through a course of such treatment as this, the former head of the Protestant party had become a changed man; his fire and energy were gone; he had taken to the study of the church fathers, and such a spirit of resignation had come over him, that, when parting with his jailer, he forced a fee upon him.

The Diet that was to settle the differences between the emperor and his princes, and between the Catholics and Protestants, was long delayed through the refusal of Margrave Albrecht Alcibiades of Culmbach-Baireuth to abide by the terms of the Passau Treaty. These terms were too lukewarm for him. He wished more decided results for the Protestant cause ; but above all no regard was paid to certain agreements which he himself had wrested at the point of the sword from a number of cities and bishoprics. While Maurice was marching on Innsbruck, Albrecht had been devastating Würzburg and Bamberg and other places in Franconia, and had calculated thus to increase his private fortune by about nine hundred thousand guldens.

There are curious facts about this revolt of " the monstrous, senseless wild beast." Albrecht began as the ally of the French; he made Worms and Spires and Treves and

The revolt of Albert Alcibiades.

Mainz, which he took in quick succession, do homage to Henry II. He wished to show the king, he said, that faith and fidelity were still to be found among the Germans. Yet, in a very short time he went over to Charles V., closed with him a most iniquitous alliance by which the Würzburg and Bamberg bishops were abandoned to their fate, and led an expedition against the French, in the course of which he captured the Duke of Aumale. Charles himself engaged in a fruitless siege of Metz, his last military undertaking. He refrained from interfering while Albrecht fought his way through Würzburg territory, laying in ashes three hundred castles and villages. He kept singularly in the background, too, when Ferdinand and Maurice, having met together in Eger, entered the lists for law and order. Perhaps, after all, this was to be the solution of his own difficulties — a war of the princes among themselves which should drive them at last to appeal to him as their arbiter.

Death of
Maurice.

Maurice and Albrecht, the former friends, met face to face at Sievershausen; in the moment of triumph Maurice fell, pierced by a bullet through the neck. He was, strange to say, mourned as a hero by the German nation, yet at the end of his checkered career he was only thirty-two years old! Albrecht still maintained himself; many Protestants in high positions, such as Maurice's own brother and successor, Augustus, still looked to him as the hope of their cause. But at last the bold condottiere, who had so long laughed the nation to scorn, met with his deserts. The ban of the empire was hurled at him by the Chamber Court, the Circles prepared to aid in carrying it out. He fled the country and soon died.

Abdication
of Charles
V.

This anomalous war had delayed, by nearly three years, the Diet that was to settle the religious differences. Charles V. had meanwhile wedded his son Philip to Queen Mary of England, and felt confident that in one direction, at least, no quarter would be shown to heretics. One by one he now divested himself of all his rights and jurisdictions; Philip received first the Italian possessions, with the title of king of Naples, then the throne of the Netherlands, and lastly the crown of Spain.

In the summer of 1554 Ferdinand was empowered to carry on the negotiations for peace with the German princes and cities, — in his own name as king of the Romans, not simply as representative of the emperor. The latter expressly declared that, for himself, conscientious scruples would prevent him now, as formerly, from making a lasting peace with the Protestants. This man, whose long reign had caused such warrings and upheavals to Germany, was at least consistent. True to the vow made at the Diet of Worms after the great hearing of Martin Luther, he had devoted his body, blood, life, and soul to wiping out this heresy. He had failed; he was ready to withdraw from the world and prepare for death. He vanished behind the walls of the Spanish monastery of St. Just, but even here the bane of his life pursued him — here in his immediate neighborhood the poisonous teachings of the Reformation took root.

Ferdinand, meanwhile, had opened that Diet of Augsburg, the rulings of which were to remain authoritative throughout the next two generations. It was here agreed that a peace should be established which might be "constant, enduring, unconditional, and forever and ever valid." Yet solidly as these men tried to rear their edifice, ponderous as were the chains by which they strove to bind posterity, the result was merely a series of faint-hearted half-measures by which, indeed, the final war of the two religions was to be staved off for sixty years, but which, in the end, were to bring upon Germany a scourge and a

The Diet of Augsburg.

visitation, longer and more deadly than has been suffered by any other nation of modern times.

The " reservatum ecclesiasticum."

So far as the Augsburg Peace had to do with the past, it was possible to come to a speedy agreement. The Protestants were allowed to continue in possession of all lands that, through change of faith in the holders, had come into their hands previously to the Treaty of Passau. But the far more difficult question, as to the future of the Reformation, still remained to be settled. Should the Protestants be allowed to continue taking away lands from the Catholics, and so, indirectly, from the empire? Some of the ecclesiastical holdings were regular principalities, owing allegiance to no one but the emperor. Might an archbishop of Cologne, for instance, by turning Protestant, keep his see, his vast possessions, and his electoral vote? Might he marry and support his family on his revenues, and, perhaps, hand them down to his descendants? The Papacy and the empire had once carried on a most desperate struggle on the matter of who should invest the bishops and abbots; the question was even more serious now. The loss of an election in any single bishopric, the conversion to Protestantism of an actual incumbent, meant the total loss of all claim to the holding.

These ecclesiastical principalities were, to quote a brilliant writer, the worst attributes of the empire's holiness. Wedged in among Protestant states, dependent politically on none of their immediate neighbors, but rather on a Pope who resided in Rome or an emperor who spent his time in Spain and Italy, they only served to perpetuate disunity in Germany, and to carry on every sort of foreign propaganda. Yet as the only possible way out of a hopeless situation, after a bitter conflict and after a deadlock in the Diet, the Protestants consented to a fatal compromise upon the subject. They allowed Ferdinand to promulgate a decree, known as the *reservatum ecclesiasticum*, or church's reservation, which declared that prelates who changed their faith should abandon their fiefs and dignities. It is true the Protestants declared at the time that they did not intend to be bound by the new measure, nor were they forced to give any guarantee or pledge in the matter. At the same time they insisted, but in turn without pledge from the Catholics, that in such "reserved" ecclesiastical holdings Protestant subjects should have free exercise of their religion. Ferdinand issued a "declaration" acceding to this demand, but in later years his party repudiated the work of their head.

A further unhallowed clause in this most disappointing peace document struck a blow at civic autonomy by requiring that, in the free imperial cities, religious affairs should remain in *statu quo*, and neither party attempt to drive out the other. In a different age such a provision would have been considered tolerant and wise; but in the present instance the fact remains that political ruin resulted for the cities. They were discriminated against in favor of the lords. The prerogative of determining the form of faith was taken away from them; no matter how hostile the one or the other party might be to all the aims and objects of the magistrates, the latter were forced by a higher power to quietly endure; they might not ostracize or expel their enemies.

Parity of religions in the towns.

So much for the shortcomings of the famous Augsburg Peace. The great achievement of the treaty was the establishment of the principle *cujus regio, ejus religio;* each potentate might establish the form of faith that was to prevail within his own domains. Full religious liberty to the individual this clause did not give, but every worshipper who did not choose to conform might move unmolested, with all his belongings, to more congenial territory.

"Cujus regio, ejus religio."

This then was the ending of the great revolt that had begun with the posting of Luther's theses. The chief loser had been the "Holy" Empire, which had renounced the claim to be the guardian of the universal faith; the gainers were the secular princes, no longer secular indeed, for now, as *summi episcopi*, or chief bishops, they had their people more than ever under their control.

CHAPTER XVI

THE ROMAN CATHOLIC REACTION

LITERATURE : Droysen, *Geschichte der Gegenreformation*, is the most readable of the accounts of this time ; Ritter, *Deutsche Geschichte*, 1555-1648, the most recent and complete. Ranke treats of the period in his book, *Zur deutschen Geschichte vom Religionsfrieden bis zum 30 jährigen Krieg*, also in his *Die römischen Päpste*. The best life of Ignatius Loyola is that by Gothein.

DURING the sixty years that followed the abdication of Charles V. and the signing of the religious Peace of Augsburg we look in vain for brilliant campaigns, for constitutional changes, for subtle diplomatic victories, for any episodes, in short, of more than local importance ; yet in view of the struggle with which it ended the period is one of great interest. The fluctuations in the mutual attitude of the two great religious parties ; the increase in the power of the one and the decrease in the power of the other ; the causes, finally, that led to their terrible locking of arms—form a guiding thread through what would otherwise be nothing but a dreary maze. The personalities of the emperors, of Ferdinand, of Maximilian II., of Rudolph II., and of Matthias need only concern us incidentally, and according as they affected the trend of religious affairs.

For twenty years following the Peace of Augsburg, the cause of the Protestants was very distinctly in the ascendent ; indeed, the Treaty of 1555 is considered by many to have saved the tottering cause of Catholicism from complete disaster and ruin. It is true that, of the seven elec-

Protestants and Catholics after the peace.

tors, four, — the emperor himself, as king of Bohemia, and
the three Rhenish archbishops, — still adhered to the old
church; but even here there were signs of a possible change.
The young heir to the throne, Maximilian II., is known to
have encouraged Protestant preachers in secret and to have
lent a sympathetic ear to the new doctrines; while Cologne,
easy of access to foreign influences, was, as we shall see,
more than once in danger of abandoning the old faith.

Heyday of
Protes-
tantism.
In the whole of North Germany only three secular
princes, Cleves, Grubenhagen, and Brunswick - Wolfen-
büttel, remained on the Catholic side; while of the so-
called imperial cities only one, Aix, could be counted on
with absolute certainty. In the south, too, although the
two largest states were in the strong hands of orthodox
Wittelsbachs and bigoted Hapsburgs, it proved impossible
to keep out the Lutheran teachings. There came a time
when the local diets of Bavaria as well as of Hungary,
Bohemia, and the five Austrian dependencies, sought and
obtained the right to receive the communion in both forms
at the hands of married priests. And worse for the church
than these out-and-out defections, was the demoralization
that spread and festered in its midst. Even after matters
had begun to mend and a board of visitors was sent to
inspect the ecclesiastical foundations, they reported that
in thirty-six Austrian monasteries there dwelt, in addition
to the normal quota of 182 monks, 135 women and more
than 200 children.

This was indeed the heyday of Protestantism; never
before or since has it been so near to becoming the universal creed of Germany. Not only was there present prosperity, but all the hopes of the future seemed about to be
realized. The youth of the land no longer sought their
instruction in Catholic institutions; the universities of
Vienna, Ingolstadt, and Cologne were forced at times to

close their theological faculties for lack of students and
professors, whereas Witttenberg and Jena, Marburg and
Heidelberg, were thronged by eager multitudes.

One would think that at least in the bishoprics the old
faith would have been strongly guarded, but such was not
the case. All the smaller sees in North Germany, with the
exception of Hildesheim, were now annexed without difficulty by the neighboring princes, who exerted such influence
on the canons, with whom lay the right of election, that in
almost every case Protestant "administrators" were chosen
in place of Catholic bishops. These canons, or chapter
monks, were for the most part younger sons of princes and
counts; only by a miracle could they have escaped infection
from the doctrines that now pervaded the upper classes.

In one quarter alone were the efforts to keep out the
Reformation in part successful. The three ecclesiastical
electorates of Mainz, Treves, and Cologne formed a nucleus
in the west for the surrounding districts, and kept a watchful eye on a whole circle of bishoprics, such as Worms and
Spires and the Westphalian sees of Münster, Osnabrück,
and Paderborn. It was evident that in these regions, which
were of strategic importance as well, because of their near-
ness to the Netherlands and France, the struggle, when it
came, was bound to be fierce. Would Catholics or Protestants win the day?

The West-
phalian
bishoprics.

Pending this struggle, however, developments were going
on within the inmost fold of each of the rival parties, which
made the issue much more doubtful than it would have
been in the first few years after the signing of the Augsburg Peace. Forces were at work which tended inevitably
to disintegrate the Protestant organization and to strengthen
and unify the Catholics.

Whatever the merits of John Calvin as a reformer, there
is not the slightest doubt but that the introduction of his

Calvinism
as an ele-
ment of
discord.

teachings into Germany wasted the energies and ruined
the political prospects of the adherents of the Reformation.
There had been none of this during Luther's lifetime;
whatever intercourse the aging Wittenberg reformer had
held with the young lawyer of Picardy had been of a
friendly nature. Calvin considered Luther a great and
good man, though, strange as such an attitude may seem
in the stern tyrant of Geneva, he saw reason to regret the
great German's intolerance. So slight were the differences
of doctrine between the two men that one marvels at the
importance they later attained; on the matters of justification by faith and the authority of the Scriptures they were
completely united, while, with regard to the real presence,
Calvin was far from adopting the extreme attitude of
Zwingli. For him Christ was actually present, but in a
spiritual, not in a bodily form. It is true he considered
belief in predestination the most important thing in the
world, and callously drove people into exile for presuming
to doubt it; but Luther, too, held this doctrine, although
making it much less prominent.

Calvin's
Institutes.

Calvin first came to the fore in connection with the persecutions which Francis I. of France, at the very time when
he was in league with the Protestants of Germany, inflicted
on the adherents of the same faith at home. In order to
appease the Germans, it was given out that the victims who
had gone to the stake belonged to the universally hated
sect of the anbaptists. It was to refute this idea that
Calvin wrote his most famous work, the *Institutes of
Religion*, which he sent with a long dedication to the king.
The latter, he declared, could not possibly know the real
character of the faith he was attempting to crush; far from
being an innovation, it was as old as the church fathers;
and he went on to give a complete statement of all the
Protestant tenets. The book of this mere boy soon ob-

tained great celebrity, going through many different editions. It is a curious fact that at the end of his life he had not altered a single view that might fairly be considered of the least importance. As much could not be said for Luther, while as to Melanchthon, his was the constancy of a weather-vane.

Calvinism would have been less dangerous for Germany had there not been connected with it a certain bareness and severity in outward observances that at once stamped its followers for what they were. Luther had been genial and human, had enjoyed the pleasures of life, and appreciated the beauties of nature and of art. The Genevan reformer, on the contrary, was stern and majestic, thinking always of God's justice and of His wrath. Although the scene of his activity was one of the loveliest spots on earth, there is never a word in its praise in his many letters. His mind was on the terrors of death and hell. By the sin of Adam all men had incurred damnation; for the glory of His righteousness God intended in all, save a few arbitrary instances, to see that the sentence was carried out. The houses in which Calvinists worshipped reflected this inward severity; altars and organs and pictures were banished from sight. Attractive surroundings were not required for a religion whose founder could cause a child to be beheaded because it struck and cursed its mother, and a woman to be scourged for singing a secular song to a psalm tune. During the term of Calvin's absolute power in Geneva, the usual punishments had been burning and strangling and tearing of the flesh with pincers. Teachings of Calvin, after marvellous successes in France and the Netherlands, found German converts in the Rhine Palatinate; not so much among the people, as among the learned doctors who taught theology in the halls of Heidelberg University. The point of chief im-

The Calvinism of the Elector Palatine.

portance, however, was the winning over of the Elector Frederick III., a man of very decided character, and the most sympathetic figure in all this period of German history. He protested, indeed, against being called a Calvinist, rejecting some of the more extreme dogmas, and maintaining that he went no further than the Augsburg Confession sanctioned and allowed.

Melanch-
thon's two
versions of
the Augs-
burg Con-
fession.
The ultimate blame for the ensuing complications rests on the head of the gentle Melanchthon. Since drawing up the first text of the Confession, in 1530, that timid theologian had changed his views on many points, and had, consciously or unconsciously, approached nearer to the standpoint of Calvin in the controversies regarding freedom of the will, the necessity of good works, and, most fatal question of all, the real presence. In a second version of the Augsburg Creed, issued in 1540, he had changed the wording of the all-important Article 10, so as to give it a broader and more comprehensive form. The change was a slight one[1] and seems, in the ensuing years, to have escaped the notice of every one save the wary Palatine elector, who saw that the amended form would leave room for the introduction of his favorite doctrine as to the spiritual presence of Christ in the Eucharist. Already doctrines preached by Melanchthon had been bitterly opposed by one Flaccius, called Illyricus, who enjoyed the protection of the dethroned Saxon line. Melanchthon's patron was the Elector Augustus, the coarse, stubborn, and unintelligent successor of Maurice.

In 1561, a year after Melanchthon's death, a number of princes came together at Naumburg to pass measures

---

[1] The original rendering was, " Quod corpus et sanguis Christi vere adsint et distribuantur vescentibus in cœna Domini." The revised version ran, " Quod cum pane et vino vere exhibeantur corpus et sanguis Christi vescentibus in cœna Domini."

which should heal all party strife, and once more to swear
a common allegiance to the Confession of Augsburg. It
was then that the matter of the two versions began to assume overwhelming importance. Frederick III. of the
Palatinate, knowing well what he was asking, urged that
the second edition be the one to receive the recognition of
all. Carefully he refrained from mentioning the real
grounds on which he based his request, simply declaring
that the earlier wording had dealt too gently with transubstantiation. Every prospect of success attended his plan
of gaining over the Naumburg assembly. The man who,
more than all others, posed as the guardian of orthodoxy,
the Elector Augustus of Saxony, had long given the preference to the second version, considering it as merely a more
careful elaboration of the Lutheran teachings. But, before
the final vote of adherence was cast, the theologians who
were present had managed to put on their guard their
respective lords. A majority of the latter signed the version of 1530, but, in order to spare the Saxon elector, appended a preface, in which they insisted on the real identity
of the two renderings. Here was a triumph for Frederick
III.! If the versions were identical, there was room for
his interpretation of Article 10, and he published now the
famous Heidelberg catechism, which has since come to be
accepted by the Calvinists, or "reformed," in all lands of
the earth. When the matter at last was fairly ventilated,
the rest of the princes who had been at Naumburg cursed
their own ignorance and made every effort to change the
obnoxious "preface"; but to this the Palatine elector, as
one of the original signers, refused his consent. Thus the
assembly at Naumburg, far from healing the Protestant
dissensions, had led to a new breach. Frederick III. came
to be looked upon as a black sheep within the fold.

Nor was this to remain a simple question of religious

Maximilian II. and the Palatine elector.

opinion, for a most vital issue was involved. The Augsburg agreement of 1555 had applied only to upholders of
the "Confession"; could Calvinists be held to belong to
this category? The Emperor Ferdinand had declared
in the negative; what the attitude of his son and successor, Maximilian, would be was a matter for much speculation. Maximilian had played a deep and double game,
often expressing his sympathy for the Protestants. At his
accession he took the communion in both forms, but not
until he had first obtained a secret dispensation from the
Pope. We know now that political schemes outweighed all
religious considerations. He aimed at the throne of Spain
for his descendants, if not for himself, and hoped to achieve
it by a series of family alliances, for which papal dispensa-
tions might well be needed. The only direct heir of Philip
II. was the feeble Don Carlos, and him Maximilian intended
to succeed. To favor the Protestants would have meant
to lose the good will of the Spanish king, as well as of the
Pope of Rome.

Spirited defence of the Palatine elector.

During the negotiations preliminary to his first Diet,
Maximilian had asked the three ecclesiastical electors what
course to pursue against Frederick of the Palatinate. They
advised him to ask the Protestant princes formally whether
they still considered the elector as holding to the Augsburg
Confession. The princes, for their own part, had already
sent the Saxon elector to demand of Frederick a profession
of faith. The latter showed at this juncture much firmness and decision. He pointed out the dangers of a schism;
the theological differences might be discussed at another
time, for the present concord was necessary against emperor
and Diet combined. None the less the princes were won
for the publication of an imperial decree, accusing Frederick
of breaking the Augsburg Peace, and ordering him to abolish his Calvinistic innovations. He was then summoned

before the emperor, and the decree was read to him in the presence of a number of princes. He was wounded to the quick at the desertion of his colleagues, and declared himself the victim of rank injustice. His defence of himself, from a different standpoint, calls strongly to mind the great oration of Luther at the Diet of Worms. He began by complaining that sentence had been passed on him without even such trial as might be claimed by the worst criminal. With regard to the religious charge, he would have their highnesses know, that in matters pertaining to the salvation of souls, he could bow to no master save God alone. Had he erred in any way, he was willing to be confuted from Holy Writ: if his imperial Majesty would like to try, a Bible was easy to procure. "Should this my most humble confidence play me false, should stern measures be taken against me on account of this, my Christian and honorable declaration, I shall console myself herewith: my Lord and Master Jesus Christ has given to me and to all his faithful followers a sure promise, that all that I lose for the sake of His name or of His honor shall be repaid to me in the other world a hundred-fold. I commend myself most humbly to the mercy of thy imperial Majesty."

As a result of the fearless attitude of Frederick, the first great attack against Protestant unity proved a signal failure. Maximilian had expected for a moment to have things all his own way. He had anticipated a declaration from the princes, not only casting off the Palatine elector, but sweepingly condemning all Calvinists and "reformed." Under the influence of the elector's eloquence an answer was returned to him that frustrated all his hopes. It was acknowledged that differences existed with regard to the communion doctrine, but these would be settled at a future meeting of theologians; there was no ground as yet for excluding Frederick from the privileges of the Augsburg

The bigoted Elector Augustus of Saxony

Peace. The Protestants themselves, and no one else, were to judge who belonged to their confession. The decree against the Elector was not valid ; it had been signed by but a few of the princes and had only been intended as an admonition. As to the general condemnation of Calvinists, it was flatly refused.

There the matter might have rested, had it not been for the jealousy and ill-feeling of Augustus of Saxony against the Palatine elector. Far worse for the Protestant cause than any harm ever inflicted by his brother Maurice, was the constant frustration, on his part, of beneficent and necessary measures. Everything tended to nourish his hatred of Frederick : the latter's "apostasy," as he called it, his constant opposition to the emperor, his efforts to force concessions by refusing help against the Turks. Augustus himself was so placed that he had everything to hope from the friendship of Maximilian. Having annexed all bishoprics within reach, he wished no further changes to be made, and frowned harshly on Frederick's great endeavor to make the Turkish assessments, as well as the recognition of Maximilian's son Rudolph, dependent on the abolition of the hated "church's reservation." Not to fight the Turks meant to risk his own boundaries. For the Palatinate, on the contrary, the Turks had no terrors, and as to church lands, there were golden opportunities for further annexations. Then, too, generous and warm-hearted as he was, Frederick would like to have helped, and did help, the Calvinists of France and of the Netherlands. He sent his son with a small army to fight with Condé and furnished subsidies to William of Orange, besides intercepting Spanish supplies on their way down the Rhine to the Duke of Alva. As for the Saxon elector, though urged not only by the Palatinate, but also by Würtemberg, Hesse, and Baden to join in a general Protestant union, which was to include the

Huguenots, he declared, with a sneer at Frederick, that he would have nothing to do with Calvinists, and actually went so far as to offer the emperor a part of his troops to be used against the Dutch by Philip II. Verily, a meaner rôle than that played by Saxony in all the great crises of German history, from the Reformation to the War of 1866, would be difficult to invent or imagine.

When, indeed, Alva's administration in the Netherlands became the worst reign of terror the world has ever seen; when the inhabitants of cities were condemned as a unit to death, and the highest nobles in the land were sent to execution; Augustus scented danger for himself, and became more friendly to Frederick, joining in a request to the emperor to endeavor to obtain the withdrawal of the Spanish troops. To the joy of the French and the Dutch, a marriage was even arranged between Frederick's son and the daughter of Augustus. As to Maximilian, he did for a moment, in consequence of the representations of the electors, rise to the height of sending his brother as an advocate of peace to Spain. But the moment was critical; Don Carlos had just died, and, even before the answer came, Maximilian sent another envoy to express his approval of whatever course the Spanish king might choose to pursue.

Maximilian the friend of Spain.

When, in October of the same year, Philip lost his French wife, the emperor, with indecent haste, sent to offer him the hand of his daughter. He hoped to arrange two other unions between Philip's daughters and his own sons.

Such being Maximilian's attitude, nothing remained for the electors and princes but to enter the war on their own account or to remain disinterested spectators. The Palatinate advocated the first of these alternatives, Augustus of Saxony, the second. The friendly relations between

Elector Augustus and the crypto-Calvinists.

these two men, which had culminated in their alliance by marriage, was of short duration. A renewal of dogmatic differences — this time between two parties in Saxony itself — aroused to a white heat the mistrust and hatred of Calvinism which Augustus had always cherished. His was a narrow and bigoted mind, and so sluggish as to be peculiarly open to deception.

The elector prided himself on his strictly Lutheran orthodoxy; but at his own universities of Wittenberg and Leipzig there existed a party which adhered to Melanchthon's later views. They were variously called: Philippists from Melanchthon's own name, synergists because they differed from Luther on the question of good works, and crypto-, or secret, Calvinists. They dissimulated and cloaked their doctrines, hoping in time to win over the elector, and, with his aid, finally to prevail. They laid regular siege to him; their agents filled his palace; his physician, Caspar Peucer, his privy councillor, Craco, his court-preacher, Schütz, were all in the plot, constantly seeking to insinuate their ideas and to undermine his faith, yet all the while assuring him of their loyalty to Luther's teachings.

But another court faction, headed by the electress, developed a keen scent for heresy, and so worried Augustus that he called upon his theologians to give a "good Lutheran proof" of their views. They drew up the "Dresden Consensus" which delighted the elector, who banished 111 persons for refusing to affix their signatures. But the play was growing dangerous; news came that at the Calvinist university of Heidelberg the "Consensus" had been joyfully adopted. Again the theologians were called to account, but once more, by involving themselves in a web of lies, they managed to disarm suspicion.

The whole plan to Calvinize the Lutheran citadel was

at last laid bare by the interception of a letter; house visitations then furnished a number of irrefragable proofs. In some of the documents were disrespectful allusions to the elector's dulness of perception, while others contained warnings against the cleverness of " Mother Anna," Augustus's wife. The duped tyrant raged and stormed, and wreaked such vengeance on the " fat, jaundiced rogue, Dr. Craco, the patron and instigator of all the rest," that, after being put to torture on the rack, he died almost immediately. Another person concerned was kept in lifelong captivity.

Flushed with the pride of victory at having routed this band of heretics, the elector caused a coin to be struck off, in which none other than he himself is represented as holding a scale where Christ on one side, waving the banner " omnipotence," weighs down four theologians with " reason" for their device. The gaping Dresdeners were treated to a display of fireworks, and were shown in flaming outlines their own valiant lord, as Hercules, slaying the Hydra of Calvinism! As a test of orthodoxy new articles were drawn up, which were supposed to combine the whole essence of the true teachings of Luther, of Melanchthon, and of the Augsburg Confession. When the Wittenberg professors refused to sign them, they were arrested and sent into exile.

With Frederick III. Augustus's ways had long since parted; he now openly repudiated him as a companion in the Augsburg Confession. Political and other causes served to widen the breach. William of Orange, who had married the Saxon elector's niece, now cast her off on the just ground of adultery, and, as fate would have it, took for his new wife Charlotte of Bourbon, the ward of Frederick and an inmate of his palace.

What the disunion of Saxony and the Palatinate meant

The breach between Saxony and the Palatinate.

for the Protestant cause, was soon to become apparent. Augustus drew closer to the emperor, visited him at Vienna, and received him at Dresden,—on which latter occasion the Saxon courtiers went so far in their servility as to attend mass with their imperial guest. Two golden opportunities arose in 1576 for forcing Maximilian to confirm the Protestant privileges — the emperor expressed on the one hand a keen desire to have his son Rudolph chosen king of the Romans, and, on the other, sent an urgent appeal for aid against the Turks, whose Sultan he had irritated by scheming for the crown of Poland. Frederick III. had drawn up a list of reforms of inestimable importance to his party; there is not the least doubt but that their acceptance could have been enforced. But Saxony willed otherwise. Thanks to Augustus, without a single counter concession, the splendor-loving but moody, arbitrary, and intensely bigoted Rudolph II. was chosen king, while, as to the reforms, and particularly in the matter of the confirmation of Ferdinand's " declaration," the elector had instructed his envoys first to support, and then to vote against, the measures of his own colleagues. He believed "that the Turkish aid should be granted to the emperor even though the latter should wish to revoke the whole religious peace."

In their respective hours of triumph and discouragement Maximilian and Frederick died. The latter's elder son, to whom fell the larger share of the Palatinate, bent his chief energies to the restoration of Lutheranism; five hundred preachers and professors and four hundred students were banished from the land. But the little principality of Pfalz-Lautern, which fell to the younger son, John Casimir, grew to be the refuge and the centre for liberal Protestantism. The "gymnasium illustre" at Neustadt became what Heidelberg had once been, and John Casimir kept in touch with all the powers of Europe in which the "reformed" religion had taken root.

That this distinction between "reformed" and "Lutheran" has perpetuated itself down to our own day was essentially the achievement of Augustus of Saxony. Policy had induced him to betray his party in favor of the emperor; hatred of Calvinism now led him to start a project for revising Luther's doctrines, and reducing all Protestant Germany to a single iron norm of faith. In February, 1576, he had called a meeting of his theologians at Schloss Lichtenberg on the Elbe, and had induced them to condemn Melanchthon's *corpus doctrinæ* and the later edition of the Augsburg Confession. They had advised him at parting to "borrow" and establish at Wittenberg a certain Dr. James Andreæ, chancellor of Tübingen, who had recommended himself in Saxony through a writing on the "ten doubtful points which have arisen among . . . followers of the Augsburg Confession." On the arrival of the great authority a meeting was held at Torgau, and a new *corpus doctrinæ* compiled, which included the Bible, the three creeds, the original Augsburg Confession, and its apology, as well as Luther's Smalkald Articles and his two catechisms. Among the notes and explanations, Andreæ managed to smuggle in a new favorite doctrine of his own, on the "ubiquity" of Christ's body; and to this he clung, although in the whirl of infinite wrangling and opposition the "Torgau Compilation" had to give place to the "Bergen book" which was the basis for the final "Concordia."

Efforts of Augustus to establish a norm of orthodoxy.

This "Bergen book," which not only condemned but "damned" all Zwinglians, Calvinists, and Melanchthonites, was now imposed on all Saxon subjects almost at the point of the sword. Andreæ was intrusted with the task of gaining signatures; and, if we may judge by a previous experience, in which he called his opponents "hogs," "fools," "dogs," and "asses," his methods were not such as to make him popular.[1]

In spite of the most violent opposition in various quarters, Augustus gained his object of imposing his "Concordia" on the greater part of Germany. By the year 1580 eighty-six estates, headed by the three Protestant electors, had introduced it into their lands. Eight thousand theologians had affixed their signatures.

The "harmony of creeds." The schism with the Calvinists was now irrevocable. The glorious hope which John Casimir of Pfalz-Lautern had so long cherished, of uniting the German church with that of the other countries of Europe, was forever frustrated. Of his own accord, John Casimir now called upon the European sovereigns to send envoys to a meeting at Frankfort. Poland and Hungary, as well as England, France, and the Netherlands, responded with alacrity, while Switzerland and Bohemia expressed their sympathy with the plan of founding a union. The final result of Pfalz-Lautern's efforts was the *Harmony of Creeds of the Orthodox and Reformed Churches*, which was published in 1581. It condemned nobody, left room for individual differences, and yet served as a strong bond; but none the less hopeless was the general outlook. Some German princes, like the Landgrave of Hesse, refused to be bound by either formulation; while the adherents of the Concordia withdrew into themselves and closed their eyes to the dangers which threatened to overwhelm all opponents alike of the Catholic Church. The latter institution had begun by this time to glory in this name of "Catholic." It saw in the dissensions of its enemies its

[1] A parody of the Lord's Prayer is extant which, as an expression of contemporary scorn, may well be inserted here : "Almighty James who art in the heaven of devils, dishonored be thy accursed name ; thy ubiquitous kingdom be destroyed ; thy devilish will be done neither here nor at Wittenberg nor at Leipzig. . . . Lead us not into thy accursed formulation, but deliver us from thy sacrilegious book !"

own opportunity of becoming universal. Inch by inch it had been gaining ground, while the Protestants had been wasting their energies in fruitless quarrels. The very Reformation which had robbed it of half its adherents had intensified its energies and awakened its dormant forces. In its recent defeats the Roman church had never really acquiesced. A private report drawn up in 1566, at the Pope's request, and concerning the validity of the Augsburg Peace, had declared that that instrument determined what actually was, not what ought to be, the case. "Properly interpreted, it remains in force only until the Catholics shall have increased in power and shall have roused themselves to the point of redemanding all their rights."

The two great levers that raised Catholicism from its slough of despond after the great blow struck by the Reformation, were the counter reform decrees passed by the Council of Trent, and the activity in carrying them out of the "Company of Jesus," or Order of Jesuits.

The early sessions of the Council of Trent.

The great council which opened in the southernmost town of Germany in the year 1545, and dragged its slow length along, like that earlier assembly of Basel, for eighteen years, was ostensibly called in fulfilment of a demand reiterated by the Protestants themselves for nearly a generation. The mere idea of it had been a constant bugbear to the church, and fine observers have noted that every time the subject was seriously broached, the price of ecclesiastical benefices went down in the market. As the result of pressure brought to bear upon him in various ways, Pope Pius IV. had agreed to call the assembly together, and to have it held on German ground; but there his forced complacency ended. The wording of the summons sent to the Protestants precluded every chance of acceptance on their parts; they were invited before a judgment seat, not

to a place of disputation. Nor was the German nation
fairly represented even by its Catholic bishops. Fearing
for the safety of their sees should they be so long absent,
the vast majority of them remained at home. The council,
therefore, was mainly composed of Spanish and Italian prelates, subservient tools of the Pope, — who was allowed to
summon whom he pleased, and did not hesitate, when it
served his purpose, to nominate and consecrate men who
would be likely to support his cause. "Daily," wrote the
emperor's envoy at the time of the third session, "daily we
watch the arrival of worn-out old men and of bishops in
their first youth, whose knowledge reaches only just so far
that they invariably see in reform a grave detriment to the
papal dignity."

It was very evident from the beginning that the Catholics lacked not only the power, but even the wish, to conciliate; they began with an uncompromising enunciation of
their own dogmas, and a positive condemnation of those of
the Protestants. The tradition of the church was declared
equal in authority to the words of the Bible; binding force
was attributed to the acts of former popes and councils. In
one of the later sessions Pope Paul III. was even allowed
to proclaim the necessity of his own consent to the validity
of any future decree, while justification by faith — a doctrine that was the very mainstay of Protestantism — was
expressly declared heretical.

The Emperor Charles V. showed no interest in the council, politically at odds as he was with various popes. His
brother Ferdinand, in whose favor, in 1555, he practically
resigned the imperial power, contented himself for a long
time with mild suggestions, which showed a misplaced reluctance to wound the feelings of Pius IV. He was a just, conscientious prince, and had shown much tact in dealing with
the Protestants, although a man of more force would have

avoided the wretched slurring over, the temporary make-
shifts, that were to lead so directly to the Thirty Years' War.
Ferdinand would gladly have seen certain privileges accorded: the use of the cup for the laity at the celebration of
the Holy Communion, the marriage of priests, a modification
of the excessive fasting. He wished such change in the
church laws as would prevent the wholesale excommunications that had so often fallen on his Austrian subjects;
he believed in the principle that councils were above popes.
He would like to have seen this particular council take
into its own hands the reform of the head and members of
the ecclesiastical hierarchy.

Ferdinand came gradually to be thoroughly disgusted at
the small results brought forth by deliberations extending
over so many years. After the sweeping condemnations of
the first two sessions, he tried to have the third held elsewhere
than at Trent, in order that it might be considered an entirely new council, unbound by the trammels of the past.
In this he failed, but he found a way to exert more influence on the course of events, and with this end in view
moved his court to Innsbruck, so as to be near the scene of
action. In common with France and Spain, he brought
forward a new set of demands, to which the council was
forced to listen. It is true the Pope made a bold move,
which, for a time, disconcerted his opponents. He carried
the war straight into the enemy's country, by threatening
to bring forward a motion for freeing the whole clergy from
the duty of paying secular taxes or appearing in state
courts. Ferdinand knew that this was no mere idle menace,
and showed himself more conciliatory. The end of the
matter was a compromise, in which some of the emperor's
demands were tacitly withdrawn.

But even the reforms that remained, and were now put
through, were of world-wide importance for the future of

The re-
forms of
the third
session.

the church. The whole ecclesiastical system was purged and rectified; all the different bonds of order and discipline were drawn more tightly, and at the same time that the church became more narrow and conservative, it grew purer, more holy, and much more powerful. The authority of the Pope, which had at one time been threatened by a proposed doctrine concerning the divine origin of the episcopacy, was immeasurably strengthened. It was distinctly decreed that he was to be looked upon as the vicar of God on earth, and supreme ruler of all bishops. His word was to be above the dictum of councils. To him was to belong not only the sole right of interpreting the Scripture, but also, until the convening of another such assembly as the present, of interpreting the decrees of Trent. The next general council, when it did finally meet in the year 1870, ably supplemented the work of its predecessor by declaring the Pope infallible.

As for the bishops, they were to be chosen henceforward from men carefully trained in ecclesiastical seminaries; their sees were no longer to be mere sinecures, but each incumbent was actually to remain in residence. Only by special papal dispensation could plurality of holdings be allowed. On entering office, the bishops were to swear an oath of allegiance to the Pope. In common with all Catholic preachers and teachers throughout Christendom, they were solemnly to promise obedience to the Trent decrees. The duties of the clergy were clearly defined, and provisions were made for a system of visitation not dissimilar to that which had proved successful among the Protestants. Steps were taken toward the education of the masses, and the strictest censorship was decreed with respect to every kind of printed production, whether old or new.

Such was the programme for the counter reformation in the Roman Catholic church. All dallying with Protes-

tantism was forever at an end. As dead branches are lopped
off from a tree, so, by the decrees of the council, these heretics had been separated from the true communion of saints.
No hope of reconciliation, no danger of further infection
from noxious doctrines. The purified church could now
proceed to fix its own usages and to live its own life.

The task of the Jesuits.

The decrees of Trent once passed, it remained to see that
they were carried out in all the lands of the civilized world.
This was the mission, this the chosen task of that body of
devoted men who, already while the council was holding
its earlier sessions, had been gathering round the remarkable Spaniard, Ignatius Loyola.   The wonderful influence
exerted by the Jesuits, the tenacious hold that they obtained
in all quarters of the globe, is a direct result of the completeness and adaptability of the order's organization and
of the spirit breathed into it by the genius of its originator.
As compared with the old Franciscans and Dominicans, the
" Company of Jesus " possessed the advantage of having a
limited task and perfectly defined goals ; it was therefore
able to array its forces so that every unit filled its place.
No drones were to be allowed in this busy hive ; men might
enter other orders for the laudable purpose of saving their
own souls, but, according to Loyola's distinct assertion,
this was not sufficient reason for becoming a Jesuit.   If
the Dominicans were the watch-dogs of the Lord, the followers of Ignatius were to be his sleuth-hounds ; they were
to chase and hunt down their fellow-men, and drive them,
willing or unwilling, into the fold.

In his own person Loyola had descended the whole scale
of life's experiences. As a proud young Spanish knight,
with no thought but for his own honor and pleasure, he
had been injured while defending Pamplona against the
French in 1521.   A bone had been badly broken, and,
when the fracture healed, the youth found, to his dismay,

The early training of Ignatius Loyola.

that one leg was so much shorter than the other as to pre-
clude the possibility of riding a horse.   Twice, in the vain
hope that it would heal differently, the joint was torn
asunder and reset; for weeks the knight lay on a bed of intolerable anguish.   He called for romances of chivalry to
while away the hours, but nothing happened to be at hand
save lives of Christ and of the saints.   These he took up with
great indifference, but they soon chained him fast and filled
his whole vivid imagination.   Immediately on regaining his
strength, he determined to mount a humble mule and ride
to Monserrat, the holy mount of Aragon.   Here he hung
his weapons on an altar sacred to the Virgin Mary, and
kept a stern vigil in the church.   Then, giving his rich
garments to a beggar and donning a hermit's gown, he took
up his abode in the Dominican monastery at Manresa.

What the cell at Erfurt had been to Martin Luther, that
at Manresa was to Loyola: seven hours a day he prayed
regularly, three times each night he rose and scourged himself.   His spiritual struggles brought him to the verge of
suicide; once he started wildly for the window, intending
to make an end of his mental agony.   Luther had been
recalled from despair by the representation of his friend
Staupitz, but Loyola was forced to fight out his battle alone
and unaided.   He conquered in the end by the aid of his
clear intelligence, and came to the final conclusion that
scruples and doubts were works of the devil.   He began
to see visions of blessedness, and feel that Christ allowed
him to come into direct communication with himself.

The
spiritual
exercises.
Here at Manresa, Ignatius invented the famous spiritual
exercises which eventually became a necessary part of the
training of every Jesuit priest.   Never was scheme more
carefully thought out or better adapted to its ends; it filled
the needs of the age for definite discipline and for an actual
series of steps by which to rise from the prevailing sloth

and torpor. If we read the exercises to-day, they seem to us a mere dry catechism; but they dawned on the sixteenth century as something almost inspired. Loyola himself describes them as a sort of athletics, a running and walking for the soul. They were a military drill, always to be gone through with under the eye of some strict master; they were a training of the imagination on scenes from Scripture, and they necessitated a constant interrogation of the individual's conscience. By various mechanical contrivances, such as jotting down, adding up, and telling over the different sins committed, by the most ingenious devices for concentrating the attention, the pupil was finally brought into a sort of hypnotized state, in which everything that had to do with the spiritual life seemed real and tangible. He was dragged through the horrors of hell, made to smell the actual smell of the brimstone, and taste its bitterness, feel the scorching flames of the fire, and hear the awful howls of the lost souls. Then came a flight to heaven, a dazzling view of Christ, a thorough partaking of his sufferings, and, finally, a full realization of the joys of resurrection. The immediate object of the exercises was, by running the whole gamut of the emotions, to evoke a strong, dispassionate frame of mind that would fit one for the blind performance of any duty. At every crisis, before every approaching struggle, they were to be gone through with anew; and always, during their progress, it was a prime necessity that the eye of the preceptor should fathom every secret thought.

In one important respect Ignatius Loyola felt that his own training was still incomplete. He coveted intellectual power, yet had never had the advantages of even a passable education. He had now reached the age of thirty-three, but, nothing daunted, he went to a school at Barcelona and sat on the bench with the smallest boys. From here he

The founding of the Jesuit order.

passed to Alcala, and thence to the University of Paris, where he studied industriously for seven years. His desire to proselytize brought him twice into conflict with the inquisition, and once he was sentenced to be whipped as a corrupter of youth. After completing his course at Paris he went on a pilgrimage to Jerusalem, and afterwards appeared in Rome, where he became prominent as a social reformer, founding refuges and associations, and procuring legislation against particularly glaring abuses. His order was established in 1540, and entered into life under the most glowing auspices, the Pope conferring upon it certain powers of which the chair of Peter had never before been known to divest itself.

Well indeed might Paul III. encourage this new creation; in addition to the regular vows of poverty, chastity, and obedience was one of absolute and unconditional fidelity to papal commands. The name " Company of Jesus " was taken in the sense of a company or troop of soldiers; the Pope, its commander-in-chief, might make use of his forces for whatever purposes he pleased; and implicit subordination to superiors was insisted upon as in no other army the world had yet seen. The workman in the garden of the Lord was to rest with but one foot on the ground; the other was always to be raised to continue the journey. This was the watchword, this the key-note of Loyola's system. In the constitution of the order, in the hundreds of separate instructions that he issued, always he harps on the same theme. A member of the order must be like the staff which an old man holds in his hand, ready to serve him when and how he pleases; he must be like a ball of soft wax, that can be twisted and moulded into any form; like a little crucifix, that can be held at will head up or head down. He must obey *perinde ac si cadaver esset*, exactly as though he were a lifeless corpse, to be pushed or turned without resistance in any direction whatever. There were absolutely no lengths to which Loyola would not go when insisting on his principle; the tendency to private judgment was to be completely and permanently eradicated. If a superior command even mortal sin in the name of the Lord Christ, it is straightway to be committed; "if the church defines as black something that seems white to our eyes, we are at once to declare it black."

The necessity of inculcating such ideas as these in early youth, if they were to prevail at all, led the Jesuits to establish seminaries for the training of future members; in connection with them were schools, which might be attended by outsiders. The devotion of the teachers, their skilful methods of instruction, and, above all, the fact that these institutions were free, ended by making them very popular; so much so that ordinary schoolmasters felt injured and jealous, and a band of them once regularly stormed the Collegium Romanum, or great central institution at Rome. Parents, too, were often alarmed lest their sons should be forced to join the order, until the Jesuits themselves at last made it a rule that no one of their scholars might become a priest without permission from his family. Except for the system of espionage and the encouragement of taletelling, the spirit that pervaded these institutions was distinctly liberal; extremes of every kind were discouraged, and Loyola himself, on visiting one of them, ordered that some boys who had taken of their own accord to fasting should be dragged from their beds and forced to eat. We hear of a hungry scholar confessing that he had stolen some figs, whereupon he was presented with a whole basketful.

The training of the Jesuit priests.

The priests of the order were chosen by a process of rigid selection. Great importance was attached to the ability to do their best in public; for silent worth there was little

recognition. When, finally, they went out into the world
on the mission for which they had been especially trained,
they were given books of instructions which regulated
their conduct down to the smallest particular. Even the
expression of countenance — what we still call the Jesuit
expression — was formally prescribed: the eyes cast down,
the brows smooth, the lips not too firmly set, the whole air
mildly gay, not sad. The new emissary was to accommodate
himself, as far as possible, to the people of the place to
which he went, and at once learn their language, and join
in their pursuits. The brothers who were sent to Munich
were especially told that they must try and acquire a taste
for beer. Among the cardinal virtues to be cherished by
all members were dispassionateness in general, and the
ability to accept insults. Invective was not to be used in
public discourses, nor were dogmas, which might arouse
opposition, to be discussed. From the very beginning
there was inculcated a certain wiliness and deception;
Satan was to be fought with his own tools. He did not
set to work by urging men at once to do what they perfectly well knew was wicked; even so the Jesuits were to
humor their flocks, to listen to their side of the question,
and only gradually to correct their faults. In fact, it was
laid down as a maxim that the other party was always to
be allowed to begin a conversation; the Jesuit was to
listen, then slowly gather up the threads, and finally remain master of the field. But the fathers were not to trust
too much to their own judgment; they were to travel, when
possible, in pairs, not only to spy upon each other, but also
in order that, if occasion demanded, responsibility could
easily be shifted.

Such were the men, mere wheels of a machine, mere pup-
pets of a policy, to whose tender mercies one country after
another, and riven Germany especially, was now handed

over; such were the future father confessors of emperors
and kings, such the teachers of the rising generation. That
Protestantism was the prime evil to be attacked was not
only evident, but was candidly acknowledged; that war,
cruel and wasting, was sure to come of their efforts, was
not sufficient reason to swerve these men from the path of
duty.

CHAPTER XVII

THE BEGINNING OF THE THIRTY YEARS' WAR

LITERATURE : One of the best accounts of the Thirty Years' War is to be found in Huber, *Geschichte Oesterreichs*. Gindeley is also good authority, and his shorter work is very readable. Gardiner's *Thirty Years' War* is an excellent short account. Ritter has not yet completed his work. Winter's book (in the Oncken Series) is a makeshift, and will doubtless make way for a monumental work of Droysen.

Active campaign of the Roman Catholic church. AT that Diet of 1576, in which Augustus of Saxony succeeded in thwarting the plans of his own party, an official of the emperor's chancery cried out, "In ten years we shall hear no more of Lutherans!" And, indeed, so audacious a campaign had already been begun that the prophecy was not unlikely to come true. Bavaria had been completely invaded by Jesuits; the Elector Albert was their stanch friend, while his younger son, Ernest, who was destined for the priesthood, had been given into their keeping. All Bavarian officials were now forced to vow allegiance to the Roman Catholic church, and Jesuits were despatched to see that they took and kept their oath. Protestant burghers were banished in crowds, and non-conforming peasants were hounded down and imprisoned. Lists were drawn up of forbidden books ; the classics were banished from the schools and supplanted by the church fathers, while even the elector's own library was ransacked and purged.

Struggle for the Western bishoprics. By this time the German nation was hurrying rapidly on its course toward war and anarchy. Never was a drama worked up to its crisis in more consistent, more relentless, progression. Stronghold after stronghold was falling; at every imperial Diet the opposition was increasing, and a deadlock becoming more and more imminent. Desperate struggles were engaged in for individual prizes, but the losers were always the Protestants. Duke William of Cleves was on the point of joining the latter when he was snatched as a brand from the burning by Spanish and Jesuit influence. The chief efforts of the Catholic church were directed to these lands on the Western boundary — to the rich duchy of Cleves-Julier, to wavering Cologne, to the bishoprics of Westphalia. Here the Protestants were largely in the majority, but with Spain, with Bavaria, and with the Jesuits, their recovery was looked upon as a matter of the utmost importance, on account of their proximity to the Netherlands. The methods of the inquisition would be severely hampered should the intended victims be surrounded with friends, and that is why Philip II. placed his troops and his gold at the disposal of the Jesuits.

Everything depended on bringing the doubtful ecclesiastical principalities into the hands of men whose power and whose orthodoxy should alike be undoubted. But among the greater Catholic princes there was only one, Ernest of Bavaria, who had chosen the church for his career. On his devoted head, accordingly, by papal dispensation, it was determined to heap as many mitres as could be wrested from Protestant control. With a train of Jesuits at his back, and with plenty of armed forces in reserve, he rapidly progressed from one dignity to another; actual incumbents were deposed by the Pope, and in the new elections that followed strong pressure was brought to bear on the different cathedral chapters. Already Bishop of Bavarian Frisingen, Ernest was made coadjutor, and then, in 1573, Bishop, of Hildesheim. One of his first acts was to encourage the Abbot of Fulda to banish all Protes-

Ernest of Bavaria.

tants from his lands.   Burial in the parish church was refused their dead, their sick were catechised before they were received into the hospitals, while the delivery of coal and wood to the lower classes was made dependent on a profession of orthodoxy.   It was in vain that the burghers drew up a protest, in which they complain of the Jesuits, that " they rest neither day nor night, but continue to plot against all the old civic liberties," that their one idea is " so to weed and thresh out a whole population that it may at last be glad to betake itself under their Baalitic yoke — which God forbid ! "

The example of Fulda was followed in the Eichsfeld, a territory dependent upon Mainz.   When the citizens of Düderstädt refused to deliver up their church to the archbishop and his two Jesuit henchmen, a blow was struck at their chief industry, the brewing of Düderstädt beer. For Ernest of Bavaria, indeed, there came a series of apparent defeats in Cologne, in Paderborn, and in Münster ; but he knew well that if he bided his time all would be well : in these very days the Protestant dissensions had reached their height.   And his defeat in Cologne had been in favor of a man who passed for a zealous Catholic, and whose appointment Pope Gregory XIII. did not hesitate to confirm.

Gebhard Truchsess of Cologne.

This matter of the choice of an incumbent for the archiepiscopal see of Cologne, was one on which there hinged immense consequences; the archbishop would be, not merely an elector of the empire, but he would be that one elector whose vote must decide whether the next candidate for the throne should be Catholic or Protestant.   Gebhard Truchsess von Waldburg, the new incumbent of Cologne, entered upon the duties of his office with great zeal.   In the lax days of his predecessors it had not been customary for these ecclesiastical princes to have a separate consecration as priest, but on this, for himself, Gebhard insisted. He promised obedience to the Trent decrees, took the side of Spain in the fruitless peace negotiations with the Netherlands, and, in various ways, rendered valuable assistance to the Jesuits. But whether it was that this powerful prelate had always been Protestant at heart, or that his faith had first been undermined by the influence of some neighboring nobles, he soon determined to leave the church and to marry the Countess of Mansfeld. On Christmas Day, 1582, he publicly announced his conversion: "God has saved me from the darkness of the Papacy, and brought me to a true recognition of His holy word." To the Pope he wrote that through his own investigations he had convinced himself of the corruption of the Roman Church, and no longer felt bound by the oaths he had taken.

Gebhard's first thought had been to retire to private life, but his Protestant friends saw here an opportunity for settling forever a momentous question. Nearly thirty years before, at the peace Diet of Augsburg, Ferdinand had promulgated the "ecclesiastical reservation"; in all the time that ensued, although the spirit of that decree had been broken a hundred times, and numberless church foundations had come into Protestant hands, its letter had remained intact. Protestants had been elected to Catholic bishoprics by the cathedral chapters, but no unmediatized Catholic prelate, no ecclesiastical prince of the empire, had attempted to go over to Protestantism and still retain the possessions he had held as a Catholic. Just this was the issue now involved; the crucial test had at last come.

Knowing well that his object could never be gained by peaceful means, Gebhard hastily levied troops and garrisoned his strongholds, choosing Bonn for his centre of operations. Everything depended for him on the attitude of the Protestant princes. Would they rise and shake

Importance of the Cologne matter.

themselves free from the slough of their own petty interests? Could their hearts once more be warmed to a general enthusiasm for their party? John Casimir, of the
Palatinate, the Calvinist, was Gebhard's warmest friend.
Would that old pillar of orthodoxy, Elector Augustus of
Saxony, ever consent to be involved with him in any common undertaking?

Defection
of Saxony
from the
Protestant
cause.

The archbishop for his part did his best to conciliate both
parties; so far did he go in his assurances to each that
John Casimir's envoy had grave doubts if "such tergiver-
sation would please our Lord God." And at first he met
with success. In outward accord the Protestant princes
sent a writing to the emperor in which they denied the
validity of the "reservation." The electors of Saxony,
of Brandenburg, and of the Palatinate, then sent envoys to
a meeting at Erfurt. But here, contrary to all expectations,
and in spite of a threatening letter that he himself had
despatched to the Emperor Rudolph, Augustus resumed his
old rôle of obstructor and general marplot. Through the
mouth of his envoys he pronounced Gebhard in the wrong,
and, contradicting his own former assertions, insisted that
the "reservation" should continue to be binding. Brandenburg upheld him, inaugurating the slack policy in religious matters, that was to cloud the glories of its ruling
house during the whole of the next half-century.

The weakness and apathy of the Protestants had reached
their climax. What wonder that Pope Gregory XIII., the
indefatigable founder of Jesuit colleges, thought the occasion favorable for regaining a hold on German national
affairs! He hurled the ban at Gebhard, deprived him of
all his dignities, pronounced the see of Cologne vacant,
and demanded a new election. It daunted him little that
the man who was now to be dismissed without hearing
or trial was one of the seven electors. Gregory was sure

of the support of Rudolph II., and, indeed, the emperor at once sent envoys to Cologne and ordered the cathedral chapter to choose a new head. Even the heart of Augustus of Saxony was stirred at this action of the Pope; in common with his Protestant coelectors he sent a protest to Rudolph, but to fight for the rights of his outraged party he had no mind. He now, on the contrary, completed the long list of his disloyal acts by permitting the elevation to the vacant see of the most dangerous enemy the Protestants had ever had — Ernest of Bavaria. In the next year, in common with Brandenburg, he formally recognized the pupil of the Jesuits as a member of the College of Electors.

Gebhard and his one ally, John Casimir, held out but for a short time; Spanish troops and Bavarian subsidies made their antagonists far too formidable. The Protestant general, John Casimir, was a poor commander, harsh, proud, and unjust, and only valiant over his cups. He had declared in his war manifesto that he was taking the field "for the protection of the true religion of the Augsburg Confession, and for the liberation of the German nation from the invading tyranny of the Roman Pope"; but when it came to action he showed himself dilatory and undecided. His troops, which he could no longer hold together, at last disbanded, at the bidding of the emperor, while Gebhard himself, a little later, was driven from Bonn and took refuge in the Netherlands.

Great and memorable was the victory the Catholics had won; they had kept their ecclesiastical reservation as well as their majority in the College of Electors; once more the voice of the Pope had been obeyed in Germany. And the fate of Cologne decided that of Münster, where, as in Liège also, Ernest was soon elected bishop. All over Westphalia the Jesuits held high carnival, founding schools and

Great victory of the Jesuits.

seminaries, and building churches. The giant proportions
of their buildings, their broad, flaunting style of architecture, show their firm belief that this their church militant
would soon become a universal church triumphant. They
had openly begun to attack the Augsburg Peace: in matters of faith, they declared, the church could alone decide;
the Council of Trent *had* decided, and all who opposed
its decrees were heretics. When, in reply to such claims,
Protestant writers spoke of " bloodthirsty plots " and
" wicked practices," some of the Jesuits candidly avowed
" that they had, indeed, made it their goal to destroy Protestantism root and branch."

The
Protestants
continue
to lose
ground.

Everything tended to force the two parties into fierce
and irrevocable opposition; the religious ties had been the
first to break, one by one there followed the snapping of
all political bonds. In the Diets, which voted by colleges,
the Protestants had enjoyed a majority among the princes
which gave them great influence; in the Chamber Court,
or general court of the empire, they had been fairly represented. Both these advantages were gradually lost. The
Catholics challenged the votes of the Protestant administrators, or heads of the secularized bishoprics, on the ground
that the latter had not been confirmed in their holdings by
the emperor and the Pope. With regard to this matter it
must be said that more than once, in order not to inter-
rupt important transactions, individual administrators had
waived their rights in the Diet, on the understanding, however, that their action should form no precedent. More
than once, on the other hand, scenes of confusion had taken
place. When, at the Diet of 1594, the chancellor of Magdeburg, Meckbach, tried to take his place in the midst of the
princes, the Archbishop of Salzburg bade him retire, and,
in his excitement, even seized him by the cloak. When
Meckbach refused to move, all the Catholics present rose

and left the hall, and the negotiations of the Diet came to a standstill.   As to the Chamber Court the manœuvre was resorted to of simply not summoning Protestant supervisors.   In case of appeal the more important cases had to be brought before another tribunal, the *Reichshofrath*, composed of Catholics and completely subservient to the emperor's will.

So bitter was the opposition in every field that the Protestants rejected a great and really salutary measure, for the mere reason that it was conceived and inaugurated by Pope Gregory XIII., who thought to impose it upon all Christendom by simply issuing a bull.   To the measure itself, the reform of the calendar, there was little to object. It is true the new calendar was not perfect enough for scientific purposes, and the old one was correct enough for ordinary use ; but the main ground of refusal lay in the fact that the Protestants would not accept a decree about which they had not been consulted, and which was promulgated by a pope whom they did not recognize.

The reform of the calendar.

For sixteen hundred years, since the time of Julius Cæsar, the Western world had made use of a system of reckoning by which the ordinary year, the time occupied by the earth in moving round the sun, occupied exactly 365 days and 6 hours.   In reality the fraction should have been slightly smaller.   The error had long been recognized, when Gregory XIII., in the year of the Cologne war, ordered the introduction of the calendar that still bears his name.   By this time the ordinary year was ten days behind the astronomical, and, which was Gregory's chief concern, the festivals of the saints no longer fell on the days originally appointed by the church.   In order to correct the past he decreed, that, for 1582, ten days should be omitted, the fifth of October of the old style becoming the fifteenth of the new ; in order to avoid future error, three times in every four centuries one of the years that would naturally assume an extra day was to return to its normal length.[1]

The further cleft that was made by the introduction of the Gregorian calendar into Germany was very real and very serious. Catholics and Protestants were no longer to have their sacred days or their feast days in common; at work and at worship they were to be divided. Employers were to be constantly at odds with their laborers, forcing them to work when they wished to rest, and to be idle when they might well have been engaged in labor. The public feeling found vent in bitter irony. " None the less," says a writing of 1584, " will the bear remain in his hole until the old Candlemas," while another pamphlet suggests that the Pope might well be anxious to have the saints' days in accord with the days of their martyrdom, for the reason that, if a suppliant should come on the wrong date, his particular patron might have gone a-walking.

Thus the Protestants adhered to the old style while the Catholics adopted the new, and the differences between them, only partially obliterated in 1700 A.D., were not finally settled until nearly the beginning of the nineteenth century.

The Donauwörth episode.

Meanwhile, actual clashes had been growing more and more frequent; a schismatic election in Strassburg had led to a secession of the Protestants from the imperial Diet of 1598; disturbances in Aix-la-Chapelle had ended in the city being purged of heretics by Spanish troops; a dispute with regard to four monasteries in South Germany caused, finally, the complete obstruction of the ordinary course of justice, the Protestants refusing to be bound by decisions either of the imperial Chamber Court or of the *Reichshofrath*, the emperor's privy council. But

[1] The year 1900 is an example of one of these frustrated leap years.

nothing that had as yet occurred caused equal excitement with the happenings in the little town of Wörth, on the Danube, between the years 1602 and 1608.

Wörth was one of those free cities of the empire in which, by the terms of the Peace of 1555, Protestants and Catholics should have agreed to live peaceably side by side. But here, as in many other towns, Protestantism had so completely gained the ascendency that the adherents of the old church numbered less than thirty persons, including a congregation of Benedictine monks. The latter rented their monastery from the city, and had long lived quietly and without ostentation, forbidden by the magistrates to perform ceremonies or engage in processions within the city limits; if a Catholic citizen died, only one priest and two monks might be present at the burial; no display was to be made of crucifixes, no incense might be used, and flags, if carried at all, were to be closely furled.

But the Jesuits had long had their eye on this monastery of the Holy Cross, and by the year 1602 all of its sixteen members were pupils from the order's university at Dillingen, while a worthy head was found in the person of a certain pugnacious Abbot Leonhard. Gradually the old ceremonies were revived, burials were more and more pompously celebrated, processions were held on every occasion. In Holy Week of the year 1605 the magistrates interfered, and ordered the monks to lower their banners while within the city limits; the abbot refused, and only yielded to actual force. But the matter did not stop here. On the ground that the religious peace was being violated, Leonhard appealed to the Bishop of Augsburg, who in turn brought the case before the emperor's privy council. Without even investigating the matter, this tribunal took the side of the Catholics, and peremptorily ordered the magistrates to refrain from further interference with the

The Jesuits in Wörth.

monks. Whereupon the abbot instituted a more noisy ceremony than before, on which occasion a general skirmish
took place with the citizens, who pursued the Benedictines
with clubs and missiles and drove them back to their
cloister walls.

Chastise-
ment of
Wörth.

In answer to a new citation from the privy council, the
magistrates declared that they had done their best to
restrain the populace, but without success — an unfortunate admission, for now the emperor commissioned an out-
sider, Maximilian of Bavaria, to see to the protection of the
Catholics in Wörth, and, of all persons, to Maximilian the
task was most welcome. He had had the same bringing up
as his brother Ernest, and was possessed with the same
zeal for the cause, and with a great ambition for the House
of Wittelsbach. Moreover, his ability was undoubted; on
the abdication of his spendthrift father, in 1598, he had
undertaken to restore the ruined finances of his land, and
had succeeded so admirably that he was later able to furnish invaluable pecuniary aid to his own party. When
Maximilian's envoys appeared in Wörth to demand an
assurance that the Catholics should not be further mo-
lested, a popular tumult arose and the commissioners were
forced to make a hasty exit; in the meanwhile a number
of Protestant estates had remonstrated against the interference of the emperor's court and encouraged the magistrates of Wörth to resist its mandates. Maximilian induced
the emperor to declare the city in the ban and to intrust the
fulfilment of the sentence to himself; he was all prepared
for the emergency, and held in readiness an army of six
thousand men. Utterly defenceless, the city surrendered
at once, — December 16, 1607, — whereupon the Bavarian
troops garrisoned the market-place, and erected a gallows.
Wörth was then treated as a spoil of war; it was completely recatholicized, and, in addition, regularly pawned

to Bavaria until the costs attendant on its overthrow should have been paid. Its very name was changed to Donauwörth, and the words, "City of the Holy Roman Empire," were formally erased from its seal.

An atmosphere heavy with storm pervaded the Diet of Ratisbon, which met at the time of these events. If Maximilian of Bavaria really believed, as he wrote to the Pope, that he "had done not a little to establish the authority of his Imperial Majesty in the Holy Empire and to inculcate respect and obedience toward him," he was to find himself strangely mistaken. The very first proposition brought forward by Archduke Ferdinand, to raise a standing army for the protection of the Hungarian frontier, met with an unbending opposition; the second, to make the renewal of the Peace of 1555 A.D. conditional on the restoration of all church lands appropriated since 1552, drove the Protestants to desperation. The only political body that could in any way have brought about a peaceful settlement of the difficulties disbanded in confusion. The importance of the moment was not misconceived; a number of Protestant estates at once proceeded to organize the so-called "Union," of which the Palatine elector was to have the guidance. Its term of duration was to be ten years. Its avowed purposes were, to defend the lands, person, and rights of each individual member, and to obtain redress for the wrongs of the party. There had been nothing like it since that unfortunate Smalkald League, which had come to such an unhappy end some sixty years before; but this time Saxony remained aloof. The Catholics, for their part, were not behindhand in marshalling their forces. Under the leadership of Maximilian of Bavaria,— the only German prince who was to keep his life, his lands, and his policy through all the long horrors of the Thirty Years' War,—an association known as the "League" came

The Protestant "Union" and the Catholic "League."

into being.   The Emperor Rudolph did not join it; on the
one hand it may have dawned upon him that his position
placed him above parties; on the other, Maximilian distinctly did not want him, preferring to play the first rôle
among a host of small ecclesiastical princes.

The
Emperor
Rudolph II.

For a time it seemed as if the question of the Cleves inheritance, of which we shall treat in another connection,
would precipitate the great struggle which all felt to be
approaching ; but the murder of Henry IV. of France by
Ravaillac turned aside the danger, and when the storm did
break it was elsewhere — in one of the hereditary kingdoms of the Hapsburgs.   In bringing about the catastrophe
the peculiarities of the heads of that house played a considerable part, and to those peculiarities, as well as to the
general policy of the Hapsburgs at home, it is needful to
turn our attention.

Rudolph II., eldest of the many sons of Maximilian II.,
and emperor since 1576, possessed no merits likely to endear him to posterity, save that he extended his protection
to learned men like Kepler and Tycho Brahe.   An ardent
lover and collector of antiquities, he filled the great palace
on the Hradchin in Prague with every kind of precious
work of art, and spent his time in the midst of his treasures,
delving into astronomy and also into necromancy.   In
character he was suspicious, yet easily deceived, shunning
the influence of strong men while falling under that of
menials, bigoted to the last degree, yet occasionally forced
to place himself in the power of men whom he knew to be
heretics.   His indecision and vacillation were almost beyond belief; time and again, for a period extending over
nearly twenty years, he negotiated with the Spanish king
for the hand of his eldest daughter, Isabella, and when at
last Philip, in despair of seeing the poor princess safely
provided for, gave her to Archduke Albert, Rudolph con-

sidered himself deeply wronged, and allowed the thought of vengeance seriously to influence his policy.

In his later days Rudolph was afflicted with attacks of insanity; he thought that his enemies were constantly pursuing him, and that magic arts were being used against him. More and more did he withdraw from the public gaze; there were times, even amid the most important happenings, when it was impossible either for foreign envoys or for privy councillors to obtain an audience. If the emperor did occasionally show sufficient energy to send representatives to the German Diet, he expressly omitted to give them full powers; they were to write to him for instructions, and often pending the weightiest decisions, interminable correspondences had first to be spun out between Ratisbon and the Hradchin. At last the bow was bent too far; a family conclave, headed by the Archduke Matthias, met to discuss the state of affairs, and to see what could be done with this sick man who could neither live nor die, who clung so fast to a power that he was completely incapable of exercising. As the breach widened, Matthias was driven into a union with the nobles and cities of Hungary and the two Austrias, while the emperor himself drew around him the estates of Bohemia, — for the most part Protestant, — which were jealous of the part played by the other Austrian dependencies, and proud, too, of having their city of Prague the imperial residence. Fairly driven to the wall by the successes of Matthias, who had now been chosen king of Hungary, and frightened by the insistence of his own adherents, Rudolph in 1609 issued the famous instrument of toleration known as the Royal Charter of the Bohemians. It granted free exercise of their religion to all persons. The Protestants were to have their own consistory or governing body, the members of which were to be called "defensors." They could call together general

The "Royal Charter" of the Bohemians.

assemblies representing the Protestants of the whole kingdom. There were restrictions indeed, in the form of supplementary treaties, that were soon to prove most galling. and
to bring about a vital issue. These related mainly to the
right of building new places of worship, and provided that
in the smaller territorial holdings the will of the lord of the
land was to be respected, and no churches built without
his permission; whereas on the royal domains the Protestants might erect such structures as they needed. But a
bitter dispute soon arose as to the meaning of this technical term, "royal domains." Did it also include the ecclesiastical estates of which the clergy had the usufruct, but
which were administered by the crown? It was pointed
out that the kings had not hesitated to draw revenues
from these lands, and even to pawn them for their own
uses.

The
bigoted
Ferdinand
of Styria.

Rudolph's concessions to the Bohemians had called forth
a strong Catholic opposition, heads of which were the
chancellor Sdenko von Lobkowitz, who to the last refused
to place his official seal on the "Royal Charter," the judge
Jaroslav von Martinitz, and the burgrave of the neighboring fortress of Karlstein, Wilhelm von Slavata, the last-
named all the more intolerant for being a renegade from
the cause he now combated. But a still more inveterate
and implacable enemy of all concessions was Duke Ferdinand of Styria, whose chances were good of one day succeeding to the crowns of Bohemia and the empire, as his
uncles Rudolph and Matthias were both old and childless,
and their brothers Albert and Maximilian were willing to
cede their claims.

Never had the Jesuits had a more devoted pupil or a
more pliant tool than Ferdinand. Of somewhat stunted
intelligence, but with a passionate love for reciting prayers,
for confessing his sins, and for scourging his own body,

his guiding principle was religious intolerance. He had once made a pilgrimage to Loretto, and had solemnly sworn on the altar of St. James to extirpate the hated creed of Protestantism. In his own domains he had succeeded so well that, in the year 1603, at Easter and at New Year, forty thousand came forward to confess their errors, — the official lists are still preserved, — while thousands more, who refused to abjure, were sent into exile.

The relations, meanwhile, between Rudolph and his powerful brother Matthias were undergoing many phases. Twice there were outward reconciliations, once, in 1610, with every pomp and ceremony. But at the very time when both parties agreed to disband their forces, the emperor was maintaining troops in Passau, which, he claimed, had been levied for service in Julier, but which, as he said, could not be dismissed until their arrears of debt had been paid. Dreams and visions now led him to make a new attack upon Matthias; astrologers had foretold the complete downfall of the latter. The Passau troops, ostensibly in mutiny for their pay, descended upon Austria. Matthias quickly reassembled his army and drove them back, but not until they had inflicted much harm. They then turned to Bohemia and even captured a part of the city of Prague, their successful progress causing Rudolph more and more to lay aside his mask. Now was the time, he thought, to become master of the Protestant estates, and to annul their hated charter. But the Bohemians were already on their guard, and had summoned Matthias to their aid, receiving from him reënforcements to the number of twenty-five hundred men. Rendered all but a prisoner in his own splendid palace, Rudolph was forced to call the Diet that was to pronounce his own fall. In vain he sought to delay the proceedings that he might the better make capital out of the general dis-

Rudolph and Matthias.

union. The first point insisted upon was that Matthias, as the choice of the Bohemian people, should be made king of that land. On the day of the pompous coronation Rudolph hid in the farthest corner of his park, lest he might hear the cries and rejoicings.

The death of Rudolph.   His imperial dignity still remained to him, and he sought to use this for the coercion of his brother and the regaining of his lost lands. No step was too extreme for him to take ; he was willing now to reverse the century-long policy of his house and to throw himself into the arms of the Protestant Union, nay even himself to turn Protestant and, old and decrepit as he was, to marry the widow of the Palatine elector. But who could now trust to the weather-vane policy of this half-crazed intriguer? His prayers, his commands, his threats, were no longer of any avail. Full of gall and bitterness, he was on the point of setting out from Prague, to try at least to circumvent the election of Matthias as his successor on the imperial throne, when a sharp attack of illness put an end to his life. Without opposition Matthias became emperor.

Ferdinand becomes king of Bohemia.   Various circumstances combined at this time to make the Holy Roman throne anything but a bed of roses. The ordinary machinery of government had ceased to act. At Matthias's first general Diet the Protestant estates formally declared that they would be bound by no majority vote in matters pertaining to religion, taxation, justice, or the prosperity and safety of the fatherland. On the eastern borders of the Hapsburg lands was a rebellion of the Prince of Transylvania, who was supported by the might of Islam. As to the Bohemian Protestants, among whom the fiercest storm was evidently brewing, Matthias, even had he wished to keep his compacts with them, would have found it a difficult matter. He himself was tottering to his grave. His chief adviser who, we are told, "thought, spoke, wrote, and acted for him," was the former imperial chancellor, Melchior Klesl, clever, industrious, and not unmerciful, but scenting in heresy the mother of rebellion, and desiring above all things to overthrow or evade the Royal Charter. But beyond and above all this, it was becoming necessary to regard the wishes of the probable successor to the throne, that Ferdinand of Styria whose bigotry and whose predilection for Jesuit practices have already been noted. Indeed, Matthias, warned that there was danger of having his house thrust aside at his death, now devoted his efforts to having Ferdinand acknowledged king both of Bohemia and of Hungary. He met with much opposition, but by sparing no means of coercion at last attained his object. In vain, at the Diet of 1617, the Bohemian estates attempted to have it stated in the protocol that they had " elected," and not merely "accepted " him as their king — a far-reaching difference, since those who had elected could also depose. They did indeed succeed in procuring from the new king a confirmation of all the rights and privileges of the land, including the Royal Charter;—with regard to the ratification of this latter instrument, the Jesuits had given him a special dispensation, in case he should be unable otherwise to obtain the crown.

The achievement of the royal dignity in Bohemia was a great victory for the house of Hapsburg, all the greater because the public mind was agitated at this time by what the Protestants considered an unwarrantable breach of this same Royal Charter. In the little town of Braunau, which belonged to the domain lands of a Benedictine monastery, the inhabitants, aided by contributions from Protestants in Germany, had built a new church of their own. The abbot of the monastery ordered it closed on the ground

The affairs of Braunau and Klostergrab.

that the land was not royal domain, and Matthias approved
the act.   Inasmuch as almost identically the same thing
occurred in Klostergrab, on the lands of the Archbishop of
Prague, there was reason to suspect a far-reaching hostile
plan of operations.   Meetings of the defensors were hastily
called and protests rained in upon the emperor from every
quarter; but Matthias, far from yielding, only inaugurated
new and harsher measures.   The judges were clothed with
new powers that they might challenge the titles of Protestant landholders, and Martinitz went so far as to command
his subjects, under penalty of eighty thalers, to attend confession in a Catholic church.

It cannot be denied that there were arguments on both
sides in this matter of the Braunau and Klostergrab
churches; but whatever the true merits of the case, the
emperor and the Catholics determined to carry their point
with a high hand.   Citizens of Braunau who refused to
hand over the keys of their church to the abbot were
seized and put in prison, — a step which gave rise to a
riotous demonstration.   In Klostergrab, the Protestants,
for fear of worse evils, were forced to help in tearing down
their own building.

The throw-
ing of the
stadt-
holders
from the
window.

The whole of Bohemia was by this time in a ferment,
and the defensors, headed by Count Matthias von Thurn,
called a general assembly of Protestant delegates at which
the fiercest and bitterest denunciatory speeches were held.
In Thurn's mind there was already ripening the project of
ridding the land of the whole hated dynasty of the Hapsburgs; some one decisive act was needed to make the
breach irreparable; consciously or unconsciously, as many
persons as possible were to be concerned in the plot.
When the Emperor, through his stadtholders, or deputy
governors, declared the assembly at Prague treasonous,
and forbade a second one that had already been summoned,

Thurn decided to carry out his plan. He had determined on the death of two of the stadtholders, the old enemies of his party, Martinitz and Slavata; they were to be disposed of in a manner commonly associated in the minds of the Bohemians with great national crises.

Ostensibly for the purpose of consulting about a new communication just received from the emperor, Thurn led an armed band of nobles to the council chamber of the castle of Prague; they filled not only the chamber but the halls as well, and blocked the stairway. Slavata and Martinitz were singled out and made to undergo a summary trial. The chief charge, enforced with fierce invective, was their opposition to the Royal Charter in 1609. Facts were adduced that roused to frenzy all who were present. A rush was made for the two stadtholders, as well as for their innocent secretary, Fabricius; they were dragged to the window and hurled to the ditch, some seventy feet below. "Jesus! Mary!" shrieked Martinitz, as he fell. "Let us see," said some one, "if his Mary will help him." "By God," he cried a moment later, "his Mary has helped him!" It seemed as though a miracle had happened.

The deed that took place in that room at Prague was one of the most important and irrevocable acts in the whole of German history; it was the official signal for the opening of the great Thirty Years' War. It is true the intended victims escaped without serious injury, their heavy wadded cloaks and a convenient dunghill helping to soften the fall. But none the less the die had been cast, the Rubicon crossed, and all the elemental passions of Europe roused into life.

The news of the uprising in Prague reached Matthias at Vienna and Ferdinand in Pressburg, where he was preparing for his coronation as king of Hungary. The emperor and Klesl were inclined to use conciliatory

The outbreak of the war.

measures; but Ferdinand, who hurried to the capital, rejoiced at the opportunity for inflicting a never-to-be-forgotten punishment upon the Bohemians. Nothing was to stand in the way of his vengeance. Klesl, on account of his tortuous policy and his slowness in making levies, was seized by stratagem and sent as a prisoner to Innsbruck. No heed was paid to the opposition of Matthias, who is said to have bitten through his bedclothes for very rage. Ferdinand's general, Count Buquoi, took the field at the head of twelve thousand men.

The Bohemians, for their part, lost not a single day in setting up a provisional government, with thirty directors, ten from each state, at its head. One of their first acts was to banish all Jesuits from the land, and to confiscate their property. An army was quickly raised; although the fatal error was committed of not putting its financial support upon a proper basis, and the plundering of its own lands was at times an absolute necessity. Great hopes were placed on foreign aid, and the Duke of Savoy, who was talked of as a possible successor to Ferdinand, actually did send the redoubtable Mansfeld at the head of two thousand men. Thurn, who was appointed commander-in-chief of all the forces, made it his chief aim to gain over the remaining Austrian dependencies, and, after a successful march into Moravia, turned his forces against Vienna. Matthias in the meantime had paid his debt, long overdue, to nature; dying, it is said, of fright at the turn events were taking. Thurn was not able to enter the capital, but within the walls were Protestant sympathizers, who gave Ferdinand momentary reason to fear for his personal safety. His confessor found him one day stretched before a crucifix. "If it be God's will, then let me be destroyed in this struggle," he said to the terrified father. He was obliged to submit to an interview with the rebels, in which the respect due to his rank was completely forgotten, one of the delegates going so far as to seize the button of his coat. Only the approach of a royal regiment rescued him from his position and caused his visitors to slink from the room. The condition of things in Bohemia suddenly recalled Thurn.

The movement begun at Prague affected the sea of European politics much as the casting of a stone disturbs quiet waters. The ripples first felt in the Austrian dependencies widened and spread until they reached the most distant lands, first Savoy and the Palatinate, then central Italy, Spain, and Flanders, Bavaria, and Saxony — not to speak of Transylvania, whose ambitious young prince, Bethlen Gabor, aided by the Porte, thought the time favorable for aiming at the crown of Hungary. Protestant and Catholic allies.

Ferdinand's first thoughts turned to the Pope, Paul V., who granted him a monthly subsidy, and handed over to the Catholic League, which reconstituted itself for the present emergency, a tithe on all church benefices in Italy. Philip III. of Spain, though almost bankrupt, was spurred on to the impossible by Ferdinand's ambassador, Khevenhiller, who threatened him, — recovering as he was from a well-nigh mortal illness, — with the terrors of the Last Judgment, should he allow the Protestants to conquer and so many souls to fall into hell fire. The most efficient ally was Maximilian of Bavaria, head of the Catholic League, who was bound, however, that a high price should be paid for his aid. Austrian lands were placed in his hands to cover all possible loss or expense, while Ferdinand promised him, should the rumor prove true that the Elector Palatine intended to accept the throne of Bohemia, that the dignity of his electoral office should be transferred to Bavaria.

To this latter possibility, the election of the Count Pala-

The young
Elector
Palatine.
tine, everything was now pointing. The Bohemians had
called together a diet to ratify the recent proceedings, and
had solemnly dethroned Ferdinand, causing a list to be
read in the assembly of all the sins he had committed in
the past twenty years. The three estates, nobles, knights,
and citizens, had voted separately for his fall. There had
been talk of choosing John George of Saxony in his place,
but some had objected on the ground of his drunken habits,
others because of his coolness and indifference to the whole
burning question. The fact that he was not chosen to
an office he would never have accepted, added to the circumstance that the leading Bohemian patriots were Calvinists, then drove this cantankerous prince over to the
side of Ferdinand, whom he helped to elect as emperor.

Well would it have been for the handsome, knightly,
young elector of the Palatinate, had he possessed some of
the worldly wisdom of his Saxon colleague. The Bohemians now offered him their crown simply because he was
their last resource. They counted on his powerful connections, for he was head of the Protestant Union, and his
wife was the daughter of King James of England. But,
although he did hesitate for a time, he finally accepted,
failing to realize that no one of the greater princes in Germany, whatever his religious convictions, could ever submit to the uniting of two electorates in one hand, and
that, however friendly the people of England might be
to his enterprise, the relations of James I. with Spain precluded the possibility of help. Others saw matters more
clearly; the elector of Cologne declared that Spain and
the House of Austria would rather sacrifice everything in
the world than give up Bohemia, and that a twenty, thirty,
or forty years' war was in prospect. He joined with Treves
and Mainz in a warning letter which declared that the
originators of such bloodshed and destruction would be

pointed at by the finger of history, so long as the world should stand.

Gathering together the riches that his ancestors had stored in Heidelberg, and followed by his beautiful English wife, Frederick set out for Prague, where he was received with the greatest enthusiasm. His youth, his agreeable countenance, his tall, slender form, made a most favorable impression. As he approached the capital, he was met by a magnificent procession of the different guilds. Fifty thousand guldens had been spent for his reception — a significant fact, and one casting a glaring light on the levity of the Bohemians, when it is considered that want of funds was daily causing a wretched loss of life in the army, the patriotism of many of the nobles having ceased at the door of their treasure rooms. At the coronation, which took place almost immediately, thousands of coins were scattered among the people, and a fountain ran wine for more than an hour. When Pope Paul V. heard of these happenings, he declared that the new monarch was entering a foul labyrinth that would surely lead to his own destruction. "He is but a winter king," said the Jesuits, sure that his reign would not last a year.

The "winter king."

And, indeed, a worse marriage of interests than that of this frivolous boy with the doomed nation that all Europe was combining to crush, could scarcely be imagined. He had not the tact, even, to try and keep the favor of his new subjects. Disapproving of their form of worship, which laid more stress on outward symbols than the Calvinism of the Palatinate, and sympathizing with his court-preacher, Scultetus, who declared that "he could not teach the gospel in the midst of accursed idols," he sacked their cathedrals, and had their images, altars, and valuable works of art hewn down with the axe. His wife, for her part, offended the people by her foreign customs, and especially

by the shockingly low cut of her dress. The general discontent increased from day to day; the nobles harped on
their rights, and the story is told that once, when Frederick called them to council, they answered that it was
against their privileges to get up so early. The fact is
certainly not easy to explain or excuse, that at the moment when the fierce battle was going on, which decided
the fate of Bohemia for generations to come, Frederick
was quietly seated at dinner within the walls of Prague,
and knew nothing until fugitives told him that all was
over.

The battle
on the
White Hill.
Maximilian of Bavaria had intrusted the command of
his numerous and well-organized forces to Baron Tilly, a
Netherlander, who had shown his bravery and capacity
in the Turkish wars. Frederick's general-in-chief was the
Prince of Anhalt, under whom were Thurn and Hohenlohe. The armies, when they met on the White Hill, a
few miles from Prague, were not so unequal in numbers,
but how different was the general spirit and courage!
Frederick had hoped at one time to gain the aid of England, France, Venice, and the half of Germany, but
nothing but disappointment had met him in all directions.
The Protestant Union declared that it could only act in
case the Palatinate itself were to be directly attacked, and
even ceased to pay the salary which Frederick had drawn
as its head. The young king's only subsidies were drawn
from Holland, his only useful allies were Mansfeld, the
Savoy commander, and Bethlen Gabor, the uncouth prince
of Transylvania. The army, then, that opposed Tilly was
ragged, unpaid, and altogether lacking in discipline; in
vain Frederick had mortgaged his jewels and the silver
from his table, and had wrung money from the Jews and
the Catholics.

The battle on the White Hill was fought and lost within

the space of little more than an hour. The Bohemians had the advantage of position, but all the daring, all the religious fervor, were on the side of the enemy. Their battle cry was "Holy Mary," the incentive to their decisive charge was given by a saintly monk, who blessed their banners, promised them the intercession of the mother of God in case of death, and thoroughly inspired with his own spirit both leaders and men alike. Anhalt, on the contrary, had relied on a calmness and courage of his troops which had failed them in the hour of need. At the very first charge they had fired wildly, and had become seized with a hopeless panic. Immediately after the defeat, Frederick consulted with his generals as to the possibility of holding Prague, but both Anhalt and Thurn had lost faith in their soldiers, and accused them of treason and cowardice; the signal was given for retreat, and Frederick and his wife left Bohemia, amid the curses of their subjects. His kingship had, indeed, vanished like the melting of winter snows.

Ferdinand, meanwhile, in Vienna, was listening to *Te Deums* and other special services. His preachers had pointed out that the gospel for the day when the battle was fought included the words, "Render unto Cæsar the things that are Cæsar's," while a Capuchin monk chose for his text the Psalmist's words, "Thou shalt chastise them with a rod of iron, and break them in pieces like a potter's vessel." Buoyed up by the consciousness of a righteous cause, the emperor initiated a political and religious reaction almost without a parallel. All important privileges relating to the Bohemians were placed in a box and sent to his palace; the parchment on which the Royal Charter was written shows to this day the savage cut that he made through its centre. The Bohemian throne was pronounced no longer elective, but hereditary, and the

The subjugation of Bohemia.

lands of all persons in any way tainted with rebellion were declared *in misericordia regis*. Courts were instituted with new and utterly unheard-of forms of procedure, evidences of evil intent being taken as a proof of the most serious charges. Not many were executed, but thousands were exiled, and the rest deprived, not only of political and religious freedom, but also of the right to speak their own language, and of the bare means of subsistence as well. Out of regard for his ally, the elector of Saxony, Ferdinand at first tried to spare the Lutheran as opposed to the Calvinist clergy; they were even told that they might keep their wives if they would speak of them in public as their cooks. When all such seductive arts had failed, and the Lutherans still persistently refused to turn Catholic, they too were banished in a body. Unremittingly, relentlessly, the reaction was carried through; the population quickly fell from 4,000,000 to less than 800,000, and Slavata reckoned that 30,000 families had wandered into exile. Starvation and torture were regular means of coercion, and in many districts there were quartered, on the refractory, bands of dragoons who in bitter mockery went by the name of angel makers.

The confiscated lands of the Bohemians.

The confiscated lands were sold to the highest bidders and could be bought for a mere song. It was by happy purchases at this dismal auction that the inscrutable Wallenstein laid the basis of his great fortune, whole cities at a time being handed over to him. To Ferdinand's credit it must be said that he afterward made partial repayments to some of those whom he had dispossessed, but whom he considered less guilty than the rest; yet the extraordinary charge is only too well founded that he made such payments in coin that he had expressly ordered debased to one-fourth of its face value, and that in reality contained but one-tenth of pure metal. This is not the least ugly of all the dark transactions of these times.   The government itself, intending to defraud its helpless subjects, was in turn the prey of a band of forgers, who, with their nearly worthless coin, bought in great quantities of the vacant lands, at nominally one-fourth, and actually one-tenth, of their already depleted cost.   Not until a later generation did the whole of this unsavory matter come to light, and the descendant of one of the coiners was fined a million guldens.   For us, the value of the whole Bohemian episode lies in the light it throws on the character of Ferdinand II. He had more difficulty in putting through his bigoted will in Germany, but his attempts were to be just as untiring and equally sincere.

CHAPTER XVIII

THE CAREER OF WALLENSTEIN, THE INTERVENTION OF FOREIGN POWERS, AND THE PEACE OF WESTPHALIA

LITERATURE : Same as in last chapter, with the addition of Ranke's *Wallenstein*, Droysen's *Gustavus Adolphus*, and Woltmann's *Geschichte des Westphälischen Friedens. Erdmannsdörfer, Deutsche Geschichte, 1648–1740*, and Ritter's work covering the same period give résumés of the results of the Thirty Years' War.

Absurd demands of Frederick V.

THAT a war which had originated in a private quarrel of the Bohemians should soon have spread to all parts of civilized Europe, was owing to two circumstances: first, that the dethroned Winter King so conducted himself as to justify Ferdinand II. in rigorously proceeding against him; second, that the emperor had made a promise to the Bavarian elector, which he could not fulfil without awakening violent opposition.

At a moment when his hold even on his own hereditary lands was growing precarious, Frederick of the Palatinate imagined that he would still be considered a dangerous pretender to the Bohemian throne. He offered to submit, but under what conditions ! The Bohemians were to be amnestied, and also to be confirmed in their right of election and in the free exercise of their religion ; the emperor was to make good the back pay of the soldiery that had just fought against him, to assume certain debts of Frederick, and to give him in addition a small gratuity or perhaps a yearly pension. The only answer to such representations was the hurling of the greater ban of the empire at this "rebel and traitor." Spanish troops under Spinola had already quartered themselves in the Palatinate, and had taken several towns; they were now reënforced by a portion of the imperial army under Tilly, the victor of the White Hill. The rest of Ferdinand's forces were kept busy in Hungary against Bethlen-Gabor. Frederick, indeed, was no longer so helpless as he had been in Bohemia. Mansfeld, who was far from Prague at the time of the great battle, had managed to escape with a considerable part of his troops. He would gladly have taken service with Ferdinand had the latter listened to his demands; but failing this, he devoted himself with real ardor to Frederick's cause, marching to the Palatinate with some fourteen thousand men. A no less important ally was the cousin of Frederick's wife, Christian of Brunswick, administrator of the secularized bishopric of Halberstadt. He was moved by a love of war which can only be described as bloodthirsty; by knightly devotion to the ex-queen, whose glove he wore on his helmet, and in whose honor his banner bore the device, "All for God and for her;" and, finally, by a well-grounded fear, that the reactionary policy of the emperor would eventually deprive him of his principality.

In one direction, indeed, from which he had a right to expect the most aid, Frederick was doomed to disappointment. The Protestant union, which had been founded in 1609 in view of just such an emergency as this, proved utterly unreliable and useless. Discord marked its deliberations, terror seized its individual members, and when, in the spring of 1621, an ultimatum was put to it by Spinola, its very existence came to an end. Out of its ruins, however, came succor for its former head, inasmuch as the Margrave of Baden-Durlach, commander of twenty thousand men, disapproving of the action of his colleagues, placed himself unreservedly at Frederick's disposal. The latter's forces had now swelled to some fifty thousand; a few

Frederick's new allies.

victories would have drawn to his banner a number of wavering princes, and a respectable balance might have been maintained even against the combined forces of Austria, Bavaria, and Spain.

But, save the one victory over Tilly at Wiesloch, where the imperial commander lost two thousand men, there came nothing but crushing disasters.   The Margrave of Baden had tried to storm Tilly's camp upon the heights above Wimpfen, and for his own defence had drawn up his wagons after the manner of an old Hussite fortress.   A fierce charge of the Spaniards under Cordova, and the accidental explosion of the margrave's own powder magazines, turned the well-fought day into a signal defeat.   A similar fate met Christian of Brunswick at Höchst.   This did not yet mean that all was lost, for the armies had retired from both fields in some kind of order; but Frederick now fell a victim to the well-meant interference of King James of England, who had endeavored of his own accord to mediate with the emperor.   The emperor's preliminary demand had been that Frederick should lay down his arms and dismiss both Christian and Mansfeld, and this James now persuaded his son-in-law to do.   The generals took service with the Dutch, whose long truce with Spain had run out in this same year, and met Cordova in the indecisive battle of Fleurus.   Christian lost his arm, which had to be amputated; but he sent word to the Spanish commander-in-chief, Spinola, to note well that the other was still uninjured; *Altera restat* was the motto he engraved on one of his coins.

As for Ferdinand, far from concluding peace as James of England had expected, he allowed Tilly to proceed without interruption to the subjugation of the whole Palatinate.   Heidelberg was taken and cruelly plundered. Maximilian of Bavaria, as head of the Catholic league.

took possession of its magnificent library, and sent it off
to Rome to become a part of the Vatican collection. This
ambitious prince, who, after years of careful management,
had brought order and system into the Bavarian administration, was now casting lusting eyes, not only on the
electoral dignity, but also on the newly conquered lands.
He had a bill of costs to present to the emperor; it proved
so enormous that Ferdinand was under the necessity of
either forfeiting the Austrian lands that he had pledged,
or of acceding to the new demands. The bestowal of a
Protestant electorate on a Catholic prince: that was a
feat that had never yet been successfully accomplished!
Maximilian, however, insisted on his claims and was ably
seconded by Pope Gregory XV., who was full of proud
plans for increasing the power of the holy Catholic
church. Spain, on the other hand, objected; she knew
better than any power in Europe what war meant, she saw
that to utterly crush the count palatine meant to prolong
the struggle indefinitely, and that the English friendship
must be forfeited should Philip IV. help to rob the son-in-
law of James I.

Even Ferdinand II. hesitated to settle the matter by
simple imperial rescript. From the beginning of the
previous century custom had sanctioned the occasional
calling together of a supplementary or deputy diet. Such
a delegation now met at Ratisbon in December, 1622, to
listen to the emperor's proposals; but the fierce opposition
that arose, even on the part of some of the Catholics,
caused him seriously to modify his intended measure. He
no longer dared now, openly and unconditionally, and for
all time, to give the electorate to Maximilian; the Bavarian
duke was merely to hold it pending negotiations with
Frederick; and he was to resign without a murmur should
the former elector "show due humility, ask for pardon, and

cease altogether from his machinations." The matter was to come up again for deliberation at a later date; the emperor, in the meanwhile, was to discuss with the electors the question of the rights of the count palatine's children. Even the Protestant Landgrave of Hesse was willing to agree to an arrangement like this, and the investiture of Maximilian took place with all form and ceremony.

But not in vain had Ferdinand been the pupil of the Jesuits. Though assuming for the benefit of the Protestants a yielding attitude, on the very day after the investiture he bound himself to Maximilian by a written agreement, to the effect that the latter should hold the electoral dignity for life; and that he, the emperor, no matter what the electors might determine concerning Frederick's children, would not consider himself bound by their decision.

Indignation at the transfer of the Palatinate.

At the first news of the deposition of Frederick, and the sequestration of his lands in favor of so orthodox a prince, all Catholic Europe was jubilant, and the Pope wrote to Ferdinand that the latter had "filled his breast with delight as with a stream of heavenly manna." But soon to the blindest eye it was evident that a storm was brewing that might shake the power of the Hapsburgs, and thus of the church, to the very foundations. Mansfeld and Christian of Brunswick appeared in North Germany, supplied with gold from England and Holland. The Lower Saxon Circle, one of those organizations for mutual defence of which ten had been formed in 1500, mustered its own army and determined to oppose the emperor, should he interfere with the North German bishoprics. Scattered here and there, their little principalities afforded to the party that held them obvious coigns of vantage.

The court of England by this time had changed its policy and was filled with hatred of Spain. The young

Prince of Wales, the future Charles I., had gone to Madrid incognito to look at his intended bride. Her religious intolerance, and the general stiffness and pride of the court, were such that the match came to nothing, and the young suitor returned home with disgust in his heart for the whole connection. The efforts of the English minister, Buckingham, brought about instead a marriage with Henrietta Maria, the sister of Louis XIII. of France. In this latter country Richelieu had just come into power, and he, although persecuting the Huguenots at home, was willing enough to encourage Protestants abroad to fight against the Hapsburgs. The Spaniards, by interfering in a local quarrel, had taken the Swiss Valtelline, as well as the province of Bormio; by which conquests the house of Austria had opened up direct communication between its German and Italian possessions. This Colossus of a house of Hapsburg was overshadowing Europe, and Richelieu, though not yet prepared for open war, was glad to furnish subsidies and diplomatic support to those who were anxious to begin the struggle.

James I. of England bestirs himself.

During this the last year of his life, the English king made up in some degree for his former lukewarmness in the cause of continental Protestantism. He bestirred himself right busily to form a coalition, that should wage war for the direct purpose of restoring to the count palatine his hereditary domains. The Dutch were easily won over; they had always sympathized with Frederick, had offered him an asylum, had paid him subsidies, and had only been prevented from doing more by reason of their own isolation.

Two other powers in Europe, Denmark and Sweden, were friendly to the cause, but England was placed in an awkward predicament of having to choose between them. Not only were Christian IV. and Gustavus Adolphus personal rivals, but in this very matter of the continental war

Treaty of the Hague with Christian of Denmark.

the policy of the one differed materially from that of the other. Christian both as Duke of Holstein, and thus member of the Lower Saxon Circle, and as uncle of the palatine electress, had his own interest in the struggle; he was, however, in every way, a pygmy compared to the Swedish king. Gustavus Adolphus, whose splendid talents had carried Sweden through glorious years of war and peace, insisted that should the struggle be begun, it should be with a large army and with ample funds; his demands, both on England and on Protestant Germany, were very high, though not higher than to a far-seeing eye the exigencies of the case demanded. But James I., and, on his death, his young successor, preferred the more modest plan of campaign of the Danish king. With him in December, 1625, Charles I. concluded the treaty of the Hague, and Gustavus Adolphus devoted all his energies to his own Polish war, and refrained from interference in Germany.

Wallen-
stein.

In spite of errors of judgment and of sins of omission on the part of his opponents, the emperor Ferdinand was at this moment in an extremely difficult and dangerous position. The sums extorted from the Bohemians had been squandered on churches and on Jesuits; the treasury was empty; to oppose the various forces that were springing up in all directions there was only the army of Tilly. Spain was occupied elsewhere for the moment, while Bethlen Gabor was making ready to help the Protestants.

It was natural that in such an emergency Ferdinand should seek assistance wherever it was most easy to obtain. Then it was that the man came to the fore who was to occupy the thoughts of his fellow-men, and to dominate his age to a rare degree — a mysterious, elusive genius, not thoroughly good but certainly not thoroughly bad. The character of Wallenstein is the more difficult to judge because of his own inveterate caution and reticence; it was his rule never to commit to paper anything that might compromise himself. Everything that we know about his motives is at second-hand, and verdicts vary according to the standpoint.

Born in Bohemia of Protestant parents, and subjected to various religious influences, Wallenstein finally counted himself a Roman Catholic, but was never fanatical or intolerant, unless it served some special turn. Superstitious we may call him, for dreams and portents largely influenced his actions, and the popular study of astrology occupied much of his time. Kepler once took his horoscope and told him that he was destined for great things; no less a person, he declared, than Queen Elizabeth of England had been born under the same constellation. With the stars in their courses in his favor, possessed of an ambition that recoiled before no step toward his own advancement, Wallenstein progressed rapidly in his military and civil career. His first wife, Lucretia Neckish, brought him a considerable fortune; after her death he looked for a connection that would afford him influence and high social position, and found it in the house of Harrach. With a sword that was always at the service of the Hapsburgs, he had risen by the year 1622 to be the highest commanding officer in Bohemia.

Early years of Wallenstein.

At the time of the great sale of lands confiscated from the Protestants, Wallenstein had been far and away the largest purchaser; the domains of the "Prince of Friedland," as he was now called, covered the whole of northeastern Bohemia. One can judge of his wealth from the homely fact that in one year alone the beer monopoly within his boundaries brought him a revenue of sixteen thousand guldens. And excellently and economically did he manage his estates; even when busy with his army in field, he is known to have sent directions about the proper food for swine, calves, and foals, and to have recommended a particular treatment for sick hens. Not altogether un-important details these, when we remember that, later, his chief occupation was not fighting battles, but providing food and clothing for immense armies, many of his supplies coming from his own lands.

Ferdinand's arrangement with Wallenstein. The arrangement was unprecedented, which Ferdinand, in his hour of need, made with Wallenstein. The latter was to raise and equip an army of twenty-one thousand men at his own expense. Once fairly in the field, the emperor was to undertake the pay of the soldiers; but they were largely to subsist by levying contributions on the lands through which they passed. The commander-in-chief, besides his regular yearly compensation, was to have as his perquisite the ransoms of all ordinary prisoners and a share of the booty, and in addition to this, he was en-dowed with political, almost sovereign, rights. He might make treaties with territorial lords, and even, if need be, grant concessions with regard to their religion.

Tilly and Wallenstein. Ferdinand little knew as yet the man with whom he had to deal, else how could he have ordered him to consult on all important matters with Tilly, the general of the league forces? The two were as opposed to each other as fire and water. Wallenstein, as he soon showed, meant to raise the ordinary prose both of war and politics to a higher plane. Protestants were as welcome in his army as Catholics, Walloons and Croats as Germans, desperadoes as honest men. His original twenty-one thousand men were growing into many times that number, and he quartered them on the lands of friends and foes alike. In Tilly's head, on the other hand, were no great political plans; he was a brave, plain soldier and a devout Roman Catholic of the intolerant and prosely-tizing kind. As the faithful henchman of Maximilian of Bavaria, his one object was to fight battles and reduce Protestants to submission. To him fell the good fortune of routing the king of Denmark in the fierce battle of Lutter, whereas Wallenstein could only point to a skirmish with Mansfeld at Dessau on the Elbe, and a long pursuit of the Savoy condottiere into Bohemia, where Mansfeld had hoped to unite his forces with those of Bethlen Gabor.

It was Mansfeld's last campaign; Bethlen, induced by the laxness of the coalition in sending him promised subsidies, made his own peace with the emperor; Mansfeld withdrew, but fell sick on the way. Whatever his faults, he was accustomed to face his enemies; and now, confronted with death, he armed himself to the teeth, girded his sword at his side, and insisted on being held in a standing position until the breath had left his body. The cause that he had espoused seemed again likely to fail, for England and France had fallen out with each other, and the Danish king, chased to the utmost limits of northwestern Europe, had little hope but in submission, and finally, in 1629, concluded the Peace of Lübeck.

Mansfeld's death.

Wallenstein's whole method of procedure had by this time raised up for him many and violent opponents, chiefly among the members of the Catholic league. What was his purpose in levying this enormous army? What was the need of it now that practically no enemy at all remained in Germany? Ferdinand himself in the days preceding Mansfeld's death had been puzzled and annoyed at the conduct of his general; he desired more activity and less recruiting, and he sent his chief minister Eggenberg to confer with Wallenstein at Bruck on the Leitha. The revelations made in this interview had fairly taken away the breath of the minister, who returned in haste — as Wallenstein's warmest adherent — to acquaint his master with the real trend of the new policy.

Wallenstein's plans for Ferdinand.

The imperial authority, it seems, was to be established not only over a few rebellious estates like the former elector

of the Palatinate or the city of Magdeburg, which refused
to accept a garrison, but over all princes and subjects alike.
As Wallenstein later expressed himself, the emperor was
no longer to be a mere image, an ornament in the general
structure.   For this it was necessary that he should have
a large and well-trained army, one indeed that should
be the terror of all Europe.   These forces were not to be
wasted in petty undertakings, nor was it wise by employing sectarian measures to make the task more difficult.
One reason for employing Protestants in the army and for
giving them some of the best offices had been to emphasize
the superior and impartial position of the nation's head.

Ferdinand
heaps
honors on
Wallen-
stein.

Ferdinand, for a time at least, was completely won over
to these ideas.   Even the tolerance towards the Protestants seems to have met with his approval.   Never before
or since has there been in Germany such a military
despotism as was now established.   The army reached
the enormous total of one hundred and thirty thousand —
an incredible number if we consider that each man was more
highly paid than are the soldiers of modern times, and that,
according to the peculiar custom during these thirty years
of war, thousands of women and children were allowed to
follow the camps and to add their maintenance to the
general expense.   The requisitions were burdensome in
the extreme; Wallenstein himself, who tried to spare
the country as much as possible, and did everything in his
power to see that the harvests were properly sown and
reaped, wrote to Ferdinand with regard to some of the
northern provinces that they were thoroughly ruined, that
the inhabitants had taken to eating cats and dogs, and that
suicides were frequent.

Yet while the dream lasted Ferdinand could not do
enough for his loyal champion and defender.   Privileges
without end were heaped upon his head.   He had formed

a plan for winning the Hanseatic towns and gaining for them a monopoly of the trade with Spain. Ferdinand accordingly appointed him "general of the whole imperial armada and of the Baltic and the North Sea." His principality of Friedland was raised to a dukedom, and permission given him to issue coins bearing his own image. He might appoint not only the lower officers of the army, but the colonels and captains as well. His pay was increased threefold, a measure which was to have retroactive force for the past three years. And all this was nothing to the final concession which even Ferdinand hesitated long before deciding to grant. The emperor by this time was millions in his great subject's debt. Wallenstein, supported by Ferdinand's Jesuit councillors, to whom he offered free play in his coveted new domains, proposed the expulsion of the Protestant dukes of Mecklenburg, and the handing over of their lands to himself in lieu of all other claims. It would be a good thing, it was argued, to make a severe example of a few rebellious princes. " I only wish," wrote Wallenstein to his field marshal Arnim, " that the Duke of Pomerania would also prove disloyal."

The " Duke of Friedland " was now an independent sovereign in all but name, with lands stretching far along the Baltic coast. The magnificence of his mode of living beggars all description. In his suite were two hundred and twenty-five chamberlains and stewards, pages, lackeys, and Jesuits ; one thousand horses were needed for their use. For his further ambitious schemes it was necessary that he should have more towns upon the seacoast, and he summoned the citizens of Stralsund to receive an imperial garrison within their walls. When the inhabitants refused the request, preferring to withstand a siege, he is said to have remarked that he would have the city, even though it were fastened by chains to the vault of heaven. Here

Wallenstein's lordly doings.

finally, however, he met with the first check in his military career, and was obliged to raise the siege on account of the aid which Danish and Swedish ships brought to the garrison.

It may well be imagined that not only the members of the league, but all the electors as well, had now become thoroughly alarmed at Wallenstein's doings. Already in 1627 a convention at Mulhausen had sent a vehement protest to the emperor, declaring that the electors themselves would take measures for "saving the sore-oppressed fatherland from final ruin." Since then, utterances had been reported to the Duke of Bavaria which roused him to the pitch of frenzy: Wallenstein intended to dissolve the league and make the imperial throne hereditary; the electors were to be made to stand on their good behavior; indeed, there would never be peace in Germany until one of them should have his head taken off and placed at his own feet; after Ferdinand's death he, Wallenstein, would make himself master with the title of "Emperor of the West." Probably the truest of all these rumors was one to the effect that Wallenstein meant to make the ruler of Germany as absolute as the monarchs of France or England. And had Ferdinand supported him, the means were at hand to have secured success.

The "Edict of Restitution."

But on this none too firm emperor there was now being brought to bear a pressure that he could not withstand. To his request that his son be chosen as his successor during his own lifetime, the electors turned a deaf ear — this finally broke his resistance. He told the representative of the Archbishop of Mainz "so truly as he desired to see God's face," he did not mean to detract from the liberty of the electors; and that if any of his subjects made the attempt, he would order his head cut off. He wrote to Wallenstein that the authority and supremacy of the imperial house were at stake, and that a large part of the army must be dismissed.

This order was in part obeyed, but the appearance of a large French army in Italy in connection with the war for the Mantuan succession, gave the general a pretext for further levies. Of far more lasting importance was the emperor's change of policy, brought about by this same pressure, in the matter of religious toleration. Without consulting Wallenstein, he put his hand to the most radical and dangerous document that has ever been issued in all the long course of German religious history. The question over which, for three-quarters of a century, diets had deliberated and courts of justice had wrangled, was now to be decided by a stroke of the pen. The cruel reaction that had taken place in Bohemia was to be attempted in Germany, and Ferdinand hoped that Tilly and Wallenstein would be his willing instruments. The strongest attack that had ever been made on the work of Martin Luther was now in progress ; but the nemesis was under way.

The act known as the Edict of Restitution, which was published in March, 1629, declared roundly that all ecclesiastical property which had come into Protestant hands since the Treaty of Passau in 1552, might now be reclaimed, and that Catholic priests should replace all Protestant holders of bishoprics. Nor should these new bishops be bound by that old, unrecorded declaration which purported to have come from the emperor Ferdinand I., and required toleration for Protestant subjects. To make the rags and tatters of the Augsburg Peace of still less avail, it was now expressly stated that the terms of that instrument had only applied to Lutherans, and that "other sects" were to be excluded from its advantages.

What a complete revolution was here intended will be seen from the fact, that the Protestants at this time held two former archbishoprics, twelve bishoprics, and five hundred abbacies, the revenues of which for two generations had been put to public uses in the different states. The Palatinate and Hesse, moreover, were full of Calvinists, to which faith belonged also the elector of Brandenburg. One might possibly think that such a general edict was meant as a mere threat or political card, but such was not the case. Ferdinand was deadly in earnest, and he set to work at once to seize churches and monasteries, and to build Jesuit colleges. A part of the spoils was to go toward the payment of the army. Goslar was fixed upon as the seat of a central Catholic university, which should spread its influence in all directions.

Dismissal of Wallenstein.

Wallenstein disapproved of the edict and refused to help in carrying it out; but little enough could he do, for his own hour had come. The princes and electors met together at Ratisbon in June, 1630, determined not to part without first having achieved the "Friedländer's" fall. Well might this struggle be called the greatest diplomatic victory of the century. Ferdinand's throne was tottering; Richelieu, whose envoys were present, had offered, if need be, to throw France's influence into the scale in favor of having Maximilian of Bavaria declared emperor. At last Ferdinand yielded, and emissaries were sent to acquaint Wallenstein with his fate. He took the news calmly; he had read it in the stars, he is reported to have said. The army, it was determined, should be reduced to thirty-nine thousand, the forces of the league to twenty-one hundred. Tilly was to be commander-in-chief.

Landing of Gustavus Adolphus.

But by this time the Edict of Restitution had called upon the stage the "strong man armed" who was to keep the house of German Protestantism. The "Lion of the North" had crouched and sprung. It was known, indeed, at Ratisbon at the very time of Wallenstein's dismissal, that the Swedish king had landed on the coast of Pomerania; but men were utterly unconscious of what that fact signified. "We have a new little enemy," the emperor is reported to have said good-humoredly in his broadest Viennese dialect. The officers of his chancery consulted their maps to find just where Sweden lay, while the Catholic princes prepared to enjoy a new division of territory, should any one be so foolhardy as to join the northern adventurer.

Wallenstein, indeed, would have known better than to underrate this danger. As "general of the Baltic and the North Sea" he had found his plans crossed at all points by the intervention of the Swedish king, and had assiduously promoted the Polish war so as to keep his enemy occupied. He had even conceived a project for striking at Sweden's trade, by building such a canal between the two bodies of water as has only been completed in our own day.

It was, in very deed, a man of extraordinary ability who had now stepped into the arena of German politics. Gustavus Adolphus, a descendant of the great house of Vasa, had come to the throne of Sweden in 1611 as rival of his Catholic cousin, King Sigismund of Poland. A mere boy of seventeen, but with keen perceptions and thoroughly trained by a watchful father, he had found himself the inheritor of three foreign wars, and of what seemed like civil anarchy. In twenty years of unremitting endeavor he had made Sweden's name thoroughly respected abroad, and had brought order and enterprise into her internal affairs. He had quelled the rebellious nobles and had made them submit to taxation. As for the Swedish army, he had completely remodelled it; combining the various disorderly squads into regular regiments, and arming these with muskets instead of spears and pikes. He uniformed and disciplined his troops, and otherwise prepared for the great tasks he had in hand. The Russians were pushed so far back from the Baltic that, as he told his estates, they would

Early years of Gustavus Adolphus

now find it hard to "spring over the little stream." By the terms of a peace with Poland, concluded in the year of the restitution edict through the timely aid of Richelieu, he gained temporary possession of a number of Prussian ports. With his "dominion of the Baltic" thus secured in the East, with his hands free for new enterprises, his next thought was to gain points of vantage on the German coast. The cry of the Protestants appealed strongly to his sympathies, but equally strongly to his political aspirations.

Reception of Gustavus Adolphus on German soil.

Gustavus Adolphus's first reception on German soil was anything but encouraging. Even the Duke of Pomerania, though he loathed the imperial garrisons that held his fortresses, lacked courage to welcome the deliverer, and only yielded to compulsion. Months passed before any power, save the cities of Magdeburg and Stralsund, made common cause with the Swedes. With some it may have been a matter of national pride, but the majority were influenced by the fear of Tilly's army. A convention of Protestant estates did take place at Leipzig in February, 1631, but the proceedings only reflected the weakness and timidity of the summons; an assembly that avowedly met for the "furtherance of peaceful negotiations," and that expressed its "friendly confidence" in the Catholic powers, was not likely to accomplish much.

Treaty of Bärwalde.

The first care of the "Lion of the North" was to rid Pomerania of the imperial garrisons; his second, to send an officer to Magdeburg to organize a systematic plan of defence, and also to announce the speedy coming of relief. Napoleon Bonaparte once declared that these early operations of the Swedish king marked him for one of the greatest generals of any age. Nor were the diplomatic achievements of less importance. By a treaty with France he secured a large subsidy without in the least compromising his dignity. Richelieu had tried to patronize this half-barbaric prince, whose father had owed his throne to the mere will of the people; he had wished Louis XIII., as " King by the grace of God," to take precedence in the wording of the document, and also to have a voice in the plan of campaign. But Gustavus had asserted himself right royally; in one copy of the Treaty of Bärwalde his name followed, in the other it preceded, that of the French king; while the only concessions he made, related to the treatment of Catholics, and the possible neutrality of the league.

Unfortunately for the besieged city of Magdeburg, Gustavus could not move from his base of supplies without first securing the allegiance of the two chief Protestant powers of the North; but two such wavering and unstable princes as George William of Brandenburg and John George of Saxony would have been difficult to find. John George's chief claim to distinction lay in his ability to consume immense quantities of wine, while the Brandenburg elector was urged in vain by his brother-in-law to declare himself either his friend or his enemy, to be one thing or the other, hot or cold; but at any rate to adopt *mascula consilia*, to show that he was a man. Gustavus finally drew up his army before the walls of Berlin, and pointed his cannon at the city—a step which caused the elector to send his mother and all the princesses to beg for mercy, and finally to appear himself and conclude an alliance. He was to deliver up the fortresses of Spandau and Küstrin for the duration of the war, and to pay a monthly subsidy. A passing cloud was cast over the reconciliation, by the fact that when the Swedes fired salvos of joy to celebrate the peace, they forgot to remove their heavy charges, and some damage was done to buildings in Berlin.

So long had these negotiations lasted, that Gustavus had seriously thought of abandoning Germany to her fate;

Negotiations with Brandenburg and Saxony.

The fall of
Magdeburg.

had he so wished he could, strange as it may seem, have joined hands with Wallenstein, who made a proposal to that effect. The worst result of the delay was the fall of Magdeburg; day after day, in hourly hope of his coming, the little garrison of three thousand had held its own against ten times that number, commanded, too, by such experienced generals as Tilly and Pappenheim. When the city at last was taken by storm, the inhabitants, determined that a point of such great strategic importance should not be of service to the enemy, applied the torch to their own houses, — an act for which posterity has given the unenviable credit to Tilly, who is represented even in engravings of the time with the flames of Magdeburg as a background. Of the whole great city, one of the proudest in Germany, there only remained the cathedral and some fifty houses.

The battle
of Breiten-
feld.

For Gustavus, indeed, from the moment of his treaty with Brandenburg, the whole horizon had begun to brighten. The queen of Sweden landed in Pomerania with fresh troops; while from England came reënforcements to the extent of six thousand men. And the emperor's own action now drove John George of Saxony to abandon his neutrality; for Tilly was ordered to try the same manœuvre that Gustavus had practised against Brandenburg, and to force the elector to a decision at the cannon's mouth. Tilly gathered all his forces at Eisleben, and put the point-blank question; but inasmuch as at the same time Saxony's demand for a reversal of the restitution edict was categorically refused — the emperor declaring that he would uphold it until not a shirt was left to his own back — the decision fell out not to Ferdinand's, but to the Swedish king's advantage. On the 11th of September, 1631, the treaty was signed, by which eighteen thousand Saxon soldiers were added to the twenty-eight thousand of Gustavus. Tilly now turned the whole fury of his attack against

Leipzig, which, unfortified and undefended, was obliged to submit to an immense indemnity, and to accept an imperial garrison. But Gustavus, with his combined army, was close at Tilly's heels, leaving him only time to intrench himself outside the city in the strongest position he could find. With his troops drawn up in a solid phalanx, ten men deep, with the cavalry on either wing and artillery in front, after the old approved fashion, Tilly awaited the enemy's attack.

Not only Tilly, but the whole German people as well, experienced that day a mode of warfare that was entirely new. In the Swedish army all was action and change; cavalry and infantry had been trained to supplement each other at every point. Instead of in dense battalions that trusted to mere weight of onslaught, the vanguard were drawn up in divisions only three men deep, the two front rows kneeling, the third standing, so that all could fire at once. In the rear was a large reserve which, in point of fact, won this battle of Breitenfeld. In spite of Tilly's superior position, in spite of the panic which seized on the Saxons and drove them, together with their elector, into mad flight, Gustavus, by a brilliant manœuvre, carried the day and almost annihilated the imperial army. From eighteen to nineteen thousand men were killed, wounded, or taken prisoners; the whole of the artillery and some ninety standards fell into the hands of the Swedes. A shout of triumph went up from Protestant Germany, and a news-leaf of the day points out in glowing words how the victory was due to God's counsel and the Swedes' undaunted courage, to justice and a good cause. The loss of Magdeburg was gloriously avenged. As no other army of any size was in the field, the road lay open to the possessions of the Catholic league, as well as to the emperor's hereditary lands.

Absolutely the only hope, now, for Ferdinand and the

Catholics, lay in the recall of Wallenstein. But the services
of the great man were difficult to obtain; all the more so,
as Ferdinand's first thought was merely to associate him in
the command with his own son. The wound to Wallenstein's outraged dignity was far from healed; the emperor
should learn, he said to Arnim, what it meant to "affront
a cavalier." He would rather, he declared to an emissary
of Ferdinand, be sent to hell than resume the command.
No, indeed, he would not take it, though God Almighty
should ask him in person. All the grain on his own lands
he removed as far as possible from the clutches of the imperialists. He did his best in these days to come to an
agreement with Gustavus, and had the latter been able to
give him eleven thousand men, he would have struck a
blow at the heart of Bohemia. In judging him for these
intrigues, it must be remembered that, in his own mind at
least, he was as free to make alliances as any other prince;
as free, for instance, as Maximilian of Bavaria, who was
even now a protégé of Richelieu's. Wallenstein had bought
his duchy for hard cash; no debt of gratitude was due to
any one.

At last, finding that Gustavus would not give him the
desired troops, Wallenstein gave way to the emperor's
pressing appeals, and agreed to "take an interest in the
imperial army." Office or pay he did not want, but he
would raise an army of forty thousand within three months,
and the emperor might then intrust the command to whom
he pleased. When the time came, as there was no one
else of sufficient prestige to keep the motley troops in order,
he yielded still further and agreed to take the field, but
only in return for dictatorial, almost royal rights. Wallenstein was to be the sole head of all the imperial armies in
the field and, save through him, the emperor himself was
to give no commands; the latter was to promise expressly

to pay no heed to anything that his father confessor or any other of the clergy should choose to say against his general. An equivalent was to be given for Mecklenburg, until such time as the Swedes should have been dispossessed; and two independent Catholic sources, a papal nuncio and a Spanish envoy, agree that Ferdinand promised Wallenstein the first electorate the latter should be able to conquer.

Meanwhile the Saxons under Arnim had taken Prague, — whence Wallenstein had no difficulty in dislodging them, — and Gustavus Adolphus in an uninterrupted succession of triumphs had marched through the "Priests' Lane," the great row of bishoprics on the Main and Rhine. Like one of the old mediæval emperors, at his headquarters in Mainz he received embassies from all over Germany. During these days of splendid repose, negotiations for peace were entered into, which are interesting as showing the conqueror's projects and his ultimate programme for Germany. For himself he claimed, in addition to a strip of territory along the Pomeranian coast, a sort of protectorship over all German Protestants; services like his, he declared, were not to be rewarded with a few months' pay, like those of any common mercenary. The restitution edict was to be annulled, and complete toleration granted; while not only was the former palatine elector to be reinstated in all his lands and dignities, but matters in Bohemia, Silesia, and Moravia were to return to the standpoint of the year 1618.

Triumphs of Gustavus Adolphus.

On the refusal of these terms, Gustavus resumed his victorious progress; his object being now to penetrate to the heart of Bavaria. The old wrong done to the city of Donauwörth was righted, when, after a two days' bombardment, the Catholic garrison laid down their arms. Tilly, with the remnants of his army, then tried to block the way at the crossing of the river Lech, but was wounded in the skirmish, and was carried to Ingolstadt to end his life. Just a year after the fall of Magdeburg Gustavus passed in triumph into Maximilian's capital of Munich, and at his side rode that same unfortunate Winter King who owed such a debt of hatred to the Bavarian duke.

The battle of Lützen.

But already Wallenstein, having cleansed Bohemia of the Saxons, had answered the appealing call of his former enemy; joining his forces with Maximilian's, he drew up his army in the neighborhood of Nuremberg, where Gustavus was intrenched. He meant, he said, to show the Swedish king, in turn, a new mode of warfare: it was that of passive resistance. Nothing could budge him from his position, though supplies for both armies grew scarcer and scarcer, and starvation bred disease. In this long game of delay he proved the master, and Gustavus, after a fruitless attempt to storm his ramparts, withdrew his troops. But when Wallenstein turned against Saxony and began ravaging the elector's lands, Gustavus followed him hard and fast, and came upon him near Leipzig. The neighborhood that had witnessed the great battle of Breitenfeld was now to see another similar sight. The fierce encounter at Lützen proved another victory for the Swedes, but it cost them dearer than a dozen ordinary defeats. Their idolized leader had never hesitated personally to face the greatest dangers; at the passage of the Lech he had even done his own reconnoitring, and once, unrecognized, had culled valuable information from one of the enemy's own pickets. Now, anxious to wipe out the repulse at Nuremberg, he seemed almost to court the most exposed positions. Riding into the very midst of a regiment of cuirassiers, he was wounded in several places and fell from his horse. Over his dead body his Swedes, led by the young Duke Bernard of Weimar, fought like very tigers; even the invincible Wal lenstein was repulsed with the loss of his best officers, of thousands of his soldiers, and of the whole of his artillery. The corpse of Gustavus Adolphus was removed to Wolgast, where an immense train of mourners followed him to the grave; there followed, too, an invisible procession of ruined hopes and lost possibilities. In all probability the death of the man in whom he had put his trust, broke the heart of the fugitive palatine elector; for the unfortunate Frederick breathed his last before the lapse of a fortnight. It might have comforted his last hours, could he only have known that his children would receive back their inheritance, and that his daughter's son would one day wear the crown of England.

As for Wallenstein, after the battle of Lützen he remained strictly on the defensive, devoting himself to the task of reorganizing his shattered army. On those of his subordinates who had been lacking in bravery, or had in any way neglected their duty, he inflicted the severest punishments, no less than eleven officers being put to death like common criminals. The difficulty of procuring cannon, not to speak of new recruits, delayed matters for several months.

Oxenstierna's difficulties.

During this time the Swedes, led by Bernard of Weimar, were able to reconquer the whole of Franconia — which was afterward given to Bernard as a separate duchy, dependent on the crown of Sweden — and also to occupy the lower Palatinate and parts of Swabia and Bavaria. The supreme direction of Swedish affairs, was given by the state council at Stockholm to the chancellor Oxenstierna, who, indeed, let fall many of his former master's projects for the Protestant cause, but clung tenaciously to the idea of securing for his country a fitting reward for all her pains and sacrifices — such compensation, he claimed, " as kings and princes, not as shopkeepers, are accustomed to give."

Oxenstierna's designs, including as they did his own continuance as leader of the German Protestants, were hampered by the attitude of the Elector of Saxony, who, although he had subordinated himself to a great king, was not minded to obey an ordinary nobleman.   The elector's private desire was for a speedy cessation of hostilities; "better," said Arnim in his name, "the worst kind of a peace than the best kind of a war."   But if the struggle must be continued, he, John George, was the proper head for his own countrymen.   So bitter was the controversy, that the question of leadership was tacitly waived, and Saxony took part in the subsequent events as an independent third party.

With the smaller Protestant powers, Oxenstierna, in April, 1633, signed the league of Heilbronn, which assured to Sweden a suitable compensation, and gave to himself the wished-for directorship.   A war council of seven Germans and three Swedes was to tender him advice, but not restrict his actions.   France agreed to continue her subsidies and sent her agents all over Germany to see that the various enemies of the house of Hapsburg should neither slumber nor sleep.

Wallen-
stein's
delays.

By the month of May of the same year, Wallenstein had a well-equipped army of sixty thousand men leisurely encamped in Bohemia and Silesia; but already the old doubts as to his ultimate purpose had begun to arise in many quarters.   What was the meaning of this lethargy and of these continued levies, when the whole hostile force in these regions only numbered twenty-four thousand men? Why did he not strike a decisive blow and then hurry to Bavaria, where Bernard of Weimar might at any moment make for Ratisbon, the key to the Danube and to the Austrian possessions?   For one thing, Wallenstein miscalculated Bernard's plans, expecting him to invade Bohemia;

he would stake, he said, his honor and his head on the correctness of this judgment. But there was, indeed, another reason for his inactivity. Political schemes, far more than war, occupied his thoughts just now; he held frequent interviews with the Saxon general Arnim, as well as with emissaries of the Bohemian exiles, who were burning to regain their lost possessions. While ostensibly conducting peace negotiations in the name of the emperor, he was striving to bring into effect his own plan for the reconstruction of Germany. If Ferdinand's views should ultimately coincide with his own, well and good; if not, it was to be a question between actual power and lofty prerogative.

From Ferdinand, Wallenstein had not received the promised reward for his intervention, nor in other ways had the emperor fulfilled his contract. In spite of all that had been said, Jesuit influences had maintained the upper hand. Spain had conceived the project of setting up an independent army in Alsace to maintain her connection with her Netherland provinces, and the emperor, without waiting for the consent of his generalissimo, had given the required permission. The Viceroy of Milan, Feria, had been appointed to the command; but Wallenstein saw in the whole move an effort to restrict his own absolute power. A still deeper offence was Ferdinand's refusal to make over to him the electorate of Brandenburg, or indeed, to assure him any other equivalent for the loss of Mecklenburg. What Wallenstein had dreamed of, was to found a third great Catholic state in the heart of Germany. The Spanish minister Olivarez had warmly seconded him in the plan, and he had arranged a combination by which, with the lands of the Hohenzollerns for a centre, his territories should stretch from Friedland to Frisia. But the emperor, longing now for a general peace, had dreaded to take so radical a step.

It must not be supposed that Wallenstein's subsequent actions were entirely influenced by a desire to be revenged upon Ferdinand. Much of his conduct must forever remain enigmatical; but enough is known to show that he was far removed from being a common traitor, influenced solely by personal motives. When the plan was broached by Bohemian nobles of making him their king, he quickly repudiated such a "piece of roguery"; when France offered her support to the same end, he broke off all negotiations. It is true he made frequent and unaccountable truces that conduced greatly to the advantage of the enemy; had his aim been perfectly single, he would have struck a crushing blow, and then made his terms.

Wallenstein's treasonable plans.

To Arnim, Wallenstein proposed that the Saxon army should unite with his own, for the purpose of dictating such a peace to Germany as should secure an equal toleration for Catholics and Protestants. All who had been unjustly dispossessed were to be reinstated in their rights. Sweden was to be pacified by being given German districts of importance. Should the emperor prove refractory, he must be intimidated. On a later occasion, in a moment of great irritation, he produced a specific plan for a campaign against Ferdinand, and the Saxon general was despatched to the Swedish camp to win, if he could, the approval of Oxenstierna. These latter negotiations were broken off by Wallenstein of his own accord; either he repented or he feared being thwarted. Perhaps he recoiled before the thought of joining with a foreigner in such an enterprise, and it is certainly significant that, in another interview with Arnim, he declared that no lasting peace could be made until all foreign powers, such as Spain, France, and Sweden, should have been "kicked out" of the empire.

So various, indeed, were Wallenstein's plans, so inscrutable his real aims, that of no power did he win the con-

fidence. Sweden, Saxony, and France were all willing
enough to urge him on; but they wished him to thoroughly
commit himself, to accept for instance the Bohemian crown,
before they could take him seriously. "Question him
searchingly and see how far he will go," was the instruction issued to Arnim by the court of Saxony. As for the
emperor, he was not at all convinced at this time that events
were not pursuing their proper course. But the capture of
Ratisbon, which Bernard now accomplished, and Wallenstein's subsequent attitude, brought matters to a final crisis;
all that had been needed completely to undermine the
great general's influence was one serious military blunder.

How often had Maximilian of Bavaria begged and implored that imperial forces should be sent to his assistance!
First General Aldringen, then General Gallas had been
stationed not far from the Bavarian frontier; but Wallenstein had instructed each in turn to remain on the defensive. His own firm conviction was that Bernard of
Weimar had no serious designs on Bavaria, but by his
puzzling marches and counter-marches merely meant to
entice away the bulk of the imperial army, and then to fall
suddenly on Bohemia. It was here that he made his fatal
error; before there was time to render assistance, Ratisbon
had capitulated.

Wallen-
stein's
failure to
relieve
Ratisbon.

Now came a series of incomprehensible moves, on Wallenstein's part, that roused the impatience at Vienna to
fever heat. He had at first written that he would march
day and night until he had driven back the Duke of
Weimar; in a council of war at Pilsen he had announced
his intention of taking one hundred companies of the best
cavalry and making an instant start. Then quickly came
the news that he had renounced the attempt, and would
go into winter quarters where he stood. Whether, as
he claimed, his act was due to the impossibility of con-

ducting a successful campaign in the severe weather that
had already set in, or whether hatred of Maximilian, or
other personal reasons, held him back, can never now be
ascertained.   In vain Ferdinand expostulated, and asked
in any case to be more frequently consulted, lest it might
seem that there was "another king in the land besides
himself."   In answer to a distinct command to march
against the enemy, or at any rate to leave Bohemia, which
was being drained dry by the constant contributions, Wallenstein sent a letter, signed by his chief officers, stating
that a winter campaign, or even the taking up of winter
quarters in an enemy's country, would mean the ruin of
the army.   The great general was growing more and more
reckless ; when Ferdinand gave some simple orders to
Colonel Suys, who was stationed in Austria, Wallenstein
countermanded them, and released the inferior officers from
the duty of obedience.

Wallen-
stein turns
traitor.

By this time Wallenstein's last friends at Vienna had
deserted him ; his appeal to the army was savagely criticised, and Maximilian of Bavaria openly urged the emperor
no longer to be dependent on the freaks, humors, and
passions of such a man.   The most active of his enemies
was the Spanish envoy, Oñate, who was embittered by the
opposition to the army sent under Feria to guard the way
to the Netherlands.

The knowledge that his fall was imminent, the determination not to bear quietly a second dismissal, drove
Wallenstein into his last and most desperate courses.
Flying messengers were sent to the French and to the
Saxons to announce that now the mask would really be
laid aside.   With feverish impatience, Wallenstein awaited
the coming of Feuquière and Arnim, the two ambassadors
on whom he had pinned his faith.   He was never to know
that Louis XIII. had taken up his cause with enthusiasm,

and had sent him an offer to pay him a million francs
yearly, from the moment when he should have struck a
blow at one of Ferdinand's provinces. The elector of
Saxony took time to consult with George William of
Brandenburg, and Arnim, also, arrived too late. As for
Bernard of Weimar, who was also approached, he refused
still to believe in Wallenstein's sincerity.

Wallenstein, in the meantime, had moved his troops
around so as to have in his neighborhood those whom he
could most trust. Among the higher officers he was absolutely sure of his field marshal, Illow, and of the generals
Kinsky and Terzky, the latter of whom was his brother-in-
law. He hoped that many more would hold to him for the
sake of their own advantage ; no one else was so able as he
to assure their back pay, and the return of the large outlays made by them for recruiting purposes. When Illow
intentionally spread the report that Wallenstein meant to
resign, there was an outbreak of grief and indignation, and
he was warmly urged to remain. He declared, apparently
reluctantly, that he would do so, if the officers would stand
by him so long as he remained in the emperor's service,
and not allow him to be put upon or insulted. The next
day, on the 12th of January, 1634, at a banquet held at
Illow's house, when the wine had passed freely, it was
determined that this agreement should be committed to
writing and should be signed by those present. Each and
all thus pledged themselves to stand by their beloved commander, and to " sacrifice for him the last drop of their blood."
But even before the guests departed the omission of the
clause " so long as he should remain in the emperor's service," was noticed ; contentions arose which led to a wild scene,
and windows, chairs, and benches were broken. Terzky is said
to have drawn his sword and threatened to cut in pieces any
enemy of the generalissimo, whereupon Piccolomini, hitherto

The
banquet at
Pilsen.

Wallenstein's warmest friend, and regarded by him with a superstitious reverence on account of some secret of his nativity, cried out in his own vernacular, "O traditore!"

The extent of Wallenstein's treason.

Even yet Wallenstein cannot be said to have descended to the lowest depths of treason. He was false to his emperor, but not false to his country. He still kept firmly in view his cherished project of imposing upon Germany a wholesome and advantageous peace. For this he labored to the last; for this, in part at least, he had sinned. Four days before the banquet at Pilsen he confided his plans to a Bohemian refugee named Schlieff, who afterward drew up a protocol of what he had been told. The French, although their money would be welcome, were not to be allowed to cross the Rhine; they were to be compensated at the cost of the Spaniards in Italy. The Swedes were to be given as little as possible, the Palatinate to be restored to the family of its former owner. The chief sufferer was to be Maximilian of Bavaria, at whose cost a number of restitutions and rewards were to be granted.

The order for Wallenstein's arrest.

The news of the happenings at the banquet in Pilsen, removed from the court of Vienna its last doubts and its last compunctions. It was determined to watch for the proper moment for informing the officers and soldiers that they were released from their obedience to Wallenstein; as yet three generals only — Aldringen, Gallas, and Piccolomini — were taken into the emperor's confidence, and told to seize the person of their commander-in-chief, if possible, and bring him to trial. The greatest secrecy was observed in the whole matter. An envoy sent by Aldringen to Vienna to ask for money to appease the soldiers, and, in general, for further instructions, did not dare to enter the city, but transacted his business through Oñate beyond the gates. After the interview, the Spanish ambassador hurried to Ferdinand, whom he found already in a state of intense fear and excitement, and wrested from him an order, which was at once conveyed to Aldringen's messenger, that Wallenstein was to be taken, living or dead. The emperor has been charged with rank deceitfulness for continuing, even after this, to correspond, cn apparently friendly terms, with the man whose death-warrant he had already issued. It can only be answered that Wallenstein's conduct was equally underhanded. In his letters to Vienna he wrote of his young master, Ferdinand's son, as his own natural successor, and told how glad he would be to raise him in the saddle and then kiss the stirrup and depart. He called his officers together a second time at Pilsen, declared that his only intention was to bring about the longed-for peace, and once more secured their promise of loyalty, on the express understanding that nothing was to be undertaken against the Emperor's person or power, or against the Roman Catholic religion. A protestation to this same effect was signed by Wallenstein and by thirty of his officers, and sent to Vienna. Yet, at the same time, the Duke of Saxe-Lauenburg, in Wallenstein's name, was urging the emperor's enemy, Bernard of Weimar, to advance his troops to the Bohemia frontier.

On one pretext or another the general-in-chief had assembled all his troops at Prague; he was about to set out from Pilsen to put himself at their head, when the news came that the imperial order deposing him had been made public, and had been generally accepted. With a thousand riders, half of whom left him under way, Wallenstein quickly made for the little fortress of Eger, where was stationed one of Terzky's regiments, under Lieutenant-Colonel Gordon, a Protestant Scotchman, whom he hoped easily to win to his side. The cavalcade was joined under way by Colonel Butler and a regiment of dragoons. Butler, a Catholic Irishman of good family, had already become convinced that Wallenstein was a traitor, and now sent word to Piccolomini that though he had joined in the march to Eger, he was one of his Majesty's truest and most upright soldiers. Piccolomini ordered him to capture or to kill Wallenstein, and to return with him to Pilsen. Butler had, in fact, obeyed the command even before the letter reached him.

Wallenstein had tried to win over Gordon and his sergeant Leslie by assuring them that Bernard of Weimar was on the way to his rescue; Illow and Terzky later summoned these two, together with Butler, to Illow's quarters and urged them to declare themselves for Wallenstein. They refused; but the two conspirators, thinking the better to persuade them over their wine, invited themselves to dine the same evening at Gordon's quarters in the castle. They appeared accordingly, with Kinsky and Neumann, the latter Wallenstein's secretary, and sat down to a feast in a niche of the great hall. Healths were drunk to the general-in-chief, and especially to his project of ceasing to be servant and becoming master.

The death of Wallenstein.

But, in the meantime, several officers and a hundred dragoons from Butler's regiment had secretly been admitted to the building. The dessert had just been served when, through two doors, they burst into the banquet room with a cry of "Long live Emperor Ferdinand!" All four of the unfortunate adherents of Wallenstein were struck down in a moment; Illow had just time to cry shame upon Gordon, and to challenge him to single combat.

From the castle the soldiers hurried to Wallenstein's own quarters, where an outdoor stairway led directly to his sleeping apartment. His steward met them at the door, and began to chide them for disturbing his master, but with cries of "rogue," "traitor," and "rebel" they broke down the door. As Wallenstein stood there, in his night clothes, leaning against a table, and saw the halberds pointed against him, he opened his arms wide, and bowed as though to receive the blows. The Irish captain Devereux stabbed him squarely in the breast. The long career was ended that had promised so much, and accomplished so little. His murderers gloried in their deed, which, according to the sentiment of the time, was a just and righteous one. They were richly and publicly rewarded by Ferdinand, who confiscated the immense wealth of Wallenstein, and bestowed it upon his own officers and soldiers. The power that had shaken the throne, and seemed about to transform Germany thus melted into nothingness. The original estates of Friedland were given to General Gallas. In the light of future events, of the unexampled misery and wretchedness to which Germany was still, by fourteen years of the most wasting and demoralizing warfare, to be reduced, one cannot help wishing, that the one man who was capable of making head against greedy and insolent foreigners, had continued to control affairs, even at the cost of the legitimate, but thoroughly incapable, Hapsburg ruler. There are things that are worse for a country than a violent change of government.

After the death of Wallenstein there is little in the purely military events of the Thirty Years' War to interest the modern reader. The young Ferdinand, aided by the Cardinal Infant of Spain, recaptured Ratisbon, and inflicted a decisive defeat on Bernard of Weimar at Nördlingen ; indeed, to the outcome of this latter battle it may be ascribed that South Germany was to remain almost exclusively Roman Catholic. "It was so bad it could not have been worse," so Bernard announced his own defeat to the Swedish chancellor. Soon afterward, in 1635, the electors of Saxony and Brandenburg withdrew from the war, and concluded with the emperor the Peace of Prague, by which

The peace of Prague.

they were to abandon the Swedish alliance and receive in return some few concessions with regard to the Edict of Restitution. Two years later the votes of these two electors turned the scale in favor of the young Ferdinand as king of the Romans, and the death of the old emperor brought him almost immediately to the imperial throne, as Ferdinand III.

France enters the struggle.

The war by this time had entered into an entirely new phase, for Louis XIII. of France had placed himself at the head of the enemies of the house of Hapsburg. After the battle of Nördlingen, Sweden and the Heilbronn league had been willing to pay Richelieu almost any price for his aid, and had agreed to let him have Alsace in return for 12,000 men and a half a million francs. In May, 1635, France formally declared war against Spain, closed a treaty with the Dutch, who were to attack the Spanish Netherlands, and prepared to throw not 12,000, but 132,000 men into the field. It will be seen how this action changed the fundamental nature of the struggle; the religious question was thrust entirely into the background, for the Catholic king had certainly no desire to see the triumph of Protestant tenets. Both France and Sweden were openly fighting for territory, and the chief occupation of their troops was ravaging and plundering Germany.

Bernard of Weimar.

Bernard of Weimar allowed himself to be regularly taken into the pay of the French king; his reward was to be a yearly salary of two hundred thousand francs, a large pension at the end of the war, and, eventually, the possession of Alsace; in addition his army was to be subsidized, and also an agreement made that, in case of his capture, no peace should ever be signed that did not include his liberation. He was treated, however, as a mere hireling, and his thraldom at last became so irksome that he cast it off. His great achievement was the siege of Breisach, where he

reduced the garrison to the necessity of slaughtering children and eating the bodies of the fallen. When the surrender of the town became known, he was hailed as a second
Gustavus, and the news of his success infused a different spirit into the whole Protestant-Swedish party.
All the greater was the gloom cast by his sudden death,
and it was darkly hinted that French poison had been at
work.

Although Bernard's death afforded a breathing space to
the emperor, it did nothing toward bringing to an end this
frightful, universal war.   The Swedish general, Banér,
had meanwhile wreaked terrible retribution upon Saxony for having concluded the Peace of Prague, and had
crowned his work by a victory over the elector at Witt-
stock; but by the end of the year 1637 he had been forced
back on Stettin.   By this time Catholics and Protestants
alike were urging that a diet be called, to settle the differences at home, and to provide for driving out the foreign
enemies.   Such a diet — the first that had been held in
twenty-seven years— met at Ratisbon in 1640, and the chief
subject discussed was that of a general amnesty.   But
from the first, it was all too plain that the worst enemy
of peace was the emperor himself, with his exclusively
Austrian and Spanish interests.   It was in vain that even
Maximilian of Bavaria urged him to change his policy
and adopt one more national, more German.   During the
progress of this diet, and by no mere coincidence, there
appeared a writing by one Hippolytus a Lapide (in reality
the Swede Chemnitz), which aroused intense excitement,
and greatly influenced public opinion.   It was entitled *On
the State of Things in our Roman-German Empire*, was a
study on the ultimate source of the supreme authority,
and wound up with the crushing conclusion, that the sway
of the Hapsburgs had always proved fatal to the progress

*The longing
for peace.*

of the country ; that no remedy could now avail; that an executioner was needed, not a physician !

For a moment it seemed as though that executioner were at the very gates. Banér was suddenly seized with the idea of descending upon Ratisbon, taking captive the emperor, and putting the diet to flight. He encamped on the opposite side of the Danube, and commenced bombarding the city; he intended on the following day to cross on the ice and complete his hardy undertaking. Even in those days of continual surprises this was a feat to set Europe agog; but it was one that, unfortunately, Banér was unable to accomplish. In the night there came a heavy thaw, the ice broke up, and the golden opportunity vanished forever. Banér withdrew to Bohemia and thence to Saxony, where he died within four months, in consequence, it is said, of his intemperate habits.

One good result the Diet of Ratisbon did finally accomplish : it was decreed that a congress should assemble at Münster and Osnabrück, and at the same time a deputy diet at Frankfort, to see what could be done in the way of a settlement. It was the first faint glimmering of the dawn of peace, though numberless small battles were first to be fought. Banér's place was taken by Linnard Torstenson, the last good general of the school of Gustavus Adolphus. In the year 1642 he marched from Brunswick to the emperor's hereditary lands, took a number of towns in Bohemia and Moravia, then turned suddenly and, joining with Wrangel and Königsmark, settled down before Leipzig. Here, on the very spot where Gustavus Adolphus had gained his first great victory, eleven years before, the imperial forces were again put to flight; according to the commanders, Piccolomini and Archduke Leopold, the whole fault lay with Colonel Mandlot's regiment, which had been the first to run. Mandlot himself, accordingly, and all the superior officers were beheaded; while of the subalterns and common soldiers every tenth man was hung to a tree by the roadside.

The outcome of this second battle of Breitenfeld placed Leipzig at the mercy of Torstenson; but, as imperial reënforcements arrived, he retired once more to Bohemia, followed by General Gallas, to whom the emperor had given the chief command. The entry of Denmark into the struggle in September, 1643, gave a new direction to events; Torstenson, bidden by the Swedish government to march against the Danes in Schleswig Holstein, cleared that whole province of the enemy, and advanced to the borders of Jutland; while Gallas, sent by the emperor to the aid of the Danish king, appeared in Holstein in the following year.

Of all the disastrous undertakings of this whole period, this campaign of Gallas was about the worst. He had started out with some eighteen or twenty thousand men, but, chiefly, through his own carelessness and hesitancy, — which can only be accounted for by accepting the report that he was daily intoxicated, — he lost all but two thousand, as many falling on the march as in the engagements at Magdeburg and Jüterbog. The remnant turned up finally in Bohemia, where they joined a new army which had been raised by the emperor's own personal efforts, and placed under the command of Hatzfeld. Torstenson defeated Hatzfeld in the fierce battle of Jankau, and Ferdinand III. s very throne seemed in jeopardy. By the end of the year 1645, Wrangel, Torstenson's successor, had in his hands the whole of northern Bohemia and a chain of fortified places extending as far as the Danube.

During all this time, French armies had been fighting with equal zeal, but with varied success, on the Rhine and Neckar, as well as in the Spanish Netherlands, where they had gained the truly magnificent victory of Rocroi. They

Shifting alliances

had been defeated at Tuttlingen and Freiburg, had then made extensive conquests, such as Spires, Mainz, and Worms, only to receive a crushing defeat at Mergentheim in the spring of 1645, when Mercy and John of Werth practically annihilated the infantry of Turenne. A few months later the blow was returned at Allerheim, in the immediate neighborhood of Nördlingen, where Mercy fell, vainly trying to retrieve the lost day.

Apart from the military events, this last period of the Thirty Years' War is remarkable for the frequent and sudden changes of allegiance on the part of almost all the powers concerned in the struggle. Only France, Austria, and Sweden stood consistently to their colors; Denmark and Transylvania proved but fitful participants; Spain, weakened by internal troubles and by the loss of her fleet in Dutch waters, could render little aid in Germany, the new elector of Brandenburg, Frederick William, who came to the throne in 1640, made a truce with the Swedes, and allowed them free passage through his lands; the Duke of Würtemberg was a secret friend of the French, and accepted a pension from them, while the Saxon elector entered into a strange agreement with the Swedes, by which he gave up Leipzig and Torgau, but was allowed to send regiments to the emperor's aid.

The campaign against Maximilian of Bavaria.

It remained to be seen what test the loyalty of Maximilian of Bavaria would withstand, and on him, now, French and Swedes alike turned and concentrated their attention. Wrangel, Torstenson's successor, had marched from Bohemia to Thuringia, thence north to the Weser, where he had taken Höxter and Paderborn; he now united at Fritzlar with Turenne, and together they started off by the most direct road for Maximilian's dominions. They took Donauwörth, but were forced to retire from Augsburg, returning, however, on a plundering and ravaging expedi-

tion, that brought them to the gates of Munich. Almost all Bavaria was in their hands, and in January, 1647, they took Bregenz, whither all the treasure and supplies from the rich Swabian monasteries had been brought together for safe keeping. Maximilian, for the moment, was in despair; he had long been listening to tempting offers from France, and he now signed a treaty by which the enemy was to vacate Bavaria in return for some Swabian fortresses. In vain had the emperor tried to deter him from this step; the elector showed that he meant his defection seriously, and when John of Werth tried to hurry with the remnants of the Bavarian army to the emperor's side, Maximilian declared him an outlaw. After a few months, however, Maximilian found that the new alliance did not bring him the peace and quiet for which he longed. The aging prince, who, directly and indirectly, had been the cause of so much evil, was under the ban of a bitter retribution from which there was no escape. The renewal of his allegiance to the emperor brought down upon him, in 1648, a fresh attack of the Swedes and French. It came to a sharp battle at Zusmarshausen, where the imperialists and Bavarians lost two thousand men, and the strong-box as well, that contained all the pay for their troops. Completely *hors de combat*, the impérial general, Gronsfeld, withdrew to the extreme eastern boundary of Bavaria, and Maximilian fled to Salzburg. The enemy rioted at will in his cities, villages, and castles, until at last, in the summer, John of Werth and Piccolomini appeared with a new army and drove them from the Inn to the Isar, eventually compelling them to cross the Lech.

Ferdinand's spirit by this time was almost broken. During the long negotiations at Münster and Osnabrück, his ambassador, Trautmannsdorf, had stood out bravely for what he deemed his master's rights. The events of the

The end of military operations

war had changed his policy from time to time, and had greatly delayed the work of peace. But of late the defeats had been growing too frequent, and now a Swedish army under Charles Gustavus of Pfalz Zwiebrücken, the new generalissimo and future king of Sweden, stood at the gates of Prague. The Hradschin and the whole quarter surrounding it had been taken, and the immeasurably rich art collections carried away; but, in consequence of the stubborn resistance of the city proper, a temporary truce had been signed. At this juncture the news came that the last signature had been affixed to the treaty of peace ; the war ceased where it had begun, under the walls of Prague, after having made the rounds of Europe.

The settlement of boundaries at Münster.

The double assembly that sat from 1644 to 1648 — the Catholic powers at Münster, the Protestant at Osnabrück — brought forth finally an instrument of peace, which deservedly ranks as a landmark in European history. It shows the end of one whole era and the beginning of modern times. It settled three questions of cardinal importance : What were to be the future boundaries of the continental states ? What balance could be struck between two faiths that had hitherto fought each other to the knife ? and, lastly, What was to be the future of Germany ?—Was an emperor to be able to inflict upon it again such miseries as it had just been through ?

The boundary problem was solved by giving to Sweden, besides an indemnity, the bishoprics of Bremen and Verden and the half of Pomerania, includings a trip on the eastern bank of the Oder, which placed the control of that stream and of all the bays and islands at its mouth, in Swedish hands. France's share was — in addition to Metz, Toul, and Verdun, which she had practically owned since 1552 — Alsace with Breisach, the Sundgau, and the right of garrisoning Philipsburg. The Rhine was thus the new boundary from the Palatinate south to Switzerland. The religious differences were settled on the basis of the Peace of Augsburg, each ruler enjoying "autonomy," being allowed, that is, to decide for himself what form of faith his subjects should follow. Germany was to continue nominally an empire, within which, however, each state was to enjoy the utmost possible degree of independence.

But what bald statement of results can possibly convey an idea of the stirring issues that were joined, and the diplomatic victories that were won and lost at Münster and Osnabrück? Ten whole months were spent in settling preliminary questions alone: such as, what powers should be admitted to the Congress; what matters should be treated; whether the papers and authorizations of individual members were in order; and what should be the rules of precedence.

The emperor had fought hard to have the empire represented at the Congress as a unit, and also to have matters which pertained solely to the internal welfare of Germany reserved for a German diet. But the Hapsburg character was too well known, and German diets, in which Catholics were apt to predominate, had hitherto been none too successful in settling religious differences. It is perfectly true, this calling in of foreign powers to sit as judges between the throne and its princes, was a humiliation such as no other of the great powers of Europe had ever been under the necessity of enduring. It was to avoid such a contingency that Henry IV. had dragged himself up the frosty slope of Canossa, and had stood barefooted, like a beggar, before Gregory VII. But now there was no remedy. Wallenstein might have helped matters; Ferdinand III. could not. By the will of Sweden and France, accordingly, each petty state was instructed to send its own ambassadors; therewith Germany's fate was sealed. The different

The triumph of the petty states.

principalities and little republics, the number of which reached to nearly three hundred, claimed, and obtained for themselves, the right to coin money, raise armies, and close alliances, besides the privilege of being consulted in matters of general government. Without their consent, the emperor might not declare war nor make peace, nor even order the building of a fortress, save on his own lands.

Etiquette.

Questions of etiquette played a great part in the Congress and led to interminable disputes, nor, absurd as they seem now, were they then without real significance. It was but one step from denying a man his due equality, to turning a deaf ear to his just demands. Disputes as to first visits, seats in the hall of assembly, titles and other marks of distinction, all received the most serious consideration. The papal nuncio demanded the loftiest place of all, nor would the imperial envoy sit on a level with the ambassador of France. The latter again was obliged to yield to the Venetian representative, who insisted, when leaving him after a visit, on being accompanied the whole way to his carriage, and not merely halfway down the path. No sooner had this weighty matter been decided in favor of Venice, than the Netherlands put in a similar claim. The right to be called " your Excellency " was urged and disputed at infinite lengths by this and that envoy. On certain such matters the French and the Spaniards failed to come to any other agreement than that, with their whole suites, they should avoid each other on every public occasion.

Close bargaining.

The difficulties as to these mere questions of form were but the mildest prelude to the haggling and bargaining, the recriminations and obstructions, when it came to active business. Each of the powers concerned had placed its demands many times higher than there was any possibility of realizing. Many months passed while Sweden was being screwed down from her ruinous demand of a twenty million indemnity to an ultimate five million. Originally, too, she had claimed for her queen a vote in the German college of electors, and the possession of all Silesia, the apple of Ferdinand's eye. The emperor, on the other hand, had done everything to save the fortress of Breisach from falling into the clutches of France. He had even suggested levelling it to the ground. But Mazarin was inexorable; not in vain had he bribed the greater number of the German princes. Nor could Ferdinand himself now afford to relinquish the proffer of the French cardinal's good offices in paring down the demands of Sweden.

Of all the clauses of the peace, none was more ambig-uous than the one relating to the French frontier. The nature of the rights to be enjoyed over Alsace, and es-pecially over the ten free cities of the empire that lay within that province, were couched in such ambiguous terms, and hedged in by so many restrictive and mutually negatory clauses, that either party might consider itself the actual possessor. Full sovereignty was to be granted to France, *saving the allegiance due to the empire!* It is be-lieved now that this vagueness was in part intentional; though few could have dreamed of the evils that were to arise in the next half century, when a French king, with very decided views as to the benefits of absolute ownership, was to take the matter in hand. *The French frontier.*

As might have been expected, the hardest questions of all to settle, proved to be those concerning religious tolera-tion, and the restoration of lands appropriated by the one church or the other. Around the old provision known as the *reservatum ecclesiasticum* a whole diplomatic battle was waged; it was finally decided to retain the measure, but to make it as applicable to Protestants who turned Catholic as it was the other way. In any case, the convert to the other faith must renounce his former holding. Long did *The Bohe-mian exiles.*

Sweden and the German Protestants hold out for a return to the state of things that had existed at the very beginning of the war. The Swedish government had practically pledged itself to restore their lands to the thousands of Bohemian refugees who had done good service in its ranks; but here the emperor remained firm — his minister Traut-mannsdorf, who was acting in his name, declared that not even the miseries of a Stockholm prison could reduce him to consider such a proposal. Nor would it have been possible, with the best of wills, to reverse all that had been done in these thirty years. The most that Ferdinand would grant for Bohemia was, that those who had been driven out since 1630 might have their lands restored.

Important measures.

For the empire at large it proved an even more difficult question to fix upon this so-called normal year whereby to test the title to property. Back of the Edict of Restitution the emperor was willing to go, but not back of that arrangement by which the upper Palatinate had been given to Maximilian of Bavaria. That would have brought Ferdinand once more to the condition of owing Maximilian the immense debt for which his father had pledged his Austrian possessions. By way of a compromise the year 1624 was finally chosen. The question of providing for the heirs of the Winter King, was solved by giving the lower or Rhine Palatinate to the young Charles Louis, for whose benefit an eighth electorate was then created, the arrangement to lapse with the extinction of either line.

Toward the end of the term of session, as the emperor, in consequence of his severe defeats, grew more and more pliant, a number of important measures were rushed through the congress without delay. The elector of Brandenburg was the successful promoter of a plan for placing Calvinists, once and for all, on the same plane as the orthodox Lu-therans; and he gained his point, even though Saxony, self-centred and bigoted to the last, bitterly opposed the measure.

Altogether, the sentiment had gained ground that there must be mutual toleration in every way. Though the rulers might choose the form of faith, they were bound to give dissenters a period of th ee years in which to dispose of their property before emigrating, and they were compelled to exercise consideration in many ways even for those who remained. In Bohemia, Moravia, and Austria, indeed, Ferdinand made no lasting concessions. He felt, and perhaps rightly, that Protestant communities would always side with his own enemies, and he was determined not to have them in his neighborhood. In Silesia he gave permission to build Protestant churches in certain specified towns.

Mutual toleration in religious matters.

Before the congress separated it gave its sanction to some important political changes that had long been accomplished facts, such as the independence of Switzerland and the Netherlands, and then struck a decided blow at the prestige of the Roman church. Although the extreme Catholic party was furious at the concessions to the Protestants, and Pope Innocent X. questioned the right of founding an eighth electorate without his sanction, the instrument of peace declared expressly that no contradiction on the part of the church or of any secular power should interfere with its validity. The Pope accordingly condemned the Peace of Westphalia, as a predecessor had once condemned the Magna Charta.

Papal condemnation of the peace.

With the signing of the great treaty on the 24th of October, 1648, the long reign of terror in Germany was brought to a close. No wonder the jubilations knew no end; no wonder that the poets of the time broke into song like so many liberated birds. Paul Gerhard, the best of them all, gives fervent thanks to God that the noble word of peace and joy has sounded, and that the murderous spear and

Ruin and demoralization caused by the war.

sword are to rest unwielded; but he cannot forget his country's ruined castles, her cities heaped with foul rubbish, her fields that are like tangled thickets, her graves so full of heroes. And, indeed, over large portions of the land there hung the desolation of the Dead Sea. It has been proved that many of the countless details of horror that have come down to us are exaggerated, are tinged with a melancholy desire to make things seem worse than they actually were. But even the most sober statistics show that men and women were reduced to the state of the lowest animals, that cannibalism was rife in various quarters, that morality was an unknown quantity. What better evidence of the utter lawlessness of the soldiery can be wanted than the famous order of General Banèr to his officers to treat the nobles, burgomasters, and other notables (from whose forced contributions he hoped to grow rich) with kicks and blows and insults of all kinds, "like dogs, slaves, and serfs!" Recruiting for the army had become the merest mercenary speculation; robbers and criminals of all kinds had flocked to the camps, where alone in the whole length and breadth of the wretched land a semblance of plenty could be found. Here, after a victory, soldiers could have been seen strutting about in gaudy clothes that had been found among the booty, or revelling with the bestial crowd of camp-followers. Toward the end of the war the proportion of these had assumed truly hideous dimensions, at the battle of Zusmarshausen, in 1648, there were present on the side of the emperor thirty-four thousand combatants and one hundred and twenty-seven thousand women, children, and useless men!

Evil results of the war. The loss of life, due directly to the war, has been placed by the lowest estimate at one-third of the whole population; some districts were turned into such total deserts that the most heroic means had to be taken to repeople them. A local diet in Franconia gave permission for every man to have two wives, and forbade any one under sixty to become a monk. A blow was struck at various industries from which they did not recover for a whole century. The grand old Hansa came to its death in these days; the exports of Danzig amounted, in 1619, to over a hundred thousand tons, in 1659, to a little more than five hundred. Had the potato not come into use at this time as an article of food, the general misery would doubtless have been even greater. The demoralization of the people at large is shown in various ways, in the decline of art, of literature, and of learning, but above all in the senseless aping of the foreigner. Each little court tried to copy Versailles, and spent the money that should have gone to healing the wounds of war, in senseless luxury; the language becomes almost another tongue, so interlarded is it with French phrases; questions of etiquette now regularly play a prominent part in the discussions of the diets. Shall the ordinary princes sit on red or, like the electors, on green chairs? Shall their lackeys wear gold or silver lace? Shall their wives be asked to take a *fauteuil* or merely a *tabouret?* At a great festival held at Nuremberg in 1650, to celebrate the progress of the measures for carrying out the different agreements, it was five hours after dinner was announced before the unfortunate guests could be seated in the proper order.

Then, indeed, at this historic feast, be it said to their credit, they thoroughly enjoyed themselves. Piccolomini, who had previously been serenaded at his house by fifteen hundred boys on hobby horses, was one of the most prominent men present; but Wrangel was also there, and many of the generals had stood over against each other in the field. Like young schoolboys, they engaged once more in a rollicking game of war, chased each other round the table, and then perambulated the town, until their colonel laughingly dismissed them, with the reminder that peace had been declared.

Childlike rejoicings

CHRONOLOGICAL TABLE [1]

[1] This table contains some facts that are not in the text.

mon penny "; wars of Maximilian in Italy and against France (1496–1517); marriage of Philip, Maximilian's son, with Joanna of Spain (1496); Maximilian's war with the Swiss cantons (1499); Diet of Augsburg establishes *Reichsregiment* (1500); Maximilian takes title of " Roman emperor elect" (1508); Erasmus, *Praise of Folly* (1509); Reuchlin's feud with the Dominicans of Cologne (1510); Pope Leo X. (1513–1521); Francis I. of France conquers Milan by the battle of Marignano (1515); the *Epistolæ Virorum Obscurorum* (1515); Luther posts his theses (1517); Philip of Hesse (1518–1567); Luther's hearing at Augsburg (1518); Duke Ulrich of Würtemberg driven out by the Swabian League (1519); disputation at Leipzig (1519); German life on the eve of the Reformation.   227–263

1519–1558   *Charles V.:* Luther's three great writings; the burning of the papal bull (1520); the Diet of Worms condemns Luther (1521); war against Francis I. (1521–1525); Francis taken prisoner at Pavia (1525); Peace of Madrid (1526); death of Sickingen and of Hutten (1523); Pope Clement VII. (1523–1534); the Peasants' War (1525); John, elector of Saxony (1525–1532); Prussia becomes a secular duchy under Albert of Brandenburg (1525); Torgau League (1526); first Diet of Spires (1526); Ferdinand, brother of Charles V., becomes king of Hungary after the battle of Mohacs, in which Louis of Hungary falls (1527); war with Francis I., which ends with the Peace of Cambray (1527–1529); sack of Rome by imperial troops (1527); second Diet of Spires, the Protestants (1529); Disputation of Marburg (1529); Vienna besieged by the Turks (1530); Augsburg Confession (1530); Ferdinand elected king of the Romans (1531); founding of the Smalkald League (1531); death of Zwingli at Cappel (1531); religious Peace of Nuremberg (1532); John Frederick, elector of

INDEX

A SHORT HISTORY OF GERMANY

THE MACMILLAN COMPANY
NEW YORK · BOSTON · CHICAGO · DALLAS
ATLANTA · SAN FRANCISCO

MACMILLAN AND CO., Limited
LONDON · BOMBAY · CALCUTTA · MADRAS
MELBOURNE

THE MACMILLAN COMPANY
OF CANADA, Limited
TORONTO

A SHORT

HISTORY OF GERMANY

BY

ERNEST F. HENDERSON

VOLUME II

1648 A.D. TO 1914 A.D.

NEW EDITION WITH ADDITIONAL CHAPTERS

New York

THE MACMILLAN COMPANY

1940

CONTENTS

CONTENTS

MAPS

A SHORT HISTORY OF GERMANY

CHAPTER I

THE RISE OF THE PRUSSIAN MONARCHY

LITERATURE : A storehouse of information for all that concerns Prussian history is the series known as *Forschungen zur brandenburgischen und preussischen Geschichte.* Eberty, *Geschichte des preussischen Staates,* must be used with caution. In Schmoller, *Umrisse und Untersuchungen,* are many valuable studies on economic matters. Tuttle's *History of Prussia* has its merits, but is partial and occasionally uncritical. Erdmannsdörfer, in his *Deutsche Geschichte,* 1648-1740, is good but does not devote much space to Prussia. Pierson, *Preussische Geschichte,* is up to date with his facts. Waddington, *L'acquisition de la couronne royale de Prusse par les Hohenzollern,* is a valuable study. Dohna's *Mémoires* are interesting. Varnhagen von Ense's *Leben der Königin von Preussen Sophie Charlotte* is charming.

LEAVING aside for a moment the general history of Germany, it becomes necessary to trace the steps by which one state rose so high above the rest that it finally became the acknowledged head and leader. Up to the accession in 1640 of that Frederick William who was later known as the Great Elector, the family of Hohenzollern could boast of no very distinguished members, and their territory consisted of scattered provinces with no real bond of union. The Mark Brandenburg had been in Hohenzollern hands for two centuries and a quarter, and the early margraves, save for fulfilling their occasional duties as electors of the Holy Roman Empire, had spent their time in conflicts with their own nobles and cities. Frederick I., on whom, at

The early margraves of Brandenburg.

the Council of Constance, the Emperor Sigismund had conferred the Mark, in recognition of his belligerent ways and administrative talents, had devoted his life and fortune to improving the land. He gained the upper hand of the Quitzows, Rochows, Alvenslebens, and other independent minded noble families by the aid of "Faule Grete," or "Lazy Peg," — a very ordinary cannon to those who view it to-day outside of the Berlin Arsenal, but an instrument of coercion without its peer in the early fifteenth century. Margrave Frederick II. tried much the same kind of argument against the citizens of Berlin, and finally built a strong fortress in their midst, which forms part of the present castle. This same Frederick II. it was who purchased from the insolvent Teutonic Order the province known as the New Mark, stretching from the Oder on the west, and the Warthe on the south, far north into Pomerania. Thus was inaugurated that specially Hohenzollern policy of widening the inherited boundaries. From that day to this, with but one or two exceptions, each ruler in turn, by inheritance, by purchase, by conquest, or by peaceful annexation, has added something to his original domains.

Joachim I.   Brandenburg's attitude in the great religious conflicts of the sixteenth century, was dubious and unfortunate ; there was no attempt to take an independent stand, and there were times when, in the larger affairs of the empire, the electorate was merely the satellite of Saxony. At the time of Martin Luther's great activity the elector was Joachim I., a stern, just man, essentially of legal mind, — the same who introduced Roman law into the land, and established at Berlin the first general supreme court for all the marks or provinces. He travelled around to see that his cities were well governed, reformed the weights and measures, tried to put down the all-pervading tendency to luxury in dress, and even organized an effective fire service. For theology he cared little ; astrology was far more to his taste ; and once, when the destruction of Berlin by lightning had been foretold for a certain day, he drove out to the Tempelhof heights to witness the spectacle. If, therefore, in spite of the fact that many of his subjects cherished Lutheran sympathies, he emphatically declared for the Catholic cause, the grounds of his action were chiefly political. He feared that a change of religion would bring about a revolution, and, indeed, laid the whole blame of the Peasants' War to the new teachings. Having once taken his ground, he maintained it with great determination, joining with those who urged Charles V. to break his safe-conduct to Luther, and threatening to put to death his own wife, the daughter of the Danish king, whom he one day discovered to have partaken of the Holy Communion in both forms. The electress fled to Saxony, where she spent three months under the humble roof of Luther and his wife, and then settled in a castle near Wittenberg.

More important than the electress's own choice of a faith, is the fact that her eldest son shared her views ; and, in truth, four years after his accession, in 1539, Joachim II. formally and publicly threw off the mask by taking the Lutheran communion at the hands of the newly converted Bishop of Brandenburg. In the course of an additional three years all the necessary changes were made, the monasteries dissolved, the chief power in religious affairs placed in the hands of a consistory. Not that Joachim II. was a man who would have followed his religious convictions, had they not guided him in the line of his advantage; it was well known to him that a very large proportion of his subjects were by this time Lutherans, and that, by taking this course, he could induce the estates to assume the heavy debts of the crown. The steps by which Brandenburg

The Reformation accepted.

became the bulwark of Protestantism in the North were not, therefore, greatly to her credit. Nor even after making his choice could Joachim II. bring himself to abandon altogether the Roman Catholic ceremonial; he loved the music, the incense, and the fine garments, — predilections which brought him more than once into conflict with his own clergy. One of them, Buchholzer, complained to Luther, who laughed at him for his scruples, and bade him, so long as his master was firm on the main points, to wear as many surplices as the elector desired, whether of velvet, or of silk, or of linen, or of all three at once. "And," the reformer went on, "if it please his Electoral Highness, he may leap and dance with harps, cymbals, drums, and bells, like David before the tabernacle of the Lord."

The Cleves heritage.

Thus far the possessions of the House of Hohenzollern had been very modest indeed; but two generations after Joachim, under Elector John Sigismund, the grandfather of the Great Elector, there came a great change. Of the acquisitions to the eastward we shall speak in another connection; for the present, it is enough to trace the steps by which Brandenburg achieved three Rhenish provinces.

The territory known as the Duchy of Cleves was, in reality, a conglomeration of small states, extending along both sides of the Rhine from Remagen to Holland, and completely surrounding the great bishopric of Cologne. In addition to Cleves proper, there were Julier, Berg, Mark, and Ravensburg, which had been in one hand for exactly a hundred years. The situation of these lands, so readily accessible from France, from the Spanish Netherlands, and from Holland, would have rendered them important, apart from the fact that they were naturally very fertile, and even then centres of a busy trade. Julier was and is responsible for much of the commercial product that is known to the world as "brown Holland." Already, for

many years before the death of the mad Duke of Cleves,
John William, who was the last male of his line, there had
been claimants to the regency, and ultimately to the crown,
as numerous as the lands which composed the heritage.
Duke William, the father of John William, had tried to
forestall the present difficulty by drawing up a document,
accepted and sworn to by all of his children, which appointed the eldest daughter, Maria Leonora, and her heirs,
the rightful successors to the childish imbecile whose reign,
it was assumed, would be but short.   Maria Leonora herself had no sons, but her daughter had married the young
Brandenburg elector, and to him she delegated all her
rights.   Immediately on hearing of the death of John
William, which took place at last in 1609, John Sigismund
sent to take formal possession of the vacant lands, with all
the pomp and ceremony that were known to the age.   In
the presence of a notary, his envoy seized the great ring
on the gate of the chancery building in Cleves, opened it,
entered, and laid claim to all the lands that could be seen
from the windows, as well as to all that had been administered from Cleves as a centre; he then nailed up the
Brandenburg coat of arms on the front of the great edifice.
It had been arranged that the same proceedings should be
gone through with in Düsseldorf for Berg and Julier; but
here, to his astonishment, John Sigismund's envoy found
on his arrival that he was too late.   Envoys of the Count
Palatine of Neuburg, Wolfgang William, son of a younger
sister of Maria Leonora, were already at work, Pfalz-Neuburg's contention being that the whole duchy was a " man-
fief," and that, in default of male heirs on the elder sister's
part, the succession fell to himself.   Thus was started a
cause célèbre of the seventeenth century, and one that was
not to be entirely settled until the Congress of Vienna, in
1815.   In view of a common danger that threatened them

from other powers, Pfalz-Neuburg and the elector came to a temporary agreement, by which the elector was to administer the affairs of Cleves, Mark, and Ravensburg — which he never after, as a matter of fact, let out of his hands — and Pfalz-Neuburg was to administer those of Julier and Berg.

The circumstance that both of these pretendants were Protestant, and that, by the provisions of the Peace of Augsburg the ruler of a land might impose his own religion on his subjects, awakened a great fear in Austria and in Spain. The loss of this territory would be a serious calamity for the Catholic church; there was risk of the neighboring Cologne, which had once or twice wavered, becoming Protestantized, and of the Spanish Netherlands being completely cut off from the Westphalian bishoprics. The Hapsburg emperor, accordingly, Rudolph II., as a last resort brought forward a claim of his own: land, the title of which was in dispute, belonged for the time being to the crown. Rudolph sent as commissioner his own brother, Leopold, and bade him establish himself in Julier and carry on the administration. To no man could such an errand have been more agreeable than to this ambitious prince, who dreamed of an alliance with Spain, the Pope, and the Catholic League, which should enable him, after completing his present task, to march to Bohemia, stifle that discontent which, as we know now, was to culminate in the outbreak of the Thirty Years' War, and perhaps place the Bohemian crown on his own head. But the Protestant holders of Cleves and Julier could also boast of strong support. Henry IV. of France — though mainly driven to make war on Spain by the mad desire to have back his mistress, whom her husband, the Prince of Condé, had placed under the care of the Spanish government in the Netherlands — was able to bring about a league between

England, Holland, Savoy, and the Protestant Union.   By
the summer of 1610, it was hoped, an army of thirty-three
thousand men would be before the walls of the town of
Julier.   Young Christian of Anhalt was to be commander-
in-chief of the combined forces, while Henry himself was
to march at the head of the French troops.

The dagger of Ravaillac frustrated all these plans; the
Catholics had raised an army against which Henry was on
the point of marching, when this fanatic, incensed at the
thought of a French king in league with heretics, put an
end to the monarch's life.   On Henry's shoulders had
rested the burden of the war, his death betokened a complete change of policy in France.   One by one the allied
powers fell away, and Pfalz-Neuburg and Brandenburg
were left in Cleves-Julier to their own devices; they drove
out the Archduke Leopold and administered the duchies
themselves, though in no great mutual concord.   One day
Pfalz-Neuburg had the hardihood to suggest that he should
marry a daughter of the elector, and that her dowry
should be the disputed provinces.   The result was a
quarrel, fierce, sharp, and full of consequences.   John
Sigismund is said to have boxed the ears of the audacious
youth, whom he considered far below himself in rank, and
Wolfgang William soon afterward, by way of revenge
and in order to gain the support of Spain and Bavaria,
turned Catholic and married the sister of the Bavarian
Duke.   John Sigismund himself, ostensibly to gain rest
for his conscience, but in reality, so far as can be judged,
in order to stand well with the Dutch, went over to Calvinism.   Here was a complication of vast importance for
the future of the electorate: the ruling house pledged to a
faith that was almost as much hated as Catholicism by the
majority of the subjects.   The bitter rivalry between the
two denominations, the "reformed," as they were called,

John Sigis-
mund be-
comes a
Calvinist.

and the Lutherans, was to endure almost down to our own day. John Sigismund himself incurred the unbending opposition of his more powerful estates. Whenever he made a demand for money, his defection from the established religion was cast up in his face. At one local diet after another complaints and resolutions on the subject were brought forward; while openly from the pulpit the elector was branded as an apostate. A tumult in Berlin ended in the storming of the houses of the Calvinistic preachers. But John Sigismund was fully able to hold his own. "A cow is liker to a windmill than your actions to your office," he wrote to the clergy of Küstrin, "and your conscience shows such gaps that a coach-and-four could drive through!"

Brandenburg in the Thirty Years' War.

The reason for all this animosity was, that Calvinism and Lutheranism had come to be the banners under which liberals fought against conservatives, and the nobles of Brandenburg resented the alliance of their king with a religious party which so directly encouraged republican ideas. Just so the Calvinism of the "Winter King" had estranged the upper classes in Bohemia. The most favorable ground that the new teachings encountered had been in the republics of Switzerland and Holland. Partly on account of her religious disunity, but also for many other reasons, the outbreak of the Thirty Years' War found Brandenburg utterly unprepared to play any rôle at all on the stage of general affairs. Her elector at the time, John Sigismund's son, George William, was one of the weakest to whom history can point. His panegyrists might say at the time that majesty "radiated from his face," but his own descendant, Frederick the Great, when drawing the sum of this life, knew better; in his memoirs he calls his ancestor "a sovereign incapable of governing, with a minister who was traitor to his country." This minister, Schwarz-

enburg, a Catholic supposed to have been in the bigoted
Ferdinand II.'s pay, frustrated every good and progressive
measure that was by any chance brought forward. He it
was who, at the time of the terrible Restitution Edict,
induced George William to dally so long with Gustavus
Adolphus; he it was who, in 1635, gathered the elector
into the fold of the Prague Peace. The shame of it all
was that scarcely an effort was made to protect Brandenburg's boundaries; every army in turn marched through
the land unmolested, or went into winter quarters, as it
pleased. There was some justification for neutrality, but
this was a weak, nerveless neutrality, during which the
country suffered the worst that unbridled enemies could
inflict. The finances went from bad to worse, although the
extravagance at court continued as before; the elector,
touched by no misfortune that did not immediately concern
himself, showed and encouraged an unseemly levity when
talking of the most serious affairs.

George William's position, it must be acknowledged,
could not well have been more difficult. Allied as he was
by family ties to Gustavus Adolphus on the one hand and
to the " Winter King " on the other, his own particular interests led him to the side of the emperor, — a complicated
state of affairs that caused him to follow his own natural
bent and adopt no consistent policy whatever. At the
time of his death, in 1640, the land was in such an utterly
wretched and hopeless condition — with untilled fields and
great gaps of ruined houses in the towns and villages — that
the estates stormed the new elector with requests to put
an end at all costs to the miserable war. This he did by
abandoning his companions of the Prague Peace, and making his own agreement with Sweden.

The young Frederick William, known as the Great
Elector, was the greatest contrast to his father that could

possibly be imagined. Strong, unhesitating, and clear-
minded by nature, he had besides enjoyed the advantages
of a liberal education in a foreign country. Sent at the
age of fifteen to the university town of Leyden, he had
remained in the Netherlands some four years, enjoying an
intellectual atmosphere far different from that of his own
impoverished, misgoverned, and unrespected land. These
were the days of Peter Paul Rubens, of Rembrandt, and
of Van Dyke; of the great jurists who had worshipped at
the feet of Hugo Grotius; and of the philosopher Des-
cartes, whose works were published in Holland when forbidden in France. Here the young Hohenzollern had
learned to know and appreciate a really flourishing state,
where manufactures throve, and where every available piece
of land was under cultivation, even if it had previously
been a marsh or a fen. On his accession to the electoral
throne of Brandenburg he was possessed of two clearly
defined aims: to build up agriculture and trade, and to
protect them with a strong army. If he progressed but
slowly in both these matters, his success in another direction, in that of diplomacy, was the more apparent. It was
in part due to him that the minor German states had independent representation in the great peace congress at
Münster and Osnabrück, and almost wholly his work that
Calvinists were allowed to partake of the blessings of the
Westphalian Treaty. His efforts, indeed, at this congress
to rescue Pomerania, Brandenburg's lawful birthright, from
the fangs of Sweden, proved of no avail; but by unfolding
all the wiliness that was one of his chief characteristics, he
obtained in compensation the bishoprics of Halberstadt,
Minden, and Cammin, the county of Hohenstein, and the
succession to Magdeburg, possessions which served as
a bridge to Cleves, Mark, and Ravensburg, and made it
easier to unite these alien districts into one great whole.

In the meantime, another Hohenzollern possession, lying
entirely outside of the boundaries of the Holy Roman
Empire, was beginning to assume immense importance.
We must consider in some detail how it became finally
so amalgamated with the Mark Brandenburg as to give its
name to the whole new state.   Prussia, or Bo-Russia, the
once flourishing land of the famous Teutonic Order, had
been, since the Treaty of Thorn, in 1466, completely under
the heel of Poland.   One half of it, West Prussia, had
been actually incorporated in that land, while, with regard
to the portion that remained, the grand masters of the
order, each in turn, were obliged to take a humiliating
oath of vassalage.   To this state of affairs, after half a
century of servitude, an effort was made by the order
itself to apply a remedy.   The cry was raised that the land
so long subject to Poland was rightfully a fief of the empire.   In their palmier days the knights would never have
acknowledged it; but now, in order to enforce their view,
they determined to elect as grand master some German
prince of influence, who would make it his chief care to
free them from the Polish yoke.   Their choice fell on
Albert, head of the Culmbach-Baireuth line of Hohenzollern, and his first step was to refuse to Poland the customary
act of homage.   In the beginning all went well; Albert
was encouraged by the Emperor Maximilian, by the other
German princes, and by many of the knights themselves,
who, grown rich and powerful, were scattered in different
commanderies throughout the empire.   But it soon became apparent that the promises had been but glittering
generalities, and that of actual assistance little or none
was forthcoming.   For eleven years Albert labored conscientiously, and even succeeded, largely by sacrificing his
own private property, in raising an army of eight thousand mercenaries, with which he attacked the immeasur-

The secular-
ization
of the
Teutonic
Order.

ably greater forces of Poland. He failed signally, was reduced to great straits, and finally, after in vain storming the empire for aid, took a step that from many quarters drew down upon him bitter opprobrium.

The Reformation had made great progress within the lands of the order; many of the knights had become convinced of the truth of its teachings, and Albert himself finally succumbed to the general trend. Appealing to Luther to know what he should do with the trust that had been imposed upon him, he was told that in its present condition the order was "a thing serviceable neither to God nor to man," and had better cease to exist. The outcome of it was that Albert pronounced the order's dissolution, reorganized it into a secular duchy with himself at its head, made the ducal dignity hereditary in his own family, and eventually did homage, but in a purely secular capacity, to Poland, whose king agreed to defend him against all the world; those of the knights who followed him were made feudal proprietors with subvassals. The German division of the order, indeed, under their own *Teutschmeister* at Mergentheim, raised a hue and cry at various diets, and caused Charles V. to threaten the author of such innovations with severe punishments, and even to put him in the ban of the empire — a weapon, however, that by this time was well blunted. Albert lived down all opposition, and when he died his like-named son succeeded him without further disturbance.

Coenfeoff-
ment with
Prussia.

Brandenburg and Prussia were now alike in the hands of Hohenzollerns, though of different branches of the family. The next step was to gain from the king of Poland coenfeoffment, or the right of the two lines to enter into a mutual-heritage compact, by which, on the extinction of the house of Culmbach-Baireuth, Prussia was to pass to the electoral branch. It was Joachim II., the sponsor of the Reformation, who at last succeeded in doing this. He had married a Polish princess, and he prevailed upon his father-in-law and suzerain, in 1568, to grant him the much-coveted reversion. Toward the end of the sixteenth century the long-looked-for contingency became more and more imminent. Albert II. of Prussia had no sons, but two daughters; of these, to make matters doubly sure, Elector Joachim Frederick married one, his son John Sigismund, for his second wife, the other. Albert II., long a hopeless imbecile, died at last in 1618, and John Sigismund, only four years after securing Cleves, Mark, and Ravensburg, fell heir also to Prussia. It remained to be seen what his grandson, the Great Elector, could do in the way of lifting the ominous shadow of Polish supremacy.

To this object, after the Peace of Westphalia, the Great Elector devoted his chief attention. If he achieved it by a tortuous and somewhat equivocal policy, the only excuse is that duplicity was the key-note of seventeenth-century statecraft, and that the only difference between Frederick William and the princes with whom he had to deal, was in point of cleverness. Well, indeed, has this elector been likened to the old familiar Reinicke Fuchs; at one moment in really desperate straits, the next moment we find him master of the situation. Nor does he ever relax his grim determination to make his land respected among the nations; unmercifully does he tax his impoverished subjects to pay for his army and his state improvements. He is reduced at times to borrowing small sums right and left; he even falls into the old and fatal error of inflating the currency. And with it all, through policy and not through love of luxury, he is obliged to keep up a magnificence at court out of all proportion to the resources of the land. Foreign princes are to be shown that an elector of Brandenburg and duke of Prussia is not in any way their inferior. In

The Polish Swedish wars.

his designs for becoming free from the yoke of vassalage, Frederick William was assisted by a war that broke out between his liege lord of Poland and that Charles Gustavus of Pfalz-Zweibrücken in whose favor the daughter of Gustavus Adolphus had just abdicated the Swedish throne. John Casimir had disputed the new monarch's right, and had been told significantly that Charles Gustavus would prove it by no less than thirty thousand witnesses. Sweden was only too glad to employ in a foreign war her *soldatesca*, withdrawn from German soil by the terms of the Peace of Westphalia, and always troublesome. An army was soon despatched to Poland by way of Pomerania. The elector, across whose lands the Swedes passed without asking leave, was in a quandary; as vassal of Poland he was bound in honor to give assistance to that power, but if he did the enemy would sack his towns. He tried to remain neutral, but that would not suffice; Charles Gustavus, whose first campaign was phenomenally successful, returned with a portion of his troops, and demanded categorically whether the elector intended to be friend or foe. Having, in his efforts to gain allies, met everywhere with a not-undeserved mistrust, there was nothing left for Frederick William but to make what terms he could. He closed at Königsberg, in 1656, the first of his long series of treaties with regard to Prussia, repudiating the Polish suzerainty, but becoming on even harder terms the vassal of Sweden. All harbors were to be opened to Swedish vessels, tolls and customs were to be equally divided, a sum of money was to be paid at each investiture, and a contingent sent to the royal army. But suddenly the whole aspect of affairs changed, and Sweden was no longer in the ascendent. John Casimir, reënforced by the Tartars and Cossacks under the hetman Chmieliecki, succeeded in rousing the Poles to one last despairing effort. War to the death was declared against this foreigner, this Charles Gustavus who blasphemed God by violating and plundering churches and monasteries; the Virgin Mary was solemnly proclaimed queen of Poland, and a day set apart on which to worship her in her new capacity. A great confidence of victory seized on the people; John Casimir boasted that his Tartars would breakfast on Brandenburgers and Swedes. With an army of sixty thousand, he marched against Warsaw, drove out the hostile garrison, and possessed himself of the rich treasure accumulated by the enemy.

By Frederick William the new crisis was welcomed as an opportunity for improving his footing with Sweden. In the treaty of Marienburg he offered to take the field on the Swedish side, if Charles Gustavus would guarantee to him Posen, Kalisch, and other Polish provinces. Then he set to work to show what his alliance was worth, and found his opportunity in the remarkable three days' battle waged for the recapture of Warsaw. Never did new troops more brilliantly sustain their baptism of fire ; by means of bold manœuvres, by changing the point of attack in the teeth of the heavy fire, the Swedish-Brandenburg army finally routed an enemy which outnumbered it four to one. Warsaw was taken and plundered, and many of its pictures and statues found their way to Berlin, not to speak of the rich columns that went to adorn the palace of the electress at Oranienburg.

Battle of Warsaw and Treaty of Wehlau

It did not suit Frederick William completely to annihilate the Polish power. He prevented the Swedes from following up their victory, and himself withdrew to Prussia, under pretext of defending that province against the Lithuanians. The Poles rallied once more, and while Charles Gustavus was absent, inflicting a severe chastisement on the Danes, retook Warsaw and Kalisch. The elector perceived how, in this emergency more than ever, Sweden would need his alliance, and took the opportunity of screwing his terms to the highest point. In the Treaty of Labiau, the third in this eventful year of 1656, he induced Sweden to recognize him as "supreme, absolute, and sovereign" duke of Prussia. But he knew well that this guarantee alone would not suffice; that the Poles, reënforced by Tartars and Russians, were quite as much to be feared as the Swedes; instead of going to war, however, he preferred to gain his end by peaceful means. Five days after the Treaty of Labiau he commenced secretly negotiating with the Poles for a similar acknowledgment on their part, offering to renounce, in return, the Polish provinces which Sweden had assured to him by the Treaty of Marienburg. It was, of course, double dealing of the rankest kind. Of the new treaty, signed at Wehlau in 1657, Sweden was to be kept in ignorance, until the elector could make sure that Austria would help him in the event of a war with his recent ally. The old Emperor Ferdinand III., had just died, and Frederick William's vote had promised to become the decisive one in the new election, for the reason that the electoral college would otherwise be evenly divided. It was his doing, then, that Leopold, who was to fill the imperial throne for the next half-century, was finally chosen, and, naturally, the favor was returned by a close alliance.

The Peace of Oliva.

The war with Sweden soon became an actuality. The elector welcomed it, for he well foresaw that it would prove the last step in securing the independence of Prussia. The emperor agreed to furnish 10,000 and Poland 7000 men. A manifesto was issued, addressed to all Germans, urging them to rise and free the Rhine, Weser, Elbe, and Oder, which were nothing else than "prisoners of foreign nations." Frederick William himself led the combined forces to a series of brilliant victories. The Swedes were driven back from every one of their recently conquered positions in Denmark; the whole of Pomerania was occupied; while at the same time the garrisons in Poland were forced to surrender.   But, much to the elector's chagrin, a new power appeared upon the scene, and, ostensibly as champion of the Westphalian Peace, ordered the cessation of hostilities.   Louis XIV. and Mazarin, having by the Peace of the Pyrenees, in 1659, concluded their long war with Spain, were able to turn their attention elsewhere. It was intolerable to them that Brandenburg-Prussia should go on with its career of conquest, and they brought about a peace congress, which met at Oliva, a monastery near Danzig.   Louis XIV. himself drew up an army of 40,000 men on the French frontier, to emphasize his demand that all her former possessions in Pomerania should be restored to Sweden.   Could Frederick William have trusted his allies, he never would have yielded; but Austria and Poland, too, were against his making territorial acquisitions.   He was obliged to content himself, therefore, with the general acknowledgment by the congress of his free sovereignty over Prussia.   In itself no mean advantage. The Peace of Oliva placed the claim of the Hohenzollerns above assault; and it marks the raising of their united territories to the rank of a European power.   Not as yet, indeed, a power that was either greatly respected or greatly feared; several architects were to work at the structure before it could reach perfection.

As yet, too, the long-coveted sovereignty had only been secured in relation to foreign powers.   Little could the elector have imagined how fierce an internal struggle remained to be carried on.   What he himself described as the hardest experiences of his life were still to be endured, for the Prussian nobles and burghers sturdily and steadfastly refused to play the part assigned them in his general scheme of government.   Little did they care for Frederick

The struggle with the estates of Prussia.

William's aspiration to shine in the concert of European rulers. They were now to learn, however, to their own unspeakable wrath and misery, the meaning of "absolutism" and "sovereign rights." In their new lord they found a man of iron, thoroughly determined to maintain the position he had taken. "I desire nothing unreasonable," he once told them, "but I mean to be master, and you must be my subjects; then I will show you that I love you as a father loves his children." No sooner had Frederick William sent his stadtholder to Prussia than the conflict broke out. The estates took the ground that the whole transaction with Poland was null and void, from the fact that their own consent had neither been asked nor given. Were they to be bartered about like so many apples and pears? They had rather enjoyed the former rule, which had left them much to their own devices; before they would consent now to do homage to their new head, they were determined to have a thorough understanding with Poland, and also to obtain a guarantee that their rights and privileges should be respected. But these same rights and privileges were such as the elector neither would nor could grant; his glance was fixed on the general good of the whole state, that of these Prussians on their own especial comfort and advantage. No taxes were to be levied, they claimed, no wars or alliances entered into against their will; in fact, in all important matters they were to coöperate, and, in order that their position might be the stronger, they demanded the right to assemble of their own accord at stated intervals. For Frederick William, a standing army, supported by regular money contributions, was a prime necessity. The estates, on the other hand, fearing that such a force might be used for their own coercion, clamored for the dismissal of the troops, the razing of certain fortifications, and, above all, the abolishment of the excise duties from which the military expenses were to be paid.

This dislike to being taxed was a deep-rooted sentiment among all the German nobles of the eighteenth century. The old feudal idea still survived, that it was dignified to fight for one's lord and master, but not to untie for him one's purse-strings except on extraordinary occasions. Characteristic on this point is the report of the elector's own privy councillors, who opposed his plan for a new property tax and a more rigid form of assessment in Prussia: "It is very hard," they say, "to treat a *liberum et ingenuum hominem* so roughly, and to force him *ad pandenda patrimonii sua arcana*," into opening up the secret places where he keeps his patrimony! When, at the local diet which assembled at Königsberg in 1661, it was announced that the elector would admit of no dispute concerning what he considered his sovereign rights; when he refused to disarm, on the ground that he would be crushed by other powers, the excitement of the people passed all bounds. Religious differences, Jesuit intrigues, and secret dealings with Poland, made the movement really dangerous. This "reformed" elector, it was said, was going to reduce the Prussians to absolute servitude. Fanatics preached from the pulpits of Königsberg that all Lutherans were to be driven from their churches in favor of Calvinists. Under the dread of such acts of violence, and under the leadership of the Königsberg demagogue Roth, a conspiracy was formed to throw off the new yoke and return to the sheltering wing of Poland; in an assembly held in the church at Kneiphof a solemn oath to this effect was taken. The land was on the verge of civil war; the Königsbergers planted cannon on their walls, while Prince Radzivill, the stadtholder, drew together what troops he could muster, and called on the elector to come at once if he would save his duchy.

Roth's conspiracy.

What the personal influence of one single, powerful man
can do, was clearly shown when Frederick William, in
October, 1662, arrived in Königsberg, and immediately ordered the arrest of the agitator, Roth, whom, on account of
his immense following among the citizens, Radzivill had
not dared to touch. This man of the people was as courageous and determined, in his way, as the elector himself.
Seized in his own house whence he had scorned to flee,
and carried on horseback at a gallop to the castle so as to
avoid the chances of a rescue, he was tried for high treason
and transferred secretly to the fortress of Peitz, near Colberg, where he was kept under arrest to the day of his
death.   Years afterward, when present by chance in Peitz,
the elector caused the prisoner to be told that if he would
ask for pardon he might go free; but Roth answered
proudly that he wanted justice, not pardon. On the
whole, Frederick William seems to have feared Roth far
less than he did Kalckstein, who now fled to Warsaw,
joined the Jesuits, and was believed to be the promoter of
every kind of treasonable plot. His person, too, was in
time secured, by underhanded means indeed, which ran
counter to the first principles of international law.   A
certain ruthlessness has always characterized these founders of powerful states.   Kalckstein was enticed to the German embassy in Warsaw, was seized, gagged, rolled in a
carpet, and placed in a wagon which drove him across the
border. He was brought to trial, put to the torture, and
finally executed — in spite of the protests of the king of
Poland, who would have made a *casus belli* out of the incident had not other considerations rendered him dependent
on the friendship of Brandenburg. Frederick William
made a scapegoat of his envoy at Warsaw, and there the
matter ended.

These two men, Roth and Kalckstein, have received

much sympathy from later generations, and have been likened to Pym, Hampden, and other martyrs of English parliamentary history. It is true they received harsh treatment, but, according to every conceivable standard, they had committed high treason. If Roth stood out and suffered for popular and class liberties, it was for liberties that would have impaired the safety of the state. It is not always best for local patriots to have their way. For Kalckstein there is absolutely no excuse; he had done his best to stir up Poland against the existing form of government, and had repeatedly, in Warsaw, threatened to take the elector's life.

It was a long and weary task, this restoring order in Prussia, but never did Frederick William display his remarkable talents to better advantage. He knew well when to be severe — of that there was no doubt; but he now showed that he also knew when to persuade and to propitiate. Nor did he spare himself any unpleasant duties. "Since I have been here," he wrote to his general, Schwerin, "I have not enjoyed one healthful hour. The whole time I am inwardly enraged, and I swallow many bitter pills." But he had the satisfaction of coming at last to an agreement, by which the Prussians, in return for concessions more apparent than real, did him homage in the most splendid manner. Never had Königsberg witnessed such a scene as on the day of the ceremony. A great platform, covered with a scarlet cloth and surmounted by a throne, was erected in the square; coins of gold and silver, struck off for the occasion, were scattered among the people; fireworks, processions, and feastings of all kinds signalized the important day.

Restoration of order in Prussia.

The yoke of the new ruler was still to bear heavily upon the Prussians; the foreign wars of the elector were frequently to tax his resources to the utmost, and heartrending complaints often found their way to Berlin. A formal request was once sent that Frederick William would consider, not his own necessities, but the bare, actual possibilities of the province. If the elector was inexorable to such appeals, it was not from lack of sympathy. The founder of the greatness of the Prussian state knew well from personal experience what poverty and hardship meant. The revenues of the Mark, when he had first taken it in hand, amounted to a paltry thirty thousand thalers; while for the province of Cleves, there was a yearly deficit of ten thousand. During the later years of the Thirty Years' War the court had frequently been obliged to borrow sums as low as fifteen guldens, that there might be something to eat upon the table. " There is practically nothing left to pawn," wrote Schwerin, the master of the household, after the Swedish-Polish War. That same war had cost some eight million thalers, which the elector was obliged to wring from his reluctant people. Almost daily in Berlin one saw wagons passing through the streets filled with the goods that had been seized for unpaid taxes, and followed by the unfortunate owners, weeping and wringing their hands.

Reforms and improvements of the Great Elector.

The quiet interval that elapsed between the Peace of Oliva and the wars with Louis XIV. gave Frederick William time to devote himself to the permanent welfare of his lands. Frederick the Great spoke the truth when he stood by the opened coffin of his ancestor, and, taking the dead hand in his own, said to those around him, " Gentlemen, this man did great things." New sources of income were gradually opened up, laws passed to govern exports and imports, factories and enterprises of all kinds started. In these enterprises the elector did not hesitate to risk his own private funds. Duties were charged on goods that passed in at the gates of the cities; and the cities, for the better protection against smuggling, were surrounded with palisades. Every encouragement, in the way of reduced taxation and free building materials, was offered to those who would restore ruined houses or cultivate waste fields. On the "domain" or crown lands no clergyman might perform the marriage ceremony, unless the bridegroom could furnish written proof that he had planted six new fruit trees and grafted six old ones. Colonists were called in from Holland and elsewhere, and everything done to induce them to stay. On the improvement of his capital city the elector expended much time and thought, devising means for replacing the thatched roofs by those of better material, and issuing orders to prevent the pigs, which abounded in the city, from running down the avenue where his wife, Dorothea, had planted her famous lindens. He succeeded so well in his various endeavors that a Frenchman could write, in 1673, "Everything seemed to me so beautiful that I thought there must be some special opening in the sky through which the sun made this region feel its favors." Before the end of Frederick William's reign Berlin had more than doubled the number of its inhabitants. Nor were greater projects lost sight of in the midst of minor affairs. An East India Company was formed, and colonies were established in Africa; but the gold dust from them, whence all the profit was expected to come, did not, according to the elector's own confession, furnish one-half the coin that was spent in the enterprise. A regular postal service was established between such distant points as Hamburg and Königsberg, notwithstanding the opposition of the great Thurn and Taxis monopoly, which had been richly endowed with privileges by the Hapsburg emperors. At the expenditure of much labor, the canal was put through which joins the Spree with the Oder near Frankfort, thus opening up an uninterrupted water course by way of the Havel and Elbe to the North Sea. It still bears the name of the Frederick William Canal. As the Spree is fifty feet higher than the Oder, it was found necessary to build a number of locks, and in the bed of one of these, on the day of the opening, the elector and his whole court dined in state. Then the gates were opened, the water flowed in, and the first ship was despatched on its course.

For the improvement of the army neither effort nor expense was spared. The chief problem the elector had to cope with was the independent spirit of the officers, who considered their regiments as their own private property. By declaring that they had sworn allegiance to the emperor and could not serve two masters, they sought to escape from the elector's jurisdiction; Colonel Rochow threatened to blow up Spandau on receiving a command that was not to his liking. Only with considerable difficulty did Frederick William manage to get rid of the worst elements in his army, and to fill their places with new men. By the year 1646, he had eight thousand good soldiers under arms; by 1655, more than three times that number. It is wonderful, considering the primitive weapons of the time, how much this army was able to accomplish, especially the cavalry, which learned to move with incredible swiftness, thus winning more than one battle over forces superior in number.

The Great Elector and Louis XIV. On the part played by the Great Elector in the wars of the empire and of Holland with Louis XIV., on the inglorious manner in which he was led about, on his humiliating Peace of Vossem, and his subsequent quarrels with Montecuculi and Bournonville, it is not necessary here to dwell. It was while he was in winter quarters in Alsace, in 1674, mourning over the loss of his eldest son, who had just died of fever, that news was brought of an inroad of the Swedes into Brandenburg. Louis XIV. had stirred

them up to this undertaking, furnishing them with the
necessary funds, and causing his resident envoy to stand
over them and see them safely embarked. The elector,
after in vain seeking immediate aid from The Hague
and from Amsterdam, put his own little army in motion
and advanced to Magdeburg, and thence, by stealthy and
rapid marches, to Rathenow. In order to hasten their
progress the foot-soldiers were crowded into wagons.
At Rathenow he managed to cut the Swedish army in
two, and when the sundered divisions tried to join, they
were overtaken at Fehrbellin, a point some fifty miles
to the northwest of Berlin. Here the elector fought one
of his most famous battles, and won a victory so signal that
his alliance was sought after in all directions, by Denmark, by Holland, by Münster, and by Brunswick. Even
the emperor, anxious to have a share in the profits of the
war, sent him a few regiments. In the following years all
Pomerania was cleared of the enemy; but the same
Nemesis awaited the elector that had overtaken him nineteen years before at the time of the Peace of Oliva. The
congress that had assembled at Nymwegen, in order to
settle the war of the empire with France, soon began to
assume an ominously friendly tone toward Sweden. The
Austrian minister announced the emperor's determination
not to endure that "a new king of the Vandals [meaning
the elector] should arise on the Baltic." Louis XIV.
finally refused to consider any general peace that did
not include the return to the Swedes of their portion of
Pomerania, and then made a separate treaty with Holland
and the emperor, leaving Brandenburg to continue a war
from which he was determined she should reap no benefit.
At the same time the Swedes made a bold effort to advance
in the dead of winter through Livonia and Prussia, and to
retake their lost German possessions.

Frederick William roused himself to do and dare the utmost; at all risks the Swedes were to be prevented from reaching Königsberg, the temper of whose inhabitants could not just then be trusted. The elector, who was known to be suffering with the gout, spread the report that he was too ill to leave Berlin, and then set out at the most rapid of paces with what troops he had at hand. A part of the way lay across the ice of the Frischer Haff, but the stadtholder of Königsberg furnished twelve hundred sleighs into which the infantry were crowded. "It was a merry sight," says an old diary, "the more so as, the whole time, they kept playing the dragoon march." The elector himself, driving swiftly by on the ice, held a review of all his forces. Later the way was lost, the soldiers had to encamp in the open, food gave out, and the whole army threatened to become demoralized. But the Swedes were in a still worse plight, and, forced to retreat, arrived at Riga with but one thousand able-bodied men out of an original sixteen thousand.

Brilliant as Frederick William's campaign had been, it helped him to no lasting benefits. His funds were exhausted, his army seriously crippled. Louis XIV. sent him an intimation that if he did not at once come to terms with Sweden a French army would be sent against him; Cleves, indeed, was actually occupied. As no help could be expected from any quarter, even the elector's former friends, Münster and Brunswick, having become pensioners of France, there was no alternative but to sign the Peace of St. Germain. At the signing of the treaty, by which he gave up all his recent conquests, Frederick William is said to have cursed the day when he learned to write. To his friend Von Buch he made the ominous remark: "It is not the king of France who compels me to make peace, but the emperor, the empire, and my own relations and allies. They shall bitterly repent it, and shall suffer losses as great as mine!" He is said once to have quoted the verse of Virgil: "Exoriare aliquis nostris ex ossibus ultor!"

The conjecture seems warranted that from this time on the elector was not wholly master of his own actions. His wrongs preyed upon him, he was tortured by the gout, and his wife, Dorothea, who tenderly cared for him, gained over him an undue influence. Things had been very different in earlier days; much as he loved his first wife, the Orange princess, he would brook no opposition from her, and had been known to enter her presence, to throw down his hat, and call loudly for one of her nightcaps, as a symbol of the rôle she wished him to play. Now Dorothea could turn him around her fingers. She was a strange, violent woman, bent on the advancement of her own children; and her hostility to her stepsons, who stood in the way of their succession, was so strong that she was almost universally believed to have tried to poison them. The younger brother fell dead at a ball in her apartments after partaking of an orange that had been handed him; whereupon the elder, the Crown Prince Frederick, immediately fled the court and went to Cassel, alleging that his life was no longer safe. A stern reprimand from his father brought him home. Dorothea's influence, as well as that of Frederick William's ministers, — who are known to have been bribed by France, — may account in part for the astonishing alliance into which the elector entered with his old enemy, Louis XIV., — at a time, too, when Louis, on the most hollow of all pretexts, was annexing lands of the empire, summoning German princes to do him homage, and endeavoring in every way to prevent Austria's success in her efforts to meet those Turkish invasions which culminated in the siege of Vienna.

This friendship cooled in consequence of the severe measures taken by Louis XIV. against the Protestants of

France.   When, in 1685, the Edict of Nantes was revoked,
when four hundred Protestant churches were torn down,
when the punishment of imprisonment and the galleys was
placed on the refusal to turn Catholic, Frederick William
dropped all the etiquette natural to an ally, and published
his famous free-hearted edict.   He spoke of the "persecutions" that were going on in France, and offered a hearty
welcome to all who might be fortunate enough to escape.
Some twenty thousand answered the call; they were
splendidly received, and given every sort of aid and encouragement.   The old church of the Huguenots still stands
in the principal square of Berlin; their school still thrives;
while their civilization, their arts, and their literature have
accrued to the lasting benefit of their hospitable enter-
tainers.   It is true, as Mirabeau once said, that the
Germans would gradually have learnt of themselves to
make hats, stockings, silk ribbons, and perfumery; but the
process might have taken a long time.   And no one can
deny the immense influence that the Huguenots exercised
in bringing in practical comforts; of gardening, for instance,
to the elector's delight, they made a regular science.

As the coolness with France grew more marked, Frederick William drew closer once more to the emperor, and
sought in especial to settle an old dispute that had been
going on between the two houses for half a century.   The
manner in which he did so was to be pregnant with results
for the future of the Prussian state.   During the Thirty
Years' War Ferdinand II. had confiscated the Silesian
duchies of Brieg, Liegnitz, and Glogau, as well as Jägerndorf, which would have reverted to Brandenburg by *Erb-
verbrüderung*, or heritage treaty with an allied house.
The Great Elector held out for the return of these lands,
but was willing at last to compromise for the little province of Schwiebus.   Even this Leopold refused until the

Crown Prince Frederick, taking matters into his own hands, and willing to sacrifice anything for the imperial alliance, signed a secret agreement to give back Schwiebus so soon as he should succeed to the electorate. How important the matter was to prove will be shown in another connection.

Frederick William died in 1688, leaving a will by which his territories were distributed among his numerous sons. So far had the electress brought the man whose whole life had given the lie to such a policy, and from whose own lips we have the positive statement that he considered subdivision the ruin of Saxony, of the Palatinate, of Hesse, and of Brunswick. The new heir, with the sanction of the council of state, suppressed the document, on the ground that it was counter to the fundamental laws of Brandenburg.

Of the personality of this new ruler, the Elector Frederick III., it is sufficient to say that, although somewhat deformed, in consequence of a fall from his nurse's arms, he was very vain, very lavish, and exceedingly fond of playing a part in pompous ceremonies. His grandson, Frederick the Great, once said of him, epigrammatically, that he was great in small and small in great things; and again, that he would probably have made a persecutor, had there been any solemnities attached to persecution. When still in the nursery he founded an order of knighthood, which not only he himself, but others also, took seriously, and with regard to which each detail was most punctiliously arranged. The sums expended in a single year of his reign for the gold and silver lace on the court liveries amounted to forty-two thousand thalers, while his daughter at her wedding is said to have worn finery which cost some four millions. On the occasion of inaugurating the new University of Halle, it was calculated that the expenses of the various festivities must have come to five times the amount

The personality of Frederick I.

of the endowment. The witty and intelligent Sophie
Charlotte, the second of Frederick's three wives, once
implied that she considered her husband a stage king, and
could not refrain on her death-bed from saying, that now
her lord would have an opportunity for one of his grand
displays. In order to raise funds for such costly predilections, it was necessary to resort to the most unique, and
even petty, methods of taxation. Scarcely an object that
was bought or sold escaped the eye of the watchful officials, and people were obliged on demand to take off in
the streets the very wigs on their heads, to make sure that
the government mark was on the inside. It was the time
when enormous wigs were a fashionable necessity; they
varied somewhat, according to the whims of Louis XIV.,
but were, on the whole, it is said, more enormous in Brandenburg than elsewhere, because the elector thought to
hide his deformity by the profuseness of his locks. In
addition to the wig tax there was a heavy tax on carriages,
on the pretext that the wheels wore out the costly pave-
ments. Permits, to be renewed each year, were needed by
those who intended to drink tea, coffee, or chocolate. No
source of revenue was left unexploited; a certain *Com-
merzienrath*, or merchant prince, by the name of Kreuz,
was intrusted with a monopoly for supplying hog bristles
to be used in the manufacture of brushes. A general
order was issued that when the swine were about to shed
their coats the bristles should be collected, wrapped in
packets as they came from each separate animal, and sent
to Kreuz's clerks. It was the custom for each owner to
mark his hog; but, under penalty of confiscation, this
marking was to be so done as not to injure the particularly
stiff hairs that grew along the spine. Witticisms at Kreuz's
expense were declared punishable by imprisonment and
mutilation.

There is a twofold marvel connected with Frederick's extravagances and with his exeessive demands on the people. On the one hand, although in addition to money payments constant contributions were required for his court festivals, his subjects were fond of him, and sincerely mourned him when he died. His very profusion endeared him to them, and many found occupation in carrying out his pageants and public works. But still more remarkable is the circumstance that at the end of his reign there was no very alarming deficit in the treasury. This is due to the fact that for his war expenses he had received large subsidies from Austria and other powers, while the regular Brandenburg revenues, administered along the lines laid down by the Great Elector, had considerably increased. The most expensive of Frederick's hobbies, costing him in all some six million thalers, was the attainment of the royal crown. It opened up a chance for unfolding unheard-of magnificence; but for that very reason it called forth all his best efforts, and brought to the surface all his latent abilities. It was his own work from beginning to end; his councillors and ministers were almost all against the project, and the difficulties in the way were very great; but he would not be daunted, and politically, as the event proved, he acted wisely and well. He joined at the right time in the upward trend of the minor European states. Hanover, in 1692, had risen to be an electorate, and her ruling house was soon to be recognized as next in succession to the crown of England; Holland had already given a king to that land; Bavaria was striving for the Spanish succession, and only the death of her electoral prince prevented her achieving it; the House of Hesse hoped to succeed to the throne of Sweden, and the Elector Palatine to become king of Armenia.

Even the Great Elector had paid great attention to

Frederick's desire for the royal crown.

questions of precedence and etiquette; carrying on long and wearisome negotiations in order to be called " brother " by the king of France, and " your Serenity " by the Spanish sovereign, and also to be allowed, like the states of Venice, Tuscany, and Savoy, to have his envoys put on their hats at the end of an interview with the emperor. If these matters were of importance to a man of action like Frederick William, they were doubly so to his punctilious and small-minded successor. Frederick declared, in 1697, at the time of the Ryswick Congress, that he had been outraged in the eyes of all Europe because, of his two envoys, only one was given a hand-shake and the title of "your Excellency " by the imperialists, whereas, in the case of monarchies, this compliment was rendered to both. Only with difficulty, at this same congress, had the title of " Electoral Serenity " been conceded to himself. But an incident that left an even greater impression, and that has often been looked upon as the starting-point for the idea of becoming king, occurred to Frederick personally on the occasion of a visit to William of Orange. Just when and where is a matter of dispute, but various writers agree that, in his capacity as king of England, William occupied an arm-chair, giving to Frederick one with only a back. " *Un fauteuil et une chaise à dos*," writes Frederick the Great, "*pensèrent brouiller ces princes à jamais.*"

Negotiations with the emperor.

The "grand project," as Frederick and his ministers always called the plan of gaining the crown, was met, when it first came up. in 1699, with objections of various kinds, the chief of which seems to have been that the assumption of the new title would bring more expense, but no real increase of power. Frederick drew up with his own hand an abstract of the reasons that led him to overrule such findings. The honor and utility of his house would be furthered. He already possessed the power:

why should he not have the name? He thought that he could reckon on the consent of his neighbors, as he desired no man's land. Now was the time, if ever, for the emperor was old, and needed his assistance. Everything turned on this consent of the head of the House of Austria and of the Holy Roman Empire, but it was difficult to obtain. Emperor Leopold, a not unkindly man, given to "hunting, music, and devotional exercises," and possessed of fine eyes, a good nose, smooth chestnut hair, and a ruddy complexion, was not without the obstinacy and slowness of his race. This was exemplified by his feeble gait, and, to quote a contemporary, by "his extraordinarily large mouth and his lower lip, so thick that it spoils all the rest of his face." As far back as 1693, negotiations had begun with Vienna for the recognition of the elector's rights in Prussia. Austria had long refused him the title of duke, on the ground that the old act by which the Teutonic Order had been invested with these lands had never been formally abrogated. At last, grudgingly, he had been reccgnized as duke in Prussia, but "without prejudice to the rights of the worthy Teutonic Order." Then had come a promise that, at least, no other elector should obtain the royal dignity in preference to Brandenburg.

The Austrian ministers were opposed to the project, chiefly on the ground that the aggrandizement of an elector would weaken the imperial authority; already electors were beginning to dispute with his Majesty on questions of etiquette. There was a religious side to the matter, too, which weighed heavily with Leopold. Should he, the natural defender of the Catholic church, help to set up a Protestant monarchy? With regard to this latter point the emperor's fears were quieted in a manner bordering on the marvellous. With his resident envoy in Vienna, Bartholdi, Frederick was in the habit of corresponding in

The Jesuits, Wolf and Vota.

cipher, names of persons especially being transmitted in numerals. Frederick received one day a message that 161 (Bartholdi himself) had better be the one to insinuate the project of royalty to the emperor. He read instead 160, which indicated a Jesuit priest, Father Wolf, who had once been at Berlin as chaplain of an imperial envoy, and with whom Frederick had had various dealings. Not greatly surprised, therefore, the elector wrote off to Wolf, who, much flattered, brought the matter before Leopold, and was not ungraciously received. Whatever scruples arose were explained away, Wolf's own hope and trust being that the new sovereigns could be induced to turn Catholic, — as Augustus the Strong had done on assuming the throne of Poland two years before, and as Ernest Augustus of Hanover had declared his willingness to do should other means fail. With this end in view, Wolf and his friend, Father Vota, laid regular siege, not only to Frederick, but to the electress as well, the latter entering with them into long theological discussions, and writing letters to Vota on so abstruse a subject as the "Authority of the Church Fathers." The hopes of the Jesuits ran high, although never for a moment did they have any chance of real success. Frederick told the English envoy that he had promised Vota " that he [Vota] should have the honor of converting him so soon as he should feel himself in the humor to become Catholic." At the cost of no greater concession than this he won two faithful allies, who did him much good service.

Austria yields. But all this would have availed him nothing had it not been for the great straits in which Austria found herself, with the war for the Spanish succession becoming daily more inevitable, and without sufficient funds in the treasury to pay for the daily expenses of the imperial household. So low did Leopold's credit fall that no Jew would lend money to him at less than seventeen per cent interest. Several regiments of the army had to be suppressed for want of means with which to pay them. "If twelve angels of Heaven were to come and ask for money, none would they get from this court," wrote Bartholdi to Berlin. And here was a power which was ready, in return for a concession costing nothing, to furnish from eight to ten thousand men, to renounce subsidies due by a former treaty, and to help secure the readmittance of Bohemia into the Electoral College. Leopold remained firm for almost a year; the correspondence on the subject fills twenty-one folio volumes. The last straw that broke his resistance was the partition treaty of March 25, 1700, between France, England, and Holland, by which Austria considered herself scandalously treated, not having been consulted on any point. Father Wolf was allowed to send a message to Berlin to the "most serene elector, and *soon, soon to be* most mighty king." The final treaty was signed only two days before the death of the childless King of Spain, an event that was to plunge Europe into a vortex of war for the next fifteen years. Much care and thought had been expended on the exact wording of the title; Frederick was determined to be no mere vassal of the empire in his new capacity, but rather to take some such name as "King of the Vandals," "King of the Wends," or "King of Prussia." To the last form objection was made by the Poles, on the ground that the whole of West Prussia still belonged to them. The wording "King *in* Prussia," was finally adopted, and a special declaration signed that no interference was intended with Poland's rights. Once at the goal of his wishes, Frederick turned sharply on the Jesuits, paid the venerable fathers in hard cash for all their services, but made it very plain that he would make no single concession in the matter of the Catholic religion.

Not even a church was handed over to them in Berlin, and so little regard was paid to the Pope that he was not even notified of what had taken place, or of the intended coronation.   Clement XII. flew into a great rage, and wrote a circular note to the Catholic powers begging them not to approve the impious actions of the Marchese di Brandenburg.   For nearly a hundred years he and his successors refused to address the Hohenzollerns by any other title, even by that of elector.

The royal coronation at Königsberg.

It remained to give an outward expression to the new honor the emperor had "accorded," and to prepare a grander and more sumptuous coronation than anything that had yet been seen.   Frederick had been very impatient for this event, had "sighed for it ceaselessly and could not sleep," wrote the French ambassador, Des Alleurs.   The crown, sceptre, and mantle had been made ready months before the time; night after night one of the gates of the city of Berlin was left wide open for the courier who was to bring the emperor's final response from Vienna.   All points of ceremonial had been carefully studied from books of etiquette and from the usages observed in Denmark and Poland.   A detailed description had even been sent from England of the coronation of Charles II. in Scotland.   There are learned discussions in the Prussian archives as to how the new king should receive the envoys of foreign countries less important than his own — standing, with his hat on, like the Emperor; or sitting, with his hat on, like the king of France; or standing, with his hat off, like this same Charles.   The procession that set out from Berlin to Königsberg, in December 1700, was of great size and magnificence; it was obliged to move in relays, as the towns through which it passed could otherwise not have stood the burden.   Thirty thousand horses had been requisitioned, in addition to those from the royal stables. The journey lasted twelve days, and the ceremonies four more; on the 15th of January four heralds-at-arms proclaimed through all the streets the elevation of Prussia to a kingdom. From this time on it was forbidden to speak of the elector save as "his Majesty"; and the English minister reports, "If any one forgets, and lets fall the words 'Electoral Highness,' he is obliged to pay a fine of a ducat for the benefit of the poor." On January 16 came proclamations from all the pulpits; on the 17th the founding of the order of the Black Eagle, membership in which forms to this day the greatest distinction in the gift of the Prussian monarch. In addition to princes of the blood, there were to be but thirty knights, well born, without reproach, and over thirty years of age. They were to wear as insignia: a band of orange color, in memory of the mother of the king; a Maltese cross; and a silver star, upon which was a black eagle holding in one claw a crown of laurel and in the other a thunderbolt, while beneath was a device, *Suum cuique*.

On January 18 took place the coronation itself, the ceremonial of which was copied from that of the imperial coronation at Frankfort, with the exception, however, that the religious element was kept in the background. Frederick did, indeed, in order that he might be called "his sacred Majesty," create for the occasion two Protestant bishops, — one Lutheran, one Calvinist; but he significantly placed the crown on his own head, and afterward with his own hands on that of his queen, the episcopal functions being confined to the consecration with the holy oil. On the splendid accessories of this whole demonstration, on the rich robes and priceless jewels, on the baldachins carried by nobles, the salvos of artillery that accompanied the drinking of every toast, the oxen roasted whole and

stuffed with animals dwindling in size, the fountains running wine, the thousands of coins scattered among the
people, it is not necessary to dwell. The house of the
governor of Prussia was decorated so as to represent a
temple of fame. The king himself composed a prayer
thanking God for having accorded him the crown, and
asking His blessing. It was characteristic of this Hohenzollern to declare an amnesty for prisoners who had not
offended against *divine or terrestrial majesty*, and to cause
a copperplate engraving to be made of the procession, in
which he himself is represented as a tall and slender youth.
The festivities lasted in all for several weeks, being renewed
on the return of the royal pair to Berlin and Potsdam.
An opera was performed called the "Struggle of the Old
and New Century." To the latter was due the palm of
victory, because it had actually witnessed the coronation;
the old century could merely make the weak defence that
it had prepared the way for the great event.

Danckel-
mann and
Warten-
berg.

By a happy concatenation of circumstances Frederick had
been able to raise the prestige of his state, and to perform
a service for his house which laid the foundation for its
future glory; but there his merits ended. He lived
merely for the present, was lamentably weak in his foreign
policy, left the business of ruling in the hands of syco-
phants, and spent what funds he could lay hold of without
attempting to organize the finances on a permanent basis.
There was, indeed, a privy council, consisting of all the
heads of the governmental departments, but it was there,
as Leibnitz said, *pour la forme et pour l'honneur*. Its head,
the grand president, held a position equivalent to that of
prime minister in other countries. One faithful and
capable president Frederick had found in Eberhard von
Danckelmann, who had been his tutor in his youth, and
had served him with much devotion during a long series of

years. But Danckelmann fell a victim to court intrigues
and to the hatred of the electress, his chief sin doubtless
being that he had opposed the idea of securing the royal
crown. He was accused of not having stood up firmly
enough for Prussia's interests at the Treaty of Ryswick, in
1697, and was finally represented as wishing to usurp
Frederick's prerogatives. " He would like to play the
elector, would he! I will show him that I am master!"
cried the irate prince, and treated his former favorite with
absolute ferocity, casting him in prison, and when no court
could be found to condemn him, keeping him there on one
pretext or another for ten years. Count Kolb von Wartenberg, Danckelmann's worst enemy, frivolous and unconscientious to the last degree, became his successor with
almost unlimited power, and with the promise that no
inquiry should ever be made into his methods of administration. His wife at the same time enjoyed the peculiar
distinction of being Frederick's official mistress, a post
which the new king had found it necessary to establish in
imitation of Louis XIV. All the paraphernalia of such a
relationship were there, — a secret staircase connecting the
two apartments, a secluded garden, in which Frederick
daily walked with his minister's wife. Yet both averred,
under circumstances leaving no room for doubt, that their
intimacy was purely platonic. The Wartenberg pair finally
fell into disgrace; the count by reason of an outrageous
misappropriation of funds, in which he and his subordinates
were concerned, the countess because of outbursts of temper and a jealous eagerness to maintain her position as
first lady at the court, which led her into a hand-to-hand
conflict and a literal tearing of the hair with the Dutch
ambassadress.

A wiser and a stronger man than Frederick would have
managed to make more capital out of the wars in which,

during almost every year of his whole reign, both as
elector and as king, his troops were engaged. On many
a field, even according to the testimony of men like Eugene
of Savoy and William of Orange, they had won the day
for the allies; yet at every peace conference Brandenburg-
Prussia played an inferior, not to say humiliating, rôle, and
came forth at the end with small rewards, which did not
begin to compare in worth with the sacrifices made. With
the exception of the tiny district in Guelders, given him
at Utrecht, Frederick bought all his territorial acquisitions
for hard cash; Quedlinburg and Elbing from the impoverished Augustus of Saxony, the small Westphalian county
of Tecklenburg from the Count of Solms-Braunfels. Far
from being the gainer, then, by the French and Turkish
wars, Prussia, bereft of her best soldiers, had been obliged
to make great sacrifices in order to raise militia armies
which should protect her boundaries against the overlap-
ping waves of the Swedish-Polish struggle. The hand of
the military recruiting officer rested like iron on the land;
many of the men who fell, bravely fighting, in Italy and
Belgium had had to be regularly kidnapped into the service. The tone of the army was incredibly low and coarse,
the punishments and general treatment such as would not
now be inflicted on dumb beasts. Slitting of the nose and
cutting off of ears were common penalties for desertion.[1]

In one respect, and in one only, can we give unqualified
praise to Frederick I.: he encouraged liberty of thought
and literary and artistic endeavor in every way. How
far this was owing to the influence of his second wife,
the witty Charlotte of Hanover, who had been educated in
three creeds so as to fit her for any husband, would be
hard to establish. Frederick the Great says of his grand-

[1] See Freytag's very interesting essay in *Bilder aus der deutschen
Vergangenheit*, Vol. V.

mother in his memoirs, "She it was who brought true
social refinement and love of art and science to Prussia,
and inspired the etiquette on which her husband laid such
stress with meaning and dignity." The *Mercure Galant*,
a newspaper of the day, gives an attractive picture of her
personality, — of her large, sweet blue eyes, the prodigious
quantity of her black hair, her well-proportioned nose,
bright red lips, and brilliant complexion. A medal struck
in her honor declared that on one throne dwelt love and
majesty. And she was more intellectual and witty, even,
than she was beautiful. It was of this queen that Leibnitz, who was like a son of the house at the Prussian
court, once declared, that she would never be satisfied
until she knew the "why of the why." "Leibnitz wishes
to teach me the infinitely little," she wrote in one of her
letters; "has he forgotten that I am the wife of Frederick
I.?" She spoke several languages, and her French, especially, was so excellent that a Huguenot refugee once
asked in all sincerity if she could also speak German.
She did not dislike magnificence and display, but would
like to have had it, to use her own words, "*indépendant
de la gêne*." The story is told that at the coronation in
Königsberg she took a pinch of snuff at one of the most
solemn moments, which proceeding so shocked her punctilious husband that he sent a lackey to warn her against
a repetition of the offence. She afterward wrote to a
friend that the whole proceeding had bored her.

Sophie Charlotte's palace at Lietzenburg, the name of
which was afterward, to honor her memory, changed to
Charlottenburg, became a rallying place for all the great
men of the day: for the versatile Leibnitz, the "father of
German philosophy and inventor of differential calculus,"
and for a host of others, philosophers and artists, Jesuits
and Pietists. Among the latter were Spener, Francke,

and Thomasius, — all of them men who, for their freedom of speech, had been persecuted in other German states, but at Frederick's court had found favor and an opportunity to teach in his new university. Thomasius, especially, is interesting as the bold and outspoken opponent of all the current nonsense of his day. He had made himself unpopular at Leipzig by laughing at what he termed the "wiggery" of his legal *confrères*, at their belief in witches, in the divine right of kings, in the efficacy of torture, and in the necessity for clothing their barren thoughts in Latin instead of in German words. Frederick received Thomasius, who had been ordered to keep silence under pain of imprisonment, with every honor, bestowing upon him a court title and a yearly stipend. Francke was the founder of the famous orphan asylum in Halle, which began with a capital of four and a half thalers, and grew to be one of the greatest institutions of its kind in the whole world.

It was with the help of these, his paladins, and especially of Leibnitz, that Frederick founded the "Academy of Sciences," which started out, among other advantages, with its own observatory. One of its first tasks was to introduce the reformed Gregorian calendar, which the Prussians, from hatred of the Pope, had in 1582 refused to accept. The discrepancy between the old reckoning and the new had by this time grown to eleven days, and this was remedied by making the first day of March, 1700, follow directly upon the 18th of February.

Frederick's death.

Frederick died in 1713, of fright, it was said, at the appearance of the "white lady," who is supposed to this day to appear whenever a great catastrophe impends for the Hohenzollern House. In this especial case the phenomenon was afterward explained. After Sophie Charlotte's death the old king, fearing that the crown prince, Frederick William, might leave no male heir, had taken to himself a third wife, Sophie Louise of Mecklenburg-Schwerin. She was always an intolerant Lutheran, and at last, being seized with religious mania, had to be confined under lock and key. She escaped one day, and passing a glass door in her flowing garments, gave her husband his death-blow.

CHAPTER II

THE TURKISH CAMPAIGNS, THE AGGRESSIONS OF LOUIS XIV. AND THE SPANISH SUCCESSION WAR

LITERATURE: Erdmannsdörfer's great work in the Oncken Series, *Deutsche Geschichte, 1648–1740,* deals exhaustively with this period and is much better than Ritter. It received a prize as the best historical production of the year in which it appeared.

Palsied state of the empire.

IF from the newly founded kingdom of Prussia we turn to the affairs of the empire at large, we shall find that, contrary to expectation, the Peace of Westphalia by no means ushered in a long period of general repose. Of that empire there was by this time little left but its outward form. What could have been more harsh than the judgment passed upon it by the clearest head of the age — the jurist and historian, Samuel Puffendorf: "It is no more a nation than was the league of Greek states which Agamemnon led against Troy; it is not a monarchy, not an oligarchy, nor yet a democracy; it is an abortion — a certain irregular body like unto a monster." As Voltaire said of it two generations later, it was a Holy Roman Empire that was neither holy, nor Roman, nor an empire. Four folio volumes, indeed, were still needed to designate all the privileges and prerogatives of its head. He was still "fountain of justice," still the supreme feudal lord from whom all power emanated. Titles and other empty distinctions he might distribute to his heart's content. But his real influence on affairs, save as head of the House of Austria, was as scant as the purely imperial revenues, which amounted in all but to thirteen thousand guldens; not enough, Charles V. had once said, to pay the expenses of the imperial kitchen. The whole institution was worn out, and Puffendorf is not sure that even the extinction of the House of Hapsburg, devoutly prayed for by another writer, would afford the desired remedy.

In the midst of this palsied state of affairs there came a series of Turkish attacks upon Hungary, as persistent, as violent, and as long-continued as those counter invasions of the Christians in the days of Godfrey of Bouillon or Richard III. That Diet of the Empire which met at Ratisbon in 1663, and which, almost from the force of inertia, remained in session until the end of all things, in 1806, had been called together to take measures for defence. A panic had seized upon the whole of Western Christendom, and, by imperial decree, in all parts of Germany the so-called Turk-bell was tolled at twelve o'clock, that the people might assemble and offer up prayers for a speedy deliverance. From all the pulpits the preachers thundered forth their warnings, while innumerable pamphlets and treatises were spread abroad.

It was no mere idle threat of the Grand Vizier Achmed Köprili, that, with an army of a hundred thousand men, he would pay a visit to the emperor in Vienna. Since the year 1527, when, through the battle of Mohacs, it came into the possession of the Hapsburgs, three-fourths of Hungary had been lost inch by inch. Budapest had become the seat of a Turkish pasha, as had likewise Stuhlweissenburg, the old coronation place of the Hungarian kings. The situation was the more perilous for the house of Austria from the condition of affairs in Transylvania, where the Turks were fostering anarchy in the well-founded hope that a prince might be chosen as ruler who would make the land tributary to the Sultan; while, as

The Turks under Mahomet IV.

time went on, the stern truth was borne in upon the Germans that their constant enemy, the "most Christian king," Louis XIV., did not disdain to send his agents among the infidels, inciting them, by bribes and otherwise, to make new attacks whenever Hapsburg victories threatened his own ascendency.

It is a curious fact that the Sultan under whom the fiercest and most formidable attacks took place was one of the weakest that even Turkey had ever had. Mahomet IV., whose reign, like that of Louis XIV., of the Emperor Leopold, and of the Great Elector, fills practically the whole latter half of the seventeenth century, — had come to the throne, in 1648, at the age of seven years. He grew up completely under the influence of women, especially of his grandmother, who was all-powerful in the palace until at last she was strangled by the party of his mother. One of the earliest sentences given to the boy by his writing master was, "Obey, or I will cut off your head." Even when he grew older, Mahomet was singularly lacking in self-will and independence. In vain his mother urged him to assert himself; when he did so it was only to make himself ridiculous, as when once he forbade any of his subjects who were not Mussulmans to wear red caps and yellow slippers, and went around, sabre in hand, to see that his orders were executed. He never commanded an army, but contented himself with handing the green standard of the Prophet to the grand vizier, and attaching the heron's plumes to the turbans of his generals. When a battle was in prospect he spent his time in consulting astrologers on the probable outcome. His chief passion, or rather his craze, was for hunting. He is known in the ballads of the time as the mighty hunter, and employed from twenty-five thousand to thirty thousand men in beating up his game. A propensity which cost him dear, for it formed one of the chief grievances of the insurgents who overthrew him, in 1687.

How came it about that, with such an unwarlike head, the Turks managed to gain such splendid victories? The answer is that, just as the old Merovingian kings had their mayors of the palace, so the Sultan had his capable grand viziers. These, during Mahomet IV.'s reign, were for the most part of the brave family of Köprili. The first of them only accepted his position on the condition of having almost absolute power, and with the express agreement that no report of evil was to be believed against him. He nominated all officials, and executed whom he pleased, the number of his victims amounting to some thirty thousand. But there was a limit to the influence even of men like these. It was absolutely necessary for them to achieve popularity by means of brilliant victories against foreign enemies, and that is what led them into their wars with the empire. Into the details of these different campaigns it is not possible here to enter. The Germans, with occasional scanty aid from other nations, fought in a number of bloody battles, often against overwhelming odds, but with such results, on the whole, that the museums of Vienna, Karlsruhe, and Dresden are full to-day of rich booty, of armor, of trappings, and of silken hangings.

It was found at the Diet of Ratisbon that, even in the face of the danger from the Turks, there was no unity among the estates of the empire, each petty prince considering his own real or fancied grievances as of more importance than a foreign war. A levy of thirty thousand men was at last voted, but the contingents were apportioned according to the long-antiquated *Reichsmatrikel*, or imperial schedule, and, in reality, not two-thirds of that number ever came together. The Emperor Leopold was obliged

The Peace of Vasvar.

to accept aid from the Rhine Confederation, which had
been formed to keep a watch upon himself, and even from
Louis XIV. — allies whom he so hated and feared that, after
they had helped him to win the battle of St. Gothard, in
which three pashas and fourteen thousand other Mohammedans fell, he hurriedly closed with the Porte the Peace
of Vasvar, in 1664. More properly speaking, this was a
twenty years' truce, and during its continuance the empire
engaged in French wars, with little molestation on its eastern borders, except from Hungarian rebels, who, in 1677,
entered into a formal alliance with France. The young
pretender to the Hungarian throne, Emmerich Tököly, in-
scribed on his coins the name of his "Protector" Louis XIV.

The siege
of Vienna.
But more important for Tököly was the winning over to
his cause of Kara Mustapha, the then grand vizier, who,
having been worsted at this time (1682) in a war with King
John Sobieski of Poland, was thirsting for a new enterprise
in order to maintain his tottering prestige. Now took place
that march on Vienna which had been threatened so many
years before. Not the one hundred thousand of Achmed
Köprili, but a flood of twice that number rolled up to the
walls of the Austrian capital, and seemed about to beat
them down. Few sieges are more famous in history; few
defences more worthy of praise. The emperor, indeed,
was better able to meet the danger of invasion than he
had been nineteen years before; and this time he rejected
the treacherous offers of Louis XIV. His warmest allies
were John Sobieski and the Pope of Rome, the latter fearing for the safety of the Eternal City itself should Vienna
fall a prey to the infidel. One friend, indeed, on whom
he had counted, the Great Elector, sent him no aid at all,
being fast in the toils of France, and having made his
offer of sixteen thousand men contingent on shameful
conditions.

The garrison which, for two long months, aided by the students and guild merchants, defended Vienna, numbered only eleven thousand men; but at the critical moment of the siege, when the subterranean mines of the enemy had already wrought much havoc, when night after night from the tower of St. Stephen's rockets of distress had been sent up in token of the last extremity, John Sobieski and the imperial commander, the Duke of Lorraine, appeared without the walls, and, after a battle which lasted from dawn until late evening, put to flight the colossal army of the grand vizier (September 12, 1683). A rich booty was secured, including Kara Mustapha's own magnificent tent. It is the same enormous silken structure which now, adorned with the weapons and other articles that were in it at the time of its capture, stands in the Johanneum, a wing of the castle at Dresden. The Sultan promptly ordered the strangulation of his unfortunate commander-in-chief, and proceeded to organize a new army; but the emperor and his allies, encouraged by their success, determined at all costs to rid Christendom of this constant thorn in the flesh. At a great sacrifice a twenty years' truce was concluded with Louis XIV., and the latter was left for the present to enjoy the fruits of his new and unprecedented policy of aggression.

All along the line now, by Austrians, Venetians, Poles, and by the mercenaries of the Pope, the struggle was taken up against the Turk, and not only in Hungary, but also in Greece. It was in the course of this war that the Acropolis of Athens was made a ruin by a Venetian bomb falling into a Turkish powder magazine. A real enthusiasm seized on Europe; a new glory, even, shone around the old institution of the empire: was not a venerable emperor, for the first time in many centuries, at the head of a really grand undertaking? Louis XIV. alone looked

Jealousy of Louis XIV.

on askance, and punished French princes who took part in the war; for it was openly acknowledged at his court that the feebleness of the empire made the grandeur of France. Gradually almost the whole of Hungary was cleansed from the invaders; Budapest fell in 1686, and in the year following a victory at Mohacs rendered it possible to presage the end of the war. A few months later a Hungarian diet, held at Pressburg, voted that the crown of St. Stephen should for all time be made hereditary in the house of Hapsburg; it was the birthday of the Austrian-Hungarian nation. The French king's jealousy rose to the highest pitch, and, isolated as he was at this time in Europe, and feeling that his only salvation lay in sudden action, he launched his forces on the borders of the empire and commenced his fierce devastation of the Palatinate. Thus Austria's old dread was realized, and she was involved in a double struggle that lasted for nearly a decade.

Louis of Baden and Eugene of Savoy.

On the eastern scene of war, which alone concerns us here, her fortunes varied with the character and daring of the heads of her armies. In Louis of Baden, who, in 1691, won the bloody battle of Slankamen, she had found a general of the highest order; but his services were needed in the west, and his successor, Augustus the Strong of Saxony, who received the chief command only in consideration of the large contingent he had brought, fought two campaigns with very small results. Fortunately for Austria, fortunately, indeed, for every one but himself, a higher honor even than that of imperial generalissimo beckoned to him in the distance and led him to resign his position. This was the crown of Poland, made vacant, in 1696, by the death of John Sobieski. Countless candidates were in the field, the strongest a prince of Condé, who was backed by all the might of Louis XIV.; but by diplomatic skill, by bribery and intimidation, by abandoning the Protestant faith, which his own land had been the first to adopt, Augustus won the day, and was crowned at Cracow in the new year. The place of Augustus in the army was taken by the talented Prince Eugene of Savoy, who thus inaugurated one of the great military careers in the world's history. A provider and husbander of resources, as well as a leader of armies, he set to work with a firm hand to organize the finances, which he found in the worst possible condition, with debts of enormous proportions, and with the whole task of provisioning in the hands of Jews, who had made their profit without fulfilling the conditions. In spite of all difficulties and drawbacks, Eugene soon gave an earnest of what might be expected of him, and set Europe ringing with the fame of his extraordinary victory at Zenta, where the Turks lost thirty thousand, the Austrians but fifteen hundred men. From the farther bank of the river the new Sultan himself witnessed this crushing defeat of his troops, and in a state bordering on madness fled to Temesvar. Even the great seal which the Grand Vizier wore around his neck fell into the hands of the Germans.

By this time the inevitable and all-embracing struggle for the inheritance of the last Spanish Hapsburg was looming nearer and nearer. The emperor needed his hands free for the new enterprise, and was glad, in 1699, to sign the Peace of Carlowitz, which ended the Turkish war for the time being, and insured him the possession of nearly all Hungary and Transylvania. In a later war, in 1718, Austria managed to extend her boundaries considerably farther to the eastward; but, later still, in the unfortunate campaigns from 1736 to 1739, she lost all these hard-earned advantages, and the final Peace of Belgrade left her almost where she was at the time of Carlowitz.

If from the Turkish wars we turn to the complications

with the "grand monarch" of France, we shall find that the key-note of the latter's policy was his claim to be rightful heir to the throne of Charlemagne; he himself, in a series of instructions drawn up for the guidance of his son, declared that the Germans had unlawfully usurped that heritage, while, to be still more definite, one of his jurists, a member of the Parliament of Paris, showed that Hugo Capet should by rights have succeeded the last Carolingian. By fair means or foul Louis XIV. intended some day to become emperor of the Romans, and at the time of the Peace of Nymwegen he could definitely count on the votes of three electors; in the meantime, on every possible pretext, he engaged in wars of conquest. His first aim was to secure the Spanish Netherlands under the pretext that, by an old law of inheritance, they had "devolved" upon his queen, the eldest daughter by the first marriage of King Philip IV. of Spain. This attempt was a failure, for Louis had to reckon with the coalition known as the Triple Alliance, and consisting of England, Sweden, and Holland; but he presently managed to sunder this union by bribes and by subtle diplomacy; to King Charles II. he promised such subsidies as would help him to realize his scheme of recatholicizing England, while in another direction, Austria, he secured neutrality and favor, in 1668, by a secret treaty, dividing up the great Spanish inheritance against the long-expected moment when the sickly young king, Carlos II., should breathe his last. Spain itself, as well as Milan and the West Indies and other important islands, were to fall to the share of the emperor, while Louis was to have Naples and Sicily, Franche Comté, Navarre, and the Philippines.

The way being thus prepared, having succeeded, too, in bribing a number of German princes, like the dukes of Brunswick, and the bishops of Treves, Cologne, and

Münster, Louis XIV. once more took the field, opposed only by Holland and by the elector of Brandenburg. To the head of Dutch affairs was now called that William III. of Orange who later became king of England. The brave little republic, which opened its dykes before the invading enemy, was not so easily crushed. Brandenburg, indeed, was a useless ally, for the Great Elector, himself an unsuspecting victim, was involved in one of the most miserable games of intrigue and deceit that policy ever prompted. Very shame had driven the Emperor Leopold to at least make a demonstration against an enemy that had wantonly broken the law of nations and disregarded the boundaries of his empire; but, mindful of his secret pact regarding the Spanish inheritance, he determined to do no real harm to his ally of France, and, while joining his forces to those of Frederick William, his general-in-chief, Montecucculi, was secretly ordered to avoid serious combat. As an Austrian minister expressed it, there was need of harnessing a tame and manageable horse to this wild and unbroken steed of Brandenburg. Foiled in every plan by which he had meant to circumvent the enemy, looked upon with scorn by the Dutch, who withdrew their subsidies from so dilatory an ally, Frederick William withdrew from the struggle and entered into the inglorious Peace of Vossem with the French (1673).

Austria's secret understanding with Louis XIV.

A year later, when events had caused Austria to renew the struggle with all seriousness, the elector once more took her side; but the unaccountable conduct of the imperial general, Bournonville, deprived the campaign of all good results. Concerted action finally became impossible. "You are neutral," said Frederick William to the Spanish ambassador, who visited the camp, "and can tell the world what is going on here; I wish to be acquitted of all blame."

Quarrels of Bournonville and the Great Elector.

At Marlenheim, through Bournonville's obstinacy, the elector lost a brilliant opportunity of surrounding the army of the French general Turenne, while the charge seems well founded that at Turkheim, contrary to agreement, the Austrian general drew off his forces, leaving those of Frederick William alone in a position of deadly peril.   It was soon after this that the Great Elector was called away by the irruption of the Swedes into the Mark. During the next years, as we have seen, he was occupied in the north, making his brilliant but fruitless conquests.

The peace of Nym-wegen.

The war on the Rhine still went on for nearly four years.   First came long manœuvring between Turenne and Montecucculi.   Then came a series of battles : at Sasbach, where Turenne was killed; at the Conz bridge on the river Saar, where the dukes George and Ernest Augustus of Brunswick covered themselves with glory; and under the walls of Treves.   The French recovered themselves for a while, but the marriage of William of Orange to Mary of England, in 1677, proved to them a severe blow; it was as bad for Louis XIV., said the English ambassador at the time, "as the loss of ten battles and fortresses." Yet none the less the Dutch people clamored for peace. Charles II. of England was as unreliable as a wavering reed; and the French king, appreciating the situation, offered to Holland an arrangement so advantageous, especially for its future trade, that the republic finally accepted, leaving the empire and Brandenburg to the French mercies.   There were those who urged Leopold to take a manly stand and continue the war on his own account, among them the Great Elector, who hoped thus to secure his Pomeranian conquests.   But the emperor, as has been said, hated the idea of a "new king of the Vandals on the Baltic," and signed for himself at Nymwegen a peace with France and Sweden, the basis of which was the condition of things in the year 1648. The wags of the time called this the peace of *Nimm-weg*, inasmuch as here were taken away all the elector's recent acquisitions. He was forced, as we know, into the distasteful Peace of St. Germain.

The French had reason enough to be proud of their diplomacy, seeing that out of a desperate military position they had known how to draw such gains. "German princes will make no more war on me," said Louis XIV. to Sophia of Hanover, who came to visit her niece, the Palatine princess who was the wife of *Monsieur*. Louis considered that now the time had come for making good those claims to the whole of Alsace which had never slumbered since the Peace of Westphalia.[1] There had been an effort at Nymwegen to bring clearness into the matter, but the French had refused to reopen it, well knowing that the ambiguous wording of those old clauses would give them the best possible pretext for the annexations they were planning.

By calmly taking possession of the defenceless lands he claimed, and by propounding a new and startling theory, in defence of which he played off the Turks and the elector of Brandenburg against the emperor, Louis now gained more territory than in many wars, and stretched the French boundaries to the Rhine. He declared that the Westphalian Peace had ceded to him certain districts *with all their dependencies*. Three "Courts of Reunion" were established, one at Metz, one at Breisach, and one at Vesançon, to determine what lands actually were, *and ever had been*, dependent on his new possessions. The cities of Metz, Toul, and Verdun, once important bishoprics, were ordered to bring in lists of lands they had formerly owned, and charters were consulted which reached

Louis XIV.'s appropriation of Alsace and Lorraine.

[1] See Vol. I, p. 493.

as far back as to Merovingian times. These so-called "dependencies" stretched far into the neighboring states, and men like the Elector of the Palatinate, the dukes of Baden and Würtemberg, and even the king of Sweden, who was of the Palatine line, were summoned to do homage to France.

Strassburg taken.

Even this hollowest of all pretexts was lacking for the French king's sudden descent on the free city of Strassburg. That most important fortress, of which Charles V. once said that, if he had to choose between losing it and losing Vienna, he would relinquish the latter, had been expressly excepted when the ambiguous rights over the other Alsatian towns had been ceded to France by the Westphalian Peace. But no care had been taken to garrison it, and only four hundred mercenaries were at hand to oppose a French force of thirty-five thousand men. After three days of negotiation the city capitulated (September 30, 1681), and three weeks later Louis XIV., in royal state and accompanied by his whole family, held a triumphant entry. Elizabeth Charlotte, Louis's sister-in-law, fairly "howled," as she wrote to her brother, at having thus to accompany the French court into a conquered German city. Poor woman, she was soon to shed still bitterer tears at the wasting and ravaging of her Palatine home, ostensibly in her own interests! For the present, Louis contented himself with the complete subjugation of Alsace and Lorraine, which were handed over to the Jesuits for the purpose of catholicizing.

The Laxenburg alliance.

That more effective opposition was not offered by the empire was due, as we know, to the attitude of the Great Elector and to the exigencies of the Turkish wars. In the agreement entered into between Louis XIV. and Frederick William, in January, 1681, it had been expressly stipulated that the elector was not to inquire into the right or wrong of any of his new ally's actions. After the fall of Strassburg the *status quo* was again confirmed, Frederick William's pension being raised from one hundred thousand to four hundred thousand thalers in order to gild the bitter pill.

After Strassburg's fall a demonstration at least was made in the shape of the Laxenburg alliance, an association of small German powers, headed by the Count of Waldeck, and finally joined by the emperor; its avowed object was to see that the peace treaties of Westphalia and Nymwegen were properly observed, for which purpose three armies were to be maintained, one on the upper, one on the middle, and one on the lower Rhine. Shortly afterward Bavaria formed its own defensive alliance with Leopold, while Saxony and Brunswick prepared to do the same.

But the advent of Kara Mustapha and the siege of Vienna took away the last lingering thought of plunging into a French war. In order to have his hands free for his new undertakings against the Turks, Leopold, in 1684, closed, as we have seen,[1] a twenty years' truce with Louis XIV., expressly guaranteeing to the latter Strassburg and all the territories acquired through the decisions of the "Courts of Reunion."

The French armies in the meantime had won Casale in Italy and Luxemburg in the Spanish Netherlands, fortresses which, with Strassburg, seemed to give them a vicelike hold on all Europe. One of Louis XIV.'s flatterers, in carving the pedestal of a column of victory, represented the German Empire in the form of a bound slave at the feet of the *vir immortalis!*

A rallying of forces against Louis XIV.

But gradually, as the Turkish war went on, and imperial victories succeeded each other, the French king was

[1] See Vol. II, p. 49.

obliged to confess to himself that a great change was coming over the political face of Europe. The young elector of Bavaria, Max Emmanuel, married the daughter of Leopold, and showed disquieting designs on the Spanish inheritance, which Louis had come to consider so entirely his own perquisite. Carlos II. himself, the childless king whose death had already been so many times discounted in the past twenty years, was enamoured of the idea of having Max Emmanuel as his successor, and openly declared in the young prince's favor; the Spanish people treated him like one of the royal family. In the empire itself one prince after another went over to the Austrian side, while the Laxenburg alliance came to life again in the enlarged form of the Augsburg League. The Great Elector, too, as already shown, grew tired of the French alliance after the revocation of the Edict of Nantes, and entered into negotiations with Leopold for the recognition of his Silesian claims; while in England, James II., Louis's faithful friend, was displaced by William of Orange, his bitter enemy, who was already in constant communication with Frederick William.

The devastation of the Palatinate.   In the end Louis XIV., hoping to nip the coalition plans of his enemies in the bud, proceeded in a perfectly ruthless and unheard-of manner to strike terror into their hearts, and began a nine years' war that started with the terrible devastation of the Rhine Palatinate. He issued a manifesto accusing the emperor of intriguing against France, and launched his armies across the Rhine. The Germans, whose vast forces had gone to fight the Turks in Hungary, were surprised in an almost defenceless condition. The fortress of Philipsburg alone made a show of resistance, and in the course of a few short weeks four electorates, Mainz, Treves, Cologne, and the Palatinate were in French hands.

Leopold answered by a counter manifesto, which the great Leibnitz is believed to have composed, and proceeded to strengthen his alliances without abandoning the Turkish war. Some scruples he had about joining with a Protestant country like Holland against a Catholic monarch; but his Jesuits drew up a remarkable document which quieted his conscience. "In a justifiable war," they said, "it is allowable to make use of horses and other beasts — consequently, also, of unbelievers!" By the Treaty of 1689, the Dutch bound themselves not only to assist the emperor in the present crisis, but also to stand by him in the matter of the Spanish succession. But already the hand of the destroyer had fallen with all its weight on the fertile Rhenish lands; the order had gone forth to throw down all the forts of the Palatinate and to level some twelve hundred cities and villages with the ground.

Louis's minister, Louvois, based his orders for destruction on purely military grounds. France was threatened on all sides — from the Channel, from the Pyrenees, and from the Rhine. Her armies could not be everywhere, and her best defence against the empire, he argued, would be a long line of desert, with not roof enough to shelter a single German soldier. It is true the French commanders had first to be educated to this policy of annihilation. One of them, General de Tessé, ordered the citizens of Heidelberg to set fire to their own houses, but promised to look the other way while they were putting out the flames. He was complained of, and received a severe reprimand from Paris. It was in these days that the first attempt at destroying the splendid Heidelberg castle was made; its treasures were robbed, its columns thrown down, its walls undermined, and great masses of straw heaped up in its halls and set on fire. The former garrison watched mournfully in the courtyard while a part of the

The castle of Heidelberg laid in ruins.

great roof fell in. A few days later the whole town of Mannheim went up in flames, and the destroyers passed on to the old, free, imperial city of Spires. Here the inhabitants were told that they might transfer their valuable effects to the cathedral, which alone would be left standing; but this famous monument, too, by chance or, as many believed, by premeditation, was also burned. The vaults containing the bones of Henry IV. and of other emperors were opened and plundered. The turn of Worms came next; the same promise with regard to the cathedral was here given, but was expressly revoked by a command from Paris. "To the inhuman delight of this mad monster" (Louis XIV.), says one of the emperor's officials in Worms, "the city was reduced to ashes within four hours. . . . Like a column of cloud the smoke rose up, wound slowly across the Rhine, and hid the light of day."

The "war of the spade and hoe."

One can imagine the feelings of Elizabeth Charlotte at hearing of the devastation in her old home. In his manifesto to the emperor, one of Louis XIV.'s grievances had been that his sister-in-law was not recognized as heiress to the Palatinate. "I cannot cease mourning and bewailing," writes "Madame" to her aunt, "that I have been, so to speak, the ruin of my fatherland. . . . Every night when I go to sleep I seem to be transported to Heidelberg or to Mannheim, and to see all the devastation; then I leap up in my bed and lie awake for two full hours. I call to mind in what a state it all was in my time, and how it is now; yes, what I myself have become — and I cannot keep from weeping. . . . They take it ill here that I grieve over these matters, but truly I cannot do otherwise." Those who look on the long line of ruined castles along that part of the Neckar and Rhine, can sympathize with "Lise Lotta."

Even from Louis XIV.'s own point of view, the devas-

tation of the Palatinate proved a failure. He had hoped
by this one bold stroke to crush the Germans, so that he
might then turn and get the better of his other enemies;
he became involved, instead, in that long, dreary struggle
along the whole length of the Rhine, which goes by the
name of the "war of the spade and hoe," because of the
insignificance of its actual engagements. The French,
indeed, except in the first and last years of the war, were
generally in the ascendent; they lost the towns of Bonn
and Mainz, but won small battles at Mons, Namur, and
Steenkirke, at Fleurus, Neerwinden, and Landen, not to
mention Staffarda and Nice. These, however, were victories which decided nothing, and their own land, meanwhile, began to groan under its heavy burdens. A French
army, too, which accompanied James II. to Ireland, was
defeated in the great battle on the Boyne; while the French
fleet, in 1692, was fairly swept from the seas at Cape La
Hogue by the English and the Dutch.

In the imperial camp matters were in a wretched condition, largely owing to the fact that the best officers and
soldiers were needed in Hungary. Year after year, too,
quarrels had arisen among the different German states
with regard to subsidies, to the requisite contingents, and,
above all, to the apportionment of winter quarters.

A general sluggishness, much inefficiency, and, occasionally, glaring cases of cowardice and treason, came to
light even among those in the highest places. Max
Emmanuel of Bavaria misappropriated Spanish funds;
Amadeus of Savoy played a most deceitful rôle, and finally
left the Germans and went over to the French with his
whole army. Heddersdorf, the German commmandant of
Heidelberg, pusillanimously allowed the French, in 1693,
to complete the work of destruction they had begun four
years earlier. The castle, to which the citizens had fled

The com-
mandant of
Heidelberg
castle.

from their own flaming houses, might well have been held
until the Margrave of Baden could come to its aid; but
Heddersdorf, in an agony of fear, shut himself up in his
own apartment, and took no measures whatever for defence.
He atoned for his cowardice by the severest punishments
that could possibly be inflicted on a soldier or a man of
honor.   The Teutonic Order, of which he was a member,
had his cross taken off and flung in his face, and then literally kicked him out of a door in token of expulsion.   By
order of the military authorities, he was then bound and
thrown into a cart, and paraded before his own regiment as
a common criminal.   His sword was publicly broken, and
he slunk into banishment, not to be heard of again until
his death, thirty-five years later, in a *nunnery* at Hildesheim!   Such was the fate of the man to whose fault was
attributable the completeness of that ruin, so famous for
many generations, which has only now, within the last
few years, been restored to its original form.

The estab-
lishment of
a ninth
electorate.
A lasting memorial of the emperor's straits and difficulties at this time, was the establishment in the House of
Hanover of a ninth electorate.   How persistently had
Leopold hitherto refused this favor!   He could not endure
the thought of another Protestant vote in the body that
had charge of the future of his children.   But Ernest
Augustus of Hanover was master of a strong state and
had, besides, warm friends at court.   No one of the German princes beneath the rank of elector could begin to
compete with him in the number of soldiers he could put
in the field.   He had brought it about that his own lands,
which only a generation back had been in the hands of
four different lines, should in the future be united; sealing
his final compact with his brother, George William of Celle,
by allowing his son, afterwards George I. of England, to
"contaminate his ancestors" to the extent of marrying

George William's legitimatized daughter, Sophia Dorothea. Of all unfortunate unions this was the worst, save
in the one particular of dynastic advantage. Treated from
the first with cold, cutting contempt, detected in a plan
to run away with the notorious Swede, Königsmark, who
was probably a spy of her husband's enemies, the princess
was relegated to the castle of Ahlden, where she lived
alone, under watch and ward, for thirty years. Ernest
Augustus was ably seconded in his long struggle for the
electoral dignity by his son-in-law, Frederick of Brandenburg; but he owed most to the skilful manner in which
he played his own cards. He knew well how to draw
every advantage from the emperor's critical situation; and
at last fairly stormed Leopold's defences by threatening
to put himself at the head of an independent third party,
to consist, in addition to Hanover, of Sweden, Münster,
and Saxony. The emperor yielded so completely that, in
return for some eight hundred men and a general promise
of support and friendship, he granted Ernest Augustus's
wish in the teeth of a strong opposition, not only from the
electoral college, but from the whole body of minor princes.
The emperor's patent was dated 1692, but not until sixteen years later was Hanover formally recognized as having
a full right to its new vote.

As the years of the dreary war rolled on, matters began
to wear a brighter aspect for the imperialists, and various
considerations rendered Louis XIV. more inclined for
peace. He lost Namur in 1695, and Casale in the same
year; a plot of the Jacobins, under his auspices, to murder William of Holland and bring back the Stuarts on the
English throne, was betrayed and failed; a severe illness
of Carlos II. brought home the fact that the moment might
be at hand when France would need every friend she
could possibly make. Under these circumstances Louis

The Peace
of Ryswick

determined to take a downward step from the pedestal on which he had placed himself, to abandon his Stuart protégés, and acknowledge William as king of England. A congress, accordingly, was called to meet at Ryswick, a village between Delft and The Hague. The sessions were held in an old castle admirably adapted for the purpose in hand. This castle consisted of a great central building, which was given over to the Swedes as mediators, and of two wings, each with its own entrance, so that the Anglo-imperial and French envoys could pass in and out without meeting or greeting each other. Not until after two months had passed in indirect negotiation, and after the momentous question had been settled as to the order in which they should enter the neutral rooms, did they come face to face.

Here at Ryswick, more cleverly even than at Nymwegen, did Louis manage to circumvent the Germans. With mathematical accuracy he solved the problem of pacifying three opponents so as to reap every advantage over the fourth. Once more the Dutch were propitiated by favorable trading privileges; the English were won by the formal recognition of their king. The Spaniards, too, were rendered harmless by the return of Luxemburg and other places in the Netherlands. Louis knew well that no one of these powers would risk its newly acquired gains in order to hinder his designs on the empire. In fact, they all three signed their own agreements without waiting to see what would be done by Austria.

The "Ryswick clause."

The negotiations at Ryswick had been entered into with the assumption that the Peace of Nymwegen should be the basis of accord, that Strassburg and all the annexations made through the Reunion Courts should be returned to the empire, and that religious toleration should prevail in the restored lands. But France, as usual, had woven around her concessions a web of saving clauses. She had promised Strassburg "or an equivalent," and even that arrangement was, after a certain date, declared to have lapsed. She had promised religious toleration "until the making of some other agreement"; but when no other agreement found her approval, she suddenly, with the treaty on the very point of being concluded, made the categorical demand that the Catholic religion should be upheld in whatever districts it had once been introduced. This was the famous "Ryswick clause" that settled the religious future of some two thousand towns and villages. It came like a thunderbolt out of a clear sky, but the lukewarm attitude of England and Holland, and the massing of 140,000 Frenchmen near the German border, made resistance impossible. Some went so far, indeed, as to say that the two Catholic sovereigns were in collusion on this point; yet this would seem improbable in view of the severity of the general terms imposed upon Austria. So humiliating were these terms that the news-leaves of the day took up the old play upon words, and declared that this was no longer a case of *Nimm-weg*, or "take away," but of *Reiss-weg*, or "tear asunder." The Peace of Ryswick was finally signed in 1697, but many believed that, at the time, it would not be permanent. It was pointed out that France had not dismissed her regiments, but, instead, was offering double pay to former mercenaries of the empire. *Latet anguis in herba*, "the snake still lies hidden in the grass," was the warning cry of an earnest patriot.

For the present, indeed, in view of the exhausted state of his finances, it was Louis XIV.'s intention to steer clear of war. He applied himself, instead, to so directing the politics of Europe that, when the long-expected crisis should come, his enemies would be disunited and he him-

The Spanish inheritance.

self master of the situation. He was determined to have, if not the whole, at least a large part, of the rich inheritance of the last Spanish Hapsburg — an inheritance embracing points as far distant as Cuba and the Philippines, and of which one could therefore truly say that on it the sun never set. But the difficulties in the way were very great. With the West Indies, for instance, England and Holland had developed an immense trade; should these islands, as well as the coasts of Spain and Italy, be appropriated by France, or should the exports to these havens, as well as the imports of precious metals and of the usual colonial products, be stopped, the Dutch and English commerce would be ruined. The only solutions of the question for these two maritime powers were the giving of the whole inheritance neither to Austria nor to France, but to some third power, or else a general division. This last alternative was accepted by Louis XIV., who saw that something must be sacrificed in order to prevent England and Holland, not to speak of Spain, from making common cause with Austria. He accordingly, after much negotiation, entered into the so-called first partition treaty with William of Orange.

Austrian and French claims.

In order to find some thread through the intricacies of this Spanish succession question, it is necessary to hold in mind the Hapsburg genealogy back to the time of Philip II., in whose favor Charles V. had abdicated his Spanish, Italian, Netherland, and colonial claims. When Philip II.'s son, Philip III., died, in 1621, he left two children besides Philip IV., who died in 1665: Anna Maria, who became the queen of Louis XIII. of France, and Maria Anna, who married the Emperor Ferdinand III. Louis XIV. sprang from the one union, Leopold I. from the other. Nor was this the only tie that bound the French and Austrian monarchs to the Spanish house, for

Louis XIV. had married the one daughter, Leopold the other, of Philip IV. It might be supposed that as both Louis XIV.'s mother and his wife were older than their respective sisters, their claim should have had the preference upon the failure of the male line; but to equalize this there came in formal renunciations of the throne, signed at the time of the French marriages, although Louis XIV. maintained that the dowry for which his wife had sold her birthright had never been paid. Philip IV., for his part, had always intended that his younger daughter should eventually inherit his crown; he even left a provision in his will that on her decease her husband should be her heir.

As now, with the waning century, Carlos II. drew near to his end, the difficulty of settling the matter became more and more apparent. The Spanish people had welcomed the candidacy of the Bavarian elector, Max Emmanuel, who had married Leopold's daughter; when, in 1694, a son, Joseph Ferdinand, was born to this pair, he, in turn, became the hope, not only of Spain, but also of England and Holland. Here was a prince, neither Hapsburg nor Bourbon, on whom, as it seemed, all could unite. It was with reference to him that the first partition treaty was made; he was to have Spain, the Netherlands, and the colonies, while France was to take Naples and Sicily, leaving for the emperor only Milan. But Louis XIV. and William of Orange had reckoned without their host. The dying king, Carlos, furious at having this disposal made of his land, mustered strength enough to appear in a council of state and to proclaim Joseph Ferdinand heir, not of a part, but of the whole, of his domains. A fleet was ordered to Amsterdam to escort the seven-year-old boy to his new kingdom. But before either France or Austria could decide, under these changed circumstances,

The partition treaties.

what course to pursue, the young prince sickened and died. It was widely believed, by his father among others, that he had fallen a victim to one of the famous *poudres de succession*, which Louis XIV. was supposed to have always on hand; but these rumors of poisoning all rest on too frail a basis. At any rate, his death was of great advantage to Louis; by the second partition treaty, which was drawn up at his instigation, in March, 1700, and with regard to which Austria was not consulted, France was to have not only, as before, Naples and Sicily, but also Sardinia and the duchy of Milan.

The death-bed of Carlos II.

Agents had meanwhile been busy at Madrid, trying to accustom the mind of the king to the idea of deeding the whole of his possessions to a French prince. The Austrian party, on the other hand, of which the head was the Spanish queen, Leopold's sister-in-law, sought to obtain a similar declaration in favor of Archduke Charles, the emperor's younger son. The death-bed of the poor monarch was made the scene of bitter strife and contention. The French party, headed by the Archbishop of Toledo and by Jesuit confessors, finally managed to remove the queen and her allies from the room, and half persuaded, half compelled Carlos, who died almost immediately after, to sign a will in favor of Philip of Anjou, grandson of Louis XIV.

It remained to be seen what attitude would be assumed by the French king. The latest partition treaty, which left to Austria half of the inheritance, had been his own work; would he adhere to it, or would he be dazzled by the prospect of the whole? In his own mind there was neither doubt nor hesitation: the partition treaty had been scarcely more than a ruse; he had been fully initiated into the plans of his partisans in Madrid, and was more than delighted by the latest turn of affairs. He declared that the Pyrenees had ceased to exist, and in the palace of

Versailles, in the presence of his whole court, proclaimed his grandson king of Spain. "Only remember," he said, in his address of congratulation, "that you are a prince of France." The worst fears of England and Holland, not to speak of Austria, were thus realized. Louis himself was confident that, with Spain a friend instead of an enemy, he could bid defiance to all Europe.

In the beginning, indeed, the maritime powers showed a dangerous apathy, out of which the Dutch were the first to be shaken by an attack of the French on the Belgian forts, for which Holland, by right of treaty, had provided the garrisons. Even then it cost William of Orange months of time and infinite pains to bring the English Parliament to a proper frame of mind. "The blindness of the people here is incredible," he wrote to Heinsius, the grand pensionary of Holland. His position was not easy, obliged as he was to humor the Tories in order to secure one of the chief aims of his life, the succession of the Protestant house of Hanover to the English throne. But with great skill he managed his affair, often concealing his own ardent wishes under a cloak of assumed coolness. In June, 1701, that final succession act was passed which made the Electress Sophia heiress to the throne of England; and, soon afterward, Parliament signed an alliance with the emperor "for the maintenance of the freedom of Europe, for the welfare and peace of England, and with the end in view of stemming the encroachments of France." Leopold was promised a " just and reasonable satisfaction concerning his pretensions to the Spanish succession." He was to have the Netherlands and the Italian possessions, while England and Holland were to keep whatever they should conquer in the colonies.

Thus, in September, 1701, was formed what is known as the "Grand Alliance." William of Orange, its chief

The "Grand Alliance."

promoter, died before it was half a year old, but it proved the instrument that was to overthrow the French Colossus and reëstablish the equilibrium of Europe. Twelve years, indeed, of furious fighting were first to pass; and, in the end, one of the very partition arrangements that had been discussed in the beginning was to be peacefully adopted.

The Grand Alliance was joined, as a matter of course, by Hanover and also by Prussia, whose newly created king went far beyond his stipulated agreements with the emperor, being eager for the latter's good will in the matter of the Orange inheritance, — lands which he claimed as heir to his mother, the Great Elector's first wife. One by one the other German powers came in, though, with characteristic tardiness, the Diet of Ratisbon did not declare war until the fighting had been fairly under way for nearly a year.

Renegade states.
One striking exception was the elector of Bavaria, who, after wavering long and weighing well the advantages on both sides, went over to the French. This ambitious prince, bereft of his hopes of sovereign influence by the death of his son, was now deluded by Louis XIV. in every way. He was to have the Palatinate if he could conquer it, or perhaps the Netherlands; a royal and, if possible, the imperial crown. Lured by such prospects Max Emmanuel, assisted by his brother, the Archbishop of Cologne, made eager preparations to crush the House of Hapsburg. Another renegade, the Duke of Brunswick-Wolfenbüttel, who with French gold had raised an army of twelve thousand men, was surprised and fallen upon by his cousins of Celle and Hanover, who appropriated his mercenaries and made them fight on their own side.

Even after signing the alliance, and after the Austrian armies had been long in the field, England was slow about opening hostilities, hoping still to accomplish something by further negotiations. But when, on the death of James II., Louis XIV. ostentatiously treated James's son with royal honors and addressed him as James III., all the reluctance of the English people to the war suddenly melted away. In the public squares of London a herald, to the sound of trumpets, formally summoned the king of France to mortal combat on the ground of "presuming to support the so-called Prince of Wales as king of England." Parliament granted forty thousand marines and an equal number of land soldiers. The chief command was intrusted to Churchill, Duke of Marlborough, who, as the "handsomest man in the world," was all-powerful at court; while his wife, too, formerly plain Sarah Jennings, had gained a great influence over Queen Anne. Not that a better choice could at that time have been made; no one had worked harder than Marlborough in bringing about the Grand Alliance, no one possessed a greater share of coolness, of daring, of all the qualities, in fact, that go to make up a perfect field commander.

The Duke of Marlborough placed in command.

Meanwhile, the Austrians had been most fortunate in finding a man of the same stamp, and one who proved able, eventually, to send new blood coursing through the flabby veins of the bodies politic and military. When the war was first decided upon, early in 1701, there was no doubt in any one's mind but that Prince Eugene of Savoy, the victor of Zenta, must be despatched to the scene of the first fighting. He, too, had spoken decisive words in favor of the war; and his initial march from the Tyrol to Italy showed the French that they had to deal with a genius of the very first order. One of Louis XIV.'s first cares had been to seize Milan, Mantua, and other places in Lombardy; and his general, Catinat, who felt assured of the route that Eugene intended to take, had posted his whole army near Monte Baldo, between the Lago di Garda and

Prince Eugene or Savoy in Italy.

the right bank of the Adige. The Austrian general, in order to keep up the illusion, sent workmen to level the main road, and then, swiftly and secretly, led his army from Roveredo over paths that were considered so impassable that not even a picket had been stationed to guard them. He reached the Lombard plains without having to fire a shot, while Catinat, not recognizing his own numerical superiority, remained on the defensive without daring to risk an engagement. The first skirmish came at Carpi, where the French, although their losses amounted to only 350 men, became so disheartened that Catinat decided to venture upon no more actions, and wrote to Louis XIV., "We are compelled, sire, to await what steps the enemy shall decide to take." This, with an army of forty thousand, as opposed to twenty-seven thousand of the Austrians! The latter were able, in sight of the French, to cross the river Mincio without molestation. Catinat was then deprived of his command and replaced by Marshal Villeroi.

To follow in detail Eugene's campaigns in Italy would lead us too far. Villeroy was defeated at Chiari and became an imitator of Catinat's timid policy; he was captured at Cremona, and the French at home could only rejoice that they were well rid of him. He was succeeded by Vendôme, "a wild, vicious genius in his personal habits, but also a genius in commanding; full of force, fire, and invention, and the very god of the French army." [1] He tried a bold attack on Eugene at Luzzara, but the latter held the field, although Vendôme's forces outnumbered his own as three to one.

But the Austrian army was greatly weakened, and reenforcements were slow in coming. Eugene complained bitterly that in four months he had received but one answer to his numerous despairing messages. Conclud-

[1] Erdmannsdörfer, II. 190.

ing that the most pressing need was a reorganization of the home war department, he gave his command to Guido Starhemberg, and hastened to Vienna, where, after months of labor, he revolutionized the military and financial management, himself becoming president of the new war council. Starhemberg was for a while in great straits, and considered himself deserted, but Vendôme gave him breathing space by turning off toward the Tyrol, for the purpose of effecting a union with Max Emmanuel of Bavaria.

Meanwhile, on the other scenes of war, events had turned out more in accordance with the usual course of Austrian and imperial campaigns. The chief command on the Rhine had been intrusted to the Margrave of Baden, once a capable commander and one who had done good service against the Turks, but now grown old and timid, and a very drag on the wheels of Eugene's policy. During two years, the siege and capture of Landau, which was eventually retaken, was almost his only successful achievement. The same inactivity prevailed in the Netherlands, where Marlborough was hampered and constantly irritated by the senilities of the Dutch war council. In August, 1702, a Dutch-English fleet set out to take Cadiz, but contented itself with the capture of a few Spanish prizes. An army of mixed Prussian, imperial, and Palatine troops did, in course of time, succeed in driving the Archbishop of Cologne from all his domains. The greatest activity in these first years of the war was shown by the elector of Bavaria. Early in 1703 he marched on Ratisbon and rendered the members of the Diet virtually prisoners, refusing them pass and safe-conduct. Then he turned against the Tyrol, took Kufstein, and made a pompous triumphal entry into Innsbruck, his head already full of plans for rounding off Bavaria with this splendid mountain province. He was preparing to cross the Brenner and join Ven-

Bavarian victories

dôme, in Italy, when a ferocious uprising of the Tyrolese peasants spoiled his plan of campaign. Driven back to Munich, he was allowed, by the lethargic Margrave of Baden, to unite with the French marshal, Villars, with whose aid he defeated the Austrian general, Styrum, between Schwenningen and Höchstädt. Villars spoke in his report of this modest engagement as "the grandest victory of which it is possible to conceive," but soon quarrelled with Max Emmanuel and was replaced by Marshal Marsin. The latter assisted in the capture of Augsburg, which was forced to pay a high contribution, to throw down its walls and towers, and to furnish winter quarters. Maximilian was greeted on his entry as "Augustus, and soon to be Cæsar"; while a medal struck in these days designated him already as "King of Bohemia." The days of the Hapsburg rule seemed numbered; early in 1704 Passau was taken, and threatening demonstrations were made before Linz.

The battle of Blenheim.

But a frightful Nemesis was pursuing the renegade Bavarian. The cause of the allies had been strengthened, in 1703, by the accession of Savoy, and also of Portugal. The young Archduke Charles, Leopold's second son, was despatched to Lisbon, where he took the title of King Charles III.. and, with Portuguese, English, and Dutch aid, prepared to march to Madrid and make good his claim to the Spanish throne. And in the meantime the Margrave of Baden had shown himself so supremely incapable in the operations before Linz, that even the old emperor Leopold was brought to ask him to resign the chief command, and appointed Eugene in his place. Last, but not least, Marlborough determined to quit the fields where he was reaping so little glory, and obtained permission to hasten to the German seat of war; he was hampered, indeed, by having to show consideration for the Margrave of Baden, who had accepted a lower command and who was to lead Marlborough's own army on alternate days. His tiresome objections to war *à la Hussara* drove both the English general and Prince Eugene, who now came up, fairly to desperation, and both were glad enough to give him twenty thousand men, and wish him Godspeed when he marched off to besiege Ingolstadt.

The union of Eugene and Marlborough brought about some of the most brilliant military achievements that are recorded in all history. Here, in the vicinity of the Bavarian frontier, they won together the battle of Blenheim, — Höchstädt, the Germans called it, — the greatest since the war began, and one in which clever reckoning and well-considered tactics played a more important part than in any battle since classic times. It was the beginning of a form of warfare that was brought to perfection by Moltke in our own day.

In the midst of the battle Marlborough performed the remarkable manœuvre of re-forming his troops under fire, and changing the brunt of attack from the village of Blenheim, about which the French infantry was massed, to a point farther to the west, where he suddenly perceived that their cavalry was weak. The operation succeeded completely, the cavalry was put to flight, the infantry surrounded and forced to surrender. Marshal Tallard was taken captive, together with the cash-box, containing the pay for his troops; twenty-eight thousand men were killed, wounded, or taken prisoner; included in the booty were fifty-four hundred provision wagons and thirty-four coaches filled with French courtesans.

Among the results of Höchstädt were the occupation of the whole of Bavaria, the flight of Max Emmanuel, the arrest of his young sons, — who were kept under Austrian tutelage for the next ten years, — and, finally, the raising

Occupation of Bavaria.

of Marlborough to the rank of a prince of the empire, with the little Bavarian principality of Mindelheim. A rebellion against the Austrian rule, which took place somewhat later, was successfully put down. In the presence of the emperor, at Vienna, Bavaria's old charters were torn through the middle and thrown on the ground, the elector and his brother were put to the ban, while the arch-chancellor of the empire publicly proclaimed that Max Emmanuel's "miserable body" was at the mercy of every one to hurt or to harm with impunity.

The battle of Blenheim was the only great engagement that took place on German soil during the whole of the succession war. In the period that followed, the Margrave of Baden was left to defend the Rhine, while Eugene resumed his command in Italy, and Marlborough, with some unwillingness, returned to Belgium. Archduke Charles, or, as he now called himself, King Charles III., succeeded in entering Madrid; but his position was precarious, and could only be maintained with the help of his army.

Turin and Ramillies.

Eugene, at first, was unfortunate in Italy, although supported by his cousin, the Duke of Savoy. He lost the field of Cassano, and was so discouraged that he thought of resigning his command. But, in 1706, supplied with funds and reënforcements, he carried out a series of most brilliant movements against Duke Philip of Orleans,—son of "Lise Lotta,"—and Marshal Marsin, neither of whom possessed the *tête de fer* which Vendôme had declared to be absolutely needed in Italy. The battle of Turin, fought in September, 1706, was another of the giant encounters of this war. For a time the chances of the day swayed backward and forward; but at last Marsin was fatally wounded, and the Duke of Orleans so seriously injured that he had to leave the field. Within two hours the

French were in wild flight, and before evening Eugene and Victor Amadeus held a triumphal entry into the town of Turin. This battle determined the fate of northern Italy, and within six months the enemy had agreed to quit the land.

No less brilliant had been the fortunes of Marlborough in Belgium, where the battle of Ramillies, fought against Marshal Villeroi and Max Emmanuel, saved the Netherlands for Austria, and took away from the Bavarian his last hope of conquering a compensation for his lost electorate. Less successful was an expedition, undertaken in the interests of the English and at Marlborough's earnest wish, against the Mediterranean port of Toulon. In spite of the assistance of Eugene the attempt failed, and the allies retired to Italy with a loss of ten thousand men.

Meanwhile the prospects were anything but bright for the emperor, Joseph I., who had succeeded his father, Joseph I. Leopold, in 1705, and who was personally one of the best and strongest of the Hapsburgs. Just as he lacked the protruding lip of his ancestors, so was his character free from the usual mixture of indecision and bigotry. In spite of the victories on distant fields, Joseph's position was highly precarious. Almost simultaneously with the Spanish Succession War there had broken out a fierce rebellion in Hungary; and, in the North, the great struggle had begun of Denmark, Russia, and Poland against Sweden. From the year 1703 on, Rakoczy had been the soul of the Hungarian revolt, and had been hand in glove with Louis XIV., who paid him enormous subsidies. A plan was on foot for giving the crown of St. Stephen to Max Emmanuel of Bavaria.

The northern war had had the effect of withdrawing Augustus the Strong, the Saxon elector and Polish king, from the cause of the emperor. The fiery Charles XII. of

Charles
XII. of
Sweden in
Silesia.

Sweden had proved a match for all his enemies,—even, as yet, for Peter the Great. In 1702 he had conquered Warsaw, and two years later had deposed Augustus the Strong and put Stanislaus Lescinsky on the Polish throne. In 1706, he determined to invade Saxony and utterly humiliate his old rival. So successfully did he carry out his plan that in the same year Augustus was forced to sign the Peace of Alt-Ranstädt; by which he abdicated his Polish claims, promised never to interfere with the Protestantism of his Saxon subjects, and agreed to give winter quarters to the Swedes, who then occupied his cities of Wittenberg and Leipzig. Here was a case where the emperor, had not his every nerve been strained to carry on the French war, was bound to intervene. A Swedish army in winter quarters on German ground, and a king who came forward with as lordly demands as though he had been Gustavus Adolphus in person! In order to reach Saxony, Charles XII. had passed through Silesia without so much as asking leave. He found there that Austria had been oppressing her Protestant subjects, and he now insisted on a number of reforms. For one whole year he remained in Saxony, keeping Joseph on tenter-hooks, lest he, Charles, should hearken to the alluring voice of Louis XIV., whose marshal, Villars, sought Charles out and is said to have proposed a common march on Vienna. But the Duke of Marlborough proved of use at this juncture, not only as a general, but also as a diplomat. He visited Charles XII. at Alt-Ranstädt, and flattered him by the prospect of having Sweden chosen as intermediary in the peace negotiations that were expected shortly to take place. On his bond, indeed, Charles XII. insisted; and the emperor was forced, in the face of an ultimatum, to sign a convention by which he conceded to the Silesian Protestants a number of religious reforms, which, strangely enough, proved permanent, — more so than the glory of the Swedish king, who, soon afterward, in the battle of Pultava (1709), received a severe punishment at the hands of Peter the Great.

Joseph I. must indeed have possessed considerable bravery not to despair utterly among the dangers and difficulties that beset him at every conceivable point. Louis of Baden, partly through his own failure to come to any rational agreement with Marlborough, had been left, in 1706, with insufficient forces on the Upper Rhine. He had been driven out of Alsace and across the river; and in the following year, while the stubborn old general lay dying at Rastadt, the whole Swabian circle was ravaged by the French. In the meantime an entirely new and unexpected enemy had arisen in Italy. Once more the world saw the spectacle of a Pope and an emperor in arms against each other; once more the ban was hurled against the godless invaders of church lands, while, in the Square of St. Peter's, there floated a banner with the device, *Domine defende causam tuam*. A coolness had existed between Joseph and Clement, owing to the latter's outspoken French sympathies and to the emperor's claim of the right to fill one vacant place in each German cathedral chapter. But when, in 1707, Joseph conceived the idea of installing Charles III. on the throne of Naples, and quartered troops in the old imperial fiefs of Parma, Piacenza, Ferrara, and Commachio, matters came to a climax. Clement raised an army and begged for assistance from France; while his adversary restored the fortifications of Commachio, and is said to have placed an inscription over one of the gates, "To Joseph the emperor, who seeks to regain the ancient rights over Italy." At Joseph's request, the king of Prussia, mindful of the Pope's refusal to recognize him, sent reënforcements, at the same time ordering his general to secure some of the larger cannon,

A new quarrel between Pope and emperor.

— with the papal arms if possible, — for the new *Zeughaus* in Berlin.   There resulted the occupation of more papal territory; a threat of sending General Daun, at the head of his troops, against Rome itself; and, finally, an ultimatum which brought Clement to his knees one hour before midnight on the day on which the term expired. The Pope agreed to disband his army, and to recognize Charles III. as king of Naples.

Lille and
Oudenarde.

As for Eugene and Marlborough, the best field for their united efforts now seemed to lie in Belgium.   It is true they had formed a different plan of campaign with the elector of Hanover, who had taken the Margrave of Baden's place on the Rhine; and so disgusted was the future king of England with their change of mind, that he threw down his command.   But the two great generals, as usual, were in the right; the French had concentrated all their forces in Flanders, and were able, in 1708, to take the towns of Bruges and Ghent.   But the allies in the same year gained the victory of Oudenarde, — a victory so signal that Marlborough for a time could think of marching direct upon Paris.   Other counsels prevailed, indeed, and it was determined instead to lay siege to Lille, which, since its conquest by Louis XIV., in 1668, had been turned into the strongest fortress in northern France.   In vain Vendôme and the Duke of Burgundy sought to bring help to the heroic Marshal Boufflers, who defended the town to the last moment, and who, even after the outer works were lost, retired to the citadel.   From here, too, he was at last driven; while, at the same time, Max Emmanuel of Bavaria, who had made a dash for Brussels, was forced back, and Belgium thus cleansed of the French.   Vendome fell into disgrace, and the new *armée de Flandres* was given to Villars; while so desperate was the general situation — the prospect of a famine in the following summer having also to be faced — that Louis XIV. sued for peace, and a conference of all the powers concerned was called together at the Hague. Here the proposals, not unnaturally, were humiliating enough for France: England demanded the recognition of the Hanoverian dynasty, and the razing of the fortress of Dunkirk; Holland, the right to garrison a belt of fortresses in Belgium; Austria, the whole of the Spanish inheritance; the empire was to recover its old boundaries, including not only Alsace with Strassburg, but also Metz, Toul, and Verdun.

Almost all of these conditions Louis XIV. was willing Malplaquet. to accept; he agreed to renounce the Spanish inheritance and even to give up Strassburg, but when, in the pride of victory, the allies insisted that, in case Philip of Anjou and the people of Spain should offer opposition, he should assist in driving out his own grandson, his cup of wrath flowed over. Neither now, nor in the following year, in the conferences at Gertruydenberg, would he treat on such a basis. "The French would be no longer French," wrote Madame de Maintenon, "if they accepted an insult like this;" while "Lise Lotta" declared that the allies had made "barbaric propositions." The conference was broken up and the war renewed.

The bloodiest of all the battles of this long struggle, and the one which, in point of the numbers participating, outranks any action of the eighteenth century, still remained to be fought. Louis XIV. roused himself to his last and most desperate effort, while the French people stood by him to a man, and many sold the silver from their table to furnish him with funds. At Malplaquet, fought in September, 1709, ninety thousand Frenchmen, under Villars, stood over against one hundred thousand of the allies, commanded by Eugene and Marlborough. With the latter were Frederick William, the crown prince of Prussia,

Schwerin the future victor of Mollwitz, and Maurice, the later *Maréchal de Saxe*.

The battle raged from early morning to late evening, with the final result that the allies maintained the field, but lost twice as many in dead and wounded as their conquered opponents. The French were not so wholly to blame for ascribing the victory to themselves: it was in these days that in all the streets of Paris one could hear the mocking song, "Marlborough s'en va-t'en guerre!" At all events, Malplaquet practically finished the war. France was on the verge of bankruptcy, and, although numerous small engagements still took place, they were only the running commentary, as it were, to the long negotiations for peace.

Death of
Joseph.

That these negotiations lasted as long as they did was largely the fault of Marlborough. The Whig party lived by war, and to it the great general was not above catering. But now a new event occurred, which changed the aspect of affairs and acted like an explosive in sundering the Austrian and English interests. In the tide of Louis XIV.'s fortunes, and not through any victories of his own, there came a wonderful rise.

In April, 1711, the young Emperor Joseph fell sick with the small-pox and died. The next of kin, and the one to whom the throne of the empire would be likely to fall, was none other than that Charles III. who was struggling so hard for the crowns of Spain and Italy. But could England and Holland now, any more than in the beginning, submit to the union of all these territories in one hand? The wheel had swung round to where it had stood eleven years before. In London, at the Hague, and in Berlin, there was but one thought, that a new Charles V. could never be tolerated; far better that France should enjoy a part of the Spanish inheritance.

Altogether, in England, a strong contrary wind was blowing. For the first time in many years the Tory party gained the ascendency. Marlborough soon found that his influence was gone; his enemies even dared to accuse him of taking a percentage from the Jews who supplied bread for his army, and of appropriating funds that were intended for the foreign troops. Queen Anne dismissed the Duchess of Marlborough from her presence, while, in the country at large, all the landowners clamored for peace at any price. Thus was England hurried into one of the most disgraceful acts in her history. Without a word to the allies, at whose side she had fought for so many years, she entered into private negotiations with France, and assured Spain to Philip of Anjou. Austria was left completely in the lurch; her minister, Count Gallas, was snubbed and boycotted in London, ostensibly on personal grounds. No other than Prince Eugene, whom the English had hitherto fairly idolized, was sent to take his place. He arrived only to learn that Marlborough had been driven from all his offices, and his command in the Netherlands given to the Duke of Ormond. After a stay of two months, Eugene was obliged to confess that for once he had lost a campaign. The command to the English army, to desist from fighting, reached it on the eve of an expected engagement on the river Scheldt, which the allies felt sure of winning. England's own soldiers all but mutinied when told to withdraw, and refused the usual cheer to their officers as they were marched off to Dunkirk. A number deserted on the way. Although fifty thousand Germans, who had been in the English pay, scorned the new orders and joined Eugene, the general discouragement was so great that Villars easily gained a succession of small victories.

The final arrangement between England, Holland, and

England deserts her allies.

France was completed at Utrecht, in 1713. Portugal,
Savoy, and Prussia joined in signing the treaty of peace.
Philip of Anjou was acknowledged as king of Spain, but
was forced to renounce any rights of eventual succession
to the French throne; while the younger Bourbons signed
a similar agreement with regard to Spain. England herself secured the invaluable Mediterranean stations of Port
Mahon and Gibraltar; and in the New World — at the cost
of France — the island of Newfoundland and Nova Scotia,
as well as Hudson's Bay Territory. Max Emmanuel of
Bavaria and his brother were reinstated in all their rights
and possessions, even Marlborough's little principality of
Mindelheim being suppressed without equivalent. On
the part of Max Emmanuel a struggle was made, in addition, for the Spanish Netherlands; but this neither England
nor Holland would allow. It was much more agreeable
to them that the Bavarian elector should have Sardinia,
which they were willing to slice off from the share they
had intended to allot to Austria. To Victor Amadeus
was given Sicily; to Portugal lands on the Amazon River;
and to Prussia, part of Guelders, with the recognition of
her right to Neuchâtel, which had belonged to the Orange
inheritance.

Charles VI., as the new emperor called himself, had
sent an envoy to Utrecht, but received such treatment at
the hands of Louis XIV. that he refused to sign the peace.
The French king sent demands, in the form of an ultimatum, which, as Charles said himself, were such as should
only have been presented to a subjugated enemy. He was
not to be acknowledged as emperor until he should have
reinstated the two Wittelsbachs; and a whole list of charges
and damages on their account was to be paid by him. He
was to give a pledge never to attempt to acquire more land
in Italy than the congress at Utrecht should have assigned.

In spite of his complete isolation and of the general
hopelessness of his cause, Charles determined to continue
the war. He would rather, he said to Lord Peterborough,
— whom in his excitement he seized by the coat-button, —
he would rather risk and lose all, than have laws dictated
to him in this fashion. The Diet of Ratisbon also was in
favor of resistance, and thanked the emperor for refusing
such "despicable and unworthy" proposals of peace, the
acceptance of which would have led to inevitable slavery.

In the campaign that followed, the French, as may be
imagined, were uniformly successful. For the fourth time in
this war, Landau underwent a siege and was captured, and
a like fate befell Freiburg. But Louis XIV., whose life
and strength were now ebbing away, was heartily anxious
for peace, and was willing, eventually, to make further
concessions than at Utrecht. It was finally agreed that
the two commanders-in-chief, Eugene and Villars, should
come together at Rastadt and discuss the question of preliminaries. The course of these negotiations was by no
means smooth. For three months the two generals, who
held their meetings in the splendid castle built by the
Margrave of Baden, wrangled as to terms. Eugene far
outmatched his opponent in the field of diplomacy, and at
last, by laying down an ultimatum and ostentatiously preparing for further hostilities, gained for Austria more
than she could have hoped. Her chief gains were the
Netherlands and, practically, all that Spain had possessed
in Italy, — including Sardinia, which was taken away from
Max Emmanuel. Three years later Austria exchanged
this latter island with the House of Savoy for Sicily.

It remained for the empire, as a whole, to make its
peace with France. For this purpose plenipotentiaries met
at Baden, and, with characteristic slowness, spent three
whole months in drawing up a document which, when it

The treaties
of Rastadt
and Baden.

was finished, differed scarcely in a single word from the Peace of Rastadt. Altogether, the part played by the empire had been one of sacrifice and self-effacement. Two questions that were vital to her were scarcely even touched upon at Baden: the rectification of the western boundary, and the repeal of the "Ryswick clause." Germany came forth from the war exactly as she had gone into it, except that she was poorer in men and money.

As for France, though defeated in every great battle, she stood there strong and aggressive as ever, having placed a Bourbon on the throne of Spain and compelled the emperor to reinstate, without punishment, his rebel vassals. Her various attempts, however, to cast a yoke upon Germany had proved a failure, and had to be postponed for nearly a century.

CHAPTER III

THE FATHER OF FREDERICK THE GREAT

LITERATURE: In addition to the general works mentioned under Volume II., Chapter I., see the memoirs of the Margravine of Baireuth, the admirable biography by Förster, *Friedrich Wilhelm I.*, and also Koser, *Friedrich der Grosse als Kronprinz.*

WHILE the empire was being defrauded at Utrecht, Rastadt, and Baden of the just fruits of its long war with Louis XIV., the state on which the hope of the future rested was entering into a new and distinct phase of its history. The process of training had begun that one day was to justify Prussia's mission as head of a regenerated Germany. Her army was to grow to be the first in Europe; her financial administration the most economical and the least corrupt; her kings were to become the most absolute, but at the same time to interest themselves most deeply in the affairs of the lowest of their subjects.

Frederick William I., who came to the throne on the death of his father in 1713, is a man whose character has been grossly misconceived by posterity. What happened on three or four famous and widely exploited occasions, when an irritable man completely lost his temper, has been made to outweigh the record of a life devoted to the interests of his people, of a phenomenal energy that never flagged from the day of this king's accession to the day of his death, of a talent for administration such as few other crowned heads have ever possessed, of a regard for rectitude and for morality that transformed the whole tone of his surroundings. For each of those violent outbursts,

The virtues of Frederick William I.

— which were seldom completely unjustified, — for each time that his cane fell on the backs of his servants or of his very provoking children, one might chronicle a hundred wise measures for the comfort and welfare of his people.

The Margravine of Baireuth.

There is a very evident reason for the misconception of this monarch's true worth, for to no other ruler has the lot fallen of having nourished in his own bosom so witty so spiteful and so unconscientious a biographer. From behind the closed doors of his own palace, from one who was with him day by day, from a daughter who professes to have loved and honored him, we have one of the most malicious pictures that was ever drawn of any man. The only excuse is that the Margravine of Baireuth could never have intended her memoirs to be published, if indeed she ever meant them to be taken seriously at all. Droysen has proved that the letters reproduced at length are not genuine, while the memoirs themselves teem with self-contradictions. Was the whole thing intended as a mere literary exercise? Wilhelmine herself speaks of a talent for pitiless satirizing very much in vogue in her century; she tells how she once read the comic novels of a certain Scarron, and with the aid of her brother applied the satires to persons at court, not sparing even the king. "I dare not even say what a rôle he played," she writes; "we showed them to the queen, who was vastly amused." Again she relates how frightened she was at losing some letters that spoke of the king in "pretty strong language," how deeply she regrets her disrespectfulness and her evil tongue; and she ends up with what gives us the keynote to the whole mystery: "I did it," she says, "more *to show my cleverness and my good ideas* than because I had a bad heart."

The Frederick William of Wilhelmine's pages is a being who carouses until four o'clock in the morning; who starves his children, and even expectorates into their food to make it the more unpleasant; who tries to strangle his son with the curtain rope, and knocks his daughter senseless by striking her "three tremendous blows in the face." Yet even if all this were true, it seems almost pardonable in view of the pictures the margravine unconsciously draws of herself and of the queen her mother. At the age of ten Wilhelmine knows all the worst court scandal, and is told by the queen to be rude to "three-quarters of Berlin." The two women, later, manage to write — in lemon juice which can only be read when held to the fire — nearly fifteen hundred letters to the young crown prince; in a moment of danger they purloin the casket in which these are contained, forge a whole series of new letters, and counterfeit the seal. Their own correspondence is carried on by notes concealed in cheeses. Both constantly simulate illness, and Wilhelmine holds balls of hot lead under the coverlet to make it appear she has a fever. Spies and villains, plots and intrigues, swoons and violence, hidings behind screens and in cupboards, meet us at every turn.

Wilhelmine's picture of her father and of herself.

The real Frederick William was a rugged genius with strongly marked peculiarities and with a determination to carry absolutism to its logical conclusion. He intended, he once declared, to establish Prussian sovereignty on a "rock of bronze"; and he considered himself accountable for his actions to God alone. "I have no money," was his usual answer to towns that petitioned for unnecessary improvements; and he once wrote to an official, "Salvation belongs to the Lord, and everything else is my affair." Strangely enough, he was unaware that his temper was violent. "God knows I am entirely too tranquil," he once declared; "if I were more choleric, I think things would go better." In addition to his children and his servants, his cane fell upon negligent soldiers and upon those of his subjects whom he discovered in idleness or wrong-doing.

The real Frederick William I.

More serious punishments he inflicted, too, which were out of proportion to the nature of the offence. He was economical to a degree that was often branded as penury, knew how to drive a hard bargain, and often insisted on his bond when common humanity would seem to have called for leniency. His manners were rough, his vein of humor coarse, his sense of the beautiful decidedly limited. Yet often we find an underlying principle of good in his acts of harshness and severity; far better err on the wrong side than fall into the spendthrift laxness of a Charles VI. or an Augustus the Strong. Frederick William's personality is constantly cropping out through the driest of his state papers; his marginal notes to the daily reports of his ministers mount up into the thousands and are a running commentary on his character. They show an industry, an attention to detail that is fairly phenomenal.

Retrench-
ments of
Frederick
William I.

Quidquid vult vehementer vult, writes a Saxon envoy of Frederick William, and this quality of impetuosity he showed from the very first moment of his accession. His fixed idea — which had come to him, doubtless, in the camp at Malplaquet where he had sharply resented the imputation that without foreign subsidies his father could not maintain a respectable army — was the necessity of making Prussia into a strong military power. For this, money was required; and the first step in the way of procuring it was economy. The old king had not been dead for half an hour when the young heir, whose pink and white complexion and friendly blue eyes had given no reason to expect such a sternness of character, called for the household accounts and drew a line through the whole list of court lackeys and pages. They appeared for the last time at the gorgeous funeral which was the final concession of a good son to the weakness of his father; they formed part in a rich tableau that represented the end of a whole era in Prussian history.

They then vanished into thin air, as did Frederick William's own great French wig and long mourning garments. The court poet, the upper master of heraldry, the twenty-five trumpeters, went the same way; while the jewels that had ornamented the late king's pall, and the countless trinkets and gewgaws that he had collected, were sold to pay his outstanding debts and to support new regiments. The household was reorganized on the simplest possible basis: three pages at ten thalers a month on which they had to board themselves; thirty riding horses instead of one thousand. The table was to be simple but good; and over against Wilhelmine's calumnies in this regard, we must place the explicit orders, preserved in the archives, that the queen and her children were to have private dishes "according to their gusto." We know of the crown prince, on good authority, that he loved *les petits plats et les hauts goûts*. Queen Sophie Dorothea was given a yearly allowance of eighty thousand thalers for living expenses and for the clothing of herself and ten children; while from the former privy purse, which was turned over to the general state-fund, the king reserved for himself but fifty-two thousand thalers. This beginning of a reform with his own person was characteristic of him throughout his reign; he held his officials to exact punctuality under penalty of heavy fines, but he himself was busy hearing reports at five o'clock in the morning. The excise duties were very onerous; but goods purchased for the royal household were not exempted, and the king's wagons were searched at the gates like those of any commoner. By medical advice, it was customary to bleed the whole army at least once a year; when the time came round, Frederick William sat out on his porch within view of his soldiers and was the first to bare his arm.

The reforms begun in the royal household **were carried**

Centraliza-
tion of the
administra-
tion.

out through the whole length and breadth of the land,
although the task was Herculean because of the many
forces that were pulling in different directions.   The more
recently acquired provinces had never been brought into a
firm relationship with the Mark Brandenburg: under the
lax rule of Frederick I., Cleves, Magdeburg, Halberstadt,
Prussian Pomerania, and East Prussia had retained their
old faulty local administration, and the proud, narrow-
minded nobility still exercised considerable influence.
The cities enjoyed a large measure of autonomy, the chief
magisterial positions remaining, by tacit consent, in the
hands of a few influential families.   The reforms of the
great elector, indeed, had not been entirely without
result: the people knew the value and need of a standing
army, and had come to see that certain public burdens
must of necessity be borne.   But the control had been
insufficient; the competency of the numerous bureaus, exchequers, and governing boards had not been clearly fixed ·
there was no economy of forces, no discipline, no routine.
What was most needed was a caste or class of trained
officials, and to procure this, the king's service had to be
made more honorable and more desirable, but at the same
time more rigid.   The first years of Frederick William's
reign mark an era in all of these matters.   The young
monarch's leading thought was so to centralize and sys-
tematize all things that he himself, as from a coin of vantage, could at any time cast his eye over the whole field.
He believed that a king, who " wished to rule with *honneur*
in the world," must do everything himself, for " rulers are
put there for the purpose of working."   And he fully lived
up to his creed.   " No one who has not seen it can believe,"
writes Seckendorf, the Austrian envoy, " that one single
man, be he ever so intelligent, could do so much and settle
so many matters in the progress of a day."

In the course of a few months, the army was reorganized on a new basis and with seven new regiments; old feudal military services, which could no longer be literally performed, were commuted for a fixed yearly sum of money which went to the paying of recruits ; a revision of the whole legal system was ordered. The king said in his edict, "one month is already gone, in eleven more the *Landrecht* (or code) must be ready for the whole land" — a command which it proved impossible to strictly carry out. The civil administration was simplified by cashiering several of the many boards. The question of taxation was next taken in hand, and it was found that, particularly in East Prussia, fraud and concealment had long been rampant — many of the nobles paying but the sixth part of what was really due on their lands. A whole new assessment for the province had to be made; and on such sound and thorough principles was this done, that the same schedule was adopted fifty years later for the new acquisitions of Silesia and West Prussia. It met all the same, at the time, with fierce opposition; and the king's own official sent a protest to the effect that the whole country would be ruined. "The whole country ruined!" ran the marginal note to the report in a hideous mixture of languages. "I don't believe a word of it, but I do believe that, as to the squires, their authority and their liberum veto will be ruined!" [1]

Not the least important of the reforms was the requirement of a budget, or previous estimate, for all public outlays in all parts of the kingdom. Not a penny was to be spent for which the king had not given his express consent; and he remorselessly cut down all demands by about one-third. He wrote on the edge of a ministerial report, which

---

[1] Tout le pays sera ruine ? Nihil kredo, aber das kredo, dass die Junkers ihre Autorität Nie pos volam (Polish) wird ruinirt werden. Ich stabilire die Souveraineté wie einen Rocher von Bronce. — F. W.

asked for three hundred and fifteen thalers to repair a toll-house in Frankfort, "Is it a castle? Twenty-four thalers!" To the governing board in the new Mark, which had petitioned for a building in Cüstrin to hold the public documents, he sent word, "There is room enough in the castle for all the archives of London, Paris, and Berlin."

The "Instruction" of 1723.

In spite, however, of all that was done in the first ten years of this reign, these were but the period of gestation for the great measure that was passed in the first days of the year 1723. The "Instruction for the General Upper Finance, War and Domain Directory" was the crown of all Frederick William's administrative endeavors, the crunching of the heel on all the "Schlendrian" or laxness of former days. It was a codification of life principles, such as only a St. Benedict, a Calvin, or an Ignatius Loyola had hitherto accomplished; and it continued to be used as a rule for Prussian officialdom until the end of all things in 1806. It was Frederick William's own most private work: he went into seclusion in his hunting-box, at Schönebeck, until he had thought it all out, then called in one of his privy councillors to put it in shape, and prepared to impose it on his unwary ministers. When his "thunder-bolt," as he called it, at last fell, he requested his friend and general, Prince Leopold of Dessau, to write him "what kind of faces the gentlemen made and whether they were *confus* or calm."

This splendid monument of absolutism bears the effigy of its founder in every one of its lines. The monarch himself is the apex of everything, "We are lord and king, and can do what we will." All the same, "We wish that any odium, however undeserved, should fall not on us, who are chary of the love and devotion of our subjects and the friendship of our neighbors, but on the General Upper Finance, War and Domain Directory, or on one or other of the members of the same, unless it shall prove possible to make the public change its bad opinion."

Under the king, is the new central governing board con- The new sisting of five ministers — each of which is head of a depart- governing ment — and of a number of councillors and secretaries. boards. Under this board, again, are the local and provincial boards and exchequers. This new General Directory replaces the old war commissariat as well as the former Finance Direc- tory, with both of which Frederick William by this time was completely out of conceit: "for one board is always trying to abstract from the other some of its special rights and revenues in order to make a parade before us and to cause us to think that our revenues are being increased by so much, when in reality we have lost just as much on the other side." And further on : "The war-exchequer belongs to no one else but the king in Prussia; item the domain- exchequer. *We hope that we are he and that we have no need either of a guardian or of an assistant.*" The new directory is to avoid everything that has to do with *Wind und blaue Dunst* — with "wind and blue vapor"; in modern parlance, with the "green table" or with "red tape." The old disputes, that took up so much time under the former boards, are to cease forever, and the new members are to live together in harmony. If they keep their minds and faculties on the king's service, they "will all have their hands full and will not need to campaign with lawsuits against each other. But the poor lawyers, poor devils, will be as *inutil* as the fifth wheel on the cart!"

The system of control inaugurated by the "Instruction" The system was one of the most elaborate ever invented, even when of control. compared with that of the Jesuits. Its weakness was, that it stood or fell with the character and predilections of the head of the state. It worked well under Frederick William I. who was determined, as he said, that all opportunity should be taken away from "undutiful rogues" of "blowing into one horn" to deceive him. The members of the General Directory were to assemble daily, in summer at seven, in winter at eight o'clock in the morning. A minister or councillor who should be an hour late was to pay a fine of a hundred ducats; for an unexcused absence of a whole day, six months of his salary. On the occasion of a second offence he was to be cashiered: "for that is what we pay them for, to work." Every evening a protocol of the day's proceedings was to be drawn up and submitted to the king, and every week reports were to be laid before him from all the provinces. Personal questions might be asked on doubtful points, provided they were couched in few words and "*nerveus*" or sinewy. The ministers, who are warned "not to be sleepy, as it were, and not to act as if they had no *inquietude*," were to be held responsible, not so much for what had been reported to them by the provincial officials as for the actual facts of the case. They were to know the *minutissima* of what went on in all parts of the kingdom, and in order to obtain this knowledge they were not only to send commissioners to supervise the work of the officials, but also to employ a large number of spies among all classes of the population, and, if need be, to send secret agents from Berlin. The provincial reports were to be carefully audited, not only by the minister whose department might happen to be concerned, but also *in pleno;* and a sharp lookout was to be kept in order to ascertain "if human intrigues and passions have not something to do with the case." Should there be a stoppage in any source of revenue, and the cause be not discernible as "plainly as the sun in the heavens," a member of the Directory was to repair at once in person to the spot.

The provincial officials themselves were to be most carefully chosen from thoroughly trained men with "open

heads," and they were to know their districts " even as we
pretend that a captain of our army knows his company and
the inward and outward qualities of each soldier that belongs to it." Every attempt at peculation was to be mercilessly struck down, death being the penalty even for
comparatively small thefts. Frederick William knew well
what was the cancerous evil of his day; it has been carefully
reckoned that in Austria in 1700, out of revenues amounting to fourteen million guldens only four million ever found
their way to their proper destination. As a particular safeguard, the " Instruction " provides that officials are not to
serve in the town or province in which they were brought
up; this will give them fewer "inducements to fraud and
deceit," and remove them from the baneful influence of
their "*Gevatterschaften* and *Connoissancen*," their gossips
and acquaintances. This king is rigidly determined that
a summary end shall be put to *alle Sudeleien*, to all dirty
and underhanded work. All irregular expenses too, and
all sudden calls on the treasury, are to be stopped: " We
are as tired of them as though they had been shovelled
with spoons into our mouth." To cover these *fluc-flac*
items, a sum of two hundred and fifty thousand thalers
is set aside, and the Directory has to see that it does not
spend a *Pfennig* more. The strictest possible thoroughness and punctuality is to be observed in making up the
budgets, which are infallibly to be ready by a certain day:
" The gentlemen will say it is not possible, but they shall
put their heads down to it, and we herewith command them
emphatically, that they shall make it possible *sonder
Raisoniren*," — without any attempt at argument at all.

No monarch since Charlemagne had personally worked
out as did Frederick William, not merely the broad outlines of a great administrative system, but also the smallest
details, such as the way to find a market for the butter of

*The re-
quirements
of officials.*

*Efforts to
increase the
revenue.*

East Prussia ; how the beer of twenty-seven other towns, which are mentioned by name, might be made as good as that of Potsdam ; how foreign weavers might be brought to Prussia by the bait of a loom, a wife, and an advance of raw material.   Many of the articles of this very lengthy document are filled with a careful explanation of how investments, which show an apparent profit, may turn out to be no real improvement — *keine Besserung, Ergo Wind.*

In two great departments, the exploitation of the crown lands and the training and equipment of the army, Frederick William outdid all the other European monarchs of his day.   The so-called royal domains — consisting of original grants, of lapsed fiefs, of purchases, secularized benefices, and heritages of all kinds — amounted in all to nearly one-third of the territory of the Prussian state.   The revenues from them were equal to those from all other sources combined, but, like private estates, they needed care and attention.   In the forests the wood must be carefully cut and not squandered, the fields were to be kept well fertilized, the meadows drained and protected by dikes.   When Frederick William took them in hand, he found them heavily mortgaged, and occupied by a poor class of tenants ; during his whole reign he devoted himself to making them flourishing and profitable.   And so well did he succeed that he raised the yearly income from them by two million thalers.   The system that he adopted of farming them out in large districts, or *ämter*, is the one that is in vogue at the present day.

Intro-
duction of
colonists.

And not only did he pay off the debts and burdens, but he settled the waste places with thrifty colonists at an enormous outlay, which returned to him later, in the form of taxes and excise duties, not to speak of stalwart men for his army.   Such wholesale damage had war and pestilence done, especially in East Prussia — where the plague of 1709–

1710 destroyed between a third and a half of the entire
population — that the colonization had to be conducted on
a very extensive scale.   Before the end of his reign this
thrifty monarch was able to look down proudly on thousands of colonists, the great majority of whom had come
to Prussia under special contract with the government.
The sums expended in the venture are calculated to have
averaged six hundred thalers for each family; while in East
Prussia alone six millions were spent in draining and other
improvements.   For a monarch whose chit of a daughter
has dubbed him parsimonious, this was a pretty fair showing.   On the occasion of his first journey through these
rescued provinces, Frederick the Great wrote to Voltaire
that there was something grand and poetical in the thought
of it; and again, "Just as the all-shadowing oak springs
from the power in the acorn, so does all my later good fortune proceed from the toilsome life and the wise measures
of Frederick William."

Of all single transactions in the way of colonization, none
was more famous at the time, and none has left pleasanter
memories,[1] than that by which nearly the whole of a persecuted community, driven from the archbishopric of Salzburg, was received into East Prussia and allowed to found
six new towns and many villages.   For two centuries, half
overlooked and half silently tolerated, the Protestant Salzburgers had lived in peace with their Catholic rulers and
neighbors; but in Archbishop Firmian, who was raised to
the see in 1727, the church found a defender of the stern
old mediæval type.   The Jesuits were called in to reclaim
the lost sheep; they decided that all the orthodox should
know each other by the greeting, "Praised be Jesus
Christ," a formula in favor with Pope Benedict XIII., who

Persecution
of the
Salzburg
Protestants

---

[1] Goethe's *Hermann und Dorothea* deals with this episode.

had promised absolution of sins to all who should answer
"Forever and ever, Amen." Against those who would not
be converted the strongest measures were employed, and
banishment and imprisonment became the order of the day.
Some of the exiles repaired to Ratisbon to complain to the
Diet of the breach of the Peace of Westphalia; but that
cumbrous body, as usual, was slow to act. Better fortune
attended two who appeared in Berlin. They refuted, by
submitting to be catechized, the calumny that they were
heretics, and managed to arouse general sympathy and interest. When, in 1731, a comprehensive edict of banishment was issued by the ferocious archbishop, and soldiers
proceeded to drive out the nonconformists in crowds,
Frederick William stepped forward as their protector, sent
commissioners with money to pay the journey of as many
as would come to him, and intimidated the archbishop
with threats of reprisal. From the moment, he declared,
that the exiles accepted his offer, they were to be treated as
his subjects; and he even obtained for them several million
thalers in compensation for their lands and houses.

Reception
of the
Salzburg
Protes-
tants in
Prussia.
The journey of the fugitives was soon transformed into
a triumphal progress. The burghers of the towns near which
they passed came out in crowds to meet them, bearing food
and presents of every kind; men and women high in rank
delighted to serve them with their own hands. The king
received them in person at Potsdam; the queen invited
hundreds at a time to her little toy castle of Monbijou.
The royal painter, Pesne, was ordered to make a portrait
of one of the maidens; while an antiquary avers that the
Berlin fashions were suddenly influenced to a remarkable
degree, — little pointed Salzburg hats and other characteristic objects coming into high favor.

It was not unnatural that, after being so fêted on the
way, many found it difficult to come down to the hard

realities of East Prussian life, — especially as they arrived
there at the beginning of a hard northern winter. In the
next few years were heard much murmuring and bitter
complaints to the effect that things were not as they had
been represented. After a time, however, the friction subsided, and the Salzburgers showed in many ways that they
were not only good citizens, but even more intelligent than
the great majority of their neighbors.

In entering upon the closer consideration of Frederick
William's military reforms, we come to the field in which,
taken all in all, he felt himself the most at home, and in
which, in the end, he was able to show the most tangible
results. Despite his untiring industry in other regards, it
is easy to see that his heart was all the while with his
army : here he was not only king, but a soldier to the core.
From 1725 on, he never appeared in public, save in his blue
uniform. He was determined that the soldiery should no
longer be looked down upon as they had been since the days of
the Thirty Years' War : if he showed them unwarranted favor
as opposed to civilians, it must be remembered that he had
a needful mission to perform, — the reconciling for all time
of the military and the national ideal. The soldiers were
to be made to feel that the country they were defending
was their own; the citizens, that there was no higher duty
than that which the soldier was performing.

The cantonal system of recruiting the army.

It is true, during the first half of Frederick William's
reign, two-thirds of the army consisted of foreigners ; there
were times when nearly a thousand recruiting officers were
busy beyond the boundaries, engaging men for high pay
and, as often as not, kidnapping those who would not
come of their own accord. But time showed the imperative need of a new system. The expense was enormous, the
violence of the press-gangs led to reprisals and to international complications; while, in spite of the heavy punish-

ments, the number of desertions was ruinous. In 1733, accordingly, the king passed a measure which has been well termed the first step on the way to general compulsory military service. The whole land was divided into districts called cantons, each one containing some five thousand hearths or families; each regiment had its own canton from which to draw its recruits, keeping a roll of the young men from whom it was to choose. It was a levelling process of very great importance, and some of the nobles opposed it bitterly; for their serfs, instead of remaining blindly obedient to them, had now other interests and other ideals. It is true there was a liberal system of furloughs, but the men who came back, wearing the king's collar and the king's cockade, were a different class of beings from the sons of the soil who had marched out. It was Frederick William's outspoken aim to make things more comfortable for them in their regiment than they were at home; they were taught to read and write, and were well fed, clothed, and lodged.

The nobles as officers in the army.

An important levelling process in the opposite direction, yet one that worked equally astounding results, was the forcing of the sons of nobles to accept military commands; they had held aloof hitherto from a service which promised little honor or emolument. In his usual radical manner, Frederick William changed all this, dismissing officers of low birth or mean sentiments, and gradually filling their places from the best elements of the population. A cry of indignation went through the land when it was found that he had sent his police and under-officers to gather in the sons of the old country families for his *Cadetten-Anstalt*, or training-school at Berlin. Many of the parents in their despair tried to prove that they were not noble at all. But the king remained firm, and continued on his way. We have a letter that he sent to the nobles in East Prussia, telling them that their sons were being brought up on Christian principles and instructed in all the necessary branches, not excepting fencing and dancing: " Twenty-four of them at a time are taught to ride free of charge; besides, they are lodged in clean rooms and have good healthy food and drink."

It was the last step in the subjugation of the old stubborn estates ; they were not only rendered docile and harmless, but they gained a new occupation, and became of the greatest service to their country.   Accustomed to com-mand at home, they easily fell into the habit of command-ing in the field — their separate interests vanished, and they have remained to this day the strongest pillars of the Prussian throne.

Apart from his efforts toward strengthening the broader framework of his army, Frederick William devoted himself to the minor details with unswerving perseverance.   His right-hand man was Prince Leopold, the " old Dessauer," who taught him much in the way of tactics and evolutions. He it was who introduced the custom of marching in step, the fixed bayonet, the iron ramrod, the quick fire.   His regiment at Halle and the king's at Potsdam were the models for the whole land.   Frederick William drilled his grenadiers in person, and allowed not the smallest irregu-larity, not even a tarnished button, to escape his notice. The men were drawn up on parade in such a way that he could pass in and out among them and bring down his cane on the shoulders of any unfortunate delinquent.   Yet his " dear blue children," as he called them, were the apple of his eye ; he was willing for their sake to make any kind of sacrifice, even to turn a deaf ear to manifest cases of in-justice and lawbreaking.   His chief pride was to have the men of the largest possible size ; and every court in Europe knew that the way to gain his heart was to send him *lange Kerle*.   We have the letter in which Count Seckendorf writes that the Prussian officers are not open to money

Frederick William's tall soldiers.

bribes, but that he *must* have more big men than the emperor has seen fit to send him.   It was Frederick William's
one folly, his one decided extravagance; he is known to
have paid as high as seven thousand thalers for one fine
specimen.   He went so far as to try by forced marriages to
influence the next generation; tall men and women were
sent to the altar, by command, who had never seen each
other the day before.   How he loved these giants!   He
talked to them personally and listened patiently to their
complaints and desires; to many of them he gave houses and
fixed incomes.   It was believed that he could never refuse
a single one of their requests, and he was obliged, at last, to
make it a law that outsiders should not employ them as
mediums in handing in petitions.   He was a little ashamed
of the sums they cost him, for on his death-bed he took the
trouble to destroy the records of his different purchases.

Frederick
William's
first war.

Viewed in the light of his administrative reforms, the
military and political events of Frederick William's reign
seem few and unimportant.   Once at the beginning of that
reign, and once at the end, Prussian troops saw active service; the period between, for all Europe, was a time of
negotiations that led to nothing, of unfruitful congresses,
of treaties and leagues made only to be broken.   The king's
first war, the only one in which he personally played an
active part, lasted but a few weeks, and scarcely rose above
the level of an execution on mortgaged property.   The
breakers of the great northern struggle, which Charles XII.
of Sweden was waging against Peter the Great, had dashed
over into Swedish Pomerania, and, in 1713, Stettin had
fallen into Russian hands.   By the treaty of Schwedt in the
same year, Frederick William induced the victors, in return
for the costs of the siege — some four hundred thousand
thalers — to withdraw, and to leave Stettin, with the adjacent territory, in his hands.   The rightful owner, Charles

XII., had been an exile in Turkey since the disastrous battle of Pultava, five years before. He returned now, after a wild and adventurous journey, and ordered the Prussian king to vacate the premises, but the latter, as a prime condition, demanded the repayment of the money advanced to Russia. Refusing to treat on this basis, and perhaps divining the eagerness with which Frederick William looked forward to annexing his territory, the impetuous Swede threw himself into a struggle with an army of Russians, Danes, and Prussians, three times the size of his own. Frederick William himself appeared in camp; and assisted in the siege of Stralsund; while Prince Leopold of Dessau commanded a force of twenty thousand men which landed on the island of Rügen. With a loss of four thousand in killed and wounded, the Swedes were defeated, and Charles fled for his life. By the final peace, which was not concluded until 1720, Prussia became the richer by the coveted Stettin, which controlled the mouth of the Oder, and by that part of Pomerania south of the river Pesne. The rest was restored to Sweden, which was forced, however, to cede to Hanover the bishoprics of Verden and Bremen. Frederick William had played a rôle which, as he confessed himself, was "not fit for an honest man," but it doubtless salved his conscience that he was obliged by the other powers to pay to Sweden an indemnity of two million thalers.

It is not too much to say, that for the remainder of his reign, the leading thought of Frederick William's foreign policy was to secure for Prussia the reversion of the Rhenish duchy of Berg — a part of that ancient Cleves inheritance which had caused so many pangs in the preceding century. By the last settlement, made in 1666, the house of Pfalz-Neuburg, which had since inherited the whole palatine electorate, was to hold Julier and Berg

The claim to Berg.

until the extinction of its male line. That contingency was now in prospect; but the house of Pfalz-Sulzbach, to whom the rest of the inheritance would naturally fall, was not minded to let slip this fairest part of it. It proved in the end a phantom that Frederick William was chasing; the last of the Pfalz-Neuburgers outlived himself, and his son and successor renounced this modest prospect in favor of larger game. But it influenced Frederick William's attitude at many an important crisis, and the failure of his plans and prospects embittered his last days.

Charles VI. and the Pragmatic Sanction.

During the same period of time, the house of Austria was chasing a similar phantom, in its desire to secure the recognition of all Europe for its so-called Pragmatic Sanction. The difference is that the pursuit of his dream only acted on Frederick William as an incentive to strengthen and unify his state, whereas Charles VI. neglected everything save the one matter in hand. With a heavy heart this prince had left Spain on the death of his brother Joseph, in 1711. He loved the stiff Spanish ceremonial, he delighted in being knelt to and treated like a demigod, and he is said once to have remarked that when he died the word "Barcelona" would be found engraved upon his heart. He had fondly hoped that he might be allowed to keep both the Spanish and the imperial crown, but that delusion had been destroyed by the peace of Utrecht. On the whole, he had not proved a bad emperor; but he possessed the traditional faults of his race, was weak and vacillating and afraid to speak his mind, conferring even with his own ministers by letter and not by word of mouth. He squandered his resources right and left, and never looked at his household accounts, which, after his death, were found to be full of imaginary items: twelve buckets of the best wine for the empress's bath; two casks of old Tokay for her Majesty's parrots, and more of the kind.

Given such an unpractical character, it is easy to understand how Charles could waste his life in seeking to gain
written guarantees for his pet project, instead, as Prince
Eugene advised him, of seeking the best of all guarantees
in a strong and efficient army and a well-filled treasury.
His aim was on the whole a just one, — to prevent the subdivision of his lands at his death and to have them pass in
their integrity, in default of male heirs, to his eldest living
daughter. This was the sum and substance of the Pragmatic Sanction, first drawn up in 1713, but not made public
until 1720, when his only son had died and there seemed
no prospect of another male heir. Had he been contented
with gaining the acquiescence of his own dependencies,— of
Bohemia, Moravia and Silesia; of the Tyrol, Croatia, and
Transylvania; of Hungary, and the former Spanish Netherlands, — one could only have looked on the Sanction as a
great gain for Austria; for, in the years that followed, all
these different states fully accustomed themselves to the idea
of having Maria Theresa as their future ruler. But when
Charles began to beg at the door of every government in
Europe, when he made and broke treaties, sacrificed commercial interests, and engaged in war as a mere act of
servility, then his policy became suicidal.

With Frederick William, Charles VI.'s relations went
through extraordinary phases. One can imagine the king's
feelings when, in 1718, a secret political agent by the name
of Clement laid before him what appeared to be conclusive
proofs of a dastardly plot, on the part of Austria and
Saxony, to fall upon him in Wusterhausen and carry him
off to Vienna. The crown prince, too, the future Frederick the Great, was to be seized and brought up as a
Roman Catholic; while the royal treasure in Berlin was to
be laid hold of and carried away. The whole conspiracy
was a fiction of Clement's, who hoped to extort money for

Suspicions
against
Austria.

his revelations; but the manuscripts were so well forged
that Frederick William was completely duped. Even after
Clement had confessed his share in the matter, the poor
king could not be convinced of its entire groundlessness.
Prince Eugene had been mentioned as one of the conspirators; to sound him, Frederick William sent a special
envoy to Vienna. "I am head of the imperial army, not
a chief of bandits," was the great leader's exclamation on
perceiving the drift of the envoy's words; though the future
was to show that Eugene could condescend to leave his
pedestal. Clement was sentenced and hung; but with
Frederick William the wound remained behind. He veered
round to Austria's enemies, concluded the treaty of Herrenhausen with England; and, even after he had returned
to his allegiance and signed the treaties of Wusterhausen
and Berlin, great efforts were needed to keep him in the
toils and to ward off the English influences.

Grumbkow
and
Seckendorf.

Now began a game of deceit and intrigue which lasted
for several years, and which finds no parallel in history.
Were it not for the evidence of his own letters one would
never believe that a man like Eugene of Savoy, who managed this affair in Vienna, could have lowered himself to
such depths. Count Seckendorf, whom Frederick William
had known and liked since the days of Malplaquet, was
sent to Berlin as a sort of perpetual envoy, and was given
funds with which to bribe the king's councillors and
attendants. He kept strict account of his outlays and laid
each item before Eugene: a yearly pension to Grumbkow,
whose voice had more weight than any other at the Prussian
court; the same to the minister resident in London, and to
the Saxon envoy at Berlin. The sums descend to mere
pourboires to the servants, and later even Wilhelmine and
the crown prince were supplied with pocket-money. Seckendorf was a man of consummate ability, and, save where

his main object was concerned, neither bad nor cruel. He
became a constant member of Frederick William's famous
tobacco parliament, where, to an accompaniment of drinking and rude practical joking, affairs of great seriousness
were often discussed and decided. Grumbkow was another
member, not utterly a villain either; but his soul belonged
to Seckendorf. The two watched their prey with feline
eagerness. He has not much time, Seckendorf writes to
Eugene, to attend to other matters, "for one is obliged to
be in the king's company from ten in the morning till
eleven or twelve at night, in order not to lose the chances
of insinuating into his mind what is right and proper."
Every now and then he enlarges his sphere of bribery; he
writes to the Chancellor Sinzendorf that his next batch of
supplies must include "some big useless giants or other
baggage of the kind . . . since from Moscow, England,
France, Denmark, and Sweden the king's good will has
been secured in this way." A medal must be sent to the
learned Gundling, who, though nothing but a court fool, is
always with the king and is apt "to instil false principles."

It must not be supposed that Seckendorf spent his time
in fighting mere phantoms of his imagination; he had a
constant and determined enemy in the queen,—"My face,"
he writes, "is so hateful to her that she will hardly answer
me at table,"— and a cause and aim, in preventing the plan
of an alliance by marriage with England, which would
have given Prussia a natural place among the enemies of
Austria. Sophie Dorothea was a strong-minded, domineer-
ing woman, greatly embittered at not being allowed to
make the display and to play the rôle in the world for which
her early training at the Hanoverian court had so well
prepared her. The foreign ambassadors at Berlin call her
"Olympia," in their reports, because of her high and mighty
bearing. She is responsible, in the last resort, for much of

Sophie
Dorothea

the misery in the royal household, setting herself like a wall of iron against some of her husband's projects, and, worst of all, estranging from him the hearts of his children. Well might her great son later set down his foot and declare, that with *his* politics women should have absolutely nothing to do.

The double-marriage project.

The great double-marriage project, by which Wilhelmine was to become Princess of Wales, and the English Amalia Crown Princess of Prussia, was first seriously considered in 1725, at the time of the treaty of Herrenhausen. Through evil and through good days the queen could never let it out of her mind, and there were times when even Frederick William looked upon it with favor. But George the First he had mildly disliked, and George the Second he utterly despised. Points of difference would come up, occasionally, which would render the mere thought of a union absolutely abhorrent : a dispute over the will of the unfortunate captive of Ahlden, who was the mother of Sophie Dorothea as well as of George II., and who died in 1726; a quarrel as to the Prussian-Hanoverian boundaries; a refusal to allow Hanover to be a happy hunting-ground for Prussian recruiting officers. Things had come once to the very verge of war, and once to a challenge for a personal duel. After this great outburst in 1729, the atmosphere suddenly cleared, and a message of the queen to London led to the sending of a special envoy, Sir Charles Hotham, with conciliatory proposals and with power to arrange the two contracts of marriage — the two, but on no account either one singly. Frederick William was ready enough to have Wilhelmine marry the Prince of Wales, but Hotham's proposition that Frederick should wed Amalia, and be made stadtholder of Hanover, filled him with alarm; he feared the luxury and the laxness of the Hanoverian court, and mistrusted with good cause the steadfastness of the crown prince. And

Grumbkow and Seckendorf had been working on him to good effect, moving heaven and earth against the English party. England wished to make a cat's-paw of him, they said; and of all things on earth that was what Frederick William most dreaded. At last, after weeks of deliberation, he answered Hotham that he considered himself honored by the prospect of Wilhelmine's marriage, but that Frederick was too young; in ten years he should like above all things to have him wed an English princess.

So far the relations with Hotham had been all that could be desired; although nothing was decided, and it was not likely that England would accept these last proposals, the door was still open for further negotiations. But, in the moment of taking leave, Hotham produced an intercepted letter of Grumbkow's tending to prove that the latter was an Austrian spy. Then Frederick William boiled over with rage, threw the letter on the ground with a forcible expletive, and declared that he had had enough of such interference. Out of the personal discourtesy, for which the king tried to atone by inviting him to dinner, Hotham made a great affair of state and departed abruptly from Berlin. Conciliatory conduct on Frederick William's part might still have bridged matters; it was not as though the letter he had so scorned had been a communication from the English court. But just at this time a long-ripening tragedy in his own household, in which England played a part, came to its climax, and cast a never-to-be-lifted shadow on the whole double-marriage project.

The insult to Hotham

Frederick William's relations to his eldest son form an important chapter in Prussian history; it is not too much to say that to the harsh discipline of his youth Frederick owed much of his later greatness. He learned reticence and self-command, he was forced to apply himself diligently to tasks which he at first despised; but above all, he learned

The antipathy of father and son.

to admire and to follow a system which originally seemed to him wrong. His directions for the education of his successor are not so different from those given by his own father; many a curb at which he himself had chafed, which he even at the time had declared intolerable, was retained in all its force.

It is a mistake to attribute Frederick William's harshness to a mere unreasoning personal antipathy or, on the other hand, purely to a contempt for the finer sides of life which the young prince loved to cultivate. What wounded and terrified the king was the thought of the shipwreck his own life-work seemed destined to endure, so soon as Frederick should come to the throne. We, who know now the true stuff of which the latter was made, are too apt to look upon him in his youth as a misunderstood genius, whose way was beset by unnecessary obstacles; as a matter of fact, he was like a wild stallion, with everything depending on the manner in which he should be tamed and broken. Without the frightful experience at the window of the Küstrin fortress, it is doubtful if we should ever have had the desperate fortitude before a world in ruins at the end of the Seven Years' War.

Iniquities of the crown prince.

On the whole, it seems not unlikely that the unreasoning antipathy had begun on the side of the son. Frederick William had at first fairly sued for the love of this boy; and we still have the instructions providing that in his childish delinquencies the latter should always be threatened with the wrath of his mother, never of his father. In all the king's plans for the improvement of the state, the thought of "Fritz" was paramount; his son at his death must find whole vaults of gold in the treasury, he once said. There were times when, for hours snatched from his toilsome days, he devoted himself personally to the child's education; his threefold aim was to make him a good manager, a good soldier, and a good Christian.

But the pupil proved singularly refractory. Was it that the blood of the Georges was struggling for the mastery? or was it that the carping jealousy of the mother instilled a contempt for all of the father's ideals? Sophie Dorothea made no secret of her dislike for her husband's Spartan surroundings, and it was not in her nature to dissimulate before her children.

Frederick began to seek flighty companions of both sexes, to commit acts of vandalism, to make debts, and to spend his money upon fripperies. Strange as it may seem, the future great commander showed a detestation for things military, and indeed, for vigorous pursuits in general. When his father took him hunting, he would hide behind a tree and bury himself in a book. His greatest delight was to put on gay clothes, to play the flute, and to write satirical French verses. He once spoke of his soldier's uniform as a shroud, and Frederick William retaliated by burning one of his gaudy dressing-gowns. But what most angered the father was a want of frankness, a tendency to conceal the true extent even of a half-discovered offence. Once by a public show of affection he fairly delighted the king. "That is good," the latter said, as he stroked the lad's hand, "only be an upright fellow, only be upright." Yet soon he had cause to think that during the whole scene Frederick had been playing him a comedy, and all the harshness of his nature rose in revolt.

One further point must be taken into consideration before joining in the unqualified condemnation to which Frederick William has too often been subjected in this matter. There was a certain purpose and policy even in the king's acts of most outrageous violence. "I have done everything in the world," he said, in one of the most affecting moments of their common lives, "by good means and by bad, to make you an honest man."

Severity to the crown prince.

Yet with all that can be said on the other side, enough remains in the prince's favor to insure him, for all time, a
goodly meed of the world's sympathy. The father's tongue
was a stinging lash; there were times when even the most
harmless incidents were interpreted to the disfavor of the
" evil wight "; there were terrible moments, such as the one
on the parade ground at Potsdam, where the boy was buffeted
and caned and forced to walk off with soiled garments and
dishevelled hair before the eyes of the common soldiers.
The same scene was reënacted in the camp at Mühlberg
during the splendid festivities at which the pair were the
guests of the king of Poland; and from that time on, the
plan of flight was never absent from Frederick's mind.
Who can blame him for not weighing carefully the consequences of such a move, for choosing ways and means that
bordered on high treason, and even for involving others in
a ruin that in calmer moments he would have seen to be
inevitable ?   Desertion and abetting desertion were crimes
which the codes of all Europe in the eighteenth century
punished with death, and when had Frederick William
been known to show mercy in such a case ?

The at-
tempt at
flight.

Immeasurably, beyond a doubt, did the crown prince
aggravate his offence by his dealings with England.   In
the face of his father's refusal to hear any more of the
double marriage, he had written to London, with his
mother's connivance, to protest that, so long as he lived,
he would take no other wife than the Princess Amalia; he
had sought to gain a promise from the envoy in Berlin
that England would grant him an asylum should he flee
from his father's court, and had negotiated for the payment of his debts by George II., placing the sum many
thousand thalers too high, that he might have funds for his
undertaking.

" In your blind obstinacy you thought to escape me,"

Frederick William said, long after the catastrophe, to his son; "but listen, my good fellow, if you were to live to be sixty or seventy, you would not get the better of me. *Bis dato*, up to date, I have held my own against every one!" Suspecting Frederick's intention, he surrounded him with watchful guardians, bound, under peril of their lives, to cut off the first attempt at flight. The golden opportunity seemed to have come when, on a journey through the empire, but a few hours' ride intervened between the camp near Mannheim and the French frontier; but in the faint glimmering of that August dawn in which Frederick awaited the page, Keith, with his horses—Lieutenant Catte, in Berlin, having agreed to meet him in the Hague, with his papers and other valuables,—he came face to face with Colonel Rochow, his warden-in-chief. The latter would not have betrayed him, but Keith, in an agony of repentance, confessed all to the king. Rochow was ordered to bring the prince, living or dead, within the limits of Prussian territory. Frederick was slow in realizing the future that awaited him; to the commissioners sent to examine him he kept saying mockingly, "Is there anything else you would like to know?" Only gradually, too, did Frederick William come to see the true bearing of the case. "I thought you were in Paris," was his caustic remark at the first sight of the would-be fugitive; but each new tidings filled him with greater alarm. The dealings with England seemed to him particularly heinous because of the consequences that would have been involved had Frederick's request for asylum been granted. "I should have invaded Hanover," he said later, "and burnt and devastated everything, even though it had cost me my life, my land, and my people."

That Frederick William ever thought seriously of putting his son to death is not likely; yet the queen feared

In fear of
the death
sentence.
the worst, and bent her pride to the extent of entreating her old enemy, Seckendorf, to obtain from the emperor a letter of intercession. And Frederick himself could scarcely be persuaded that a clergyman who visited him in his prison at Küstrin, was not there for the purpose of preparing him for his last hour. At the best, he could hardly have hoped, now, ever to succeed to the throne ; he had been repeatedly interrogated as to whether, from a sense of his own unworthiness, he would not resign his claims.

As for the king, it must be said that there was nothing in his conduct, at this juncture, of blind rage or vindictiveness. He himself suffered intensely, and at night walked the floor in sleepless wretchedness, wrestling with the problem of how to make his son *ein honnête homme*. He felt that the mocking spirit, of which Frederick was even yet possessed, must be subdued at any cost, and a sense borne in upon him of the earnestness of life. The boy needed, Frederick William wrote a little later to Leopold of Dessau, to have a taste of real danger, to perform reconnoitring duty where war was going on, to work in trenches or on redoubts : "Should he do this with a good grace and remain steadfast, I would pardon him fully," he said.

The execution of
Catte.
As a present means of discipline, the king contrived an ordeal, compared to which any conceivable danger in the field must have seemed a welcome alternative. The cases of all persons directly concerned in the plan of flight had been submitted to a court-martial of higher officers. They had pronounced the heir to the throne beyond their jurisdiction, but had sentenced Lieutenant Catte to life-long imprisonment. This verdict Frederick William changed, with full right as chief justice of his land, to death on the scaffold. To Catte he sent expressions of regret, but declared it better that he should die, than that justice should perish in the land. Then came the day when the young

Frederick was informed that in two hours his friend must be beheaded before his own eyes. " What awful news is this you bring?" he cried; "Lord Jesus, rather take my own life!" But no one listened to his prayers, and soon the gloomy procession turned the angle of the fortress wall. The escort drew up in a circle with Catte in their midst, and Frederick had only time to rush to the window and throw a despairing cry for pardon to his unfortunate accomplice. The latter, full of love and devotion to his prince, answered that he had nothing to forgive; later a writing of his was brought to Frederick in which the latter was urged to give his heart to God and not to bear malice against the king. As the blow fell, the prince lost consciousness, then stood for hours with his eyes glued to Catte's corpse, which Frederick William, as an aggravation of the punishment, had ordered to be left where it fell, from eight in the morning until two o'clock in the afternoon.[1]

It speaks well for the penetration of Frederick William The disci-
that not only did his rough experiment do Frederick no pline at
harm, but that it really seemed to strengthen and steady his Küstrin.
character. The same may be said, in a still higher degree, of the year of probation that the prince was obliged to pass through in order to regain his father's favor. " The school of misfortune," he once himself declared, " makes one circumspect, discreet, and sympathetic. One carefully weighs the possible consequences of each smallest step." Three days after Catte's execution, Frederick was given the freedom of the fortress and town of Küstrin; but was not to be saluted by the guards, nor even by the officers of the garrison. He was to work daily in the War and Domain office as *Auscultator* or assistant clerk, the king commanding that " on a lower level there should be placed

[1] " Cruel as the grinding of human hearts under millstones," writes Carlyle of this episode, " but was it only that?"

for him a little table and a chair, and on the table ink, pen, and paper." Here, month after month, the prince worked not only faithfully but cheerfully ; learning the lesson of governing in all its smallest details, and often luring a smile from the friendly judges and councillors by the wit that would flash out from his legal reports. He bore no malice to any one, and, strange to say, Grumbkow, whose machinations against the English marriage had largely contributed to his misfortunes, became, to all outward appearances, his warmest friend. The king persistently refused to see him, or to grant him the right to wear his uniform. "Had I done what he has," Frederick William wrote to Wolden, the young man's special mentor and guardian, "I should be filled with a deadly shame, and never allow myself to be seen at all."

The restoration to favor.

But at last Wolden received a message to say that the king was coming to see the culprit. "So soon as I look him in the eyes," he declared, "I shall know whether or not he has really improved." On the day of the visit — we have Grumbkow's protocol of all that took place — Frederick was called to strict account for every one of his past sins ; but his eyes told the tale that his father wished to read. Frederick William began to relent, and the interview at last grew extremely affecting. The king ended up with a declaration of forgiveness, and Frederick, dissolved in tears, knelt and kissed his feet. Then, as Frederick William was about to enter his carriage, he turned, and embraced his son before the eyes of an eager throng. "I never believed before," said Frederick, when he was gone, "that my father cherished for me the least spark of affection." A few weeks later came another affecting scene in the ball room of the Berlin castle, where the king, who had arranged that the crown prince's coming should be a complete surprise, led him by the hand through the crowded hall straight to the queen, "See, madam, here is our Fritz again!" Soon afterward, on petition of all the generals who were present in Berlin, he was reinstated in the army, and promised the command of a regiment in Ruppin.

Even now it was only by walking the narrowest of paths that he could keep his father's favor. He often fretted and chafed, and once, on the occasion of the king's illness, wrote ugly words to his sister to the effect that "the Turk" had no intention of dying. But he had learned to bow to a will that was stronger than his own, and he thought no more of open insubordination, — not even when a question arose which concerned nobody so much as himself, affecting as it did his whole future. The crown prince's dealings with England had put a final end, in Frederick William's mind at least, to the double-marriage project. "In all my days, neither single nor double," he declared; "I will not have their princesses in my house, nor will I give them one of mine, even under the best of conditions." The outcry over Catte's judgment and execution had widened the breach. "Had I a hundred thousand such Cattes I would behead them all together," was the message he sent to the English people through his ambassador. He meant, he said, to *souteniren* himself as *Herr despotique*, and the English were to know that he would suffer no co-regent at his side.

The men who had most reason to rejoice at this attitude were Seckendorf and Grumbkow. Fully in possession of the ear of the king, they now arranged a marriage between Frederick and the Princess Elizabeth Christine of Bruns-wick-Bevern, a niece of the empress. Grumbkow, for his services in the matter, received a present of forty thousand guldens, in addition to his yearly stipend, from the Austrian court: "for if ever any one in the world deserves favors, it is this man," wrote Seckendorf to Vienna. It mattered little that Elizabeth Christine was person-

The forced marriage.

ally distasteful to Frederick; he felt indeed that any marriage would be a relief from the strict discipline and supervision under which his father still kept him; but he declared from the first that there never could be any sympathy between this woman and himself. "I pity the poor thing," he wrote to Grumbkow, "for now there will be one more unhappy princess in the world." His letters grew more and more desperate. "My God, is not one such case enough?" he cries, referring to the unfortunate marriage of his younger sister with the Margrave of Ansbach. And again, "I would rather marry the commonest piece of female baggage in all Berlin than this praying nun, with a face like a half-a-dozen flies all rolled into one." Finally, "I will keep my word, I will marry her; but then, enough: *Bonjour, Madame, et bon chemin!*"

The futility of the marriage.

Nor was there to be spared to the young bridegroom the saddest and bitterest of all considerations — the needlessness of the whole sacrifice. The marriage had been brought about chiefly for the sake of Austria; Frederick William's policy for years had been that of absolute trust in the emperor. "He will have to spurn me from him with his feet," he once said; "I am his unto death, faithful to the last drop of blood." But that spurning process had already begun.

England's guarantee of his Pragmatic Sanction had always seemed to Charles VI. one of the most necessary to obtain. After years of enmity, he had achieved his wish, in 1731, at the sacrifice of his Ostende Company, Austria's one great commercial enterprise, which interfered with the English trade in the East Indies. Surely complaisance to a new ally never went further than when now, just before the wedding with the Prussian crown prince, Seckendorf was instructed to break the match he had so carefully arranged and to bring about that old, so often mooted union between Frederick and the English Princess Amalia.

He received his instructions and acquitted himself of his mission only twenty-four hours before the ceremony was to be performed, and after the guests had already arrived. Frederick William was unnaturally calm; he thought Seckendorf must be dreaming, he said, and refused utterly to besmirch his honor and his parole by countermanding the festivities. So Frederick went to the altar to no one's benefit; while Frederick William was hurried along from one bitter experience with Austria to another.

More and more it became evident that Charles had no intention of keeping the agreement with regard to the duchy of Berg, which he had made in 1728. We know now, that he was bound by contrary promises to the other party, the house of Pfalz-Sulzbach. He began, soon after the *entente* with England, to declare that the town of Düsseldorf must be excepted in any case; and finally tried to force Frederick William to accept the intervention of a congress of nations. This proved in the end a foolish policy, which freed Prussia from the trammels of the Berlin treaty. Frederick William was deeply pained, too, by the manner in which the emperor treated his offers of aid in the war that broke out with France, in 1735, with regard to the Polish succession. Louis XV. fought for his son-in-law, Stanislaus Lescinsky; Austria and Russia for Augustus III. of Saxony,—who finally won the day. But the campaign on the Rhine, though led by the old Prince Eugene with the young Frederick in his camp, was a series of wretched blunders. Frederick William would gladly have sent fifty thousand men; but Austria feared that he would seize Berg, and required him to send no more than his bare contingent. The emperor made light in every way of the value of Prussia's aid. A common indignation against Austria seems to have broken down the last barriers that remained between the father and son. Frederick

Austria's treachery

William was repeatedly heard to remark, "There stands one who will avenge me!" Once he poured out in writing his wrath at the emperor's ingratitude and ended up with, "The reflections which must result from what I tell you may give you an opportunity to be on your guard in the future;" while Frederick himself, as far back as 1737, prophesied, in a letter to Grumbkow, that pride in Austria was going before a fall: "Should the emperor die to-day or to-morrow, what changes will not the world experience!" "The king treats me now as I always wished he would," writes Frederick in 1739. It was in these days that his eyes were opened as to the magnificent results achieved by his father in the work of reclaiming East Prussia. One painful scene still took place when, a few weeks before his death, the old king was holding his tobacco parliament, and, on the entry of the crown prince, every one in the room rose and saluted him. It had always been a principle that no ceremony of the kind should be observed. Full of bitterness of heart, the old invalid caused his chair to be wheeled into another room, and sent back the command, that those who had "worshipped the rising sun" might disperse to their homes.

In his last days Frederick William summoned strength to review for Frederick's benefit his whole foreign policy, and to warn him against Austria's invariable efforts to hold down Prussia. He had again grown very loving, very tender. Once, in the presence of the crown prince, he turned to a number of officials and cried out, " Has not God shown me too much favor in giving me so strong and worthy a son ? " and again, locking him in a warm embrace, his voice choked with sobs, " My God, I die happy in leaving so worthy a son and successor ! " The Nemesis of the past had been propitiated, and, in the account which Frederick wrote of his father's life, there is not a word of blame save in the one point, that he had forced him into an unhappy marriage.

Father
and son.

CHAPTER IV

THE WARS OF FREDERICK THE GREAT

LITERATURE : Schaefer, *Der siebenjährige Krieg*, is still the great
authority for the Seven Years' War. Longman, in the *Epoch Series*, is
simply a condensation of Schaefer. Tuttle, *Frederick the Great*, extends
only to 1757. Koser, *König Friedrich der Grosse*, is also incomplete,
but excellent as far as it goes. Koser is the greatest living authority on
Frederick.

WHEN first confronted with the prospect of his father's
death, young Frederick of Prussia complained bitterly
that he was being thrust out into the midst of storm, that
a relentless fate was forcing him to mount Fortuna's car,
that the peaceful, pleasant, and industrious days he had
latterly been enjoying at Rheinsberg, his small palace near
Ruppin, were at an end forever. Not that he meant to
make any radical change in the system of administration ;
with the old king's methods he had of late become completely reconciled,— with his economy, his attention to detail, his diligent care for the army. But events were to
assume a quicker tempo, the instruments at hand were
to find their use, the millions lying idle in the vaults
of the treasury were to be put into circulation, the ninety
thousand soldiers were to show of what deeds and what
exertions they were capable. In his very first address to
his officers, Frederick told them that their regiments were
expected to be useful as well as ornamental ; immediately
after his father's funeral he dismissed the tall, showy grenadiers, and formed new regiments of better and less costly
material. To the surprise and disappointment of many he

Frederick's firm grasp of the reins of government.

123

proved as stern, decisive, and absolute as ever Frederick William had been; haughtily reprimanded the Prince of Anhalt, the "old Dessauer," who spoke of "exercising authority"; and sent General Schulenburg, who had come to Berlin to congratulate him on his accession, flying back to his regiment with instructions not to leave it again without permission. Yet Schulenburg, if any one, deserved well of his new master, for he had been president of that court-martial which had, eight years before, firmly declared the case of a crown prince to be beyond its jurisdiction.

The Heristal matter.

In the matter of a dispute with the Bishop of Liège concerning the little Prussian principality of Heristal, — a part of the Orange inheritance, — Frederick in these days called for the advice of his ministers; but, angry at their pacific injunctions, and at their evident awe of the Emperor Charles VI., who was ready to take the bishop's part, he wrote on the edge of their formal report: "When the ministers talk politics they are clever men, but their ideas on war are like the opinions of an Iroquois on the subject of astronomy." By marching three battalions of grenadiers and a squadron of dragoons into the bishop's territory he brought the latter to terms; while Charles VI., struck by the young king's perfectly fearless attitude, thought best to suppress a *dehortatorium*, or formal admonition, that was already under way. Podewils, Frederick's minister of foreign affairs, declared to Charles's envoy, that his master considered himself fully on an equality with his Imperial Majesty, who, he would have him understand, was only *primus inter pares*.

The death of the emperor.

A few weeks later, while Frederick himself was lying sick of a fever, a messenger brought the news of Charles's sudden death. The very same day Frederick wrote to Voltaire: "The time has come for an entire change in the old political system, the stone has again broken loose which once descended on the four-metalled image of Nebuchad-nezzar and destroyed it utterly. . . . I have cast off my fever [with the aid of quinine, which had hitherto been considered too dangerous a remedy], for I shall need to put my body to every conceivable use." Yet, as Frederick said himself two days later, there was no reason why a bagatelle like the death of the emperor should greatly excite him; "It is only a matter of carrying out plans which I have long had in my head."

Almost immediately, the army was commanded to hold itself in readiness; by November 15, Frederick was able to write from Rheinsberg to his minister, that he had given his Berlin regiments a false order of march in order to throw the "tattlers" off the scent, and that Podewils must keep his eyes open. "If heaven is not absolutely against us, we have the finest game in the world. . . . I think of striking my blow on the 8th of December, and thus inaugu-rating the boldest, most rapid, and grandest undertaking in which a prince of my house has ever been engaged."

To the last moment Frederick kept his plans secret. First at Rheinsberg, then at Berlin, he filled the palace with guests, for whom he arranged comedies and balls. The very evening before his departure for the army, was filled till far into the night with a double entertainment — a mas-querade and a supper. The next morning at nine he mounted his coach and drove off to Frankfort-on-the-Oder, and three days later wrote to Podewils: "I have crossed the Rubicon with banners waving and to the sound of trumpets; my troops show the best of wills, the officers are full of ambition, and the commanders thirst for fame. . . . Either I die or I reap honor from this enterprise." To Jordan he wrote: "Be my Cicero and show the justice of my cause. I will be thy Cæsar and carry the matter through."

The descent on Silesia.

No act in history has been more variously judged than the sudden descent of the Prussian king on the Austrian province of Silesia; apologists and accusers at once sprang up, and the dispute thus inaugurated never has been, and never can be, entirely laid at rest. Undoubtedly, it was barbarous practice to thus invade a friendly country without so much as a declaration of war, unchivalrous conduct for a strong king to throw down the gauntlet to a young queen struggling, in the midst of bereavement, to maintain her endangered inheritance; and all this out of motives in which, as Frederick confessed himself, ambition and the "desire to make a name" played a conspicuous part. On the other hand, Frederick had long known that the death of the last male Austrian Hapsburg would be the inevitable signal for just such a struggle as had followed on the extinction of the Spanish line. In spite of the Pragmatic Sanction, the succession of a woman was likely to be disputed by no less than four rulers: by the kings of Spain, Sardinia, and Poland, and the elector of Bavaria. Frederick's own house had claims against the greater part of Silesia, which had been hoarded up for three generations against this very day; the old Chancellor von Ludewig, in Halle, had for forty years been collecting proofs on the Prussian side, while, before him, Ilgen, minister to the Great Elector, had warned his master to be on the lookout for a favorable opportunity. A plan for the conquest of Silesia had been drawn up at that time; it was once shown to Frederick William I., who declared that it was worth to him a hundred thousand thalers; its existence was well known to the young Frederick.

Ground for the claim to Silesia.

There is no need here to recapitulate the grounds upon which Prussia based her claims; even Austria had, to some extent, acknowledged their justice by agreeing, before the Great Elector's death, to give up Schwiebus in return for a safe title to Brieg, Liegnitz, Wohlau, and Jägerndorf. It is true the emperor had stipulated in secret, with the then electoral prince, that Schwiebus should be returned to him without equivalent so soon as the old elector died; but Frederick I., when later fulfilling this condition, laid stress on the advantage taken of his youth and inexperience, and expressly refused to ratify that former renunciation of his father to the larger duchies. Frederick II. maintained that by the retrocession of Schwiebus those older claims had regained their former force and vigor.

Apart from the justice of the claims themselves, it is urged that Frederick should first have tried the path of peaceful negotiation; but here Austria reaped the harvest of her own previous perfidy. When had negotiations with her ever led to tangible results? when had her means been anything but false and underhanded? Frederick was willing enough to negotiate, but he wished to do so from a coign of vantage, and for that reason he threw his armies into Silesia. More than this, the result proved that he was stronger than his antagonist; but who at the time could have foreseen this? Austria was three or four times the size of Prussia, among her troops were veterans of two wars, and she had numerous allies; nor was Maria Theresa personally so helpless and alone as many have supposed. Her strength of character brought her to the fore and made her a redoubtable enemy for Frederick; but the latter could not know that her husband, Francis of Lorraine, would prove so complete a nonentity. It was with him that all Frederick's thoughts were at first busy, with him that negotiations were carried on. The tragedy of Maria's situation lay not in the fact that she was a beautiful young woman thrown entirely on her own resources, but in the circumstances that her country had been wretchedly mismanaged, that of the list of soldiers on paper not half were fit to take the field, that luxury and extravagance had emptied the treasury, that rottenness and corruption ruled in all the public offices. A state that has thus sown to the wind is sure to reap the whirlwind.

Pleasure of the Silesians in being conquered.

Frederick's task was rendered immeasurably easier from the fact that the Silesians, groaning under bad government and religious persecution, showed very little aversion to being conquered. With the exception of the three fortresses of Brieg, Glogau, and Neisse, in which the regular Austrian troops took refuge, the whole land submitted without a blow. When the Austrian minister, Bartenstein, confessed that "an excessive zeal in religious matters had made the number of malcontents very large," he was stating the case far too mildly. The Treaty of Alt-Ranstädt, by which Charles XII. of Sweden had wrested a promise of toleration for the Protestants from the Emperor Charles VI., had been robbed of all its value by the intrigues of Jesuit confessors. Under the head of "apostates" were included many whose only sin consisted in having Protestant relatives. Frederick, at his coming, found the prisons full of those who were suffering for their faith; and one of his first and most popular acts was to send to Berlin for a batch of preachers.

Entry into Breslau.

With the citizens of Breslau, the capital of Silesia, Frederick treated as with an independent power, securing their neutrality and promising not to burden them with a Prussian garrison. Then he held an entry into the town the like of which, under similar circumstances, has rarely been seen. A company of militia received him at the gate; the garrison formed in two lines, down which he rode on horseback, followed by a long train of officers, pages, and lackeys. His coach of state, empty save for his ermine and velvet mantle, preceded him; even the car containing his belongings was drawn by gayly decked mules. No lord returning to his own could have been greeted with more enthusiasm; never-ending cheers followed him to his quarters, and he was finally called out to his balcony to bow his thanks. All the chief officials and grandees accepted his invitation to a dinner, at which he drank to the town's prosperity, — his soldiers the while moving peacefully about the streets as objects of admiration to every one, especially, writes a Breslau diarist, to "our Silesian womankind." A few days later came a grand ball, and the civic chroniclers took the trouble to note the names of each and all of the ladies whom the handsome young king favored with a dance.

Far from joyous, as may be imagined, were the feelings of the queen of Hungary and archduchess of Austria at being robbed of the province which she considered the "fairest jewel in her crown." Maria Theresa was not the woman to take lightly a blow like this; piety toward her father's memory, if nothing else, made it a sacred duty to her to maintain his possessions intact. And she was possessed of every quality that could rouse her people to risk all in her defence; men praised her lovely voice, her dramatic abilities, her grace, her tact, her skill with the bow and arrow, her horsemanship, her fluency in languages. "Oh, if she were only a man, with just the qualities she actually possesses," sighed old Chancellor Sinzendorf to the English envoy, Robinson. On two occasions the Hungarians were roused by her to a perfect fervor of enthusiasm: once when she appeared in their Diet, accompanied by her child, and pleaded for their aid; and again when, at her coronation, she rode up the Mount of Defiance and swung her sword to the four winds of heaven as a challenge to all her enemies.

Her husband, on the other hand, was almost universally

Personality of Maria Theresa.

despised. Four years before, as generalissimo of all the
Austrian forces, he had failed to gain credit or renown in
the Turkish war that had ended so miserably with the
Peace of Belgrade; the bitterest and most hateful complaints were later brought against him. His wife, though
devoted to him, was not blind to his faults; there were
times in these wars with Frederick when she begged and
pleaded with him not to take a command. "I at last took
refuge," she once wrote to her sister, "in our usual resources of caresses and tears; but of what effect are they
on a husband of nine years' standing? . . . At last I
became very angry, which served me so well that both he
and I were taken ill."

Almost immediately, on her own accession, Maria had
insisted that Francis be declared coregent; and it was to
him, as we have seen, that Frederick's envoys directed
themselves. In return for the coveted province, they
offered every advantage of alliance and friendship — support against all enemies, the Prussian vote at the impending imperial election, even a large sum of money. The
grand duke on the whole was firm, and took a lofty tone.
"Rather the Turks before Vienna," he cried out, "or the
surrender of the Netherlands to France, or any concession
to Bavaria and Saxony, than the abandonment of Silesia."
On two separate occasions, however, when Francis had
just made utterances that sounded somewhat more conciliatory, there came a light knock at the door, and the
queen appeared with an innocent question. The envoys
were at last dismissed with the haughty remark, "Go
home to your master and tell him that, so long as a single
one of his soldiers remains in Silesia, we have not a word
to say!" It was in vain that Frederick finally offered to
content himself with a part, instead of the whole, of
Silesia; in vain that he tried to win the support of the

Austrian councillors by the promise of enormous bribes.
All offers were scornfully and categorically refused. The
"woman with the heart of a king" remained obdurate, in
spite of her desperate circumstances.

For the present, Austria's expected allies had failed to
make their appearance. In Russia, indeed, amid palace
revolutions like those of the most benighted Oriental
monarchy, a party came to the fore that was distinctly
hostile to Prussia; and Podewils, when he heard of the
fall of Frederick's friend, the prime minister, Münnich,
wrote to his master, "Pandora's box is opened; we are
entering into the most terrible crisis that ever impended
over the house of Brandenburg." But Podewils was
always over anxious. "Gently, gently," Frederick had
been obliged to say to him shortly before, "you are get-
ting too excited." Again, on another occasion, "I am
sorry to have to tell you that I don't know a more chicken-
hearted man than you." Russia, as it turned out, had
enough to do to attend to her own troubled affairs, and
the same was true of England, which had more real sympathy with Maria Theresa, and, on account of Hanoverian
jealousies, more real hatred of Frederick than any other
power. "We must clip this prince's wings," said George
II. to the Polish-Saxon envoy; "he is too dangerous for
both of us;" but there were more factors to be reckoned
with in England than the mere will of the king. And
Saxony, though dreading above all things the aggrandizement of her Prussian neighbor, and in every way secretly
conspiring against Frederick, was in too weak hands to
accomplish much; her elector, from the first, offended Austria by his rapacious demands for eventual compensation.

Frederick's own determined attitude did as much as
anything to keep outsiders at bay and to give his first
encounter at arms the form of a gigantic duel with Aus-

Austrian
sympa-
thizers.

tria. "I shall perish rather than give up my project," he said to the English envoy, Guy Dickens; "the other powers need not think that I am to be intimidated by threats. . . . If the worst comes to the worst I shall join with France and beat and bite and devastate in all directions!"

Austrian delays.

As for Maria Theresa, many a weary day passed before she was able to despatch an army to Silesia; she could do nothing to hinder the fall of Glogau, which surrendered, after a desperate storm, to young Leopold of Dessau. Frederick in the meantime had had narrow escapes from attempts on his life; once, when he himself chanced to have ridden ahead, his carriage was shot at and two persons in it killed. An Austrian who was captured declared that he had been hired by the Grand Duke of Lorraine to assassinate the king; and Frederick, though not in the least believing this assertion, was not above making use of it for political purposes. For the world's benefit Podewils was ordered to "paint the unworthy proceedings of the Vienna court in suitable colors." The risks that he was constantly running caused the young king at this time to issue directions for the eventuality of his death or captivity. "Should I have the misfortune to be taken alive," he wrote to Podewils, "I command you unconditionally — and your head shall answer for it — that during my absence you obey none of my orders; that you serve my brother with your counsels; and that no unworthy step be taken by the state to secure my release. . . . I am only king so long as I am free." In case of his death his body was to be burned after the manner of the Romans, his ashes to be deposited in a vase at Rheinsberg, and a monument to be raised to him like that of the Horatii at Tusculum.

When the Austrians did at last cross the Giant Mountains, their coming was in the nature of a surprise. Their commander, Neipperg, in so far justified his boast of having learned the art of war under Prince Eugene, as to succeed in conducting his army quickly and safely over an unguarded pass; but soon he was obliged to send word to Vienna that "to tell the truth he had not yet decided whether to turn to the right or to the left." He could not know that Frederick was obliged to make superhuman efforts to bring together his troops, which were scattered in half a dozen different camps. The Silesians proved bad informers, and Neipperg, stationing his army at Moll-witz and the neighboring villages, was forced to remain on the defensive and await the course of events. Here at Mollwitz, Frederick determined to attack him, although, in spite of its being the month of April, the snow lay two feet deep upon the ground. His infantry was superior in numbers to that of the Austrians, whose cavalry, on the other hand, was stronger.

Mollwitz was one of those battles on the result of which everything depended; not only did alliances hang in the balance, but the enemy, if successful, could have barred the way to Breslau and Berlin, which were Frederick's bases of supplies. And the result seemed very doubtful. The Prussian troops, thoroughly as they were exercised in all the arts of the parade ground, were utterly unused to real war; before the crashing cavalry charge of the Austrian generals, Römer and Berlichingen, their line was pierced in several places, and Schulenburg, whose slowness in taking his position had given the enemy their advantage, was mortally wounded while trying to retrieve his error. To add to the confusion the second battle line, seeing nothing but Austrian cavalry before them, fired into the rear of their own first line. On the verge of despair, Frederick sent one of his lieutenants to the old Dessauer with the news that the battle was lost; he himself, by the advice of Schwerin, — who, indeed, had not yet abandoned hope, — left the field with a few followers and rode through the gathering darkness to Oppeln. Here he fell in with Austrian hussars, and nothing but the extraordinary speed of his horse saved him from capture.

Victory snatched from defeat.

Not until two o'clock the next morning, did Frederick learn that he had fled from the most brilliant of victories. Schwerin, after a peremptory order to young Leopold of Dessau to stop the suicidal firing of his men, had ridden up to the standard of the first battalion of the guards, had ordered the music to play for an attack, and then, with the whole right wing, had fallen upon the Austrian infantry. His muskets were better than those of the enemy, while the iron ramrods enabled his men to load and fire more quickly. The Austrian foot-soldiers were soon taking refuge one behind the other; while the cavalry skulked far in the rear, refusing to advance even though General Berlichingen, in his rage and despair, clove the skulls of two of his men and swept several from their horses with his sword. The last great act of the battle of Mollwitz was an advance of the whole Prussian left wing, at double-quick time and with an absolute precision that would have gladdened the heart of Frederick William I. and justified all his minute care. Never in his life, wrote one of the enemy's own officers, had he seen anything so superb. The tables were completely turned, and Neipperg was soon in full retreat. In his own account of this battle, Frederick speaks of his infantry as "Cæsars and heroes," but of his cavalry as "not worth the devil's taking"; while his own absence from the field is too bitter a memory even to find mention.

The French alliance.

While Austria was recuperating her bruised and beaten forces, Frederick had time to attend to the matter of alliances. His camp at Mollwitz was sought out by envoys from all the powers; it was immediately evident how much higher he had risen in the general scale of estimation. The fate of Europe hung on his decision; for Belle-Isle, the French envoy, had appeared, with all the pomp and magnificence of a reigning prince, to advocate a scheme for the thorough despoliation of Austria. Her provinces were to go to pay the electors for discarding the traditions of three centuries and putting a Wittelsbach on the throne of the empire. Frederick wavered long, coquetting with England; but at last, by a treaty signed at Breslau on June 4, 1741, accepted the French programme. In a number of secret articles, France guaranteed to him Lower Silesia, with Breslau, and promised not only to vigorously prosecute the war on her own account, but to assure the non-interference of Russia by stirring up Sweden to war against her. In spite of dissensions between Belle-Isle and his chief, Cardinal Fleury, an allied French and Bavarian army was soon in the field, and succeeded in taking Linz, the capital of Upper Austria. It would have been easy to fall upon Vienna, which was ill garrisoned and ill fortified; and Frederick did his utmost to induce the French to undertake the task. He burned with impatience, he wrote to Belle-Isle, to embrace him as victor before the gates of the city. "This Austria must be struck to earth," he said to Valory; "incurable wounds must be inflicted upon her before she is in a condition to parry the blows!" But Belle-Isle preferred to march on Prague—ostensibly from military considerations, but in reality because the French feared to do too much for their emperor elect, Charles Albert of Bavaria. "If we make the elector master of Vienna, we shall no longer be master of the elector," a French diplomat is said to have remarked. Frederick found that his own counsel weighed for nothing.

The truce
of Klein-
Schnellen-
dorf.

Prague fell through the tardiness and bad generalship of the Grand Duke Francis; and Maria's situation was growing more and more desperate, when a voice called to her, as it were, from the deep, and a hand was stretched out from the least expected of quarters. Frederick had once said to Podewils, "If honesty will help us, we will be honest men; if duplicity is needed, then let us be rogues." Now, discontented with the French proceedings, aware that it was to his advantage not to have a protracted war, anxious, above all things, to get Neipperg's army, — which was safely under the shadow of the fortress of Neisse, — out of Silesia, he closed, through the medium of the English Hyndford, the secret agreement with Austria, known as the truce of Klein-Schnellendorf (October 9, 1741). Everything was done to deceive the French. Valory, who was in the Prussian camp at the time, knew nothing of what was going on. A number of articles concerned themselves with measures by which appearances were to be preserved: there were to be several skirmishes and a sham siege of Neisse, which was to capitulate at the end of fifteen days.

The
Emperor
Charles
VII.

Comment is superfluous when delving into this slough of intrigue; many a diplomatic move, especially in the eighteenth century, will not bear the test of plain morality. Small consolation that in this matter one country was as bad as another! But, even from a political standpoint, the truce of Klein-Schnellendorf was a false move on Frederick's part; for the benefit to Maria Theresa of having Neipperg's army for use against the French, far outweighed the disadvantage of losing the one fortress of Neisse. Frederick, indeed, on the pretext that the promise of secrecy had been violated, soon repudiated his agreement and occupied the Austrian province of Glatz; but from this time on the fortunes of Maria Theresa were on the mend.

The French were dislodged from Linz; the Austrians were able to carry the war into Charles Albert's own dominions, and, in the very days when, as Charles VII., the elector was being crowned emperor of the Romans at Frankfort, his Bavarian possessions were wrested from him. A witticism against his field marshal, Count Törring, to the effect that he was like a drum because only heard from when beaten, went the rounds of friend and foe. A medal was struck with two images of Charles himself, the one as elector, with "Aut Cæsar aut nihil," the other as emperor, with "Et Cæsar et nihil."

Meanwhile the Austrian commander, Prince Charles of Lorraine, had come upon the Prussians at the village of Chotusitz, not far from the Bohemian town of Czaslau; but, through an error of judgment, had allowed Frederick time to unite with the young Dessauer and to draw up his army in good order. Then, indeed, the Austrians fought like tigers and carried the struggle into the narrow village streets, from which, by setting fire to the straw-roofed houses, they finally dislodged the Prussian occupants. Twice Frederick's wavering troops had to be urged back to their duty: once by a brave officer, who seized a banner and threw himself into the breach; again, "in the name of God and of the king," by a fiery young field chaplain. The Austrians attributed their own final defeat to the fact that their cavalry had stopped to plunder the Prussian camp. *The battle of Chotusitz.*

"Who could have foretold," wrote Frederick a few days later to his friend Jordan, "that Providence would choose a poet to overthrow the European system and cross the calculations of kings!" Yet in reality there was little of pride or exultation in his heart. He had once more determined to make a private peace with Austria, even on less advantageous terms than he had demanded before the battle. At that time, he had asked for two Bohemian counties; these Maria Theresa still refused to relinquish, preferring, as she said, to perish in the ruins of Vienna. "If the gates of hell should open," she would not give up Königgrätz. By the treaty of Breslau, signed in July, 1742, she saved for herself not only these districts, but even a small part of Upper Silesia.

The Peace of Breslau.

The reason for Frederick's second defection from the French was, as before, their arrogance and uselessness as allies; in these very days the Duke of Broglie's incapacity had brought about a disastrous defeat — a new "imbroglio," said his enemies. But the young king's conscience was not clear; it was in vain that he armed himself with a sardonic smile when talking to Valory, and spoke of the "little goading speeches" of the Parisians as parrot-like utterances which they themselves did not understand. He really did feel sore and sensitive, especially when the sentiments once expressed in his writing against Machiavelli were ruthlessly submitted to the test of his own conduct. He went so far as to write a pamphlet in self-defence — which Podewils would not allow him to publish — and a letter to Fleury, in which he threw the whole blame upon Broglie. He likened him to a Penelope, who was undoing all his, Frederick's, work: "Can I be held responsible for Broglie's not being a Turenne? Out of a night owl I cannot make an eagle."

Having secured by the Treaty of Breslau a territory equal to one-third of the whole former Prussian state, and having been recognized by the voice of his people as "the Great," Frederick could afford to stand aside and watch the European war. With feelings far from pleasurable he saw Austria extricate herself from her difficulties, make favorable treaties and alliances, and gain military advantages. His contempt for the French grew to withering

scorn when he heard that Maillebois had abandoned an
attempt to relieve Prague; that Belle-Isle, in consequence,
had been obliged, in the dead of winter, to make a disastrous retreat; and that the main French army of seventy
thousand men had been pushed out of Bavaria almost
without striking a blow. "I must confess," Frederick
wrote, "that bad as was my opinion of old Broglie, his
present conduct exceeds all expectations in the way of
cowardice and folly." After the battle of Dettingen, in
which the so-called Pragmatic army, consisting largely of
English, defeated the Duke de Noailles; and which was
considered in London so brilliant a victory that Handel
composed a *Te Deum* in its honor, Frederick declared that
he never again wished to hear the name of a Frenchman.

England, on account of her own enmity to France, had
become the stanchest supporter of Maria Theresa. The
"firebrand," Lord Carteret, had introduced an entirely new
spirit into her policy, and showed activity in all directions.
It was largely his doing that Austria, in September 1743,
signed with the king of Sardinia the Treaty of Worms, by
which, in return for land cessions in Lombardy, Charles
Emmanuel agreed to fight the French with forty-five thousand men. Frederick noted with alarm that this Worms
agreement, — which guaranteed Austria's possessions on the
basis of former treaties, — passed over in silence the recent
Breslau provisions. Maria Theresa was becoming aggressive; she spoke openly of "the unfree election by which
the elector of Bavaria (Frederick's protégé) is said to have
become emperor," and sent a protest to the Diet to the
effect that the Bohemian vote belonged to her and had
not been properly cast. The interference of the English,
too, seemed to Frederick full of menace. He wished, he
declared to Podewils, that the devil would take his uncle,
George II. "Listen, my lord," he said to Hyndford, "I

The second
Silesian
War.

don't care what happens to the French, but I shall not allow the emperor to be ruined or dethroned." A treaty, concluded between Saxony and Austria, in January, 1744, finally determined him to reënter the arena; and, what was more, not to withdraw from it empty-handed. By an agreement made at Frankfort he secured the help of the young Elector Palatine and the Landgrave of Hesse-Cassel, and then so far conquered his own repugnances as to sue for an alliance with France, — even condescending to write a personal letter to the Duchess of Châteauroux, the all-powerful mistress of Louis XV. Largely by her influence, a treaty was drawn up by which the prospective spoils were apportioned between Prussia, France, and the emperor. Louis XV.'s share was to be some coveted fortresses in the Netherlands; Frederick's, three Bohemian counties, in addition to the whole of Silesia; Charles Albert's, the rest of Bohemia.

Failure of Frederick's Bohemian campaign.

Thus the struggle began anew. As general of the emperor, Frederick demanded and enforced the right of free passage through Saxon territory; made a dash for Prague, which he captured without difficulty; and then pushed farther south, with some thoughts of reaching Vienna. Maria's army was in the midst of a victorious advance into Alsace when the news came of the fresh invasion. Prince Charles hastily recrossed the Rhine, and now all the worthlessness of the French as allies once more came to light. Regard for one of the first rules of joint warfare should have led them to hold fast the Austrian army, which was retreating from them and which their own forces outnumbered as two to one; instead, they allowed it to return unmolested, while their own troops marched off to the Netherlands. Frederick, as may be imagined, was soon in sore straits — the more so as twenty-two thousand Saxons marched to Maria Theresa's

aid.   Far from carrying out his threat of "setting his foot
on the throat of his enemy" in Vienna, he was reduced to
a strict defensive and was compelled to retreat to Silesia
as best he could.   Gladly enough would he have risked
an engagement; but the policy of the Austrians, now led
by the gifted Traun, whom even Frederick acknowledged
as at this time his own superior, was to delay and to
annoy.   As post after post was relinquished, as provisions became scarcer and scarcer on account of the
hostile attitude of the Bohemian peasants, a demoralization spread among the soldiers such as a royal Prussian
army had never yet known.   The Austrians maintained
that they had actually counted nineteen thousand deserters; and certain it is that the army of eighty thousand
men soon dwindled to half its original size.   Maria Theresa
felt sure of the future, and issued a proclamation to the
Silesians, promising them speedy liberation from the "unbearable yoke" under which they were languishing.

As for Frederick, who blamed himself greatly for many
of the misfortunes that had occurred, and confessed frankly
that "no general had ever committed so many blunders in
a single season," he was determined to strike some signal
blow, to risk *le tout pour le tout*, and to return to Berlin
as victor or not at all.   Strangely enough, the image of
Maria Theresa, fearless among overwhelming dangers,
rose before him and steeled him to new efforts: "Think
of this woman who did not despair when the enemy stood
before Vienna and flooded her richest provinces," he wrote
to Podewils.

Frederick had purposely left the passes of the Giant   The battle
Mountains unguarded, in the hope that the enemy would   of Hohen-
cross them and attempt to recover Silesia; but he was   friedberg.
hardly prepared for the haste with which the Hungarian
pandours and hussars swarmed into the land.   He was

completely cut off from a part of his forces, which the
Margrave of Schwedt commanded in Jägerndorf ; and
only a desperate ride of General Ziethen to bring Schwedt
his instructions, and a splendid return march of Otto
Schwerin through the midst of the enemy, prevented a
grave catastrophe.   "Kiss Schwerin for me a thousand
times," wrote Frederick to the margrave, "and tell him
that as long as I live I will never forget his bravery and
steadfastness."

The Austrians had underrated the Prussian forces.
Taking the failure to guard the passes for a sign of weakness, they determined to attack Frederick at Hohenfriedberg, not far from Schweidnitz.   "There can be no God in
heaven if we do not win this battle," said Prince Charles
of Lorraine to one of his adjutants.   Free from anxiety,
the Austrian leader — the man who had felt so superior to
Traun that he had forced him out of the command — lay
quietly down to sleep within sight of the Prussian camp,
having been assured by his scouts that the attack might
safely be postponed until the following day.   But, leaving his fires burning and his tents standing, Frederick,
with his whole army, stole softly out into the night and
took up a more favorable position.   At early dawn the
Saxon contingents were attacked and put to flight before the Austrians were ready to begin their fire; Prince
Charles's right wing was easily thrown into confusion,
and a magnificent charge of the Baireuth dragoons, under
Gessler, completed its ruin.   Sixty-six standards were
captured and twenty-one battalions routed — numbers
which, by Frederick's command, were later incorporated in
the Gessler coat of arms.   The rest of the beaten army retreated as best it could, leaving sixteen thousand men on
the field and losing nearly nine thousand stragglers and
deserters.   "Never did the old Romans do anything more

brilliant," wrote Frederick to Podewils; and then set to work to compose a commemorative march, which is played in the Prussian army to this day.

Frederick hoped to have achieved from Hohenfriedberg "a good peace and a long rest," but he was doomed to disappointment. Maria Theresa was by no means reduced to desperate straits. She still had the Saxons, English, and Dutch on her side ; and when, in these days, the Emperor Charles VII. died, she came to terms with the new Bavarian elector by the Treaty of Füssen. The French conveniently confined their efforts to the Netherlands; where, indeed, they had succeeded in winning the brilliant victory of Fontenoy. Maria's own courage was as unbroken as ever; even, she declared, though she were sure of making peace with Frederick on the following morning, she would risk a battle the evening before. The satisfaction was hers of having her husband declared emperor at Frankfort; and, in the festivities that followed, she remained in the background and refused to be crowned, that he might have the more honor. With Saxony, she formed a bold plan for striking a blow at the heart of Frederick's possessions and for despoiling him of parts of Brandenburg. Russia, too, was to be included in the arrangement, and to be allowed to cede to Poland certain provinces of East Prussia.

New victories of Frederick frustrated the tempting plan. He had been attacked at the village of Sohr, not far from the Bohemian border, by an Austrian army nearly double the size of his own — the enemy trying the same manœuvre that he himself had so successfully executed at Hohenfriedberg, and taking a new position under cover of the night. Only with the rising sun did he see the extent of the danger, and the impossibility either of retreating or of remaining in camp. There was no alternative but to

The battle of Sohr.

form in line of battle under the heavy fire of the Austrian batteries, and then to storm the heights on which they stood. The deserted camp was plundered by hordes of Hungarians, Frederick's horses and dogs, his clothes, his books, and even his flute were carried off; but none the less his courage and coolness won the day. The enemy were driven from height to height with terrific losses. He was "beaten, yes, well beaten," Prince Charles confessed in a letter to his brother. The prophecy of King George of England that, "the king of Prussia would do more in one day than Prince Charles in six months," had been richly fulfilled.

The battle of Kesselsdorf.

But still more decisive than Sohr, was an action that took place a few weeks later at Kesselsdorf, near Dresden. On hearing of the plan to dismember Brandenburg, Frederick had sent an army into Saxony, intrusting the supreme command to Leopold of Dessau — who undertook it unwillingly, complaining of his age and infirmities. The old companion in arms of Marlborough and Prince Eugene, himself the hero of twenty-one battles and twenty-seven sieges, had been out of conceit with the whole Silesian war, in which his advice had not been freely asked. But Frederick urged him on to his duty; and when his movements seemed too slow, did not hesitate to reprimand him in the sternest manner. "My field marshal," he wrote, "is the only person who either can not, or will not, understand my plain commands." He fairly goaded him into an engagement, knowing that all depended on frustrating a union between the Saxons and the Austrian army that had been defeated at Sohr. The "old Dessauer" did finally rise to the occasion; his last fight was one of the grandest he had conducted in all his half-century of service. With 22,000 men, he stormed the heights at Kesselsdorf, on which stood 34,000 Saxons — while Prince

Charles's army of 46,000 men had advanced to a point only five miles off. As Frederick was ready by this time to unite with his victorious general there was nothing for the Austrians to do but to sue for peace. They expected, indeed, a hard diplomatic struggle; Maria's envoy, Harrach, had, he said, "wished to tear out his eyes because, through negotiations with this Tamerlane, he would be compelled to forge for his mistress chains of everlasting servitude."

But Frederick showed himself remarkably lenient; by the Dresden Peace, which was signed on Christmas morning, 1745, he gained neither more nor less than he had enjoyed by the Peace of Breslau, except that Saxony had to pay a war indemnity of a million thalers.

The Peace of Dresden.

For Maria Theresa, indeed, although Frederick acknowledged her husband as emperor, this second renunciation was more painful than the first had been, and would never have been signed had her instructions reached her envoy, Harrach, in time. In 1742 she had seen her way to wresting Bavaria from Charles VII.; now, while abandoning Silesia, she had to be content to part with a million and a quarter of Germans with no compensation to balance the preponderating Slavic elements in her heterogeneous domains. Austria's rôle as the first German power had been played to the end.

"Happy are they," wrote Frederick a few weeks after the conclusion of the Dresden Peace, "happy are they who, having secured their own safety, can tranquilly look upon the embarrassment and anxiety of others." And again, in the following year, "I continually bless my present situation, hearing the storm rage and seeing the lightning split the finest oaks, without being myself affected. It is a sensible man who keeps quiet and learns moderation by experience. Ambition in the long run is a virtue for fools, a guide that leads us astray and lands us in an abyss hidden by flowers."

Once more a peace with Frederick meant anything but a season of quiet for Maria Theresa. For two years and more her war with France continued, and Marshal Maurice de Saxe, one of the numerous irregular progeny of Augustus the Strong, succeeded in wresting from the incapable Charles of Lorraine every single stronghold in the Netherlands, save Luxemburg and Limburg. Even the presence in camp of Louis XV. himself could not, as Frederick with biting sarcasm declared, prevent the progress of the French arms. The pitched battle of Rocoux, fought in October, 1746, ended in the total defeat of the allies. In Italy, it is true, the Austrians were more fortunate; while the English were able, in America and on the ocean, to find vulnerable points in the armor of their enemies. For the campaign of 1748, preparations had been made on a hitherto unheard-of scale. The forces in the Netherlands were to be raised to a total of 156,000 men, while 90,000 Austrians and Sardinians were to operate in Italy, and a corps of 50,000 Russians in the English pay was to advance to the Rhine. But, before all these armies could come into action, the general desire for peace and the progress of diplomacy had led to the summoning of the Congress of Aix-la-Chapelle; where, in spite of the reluctance of Austria, — which alone was called upon to make serious sacrifices, — a peace was finally arranged. The French gave up their conquests in the Netherlands, and Maria Theresa ceded to Don Philip of Spain, Louis XV.'s nephew, the duchies of Parma and Piacenza.

Although a separate clause in the Treaty of Aix — forced through by England and France in the hope of securing the future peace of Europe — guaranteed to Frederick the possession of Silesia, it is doubtful if in her heart of hearts

Maria Theresa ever really for a moment acquiesced in her fate. "She forgets that she is queen, and breaks into tears like a woman, whenever she sees a Silesian," an English envoy had written in 1743. Of the efforts she now made to increase her revenues and to place the administration of her lands on a firmer basis we cannot here speak. Her surest hope for the future seemed to lie in the acquisition of strong allies, and in this she was helped by the natural isolation of Prussia and by the personal unpopularity of Frederick. France could not forgive him for twice deserting her cause and making his own advantageous terms with the enemy; at the Congress of Aix the French envoy-in-chief, Severin, had spoken of him as a "filigree king," as a regular *fripon ;* and, on his return to Paris, had refused to visit the Prussian ambassador. As for Russia, the Czarina had been on the point of invading Frederick's lands when the battle of Kesselsdorf turned the scale in his favor; even after the Peace of Dresden Elizabeth had offered to furnish ninety thousand men if Austria would resume the war. This wild, passionate Czarina, who spent her nights in drunken orgies, and who was egged on by Frederick's bitter enemy, Bestucheff, hated the Prussian king with an unholy hate. Sarcastic and malicious enough were the remarks he had often made about her; and Bestucheff, who was at the same time her prime minister and the father-in-law of her unacknowledged daughter, found it to his interest to have his agents carefully retail them in her ear. Two lackeys who had left Frederick's service for that of the Russian court were among the tale-bearers, as were also the English and French ambassadors. More self-respecting men, indeed — like Count Kayserling, the Russian envoy to Berlin — would not be concerned in the foul business, and flatly refused to obey the orders which bade them act as scavengers for stray bits of personal gossip and slander

In the year after the Treaty of Aix, an attempt, on Bes-tucheff's part, to set aside the succession of Frederick's brother-in-law, the crown prince of Sweden, — who, in-deed, under altered circumstances, had had Russia herself to thank for his elevation, — led to the very verge of a Prus-sian-Russian war. "My Swedish sister awaits a visit this year which will not be very agreeable to her," wrote Fred-erick in the spring of 1749; and again, to Frederike Ulrica herself, "We must do our best to keep on our guard and to be prepared for the worst that can happen." His energy in mobilizing his forces did much to avert the catastrophe; and Elizabeth, finding that France was inclined to help Sweden, and that Maria Theresa would only join in the struggle on conditions dictated by her own interest in Silesia, desisted from her warlike plans at the eleventh hour. But Frederick knew well that the danger was only temporarily averted; four or five years of peace, he de-clared, and he should find himself once more attacked. He little knew what a general avalanche the Russian-Austrian intrigues — aided by that French-English struggle which had started with the American boundary disputes and was resolving itself, in Europe, into a fight for Hanover — were to bring down about his ears.

In the interval the world was to see a shifting of alli-ances which belongs to the seven wonders of diplomatic history. Austria, for two hundred years, had been the constant enemy of France. The Emperor Charles V. had fought against Francis I. and Henry II.; Ferdinand II. and Ferdinand III. against Richelieu's generals; Leo-pold I., Joseph I., and Charles VI. in repeated wars against Louis XIV.; Maria Theresa herself, for seven years, against the present king. To Prussia, on the other hand, from the days when Frederick William I. broke off the double marriage project and expressed his opinions

so freely about George II., England had been an object of
hatred.   In the Austrian succession war, George's subsidies, his armies, even his own mediocre military talents,
had been at the service of Maria Theresa.   Even after the
Peace of Aix it had more than once come to the verge of
a rupture with Frederick: the latter, in 1751, in spite of
Podewils's frightened "What will your uncle say?" had
chosen one of the heads of the Jacobites, a man whom the
English government had pronounced a rebel and an outlaw, to be Prussia's official representative in Paris.   And
when England, which, in the previous war, had captured
Prussian vessels carrying French merchandise, persistently refused compensation, Frederick, in 1752, retaliated by retaining the interest on the Silesian debt, which
an English syndicate had assumed.   In London the excitement was intense; the wildest rumors gained ground, and
active preparations were made for the defence of Hanover
— which, it was believed, would be immediately attacked.
Indeed, in the following year, when, after the defeat of
George Washington at Fort Duquesne, the prospect of a
long and bitter struggle between England and France
became assured, Frederick urged this very measure on the
French ambassador, Latouche.   "That is the surest means
of making this —— [George II.] change his tune," he
said; employing a "cavalier-like epithet," with regard to
his uncle, which Latouche found too strong to report to
his own government.

And yet, after all, toward the autumn of 1755, Frederick began to veer round to the side of England: his
reasons for so abrupt a change of policy being, firstly,
that the French expected too much of him — that, in fact,
they wished "to pile upon their allies the whole burden
of the war and keep their own hands free"; and, secondly,
the circumstance that Russia was making dangerous over-

The Convention of Westminster.

tures to England. The time had not yet come when Frederick could face the idea of having Prussia, with its scanty population of five millions, carry on a war against three great powers, with only one single slippery ally like France. It was probably true, what Lord Hyndford had once said, that he feared Russia more than God. In proportion, therefore, as the Russian-English relations grew warm or cold, he regulated his conduct toward George II.; well knowing that, by her position, Prussia was better able than any other power to accomplish the English king's desire, and insure the safety of his Hanoverian possessions.

Finally, early in 1756, after Russia had already agreed to furnish seventy thousand men, who were to be supported by English subsidies, Frederick closed an alliance with George. The Convention of Westminster provided for firm peace and friendship between Prussia and England, and stipulated that each should turn against any enemy attacking the lands of the other. A united army was to oppose any foreign power that should presume to force its way on to German ground. This agreement, this one little stroke of the pen, Frederick hoped, would reduce "the queen of Hungary to madness, Saxony to insignificance, and Russia to despair."

The first Treaty of Versailles.

Parallel with these English-Prussian negotiations had gone those of Maria Theresa with France. The bait offered to the latter power was a part of the Austrian Netherlands for Louis XV.'s nephew, — who would then be asked to renounce Parma and Piacenza, — and the support of another relative of the French king, Prince Conti, as candidate for the Polish throne. In return for these favors, the French court was to help the empress to gratify the ruling passion of her life, and reduce Prussia to the limits it had occupied before the Thirty Years' War. The hated

king was to become once more a mere margrave. All that
was needed was French subsidies; fighters enough could
be gained by allowing Frederick's natural enemies to rend
and rive at the body of his doomed state. Saxony was to
have Magdeburg; Sweden, Stettin and Further Pomerania; the Palatinate, Cleves and Mark; the Franconian
Circle, Ansbach and Baireuth.

The news that Frederick had signed the Treaty of Westminster found France still undecided, but soon weighed
down the balance in Austria's favor. Kaunitz, the dashing new minister, whose progressive policy was so hated
at Vienna by all save the empress herself, had done his
work well at the Parisian court. No means had been left
untried of influencing the weak voluptuary who sat on
the throne of the Bourbons. Kaunitz and his successor in
Paris, Starhemberg, had succeeded in winning the favor of
Madame de Pompadour, — the graceful and beautiful, but
coarse-minded and unscrupulous, mistress of the king. It
is not true — at least the empress herself indignantly
denied the rumor — that Maria Theresa went so far as to
write to the Pompadour a personal letter and to address
her as "sister" and "cousin"; nor is it true, in spite of
anecdotes which seem to prove the contrary, that Frederick had systematically neglected this person of ignominious birth. But certainly the empress had sent presents
and polite messages, while Frederick in some way or other
had incurred the Pompadour's dislike. The latter boasted
herself, and probably with right, that the preliminary
treaties signed at Versailles, in May, 1756, were essentially her own work. To be sure, Austria had not as yet
gained all that she desired. The treaty was merely defensive; and Louis XV. objected to depriving Prussia of
more than Silesia, besides desiring the whole of the
Netherlands for France.

Frederick
learns the
designs of
his enemies.

Frederick had hoped that her own treaty with England would prevent Russia from making war on a power that had just become the closest ally of the English, but he was mistaken. Elizabeth was more eager to attack him than was even Maria Theresa. When the latter's envoy broached the subject the Czarina replied that she had been on the very point of suggesting an offensive alliance. Her disappointment was great when Austria, for the reason that France had not yet been won for an aggressive policy, determined to postpone the campaign until the following spring. Bestucheff, indeed, was not so warlike as his mistress. Elizabeth was ill with strange maladies. It seemed not unlikely that she would soon die; and regard for the "rising sun" prompted the wary minister not to strike too hostile an attitude either toward Prussia or toward England.

Frederick was well informed of all the schemes that were being forged against him: he had in his pay a member of the Saxon chancery — a trusted member, who supplied him with copies of the most secret documents. From various directions, too, he received words of warning and advice; nor did he scruple to have the Berlin post-office open letters on their way from St. Petersburg to England and Holland. At last a Dutch ambassador, whose correspondence had been read, but only half understood, volunteered the positive information that Austria was preparing to put eighty thousand, Russia one hundred and fifty thousand, men in the field. On one point at least Frederick was fully determined: he would not meet his fate like a lamb led to the slaughter. When hostilities should open he meant to make the first move. "There is no help for it," he declared to Mitchell, the English envoy; "if this lady" — pointing to a portrait of Maria Theresa which hung on the wall — "wishes war, she shall have it soon." "Look into my face," he had said a moment before to the same personage; "does my nose look like one at which fingers can be wagged? By God, I will not stand it!" Mitchell had answered, in a manner not displeasing to the king, that indeed patience and submissiveness were not exactly to be counted among the qualities for which he was distinguished.

In order to bring matters to a climax, Frederick despatched one messenger after another to Vienna with categorical questions. First, what was the meaning of the movements of the troops in Bohemia and Moravia; were these preparations being made with a view to an attack upon himself? Maria's answer was purposely evasive and unsatisfactory; she wished to provoke Frederick and make him the aggressor; only then could she hope for the full benefit of her treaty with France. Hard and fast on the heels of the first envoy, came a second, requesting a straightforward answer as to whether the empress intended to attack the king of Prussia either in the present or the following year. A few days later, Frederick wrote on the margin of his military instructions to Duke Ferdinand of Brunswick: "The answer has come and is good for nothing." For the third time, he sent to say that he was certain now of the evil intentions of the Vienna court; his troops were already on the march, but he would order them to turn back if the empress would give him the assurance he had latterly demanded.

An ultimatum sent to Vienna.

One imperative duty Frederick felt called upon to perform before throwing his forces against the main Austrian army: the Saxon court which, as he knew from the testimony of its own archives, had tried to egg on all the other powers against him, and which, beyond a doubt, meant to follow Bestucheff's advice and take part in the struggle "so soon as the rider should begin to waver in the saddle,"

Frederick's occupation of Saxony.

was first to be rendered harmless. Only by occupying the electorate could proper communications be kept up with Berlin; in no other way could the forces Frederick meant to throw into Bohemia and Moravia be secured from ugly surprises. The only misfortune was that the cowardly king, Augustus III., did not succeed in making his escape from the land. The commander of the body-guards had been asked if he could guarantee that no spent ball should strike the royal person; and, on his giving a negative answer, the attempt was abandoned, and Augustus, with his army, withdrew to an almost impregnable position in Saxon Switzerland, between Pirna and the Königstein. Prussian troops marched into Dresden, and, in spite of the fierce resistance of the queen, Maria Josepha, who actually threw her person in the way, forced open the door of the room in the palace where the archives were kept, selected three bags full of compromising documents, and sent them off to Berlin to be published for the benefit of Europe. An ultimatum was sent to the commanding general, Arnim, to the effect that the whole Saxon army must take the oath of allegiance to the Prussian king. To Arnim's objection that no example of such a thing could be found in history, "Oh, yes, there can," Frederick answered; "and even if there could not, I would like you to know that I pride myself on being somewhat original."

Capitulation of the Saxons.

An Austrian army, under General Browne, who proposed to relieve the Saxons in Pirna, was met on the left bank of the Elbe, at Lobositz; and a battle took place among the steep vine-clad hills (October 1, 1756). The Prussian troops, to use Frederick's own expression, performed "miracles of bravery," but the enemy, too, proved that they were "no longer the old Austrians." The chief advantage of the slight victory was that the beleaguered army lost hope and was soon brought to submission, the capitulation being signed on the 15th of October. The officers were released on parole and the common soldiers incorporated in the Prussian army, — whereby the fatal mistake was made, as Frederick himself confessed, of not dissolving the regiments and apportioning the men among loyal battalions, but of simply placing them, as they were, under Prussian commanders. No wonder they deserted by thousands, and thus belied the expectation that, being Protestants, they would serve more willingly under Frederick than under their own Catholic king. On the whole, this Saxon campaign had been unfortunate. Seven precious weeks had been wasted in starving out a camp that could only have been taken with great loss of life; and the great advantage of keeping the members of the coalition as far apart as possible had thus been forfeited. Now, the season was so advanced and so uncommonly cold that nothing remained but to go into winter quarters, — Saxony, meanwhile, being placed completely under Prussian administration, and the taxes of her subjects going to the uses of her conqueror.

The king of France had heard the news of the humiliation of his friend, the king of Poland, with rage and with oaths of vengeance. Yet Louis XV. wavered long before committing himself finally to Maria Theresa's scheme of destruction. It was one year to a day from the signing of the first Versailles Treaty, before the second, offensive, one was concluded. Then, indeed, greed of Belgian land, the Pompadour's intrigues, and Louis's own ridiculous pretension to be the champion of the true religion against the assaults of a heretic and madman, induced France to go to the greatest lengths that even Austria could have desired. Instead of mere subsidies, Louis was to furnish one hundred and fifteen thousand men. Prussia was to be dismembered and the spoils divided in all directions.

The second
Treaty of
Versailles.

The very least of the demands of the allies were to include
the whole Cleves heritage, Silesia, Crossen, Magdeburg,
Halberstadt, and the share of Swedish Pomerania acquired a generation before by Frederick William I.
Maria Theresa and Elizabeth had arranged, in addition,
that Frederick should lose the very nucleus of his royal
power, — the province of East Prussia; it was to go to
Poland, which, in turn, was to cede to Russia Courland
and Semgallen. To be sure, Maria's envoy, Esterhazy,
was reminded in St. Petersburg of the homely proverb,
"Catch your hare before you skin him"; but so completely
did Frederick seem to be rushing into the toils that a little
confidence was pardonable. Russia was not only to send
an army through Poland, but her fleet was to operate in
the Baltic; while Sweden, Frederick's only hope in the
North, was now drawn into the alliance against him, and,
in return for French subsidies, agreed to furnish twenty
thousand men. Moreover, Austria, at the Diet of Ratisbon, succeeded in drawing over to her side sixty out of
eighty-six of the estates of the empire, by which majority
the Diet voted "imperial execution" against the wanton
invader of Saxony.

Frederick
isolated.

Prussia's only hope seemed to lie in the prospect of
English aid,— a prospect which, for the present at least,
proved completely illusory. England had wars to wage
in all parts of the world; and in this very year was hard
pressed both in India and in America. Frederick was
keenly alive to the perils of his situation. He likened
himself to a stag on which a "pack of kings and princes"
had been let loose, or to Orpheus pursued by Mænads —
represented by the two empresses and the Pompadour.
Once more, as in 1740, he issued the most stringent commands as to what should happen should he die or fall
into captivity; in the latter case even his own letters and

entreaties were to be disregarded. But his danger heightened instead of dulling his intelligence, and he well deserved what Napoleon Bonaparte considered "the highest praise that one can pay to his character," namely, that he "was especially great in decisive moments." In public he never repined; "the whole army reads the face of its commander," he once wrote; "a general must be like an actor." But even in his heart of hearts he seems to have possessed a steady beacon-light of hope. " *Un certo non so che*," he wrote to the Margravine of Baireuth, "seems to tell me that all will go perfectly well." And again, at the time of the last visit he was destined to make to his own capital for the space of more than six terrible years: "I have a presentiment that I shall neither be killed nor wounded; I confess, however, that, should things turn out badly, I should a hundred times prefer death to the fate that would await me. You know my enemies; you can judge what I should have to swallow in the way of humiliations!"

One great advantage Frederick possessed which outweighed much numerical superiority: he was absolute lord and master, not only of his army, but also of the resources of his land. He could, and did, make forced loans, anticipate taxes, and even inflate the currency to meet immediate needs. Every plan of the Austrians, on the other hand, had to be made with reference, not only to Charles of Lorraine, the incompetent commander-in-chief, but also to Maria Theresa, to her husband, and to a permanent war council in Vienna. And at the side of the Prussian king, himself assuredly no mean general, there stood the bravest and most experienced commander in Europe, — Curt von Schwerin, the victor of Mollwitz, once the companion in arms of a Marlborough, a Eugene, and a Charles XII. The queen of Hungary will have two "nice boys" to deal

Advantages of absolutism.

with, Frederick had said, meaning himself and Schwerin. So widespread was the latter's fame that, in 1745, Louis XV. had offered to place him in command of one of his armies. Not the least of Schwerin's merits was his zeal in attending to the needs, wants, and comforts of his soldiers, while at the same time preserving the strictest order and discipline. "Never will the army forget," wrote Frederick, sixteen years after his great general's death, "that it has been under the command of a Marshal Schwerin."

The battle near Prague.

In the enforced idleness of the winter quarters in Dresden, Frederick spent his time in studying the great campaigns of Turenne, Eugene, and Marlborough; he visited the field of Lützen, where Gustavus Adolphus had found his death. All his thoughts and energies were bent on how to *abimieren* the Austrians — to drive them into an abyss of ruin and despair before the advent of the French and the Russians. After long consultations with Schwerin and with one whom he esteemed almost as highly, Winterfeldt, he determined to make a dash at the enemy's camp near Königgrätz, — a daring resolve considering that the supplies were insufficient and that, on account of the earliness of the season, not even grass could be obtained for the horses.

The Austrians had received warning of Frederick's intention, but, in their blindness, had held the report for a ruse of war. Now, their sole alternative was to retreat to the hills near Prague, leaving behind them stores of inestimable value. They took up a strong position on the crest of the Ziscaberg, the approach of the Prussians being rendered more difficult by the steepness of the ascent, on the one side, and by the slimy and treacherous nature of the ground upon the other. But on they came, floundering through the beds of empty fish-ponds; and finally, with desperate bravery, they put the enemy to flight, mortally wounding the most capable Austrian general, Browne, and driving Prince Charles into such a panic that he fell unconscious with a spasm of the heart. But the Prussian losses, too, were terrific: fiery old Schwerin himself, who, with a cry of "This way, my children!" had seized a flag and ridden in front of his battalion, was fatally pierced by a bullet — a costly sacrifice that filled Frederick with pain, and that, to use his own words, "withered the laurels of victory." Rather, he declared, would he have lost ten thousand men.

Had the old hero lived a few days longer, he would doubtless have hindered his beloved king from one of the most disastrous steps of his life. Leaving the bulk of his army to coop up the Austrians in Prague, Frederick moved, with a small detachment, to join the Duke of Bevern, and cut off General Daun, who was marching to the city's relief. He would not believe the reports as to the strength of Daun's army, and determined to give him battle at once. When he drew up against him, near the small town of Kolin, he found himself outnumbered by two to one. Even then, the Austrians were all but driven to retreat; the day would not have been lost but for disobedience to Frederick's distinct command that one whole wing should remain in reserve. "With four fresh battalions," he declared later, "I could have won the engagement." As it was, out of all his flying soldiers he could only rally some forty men, with whom he attempted to make a charge. "Will your Majesty try to take the battery alone?" cried one of his adjutants, inducing him finally to desist from the attempt and to give the order for a general retreat. Nearly two-thirds of his infantry were dead or wounded, or prisoners in the hands of the enemy.

Never were hopes more completely crushed than by the outcome of this battle. The army before Prague would not

The defeat at Kolin.

believe the news, until they saw the dejected bearing and sunken eyes of their king. Well might the victorious enemy chant their Ambrosian hymns; and well might Maria Theresa decree rewards to her soldiers and found an order, in her own name, of which her successful general was the first recipient. Kolin decided the whole Bohemian campaign. Crestfallen to the last degree, Frederick determined to retire to Silesia; and when, at last, he rallied his army in a place of safety, some 40,000 men failed to answer to the roll-call. A corps, which he had intrusted to his brother, Augustus William, the heir apparent to the Prussian throne, had suffered terrible losses on account of the indecision and incapacity of its leader: stinging and cruel were the rebukes that Frederick administered; he could be as harsh as ever his own father had been when occasion demanded. "You may, if you like, command a harem," he wrote, "but so long as I live I will never trust you with the command over ten men!" He bade his own soldiers hold no intercourse with those which his brother had been leading. Fairly crushed, mentally and physically, the poor prince wasted away, and died broken-hearted within a few months.

The Convention of Kloster-Zeven.

It was, indeed, no time for leniency, for the general situation seemed absolutely hopeless. "In these unhappy times," wrote Frederick to D'Argens, "one needs entrails of iron and a heart of bronze." To meet nearly 100,000 Russians in East Prussia only 24,000 men were available; Marshal Lehwaldt gave battle at Gross-Jägerndorf, but his defeat was a foregone conclusion. It was much to his credit that he was able to beat an orderly retreat, and Frederick had nothing but praise for his endeavors; to reënforce him in any way was beyond his power. Against the Swedish battalions that gathered in Stralsund, some 22,000 strong, there could only be opposed some few volunteers. The fortress of Peenemünde was soon forced to surrender, while the fate of Stettin hung wavering in the balance. Thus from all quarters the tide of invasion rolled relentlessly in. The enemy could recruit its armies from a population of some 60,000,000, while 4,500,000 was all that Prussia could boast. England, indeed, was Frederick's ally; but no British soldiers were despatched to his aid. An army of nearly 50,000 Hanoverians and Hessians had been placed under the Duke of Cumberland for the sake of protecting the electorate against the attack of three times as many French; but this favorite son of George II. was absolutely lacking in military talents, and withdrew, in a panic, from his only serious engagement, at Hastenbeck, at a time when the advantage was all on his own side. Driven from point to point, he finally ran his army into a regular *cul de sac*, where he was forced to surrender and to sign the disgraceful Convention of Kloster-Zeven. Fortunately, to spare his feelings, the French commander had called it a convention, and not a capitulation, — the difference being that the one required ratification, the other not.

It was in Frederick's favor that, although the empire, as a whole, had brought some 60,000 men into the field, these forces were of the worst possible material, and not over loyal to their cause. Large as was the majority of the delegates that had voted for imperial execution, the people of Germany, as a whole, sympathized with Frederick. The latter's envoy at the Diet, Plotho, became a popular hero for the courageous manner in which he received the imperial notary who tried to serve upon him the formal citation by which his master, the "Margrave of Brandenburg," was bidden to appear within two months and show cause why he should not be placed in the greater ban of the empire and lose all his fiefs, privileges, liberties, and

Sympathy of Germans for Frederick.

expectations. The notary himself has left a description of how Plotho seized him by the robe, stuffed the citation "between his coat," forced him backward out of the room, and called to two of his lackeys to "pitch him down the stairs." Goethe has told how, seven years later, at the coronation at Frankfort, Plotho was still the cynosure of all eyes, and how respect for the Hapsburgs could scarcely prevent the murmurs of approbation from breaking out into open applause. The ban against Frederick was never formally published, nor was the emperor even in a position to procure Plotho's removal.

The great battle of Rossbach.

Frederick, in the meantime, leaving the Duke of Bevern, with the bulk of the army, in Silesia to keep the Austrians in check, had marched off to Thuringia. He tried to entice Soubise, who commanded a second French army, and Hildburghausen, under whom were the contingents of the empire, to give him battle. He would gladly in these days have made peace with the French on any honorable terms, and his agents were instructed to offer Madame de Pompadour half a million thalers, or even the principalities of Valengin and Neuenburg, if she would use her good offices in Prussia's favor. But nothing came of the endeavor, as Louis XV. refused to treat without his allies. Soubise and Hildburghausen kept out of the path of Frederick, who was forced to waste his time in marches and countermarches, while one piece of bad tidings after another rained upon him. In a skirmish near Görlitz, his best-loved general, Winterfeldt, was killed; while a small corps, under the Austrian Haddik, entered Berlin and laid it under contribution. A mere fleeting visit, indeed, in which little damage was done. From some unknown cause, Haddik refrained even from blowing up the Prussian powder magazines, and his withdrawal the next day furthered Frederick's cause in an unexpected manner.

The latter's endeavor to intercept Haddik was looked upon as a retreat by Soubise and Hildburghausen; they came out from among the Thuringian hills, intending to liberate Saxony.   Then Frederick turned, eager to give them battle, and took up a strong position at Rossbach — not far from the great Leipzig plain, where the battles of Breitenfeld and Lützen had been fought.   From a hole in the roof of the town hall, made on purpose by removing pieces of slate, he watched the enemy's movements for hours.   Confident in their overwhelming numbers, — some 43,000 against 20,000, — the combined army tried the daring manœuvre of marching completely around the Prussian flank; their one dread and fear was that Frederick might escape.   But, for him, one of the great chances of his life had come; under the shelter of the Polzenberg and Janusberg he changed his whole position, and, when thought by the enemy to be in full retreat, swept down upon them from the crest of the hills.   Those were a kind of tactics of which the world till then had little dreamed.   In the course of an hour the battle was decided, at a sacrifice in all of 530 men.   Frederick killed and wounded 3000 and took 5000 prisoners.   The rest fled precipitately, and the mere rumor, "The Prussians are coming," was enough to make them march the whole night through.   The roads were strewn with hats, cuirasses, and heavy riding boots; while the Thuringian peasants earned handsome sums by dragging fugitives from the villages and forests and delivering them up at so much a head.   Voltaire, in far-off Ferney, was in despair.   "This is no favorable time for Frenchmen in foreign lands," he wrote; "they laugh in our faces as though we had been adjutants of M. de Soubise."   As for Frederick, he poured out his heart in rejoicing to the Margravine of Baireuth: "Now I can descend to my tomb in peace, for the fame and honor of my people are saved!" He wrote grotesque odes to the "perfumed heroes" and to the *écraseurs*, who had themselves been crushed.

Austria
nearly
recovers
Silesia.
Yet one such victory was not enough; still another fierce encounter was needed to equalize the earlier losses of this wonderful year of warfare, and to extricate the caged lion from his perilous position. And the brightness of Rossbach was to prove the merest foil to the splendors of Leuthen.

The scale in the meanwhile had leapt up in favor of the Austrians. Far from being daunted by the defeat of the French and of the troops of the empire, Maria Theresa is thought to have heard of it with a certain satisfaction. These allies had been difficult to manage of late and had followed too much their own purposes and inclinations. And Silesia, in spite of Rossbach, was in a fair way of being won back. The Duke of Bevern was proving too timid; he hung on the commands of Frederick and waited for the royal approval of measures which could only be successful if carried out at once. Thus Schweidnitz, Frederick's new fortress, fell, after a siege of seventeen days, without a battle having been offered to the besiegers; and 5800 Prussians were made prisoners of war. When finally an engagement did take place, near Breslau, the circumstances were far less advantageous; and the defeated Prussians were obliged to retreat into the town. Bevern himself was taken captive, — voluntarily, as Frederick at first believed, — and when, soon afterward, Breslau fell, the fate of Silesia seemed sealed. Some 4000 men who had fought on the Prussian side went over to the empress. Charles of Lorraine was instructed to hasten and give the *coup de grâce* to Frederick's disorganized army.

But the latter had become a new man since the battle of

Rossbach.   He steps forward now, at the very height of
his extraordinary genius, full of self-confidence, the inspirer of others, the very God of his troops.   "His heart
is torn, but his head is clear and cool," declares his secretary, Eichel.   He found the Silesian army in an incredible
state of demoralization, but his presence in camp worked
a marvellous transformation.   The sight of his determined
face, — which had taken on entirely new lines in the course
of this awful war, — the glance of the great, earnest eye, the
sound of the sympathetic voice, did as much to restore order
as the brief, emphatic words with which he addressed his
officers.   Whoever wished to abandon him might go at
once without fear of punishment; the situation was desperate, a battle must be risked at any cost.   The enemy
favored him by quitting a strong position in order the
more quickly to dispose of this "Potsdam parade guard" —
this tiny force from one-half to one-third the size of their
own.   "The fox has crept out of his hole," cried Frederick,
in boundless glee; "now I will punish his audacity."

Here at Leuthen this royal commander tried, with phenomenal success, his most famous devices; — he played
with his army as though it had been some instrument,
some carefully graduated machine.   Making a feint against
the enemy's right wing, he hurried the bulk of his forces
obliquely across their whole line of battle, and fell with
terrific impetus upon their more exposed left.   No clever
pugilist ever more completely broke down the guard of his
unwary antagonist.   The slaughter was appalling; the
retreat so disastrous that only 35,000 starving and ill men
out of an original 60,000 or 70,000 found refuge in Bohemia; while, by the capitulation of Breslau, 18,000 more
became prisoners of war.   Napoleon Bonaparte said of
this battle: "It was a masterpiece in the way of evolutions, manœuvres, and determination, and would alone

have sufficed to make Frederick immortal and to rank him among the greatest generals. He attacked a vastly superior and victorious army, already drawn up in line of battle, with an army consisting in part of troops that had just been beaten, and carried off a great victory with comparatively small losses."

English aid.   With the exception of the fortress of Schweidnitz, all Silesia was once more in Frederick's hands. The Russians, too, on the strength of a report that the Czarina Elizabeth had died, — or possibly because their leader, Apraxin, was mixed up in a conspiracy to supplant her, — had already turned homeward; and Lehwaldt, thus set free, had practically purged Pomerania of the Swedes. England, moreover, had awakened to her responsibilities, had repudiated the Convention of Kloster-Zeven, and voted four million pounds sterling in the way of subsidies; besides placing the control of the Hanoverian forces under a general in whom Frederick had the fullest confidence, Ferdinand of Brunswick, who had served from youth up in the Prussian army. New indeed was the spirit which William Pitt had infused into the government of the English nation; he it was who had cried out in Parliament, " I feel the most grateful sentiments of veneration and zeal for a prince who stands, the unshaken bulwark of Europe, against the most powerful and malignant confederacy that ever yet has threatened the independence of mankind."

But Frederick had gained a breathing space only to be plunged more deeply into a sea of dangers and difficulties. He had hoped for peace after his great victories, but he soon realized, as he wrote to his brother Henry, that he must "continue his rope-dancing." Year after year he was to experience more bitterly what it meant to sustain a war against enemies on all of his boundaries; year after year he was to find it more difficult to raise men

and money.   Nor was it a question of numbers alone;
the material, too, of his army was rapidly degenerating.
The recruits were less well trained, while no suitable
officers could be found to take the place of the devoted men
who had fallen at their posts.   It could not be otherwise,
when the Prussian state was so infinitely smaller in area
than the domains of any one of its principal antagonists.

In the spring of 1758, Frederick managed to take
Schweidnitz; while Ferdinand of Brunswick, with great
energy, forced the French to evacuate Minden, and drove
them across the Rhine.   They had suffered much, these
troops of Louis XV.; badly cared for, sickness had broken
out in their camp, and, in the month of January alone, some
ten thousand had died in hospital.   Later on in the summer, Ferdinand defeated Clermont, who, to repeat a Parisian witticism of the time, "preached like a soldier and
fought like an apostle"; and took Düsseldorf.

But the Czarina Elizabeth had meanwhile discovered
and put down the conspiracy against her, Apraxin had
been removed from the command, and Bestucheff disgraced, threatened with the knout, and even sentenced to
death — a penalty which was then commuted to banishment.   With more determination than ever the campaign
was carried on in East Prussia; and General Fermor,
Apraxin's successor, brought the whole land into his
hands.   All the cities, as well as the chief nobles, were
forced to swear allegiance to Russia; they did it with an
apparent willingness that the Prussian king never forgave.

Frederick himself had marched into Moravia intending
to reduce the fortress of Olmütz; but his engineers miscalculated the proper distance at which to throw up their
intrenchments, and, while they were making good their
fault, some four thousand valuable transport wagons fell
into the hands of the Austrian general, Laudon.   Fred-

Frederick's
retreat from
Moravia.

erick, short of ammunition and in every way crippled by the loss, was nearly hemmed in between two formidable armies. Daun had some seventy thousand men, while in Laudon, whose services he had once rejected when offered to himself, he found the most formidable general with whom he had ever yet had to contend.

His own determination was now quickly made. Calling his officers together, he appealed to their loyalty and bravery, threatened to cashier any one of them who should say that all was lost, or even show a crestfallen countenance, and then, abandoning the field, made one of the memorable retreats of history, and reached Silesia with his army safe and sound. From here, after only two days' rest, he started off with fourteen thousand picked men to give battle to the Russians, who had advanced as far as the river Oder and were threatening to overwhelm the whole Mark Brandenburg. "Say to all your officers," he wrote to Dohna, to whom he had intrusted the defence of the Mark, "that my device is 'conquer or die,' and that, if any one thinks otherwise, he can stay on this side of the Oder and go to the devil!"

The battle of Zorn-dorf.

In ten days, through the hottest of August weather, Frederick marched 150 miles to Frankfort on the Oder; then he joined forces with Dohna before Küstrin, obliging Fermor to abandon the siege of that fortress. Soon after, at Zorndorf, was fought one of the bloodiest battles of the whole war, if not, indeed, of the whole century. Frederick had been sadly mistaken in these Russians; he considered them bad fighters — and he was right as regarded their capacity for executing swift manœuvres. But they stood their ground in the grim jaws of death as well as any troops in Europe. Frederick conquered them here at Zorndorf — conquered them so completely that they could not make their projected junction with the Swedes, and were obliged

soon to abandon the campaign.   But the fierceness of the
ten-hour fight had been unprecedented; maddened by the
cruelty and wild excesses of these half-barbarians, Frederick, for the first and only time in his life, had commanded that no mercy be shown, no quarter given.   When
ammunition grew scarce, the fight was continued with
bayonets, sabres, and the but-ends of muskets; dying
men clasped each other in a last hostile embrace, and a
Russian, mortally wounded, was found gnawing the flesh
of a Prussian.   Frederick's losses were about eleven
thousand, those of Fermor nearly twice that number.

Twice during this battle, the dashing cavalry general,
Seydlitz, had saved the wavering fortunes of the day by
unexpected charges.   At first Frederick had been alarmed
at his unwonted independence and had sent him a command, followed by a stern warning that he must answer
for his actions with his head.   But Seydlitz had seen his
opportunity, and sending word, "After the battle my head
is at my king's service," had gone his own way.   His
head was safe enough when, later, at the door of his tent
Frederick received him with a warm embrace and acknowledged him the real victor.

If any one advantage could outweigh the numerical
superiority of the allies, it was Frederick's capacity for
swift movement and sudden action.   The dead that fell
at Zorndorf could scarcely have found burial before he
started off for Saxony, the defence of which he had left in
the hands of Prince Henry of Prussia—that one of all his
brothers in whom, in spite of the difference of their characters, and, on Henry's part, of a lack of sympathy and
comprehension, he placed the most confidence.   And here
in Saxony, Henry had fully justified it.   Daun had taken
advantage of Frederick's absence to invade the land, and
Henry had held him at bay and avoided disaster, although

The defeat
at Hoch-
kirch.

the different forces against him outnumbered his own by four to one.

For the present, indeed, the days of signal victories were over; and, for the three defeats which followed, Frederick had no one but himself to thank. At Hochkirch, near Bautzen, he had encamped in a position which he knew to be dangerous, seeing that a vastly superior force of Austrians held the hills all around. Marshal Keith had said to him, "If the Austrians leave us unmolested in this camp, they deserve to be hanged;" but Frederick had merely answered, "It is to be hoped that they fear us more than the gallows." He despised this Daun, this Fabius Cunctator, who always remained on the defensive. But in the present case Daun listened to good advice and made a night attack upon the Prussians. The latter rushed to arms half-naked and confused by the din and uproar; so dark it was that they could only distinguish friend from foe by feeling for the fur caps of their antagonists. For five hours they made a stubborn resistance, and then retreated, beaten, and with losses much greater than those of the Austrians, but in good order. Frederick, who fortunately had not yet received the news of the death of his favorite sister, Wilhelmine, which took place in this very night of Hochkirch, remained calm and cheerful. He did indeed write to his brother Henry, "Unhappily I am still alive;" but on the very same day he also wrote to Schmettau, the commandant of Dresden, "I am determined not to retreat a single step, but rather, standing firm, to await the enemy and give him battle a second time."

The battle of Kunersdorf.

But Daun furnished him with no opportunity; intrenching himself with as much care as though he had never won a victory, the Austrian commander considered that he was doing enough for his mistress by guarding the road

to Silesia, where a second Austrian army was besieging
Neisse. Frederick slipped by him, relieved Neisse, and
was soon back in Saxony.

In the following summer the Russians again advanced
to the Oder. Elizabeth's zeal had slackened after Zorndorf, but the courts of Vienna and Paris had taken care
that she should see an official report in a Berlin newspaper
in which the Russians were spoken of as "barbarians."
She had fallen into a violent rage, and informed Maria
Theresa, through Esterhazy, that she would risk her last
rouble and her last man for the sake of annihilating the
king of Prussia. Her own guard regiments had been
despatched from St. Petersburg, and, in July, 1759, the
reënforced army won the battle of Kay, near Züllichau,
and took the important town of Frankfort-on-the-Oder.
For the first time in the war, a supplementary corps of
Austrians, under none other than Laudon, was sent to
Prussia, and Frederick's downfall seemed assured.

Nothing daunted, he attacked the combined army, nearly
double the size of his own, on the heights of Kunersdorf,
routed the Russian left wing, and took seventy guns and
several thousand prisoners. Had he been willing to rest
on his laurels and to give a breathing space to his army,
which had been marching and fighting for twelve hours,
he would have saved himself the most awful, the most
overwhelming, of all his defeats. But he wished to annihilate the Russians by cutting off their retreat; and, failing
in this, drove them to make a last desperate stand. They
held the Spitzberg against all his assaults; although the
Prussian infantry stood there, hour after hour, suffocated
by the heat and tortured by the thirst —which they had
been unable to quench on their long, dusty march. They
hoped to the last that Seydlitz would sweep down to their
rescue as he had done at Zorndorf; but Seydlitz was

lying wounded and could bring them no help. A right instinct had led him to delay carrying out one of Frederick's commands, but when the order came a second time he had fallen in attempting to obey.

The king himself had shown a never-failing courage, and at the last could scarcely be drawn from the lost field. Two horses had been shot under him; his clothes were riddled with bullets, one of which would certainly have wounded him had it not flattened against a golden *étui*. The outcome of the battle procured him the darkest moments of despair that he had ever known in his whole life. "Of an army of 48,000, there are not at this moment 3,000 left," he wrote to Finkenstein. "The consequences of the battle will be worse than the battle itself; I have no more resources, and, not to hide the truth, I consider that all is lost. I shall not survive the ruin of my country. Farewell forever!" So completely did he consider his career ended that, under pretence of illness, he resigned the command to General Finck, bidding him make a last effort to save Berlin should Laudon march in that direction. But, a few days later, he was able to write to his brother Henry: "You may reckon upon it that so long as my eyes can open I shall do my duty and serve my state." And again, after the lapse of a fortnight, overjoyed at hearing that the Russians had retired from the Mark: "I have to announce to you a miracle that has happened in favor of the House of Brandenburg!"

Frederick found that his losses were not so great as he had feared — some 18,000 or 19,000 against 16,000 of the enemy; and in this same month Ferdinand of Brunswick had won the great battle of Minden against the new French commander, Contades. Here at Minden, the enemy would have been as completely routed as was Frederick's army at

Kunersdorf, had it not been for the cowardice and folly of the English Lord Sackville, who, at a decisive moment, refused to join in the engagement. "For God's sake," a lieutenant colonel had said to Ligonier, Ferdinand's aide-de-camp, "repeat your orders that that man may not pretend he does not understand them; for it is now over half an hour since we received orders to march, and yet we are still here. For you see, sir, the condition he is in." Sackville was later court-martialled, and declared "unfit to serve his Majesty in any military capacity whatever."

There is no doubt but that, had Daun and the Russian general, Soltykoff, acted in concert, Frederick's worst fears would have been realized. But the Russians were angry because, save for sending Laudon's corps, the Austrians had done little to support them. They themselves had lost 27,000 men since reaching the Oder; it was time, Soltykoff thought, that Daun should bear more of the burden of the war and allow his, Soltykoff's, army to rest. Moreover, the Austrian field marshal, instead of furnishing long-promised provisions and supplies, now offered a mere money payment. "My soldiers do not eat money," answered Soltykoff, in a rage; and the friction at last precluded all common action. *The surrender at Maxen.*

For Frederick, indeed, fate still had blows enough in reserve. Immediately after Kunersdorf, he had ordered Schmettau to make what terms he could for Dresden. The commandant surrendered within a fortnight, convinced that without hope of succor a garrison of 4000 could accomplish nothing against six times that number. The first fruits of the war, the Prussian centre of supplies, was lost; and soon came the surrender at Maxen of 12,000 men under General Finck, who, in too literal obedience to commands, had allowed himself to be surrounded, and then, instead of fighting his way out, had

laid down his arms. "That cuts me to the marrow,"
Frederick said when he heard of the disaster; and, a whole
year later, he declared: "If we are conquered, we shall
have to date our ruin from the day of that wretched occurrence at Maxen." Finck was disgraced and placed under
arrest.

Frederick's dwindling resources.

It seemed, indeed, in the two years that followed, as if
even Frederick's superhuman efforts must meet with failure. With breathless interest all Europe watched him
extricate himself from one hopeless situation after another.
What saved him was his own activity and courage; the
capability and bravery of generals like Ziethen, Seydlitz,
Ferdinand of Brunswick, and Prince Henry of Prussia;
and, lastly, the fact that at home the affairs of the allies
were managed, in the final instance, by three capricious
women. How long had Maria Theresa clung to Charles
of Lorraine after all the world knew that he was nothing
of a general! It was the same with Elizabeth and Fermor.

All the same, the iron ring was being drawn closer and
closer around Frederick. In the spring of 1760 he could
oppose but 90,000 Prussians to 200,000 Austrians; for
the first time since the war began, Laudon could open a
campaign on Prussian territory. He took Glatz and appeared before Breslau, after having fairly annihilated a
corps under General de la Motte Fouqué at Landshut.
Fouqué himself, the Prussian Bayard, was wounded and
taken prisoner, but not until the bravery of his resistance
had filled even the enemy with admiration. One of the
Austrian colonels, Voit, would have lent him his own
horse: "I should only soil your fine trappings with my
blood," he said, refusing the offer. "My trappings will
be worth infinitely more," was the generous response, "if
they are spattered with the blood of a hero."

Frederick himself, after bombarding Dresden to no

effect, marched to Silesia, where he found himself surrounded by no less than three Austrian armies: those of
Lacy, Daun, and Laudon; while a large Russian corps
was not far off.   These, according to his own verdict,
were the most perilous days through which he had ever
passed; only the most extreme wariness and agility saved
him from destruction.   Night after night, he changed his
camp after the enemy had already made their dispositions
for an attack.   At Liegnitz, at last, they felt sure of
securing him; Daun and Lacy were to fall upon him
simultaneously, while Laudon was to cut off his retreat.
He was told of the Austrian boast, "The sack is open,
we need only to pull the string and the king and his army
are caught!"   "They are not so wrong," was his comment,
"but I hope to slit their sack!"   Under cover of the night
he caught Laudon on the march before the latter could take
up his appointed position.   Daun, with his usual indecision, did not come to the rescue until the last moment;
and Ziethen received his advance guard with a volley from
the heaviest guns.   Lacy was held back by swampy ground,
though Laudon believed that he had purposely left him
in the lurch.   The latter's losses were nearly 11,000 as
compared to 3500 of the enemy.

As for Frederick, he evaded the Russian general, Czernitscheff, and threw him into a panic by the simple subterfuge of allowing one of his own letters, with a greatly
exaggerated account of the victory of Liegnitz, to fall, as
if by chance, into Russian hands.   But Czernitscheff,
later joining with Totleben, appeared before Berlin, and
forced it to capitulate and to pay a heavy ransom.   Lacy
occupied Potsdam and Charlottenburg, in which latter
place much wanton damage was done.   On the news of
Frederick's approach, the Russians withdrew to the Oder,
and Lacy to Torgau, where he joined Daun.   The circle

had narrowed until it enclosed the very heart of Frederick's own domains.

Here at Torgau, Frederick, with 44,000 men, stood over against the 60,000 of Daun, determined, as he wrote to his brother Henry, "to conquer or die." He had called his generals together and told them that he "did not wish the opinion of any one of them, but would merely tell them that Daun must be attacked on the following day." Ziethen was intrusted with the whole right wing, and was ordered to outflank the enemy and cut off their retreat to the south. The strength of the Austrians lay in the number of their heavy guns, which almost doubled those of the Prussians; and Frederick's first attack was greeted by the most murderous fire he had ever experienced. Indeed, the Prussians soon found that they had before them a task of unwonted seriousness. In the midst of the engagement Frederick himself, who had hitherto borne such a charmed existence, was struck in the breast by a bullet and fell unconscious from his horse; fortunately, the ball was almost a spent one, and during a part at least of the remainder of the battle, he was able to retain the command. Wearied, indeed, and weakened, he at last repaired to a little church near by to have his wound bound and to formulate his plans. Darkness had come on and no one knew which side had won. Austrian and Prussian soldiers sat down peaceably together, after mutually agreeing to surrender themselves the next day to the army which should prove to have been victorious. The Austrian commanders, indeed, considered the field theirs, and sent off the news to Vienna; where it was proclaimed in the streets and imparted by special envoys to the foreign powers. But they had counted without Ziethen's hussars. From the opposite side, after night had already fallen, he had started to storm the heights of Supitz, which the

Austrians had maintained the whole day; and by midnight had forced Daun to order a retreat.

Except for the fact that defeat would have meant ruin, Frederick gained little by dearly bought victories like Torgau. Ten thousand more of his sadly dwindling army were incapacitated for fighting. He himself was growing very bitter and savage against those who forced him to continue the war, and who had just plundered his capital. He sanctioned now so merciless a sacking of the castles of Torgau and Hubertsburg, that one of his generals, Saldern, refused to carry out his commands. *Frederick on the defensive.*

In the following spring, Frederick was able to oppose only 96,000 men to three times that number of Austrians and Russians; while Ferdinand of Brunswick had to contend as usual with a French army nearly double the size of his own. The war enters now into a somewhat slower *tempo;* the year 1761 is the year of sieges and camps, and, on the Silesian scene of war at least, is not marked by a single pitched battle. For the first time in the course of the war, Frederick devoted his whole energies to intrenching himself as strongly as possible; and his camp at Bunzelwitz, north of Schweidnitz, proved marvellously strong and effective. The Austrians, on the other hand, besieged and took Schweidnitz, while, at the same time, Colberg, after a long and glorious resistance, fell into the hands of the Russians.

Thus again the field of action was narrowed; thus again Herculean efforts were needed to raise the Prussian army, which had shrunk to a meagre 60,000, to its normal size. Any other man than Frederick, indeed, would have been completely brought to bay by the sickening news that now came from England: how the courageous and warlike Pitt had fallen and been replaced by the favorite of the new king, the pacific Bute; how the mili- *Lord Bute's abandonment of Frederick.*

tary convention with Prussia had not been renewed, and the English subsidies, which of late years had been very considerable indeed, were henceforward to cease; how Frederick was advised to make peace, even at the price of some of his lands. So far did Bute go in his desire for peace and quiet, that he was willing to renounce Newfoundland and other English conquests in North America; and drew down upon himself, in consequence, in his own land, a flood of satiric sheets, in which he was most unfavorably compared to the idolized Pitt. Nay more, Bute so far forgot the long Prussian friendship as to send an envoy to urge the Russian court to continue its armies in the field against Frederick, on the ground that otherwise Frederick would have free play against Maria Theresa, and thus the war might be prolonged indefinitely! The English treason to the German cause at Utrecht was nothing to this base attempt at crippling a former ally. Bute's own envoy, Mitchell, was outraged at such conduct and at his chief's whole attitude. He begged Frederick not to confound the English nation with a madman, who was rushing to his own destruction and would surely end upon the scaffold. "I am tired of my accursed trade," Mitchell wrote to Keith, the envoy at St. Petersburg.

To Bute's surprise, Frederick accepted the withdrawal of the subsidies with a certain equanimity; the demand that he should rush head over heels (*à l'hurlu-burlu*) into a peace he declared impossible of fulfilment. "The English thought," he wrote later, "that money did everything and that there was no money except in England." But he never forgave this desertion; one of his favorite horses, which he had named after Bute, was condemned to haul wood with base mules. When England's war with her American colonies broke out, all Frederick's sympathies were with the latter; and on the Hessian soldiers who were sold to fight across the water he placed the same tax, when they crossed his domains, as on cattle going to slaughter.

Frederick was kept from despair and, so far as human judgment reaches, from utter ruin, by events which were occurring simultaneously in Russia. His old, indefatigable enemy, Elizabeth, died on January 5, 1762; and was succeeded by her Holstein nephew, Peter III., who had always cherished a romantic attachment for Frederick. In the very night after the Czarina's decease, couriers were sent off to the army, bidding it advance no farther into Prussian territory and to refrain from all hostilities; within a week, a secret messenger had been despatched to Frederick himself, assuring him of the new Czar's firm friendship. The Prussian king answered by freeing Peter's little German principality of Zerbst from all levies and imposts, and by returning all the Russian prisoners of war. In the month of May, a formal peace was signed at St. Petersburg; and the event was celebrated with the utmost rejoicing in every city of the Mark. "Heaven still stands by us," wrote Frederick to Ferdinand of Brunswick, "and everything will turn out well." He had grown as tired of this struggle, as tired of life, to use his own favorite simile, as the Wandering Jew himself; but now the end was in sight. The peace with Russia was followed by one with Sweden, with which power, indeed, Frederick said contemptuously that he was scarcely aware of having been at war: one of his generals, Belling, had had a little trouble with these Swedes, but would probably settle it by himself. *Russia changes front.*

Peter III.'s enthusiastic demonstrations of friendship went so far, that he had himself chosen colonel of a Prussian regiment, and that he also sent Czernitscheff back with eighteen thousand men to fight on the side of this former enemy. The Russian general joined Frederick when the latter was *The battle of Burkersdorf.*

preparing to fight a battle for the rescue of Schweidnitz; but the brave Prussian king was none the less destined to finish this war without the aid of foreign troops. Just as the attack was about to commence against the Austrians, who were posted on the heights of Burkersdorf, news came that Peter III. had been deposed by Catherine II., who, though willing to ratify the recent peace, was not minded to shed the blood of her Russians in an indifferent cause. So much was gained by Frederick, that Czernitscheff agreed to keep secret from the Austrians the order for his recall; his soldiers, though lay figures in the battle of Burkersdorf, helped greatly to decide the day in favor of the Prussians.

The long struggle of years was ending where it had begun, as a stern duel between Austria and Prussia. George III. of England, in November, 1762, closed the treaty of Fontainebleau with France on the understanding that each power should abandon its former ally.

The peace of Huberts-burg.

But how could even a Maria Theresa hope to compete, alone, with an enemy whom she had failed to crush when in bond with nearly the whole continent of Europe? She offered to accept the mediation of the electoral prince of Saxony; and, when Frederick refused, sent her own envoy direct to the castle of Hubertsburg with directions to agree to a peace on the basis of a return to the condition of things before the war — a solution of the difficulties which Frederick himself had proposed. Yet, even then, the negotiations, which were conducted on the Prussian side by the minister, Hertzberg, occupied a full seven weeks, many of the questions raised being merely incidental. The Viennese envoy insisted, for instance, that in both copies of the treaty the name of Maria Theresa should come first; and negotiations had to cease until word came from Frederick that the matter was wholly indifferent to him.   The peace was signed on the 15th of February, 1763, a *status quo* in every particular.

This, then, was the end of the great struggle that had cost a million lives and loaded every state of Europe, save Prussia, with such a national debt as they have never yet been able to liquidate.   Unlike the majority of peace treaties, it seemed to satisfy every one; although the undoubted victor was Frederick, who retained Silesia, after having warded off from the Prussian state an almost certain destruction.   The English envoy, Mitchell, immediately on the receipt of the news, wrote to the Prussian king that he had long considered him the first of warriors, but must now admire him as the most able negotiator that had ever lived.

CHAPTER V

FREDERICK THE GREAT IN TIME OF PEACE

LITERATURE : Koser has excellent chapters on various phases of Frederick's reign. See also the learned biography by Preuss. Reimann, *Neuere Geschichte des preussischen Staates*, deals exhaustively with the period from 1763 on. Dohm's *Denkwürdigkeiten* are an interesting treatment of the last twenty-five years of the eighteenth century, by a contemporary. Tuttle is at his best when treating of Frederick in time of peace. Oncken's *Friedrich der Grosse* is not remarkable for any merits. See also Pierson and Eberty. Some of Schmoller's excellent studies include Frederick's time.

Frederick a national hero.

IF the happenings in Prussia occupy considerable space in our pages, it is not merely because these matters are intrinsically of great interest, but also because that state was now actually assuming the leadership in Germany. When once an elector of the empire, in a seven years' struggle, had succeeded in defeating, not merely the house of Austria, with four times the territory and six times the population, but, at the same time, the might of Russia and France combined, — not to speak of the whole of the rest of Germany, — there was no doubt as to where lay the centre of national gravity. Frederick the Great is looked upon to-day, not as the special hero of the Prussians, but as the hero of the whole German people. His portrait was hung in the huts of peasants all over the land, and was sold in so many impressions that at this day contemporary copies can be obtained in the print shops for a mere song.

In person, Frederick was a typical German, fair-haired and with blue eyes of wonderful brilliancy — we are told by one who saw him often, that none of the portraits could do justice to those eyes. In stature he was very short, measuring not more than five feet five. In his personal appearance, as well as in all his habits and ways of thought, he changed greatly in the course of the Seven Years' War; one has only to look at the engraving by Wille, taken in the year of his accession, and to compare it with one of the later ones, like that of Bartolozzi, to appreciate the difference. In the one the features are well rounded, handsome, radiant, and rather pleasantly arrogant; in the other they are grim, determined, foxy, and deeply lined with care. He writes himself in one of his letters about those wrinkles and their cause, and we can trace the change in other ways. No more striking contrast can be imagined than that which appears in the whole tone of his correspondence. "My youth, the fire of passion, the longing for fame," he writes to Jordan, in 1740, "yes, to be frank, curiosity and, in the last instance, a secret instinct, have driven me from my quiet rest; and the wish to see my name in the news-leaves and in history has led me astray. Come to me here, philosophy maintains its rights, and I assure you I would think only of peace and quiet had I not this accursed desire for fame." "Yes, experience is a fine thing," he wrote in 1762; "in my youth I was buoyant as a foal that springs around a meadow without a bridle, now I have grown as cautious as old Nestor. But more than that, I am gray, furrowed with grief, bowed with bodily ills — only fit, in short, to be thrown to the dogs."

Personal characteristics of Frederick.

The price of this king's victories had indeed been a terrible one to pay. No language can do justice to the steadfastness with which he had met every kind of onslaught; but the man within was filled with thoughts of bitterness and despair. "Death is sweet in comparison to such a life," he wrote in 1760. ". . . Never will I outlive the moment that obliges me to sign a disadvantageous peace.

Terrible strain of the Seven Years' War.

. . . I have lost all my friends and my dearest relations; my unhappiness has reached the limits of possibility; I have nothing left for which to hope."

As early as 1758, he had written that he had lost everything he loved and honored in the world. It would be hard to equal in bitterness and cynicism the terms in which he speaks of his prospects in 1761: "Next year, too, I shall have to go on rope-dancing and making dangerous bounds whenever it pleases their very apostolic, very Christian, and very Muscovitic majesties to call, 'Jump, Marquis!' . . . Ah, how hard-hearted men are! They say to me, 'You have friends.' Yes, fine friends, who cross their arms and tell me, 'We really wish you all success!' — 'But I am drowning; throw me a rope!' — 'Oh, no, you will not drown.' — 'Yes, I must sink the next moment.' — 'Oh, we hope the contrary. But if it should happen, be convinced that we shall place a fine inscription on your tomb!'" Shortly before the end of the war he wrote to Frau von Camas, "You speak of the death of poor F. . . . Ah, dear Mamma, for six years now it is no longer the dead, but the living I bemoan."

Frederick's coldness to his wife.

Beyond a doubt, the halcyon days of Frederick's life fell in the period between the Peace of Breslau, in 1745, and the beginning of the Seven Years' War, in 1756. It is true that his marriage had turned out fully as unhappily as he had prophesied. He had declared, at the time, that he would put away his Brunswick bride on the day of his coronation; but there was no formal proceeding of the kind. There had been a period, indeed, when, at Rheinsberg, they had lived together quite happily. When he first went off to the Silesian wars he wrote to her, if not warmly, at least in a friendly strain; he counts on the pleasure, he declares, of seeing her again after the peace. But he gradually grows colder and colder; and when her brother dies

he waits a long time before sending her a word of regret.
Their relations were at last established on the most distant
and formal of footings. Frederick always insisted, indeed,
that she should receive to the full the honors due to a
queen; and her court, at Berlin in the winter and at Schön-
hausen in the summer, was the centre of considerable
activity. Ambassadors were punctilious in paying their
respects; her birthday was a brilliant festival; while
parades and other expressions of rejoicing were inaugurated in her honor. The king made her formal visits at
long intervals; but to Potsdam, where he resided for half
the year, she might never come — not even when her husband was desperately ill. It is doubtful if she ever even
laid eyes on Frederick's exquisite little palace of Sans
Souci. Once when her brother Ferdinand came to Berlin
and Frederick was absent in the wars, the latter wrote to
Ferdinand that he would be pleased to have him visit the
palace, and, if the queen should choose to accompany him,
everything would be ready for her reception. But Elizabeth Christine proudly refused. She would not choose the
time of her husband's absence to visit his abode.

Frederick was right when he said, at the time of his
marriage, "There will be one more unhappy princess in
the world." Elizabeth Christine would have liked nothing better than to be a faithful, loving, and devoted wife.
She repeatedly declared that she was ready to die for the
king, and she waited in hope and expectation that time
might bring a change. Once, when she knew that he was
coming to Berlin, she rose from a bed of sickness, declaring that, living or dead, she must be there to receive him
on his arrival. Yet all this devotion and humility never
softened the heart of the man who was its object. Frederick had once said of his intended bride, "Let her be as
frivolous as she pleases, only not simple;" perhaps all

Unhappi-
ness of
Elizabeth
Christine.

this affection bordered on simplicity. Yet there were other, worse qualities, such as a proneness to suspicion, a moodiness of temper, a certain discontent. At all events, Frederick thoroughly detested her. Once, when he had arranged a little journey and a festival for his mother, Elizabeth Christine sent word through her brother that she would like to take part; but Frederick refused, on the ground that she was a simpering marplot and would spoil the whole occasion.

Death
of Wil-
helmine.
Thus it came about that Sans Souci was scarcely ever graced by the presence of a woman. With his sister Wilhelmine, Frederick had quarrelled at the time of the election, as emperor, of Maria Theresa's husband. The Margravine of Baireuth had not been able to refrain from paying her respects to the new empress and from taking part in the Frankfort gayeties. But the breach had been healed and Wilhelmine for a time had been her brother's guest at Potsdam. Her death, on the night of the battle of Hochkirch, was one of the most terrible blows of these terrible times.

Frederick's
guests at
Sans Souci.
Frederick found consolation for the lack of a normal household in his dumb beasts and in his literary men. To his dogs he was perfectly devoted; they were allowed the utmost liberty, were fondly inquired after when the king was absent, and were finally buried in the tomb he had intended for himself. With his horses it was the same; some of them were allowed to roam about at will, and one, the famous Condé, was even invited into the hall of Sans Souci, where, according to tradition at least, he wrought havoc to the pavement with his heavy feet. The broken tile was long shown to visitors, until, in common with the chair-cover torn by the dogs, it was repaired by the present ruler.

One of the first acts of Frederick's reign had been to

issue invitations to foreign celebrities to come and grace
his court.   Many, like Vaucanson and Gresset, had been
obliged to refuse, but Maupertuis — at the height of his
fame as Arctic explorer and discoverer of the flattening of
the poles of the earth — had accepted the presidency of the
Berlin academy.   Many of the newcomers received sti-
pends, and had, therefore, to be at the king's beck and call.
A constant guest for a time was the Scotchman, James
Keith, who had been a general in the Russian service and
was now made Prussian marshal.   He writes to his brother,
in 1747: "I enjoy here the distinction of eating with him
[the king] almost every afternoon and evening.   He has
more intelligence and wit than I can describe, and speaks,
with thoroughness and technical knowledge, about the
most varied matters.   He has surrounded himself with
men whom he treats perfectly informally, almost like
friends, yet there is no favorite."   Keith praises the king's
habitual politeness, but finds him somewhat inscrutable.

In this familiar circle Frederick passed merry evenings,
playing the flute and reading aloud his own odes, satires,
and epistles.   The want of restraint, however, was not
allowed to turn into license — once Voltaire was roundly
snubbed, but wittily turned it off with a "Silence, gentlemen; the king of Prussia has just come in."   Frederick's confidence in these friends went so far, that he had
twelve copies struck off for their benefit, by his own secret press, of a somewhat scandalous production, entitled
Works of the Philosopher of Sans Souci, which ridiculed
the church and caricatured half the crowned heads of
Europe.   Voltaire's criticism was, that the king had
worked too fast to have created a real work of art; that
while he, Voltaire. was trying to better some fifty old
lines Frederick had composed four or five hundred new
ones.

First meet-
ing with
Voltaire.

Frederick's first meeting with the great French poet, wit, and historian had been in the year of his accession, although letters had previously been interchanged. The young king had written that he could neither live happily nor die quietly until he should have embraced this friend; while Voltaire had answered: "Simeon shall behold his salvation; the French are Prussians one and all; my heart proclaims to me that the hour is nigh when, from the lips of the crowned Apollo, I shall hear speeches which would have been admired by the wise men of old." It would have been hard for even a crowned Apollo to continue on such a level, and it is no wonder that there was disappointment on both sides at the first interview. Frederick was suffering from a violent fever, yet, as he wrote himself afterward, "with people of that stamp one has no right to be ill." Voltaire was fatigued from his journey, — the meeting took place in Cleves, — he had expected more magnificence, and he adopted an unpleasant tone. Yet his *Mahomet*, which he read aloud, pleased the king greatly; it seemed to him scintillating with ideas.

Voltaire
at Rheins-
berg.

Voltaire was invited to Rheinsberg, where the two made verses, feasted, gambled, and *danced* together; yet here, too, there was a slight trail of the serpent over the whole. A witticism at the expense of his dead father was taken very ill by the king; Frederick gained the impression that his guest was collecting material with which to make the Berliners ridiculous; lastly, the bill for travelling expenses, three thousand thalers, seemed exorbitant, — a good deal to pay for a court fool, wrote Frederick in wrath. But, worst of all, the man of letters had agreed to play the political spy for the French king; though to worm a secret from this young Hohenzollern was more even than a Voltaire could accomplish.

In spite of all this, we see Voltaire frequently receiv-

ing and refusing invitations to the Prussian court, — the
secret of the refusal being, however, that the "divine
Emily," the Marquise du Châtelet, had not been invited
to accompany her famous adorer. To a hint in that direction Frederick had answered, that two such divinities
would dazzle his eyes out. He had once sarcastically remarked of this woman's literary efforts, that she always
started to write, the moment she began her studies; and
that her friends should advise her to educate her son and
not the world.

But in 1749 Emily died in childbirth; Voltaire's position as regarded the French court was not all that he could
have wished, and, after some hesitation, he accepted Frederick's renewed offer. The latter was too shrewd not to
know by this time with what kind of a man he had to
deal; in a letter he calls Voltaire an ape who deserves
to be chased from the temple of the Muses. But he longed
to have this acknowledged master of the French language
correct his own verses. "I need his French," he wrote;
"why should I trouble about his morals?" Moreover, he
really worshipped Voltaire's genius, which, he was sure,
would prove immortal. He burned to be able to catch from
his very lips the words that must seem so much colder
when transferred to paper.

Voltaire at Sans Souci.

At a hint concerning the travelling expenses, Frederick
sent a poem to announce that a golden shower was about
to descend upon his Danaë; and was told in return that
this special, antiquated Danaë loved her Jupiter and not
his gold. All the same, the travelling expenses were
reckoned at four thousand thalers, and a salary accepted
of five thousand more — besides board and lodging, and the
ordre pour le merite. Further advantages — not to speak
of the joy of living in such a lovely jewelled nest as
Sans Souci — were the king's delight in prose and poetry;

his friendly attentions, "which were enough to turn one's head;" and the perfect freedom of intercourse. "I am so presumptuous as to think," Voltaire exclaims, "that nature created me for him." "I forget," he goes on, "that he is the ruler of half Germany and that the other half trembles at his name; that he has won five battles and is the greatest general in Europe. . . . The philosopher has reconciled me to the monarch."

> "*Il est grand roi tout le matin,*
> *Après dîner grand écrivain;*
> *Tout le jour philosophe humain*
> *Et le soir convive divin.*"

Voltaire's escapades. Others received Voltaire well beside the king. As he walked to the royal box on the occasion of a great running at the ring, held in the square before the Berlin castle, the Frenchman could hear the murmurs of admiration, and his own name passing from lip to lip. Well might he write home that he seemed to have reached port after thirty years of storm. That this idyllic state of things did not continue longer was the poet's own fault. He was like a kangaroo (the simile was Frederick's): there was no knowing where his next leap might land him. One of his escapades was to employ the pawnbroker Hirschel to buy up bills in Saxony against the Saxon exchequer — the Peace of Breslau having provided that, when owned by Prussians, these notes must be honored in full. To make the affair still more scandalous, there followed a lawsuit with Hirschel, in the course of which Voltaire was generally believed to have falsified records, and to have substituted paste for real diamonds left with him as security. "Voltaire is outswindling the Jews," wrote Frederick, and bade him have no more dealings of the kind "either with the Old or the New Testament." If he is to continue at Sans Souci he must control his passions and live more like a philosopher.

The jealousies of the coterie of learned men made matters more than lively at the Prussian court. Voltaire had procured the banishment of a certain D'Arnaud, whose only apparent crime was, that Frederick had saluted him, in a poem, as the rising sun that was to take the place of the waning Apollo of France. The scientist La Mettrie caused that same waning Apollo moments of the bitterest anguish, by declaring that the king had compared him to an orange, which, in another year, he would squeeze dry and throw away. Voltaire comes back to the matter again and again; he broods over it, he writes about it; and, when La Mettrie unexpectedly dies, his one grief is, that now the truth about the orange will never be fully known.

Jealousies at Sans Souci.

The crisis was brought about by a quarrel between Maupertuis and one König, in which Voltaire was the violent partisan of the latter. König maintained that one of the vaunted discoveries of the scientist — it concerned the minimum of force — was one that the great Leibnitz had written about, only to show its hollowness. His authority, he said, was a private letter of Leibnitz; which, however, though it really did exist, he was unable to produce when called upon, and was, accordingly, expelled from the academy. Voltaire upheld him with fiery enthusiasm and perpetrated a number of scurrilous satires against the "globe-flattener," Maupertuis, which culminated in the famous *Diatribe du docteur Akakia*.

Furious at having one-half of his intellectual household thus arrayed against the other to the delight of the outer world, Frederick ordered the edition of Dr. Akakia suppressed; and when another appeared in Dresden, commanded that the volume should be burnt by the common

Arrest of Voltaire.

hangman in front of the door of its author. This was too
much even for the small-souled Frenchman, and Voltaire
tendered the resignation of all his dignities. The king
finally let him go, but requested him to leave behind that
pledge of a former intimacy, the *Œuvres du Philosophe de
Sans Souci*. Whether by accident or by design the order
was not obeyed; and Frederick, just starting off for East
Prussia, ordered his representative in Frankfort to seize
the favored son of the Muses, and take the book from his
baggage. The order was too literally obeyed. The volume
was among the effects that Voltaire had left behind him
in Leipzig; it was weeks before it could be procured, and
even then the poet was held still longer on a charge of
attempt at flight. A trying ordeal indeed for a fiery character like Voltaire! All his pent-up bitterness finally
found vent in the *Vie privée du roi de Prusse*, a writing
well designated as "one of the most malignant and men-
dacious, yet one of the most deadly, satires in the whole
range of literature."

Frederick
as a
musician
and as an
author.

That Frederick, in spite of such episodes, found time
and inclination to attend to his own musical and literary
labors argues well for his powers of concentration. He had
learned to play the flute under the famous Quantz; a part
of his morning was regularly devoted to practising, and
nearly every evening he played in concert. He has left
behind him 121 flute sonatas of his own composition,
beside a number of military marches, which are so tuneful
as immediately to attract attention when played by modern bands. Besides this, Frederick's literary works of
different kinds fill twenty large printed volumes. His
Histoire de mon temps, written, like all his other productions, in French, is considered the most remarkable production of its kind since Cæsar wrote his commentaries. It
is partisan, of course; from first to last Frederick is writing

a sort of glorification of himself, his house, and his work. But, apart from this, Frederick writes as only a chief participant ever can write, and tells us much that could never otherwise have become known. Within his general limits, he is just, fair, frank, and outspoken.

Nor must it be imagined that these matters took up even the principal part of the time of this most indefatigable of all monarchs. By rising at three and four o'clock, he was able to transact the current affairs of a great and important state and to receive each day a number of humble petitioners, whose cases were almost always disposed of within the twenty-four hours. "You are correct," he writes to Jordan in 1742, "in thinking that I work hard; I do it to live, for nothing is more like death than idleness." "The people are not there for the sake of the rulers, but the rulers for the sake of the people," he writes in one of his essays; nor was it a figure of speech when he declared that the king was merely the first servant of the state. He objected at all times to being placed on a higher plane, and caused the prayer for himself in the church service, which asked favor for "his Majesty," to be changed to: "O Lord, we commend to Thee, Thy servant our king."

Frederick's great industry.

This man was the very incorporation of the German "*Pflicht.*" Among the effects of one of his cabinet councillors, and only for the years 1746 to 1752, there were found some twelve thousand royal decisions. The position of these councillors, as may be imagined, was no sinecure; obliged to appear at five and six in the morning, they remained standing until the last bit of business was transacted. One of them fell down dead in this fatiguing exercise of his duties. Ministers, councillors, and officials of all kinds were, to a large extent, automatons, and were often treated and scolded like children. "You are all of

Frederick's councillors.

you first-rate cheats, and not worth your bread," Frederick writes to a board of magistrates. " You ought to be driven out; just wait till I get to Prussia!" He calls his general directory impertinent, corrupt, ignorant, even out and out *canaille;* he threatens to cut off Podewils's head. An official who wished for leave of absence in order to go to a watering-place, is told that he is a fool to throw away his money.

When it so pleased him Frederick transacted the most important business — issued manifestoes or treated concerning war and peace — without consulting or even informing his ministers. It was paternal government carried to its utmost lengths; every official knew that at any moment the king's sharp glance might be prying into his affairs and detecting the weak points of his administration. There was no mere routine work about it, for Frederick was a born reformer, never contented with existing conditions. His activity extended in all directions — to criminal and civil justice, to the army, to the finances, to the betterment of social conditions, to the improvement of agriculture and trade.

Humane measures.
But four days had elapsed after his father's death, before he had issued an edict to his judges that torture was no longer to be employed in criminal investigations — though, strangely enough, he considered it more salutary for the people not to know of the change. Judges were instructed, always to weigh the question as to whether this form of proof should be resorted to, but always to decide in the negative. Frederick abolished, too, the barbarous custom by which women convicted of slaying their offspring were to be drowned in leather sacks of their own sewing. Certain arbitrary hindrances to marriage were also to be laid aside. At the same time religious toleration was enjoined in the strictest terms:

"If Turks and heathen should come to populate the land, we would build them mosques and churches;" and again, "All religions must be tolerated . . . here every one shall get to heaven in his own fashion!" Catholics were told that they could build their churches "as high as they pleased and with as many towers and bells." Yet, in practice, against the Jews Frederick made an exception: not because of their beliefs, but because of qualities that he considered inherent in the race. Each head of a family was obliged to have a written permit to live in his district, and a given total was never to be exceeded. The poor wretches were pushed about, expelled from this or that locality, encouraged where it was thought they might prove useful, and burdened with a number of galling conditions. Each new settler was made to buy a certain amount of porcelain from the royal manufactory; nor might he use his own judgment, but must needs take what was allotted to him, and at a fixed price. Even then, he might not enjoy his own purchase, but was bound to send it out of the country.

In the matter of civil lawsuits Frederick employed the learned Coccei to make a clean sweep of abuses that had turned the Prussian courts into a perfect Augean stable. Barristers, advocates, and notaries had been fattening on the fees of cases that had been allowed to drag along for ten, twenty, yes, for two hundred years. The acts in a dispute concerning one little village boundary filled seventy folio volumes. Coccei was sent from town to town and from district to district, and in Pomerania alone, in the course of eight months, had settled some twenty-four hundred old cases. No case in future was to occupy, at the utmost, more than one year.

Reform in law procedure.

Unlike his father, Frederick made it a rule not to interfere with sentences passed by the regular courts; he had once declared that no one was to obey him should he

take such liberties with the law.   He was rather pleased
when a man, whose mill adjoined Sans Souci and who had
refused to sell at the king's price, told him to his face, in
answer to his half threat of dispossession, that there were
courts of justice in Berlin.   But in one famous case, —
that of the miller Arnold, — Frederick, suspecting that
a bench of aristocratic judges were denying justice to a
poor man, threw himself heart and soul into the cause
and constituted himself supreme judge.   The judges
of the New Mark, by whom the case had first been
decided, were told that they were not worth a charge of
powder and that they might all go to the devil.   When
the Berlin court rendered a similar decision, the grand
chancellor and three of his associates were summoned to
the palace, where they found themselves in the path of a
cyclone.   How in the world, thundered the king, could a
miller earn his living if the water was shut off from his
mill?   When the *canaille*, as he called them, tried to
explain that no possible injury had been done to Arnold,
they were told to hold their tongues; while the grand
chancellor was suddenly dismissed from the office he had
held for years with a curt "Get out!   Your place has been
given to another."   Cruel indignities were then inflicted
on all concerned.

In all this Frederick was absolutely and entirely in the
wrong, although he would never publicly acknowledge it.
That was his way; it would be bad for the people to think
him capable of error.   But in private he wrote, "I have
been too hasty — curse the fellow!"

The country benefited indirectly from the incident from
the fact that the expelled chancellor's successor was that
Carmer who codified the Prussian common law, giving it
the form it was to retain until the introduction of the
German common law in the year 1900.   This matter, as well

as Frederick's other endeavors for the good of his people, had been sadly interrupted by the Seven Years' War. The country had been at the mercy of invading armies; anarchy had taken the place of order; whole cities had been plundered and burned. Frederick himself reckoned that thirteen thousand houses had vanished without leaving a trace. He likens his land to a man covered with wounds and exhausted from loss of blood. The condition of the people was indeed appalling — how appalling may be gathered from the fact that in the city of Berlin, which had scarcely been touched by the enemy, one-third of the inhabitants were forced to live on the charity of the rest.

But paternal government has its advantages; never did any man more thoroughly accept his responsibilities than did Frederick at this crisis. He set himself the definite task of freeing his country, within two years, from every trace of the war; even before he reëntered his capital, after an absence of six years, he had made arrangements for the provinces through which he passed. With an iron determination never to cease fighting until an advantageous peace should have been secured, he had made himself entirely ready for a new campaign, and had in hand a fund of 20,000,000 thalers, besides thousands of horses, and stores of provisions and grain. Right and left, now, he distributed this wealth — never rashly, never thoughtlessly, but always after the most searching inquiry into the nature of the needs. "I must look through and correct still more accounts," he writes to his brother in July, 1763. ". . . It has been going on like this without interruption for four months. . . . I have also to provide Berlin with wood for the coming winter." In Silesia, where the ravages of war had been most constant, he freed the people from their taxes for six months, rebuilt

8000 houses, and gave 17,000 horses for agriculture, besides an immense amount of grain for seed. Applicants who seemed to Frederick undeserving went empty away. "I won't give the low-lived rabble a groschen," he said of the burghers of Potsdam; and to a landrath who wanted compensation for personal losses: "At the day of judgment each man will regain what he has been deprived of in this life." One of his most salutary acts was to dismiss to their homes some 30,000 soldiers, that they might aid in the cultivation of the fields.

Frederick's inflation of the coinage.

The most arbitrary, and perhaps the most characteristic, of Frederick's measures at this time, was his treatment of the currency and of the obligations of the state toward its creditors. His strategy in this respect was as brilliant, and involved as much immediate suffering, as in the case of any of his battles. It is surely an all but incredible record for Prussia to have emerged from this unequal war practically freed from debt; at the very darkest hour the taxes had not been raised, no loan negotiated. Yet almost as incredible were the means that had been employed to achieve this end. The war fund left by Frederick William I., the English subsidies, even the heavy contributions levied on the conquered lands and provinces, had not nearly sufficed for the never ending outlays; the remainder had to be raised by holding back the salaries of the civil officials and paying them in promissory notes, and by inflating and adulterating the coinage to the last degree. And when the moment for redemption came the doors were closed. Simple edicts restored the coinage to its normal basis; the promissory notes were paid in the old currency; but that currency itself was redeemed at but one-fifth of its face value. The hard-worked servants of the state were those on whom the heaviest burden fell. It was cruel and unjust, a practical declaration of bankruptcy;

yet Prussia stood thereby at an immense advantage over her debt-laden rivals.

To bettering the general conditions of his lands Frederick now bent every energy. Those gay suppers in Sans Souci had ceased forever; it was even noticed that the king showed less care for the neatness of his person. His head was full of plans for draining and settling new lands, and for furthering agriculture and commerce. The number of colonists that were induced to come to Prussia during his reign has been carefully estimated at nearly 300,000; 900 new villages were founded. Add to this, that the army contained some 80,000 to 90,000 foreigners, many of whom remained permanently in the land. This so-called colonization was carried on with the utmost system and regularity. Frederick followed every rise of taxes, every national calamity that occurred in neighboring lands; when the town of Grossenhain burnt down, his agents were sent to the spot to lead the sufferers to the land of promise. The underlying idea of all this was, that Prussia must be made to produce at home all, and more than all, that the people needed; if artisans of a certain kind were wanting search was made for them far and wide. Butter-makers from Holland were in great demand, as were also persons who had had experience with the manufacture of silk.

This latter industry, the most exotic that Prussians had ever undertaken, was actually made to flourish; although but one-sixth of the raw material could be grown in the land itself. Frederick tried to make it a part of the occupation of preachers and sextons, in their cemeteries, and schoolmasters, in their yards, to grow mulberry trees for the cultivation of the worm; and he issued comprehensive edicts on the subject. It would be so simple, he declared, if only the wives and children would look after the cocoons.

In spite of the rivalry of France, where climate and the price of labor were far more favorable, it was calculated that, in 1796, no less than 12,000 Prussians were engaged in the manufacture of silk.   Colonists were paid so much for every loom they set up, and were protected, besides, by heavy duties placed on foreign importations.   Frederick considered every penny that went out of the land as wasted.   "If a man has a purse of five score ducats," he wrote, "and draws one out every twenty-four hours, without putting anything back, — at the end of a hundred days he will have nothing left."

Reclaiming of waste lands.

The greatest privileges and inducements, indeed, were offered to all these newcomers, Frederick expending on them directly some 25,000,000 thalers.   A part of the travelling expenses, proportioned to the distance and to the size of the families, was regularly paid; aid in the shape of building materials, or even of money, was furnished; while exemptions were granted from customs duties, from state and communal taxes, and from liability to military service.   The farmer received his cattle, his seed, and his tools; the manufacturer was encouraged to start new industries.

On the fertile land along the Oder, which was reclaimed by draining and by building dams, some 1200 families were established.   "I have won a province," Frederick exclaimed as he gazed on the 225,000 acres that were thus rescued from the waters.   Along the Warthe, the Vistula, and the Netze operations were undertaken on the same gigantic scale; and it may be roughly estimated that, in all, from 1500 to 2000 square miles were thus recovered.

Protective duties.

The desire to protect home industries and to cut off every chance of competition from foreign markets, led Frederick into passing the most unpopular measures of his whole reign.   Heavy duties were placed upon almost every article, and the pettiest means resorted to in order to prevent smuggling. People were stopped, not only at the city gates, but also in the streets; their houses were entered at will and every corner searched; while the burden of proving that the goods were not contraband rested with the owners. Moreover, when the duties, although levied on some 3000 articles, failed to produce the expected revenue, Frederick chanced on the evil idea of putting the direction of the whole matter into the hands of a board of Frenchmen. With a horde of subordinates, they fell upon the land; in addition to their salaries they were to have five per cent of all profits which should exceed the estimates of 1765 and 1766. Their official title was, *administration générale des accises et péages*, and they unfolded a system of espionage which was perfectly odious to the Germans. Coffee was one of the articles most generally used and most frequently smuggled: Frederick, in his paternal fashion, told his subjects that it was not good for them to drink it; that he himself had been raised on beer soup; that if they would persist he should feel obliged to impose a duty of 250 per cent. In order more absolutely to control its use, it was decreed that no one should burn it or grind it at home, but only in the royal mills; where, as a matter of fact, it was sold at treble its worth. Regularly appointed "coffee-smellers" went from house to house, to see that the command was obeyed. Nor did the new system help matters in the least: as nearly as we can estimate, two-thirds of the coffee used in Prussia was brought in by unlawful means; and disorders of every kind resulted, culminating in violence and murder.

Only the boundless love and devotion the people felt for the person of their "Fritz" prevented more serious outbreaks. Once, on an afternoon drive, he came upon an excited crowd grouped around a caricature of himself in which he was represented as holding a can of coffee on his knee. Stopping his horses he bade them lower the picture that it might be the better seen — whereat the scowls melted into rapturous approval.

Frederick would not have been a Hohenzollern had not the army, in the ultimate instance, been his chief care. Like his father, he managed everything about it in person, himself training and drilling the troops that he led to battle; he caused minute reports to be drawn up, from which he learned the capacities and the special good and bad qualities of every regiment. Officers and soldiers alike were subjected to hard, serious work, and were given but small pay. Nor were there any regular pensions even for those who had distinguished themselves, or been wounded, in the field. The king's chief device was, to appoint his retired subalterns to positions as country schoolmasters, irrespectively, it would seem, of their qualifications. Here they would be sure, at least, of a beggarly pittance for the rest of their days. The common soldier, under this reign, was a mere part of the machine; and, being usually of poor stuff at the outset, had too often to be flogged into shape. The discipline was extraordinarily severe; running the gauntlet proved fatal in dozens of instances, and it was expressly made known that a certain amount of harshness was considered no discredit to an officer. It was the king's wish that the rank and file should dread those in command more than they did the enemy.

Frederick spared himself as little as he did his men; during the manœuvres he would rise at two o'clock. Before the end of his reign he had increased the total of his soldiers to two hundred thousand, an enormous ratio to the small number of Prussia's inhabitants. Going the rounds of his provinces every year, he inspected each separate regiment, introducing a number of reforms — such as

lightening the cavalry and infantry,— and providing a new
trigger that enabled the men to shoot as often as six times
in the minute.

The officers of the Prussian army were almost exclusively nobles; they alone were supposed by the king to
have a well-developed sense of honor.   Frederick believed,
and said openly, that on them depended the security of the
state.   All able-bodied nobles were, therefore, practically
obliged to become officers; and there were times in the
Seven Years' War when, even then, there were not enough.
Commoners were taken in, but were dismissed or degraded
as soon as the war was over.   This sacred caste of men of
high birth was to be fostered in every way.   Frederick
gave millions to pay their debts and prevent the alienation
of their lands; he exempted them from the excise taxes
and from the odious presence of the coffee-smellers.   On
the other hand, the noble was never to disgrace his rank
by engaging in trade, nor might he marry out of his own
sphere.   Hussar officers were never to marry at all; while
others had to beg permission, which was not always
granted.   The king did not wish, he said, to see a regular
"weepy weep" every time the troops marched out to war.
The observance of the difference in rank went so far that
a noble might never acquire a farm or peasant estate; he
alone was entitled to wear a feather in his cap; at public
festivals his end of the room was barred off from the common herd; while, at masquerades, he alone might wear
the pink domino.

The peasants, who formed the bulk of the army, were
not exactly slaves; for they could not be arbitrarily bought
and sold, except as a part of the lands on which they
dwelt.   But they still had to give to their lords a very
large proportion of their time and of their produce; while
the lords, in turn, had many ways of inflicting hardships

Nobles as
officers.

Hardships
of the
peasants.

and punishments upon them.   Their children were forced
to be household servants for the term of five years, and
without pay.   Frederick recognized the existence of great
evils in this regard, but tried in vain to remove them.   A
decree abolishing serfdom in Pomerania was rescinded because of representations on the part of the nobles; and the
matter remained in abeyance until the days of Baron Stein.

The first
partition of
Poland.

Although the first half of Frederick's reign was almost
wholly warlike and the last half almost wholly peaceful,
the amount of territory acquired in each was very nearly
equal: fierce struggles against a world in arms had gained
and kept Silesia, while, eleven years later, a stretch of
land of similar dimensions was won by purely diplomatic
arts.   By the first partition of Poland, in 1772, there came
to the share of Prussia that portion of the land of the
Teutonic Order which had fallen absolutely to its Slavic
conqueror by the Treaty of Thorn, in 1466.   This territory
had been known by the name of West Prussia — in con-
tradistinction to East Prussia, which, though in feudal
dependence to Poland, had yet remained the property of
the order, and had eventually found its way into the hands
of the Hohenzollerns.   On the whole, it may be doubted
whether, for Frederick the Great, West Prussia was not a
more valuable acquisition than even Silesia.   To be sure,
the natural resources of the land were infinitely inferior,
and the important towns of Danzig and Thorn were excepted from the cession.   But West Prussia had hitherto
completely cut in two the possessions of the Hohenzollerns,
which now stretched in an unbroken line from the borders
of Hanover to the river Niemen.   And the new lands
along the rivers Netze and Vistula were capable of great
improvement; for, when properly drained and protected,
the soil was extremely fertile.

This division of parts of Poland by the mere right of The Polish
the strongest has been generally cried down as one of the nobility.
most iniquitous acts in history; a satiric artist of the
time has drawn an apt picture of the poor Polish king
tearing his hair, while Frederick, Catherine, and Joseph
coldly point to the map of Europe, which they are cutting
up to suit themselves.   But it must be said, on the other
side, that if ever a people had been proved incapable of
self-government it was these Poles.   Frederick was not
exaggerating when he declared, on his first visit to these
parts, that Canada was in a better state of cultivation, and
that he had acquired " a piece of anarchy."   A nation of
savages could not have acted more lawlessly or taken less
heed to their own advantage than did the Poles.   For
more than a century the cruelest kind of civil warfare had
been the order of the day; and even such national institutions as there were, could at any moment be put out of joint
by the *nie pos walam*, or *liberum veto*, of a single noble in the
Diet.   One-fourteenth of the whole population belonged to
the nobility, for all children inherited the title alike; and
it was, furthermore, the custom to create new nobles *en
masse*.   After the relief of Vienna, in 1683, John Sobieski
had conferred this distinction on the whole of his cavalry.
These *Szlachcicen*, as they were called, held all the public
offices, and ground down the lower classes — who often lived
in earth huts and were little better than brutes.   The business of ruling was ostensibly performed by an elected king
and by a Diet of some two hundred members; but, year
after year, there were bitter conflicts of interest, which
not infrequently ended in the formation, all over Poland,
of confederations for mutual aggression.   Incredible as it
may seem, it has been reckoned that, out of fifty-two diets
held between the years 1652 and 1704, no less than forty-
eight broke up in disorder.   At the Diet of 1746, one party

refused to allow the signing of the very laws it had just helped to pass, and, throughout one whole evening session, lasting several hours, blew out the candles every time they were brought in.

Degeneracy of the Poles.

No wonder Jean Jacques Rousseau could say of the Polish nation, "It is a body that has a stroke of apoplexy every time it moves." Even the loyal primate, Lubienski, — in summoning to the election of 1764, — declares that the laws are disregarded, that commerce has ceased, that the boundaries are unprotected, and the treasury empty. "In all history," says his proclamation, "no example can be found of such disorders;" and again, "A kingdom so miserably constituted must of necessity either become the prey of an enemy or relapse in time into Tartar steppes." King Stanislaus Lesczinsky had once written, "Our turn will surely come, and we shall be the prey of a great conqueror; *perhaps the neighboring powers may decide to divide our territory.*" It is evident that, whatever fate was to strike Poland, her condition could not have been changed for the worse; moreover, if an excuse is needed for Frederick the Great, it is to be found in the fact that Russia would have absorbed the whole had he refused to take his share, and that, by accepting this solution of a difficult problem, he averted a general European war.

Stanislaus Poniatowski.

The Polish question had just become important at the time of the death of Augustus III., in 1763. Frederick, isolated, and estranged from all the other great powers, had determined to cultivate the friendship of Catherine II., and aided her in bringing on the vacant Polish throne her former lover, Stanislaus Poniatowski. To him it was roundly intimated that he never could have become king by his own efforts, and that he would be expected to show his gratitude by subserviency to Russia. The utmost pressure had, indeed, been exercised upon the electors:

the Russians had camped before Warsaw and had sent bands of Cossacks at intervals to parade the streets; the primate, Lubienski, had been bribed by the gift of a splendid piece of fur worth twenty-four thousand roubles and by the promise of eighty thousand more after the election. At Catherine's request, Frederick had sent Prussian troops to Poland; and, on the news of the success of Poniatowski, he congratulated his ally in the most glowing terms. "God said, Let there be light, and there was light," he wrote; "as far as the Ottoman Porte your Majesty forces from all a recognition of the excellency of your system. You speak, madame, and the world is silent before you." Frederick might well express his admiration for Catherine, inasmuch as, in the treaty signed with himself shortly before the election, she had secured all the advantage for herself, — he promising to interfere in Poland for the sake of purely Russian interests. It had been hinted, indeed, even then, that in case of war he might hope for compensation.

The Poles rushed blindly on to their own ruin. This forcible imposition of a king did not seem to greatly worry them, but they could not be brought to keep peace among themselves. The main body of the people, fanatic and Jesuit-ridden to the last degree, would grant no concessions whatever to the so-called dissidents, — members of the orthodox Russian and of the Lutheran church. Not only might they hold no office, but they might not even partake of their own communion or bury the bodies of their own dead without first receiving permission of the Catholic authorities. Forbidden to build new churches, or even to repair the old ones, their schools, too, were shut up and their children lured into Catholic establishments; while, over the dying, the Jesuit priests hovered, trying to make converts at the last moment.

The Polish nonconformists.

Here was a matter that gave Prussia and Russia constant pretexts for interference; while Austria, becoming alarmed for the very existence of Poland, began to assume a threatening attitude toward these two powers. By a new treaty, in 1767, Frederick promised Russia that, under certain circumstances, he would throw an army into Austrian territory; but, in such a case, he fully intended to compensate himself at the cost of Poland.

From this time on, Frederick's thoughts were constantly busy with the project of acquiring West Prussia; though the actual suggestion seems to have come from Russia, and the actual impulse did certainly come from Austria. The affair of the dissidents involved the Czarina in a war, not only with the Poles, but also with the Turks — whose territory had been inadvertently violated by the seizure of Polish refugees. Moldau and Wallachia were soon in Russian hands; Austria, greatly alarmed, made advances to Turkey and also to Prussia — an interchange of visits taking place between Frederick and Maria Theresa's son and coregent, Joseph.

Folly and superstition of the Poles.

The Poles, meanwhile, acted more and more like irresponsible children. In 1768, they had made concessions and signed agreements which they later refused to carry out. They were perfectly blinded in their hatred of the Russians, and, in the face of the tremendous superiority of the latter, pinned their faith upon the supernatural; they believed that the halos from the heads of the risen dead would blind their enemies, and that the Mother of God would direct the bullets of a people that had chosen her to be their patron saint. It was seriously reported that Joseph and Mary, together, had stocked the Cracow arsenal with much-needed ammunition.

A Russian-Austrian war was now on the very point of breaking out; and Austria, in 1771, signed an alliance with the Turks. Frederick by the terms of his treaty was bound to aid Russia. But Austria's occupation of the Polish district of Zips — on the ground of an old mortgage which she meant now to redeem — and her subsequent seizure of adjoining territory, brought about a solution of the difficulties which was unexpected to the party most concerned. Catherine's remark to Prince Henry, Frederick's representative, on hearing of this action, was a seemingly innocent question as to why others, too, should not do the like. The result was a race for gain and a staking out of ever increasing claims, which culminated in the famous Treaty of Partition of 1772. Of all the contracting parties, Austria seems to have had the least right on her side; and, had it rested with Maria Theresa alone, the transaction would never have been consummated. But Joseph II. was the incarnation of greed, and Kaunitz well supported him.

The conscience of Maria Theresa.

The poor empress, though she eventually consented to everything, was more unhappy than ever in her life before. "I have but a very poor opinion of our right," she declared. And indeed Russia and Prussia had at least the excuse, that the Polish war had caused them heavy losses, for which they were now seeking indemnity. In February, 1771, Maria Theresa wrote: "When claim was laid to all my lands I buoyed myself up with my good right and with the help of God; now, when not only is the right not on my side, but obligations, justice, and fairness are against me, I have no peace left." She could not bear, she said, the reproaches of a heart unaccustomed to deceive itself or others. When the Swedish envoy, Count Barck, once tried to comfort her by declaring that she was accountable for her actions only to God: "Yes," she cried, solemnly raising her hands to heaven, "that is the very judge I fear!"

Yet, all this time, her government was fairly insatiable

Austria's
greed.

in its demands. Frederick the Great, who complained
bitterly that Austria was acquiring so much more territory than himself, remarked of Kaunitz that he was pretty
well imitating the greed of the double eagle on the coat
of arms of his court; and, in talking to Zwieten, the Austrian envoy, he suddenly broke out with: "*Potztausend!*
you have a good maw!"

In the final settlement Austria's share was, as a matter
of fact, three times the size of Prussia's, and much more
fertile and populous; although, as Kaunitz pointed out, it
was less favorably situated, being separated from the rest
of the monarchy by the Carpathians. The Russian portion
was larger still; but contained only half the number of
inhabitants and consisted mainly of woods, marshes, and
barren stretches of sand.

Despair and
levity of
the Polish
patriots.

Poland herself had less than no voice in this whole
matter of partition. When the grand chancellor, Czarto-
riski, told the Russian envoy that, in the forty years of his
administration, he had never dreamt of such a possibility,
"Yes," was the insolent answer, "the older one grows, the
more one learns!" The Diet was commanded, in the most
peremptory manner, to assemble — to begin deliberations
on the 19th of April and to end them on the 7th of June.
The annexed districts were allowed no representation,
while many other provinces, in despair, refused to send
delegates at all. Those who did come together to this
most maimed of assemblies, were obliged to sign allegiance
to a "confederation" before being allowed admittance to
the hall; it was made generally known that the least
opposition would cause the allies to increase their demands; while Prussian and Russian soldiers were drawn
up in rank and file, ready to be quartered on the recalcitrant. The Bishop of Luck but narrowly escaped being
made to share his sleeping apartment with twelve hussars.

The poor king of Poland was in the depths of despair. "I am completely in the hands of the three courts," he wrote to a lady in Paris. "I am dying of hunger; they have attacked all that I hold most dear." He cursed the day that had brought him to this unhappy spot, which he nevertheless was debarred from leaving. The treaty was ratified in September, 1772, after Frederick and Joseph had made unworthy attempts still further to increase their holdings. The Polish delegates signed with actual tears and wailings; before he could be prevented, one of them had written the word "farewell" opposite to his name. Yet the childishness of these patriots was simply unconquerable. The papal nuncio is authority for the statement that frivolity, corruption, and unbridled extravagance were displayed as never before. On the night before handing in the formal renunciation of thousands of square miles of their territory, many took part in a great festivity at the Brühl palace. Fireworks were set off and King Stanislaus Augustus Poniatowski himself opened the ball with the Princess Sapieha!

For Frederick, the acquisition of West Prussia was the incentive to unprecedented efforts in the way of reclaiming waste lands and of regenerating a fallen people. His first visit to his new territory had not disappointed him. "It is a very good and very advantageous possession," he wrote to his brother Henry; "but in order that fewer persons may be envious, I say to every one who will listen, that I have seen nothing but sand, pines, moorland, and Jews." On September 27, 1772, the estates did him homage in the great hall of the ruined Marienburg; they were feasted at his expense, and gold and silver medals were distributed among them; while coins to the amount of 2000 thalers were flung to the people. From now on, he exchanged the old title of "king *in* Prussia" for the fuller

Frederick's reforms in West Prussia.

"king *of* Prussia"; and ceased to complain that his kingdom was an anomaly, belonging neither to the small nor to the great powers. He drew colonists by the thousands into poorly settled districts; spurred the farmers on by setting prizes on the best results of agriculture; founded public schools, and did away with the superabundant Catholic holidays that had done so much to encourage idleness. The whole apparatus of a well-ordered administration was introduced: military divisions, judicial courts, rapid postal communication, commercial regulations. The Bromberg Canal between the Netze and the Brahe, constructed at a cost of 740,000 thalers, opened up a direct path of trade to the Elbe and to the Oder. The revenues from the new province soon rose to 5,000,000 thalers; besides which, 25,000 men were added yearly to the Prussian army.

The Bavarian succession war.

The military establishment went on increasing until the day of Frederick's death, and, at the last, numbered nearly 200,000 in all — an enormous total for a state with a population of but little over 5,000,000. One small disastrous war came to mar the end of a glorious reign — a war, as usual, with Austria, and one in which, although no battle was fought and no siege undertaken, some 20,000 Prussian soldiers succumbed to sickness and the treasury was depleted by 17,000,000 thalers. This Bavarian succession war is one that historians delight to ridicule, and that contemporaries nicknamed the "potato war," because the chief occupation of the troops was hunting for food in the fields. Frederick's military reputation suffered, too, inasmuch as he failed to accomplish what he attempted, and showed, in general, the effects of old age and of a broken constitution. Yet if Austria was to be prevented from holding the leadership of Germany, the war was necessary and, indeed, unavoidable. With the Emperor Joseph II., the acquisition of new lands had come to be an inveterate passion; he had taken all that he could possibly lay hands on in Poland; he had wrested the province of Bukovina from Turkey; and now he was lusting for the whole of Bavaria. One is tempted to think that he had learned his lesson from Frederick the Great; for his methods were very similar. Old claims to Bavaria, dating back to 1426, were raked out; and, before they could be acknowledged, armies were sent to enforce them. It mattered little that the claims were baseless, and that the very emperor, Sigismund, who had made the grants in question, had reversed them in 1429, with the consent of the parties concerned.

The family of Wittelsbach, divided into three lines, held at this time Bavaria, the Palatinate, and the Duchy of Pfalz-Zweibrücken. The Elector Maximilian Joseph, however, and the Count Palatine Charles Theodore were both childless and together had signed an instrument — the names only being left blank — by which, when one died, the other was immediately to be proclaimed heir to his lands. United, this would make a territory nearly equalling Prussia as it had been at the time of the accession of Frederick the Great; and Emperor Joseph had once said of Charles Theodore, "God grant that he do not also inherit the mind of a Frederick, for to him alone will he be second in power and possessions in Germany." *Austria lusting for Wittelsbach lands.*

The sequel showed that on this point at least there was no ground for fear. On the death of Maximilian Joseph, in 1777, Charles Theodore, far from displaying the mind of a Frederick, proved as clay in the hands of Austria. Only let him have peace and quiet, and comfortable possession of what was left, and he was willing to sign away almost any part of his inheritance. He was afraid, indeed, to show the agreement with Austria to his heir, Charles of Zweibrücken, and tried to obtain the latter's signature without having him read the document; Austrian troops in the meantime had taken possession of Lower Bavaria and the Upper Palatinate, and were encroaching in all directions. It was at this juncture that Frederick the Great awoke to a sense of what a preponderance in Germany success would give to Austria. Moreover, in thus trying to absorb an electorate, Joseph II. was acting contrary to the Golden Bull, to the Westphalian Peace, and to his own electoral concessions. Yet it seemed to Frederick that the impulse should come from the injured parties, and he tried to galvanize the person most concerned, Charles Theodore, into a posture of resistance. Failing in this endeavor, he sought to prop up Charles of Zweibrücken, who needed much encouragement. The only manly member of the family was the Princess Maria Anna, a sister of the dead Maximilian Joseph, who of her own accord appealed to the Prussian king. "Ah, why were not you elector?" Frederick wrote to her; and together they did finally induce Duke Charles to send a formal appeal for aid to Prussia and to France, and, in March, 1778, to bring the matter before the Diet at Ratisbon.

Prussia and Russia cry halt to Austria.

Frederick was now in a position of great strength. For the first time Prussia headed a movement for the protection of a minor German state against Austrian aggression: the emperor was to learn that he could not rule like a Turkish sultan and break all privileges and compacts. Saxony, too, had well-grounded claims to a small part of the Bavarian inheritance, the Saxon electress having been a sister of Maximilian Joseph. It was likely that Catherine of Russia, being Frederick's ally, would interfere in his behalf; while Maria Theresa, grown old and timid, was openly out of sympathy with her ambitious son, whom she warned against irritating Frederick — for, from this "monster," the worst was to be expected. The armies

had been in the field some months when, without consulting Joseph, she sent Baron Thugut to the "monster" with
overtures of peace; this led to long negotiations, during
which military operations were carried on without spirit, —
the hardships of the approaching winter compelling Frederick at last to beat an inglorious retreat into Silesia.

A word from Catherine of Russia proved more decisive
than arguments or manœuvres in other directions.   In the
spring of 1799, she declared that she considered Austria's
claims groundless, and that, should the emperor persist in
his designs, she would feel compelled to fulfil the terms
of her alliance with Prussia.   Unable to resist such a combination as this, the emperor consented to the calling of a
congress at Teschen, where peace was finally signed on the
13th of May, 1779.   A miserable war and a miserable
peace!   Whereas Frederick had fought for the principle
that Austria had no right to an inch of Bavarian territory,
he was obliged to consent to the cession of the rich district, between the Inn, the Danube, and the Salzach, containing some sixty thousand inhabitants.   His own reward
was nominal: the right to incorporate Ansbach and Baireuth as a part of Prussian territory — a right which had
never been seriously disputed.   To accomplish this small
result, he had submitted to the calling in of Russia in a
purely German question — a precedent for the future of
which that power was often to take advantage.

The future proved that a simple treaty of peace was not
sufficient to bar the progress of the "Cæsar possessed by demons," — as Frederick affectionately denominated Joseph.
No emperor since Charles V. had shown such activity both
for good and for bad.   In his own Austrian lands Joseph
established religious toleration, abolished all the harder
features of serfdom, took away all inquisitorial power from
his criminal courts, dropped from the code such crimes as

Joseph II.'s ambitious plans.

magic, apostasy, and marriage with infidels, and introduced compulsory education. But, in the empire at large,
he encroached more and more on the liberties and on the
possessions of the estates, proving himself, by his methods,
a political Ignatius Loyola, — with spies everywhere and
with complete carelessness as to the means by which his
good ends were to be accomplished. The Westphalian
bishoprics were his first object of attack. His brother
Maximilian was elected coadjutor of Cologne and Münster, and, like that Ernest of Bavaria of Reformation times,
sought to bring adjacent sees into his own hands. From
the Catholic clergy in general an attempt was made to raise
obsolete revenues; the Austrian police interfered beyond
their own boundaries; claims were laid to Würtemberg
and an exchange proposed with Baden.

The league
of princes.
Most serious of all, was a new attempt to gain Bavaria,
made in 1784, this time not by war or by encroachment,
but by diplomacy. Charles Theodore was invited to renounce his electorate, in return for the Austrian Netherlands and the title of king of Burgundy. To Austria, this
meant the control of all South Germany and the absorp-
tion of an important electoral vote. And Charles Theodore was not unwilling to make the exchange, although
the Duke of Zweibrücken declared that he preferred to be
buried under the ruins of Bavaria. This answer, said
Joseph, "smacked chiefly of Potsdam," nor was he far
wrong. Frederick by this time had completed a long
projected *Fürstenbund*, or close association of princes, for
mutual protection. The confederates were to act as a unit
at the diets, to strive for a reform of the imperial Chamber
Court, to guarantee to each other the safety and inviola-
bility of their territories. As there were three electors,
Hanover, Saxony, and Brandenburg, in the league, and
as all agreed to act in unison at a future election, an enor-

mous pressure could be brought to bear upon the Hapsburgs.

This first confederation of German states, under the
leadership of Prussia, was temporary in character and
looked to the attainment of a single object — the frustration of the Austrian designs on Bavaria. This object it
achieved, but it played no further rôle. Yet the *Fürstenbund* has its great importance as the presage of what was
to come; and, also, for two other reasons: for the first time
Germans tried to settle their own affairs without calling
in foreign aid, and, for the first time, in the composition
of such a league, religious differences played absolutely
no part. "It is time to get out of the old rut," a warm
defender of the project had written; "be you Catholic or
Protestant, you are a free German man whose forefathers
would rather have died than serve!"

The *Fürstenbund* was the last political achievement of
Frederick the Great; the time had come for him to throw
off what he himself called "the worn-out cover of his
soul." His last years seem to have been miserably
unhappy: all his pleasures and resources had come to an
end, and the loss of his front teeth prevented him even
from playing the flute; while oppressive taxation had cost
him much of his popularity. "Old sour-mug" was the
nickname given him even in his own family. For the
person of his heir, — his nephew, Frederick William, —
he had neither love nor respect; he doubtless felt a presentiment of the coming wreck and ruin of his country.
The "wonderful man of war," as Pitt once called him,
had become a sad misanthrope. "I am tired of ruling
over slaves!" he once said; and he interrupted a pedagogue, Sulzer, who was telling him didactically that
man inclined rather to the good than to the bad, with:
"Inclines more to the good? Ah, dear Sulzer, you don't
know this damned race as I do!"

Death of
Frederick
the Great.

More and more he withdrew into himself, working the more feverishly the nearer he saw his end approaching. Though racked with pain he continued to receive his councillors at four o'clock in the morning. When, indeed, he appeared at parade, everything else was forgotten but the former military glory, and wave after wave of applause was wont to greet the old hero. It was a rare occasion like this that hastened his death; six hours in the saddle, with no protection from the rain, proved too much for the broken septuagenarian. On the 17th of August, 1786, he passed away in his arm-chair, at Sans Souci, and a new era broke over the Prussian state.

CHAPTER VI

THE FRENCH REVOLUTION, THE DISRUPTION OF GERMANY, AND THE DOWNFALL OF PRUSSIA

LITERATURE : In addition to the general histories of Prussia we have Treitschke's *Deutsche Geschichte im XIX Jahrhundert*, the most brilliantly written history in the German language. It does not altogether supersede Häusser, *Deutsche Geschichte, 1786–1815*. Fyffe's *Modern Europe* is based largely on the latter work for this period. Boyen's *Erinnerungen* is a contemporary source of high value. We have also a number of splendid biographies which partly fall into this period : Seeley's *Stein*, Droysen's *York*, Delbrück's *Gneisenau*, Lehmann's *Scharnhorst*. The Countess Voss, mistress of ceremonies of Queen Louise, has left famous memoirs which, however, display a certain aridity of mind. Nettlebeck's *Lebensbeschreibung* is very interesting. Fournier's *Napoleon* is good.

AT the end of the eighteenth century there were in Germany no less than three hundred independent sovereignties, ecclesiastical states, or free cities; not to speak of fifteen hundred imperial knights with jurisdiction over their subjects. The territory of modern Würtemberg alone, was divided among seventy-eight different rulers, under the almost nominal headship of the emperor. Some of these principalities were infinitesimally small, even when compared with domains like those of a modern prince of Waldeck, which one can traverse in the course of a morning's stroll. The abbess of Gutenzell was down in the *Reichsmatrikel*, or military schedule of the empire, for one-third of a horseman and three and one-third foot soldiers; the barony of Sickingen for two-thirds of a horseman and five and one-third foot. The burgravate of Reineck could boast of one castle, twelve poor subjects, one Jew, and a couple of farms and millwheels.

Germany a conglomeration of small principalities.

The rulers of these petty states wasted little thought on problems of good government. The bishoprics and abbacies, not being hereditary, were subject to a total change in the methods of administration with every change of incumbent; there was no temptation to introduce far-reaching reforms, to further industry, to secure colonists. If by chance, as occasionally happened, one of these principalities came into the hands of a really progressive man, his work was almost invariably undone by his successor. The great majority of the bishops settled down to the enjoyment of the moment, and their lands became the paradise of idlers; of the population of Mainz one-quarter were priests or beggars. The bishops themselves were as worldly as any secular princes, and spent, in drinking, most of their time, and a good part of their revenues. During a week that he spent at the court of Würzburg, Pöllnitz, the memoirist, declares that he never once left the table in a conscious condition; yet he innocently gives the palm in these matters, not to Würzburg, but to Fulda. A whole string of these bishoprics, — Mainz, Cologne, Treves, Worms, Spires, and others, — extended along the Rhine, forming the boundary against France: a weak bulwark they were now to form when the waves of the French Revolution came surging into Germany.

As to the free counts of the empire, who were also particularly numerous on the Rhine and in Westphalia, it would seem as if no effort of satire or caricature could approach the sober reality. Never in all history have pretensions so vast been coupled with territories so small. Dozens of states were able to boast of not more than seven or eight square miles apiece, yet their rulers invariably spoke of themselves as " we, so and so, by the grace of God "; and the number of " excellencies," of ministers, of marshals, of privy councillors, of *real* privy councillors, and of chamberlains, would seem almost to outnumber the male population, did we not know that many of these pompous offices could be held by one and the same man. To hide the paucity of subjects heroic efforts were often made: in one principality we find a law reducing the salary of any chancery official who does not appear at the carnival with his wife and grown-up daughters; in another, we learn that the prince provided three uniforms for his guards, so that at different times of the day they might appear as cuirassiers, as grenadiers, or as Uhlans.

There is a darker side, too, to the goings-on of these proud but impecunious lords, whose finances were often in such condition that a chief source of revenue was the lottery. Their subjects were treated like abject slaves and money wrung from them under every possible pretext. The great jurist, Moser, who has left us the best contemporary picture of constitutional matters, speaks of the code of laws of one principality as a "text-book of Christian sultanism." Resort was had to the pettiest oppressions, as when, in Wittgenstein, each house-owner was obliged to catch twenty sparrows a year and to pay a forfeit for every one short of that number. The prince of Anhalt-Zerbst made it a penal offence for any of his subjects to annoy him with complaints. There seems to have been no depth, even of crime, to which these free counts would not descend. In extreme cases the emperor's court mustered up energy to interfere; and we hear, among others, of a Count of Leiningen who was arrested and deposed on a charge of "horrible sacrilege, attempted murder, poisoning, bigamy, high treason, oppression of his subjects, unpardonable mishandling of strangers and, also, of clerical personages." A Count of Wolfegg was banished for "deceptions practised against widows and orphans."

Free
knights and
free cities.

The free knights of the empire, — descendants of the
Ulrich von Huttens, Franz von Sickingens, and Götz von
Berlichingens of Reformation times, — differed from the free
counts in not having a seat in the Diet, and in not being
obliged to aid the empire save with their own good swords.
The emperors were usually their friends, and Ferdinand
III. had caused to be inserted in the Westphalian Peace
an acknowledgment of their freedom from other jurisdiction than his own, besides other privileges that made them
hated and envied by the counts.   On the other hand, their
voluntary subsidies were the largest single item of the
emperor's scanty revenues.   Their character, as a whole,
was bad; and we have remarkable compacts, entered into
by whole bodies of them, for the observance of the most
elementary laws of good conduct, such, for instance, as
the non-committing of forgery!   By the more advanced
estates of the empire they were hated for their unprogres-
siveness, being only outdone in that respect by the degenerate free imperial cities.   These latter, of which there
were still some fifty, had been on the downward path ever
since the fifteenth century; at the end of the eighteenth
they entered a protest against the broader postal system
that the larger states were trying to introduce, on the
ground that their local messengers would lose their employment!   It may be said here, with regard to all these
little anachronisms in the way of ecclesiastical and lay
sovereignties, that, even before the French Revolution
and the power of Napoleon gave the final impetus, the
idea of secularization and annexation had long been in
the air.   When that time did come, there was very little
sympathy for them in any part of Germany.

The im-
perial Diet.

The only institutions reflecting what still remained of
the unity of the empire were the *Reichstag*, or Diet, the
imperial *Kammergericht*, or Chamber Court, and the em-

peror's own Austrian court, the *Reichshofrath*, at Vienna. The first of these, the Diet, had its headquarters at Ratisbon and formed, since 1666, a permanent or perpetual body. Moser thinks it fortunate in having sat so long, as a new one could never have been brought together. Vastly it differed, indeed, from those famous old assemblies of Hohenstaufen or of Reformation times, when the emperor and his princes rode in with such retinues that the walls could not contain them. So low had the prestige of the empire now fallen that its chief business was in the hands of half-paid underlings; scarcely one of the states had an envoy entirely its own, but rather banded together with eight or nine others to save expense and trouble. There were years when all three colleges combined — the electors, the princes, and the free cities — could boast of but twenty-nine delegates among them. Even then the machinery of government was uncommonly slow and unwieldy; each imperial proposition had first to be agreed to in each of the three colleges, which then negotiated one with the other; while in default of unanimity no conclusion was arrived at at all. This frequently happened, for the interests represented were often European rather than German. The envoy from Hanover voted in the interests of England; Brandenburg signified Prussia; Saxony, Poland; Austria, Hungary and Flanders; Alsace, France; and Oldenburg, Russia.

But what most hindered the progress of affairs at Ratisbon and what made the assembly the laughing-stock of Europe was the extreme sensitiveness with regard to etiquette and precedence. Once or twice such matters almost led to war between small states, and an incident with regard to the taking in to dinner of the wife of the Austrian envoy was not settled until after ten formal writings had been drawn up and published. If this same Austrian commis-

Attention to etiquette.

sioner was to be visited by the envoy of an elector, it was immutably prescribed just what courtesies should be rendered, and just how far the legs of the electoral representative's chair should be placed on the red carpet where sat the emperor's agent. The envoys of the ordinary princes had advanced a claim that the front legs of their chairs should at least be allowed to rest upon the fringe. Once, when, after a dispute as to who should sit on green and who on the more august red chairs, it had been decided that all should sit alike on green, one of the electoral members brought in a red cloak and placed it so as to cover the whole seat, — considering that thus, as he wrote to his home government, he had vindicated the honor of his master ! It was the same with regard to eating off gold or silver plate, and particularly with regard to the liveries of the servants.

The imperial Chamber Court.

With the imperial Chamber Court matters were worse if possible than with the Diet ; from the beginning, in 1495, the emperors had looked upon this institution as a curtailment of their own prerogative and had drawn all the cases they could before their own Austrian court, the *Reichshofrath*, of which the members were imperial satellites. Long without a fixed abode, the Chamber Court had, in 1576, settled at Spires, whence, in 1689, it had fled from the armies of Louis XIV. It was four years more before it could find a town to harbor it; and, when insignificant Wetzlar at last opened its gates, it remained there contentedly to the end of its existence, although for more than fifty years there was no building large enough to hold its records, which were stored in other towns. If the members of the Diet quarrelled about precedence and etiquette, still more did this highest court in the land wrangle over form and procedure : a quarrel begun in 1704 hampered the transaction of business for seven years, while another, fifty years later, caused a suspension of all activities. The want of a fixed income was so serious that, out of the fifty judges originally contemplated, but seventeen could be employed; and the proposal was made to raise revenues by lottery. The number of unsettled cases was very great: Goethe, who was employed in his youth at this court, speaks of twenty thousand and declares that they are yearly increasing at the ratio of two to one. No wonder, when we hear that a single suit had been going on for 188 years, and that, in another, 684 witnesses had been heard, whose testimony filled no less than 10,864 pages! The Emperor Joseph II. had tried to cope with these magnificent arrears of injustice and had established a revisory committee; but, after nine years of labor, the members had gone apart in despair, and, we are told, " with mutual bitterness."

The old empire of Charlemagne, of Otto the Great, and of Frederick Barbarossa was paralyzed to its very marrow, and the best minds of the age had no sympathy or loyalty left for it. "I have no conception," writes Lessing, " of the love of fatherland, and it seems to me at best a heroic weakness which I can very well do without." Goethe was made happier by an interview with Napoleon than by any victories of German arms. The most real patriot of the day was Baron Stein, the last and best of the imperial knights; but even his loyalty was not to a present but to a future Germany, that he himself was to help to build. *No patriotism among the Germans.*

Over against all this disruption there might, at any time up to the death of Frederick the Great, have been placed the power of the Prussian state. Here at least it seemed as if a great integral part of the empire had been built up upon a rock of bronze. How else could a Prussian king have so long held at bay the rest of Germany and the whole of northern Europe? And when Frederick founded *Decline of Prussia.*

his *Fürstenbund*, it seemed as though a bulwark had been set up that would withstand almost any possible shock.

Yet scarcely had this iron-sceptred rule come to an end when the state for which the watchful old king had done and suffered so much, began a surprisingly rapid downward career; within a period of ten years it had engaged to maintain a dishonorable inactivity, within twenty it had to face, not only financial bankruptcy, but moral and intellectual, political, and military ruin. How Frederick would have writhed in his coffin to see the Prussian government conducted on sentimental-mystic principles, and to find a grand commander of the Rosicrucian Order consulting images in magic mirrors as to future policy!

Frederick William II. and the Rosicrucians.

Even outside of Prussia, the end of the eighteenth century was a halcyon time for spiritualists, alchemists, and all sorts of secret and mysterious associations. Freemasonry flourished in various forms, and one outcome of it was this Order of the Rosicrucians, — in the ninth or highest degree of which, a brother became as wise as Moses or as Aaron, and could command implicit obedience from all underlings. The occupation of the brethren was the mystic interpretation of the Bible and of natural occurrences, and the communing with spirits. Attempts were also made to create men by chemical processes, to find the philosopher's stone that would turn everything to gold, and to provide an elixir of youth. A professed object of the Rosicrucians in Prussia was " to further the honor of the Almighty in a fallen world as a means to the happiness of the human race " ; and all this was to be done " by means of the exalted knowledge and powers bestowed by divine mercy on the highest officers [of the order] and on them alone." A severe reprimand was bestowed on a sceptical brother who refused to believe that his superiors could hatch chickens from boiled eggs.

It was into such an order as this that the Prussian king caused himself to be initiated as Brother Ormesus Magnus; and one of the "highest officers," Wöllner, almost immediately recommended himself to him as "an unworthy instrument by which to save millions of souls from ruin, and bring back the whole land to faith in Jesus." Wöllner gradually made himself head of various departments, and declared war on the old system of enlightenment. When Ministers Herzberg and Hoym opposed a certain taxation project, Wöllner complained sadly that they "still had Satan in their hearts." In 1788, he succeeded in ousting the old minister, Zedlitz, and himself assumed the whole direction of Prussia's spiritual affairs. The king declared his intention of no longer permitting "that the religion of Christ be undermined, the Bible made a laughing-stock to the people, and the banners of infidelism, of deism, and of naturalism be openly set up." Candidates for the ministry were put through most rigid tests; a censorship was established forbidding all discussion of religious or dogmatic questions; and even the great philosopher Kant was taken to task for one of his writings, and warned either to make a better use of his talents or to suffer the consequences.

Such measures were unwise enough in themselves; but when it was found that behind it all there existed in the royal household an almost unparalleled immorality, the result was disastrous alike to the prestige of the throne and to the good conduct of the people. Frederick William had not only divorced one wife, Elizabeth of Brunswick, and kept a second, Louise of Hesse-Darmstadt, in seclusion; but there was no secrecy about his connection with the wife of his chamberlain, Rietz, whom he raised to the rank of Countess Lichtenau, and who influenced him throughout his whole reign. Moreover, on the plea that

Immorality of the court.

Martin Luther had excused such conduct in Philip of Hesse, he contracted bigamous marriages, sanctioned by unworthy priests, first with the charming Julie von Voss, niece of the old countess; then, on her death, with Sophie Dönhoff.

For a time, Frederick William had made a successful bid for popularity by reversing many of the more hated measures of his predecessor. The French tax-gatherers and coffee-smellers were packed off in disgrace without even the salaries they had well earned; life was made more easy for many citizens, and particularly for the widows and orphans of soldiers. The Miller-Arnold decision was reversed, and Blücher and York, officers who had been under Frederick's displeasure, were reinstated in the army.

Frederick William's lax rule.
Real wrongs may thus have been righted, real generosity exercised; there is no doubt but that Frederick William sought the happiness of his subjects, but his tender-heartedness did them more harm than good. The taxes abolished were not replaced by other revenues; aged officers were left in the army, when, for the sake of the service, they should have been placed on the retired list; land grants were recklessly made. Frederick the Great had left an accumulation in the treasury of more than fifty million thalers: it took but nine years to exhaust this, and a debt was begun which soon ran up to fifty millions more.

It is difficult to name a department in which there was not some break with the former policy. The minutiæ of drill wearied the king, so he handed over the direction of military matters to a newly constituted board. Frederick had allowed outsiders to have little influence either on his internal or his external policy; his successor was in the hands of Wöllner and of another Rosicrucian, Bischoffs-werder, who had once cured him of a disease, and with whom he spent much time in calling up the spirits of the dead.

Frederick had made it a principle not to thrust himself into European politics where the interests of Prussia were not directly concerned. " Were I to interfere in the case of every tiff in my family," he once said, " I should soon be at odds with half of Europe." His successor, on the contrary, almost immediately became involved in a struggle between the patriotic and the aristocratic parties in Holland, for no other reason than that the wife of the Prince of Orange was his own sister. Twenty thousand Prussians marched into the country, and, almost without bloodshed, restored order ; but no effort was made to recover even the actual costs of the expedition, which amounted to six million thalers ; while soldiers and officers alike, having to face but small opposition, gained an exaggerated idea of their own prowess. *A weak foreign policy.*

The same inability to make capital out of a favorable situation showed itself in a more serious degree with regard to Austria. The past had proved conclusively that here for all time was Prussia's natural enemy and rival in Germany ; even a tyro could have seen that the only proper policy was to strengthen and extend that *Fürstenbund* which had cried halt to the house of Hapsburg in the matter of the Bavarian succession. There were golden opportunities only waiting to be seized; for Joseph II.'s reign was ending in fiasco and revolt, and the *Fürstenbund* possessed a majority in the electoral college sufficient to altogether exclude the old imperial line. Moreover, Joseph's latest acts might well be regarded as a challenge to Prussia; for his friendship with Russia had culminated in a common attack upon Turkey which was intended as a preliminary to further aggressions in the empire itself. This threatening of the balance of power led to an alliance *Prussia, Austria, and Turkey.*

between Prussia, England, and Holland, and to a demand that Austria should cease hostilities in Turkey. Frederick William was eager for war, and drew his troops together; but his minister, Hertzberg, thought to achieve his ends by a series of diplomatic moves, and by changes of territory that would have given Moldau and Wallachia to Austria, Galicia to Poland, and Danzig and Thorn to Prussia.

In the end Austria was compelled to cease hostilities in Turkey and to render back her conquests; but Prussia once more reaped nothing for herself but a harvest of debts. Leopold was allowed to succeed Joseph without any counter concessions being asked or offered; the new emperor was most adroit in appeasing the wrath of the truculent Prussian king; and, although the Treaty of Reichenbach, signed in 1790, was an apparent humiliation for Austria, it was in reality a brilliant victory. The Turkish conquests that were abandoned could never have been maintained without great difficulty; while Prussia's new, peaceful attitude allowed Austria to settle her own difficulties with the rebels in her Belgian provinces and in Hungary.

The Congress of Reichenbach.

Moreover, in the midst of the negotiations, Frederick William had shown his weakness of character to the whole world; at the congress that was held in the little Silesian town of Reichenbach one set of demands was on the point of being acceded to, after long deliberations, when others of a quite different nature were suddenly brought forward. These, too, Austria was obliged for the moment to accept, but she neither forgave the insult nor did she ultimately fulfill her agreements. Prussia had been wasting her forces; she had gained no material advantages, she had exacted no valid pledge for the future. Worst of all, a recognition of the *Fürstenbund* had not been made a condition of the peace ; and the one chance of forming a permanent counterpoise to Austrian aggressions had been weakly forfeited.

Meanwhile, to the Prussian state, the French Revolution had brought new dangers and difficulties, to its head, new opportunities of squandering treasure and prestige ; while the stirring events that were going on in Poland caused Frederick William's attention to oscillate between his eastern and his western boundaries, with the result that little was accomplished in either direction.

Theoretical enthusiasm for the French Revolution.

The earlier events of the French Revolution had aroused a certain amount of enthusiasm in Germany, though not of the kind that leads to action. Philosophers like Kant and Fichte imagined they were witnessing a practical working out of their own teachings, the triumph of the sovereign ego. The former is reported to have cried out, " O Lord, now lettest Thou Thy servant depart in peace, for mine eyes have seen Thy salvation "; while the latter openly defended the right of a people to change its form of government, when necessary, by violence. The poet Klopstock wrote an ode to the Revolution and dressed himself in mourning when Mirabeau died. In Mainz, in Hamburg, and in a few other places, liberty poles were erected and celebrations held in honor of the storming of the Bastile ; in Berlin women wore in the streets the tri-colored badge of liberty, equality, and fraternity. There were few actual disturbances, and it mattered little to Germany at large that an abbess of Frauenalp was driven from her tiny domains. Moreover, when blood began to flow so freely in Paris, all other feelings gave way to horror and disgust. " Cancers are not cured by rose-water," wrote one apologetic news-leaf of the day ; but, fortunately, in Germany, the more radical remedy was **not** popular and was not employed.

Friction
caused
by the
Revolution.

The Revolution could not be kept within the boundaries of France for several reasons; in the first place the rights of the empire had been infringed upon when, on August 4, 1789, all feudal, and, in June, 1790, all ecclesiastical, jurisdictions were sweepingly abolished. Much of the land in Alsace belonged to German bishops and princes; their rights had been acknowledged by the Peace of Westphalia, as well as by later treaties, although their status had never been clearly established. France was willing now to pay some indemnity, but not to restore the confiscated territory. The Diet of Ratisbon made recriminations, but, with characteristic dilatoriness, allowed the matter to drag on for two years. A further leaven of discontent lay in the fact that the dispossessed French nobles sought refuge on German territory, — notably at Coblenz, in the archbishopric of Treves, — where it soon became evident that they had forgotten none of their extravagances and follies. Upheld by the archbishop, they set up a gay, dissipated little court and commenced to muster and drill an army, — using the public buildings, and even the weapons from the arsenals, for their own purposes. Naturally, such doings aroused the wildest indignation in France and made matters ripe for war.

The decla-
ration of
Pillnitz.

But the chief cause of Germany being drawn into the maelstrom, was the sympathy of the Emperor Leopold and of Frederick William for the luckless king and queen of France. Leopold was the brother of Marie Antoinette, and, though long deaf to her prayers and entreaties, prepared for emergencies by forming an alliance with Prussia — an alliance for which Bischoffswerder was responsible and in which all the advantage was on Austria's side. This Treaty of Vienna was signed in July, 1791, contrary to instructions and contrary to the trend of opinion in Prussia; but the Rosicrucian knew his royal master and

easily procured his sanction.   In an encyclic letter, dated
at Padua, Leopold had already called upon the powers of
Europe to prepare to avenge any insult that might be
offered to Louis XVI., and to refuse to recognize any
French constitution not voluntarily accepted by the
crown.   The emperor and the king of Prussia then met
at Pillnitz, in Saxony, and issued the meaningless declaration that they considered the affair of Louis XVI. the
common concern of all sovereigns — meaningless because
all action was to be unanimous, and it was known beforehand that England would not act at all.

The excitement was quelled for a time by the reinstatement of Louis XVI. in his dignities, and by his voluntary
oath to observe the constitution.   Leopold modified his
demands with regard to the confiscated lands in Alsace,
and joined with Prussia in ordering the Archbishop of
Treves to desist from favoring the *emigrés*.   But, by this
time, the wilder Girondins had gained the upper hand in
the French assembly ; men like Brissot and Condorcet
were convinced that war alone, by making the republic
acceptable to a reluctant majority and by filling the
empty coffers with booty, could save France.   To this
end they exerted all their eloquence : " A people that
has conquered its freedom after ten years of servitude
must have a war," cried Brissot in a Jacobin gathering.
The designs of the foreign powers were painted in the
blackest colors ; and whereas, at Padua and Pillnitz, the
emigrés had in reality been pushed aside, they were now
declared to be at the bottom of a great conspiracy.   A
demand, in the form of an ultimatum, was put to Leopold ; under penalty of immediate war he was to promise
to renounce his plan of a European alliance and to show
his readiness to support France.   In answer to his dignified reply, war was declared on the 20th of April, 1792, —

The
Girondins
bring abou,
war.

the unfortunate Louis XVI., already more a corpse than a man, being forced to appear in the legislative assembly and read the fateful words.   The terrible era of bloodshed began, that was not to end for twenty-two years.

The march
of the
allied
armies
under
Brunswick.
In spite of occasional small victories like those which led to the composing of "Heil Dir im Siegerkranz" in 1793, and to the erection of the Brandenburg gate as an arch of triumph, the next three campaigns were in reality full of disasters for Germany.   The reasons of this are to be found in the misconception of the strength and determination of the French, in the unfortunate choice of a commander-in-chief, and, finally, in the differences of aim and policy between Prussia and Austria.   In this latter country Francis II., a man of the feeble stamp of Charles VI., had succeeded the capable Leopold.

At the beginning there had been real enthusiasm for the war : "To Paris, to Paris !" was the cry of the Prussian officers ; "a mere hunting party ! Rossbach ! Rossbach!" "Don't buy too many horses," Bischoffswerder said to Colonel Massenbach, "the comedy won't last long !"   But it soon became evident that the *emigrés* had told outrageous lies about the numbers, discipline, and spirit of the French army ; as a matter of fact there were in 1793 nearly a million sturdy men voluntarily in arms, — among them dozens of the future generals and marshals of France — while, from the people at large, instead of the expected cries of *vive le roi*, the advancing army heard everywhere *liberté et égalité*, varied by the mocking *ça ira !*

Valmy and
Jemappes.
The forces of the allies, numbering a hundred thousand men, were ridiculously insufficient for the invasion of a land like France.   The Austrians had sent but a corps where they should have sent an army ; the arrangements for provisioning were so poor that halts were made for no other purpose than to bake bread ; while the commander, Duke

Charles Ferdinand of Brunswick, who was hampered besides by the presence of Frederick William II. in camp, displayed an unparalleled hesitancy and want of daring. One who was under his command at this time accords him "great talents, deep insight, but, at decisive moments, a total want of character." He inaugurated his first expedition by one of the most blatant and unwise manifestoes that ever was devised; in it the inhabitants of Paris were ordered to show due respect to the king and royal family, else the members of the assembly, of the municipality, and of the national guard would answer with their heads, without hope of pardon, while the city of Paris itself would be delivered over to military execution and total overthrow. This from a man who turned his back and withdrew from renewing the charge, when on the heights of Valmy there offered itself a first great chance of an almost certain victory! His own excuse for retreating was that he feared lest Frederick William, with insufficient forces, should insist upon marching on Paris! Almost contemporaneously with this shameful episode at Valmy, of which Goethe said that night, "to-day begins a new era in the world's history," came the defeat of the Netherland army of the Austrians, at Jemappes, and the rounding of the Prussian flank by Custine, who fell on the defenceless Rhine bishoprics. The elector of Mainz and his nobles instantly took to flight with all their treasure, — "for once," writes a contemporary, "our beautiful, venerable Rhine furnished a pleasing spectacle of busy traffic," — but to the lower classes there was issued an archiepiscopal edict ordering them to stay where they were under pain of the highest displeasure!

The year 1793 was marked by the death on the scaffold of Louis XVI., and by the formation of the first great coalition of the indignant powers. Prussia accomplished the

Frederick
William
hesitates
between
France and
Poland.

reconquest of Mainz ; but, in the midst of the campaign, events in Poland brought about a great division in Frederick William's interests, and fanned the jealousy of Austria to a white heat.   From now on, neither on the eastern nor on the western frontier, were matters pushed with sufficient emphasis.   At the end of his own resources, the successor of Frederick the Great begged in vain for subsidies from the other German states, and finally entered his whole army into the pay of the English ; but, according to their notions at least, fulfilled his part of the contract so badly that the supplies suddenly ceased.   He had thought to accept their money while yet retaining his position as head of a great power and choosing his own scene of war ; whereas Pitt treated the Prussians as the Hessians had been treated in the American war, and ordered his new hirelings off to Belgium.

The
"dumb
session" of
Grodno.

In Poland, in 1791, a liberal constitution had been set up that had the disadvantage, from a Russian and Prussian point of view, of promising to make the country strong and united ; on the plea that the dangerous ideas of the French Revolution were here taking root, Catherine II., with the help of the confederation of Targowicz, overthrew this constitution and prepared for a second partition.   Austria was not consulted at all, and Frederick William was forced to take what was offered, or see the whole absorbed in Russia.   His thoughts had been busy in this direction far more than with France, and his army pressed in to complete the iron chain around Grodno, where the Diet was ordered to meet.   Then followed the famous " dumb session," where absolute silence followed each demand to sign the Prussian title-deeds.   After midnight had passed, the presiding officer, Count Ankwicz, declared that silence gave consent ; and, when silence still followed a threefold putting of the question, Marshal Bielinski pronounced the motion passed. We know now, in the light of new evidence, that the whole was a concerted comedy, designed to protect the members, who had all been bribed, from the wrath of their constituents, — Ankwicz and Bielinski both accepted rich rewards from Russia. But the falseness and levity of the Poles themselves does not alter the shamefulness of the entire proceeding. Prussia's share of the robbery consisted of Danzig and Thorn, besides Posen, Gnesen, Kalisch, and other districts, — containing in all some twenty-five thousand square miles and one million inhabitants. The whole was given the name of the province of South Prussia, and filled up a great gap between Silesia and West and East Prussia. To Poland there was still left about one-third of her territory ; but her tenure of that was none too secure.

The second partition of Poland still further widened the breach between Frederick William and Francis of Austria ; all the more as the latter's counter demand of the right to exchange the Netherlands for Bavaria — a demand encouraged so long as it suited Prussia's interests — was now refused. As a result of all this hostility, the war on the Rhine was conducted with more laxness than ever ; the generals, Kalckreuth and Möllendorf, remained inactive at important moments ; and, in July and August, 1794, Jourdan, Michaud, and Moreau were able to conquer Aix-la-Chapelle, Coblenz, and indeed the whole left bank of the Rhine with the exception of Mainz.

The second and third partitions of Poland.

Meanwhile the curtain had risen for the last act of the Polish tragedy. Russian oppression led to a final struggle for freedom, of which Kosciusko was the intrepid hero. Frederick William's troops had a chance to quell the revolt before the Russian troops could come up. At the head of his army he did conquer Cracow and turn against Warsaw; but his evil genius, Bischoffswerder, urged him not to risk his forces in an attack ; and it was reserved for the Russian Suvarov to defeat Kosciusko's army and carry off its leader. It was Russia and her new ally, Austria, that now dictated the terms of the final partition, — forming in January, 1795, a secret compact with regard to Prussia, which was to be given Warsaw and a strip adjoining East Prussia, but this, only in the event of her acquiescing in Russian and Austrian aggrandizement at the expense of Turkey. At the risk of losing the share that he already possessed, Frederick William was forced to submit and to sign the treaty.

Bad administration of the new provinces.

It may be thought that, having by these two partition treaties of 1793 and 1795, nearly doubled its territory, he had not done badly for the Prussian state; yet nowhere is the contrast to the policy of Frederick the Great more clearly to be seen. The province of West Prussia, all surrounded by Prussian territory, had been a great gain ; and by Frederick's wise and liberal measures had been raised to the level of the rest of the kingdom. The two new provinces of South Prussia and new East Prussia, on the other hand, introduced a thoroughly discordant element and one that could not be assimilated. The masses continued priest-ridden and ignorant, and contributed nothing to the common store; nor was Frederick William the man to carry out the needed reforms. On the contrary, he regarded these lands merely as a means of enriching his faithful supporters ; and he deeded away vast estates, right and left, without care or thought for the future. While other countries, in these troubled times, were doubling their military forces, he contented himself with a very slight increase of the army.

As a matter of fact his resources were at an end, his friendship with Austria broken, his zeal for the French campaign extinguished. He could not even say with truth, "all is lost save honor," for that, too, was seriously The sepa- compromised. Prussia had become the least respected of rate Peace states, and it is scarcely to be considered a step downward of Basel. when now, at Basel, she made a separate peace with France, one secret clause of which boldly faced the prospect of the left bank of the Rhine remaining in French hands. It is true, Frederick William hoped that the rest of Germany would follow his example; indeed, as it was, the Peace of Basel was to apply to all the states behind an imaginary line of demarkation, including Hanover and Saxony. But the fact remains that he left others to fight his battles, and that he was willing to sacrifice German lands, — merely stipulating that, if Prussia should lose her own outlying provinces, she should be indemnified at the expense of some power or powers on the right bank of the Rhine.

There is a great difference of opinion between the con- The Treaty temporary observer and the modern historian as to the of Basel a merits of this treaty. Frederick William wrote to Cath- grave error. erine that he considered himself as merely following in the footsteps of Frederick the Great, by first securing his territory, and then preserving it in peace. Hardenberg, the future reformer, approved the step; and Kant was moved by the news to write his treatise on perpetual peace. A transient era of commercial prosperity beguiled the masses. But, seen in its right perspective, this peace unmasks itself as the beginning of the end, as an abdication on the part of Prussia of all her rights and privileges. Her most passionate lover and advocate of to-day, the late court historian, Von Treitschke, considers that no defeat in battle could have humbled this state as she now humbled herself, that an open alliance with an enemy would have been preferable to this pusillanimity, that here at Basel was committed the most serious political error of modern German history, an error that had to be atoned for through two decades of unparalleled misery.

Napoleon
Bonaparte
in Italy.

Prussia stood aside, now, while Austria continued the war, — continued it, with little help from the empire, against five French armies, one of which was commanded by the rising genius of the age, Napoleon Bonaparte. The latter was sent to Italy in the spring of 1796, and soon began to display his marvellous abilities, — showing to the world a new and wonderful kind of strategy that required no base of supplies, and, indeed, that bade defiance to all the old rules of warfare. He attached his soldiers to his own interests by furnishing them with booty in plenty : " I will lead you into the most fruitful plains in the world," he had said to them; "flourishing provinces, great cities, will be at your disposal." In return, he demanded courage and steadfastness and a willingness to die by thousands in pursuit of great objects. His design was to master Mantua and control the passes of the Tyrol; then to join with the Rhine army under Moreau and Jourdan and completely crush the enemy. As far as the Italian scene of warfare was concerned, he was successful : making a separate peace with the emperor's Sardinian allies, taking and holding Mantua against four attempts to relieve it, gaining the battles of Arcola and Rivoli, and bringing Lombardy, Venice, and the papal states to terms. But Moreau and Jourdan, after achieving several victories, were forced back across the Rhine by the brave young Archduke Charles; and the principalities of Würtemberg and Baden, which had gone over to the French, thought best to renew their allegiance to the empire.

The Treaty
of Campo
Formio.

Napoleon, from political motives and from a desire to have the peace all his own, had made overtures to Austria even while preparing to deal further blows. Professing to be animated by the most humane of motives, he wrote that he would feel prouder of the humble crown to be earned by saving a single human life, than of all the

mournful glory that could come of success in war. He
was willing that Austria should emerge from the long
conflict nc poorer in territory than she had entered it ;
but the map of Europe was to be cut according to his
own pattern, and Austria was to definitely abandon the
cause of the empire.   Baron Stein, with whose grand
character we shall soon become familiar, calls the treaty
that was signed on October 17, 1797, "the black and
complete treachery of Campo Formio "; yet it was scarcely
more black than the Peace of Basel of 1795, or than a
subsequent treaty of August, 1796, that gave Prussia
definite compensation in case of the sequestration of Cleves
and Guelders.   In the new treaty of France with Austria,
as well as in that with Prussia, the clauses regarding the
left bank of the Rhine were secret; in both cases the
leading powers in Germany promised to abandon to their
fate provinces that contained the coronation place as well
as the first archiepiscopal see of the old empire.   Austria's
reward was to be the dismembered republic of Venice, —
for which she had long lusted, — the archbishopric of
Salzburg, and, possibly, Bavaria as far as the river Inn.
Belgium, on the other hand, was to fall to France; while
Lombardy was to be allowed to join the Cisalpine Republic, one of Napòleon's new vassal states.   The conqueror
himself has said of this Treaty of Campo Formio, that he
considered it one of the most advantageous that France
had signed for centuries ; while the emperor, too, had
every reason to be satisfied, although, by secularizing
Salzburg, he gave the signal for a descent upon the lands
of the clergy in Germany.

As Austria had no possible right or authority to deed
away territory of the empire, it was necessary to call a
congress for that purpose.   With characteristic duplicity
the summons invited the different states to send repre-

The Con-
gress of
Rastadt.

sentatives to the town of Rastadt who should treat of
constitutional affairs *on the basis of the integrity of Germany*. Matters pertaining to the public weal were to be
settled so as to conduce for centuries to the lasting joy
of peace-loving humanity. The withdrawal of the emperor's forces from Mainz, of which the French were
allowed to take possession, and the simultaneous entry
of the Austrian troops into Venice, gave the first official
betrayal of the whole scheme. France's plenipotentiaries
at the congress now came out with their unvarnished
demand for the left bank of the Rhine, and the German
princes whose lands were to be taken began to clamor for
compensation and to throw themselves upon the generosity of the national enemy. It was the beginning of
an ignoble race for gain, inasmuch as each power, Prussia
included, thought by French influence to greatly better
its previous condition. Even the Poles when robbed of
their fatherland had acted with more dignity. It was
during a hasty visit to this congress that Napoleon Bonaparte gained his first insight into German politics and
German character, which may well account for the con-
temptuousness with which he always treated this people.

Weakness
of the
empire.

And, indeed, the empire of Charlemagne was nearing
the last stages of paralysis. In January, 1798, the witty
publicist, Görres, drew up its last will and testament, recommending that its latest committee or deputation, here at
Rastadt, should become permanent and conclude a perpetual peace, each article of which should be discussed in
at least fifty thousand sessions; that its army be handed
over to the Landgrave of Hesse to be sold out to the
highest bidder, and its archives turned into smelling-salts
in case the heirs should be attacked with faintness.
Although the Congress of Rastadt continued in session
for more than a year, the last months were spent in fruit-

less controversy, and Austria was already treating with England and Russia for the formation of a second great coalition. The conduct of the French had become unbearable to Austria; instead of assisting the emperor to his promised portion of Bavaria, instead of excepting Prussia's provinces from the general annexation of the left bank of the Rhine so that she might have no claim to compensation, they were growing more and more friendly to this arch-enemy. And their demands at the congress kept increasing beyond rhyme or reason. Germany was to assume all debts of the annexed districts and pay them out of the revenues of ecclesiastical territory; the islands of the Rhine were to be included in the cession. What good, it was finally argued, would the left bank prove to France if controlled by forts across the river? Kehl and Castel must be handed over, and the impregnable Ehrenbreitstein completely demolished. Hostilities were precipitated by the action of Bernadotte, who was acting as envoy in Vienna. In scorn of a local military celebration, he threw out a great tricolored flag from his balcony, and when it was torn down demanded his passports and returned to Paris.

The time for a general attack by the other great powers of Europe on France and her daughter republics seemed well chosen : Napoleon Bonaparte was absent, having been sent to Egypt to strike a blow at England in the East; Hoche, the next commander in ability, had just died; the new Czar, Paul, was as much in earnest as his mother had been the contrary. It is true, Prussia held aloof entirely, but Prussia was now regarded, even by her own new ruler, as an unimportant factor. *The second coalition war.*

The hero of the first period of this second coalition war was undoubtedly the Russian, Suvarov; in a series of brilliant marches and actions he recovered nearly the *Suvarov.*

whole of Italy; while Archduke Charles, by the battle of Stockach, stopped Jourdan and drove him back across the Rhine. Meanwhile the French envoys at Rastadt, who, even after the coalition had begun its military operations, had continued to treat with the minor German powers, were ordered to withdraw, and then foully set upon, — by order, it is believed, of the Austrian prime minister Thugut, whose object was to procure certain valuable state papers of which they had possession. The outcome of the mêlée, fatal in the case of two of the envoys, increased the hatred felt by the French, who, however, as yet were powerless to requite such evil. It was the good fortune of France, however, that in not one of these great coalitions was any single power willing to subordinate its own interests to those of the common cause. Austria expected Suvarov to lay Italy at her feet; Russia desired to reëstablish the sovereignties that Napoleon had abolished, and her general, at last, thwarted at every point, downrightly refused to besiege Genoa, which was the last stronghold of the French. At England's suggestion, and hoping to be more free from restraint, he left the scene of his victories and started through Switzerland to meet additional Russian forces that were coming from the North, but — as he himself believed, through Austrian treachery — accomplished nothing beyond a series of phenomenal Alpine marches. Toward the end of the year 1799, in deep disgust, the Czar, who fully shared Suvarov's suspicions as to Austrian duplicity, called home his forces.

The peace of Lunéville.

At the same time Napoleon Bonaparte returned from Egypt, joined with Sieyès in a successful attempt to overthrow the existing constitution in France, and then, as First Consul, clothed with absolute power, prepared by a theatrical march across the St. Bernard to alter the complexion of affairs in Italy. The unrivalled victories of

Marengo and of Hohenlinden soon brought Austria back to the position she had occupied at the time of the Treaty of Campo Formio; and the Peace of Lunéville, signed in February, 1801, was a practical repetition of that earlier agreement, except that the last veil of secrecy was withdrawn from the cession of the Rhine provinces, and that France was conceded a voice in the matter of compensation. Moreover, in accordance with Napoleon's peremptory demand, the agreements were signed by the emperor not merely in the name of Austria but also of the whole empire; the cession of land which, including Belgium, aggregated some twenty-eight thousand square miles and contained three and a half million inhabitants, was thus finally consummated and the Rhine became the boundary between France and Germany. The new acquisitions were divided into departments after the manner of the rest of the territory of the French republic, while the question of the indemnities was reserved for further negotiations.

Meanwhile, in Prussia, soon after the peace of Campo Formio, there had been a change of ruler; for Frederick William II., in spite of the *aurum potabile*, or liquid gold, administered by his Rosicrucian brethren, had died of dropsy. The hearts of the people had gone out to his virtuous young successor, and especially to the latter's beautiful and charming wife, — Queen Louise, a Mecklenburg princess, — who rewarded their adoration in this very year, 1797, by giving birth to that William who was one day to become the consummator of German unity. So good were Frederick William III.'s intentions, so free and liberal his promises, that nothing but plaudits were heard on all sides. "This prince spoils our revolution," a French Jacobin complained; while an eloquent German exclaimed joyfully, "Pure reason has descended from heaven and taken its seat upon our throne." An enthu-

Death of Frederick William II and enthusiasm for the new king.

siastic band of admirers founded a set of Prussian year books in which to chronicle the expected reforms.

Incapacity of Frederick William III.

But if Frederick William III. possessed all the piety, all the morality, and all the sense of duty that could be required from any Christian man, he was, nevertheless, absolutely incapable of guiding a state like Prussia through a period of storm and stress. Timid, ill-trained, and inexperienced,— a mere pygmy compared to Frederick the Great,— he was yet called upon to govern a greatly enlarged state and to face an enemy like Napoleon Bonaparte. With his full share of Hohenzollern obstinacy, he clung to his absolutism and refused to set up competent ministers; the consequence was that his cabinet secretaries, petty men like Lombard, Beyme, and Haugwitz, assumed undue influence, insinuated where they had no authority to advise, and finally landed the ship of state on the rocks of Tilsit.

Division of the spoils of Germany.

The worst of the political faults was the continued complaisance shown to France. The scheme of that power for compensating with ecclesiastical lands on the right bank of the Rhine those princes who had lost possessions on the left, was not only acquiesced in but warmly advocated; indeed, Prussia went so far as to accept for herself five times the amount of territory she had forfeited. Although nominally in the hands of a committee of the Diet known as the Imperial Deputation, the work of dividing the spoils was really carried on at Paris. Thither, as suppliants, went the dispossessed in person:— the Solms, Laubachs, the Leyns and Leiningens, the Isenburgs and Hechingens, and a number of others. Treitschke calls them a swarm of hungry flies feasting on the bloody wounds of their fatherland. Gagern, the envoy from Nassau, relates how unworthily they sued for the favor of Talleyrand and of his secretary, Mathieu; how they caressed the minister's little poodle and played blind-man's-buff and drop-the-handkerchief with his favorite niece. It rained snuff-boxes, rising in value to 20,000 guldens, while Hesse-Darmstadt offered a bribe of a round million.

When all had been happily arranged, the act which is known as the Principal Decree of the Imperial Deputation (February 25th, 1803) annihilated 112 German states, in addition to the 97 ceded to France, and divided up 50,000 square miles of territory with more than 3,000,000 inhabitants. When the decree was referred to the Diet for ratification, that body acted with characteristic regard to ceremonial : in order to make the vote valid, the dispossessed members were ordered to be present, but, as each answered to his name, he was formally entered as "absent" in the roll. By this extensive confiscation of church and civic property, the number of ecclesiastical princes was reduced to three, that of the free cities to six. Mainz retained the archchancellorship, but was forced to exchange its lands; in place of Cologne and Treves four other principalities were raised to the rank of electorates: Salzburg, Würtemberg, Baden, and Hesse. Upon the last-named three states, as well as upon Bavaria, it had been Napoleon's policy to heap all the benefits in his power, in order to have a "Third Germany" to make use of against Prussia and Austria. For that reason Baden was given in compensation for her lost territory ten times as much as was her due ; Prussia's acquisitions, on the other hand, though not inconsiderable, were to be as far as possible away from France.

After the passing of the Principal Decree of the Imperial Deputation, the events that led to the ending of the Holy Roman Empire and to the extraordinary catas-

The Principal Decree of the Imperial Deputation.

trophe of Prussia, followed each other in rapid succession.
Frederick William had been in the enjoyment of his ill-
gotten gains but a few months when he was awakened
from his dream of being the protector of North Germany
by the announcement that Napoleon meant to strike England "wherever he could reach her." Soon afterward,
French forces under Mortier were entering Hanover. It
cannot be said that there was much love lost between the
Prussian and Hanoverian, or between the Prussian and
English governments, but every instinct of self-preserva-
tion should have driven the king to an energetic protest,
and, if necessary, to war. Even Haugwitz recommended
the immediate despatch of an armed force. Here was
the enemy whom Prussia had most reason to dread at
her very throat; Hanover almost cut her domains in two,
and the French army was encamped close to the walls
of her chief fortress of Magdeburg. Yet Frederick William remained inactive while the whole Hanoverian army
capitulated, while all the wealth of the land was appropriated, and even the forests were cut down and carried
off to France to furnish masts for the conqueror's ships.
Even when Napoleon proceeded to block the mouths of
the rivers Elbe and Weser, and thus strike a deadly blow
at Prussian commerce, this king could think of no other
expedient than to send to Brussels the self-sufficient Lombard with a few sentimental reproaches. He was sure,
Frederick William wrote, that in occupying Cuxhaven
Napoleon's general had exceeded his commands. Lombard was delighted with the suavity of his reception by
the powerful First Consul. "What I cannot reproduce,"
he wrote in his report, "is the tone of kindness and open
frankness with which he expressed his regard for your
rights." Dazzled, blinded, by Napoleon's greatness, he
could not praise enough the truthfulness, the loyalty, the

friendship that rang out in every word, and he returned from his mission without having obtained the fulfilment of one single demand.

, And Frederick William had no wrath to vent upon this empty head. "The king is determined once for all," wrote Haugwitz, who himself was soon to emulate the conduct of Lombard, "to show to all Europe in the most open manner that he will positively have no war unless he is himself directly attacked." Yet the time was not unsuitable; the political constellation was favorable, while Napoleon was too full of his intended invasion of England, for which he was massing his troops on the Boulogne shore, to wish for a struggle with Prussia and Hanover combined.

Following quickly on the occupation of Hanover came the outrageous violation of German territory involved in the murder of the Duke of Enghien, — a member of the House of Bourbon, who was declared to have taken part in a royalist conspiracy against the life of the First Consul. Enghien was seized in his own house, at Ettenheim, in Baden, by bands of French soldiers, who had marched up in the silence of the night; he was dragged to Vincennes, and, within the shortest possible space of time, tried before a court-martial, sentenced, and shot by his own open grave. Scarcely an attempt was made to excuse such conduct, though Baden and the empire were at peace with France; and Germany had sunk so low that there was no remonstrance at the flagrant breach of international law. The servile elector of Baden, when driven to the wall, pretended that Napoleon had asked his consent. When Russia tried to stir the Diet to action, the elector wrote, at his master's dictation, that he thanked the Czar for his interest, but had full confidence in the friendship and good sentiments of the French court. And the Diet

The murder of the Duke of Enghien.

itself escaped responsibility by flight, entering upon its holidays before it was time.   In the popular mind, indeed, the incident engendered intense bitterness ; Beethoven turned the slow movement of his new symphony into a funeral march, and dedicated it to the dead hero, rather than exalt, as he had intended, the great conqueror.

Servility of the South German states.

To Frederick William's tender heart the murder of the Duke of Enghien was such a blow that it put an end for the time being to the project of a Franco-Prussian alliance; although Napoleon of late had been overflowing with kindness, and had significantly hinted at a plan of forming a North German empire with the Hohenzollern at its head.   The South German states, indeed, did not waver in their subserviency;   and when, on May 18, 1804, their patron was proclaimed emperor, they outdid the French themselves in the warmth of their congratulations and in the fulsomeness of their flattery,—declaring that this new Cæsar was most like to their own first emperor, Charlemagne, and recommending themselves for further favors, should there be any more lands to divide. Nothing could have exceeded the jubilation with which Napoleon was greeted on the occasion of a journey through the Rhine provinces.

Austria becomes an empire.

Austria at this juncture considered it time to get to cover, as it were, well knowing that at the next election a Protestantized and secularized electoral college would not be likely to favor the Hapsburg dynasty.   With the consent of Napoleon, and after having, in return, recognized the latter's new dignity, Francis II., in this same year 1804, adopted the title of hereditary emperor of Austria, without as yet formally divesting himself of that of emperor of the Romans.   He grounded his action on the greatness of his house, which, as he declared,—although divine providence and the vote of the electors had brought it to such a pitch of glory that its head personally needed neither added title nor prestige, — ought not to be behind any European power in outward rank.

Meanwhile, Alexander of Russia, still indignant over the murder of the Duke of Enghien, for whom he ordered his court to wear mourning, and displeased with the result of his protests in Paris, — convinced, too, that Napoleon was cogitating a general European war, — had begun to treat in London and Vienna for the formation of a third coalition. In November, 1804, Austria closed with him a defensive alliance in the event of the French endeavoring to extend their sphere of influence in Italy. In April, 1805, England agreed to aid Russia in raising a European army of half a million of men with which to restore the threatened balance of power. Napoleon in the meantime had demeaned his greatness — so he wrote to the Czar — to the extent of accepting the Italian crown. The incorporation of Genoa in the French empire, and the excessive jubilations over former French victories in Italy, then forced Austria into open hostility. *The forming of the third coalition.*

Both France and the coalition worked hard to secure an alliance with Frederick William III., whose army of two hundred thousand men was likely to be an important factor in the struggle. William Pitt suggested as as inducement to Prussia the proffer of the left bank of the Rhine, and, if need be, of Belgium; while Napoleon held out the bait of Hanover, which, however, could only have been maintained at the cost of a war with England. Yet between these two possibilities, Frederick William wavered and pursued a zigzag policy; and finally, angered at the Russian threats of violating his territory, sought his usual refuge of feeble neutrality. Out of this he was roused by the news that France had actually committed the act that Russia had only threatened; full of righteous indig-

nation he mobilized his army, yet, even then, sent Haugwitz to carry on further negotiations with Napoleon, and
allowed his commander-in-chief, the Duke of Brunswick,
to fix the latest date possible for effecting his junction
with the Austrians.

Napoleon and Mack.

To Napoleon the news of the arming of the coalition
came very opportunely; for two years he had been per-
fecting and drilling his army for the ostensible purpose of
crossing the channel and "avenging the disgrace of six
centuries" against England. His admiral, Villeneuve, had
succeeded in luring Nelson's fleet to the West Indies, but
not in keeping it there; and the prospect for Napoleon of
achieving his design of invasion, if he really ever seriously
cherished it, must have seemed more distant than ever.
Instead, that alternative which had always been present in
his mind now presented itself with redoubled force. He
knew the Austrians better than did Pitt, although the
latter had complained of these "gentlemen in Vienna"
that they were always one year, one army, and one idea
behindhand. Napoleon had even had personal dealings
with the general-in-chief, Mack, who in 1799 had been a
prisoner in Paris. The opinion there formed had been
extremely unfavorable; this was just the kind of enemy
the French Emperor longed to have his generals meet.
"He is certainly one of the most incapable men in existence," he declared; "and, moreover, he has bad luck."

**The sur-
render at
Ulm.**

Mack had been chosen for his present position, to the
detriment of the Archduke Charles, not because of any
achievements in the field, but rather by reason of the
fertility of his brain in making brilliant plans. Unfortunately there was wanting a basis of caution and foresight.
While Napoleon was informed of every slight move of his
enemies, while his spies circulated freely in the Austrian
camp in the guise of wine-dealers, Mack did not have the

least conception that already, for three weeks, armies had
been marching from all directions to surround him. He was,
to use his own subsequent words, in a "complete dream";
he had expected to meet thirty thousand men, when, in
reality, there were nearly seven times that number against
him : all within the space of one short week, Marmont
nad crossed the Rhine at Frankfort; Bernadotte at
Würzburg; Ney, Lannes, and Murat at Kehl; Soult
and Davoust at Spires, and Napoleon himself at Strassburg. "Soldiers," cried the latter to his army, "your
emperor is in your midst ! You are now the vanguard
of the grand nation."

How different was the spirit in the army of the coalition !
When Mack drew his forces together at Ulm everybody
but himself saw that he was recklessly perilling their
safety; and the next in command, Archduke Ferdinand of
Modena, withdrew with twelve battalions in disgust, and
made his way through, though with heavy losses, to
Bohemia. But Mack was blinded by the delusion that
the rumored landing of the English in Boulogne, the
expected joining of the coalition by Prussia, and an
imaginary insurrection in Paris, would require the emperor's presence, and that Napoleon was even now beating
a retreat. There were persistent reports at the Austrian
court that the "star of the tyrant was waning"; that,
after all, he was merely a stage-monarch; and that
adulation and luxury had weakened his powers. The
rude awakening from the "complete dream" came on the
20th of October, 1805, when Mack, almost immediately
after having exhorted his troops to hold out to the last
man, surrendered them all, to the number of twenty-three
thousand, without striking a blow. "The shame that
oppresses us," wrote an Austrian officer, "the filth that
covers us, can never be wiped away !" It made no differ-

ence in the struggle on the continent that, four days later, Nelson, at Trafalgar, obliterated the sea power of France for a generation to come.

The Treaty of Potsdam.

As Napoleon swept on, accompanied by his German vassals, — and making, as was his wont, straight for the enemy's capital, — the Russians and the remnant of the Austrians withdrew to Moravia. All was not yet lost, for the French were moving farther and farther from their base of supplies; while, for the allies, reënforcements were on the way from the northeast, and there was every reason to hope that Prussia, whose armies had quickly been mobilized, would now definitely declare for the coalition. The news of Bernadotte's march through the Prussian territory of Ansbach, by which, as the allies claimed, Mack's surrender was effected, had roused Frederick William to unwonted energy, and he is said to have cried out, "I will have nothing more to do with the man !" — meaning Napoleon. He had at once notified the Czar that the Russians might cross Silesia; within ten days after Mack's capture Alexander had come to Berlin, and on November 3 had signed the Treaty of Potsdam, by which Prussia agreed to throw an army of 180,000 men into the field should Napoleon not agree, within four weeks, to relinquish all his conquests in Holland, Switzerland, and Naples. On the whole transaction the seal of sacredness had been set by a midnight visit of the Czar, the king, and the beautiful Queen Louise to the last resting-place of Frederick the Great, and a kiss imprinted on his coffin.

The battle of Austerlitz.

Napoleon, meanwhile, had taken Vienna and sent off her works of art to enrich his collection in Paris; as he advanced into Moravia, however, the position of affairs became less encouraging. Every day that passed meant a gain to the allies, a loss to himself, — a fact of which

Kutusoff, the Russian general, was well aware. But a rash decision of the Czar, impelled, it is said, by the sight of his own splendid regiments marching in review, gave to the French emperor the longed-for chance of gaining what proved to be his most splendid victory. He could not believe his ears when the report reached him that the enemy had left a strong position to try and cut him off from Vienna ; one who was with him reports that, trembling with joy and clapping his hands, he cried out to those around him : "That is a wretched move ! They are going into the trap ! They are giving themselves up ! Before to-morrow evening this army is mine !" And after the battle to his soldiers, "Soldiers, I am satisfied with you !" As well he might be, for the losses of the allies at Austerlitz were twenty-six thousand, not to speak of nearly all the guns, all the ammunition, and all the baggage.

A few days before this battle of the three emperors, Haugwitz had arrived in Napoleon's camp at Brünn with the demands of the Prussian king. He had travelled as slowly as possible, he allowed Napoleon to dally with him and send him from pillar to post, and finally, after Austerlitz, ended up a course of the most incomprehensible behavior by concluding a treaty of alliance instead of presenting an ultimatum. By the Treaty of Schönbrunn, Prussia was to receive Hanover, and, in return, to cede the remainder of Cleves, the fortress of Wesel and the principality of Neuchâtel to France, as well as Ansbach to Bavaria. On the surface, it seems incredible that any man on his own responsibility should have dared such action as that of Haugwitz ; still more incredible, that Frederick William should have ratified these engagements and treated their sponsor with respect and consideration. But underneath it all, as a recently discovered letter has proved,

The mission of Haugwitz

lay the bitter fact that the king's own courage had given out at the last moment, and that he had secretly instructed Haugwitz on no account to let it come to war !

The Peace of Pressburg.

Truly, with all sympathy for Prussia, with a knowledge of all the good forces that were even now slumbering within her, one can only say that she richly deserved her fate. Now that time has cleared the mists away and given us a larger point of view, it seems incomprehensible that this Hohenzollern should have failed so utterly to recognize where his true interests lay. Even after Austerlitz there were enough Russians at his disposal to bring the total of his army up to 300,000 men. But instead of fighting France, he deliberately agreed, in a supplementary treaty signed at Paris with Napoleon, to expose himself to a war with England for the sake of Hanover; and then, as a climax of folly, reduced his army to a peace footing ! Austria, in consequence of Prussia's action, was driven to sign with France the Peace of Pressburg (December 26, 1805), by which she was divested of 28,000 square miles of territory, 3,500,000 inhabitants, and 14,000,000 guldens of yearly revenue. On the east, on the south, and on the west her provinces were cut from her; and the man who was still head of the Holy Roman Empire was forced to acknowledge the kingship and full sovereignty of Na-

The Rhine confederation and the end of the Holy Roman Empire.

poleon's satraps, Würtemberg and Bavaria. These parvenu kings now set the crown on a long succession of misdeeds, by forming, with fourteen other princes, the Rhine confederation and repudiating the jurisdiction of the empire. At the Diet, eight envoys handed in the declaration that their masters saw fit, "commensurably with their dignity and the purity of their goals," to renounce allegiance to an organization that had practically ceased to exist, and to place themselves under the protection of the great monarch " whose views had always shown

themselves in accord with the true interests of Germany."
As for Francis II., one of the least sympathetic scions of
an unlovely race, he took occasion to write to Count Metternich, whom he sent to Paris to bargain with Napoleon,
" The moment for resigning the imperial dignity, is that
when the advantages which accrue from it for my monarchy shall be outweighed by the disadvantages that
might arise from its further retention." Metternich is
to place the price of imperial dignities very high in the
market, and to show " no disinclination to the resignation
of the said dignity, but rather a readiness — but only in
return for great benefits to be acquired by my monarchy."
" With such sentiments," writes the scourging pen of
Treitschke, " did the last Roman-German emperor bid
farewell to the purple of the Salians and the Hohenstaufens ! " The formal abdication was drawn up on the 6th
of August, 1806, and the chief ground assigned was the
defection of the Rhine princes.

Swiftly and heavily Prussia's retribution for all the
faults and errors of the past now fell upon her. Through
Napoleon's intrigues, she failed in her effort to found a
North German confederation and thus collect the last
Germans under her banner ; while, as was to be expected,
her dealings with regard to Hanover involved her in a
war with England. Hundreds of her merchant vessels
were captured in British harbors and her commerce ruined.
For Hanover she had suffered all this, for Hanover she
had violated every precept of consistency and of political
probity. And now, casually, at a dinner, her envoy learned
from the British envoy, Lord Yarmouth, that Napoleon,
who was treating for peace with England, had offered, as a
basis of negotiation, the retrocession of this same Hanover !
The English negotiations failed and Pitt's dying prophecy,
" Roll up the map of Europe, it will not be needed these

Napoleon's perfidy with regard to Hanover.

ten years!" eventually proved true. But the perfidy of
the man whom he considered his ally, and the final con·
viction that Napoleon really intended Prussia's ruin, induced Frederick William to listen to the war party at
Berlin, to which his courageous wife and even Haugwitz
belonged. He mobilized his forces, entered into an agreement with Russia by which the Czar was to furnish him
with 70,000 men, and, finally, sent an ultimatum to the
effect that the French must retire entirely from Germany
and place no hindrance in the way of the projected North
German confederation. In a proclamation to his people
he declared that he was taking up arms to free unhappy
Germany from the yoke under which she was languishing,
for: "over and above all treaties nations have their rights!"

Enthusiasm   The war was sure to be popular, for the weight of Na-
for the   poleon's tyranny was beginning to be widely felt; shortly
war.   before, he had again-shocked all Germans by the execution
of Palm, a bookseller of Nuremberg, whose only crime was
having sold a patriotic pamphlet called *Germany in the
Depths of her Humiliation* — the most revolutionary advice
in which seems to have been, "lift up your voices and
weep!" It has been said of this murder of Palm, that its
effect on the people at large was like that of the Enghien
tragedy on the crowned heads. In Berlin there had
already been demonstrations; young officers had sharpened
their swords on the window-sill of the French ambassador,
and had joined in the theatre in the chorus in Schiller's
Wallenstein, "Up, comrades, up ! to horse, to horse !"

Unpre-   But a campaign on which the very existence of a nation
paredness depended should have been inaugurated with more care
of Prussia. and caution. Frederick William III. has justly been
blamed for not entering the war before ; now he entered
it too soon. Thousands of his soldiers had been granted
leave of absence ; whole regiments had been sent back to

their distant garrisons; while, on the other hand, large French forces had remained stationed in South Germany. And the condition of the army was deplorable, its general spirit unwarlike to the last degree. The chief commands were in the hands of self-satisfied old graybeards, who had done good service in the time of Frederick the Great, but had since grown weak and pampered on account of the comforts that their sinecures offered. It would be hard to imagine a more baneful arrangement than that which allowed officers to reap advantage from issuing leave of absence to their men; the sums economized from food and maintenance flowed in such streams into the pockets of the captains, that their income in time of peace was double what it was in time of active service. The forms of the past had survived, but not the spirit; even on the march, the most promising young officers were held down to clerical work when they should have been scouring the country for information. The importance attributed to minor matters, to the length of the pigtail, to the manner of giving out the parole, bordered on the ridiculous if not on the insane. Just before the battle of Jena, Frederick William met Captain Boyen, who all the morning had been engaged in desperate efforts to clear an obstructed road for the troops, and sent word to him — that his hair was out of order.

It is doubtful if too much blame for the catastrophe of his country can be thrown on the shoulders of this weak king. His lovable personality, his perfect uprightness, his martyr-like attitude in misfortune, the final triumph of his cause, endeared him to his subjects and have blunted the pen of censorious historians; yet, as head of a nation rigidly trained for nearly a century to look to its king for everything, he had proved a most lamentable failure. At each critical moment he wavered like a broken reed.

Folly and weakness of the king

His own last ultimatum to Napoleon is a marvel of feeble self-exculpation, full of allusions to France's glory and to his own good services on her behalf. " I was the first to recognize you," he wrote. " I have been insensible to threats as well as to promises when it was a question of making me false to our good relations." Sentimental reminiscences at a moment like this when the stake was nothing less than national existence, and when most positive proofs had been furnished of the enemy's perfidy! Others saw what Frederick William could not even yet be brought to see, that nothing whatever was to be hoped for from this man, that the wheel of destruction was relentlessly advancing, that the sins committed ten and five years before were to be bitterly atoned. Ernst Moritz Arndt, the inspired prophet of liberty, draws a frightful picture, at this time, of the ruin to come, of the terrible destroyer hurling his legions from the ocean to the Rhine, of the soil stamped by the feet of hundreds of thousands, of the plunder, the starvation, the shame: " Unhappy princes, could you suffer more than you now suffer? Certainly you could not suffer more unworthily." And Jena was not yet fought, Tilsit not yet signed! An incredible blindness prevailed among the officers of the army as to the shortcomings of that institution. General Rüchel on the public occasion of a parade declared that Prussia had " several commanders equal to General Bonaparte "; Blücher, even, expressed his perfect satisfaction with the present condition of the military forces. After the campaign had already begun, a certain Captain Liebhaber was heard to say at mess: " As yet the enemy has taken no step that we had not previously prescribed to him. . . . Napoleon is as certainly ours as though we had him in this hat," whereupon many officers rose on tiptoe and looked into the hat.

Of all Frederick William's faults and imperfections none proved more fatal than his inability to recognize and make use of great men. He clung to his Beymes, his Lombards, and his Haugwitzs to the very last moment; his chief military adviser, General Köckeritz, once confided to General Boyen that he did not like to have two opposing parties approach him on a matter at the same time, "for they always know enough to put the case in such a form that I cannot tell which is right!" With the Duke of Brunswick, commander-in-chief of all the forces that were to fight against Napoleon, matters were still worse. Brunswick in his youth had been a brave leader, fearless of danger. Frederick the Great had once likened him, in verse, to the Turennes, the Weimars, the Condés. His reputation had extended beyond Germany, and, at the outbreak of the French Revolution, the Jacobins had wished him for their own commander. His achievements, indeed, on the German side had, as we have seen, been far from glorious. He was still brave in battle, but weak as his master when it came to making a decision. When the army started out in September, 1806, to meet the French in the Weimar-Jena-Erfurt region, Frederick William accompanied it. "What shall we call headquarters, royal or ducal?" wrote Scharnhorst, the only thoroughly trained soldier of them all. No single step was taken without hours of polite discussion—Frederick William and Brunswick both shunning responsibility and at last taking refuge in frequent councils of war. Had it not been for one of these latter, that lasted for eight priceless hours, Prussia might still have escaped the catastrophe of Jena. There was no concealment of the dilemmas of those highest in authority. Boyen tells of a door left open, so that a room full of young officers could hear Brunswick and the king declare their total ignorance as to the enemy's position.   All trust, all confidence, in such leadership was gone.   A deputation of officers appeared before Kalckreuth and urged him to save what was still to be saved and himself take command.

Jena and
Auerstadt.

As at Ulm, the French came upon their enemy utterly unawares and found them in a long, straggling line.   On one and the same day, Hohenlohe was defeated at Jena, and Brunswick himself, twelve miles north, at Auerstadt. Hohenlohe succumbed to superior numbers and to his own folly in camping on a plain without attempting to seize the adjoining heights, — up which, torch in hand, Napoleon himself had led his troops under cover of the night.   At Auerstadt, Brunswick's forces actually out-numbered the French by several thousands; but early in the fight he himself was blinded and mortally wounded, and could no longer direct the battle.   The other generals were ignorant of what plan of operations he had intended. Frederick William, though present, could neither make up his mind to take command himself, nor did he appoint another general-in-chief.   The different divisions of the army waited in vain for their orders, and Kalckreuth's sorely needed reserves were not called up.   Scharnhorst led a forlorn hope, and almost succeeded in saving the day.   Forced at last to retreat, he drew out his right wing in some order; but as fate would have it, the two simultaneously defeated armies pursued the same line of retreat; and unexpectedly, in the darkness of the night, came upon each other.   All discipline was at an end. Baggage, artillery, horses, and men, all were involved in one horrible moving snarl.   The king himself, with Blücher at his side, rode for fourteen hours in momen-tary danger of capture.

The worst result of the battles of Jena and Auerstadt was the sudden revulsion that they brought about, from the most arrogant over-confidence to the most extreme despair and discouragement. After one single day of battle, all power of resistance was at an end. To use the language of Napoleon's own twenty-second bulletin, the great beautiful army of the Prussians had vanished like an autumn mist before the rising of the sun. But most astonishing of all, was the manner in which one fortress after the other, hitherto deemed impregnable, fell like a house of cards. Two days after the battle of Jena, Erfurt, with eleven hundred men and great stores of provisions, capitulated ; nine days later, Spandau followed suit ; then Stettin, then Küstrin. Great hopes had been placed on Magdeburg, in which was stored a million pounds of gunpowder, and which sheltered twenty generals, eight hundred officers, and twenty-two thousand soldiers ; yet this great fortress, though besieged by a force less in numbers than its own garrison, surrendered after the twelfth shot. The blame for such occurrences falls almost directly upon the king, in whose hands had lain the appointment of the chief officers. The commandants of Magdeburg and of Küstrin were both men who had previously been punished for cowardice before the enemy ; while the commandant of Stettin had frankly told Frederick William that he was too old and too feeble for the position, and had only accepted it as a sort of sinecure.

Meanwhile, Hohenlohe, with some twelve thousand men, surrendered at Prenzlau, in the Ukermark, to a much smaller force. He was deceived by the false assertion of Murat that he was opposing him with sixty-four thousand men. Blücher, York, and Scharnhorst, who had intended to join Hohenlohe, cut their way through to Lübeck, where, after desperate fighting, and after food and ammunition had come to an end, they were taken captive. Boyen had been seri-

ously wounded.   Only in Silesia, and in one little Baltic
fortress, was there any thoroughly successful resistance
west of the Vistula; when the commandant of Colberg,
Lucadou, spoke of surrender, the brave old sailor, Nettelbeck, defied him to his face, and organized a band of citizen
defenders.   The country around was flooded, the walls
strengthened, and supplies ordered by sea from England
and Sweden.   An eloquent letter from Nettelbeck induced
the king to recall Lucadou, whose place was given to
Gneisenau.   These two heroic men, Gneisenau and Nettelbeck, played well into each other's hands, and each has
done full justice to the merits of the other; each was tireless in his activity, wonderful in his courage and patriotism.   To both in common it is due that Colberg held
out — though, after superhuman efforts, on the very point
of falling — until peace was at last declared.

Napoleon
in Berlin.
Napoleon had so well appreciated the meaning of the
victory at Jena that, only a few hours later, he imposed a
contribution of one hundred fifty-nine million francs on all
the Prussian provinces west of the Vistula; within a week
he had incorporated those to the left of the Elbe in the
French empire.   He himself had begun a triumphal progress toward Berlin; while Frederick William and his
court fled to the extreme northeastern part of Prussia.
Baron Stein, who for a short time had been minister of
finance, managed to secure the money boxes of the state
and convey them to a place of safety — a wise precaution if
a new army was to be raised.   In Berlin, Napoleon gave
full swing to the dictates of his thoroughly vengeful
nature.   On the walls of her own palace he wrote insults
against Queen Louise, whom he considered largely responsible for Frederick William's declaration of war; from the
grave of Frederick the Great he carried off the scarf and
sword and presented them to the *Invalides* in Paris; he

caused the obelisk on the battlefield of Rossbach to be broken in pieces and thrown in the dust; the figure of victory with her prancing steeds was lowered from the top of the Brandenburg gate and relegated for the next eight years to a shed on the banks of the Seine. Down the broad avenue *Unter den Linden* was driven like a herd of cattle the famous *gens d'armes* regiment, whose officers had been the gilded youth of the town, had engaged in wild notorious escapades like that summer sleighride over salted roads, or that chase of Catholic priests after one disguised as Luther, had graced the salons of those intellectual Jewesses, Rahel and Henriette Herz. It was to be many a long day now before a Prussian officer might dare even to show himself upon the streets in his uniform. The frivolous, self-conceited Berliners had a hard lesson to learn; the better-minded among them had to struggle not merely with misfortune, but also with shame, treason, and disgrace. Frenchmen themselves turned away in disgust from the cringing fear with which they were met. "Let it lie," said one of them, to whom had been officiously pointed out a goodly supply of timber; "let it lie, that your king may have something on which to hang you rogues!" Low-minded men were found who were willing to edit the newspapers in the interests of the French, and to cover with insults the Prussian royal house; a considerable number of Frederick William's old officials worked quietly on under the new régime. Even distinguished scholars like Johannes Müller and the philosopher Hegel were willing to bend their knee to the hero of the age.

For a while, even after the battle of Jena, Frederick William III. had retained his optimistic view of Napoleon's character. On the day following that event, he had sent to the emperor and asked for a truce and for

Napoleon's demands.

conditions of peace; he was sure, he wrote, that a man so loyal, with such nobility of soul, would demand nothing against his, Frederick William's, honor and the security of his territories.   Napoleon refused the truce, and his conditions for peace kept growing more severe with each new capture and surrender.   After the fall of Stettin he demanded, not merely the cession of all Prussian lands west of the Elbe, but also an abandonment of the alliance with Russia, and an agreement in certain contingencies to go to war against her; after the disgraceful capitulation of Magdeburg, nothing would satisfy him but the withdrawal of the last remnants of the Prussian troops beyond the Vistula, and the abandonment of the forts that still stood firm in Silesia, as well as Thorn, Danzig, Graudenz, and Colberg.   A treaty to this effect had already been drawn up, and a majority of the council called to debate upon the matter at Osterode had voted to ratify it, when the king, supported by Stein and Voss, found the courage of desperation and determined to fight to the death.   Particularly horrible to him had been the thought of abandoning this faithful Russian ally, this Czar to whom he felt bound by the most intimate ties of personal friendship.

Servility of Saxony.

Napoleon had experienced in this campaign the value of the Rhenish princes as allies; their soldiers had fought as bravely as the French themselves, and are said to have acted with even greater brutality.   Their confederation was now joined by Saxony, which was forever estranged from Prussia by the promise of Prussian land and the gift of a royal crown.   The new king, Frederick Augustus, who, shortly before, had been treating with Frederick William III. for entry into the proposed North German confederation, now outdid even Bavaria and Würtemberg in cheerful submissiveness.   While Prussia was in the last agonies, a great festival was held in Leipzig, where the sun, the emblem that Napoleon had borrowed from Louis XIV., was the most prominent decoration. An inscription over the anatomical room in the university proclaimed that "The dead, too, cry long life!" "Saved is the fatherland" was the favorite refrain. In Poland, too, Napoleon fostered a revolt, causing weapons to be distributed among the insurgents and expressing his deep interest in their aims.

Prussia's one friend, drawn closer by these very Polish troubles, was the handsome, blue-eyed young Czar Alexander; his forces under Benningsen joined the last remaining Prussian corps, that of Lestocq, in which Scharnhorst was the leading spirit; and together they prepared for Napoleon the first check that he had ever experienced in his victorious career. The battle of Eylau was bloody in the extreme, — some forty thousand men are said to have fallen in all, — and, though not entirely defeated, the French were forced to retire into winter quarters. The emperor made overtures of peace which Frederick William in turn refused. The prospects seemed brighter, though still far from encouraging. The Czar treated the Prussian king with the utmost friendliness, and once exclaimed fervently, "Is it not true, neither of us two shall fall alone?" In a treaty signed at Bartenstein, April 26, 1807, the two powers bound themselves not to lay down their arms until Germany should have been freed and the French driven back beyond the Rhine. *The battle of Eylau.*

But the battle of Friedland — entered into reluctantly by Benningsen after months of delay, during which Napoleon was reënforcing his army — proved a second Austerlitz; without even notifying his ally, the frightened Alexander accepted his defeat as final, and promised to sign a truce. From an enemy of Napoleon, he became his warm and *Friedland.*

affectionate friend, revelling in the thought of sharing with him the rule of the Western world.

The three
monarchs
at Tilsit.
The final doom of Prussia was spoken at Tilsit, where interviews between Napoleon and his two royal antagonists were held in the most romantic of trysting places, — a pavilion erected on a raft in the river Niemen. The whole scene was well calculated to work on the impressionable spirit of the young Czar; he was lured, not torn, from his loyalty to Frederick William. Napoleon made it appear, and indeed it was true, that only as a favor, and out of regard for the emperor of all the Russias, were any of his territories at all to be returned to the Prussian king; the latter was not called in until after two days, when he was treated with contempt and covered with reproaches. Frederick William had spared himself no personal humiliation that could better the terms for his country; he had even induced the beautiful queen to pay her humble respects to the man whom she regarded as the incarnation of the devil. She was treated politely, and returned under the impression that her visit had done some good; but, as Napoleon himself later wrote, her entreaties slid off him like water from oiled cloth.

The Treaty
of Tilsit.
In the formal document of the Peace of Tilsit the clause regarding the favor to the Czar was inserted — a wanton insult such as is rarely to be found in a great treaty. But, worse still, Alexander did not scruple to accept part of the spoils, the Polish-Prussian district of Bialystok. An English cartoon that is said to have been much enjoyed in Leipzig, and that well characterizes the situation, shows " Bony " and the Czar embracing so violently that the raft takes to rocking and throws Frederick William into the water.

The poor Prussian king lost all the districts west of the Elbe, and almost all that had been acquired from the last two Polish partitions, not to speak of isolated provinces like Baireuth and East Friesland. In actual square miles, as well as in population, there was taken away from him more than half of his possessions. These went to form the kingdom of Westphalia for Jerome Bonaparte, and the duchy of Warsaw for the faithful king of Saxony. What was left was spread out in the form of three clover leaves, at the mercy of every enemy; while for Frederick Augustus there was reserved in addition a right of way, a *via regis*, straight across Silesia.

Forced to accept this complete maiming and mutilation of his fatherland, Frederick William, in a formal proclamation, released his lost subjects from their allegiance. "That which centuries and worthy forefathers," he wrote, "that which treaties, love, and confidence once bound together, must now be sundered. Fate commands, the father parts from his children; no fate, no power, can tear your memory from the hearts of me and mine." The peasants of the county of Mark wrote back in their coarse dialect: "Our hearts almost broke when we read your message of farewell; so truly as we are alive it is not your fault!"

The lost provinces

CHAPTER VII

THE REGENERATION OF PRUSSIA AND THE WAR OF LIBERATION

LITERATURE : Same as for previous chapter.

The realization of the truth in Prussia.

THE unparalleled misfortunes which had fallen upon Prussia, paired as they were with shame, cowardice, and dishonor, had worked at least one salutary result: the eyes of the king and of those around him were opened, the era of complacency and self-satisfaction was at an end. Soon after the events at Tilsit, Queen Louise wrote to her father that what had happened had been inevitable, that the old order of things had outlived itself and crumbled of its own weight. " We have gone to sleep," she declared, " on the laurels of Frederick the Great, the lord of his age, the creator of a new era. With that era we have not progressed, therefore it has outdistanced us. From Napoleon we can learn much, and what he has accomplished will not be lost. It would be blasphemy to say, ' God be with him,' but evidently he is a tool in the hand of the Almighty with which to bury what is old and lifeless, closely as it may be welded with the things around us."

So firmly was reverence for monarchical rule still grafted on the Prussian people that reform without the king's assistance would have been impossible ; of the greatest importance it was, therefore, that Frederick William took up the work bravely and conscientiously. He could not, indeed, entirely conquer his ingrained faults of character; his indecision, his bluntness of perception, were still to drive the best of his advisers almost to despair; the state, before it could rise, was to sink to even lower depths. But, all the same, the king dimly saw the right path; and he held to it until his good fortune, finally, led him into the open.

The fate of all Germany hung on this regeneration of Prussia: low as that power had sunk, there was no other to assume the leadership. Austria, indeed, under the guidance of Stadion, was to make the attempt; and the year 1809 was in many ways to prove the most brilliant in her whole history. But she was to fail after staking her all, and her collapse was to be final. The kingdoms of Bavaria, Würtemberg, and Saxony, and the grand duchy of Baden, were utterly lacking in national patriotism; they continued to bask in the sunshine of Napoleon's favor until the storm-clouds rolled up and forced them to ignominiously run elsewhere for shelter.

Prussia still the natural leader.

One of Frederick William's most praiseworthy acts was to send for a man whom, just before Tilsit, he had loaded with reproaches and dismissed from office for having refused to compromise in any way with the old evils of cabinet government. Baron Stein — one of the last remaining free knights of the empire, with estates and a ruined castle on the Rhine — had been a trusted servant of Frederick the Great, and, in 1804, at the age of forty-seven, had become minister of trade and commerce. A stern, terrible, yet very just official, he had never learned to cringe to royalty, and felt himself fully the equal of any of the petty princes. Better than most men he knew the evils of divided rule; from the bridge over the Lahn, near his own home, he could look into the territories of eight different potentates. His own political views had become broad, liberal, and essentially national. "I have but one fatherland," he once wrote, "which is called Germany. . . . With my

Baron Stein.

whole heart I am devoted to it, and not to any of its parts."

Ruthlessly outspoken where he scented evil, Stein had doubtless gone too far in his denunciation of the king's favored councillors. Immediately after Jena, he had drawn up a memoir which was laid before the queen, and in which those in power were savagely and relentlessly criticised. Beyme was treated more leniently than the others, but was spoken of as totally lacking in the knowledge requisite for his position. Lombard was called a French poetaster, who idled away his time in play and debauchery with empty-headed people. Haugwitz's life was declared to have been an unbroken series of disorders and corruptions, that of a shameless liar and enfeebled *roué*. Soon afterward, Stein had joined with the king's own brothers in a new remonstrance, which accused the cabinet of playing into Napoleon's hands; but, when Frederick William had tried to compromise and to retain both Stein and Beyme, a misunderstanding had arisen which caused the king's wrath to completely boil over, and led him to write his opinion, as he expressed it, in plain German. He drew the pen, indeed, through certain passages of the letter relating to possible imprisonment; but he had used the words insolent, obstinate, refractory, and disobedient, and when Stein wrote back that a man with all those blemishes was not likely to be of much service to the state, he had received answer, " Baron Stein has passed judgment on himself."

The matter of the Prussian indemnity.

Now, at the king's call, acknowledged as the only man who could save the state, Stein came without hesitation — disdaining to make conditions like Wallenstein of old or even like Hardenberg to come. He had a most thankless task to perform, and he himself did not as yet know the worst. Never was a state to be so badgered and tortured

as Prussia during the next two years. The amount of
the indemnity had not been fixed at Tilsit; Daru, Napoleon's representative in Berlin, had mentioned one hundred million francs, which Frederick William had declared
it a physical impossibility to pay. A month later, Napoleon
demanded, not merely the original hundred million, but
also a sum equivalent to all the state revenues for the
eight months preceding the peace. The negotiations on
this matter, as well as on the manner of payment, went on
until September 8, 1808, when a supplementary treaty
was signed at Paris. The exhausted land in the meantime — the revenues of which for 1808 were 386,000 thalers,
the necessary expenditures 2,200,000 — had been forced to
submit to the presence of 160,000 Frenchmen, and had
been torn by doubts whether it would not have to sacrifice Silesia, or cede to France the royal domains. Extortionate charges of every kind had been trumped up and
sources of revenue sequestered; Napoleon had even seized
a fund set aside for the support of widows and orphans —
which act greatly incensed against him the women of the
land. More than a billion francs in all flowed into the
French treasury, and many a bitter experience was thrown
into the scale. Prince William, the brother of the king,
felt obliged to appear in Paris to haggle for better terms.
He offered himself as hostage if only the troops might be
removed: " Very noble, but impossible," was Napoleon's
reply. A proffered alliance was scorned until full payment should have been made. To all complaints the
emperor invariably answered, "The king has money
enough, why does he need an army when no one is at
war with him?"

The Paris Treaty was even more galling than the forced
agreement at Tilsit. The amount of the indemnity had
again been increased; the fortresses of Glogau, Küstrin,

The Treaty
of Paris.

and Stettin were still to be held by French garrisons;
rights of way were to be granted in all directions; for the
next ten years the Prussian army was not to number more
than forty-two thousand men, and, in case of a war with
Austria, sixteen thousand men were to fight on the side of
the French.   Frederick William would never have ratified such engagements had there been the least hope of
support from the Czar, who might well have protested
against this aggravation of the Peace of Tilsit.   But
Alexander, although at this time he visited the royal pair
in Königsberg, on his way to the brilliant congress at
Erfurt, was fast in the toils of Napoleon, whose favor he
needed in his designs on the Danubian principalities.   He
promised to do what he could for his luckless friends, but
his only sincere advice was submission.   In Erfurt, Napoleon received the Czar with the utmost magnificence;
though he did not grant his desires, and more than once
offended him by a total want of tact — as when, for instance, he invited Prince William of Prussia to join in a
hare-hunt on the battlefield of Jena, or again, when he
decorated with the Cross of the Legion of Honor soldiers
who had especially distinguished themselves against the
Russians.   Doubtless Napoleon's real motive at Erfurt was
to show himself in all his magnificence as the equal of the
Czar; and for that reason he summoned his German satellites, without, however, granting them a voice in the serious
deliberations.   The actor Talma could boast that he had
played to a parterre of kings, though very new and very
timid and very badly treated kings : " *Taisez-vous ce n'est
qu'un roi*," said the master of ceremonies to the chief
trumpeter, when the latter was about to strike up in
honor of one of them.   The princes of the realm of literature fared better.   "You are a man," Napoleon said
to Goethe, with whom he talked about the sorrows of

Napoleon at
Erfurt.

Werther, and whom he requested to write a tragedy on
the theme of how happy Cæsar would have made his
people if they had only given him time. Wieland, too,
was urged to implant in the public mind a more favorable
opinion of the Roman emperors. As for the Czar Alexander, all that he accomplished for the Prussian king was
to gain a rebate of twenty million thalers from the total
of the indemnity, half of which Napoleon made up by
charging four per cent interest on what remained.

Meanwhile the great reforms in Prussia were well
under way; they were to fall into four great categories:
social reforms, administrative reforms, reforms in the army,
and reforms in public sentiment. What the French Revolution had done by force and by shedding rivers of blood,
was now to be accomplished by the magic of strong men's
names and the issuing of a few edicts. Feudal tyranny
was to be done away with, the spirit of caste exorcised,
local self-government introduced, the army to be cleansed
and rejuvenated; a wave of patriotism, finally, was to be
aroused, that would sweep away all the sins and errors of
the past.

Stein and his fellow-reformers.

Immediately on receiving his summons, Baron Stein had
hastened to Memel, where, to quote his own words, he had
found the king " deeply depressed, believing himself pursued by an inexorable fate, and thinking of abdication."
The queen was " gentle and melancholy, full of anxiety
but also of hope." Stein soon discovered that his own
position was as nearly that of a dictator as was possible
under a monarchical form of government. Yet he did
not stand alone, for ready to help him was a devoted band
of earnest, talented, and progressive men, who had come
to the front in this time of dire need. Strangely enough,
almost all of them, like himself, had been born and brought
up outside of Prussian territory : Scharnhorst and Har-

denberg were Hanoverians, Blücher a Mecklenburger, Arndt from the island of Rügen, Gneisenau and Fichte from Saxony, the gentle, scholarly Niebuhr a Dane. The latter, together with Schön, Stägemann, and Altenstein, was a member of what is known as the Immediate Commission, in which, with Hardenberg's aid, there had already been worked out a scheme for an entire change in social relationships and in the manner of landholding in East Prussia. Within a week after his arrival, Stein applied this to all Prussian territory, and published his famous emancipating edict.

The emancipation of the Prussian serfs.

Difficult as it is to realize, up to this moment two-thirds of the population of Prussia had consisted of unfree persons, — not slaves in the full sense because protected by law from many acts of oppression, yet unable to leave their homes of their own free will, and bound to personal, often menial, services. The evils of the system had long been apparent, but Frederick the Great, as well as his successors, for fear of disorganizing the army, had shrunk from violent interference. Now, by the edict of October 9, 1807, which was recognized at the time as comparing in importance with Magna Charta and the Habeas Corpus Act, all this was changed : " From Martinmas, 1810, ceases all villainage in our entire states. From Martinmas, 1810, there shall be only free persons, as this is already the case upon the domains in all our provinces ; free persons, however, still subject, as a matter of course, to all the obligations which bind them as free persons by virtue of the possession of an estate or by virtue of a special contract."

Other paragraphs of the edict, those relating to freedom of exchange in land, and to free choice of occupation, are almost equally important, and aided equally in transforming a ground-down nation into one of joyous patriots.

Every pressure had hitherto been brought to bear that could keep a man in the station of life to which he had been born. It was against the law for a noble to become a citizen, or to hold citizen or peasant lands; equally against the law for a peasant or citizen to purchase or assume mortgages on the estates of nobles. As a consequence, bankrupt nobles had almost no market for their lands, and could raise no capital with which to cultivate them. Forbidden to engage in trade, their only alternative, their only hope, was in the capricious bounty of their sovereign. *Removal of class and property distinctions.*

It betokened indeed a great social revolution when now, in the king's name, Stein declared, "Every inhabitant of our states is competent, without any limitation on the part of the state, to possess, either as property or pledge, landed estates of every kind"; and again, "Every noble is henceforth permitted, without any derogation from his position, to exercise citizen occupations; and every citizen or peasant is allowed to pass from the peasant into the citizen class, or from the citizen into the peasant class." An ordinance concerning the cities, a few months later, bestowed practical self-government, with merely a right of oversight reserved for the crown.

Such radical changes as these presupposed and rendered absolutely necessary corresponding changes in the whole military system; and here Scharnhorst, as head of a re-organization committee, played, and with equal success, the part of Stein. The same object was kept constantly in view: the army was to consist no longer of slaves kept in order by fear, but of devoted, enthusiastic patriots; it was to be the "uniting point of all the moral and physical powers of all the citizens of the state." First, a signal example was to be made of all who had been to blame for the recent disasters, then a thorough inquiry *The character of Scharnhorst.*

instituted into the causes of weakness and inefficiency, —
and the proper remedies applied.

Both Stein and Scharnhorst were fortunate in having a
definite end for their reforms in view. The land was to be
liberated as soon as possible from under the heel of the
oppressor. In everything else indeed, save in their devotion to a common cause, the men were as different as possible : Stein, of commanding presence and aristocratic
ways, sudden, impulsive, fearless of consequences ; Scharnhorst, unmilitary, almost slovenly in appearance, with no
objection to munching his evening meal in the streets or
parks of Hanover, yet, by virtue of necessity an ideal conspirator, with as many folds in his conscience, Treitschke
has said, as wrinkles on his simple face. He became,
eventually, a master in the art of throwing people off the
scent, and reminded his contemporaries of that William of
Orange who earned the name of the Silent by dissimulat-
ing his knowledge of the devilish plots of the Spanish king.
So simple was his manner that even the king was at ease
with him, a distinction of which no other really great man
could ever boast.

Gneisenau.   Associated with Scharnhorst in the work of reforming
the army were Gneisenau, Boyen, Grolman, and Clausewitz, — the first-named of whom had offered the only heroic
and successful resistance of the campaign. His defence of
Colberg had been of far more than momentary importance ;
he had kept open to the last the only means of communication by sea with England and with Sweden ; he was the
first to make systematic use of the weapon that was to
overthrow Napoleon — a citizen army with courage to fight
to the death. His methods in Colberg had been counter
to all military precedent ; he, the head of a besieged
garrison, had been the constant aggressor, not confining
himself to protecting his own walls, but throwing up

in the open field earthworks that took the enemy many weeks to storm. These doings had been watched with breathless interest throughout Prussia; and Gneisenau was already the hero of the hour when he was called to act on the new committee. Boyen, too, was a man of great ability, and was later to become famous as the founder of the modern Prussian army organization.

These men went about their task with an inspired zeal that was to recoil before no personal considerations whatever. An investigation was begun into all the surrenders that had taken place, either in the field or behind the walls of fortresses. In order to find a severe enough punishment recourse was had to the statute of the Great Elector: " When a fortress is given up to the enemy without extreme necessity, its governors and commandants shall be punished with death; " and seven officers were condemned to the severest penalty of the law. The king pardoned them, indeed, doubtless realizing how much of the unreadiness of the fortresses was his own work, and how often he had implied to the old generals that their positions would be sinecures. In general, for the future, the burden of proof was to rest with the officers; they might receive no position, enjoy no pension, without bringing testimony as to past good conduct. Age and incapacity were not spared. Here the gentle Scharnhorst was stern and implacable: of the 143 generals belonging to the army in 1806, but two served seven years later in the war of liberation.

The old life of ease for the officer had become a thing of the past. He might no longer take with him from one to five pack-horses to carry his tent, his bed, his table, his chair, and a hundred other luxuries; of the thirty-two thousand extra horses five-sixths were now discarded and the number of servants reduced by one-half. Nor were the nobles, for the future, to have the exclusive right to

Punishment of the cowardly commanders.

Curtailment of luxuries.

all the commands; in time of peace technical knowledge, in time of war bravery, activity, and circumspection were to be the criterions of advancement. As a matter of fact the nobles continued and still continue to hold the chief positions, but their training has become rigid and thorough.

The treatment of the common soldier. Above all, there was need that the calling of a soldier should be made respected and desirable; that the old system of recruiting, which had gathered in thieves and cut-throats by the hundreds, should be abandoned; that respectable parents should be proud to have their sons in the ranks. Infamous indeed, and suitable only for an army of convicts, had been the old manner of cursing and whipping the troops into shape. It had been in the power of each insolent young ensign of sixteen to flog old soldiers half to death for the slightest involuntary breach of discipline; the common punishment for more serious offences had been the horrible running the gauntlet, which brutalized alike those who received, those who inflicted, and those who witnessed it. With his hands bound so that he could do no harm, with his feet ironed so that he should proceed but slowly, with a ball of lead in his mouth that he might not bite off his tongue for agony, the culprit was driven again and again down the line of two hundred men, who beat him with rods of birch or hazel that had been steeped in salt! When too weak to proceed he was bound to a stake and the whipping continued, and not rarely, but frequently, the punishment proved fatal. The chief innovation of the committee of reorganization was to form what we may call a moral awkward squad for the incorrigibles, who might still on occasion be flogged. The rest were to be treated as self-respecting men, and minor breaches of discipline were to be punished with detention in barracks under word of honor.

This new army was to be essentially for use and not for

display. The tricks of the parade ground were now abandoned, and serious work and target shooting took their
place. Wigs and pigtails were discarded, the uniforms
made more comfortable, the amount of baggage decreased.
Every regiment that had been concerned in a surrender
had been permanently disbanded, so that no old prejudices or traditions stood in the way. The Treaty of Paris,
of September, 1808, had required that the numbers of the
army should never exceed forty-two thousand; — a poor
showing if we think of the six hundred and fifty thousand
men that Napoleon was able to lead against Russia. But
the fertile brain of Scharnhorst had evolved a plan by
which the letter of the law might be kept, but the spirit
evaded. By his famous crimper system, so called from
the spare horse that was kept in reserve, recruits were
given leave of absence after a month of rigid drilling in
the most essential points. While the army at any given
time might not exceed in numbers the allotted figure,
there were thus trained in all some one hundred and fifty
thousand men ; when the troops marched out to parade, a
number of them invariably remained behind in the barracks, so that there might be the less ground for suspicion and inquiry.

The "crimper" system.

In other fields besides the administration and the army,
men were busily working for the regeneration of Prussia.
The so-called *Tugendbund* was a widespread secret society with the object of inculcating patriotism. Some of
the great men of the time belonged to it; others made use
of it without joining; others, still, held entirely aloof.
Stein condemned it as a sort of modern *Vehmgericht*.
There was, all in all, a considerable amount of conspiracy
in progress — secret buying and transporting of weapons,
meetings of patriots in the woods at night, travelling
under false names and in disguise, writing of letters with

The rousing of public sentiment.

sympathetic ink. The idea of murdering Napoleon was in many minds; the poet Kleist carried it around in his disordered brain. The Countess Voss, court mistress of ceremonies, was reported to have formed a definite plot; and actual attempts at assassination were made. Poets, preachers, and philosophers kept urging the inner revolution that alone could save the state. Old Father Jahn invented modern gymnastics; apparatus was put up in parks and public places; moral and political teaching accompanied the exercises, and a most wholesome change was immediately apparent in the youth of the land. Ernst Moritz Arndt, the most stirring poet of the time, threw all his talents into furthering the cause; while John Gottlieb Fichte held discourses in the Academy, in the same building as the French garrison, and dwelt upon the oppression of the foreign yoke and the shame of the present situation. So lofty were his ideas, indeed, and clothed in such philosophical language, that the French censor saw in them no harm, and allowed the lectures to be published. The stupid man never dreamt what a bugle call they were to prove to national revolution, nor to what depths they were to stir the German nation. It was a campaign of education that Fichte advocated; and he looked for results at the end of twenty-five years. "No man, and no God, and no possible event can help us," he declared; "we must help our own selves if we are to be helped at all." And in similar strains Schleiermacher talked to the crowded congregations in his little church in Berlin.

The effect of the Spanish uprising.

Both Stein and Scharnhorst were eager to start an uprising of the whole people at the first favorable opportunity; that opportunity seemed to them to have arrived when, in 1808, the Spaniards began to show what a purely national, as opposed to a royal, army could accomplish.

The effect of this Spanish rebellion was incalculable; here was a people weaker, more demoralized, than the Prussians themselves, holding their own against the world-conqueror and requiring his presence with three hundred thousand men. It is no exaggeration when Seeley calls this, "the greatest European event which had happened since the French Revolution, the beginning of a new and grand chapter in European history." On England, which was already helping Spain, Prussia could have relied for aid ; also on Austria, which was on the verge of her own desperate revolt, and which could now boast of a general second only to Napoleon himself. But Frederick William would call no *levée en masse* so long as Russia would not help him; and Alexander, though beginning to detest Napoleon, still hoped to make use of him against Turkey, having already, by his countenance, acquired Finland. The question has often been raised whether the Prussian king was right or wrong in his firm, not to say obstinate, attitude. As events turned out, he gained more by waiting; but only because a miracle happened. What human intelligence could have foreseen the ruin of Napoleon's army in the Russian campaign? What statesman in his senses should have counted upon it? Stein was perfectly right when he argued that Prussia had little to lose and everything to gain by acting at once.

But Stein's own days in office were now numbered. By an incomprehensible lack of caution on the part of a conspirator who stood so high, and on whom so much depended, in September, 1808, a most compromising letter had been intercepted and forwarded to Napoleon, who published it in the Paris *Moniteur*. The missive, not even written in cipher, was addressed to Count Wittgenstein at the court of the elector of Hesse ; Wittgenstein himself was none too reliable, and Stein's messenger, Koppe, seems not to

Stein's intercepted letter.

have used even ordinary care. Yet the prime minister of Prussia spoke openly of fanning the spark of revolt, of spreading the news of the Spanish successes, of forming connections in Hesse and Westphalia.

Timid
counsels.

Napoleon had referred directly to this letter when increasing the severity of his terms in the Treaty of Paris : could Frederick William have taken a firm attitude, acknowledged the discontent that was rife among his subjects, and made the most of it, all the advantage would have been on his own side. Napoleon was in no condition to cope with two popular insurrections at the same time ; he was even now withdrawing his troops from Prussia. But the king, as usual, pursued a half-hearted policy, neither boldly resisting nor frankly conciliating the French emperor. Stein's position became untenable, not so much because of the threats from France, as of the bitter opposition of the anti-reform party at Berlin, a party to which not only the contemptible Kalckreuths and Köckeritzs belonged, but even a man like General York, who was in the end to prove himself capable of a grand and patriotic act. York's present attitude was supremely pessimistic. "The French have Argus eyes," he wrote. " For a Sicilian Vesper or for war in the Vendée fashion the German is not at all suited. Besides, in our flat land how could anything of the kind be possible ? In our present circumstances, the wisest and safest course is quietly to watch the progress of political relations, and it is real folly to provoke the enemy at our own risk." Such language was in keeping with Commandant Schulenburg's famous remark when the French entered Berlin: "To be quiet is the citizen's first duty ! "

Stein goes
into exile.

When, by ratifying the Treaty of Paris, the king sided with this more timid party, Stein's retirement was inevitable. Men of good judgment believe that he would have been forced to go even if the famous letter had not been

intercepted. It was three months after that event before
Napoleon proscribed him and confiscated his property;
but the estrangement with the king had been increasing
from day to day. The poor queen, too, was bitterly
disappointed at Stein's opposition — partly on political,
partly on financial grounds — to a projected journey to
St. Petersburg, whither the royal pair had been invited
by the Czar. In short, by the end of November, Frederick
William had decided to part with his minister, — first declaring himself, indeed, in full sympathy with his scheme
of administrative reform. On the day of his dismissal,
November 24, Stein drew up a programme for still
further changes, many of which did not go into operation until years had rolled by — among them the recommendation of a universal national representation. A few
weeks later, he was fleeing through the winter night, with
a price set on his head, for the Austrian frontier — still to
work for his adopted country and to witness its redemption after four more years of enslavement. But the
interval was very bitter; during his three years' stay in
Austria he was allowed to play no part in public affairs,
and he thought seriously of emigrating to America —
Kentucky and Tennessee attracted him most; there, he
considered, were to be found the finest climate and the
finest soil, as well as glorious rivers like his own Rhine.
There he would find rest and pleasant intercourse.
Stein's successor in office was Altenstein, a man of
feeble powers and not likely to oppose the king. The
journey of the royal pair to St. Petersburg took place;
the Czar's hospitality was lavish, his personal attentions
sincere and well meant, and, moving about in his splendid
drawing-rooms, the poor crushed Louise felt herself once
more a beauty and a queen. It was the last gleam of
sunlight that was to fall into her life; she died in the

following year of a broken heart, if ever such a thing is possible.

Napoleon
invades
Austria.
Without Prussia's aid, Austria entered upon her momentous struggle, — driven to it, not so much by any one act of Napoleon against herself, as by indignation at the French emperor's doings in Spain, and by fears for the future. She was better equipped than four years previously, having found in Stadion and Archduke Charles her Stein and Scharnhorst, and having already organized a *Landwehr*, or professionally trained reserve. For once, too, the emperor assumed a really patriotic tone, — pointing out, in his war manifesto, the difference between the Spaniards dying for their country and the Germans acting as vassals to the French oppressor.

Had the Danube become a river Lethe, Napoleon asked, that the people of Vienna should so soon have forgotten their former disasters? He now sent one large army from the direction of France, while another, under Davoust, descended from Prussia. He himself waited at Paris until the sun-telegraph brought him word that the Austrians had crossed the Inn ; and then, travelling night and day, made his way to Bavaria. In a week of skirmishing, he inflicted such injury on the army of Archduke Charles that the latter abandoned the offensive, beat a retreat toward Vienna by the roundabout way of Bohemia, and counselled the Austrian emperor to begin negotiations for peace. These operations at Abensberg, Landshut, Eggmühl, and Ratisbon are among Napoleon's supreme achievements. On arriving at Donauwörth he had found the position of his own troops very unfavorable, the enemy well concentrated ; in a few days he had not only changed all that, but was able, unmolested, to march on Vienna. There is no doubt but that the troops of the Rhine Confederation had been of the greatest assistance

to him in gaining this series of victories; it was their
doing that he won this campaign, the last in which he
was ever to enjoy continuous success

It may be said, on the whole, that the Austrian *people*   Dörnberg
fought with the utmost bravery and that the entire fault   and Schill.
lay with their leaders. The Archduke Charles, especially,
disappointed all hopes. He had had a chance to cut off
Davoust's army, but had failed to make use of it; he had
taken six days to perform a march which the French
afterward accomplished in two; he had given Napoleon
all the time he needed to reconcentrate his forces. One
of the worst results of his defeats, worse even than his
loss of fifty or sixty thousand men, was the discouragement that spread through Europe. There were parts of
Prussia where, with or without the king's sanction, a little
success would have provoked a general uprising of the
people. As it was, there took place in these days two
notable attempts, foredoomed, however, to utter failure:
that of Dörnberg, who tried to raise an insurrection in
Westphalia; and that of Major Schill, one of the heroes
of Colberg, who induced some five hundred peasants to
follow him, and set forth from Berlin to "win back for
his beloved king his last village." He had meant to join
with Dörnberg, but arrived too late, and expiated his act
of madness by a brave death in the streets of Stralsund.
His head was severed from his body and was made to
grace an anatomical museum; his officers were shot, his
men sent to the galleys to labor in chains, in common with
French robbers and murderers.

In the valleys of the Tyrol, meanwhile, there had actu-   The upris-
ally taken place just such a popular uprising as Stein and ing of the
Scharnhorst had desired for Prussia. This strong and   Tyrolese.
sturdy, but narrow and superstitious, people had been
forced, by the Treaty of Pressburg of 1805, to transfer

their allegiance from Austria to Bavaria; their revolt now had nothing of a German national character, but was directed against these new masters, and especially against a number of innovations that in themselves were not at all unsalutary. Such were the conscription, the restriction of the number of church holidays and the secularization of church property. It was the clergy whose liberties were most attacked, and it was the clergy who poured the flame of sedition into the hearts of these, their blind followers.

From the first, Austria had fostered and stirred up this revolt; Archduke John, — particularly beloved by the Tyrolese, — kept closely in touch with the patriot leaders; Austrian troops moved to join them, and Andreas Hofer, the brave innkeeper of Innsbruck, was honored with a golden chain from the emperor. The fighting was carried on with unexampled bitterness. Hofer, Peter Mayr, Speckbacher, and Haspinger showed themselves heroic leaders; and the town of Innsbruck was three times captured and three times lost. In this part of the world men were doing their duty, no matter what might be happening on the larger field of war.

The battle of Aspern.

Meanwhile, at Aspern, on the northern bank of the Danube, four miles below Vienna, Napoleon suffered a defeat such as had never yet been inflicted upon him. With a loss of fifteen thousand men he was forced to retreat to the little island of Lobau, where his troops passed two days in abject misery, with no food and only the polluted waters of the river for drink. Such was the real course of events; officially it was different. "The enemy withdrew within its lines," ran Napoleon's bulletin, "and we remained masters of the battlefield."

It was a golden opportunity to trap the whole French force; but the Austrians, too, had suffered heavily and

did not return to the attack with sufficient energy ; indeed,
Archduke Charles hoped now that diplomacy would take
the place of further battle.   The victory of Aspern
undoubtedly made a deep impression on Europe, as did
also the bravery of the exiled Duke of Brunswick, who
of his own accord raised a little band, fought at the side
of the Austrians, and eventually cut his way to the sea,
and took ship with his men for Helgoland.   It is thought
that even Frederick William would have allowed himself
to be carried away by the current of enthusiasm if only
Austria had been willing to grant his reasonable terms, —
to promise to make no separate peace, and to engage
to help Prussia to secure her former boundaries.   But
with the blindness of the Hapsburg court there was no
reckoning.

The battle of Wagram, — which proved a defeat, though
not an overwhelming one, for Austria, — was like Austerlitz
before the Treaty of Pressburg or Friedland before Tilsit.
The emperor was tired of the war, the more so as an intended English expedition to the Baltic coast proved a
miserable failure.   The armistice of Znaim was followed
by the Treaty of Vienna which brought Austria, comparatively speaking, almost as low as Prussia ; she lost territory containing nearly four million souls and was thrust
far back from the Adriatic.   In some ways, her position
was even worse than that of her rival, for, as has been well
said, she had played her last card and failed.   She had had
her Stein and Scharnhorst, had tried regeneration, reorganized her army, and passed liberal measures.   Now, all
was changed ; she had fallen forever from her high pedestal, and there followed the most complete reaction.
Stadion resigned, and Metternich, the incarnation of conservatism, took his place.   One of his first acts was to bring
about the union of Napoleon with Marie Louise, the

The
collapse of
Austria.

daughter of the Emperor Francis. The emperor's admirers
compared him to the Deity who had given His only begot-
ten Son for the good of His people ; but there was in
reality little that was divine about this cold-blooded Hapsburg. It was once said of him that he had perfectly political bowels. If there was one man who had deserved well
of him it was Andreas Hofer, the brave leader of the Tyrolese ; yet Francis abandoned him to his fate. Between
the time of the betrothal and the wedding-day Andreas
was court-martialled and shot. As for Marie Louise herself, she needs little sympathy ; there was nothing in the
conduct of this frivolous woman to remind one of a sacrificial victim.

Napoleon's
breach with
Russia.

One great result of the new policy of Napoleon toward
Austria, was to drive into the camp of his enemies the power
that was destined at last to bring him to his knees. Napoleon had negotiated for the hand of a Russian princess, and,
when Alexander temporized on account of the youth of the
lady in question, had abruptly let the matter drop. Indeed
the French emperor's only intention seems to have been to
frighten Austria into the more desired match. But, apart
from this blow to the Czar's *amour propre*, there were causes
enough to foment dissension. Alexander was not sufficiently pliant in the matter of the continental blockade by
which Napoleon was endeavoring to destroy the commerce
of England ; he would not agree to seize neutral ships that
came near his coasts, and thus defeated the whole of Napoleon's gigantic scheme. Negotiations on the subject only
led to more friction. Then, too, the French were encroaching more and more along the Baltic, and had driven out
the Duke of Oldenburg, who was a relative of the Czar.
But what touched the latter most nearly, was the fact that
Napoleon, by his treaty with Austria, was bestowing more
territory on the duchy of Warsaw, with the intent of mak-

ing it fully subservient to himself. The French emperor refused to ratify an agreement drawn up by his own envoy, Caulaincourt, to the effect that the dead Polish kingdom was never to be resuscitated, and that even the word Poland was to be carefully avoided in public documents. The idea of a Russian invasion had now taken shape in Napoleon's mind, and to Alexander's accusation, that he was plotting to restore Poland, he simply answered, "I do not intrigue, I carry on war with four hundred thousand men." By 1811, the Czar had expressed his fear to the French envoy that the world would not be large enough for himself and the emperor ; and in that same year Napoleon declared the alliance at an end, writing with unusual frankness, "Your Majesty has no more friendship for me." His last step, his usual method in prefacing a war, was to publicly insult the Russian ambassador.

There was no question but that, in the pending struggle, all the newly made kings, indeed all the members of the Rhine Confederation, would remain on Napoleon's side. The latter wrote, in April, 1811, to Frederick of Würtemberg: "If the allied princes shall inspire me with even the slightest doubt of their inclination for a joint defence, I freely declare that they are lost. For I prefer enemies to uncertain friends." Austria, too, so recently allied by marriage with the great emperor, and at odds with the Czar on various grounds, agreed to furnish the grand army with thirty thousand men. As for Prussia, wedged in between the hostile powers, her position was fairly pitiable. At best her land was to be trampled over by immense armies, and requisitions to be imposed upon an almost starving people. Her sympathies, naturally, were all with the Czar, but her momentary interests drove her to the side of the French. And Napoleon, although he adopted a friendly tone, would stand no trifling ; when

Napoleon intimidate, the Germans.

the Prussians, not yet certain of the future, commenced to mobilize their forces, and to double the permitted numbers, he sternly bade them halt and keep within bounds.

Harden-
berg's ad-
ministra-
tion.

After the fall of the feeble Altenstein, there came to the head of affairs the second of the two men whose names are chiefly connected with great legislative reforms. Hardenberg differed from Stein in almost every particular, and his character as a whole is less admirable. In curious contrast to his devotion to the state, and his willingness to accept responsibility, was a youthful frivolity that caused him to chase forbidden pleasures and adventures, even in old age. His knowledge of the world stood him in good stead; he was more affable, more diplomatic, than Stein, and he won, occasionally, where the latter would assuredly have failed. The great problem of his administration was to stave off the bankruptcy that so constantly threatened the state; and, though many of his separate measures failed through inherent weakness, in the main he fulfilled his task. In the spring of 1812, there were, indeed, some thirty-seven million thalers still due to France, but no province had been forfeited, nor had the royal domains fallen into French hands.

While taxing them very heavily, Hardenberg had, in other respects, done what he could to improve the condition of the people. At the cost of the nobles, the liberated serfs were fitted out with small farms of their own. The Jews, for the first time in centuries, were given equal legal rights with Christians. They were no longer to be known as the Jew Isaac or the Jew Abraham, but were ordered to provide themselves with second names. Those that they chose reflect the romantic spirit of the early nineteenth century; the mountain, the valley, the rose, the lily, the lion, the wolf, the golden stars, were all called into requisition in countless combinations.

But all the struggles with adversity, all the reforms since Jena, seemed now to have been made in vain. Though Napoleon might spare Prussia in his hurry to strike Russia, there was every chance that, on his victorious return, he would obliterate her territory from the map of Europe. Many considered it the duty of the nation to fight to the death and fall with honor. Even Frederick William turned longingly to Russia and prayed for a close alliance. The Czar, however, announced his intention of fighting as Wellington was fighting in Spain, and avoiding close contact. Space, illimitable space, was the chief weapon at his command, and he meant to use it to the utmost. He agreed that Prussia would necessarily be submerged for a time, but declared his hope that, in the end, all would turn out for the best.

Thus, driven by force of circumstances, Frederick William began to negotiate with France. He hoped, since he had been so near joining Napoleon's enemies, that he would be able to obtain favorable conditions; he even found courage to utter a few threats. But the emperor, in his blunt, characteristic manner, made no concessions at all; but laid down a hard and fast ultimatum, and gave but twenty-four hours for its acceptance or rejection. The Prussians were to owe military service to Napoleon everywhere save in Turkey, Spain, and Italy; twenty thousand of them were at once to join with him in fighting their former best friend; twenty thousand more were to garrison Prussian fortresses in the interests of France; requisitions of forage, bread, etc., were to be made at once, but payment was to be a matter of future agreement, — such were the galling terms by which this thoroughly isolated government was forced to bind itself over. The work of the patriots was undone, and nearly all of them, with sorrowing hearts, asked for and received their dismissal. Gneisenau, Scharnhorst, and Boyen all resigned, but still labored in secret for the cause; some twenty-one officers entered the Russian service.

Stein himself, at this time, received a summons to St. Petersburg. Alexander's first act was to apologize for the shameful Treaty of Tilsit; already, in his summons, he had invited the great political reformer to aid him in the struggle against the enslavement of Europe. Stein's definite task was to win over Germans for the Russian alliance. Aided by Ernst Moritz Arndt he inaugurated a regular campaign of enlightenment; a German commission and a German legion were established in Russia; bands of men were detailed off to intercept Napoleon's couriers; journals were established and pamphlets struck off from secret presses.

Once more, as at Erfurt, the French emperor held brilliant court on German soil, and the Austrian emperor and the Prussian king came to Dresden to do him honor. The customary salute of cannon was omitted in Frederick William's case, and Hardenberg tells in his diary how Napoleon's first words were a gruff "You are a widower?" Francis was invited every day, Frederick William, as a person of less distinction, only every other day, to the imperial table.

Meanwhile the grand army, the largest that had ever been mustered since the days of Xerxes — it is computed to have numbered six hundred and fifty thousand men — came rolling on, and a large part of it soon crossed the Russian frontier. The colossal failure of this campaign was due to two causes: first, to a slackness of discipline arising from the youthfulness of the recruits, and to their having been allowed to plunder on the way; and second, to the difficulty of procuring supplies in these new and strange surroundings. A sufficiency of stores had been gathered together, but the arrangements for carrying them were inadequate; through the death of horses and the breaking down of wagons immense quantities were lost, and hunger and thirst began their fatal work. Long before the winter set in, thousands were dying every day. Then came the usual dash for the enemy's capital, the bloody battle of Borodino, the entry into silent Moscow. Napoleon carried off the great cross on the Kremlin because he thought it was gold; just so the brilliancy of this easy victory was to turn to dross. Flames broke out, and, when engines were sought with which to quench them, none could be found. So far as is known, it was the Russian commandant himself who set fire to the houses in Moscow, liberating prisoners for the special purpose. On the dreadful retreat, the ghastliest in all recorded history, there is no need to dwell; but seven thousand of the original advance army ever returned to the frontier, to be joined by twelve or fifteen thousand more who had been stationed nearer home. Napoleon had the courage to instruct General York, in command of a Prussian force near Riga, to protect the retreat of the French; and to write to Frederick William from Riga to increase his stipulated contingent. He himself hastened to Paris to raise fresh troops. Inexhaustible were the resources of this man, who could almost immediately replace an annihilated army of half a million men; it is true the majority of the new soldiers were half-fledged boys whose natural term of service would not have begun until two years later.

While hurrying homeward from Moscow, Napoleon had given out that the grand army was returning at his heels in vast numbers; but the whole extent of the terrible catastrophe became apparent to the Germans when the fugitives began to pass through their cities without the least vestige

The return of the remnants of Napoleon's army.

of organization. It was hard to believe that these were the allies that had marched out with drum and trumpet but a few months before, haughty and insolent in all their ways; it seemed rather a procession of penitents, silent, in sackcloth and ashes. They were hollow-eyed with suffering, disfigured with frostbites, and they wore, for the most part, only such garments as the peasants, and even the women, could furnish them. Around their shoulders hung pieces of carpet, old shawls, even skins of cats and dogs; on their feet were every kind of substitute for shoes. The vastly greater number of those who had fallen in battle or by the wayside seemed more to be envied than such survivors; yet these poor remnants of humanity were soon to be driven into new wars, being almost the only veterans capable of drilling and commanding the young recruits. Frederick William had been advised not to harbor them in Prussia, but to such severity he could not bring himself; the French were nursed in Prussian houses, and suffered nothing worse than that an occasional schoolboy tried to frighten them with shouts of " The Cossacks are coming ! " Besides they were Prussia's allies, and Frederick William could not make up his mind to renounce them; if he hated Napoleon, he also distrusted the Russians and Austrians. It is also to be feared that he distrusted himself and his own people.

The treason of General York.   There was one man whose dilemma was even worse than that of the king, because immediate action was needed. General York, in command of the only Prussian army in the field, — not yet knowing the extent of the disaster, but ordered by Napoleon to protect his fleeing forces, — was at the same time approached by the Russians, who had never really looked upon him as their enemy. The Czar himself sent a promise not to desert Prussia till her old boundaries should have been fully restored. York, a rough character who said that he never could feel at home with the " damned *michs* and *mirs* " of his own language, was personally one of the most upright of men, with the strictest ideas of military duty ; he was the officer of a king who was bound by a solemn treaty and who seemed inclined to keep it. Yet the trained eye of the observant general saw that now, if ever, was the time for breaking loose from an unbearable yoke. He fought and wrestled with himself, entered into negotiations with the enemy, and at last said to Clausewitz, who came to meet him at Tauroggen in the name of the Russian general Diebitsch, " You have me ! Tell General Diebitsch that to-morrow morning early I will come within the Russian lines. Time and place I leave to him." Assembling the officers of his corps, he asked those to join him who were willing to risk their lives for freedom and for fatherland ; and, when the shouts of joy and acquiescence had died away, he said solemnly, " Then with the help of God may the work of our liberation begin and be carried to a finish." To the king he had already written, " If I am doing wrong, I will lay my old head without a murmur at your Majesty's feet." On the 30th of December, 1812, he signed the famous Convention of Tauroggen, according to which his whole force was to remain neutral until further commands should arrive from the king, and in no case to fight against Russia during the next two months.

Exactly what view Frederick William took of York's action is impossible to determine ; there is reason to believe that his feelings and his actions were at variance. He repudiated the Convention of Tauroggen and dismissed York from his service, but the messenger who bore the order was apparently instructed to fall into the hands of the Russians, and even to encourage the latter. If such

Frederick William and General York.

was the case, York himself was not in the secret ; deeply depressed, he wrote to General Bülow to know if those in power in Berlin had sunk so low as not to dare to burst the chains of slavery they had worn so long. " With bleeding heart," he continues, " I tear away the bonds of obedience and wage war on my own account. The army wishes war with France, the people wish it, the king wishes it ; but the king's will is not free." Frederick William's upholders maintain that he was absolutely forced into double dealing from the fact that the French troops on German soil still outnumbered the Prussians by five to one, and that in Berlin itself he was helpless in the midst of a large French garrison. The king certainly desired the alliance with Russia, but, as Hardenberg wrote to Stein *à propos* of "dear Amalia's marriage" : "Father wishes everything to remain secret until uncle has settled matters properly," wherein, of course, "Amalia" stands for Prussia, "father" for the king, "uncle" for the Czar.

Frederick William at last gives way.

Frederick William, in short, was going through another of his terrible crises of indecision. On the one hand, he seems to have hoped that by remaining friendly to Napoleon he could procure a remission of the remainder of his debt and the removal of all French troops ; on the other, Russia threatened, in case of the refusal of an alliance, to practically annihilate Prussia and merge it in a new kingdom of Poland. England, too, alternately urged and warned. At home, petitions from the people poured in from all sides ; and conservatives and liberals alike joined in the cry. Once, Hardenberg, after a long conference at Potsdam, in which he urged Frederick William to strike, went down on his knees and wetted the king's hand with his tears. Stein, in East Prussia, as agent of the Czar, was moving heaven and earth to provoke a rupture. Calling together the provincial estates, he induced

York to appear and propose a scheme, which was adopted, for calling out the *Landwehr*. Frederick William began to cower before this new Simon de Montfort, who summoned parliaments without his leave. Almost worse than the French he hated these strong men who seemed to be shaking at the prerogatives of his throne. At Scharnhorst he scolded behind his back; Boyen he caused to be watched by the secret police; once, when Stein lay at the point of death, he failed to visit him. So much the war party at last accomplished — partly, indeed, by spreading a report that the French intended to seize the king's person — that Frederick William consented to leave Berlin, where he was surrounded by hostile influences, and take up his residence in Breslau, where he would be nearer to the Czar. Here, at Breslau, he at once began to show more spirit and determination; all exemptions from military service were declared removed, and for the first time in Prussia's history men of gentle birth served in the ranks, — regiments of chasseurs being formed for them, in which, indeed, they were treated with leniency and consideration. Soon, by Stein's mediation, the Treaty of Kalisch was arranged with Russia; and the Czar agreed to continue in arms until Prussia should have regained her former possessions or their equivalent.

Finally, on March 16, 1813, war was declared against the French. On the following day the king issued a stirring call to his people. Article 8, of a convention signed on March 19, decreed that there should at once be established an army of the line (*armée de ligne*), a *Landwehr* (*une milice*), and a *Landsturm* (*levée en masse*). Now at last people and king were united; the long period of mutual doubt and suspicion was past, and the Titanic struggle for liberation had begun. A wave of enthusiasm like to that at the time of the crusades swept over north-

Wild enthusiasm for the war with France.

ern Germany; honest peace or glorious death was the watchword, and more answered the call than could be accepted. Nothing could exceed the spirit of self-sacrifice shown by the masses; even a Frenchman wrote that the Prussians had restored the human countenance to honor. Women were busy night and day turning their husbands' blue Sunday coats into the simple uniform required for the *Landwehr;* mothers allowed their young boys to leave school and enlist; and nine of the scholars of the " gray cloister " in Berlin found death on the field of battle. Young men who sought excuses for not serving were flouted by their girl friends. Whole classes from the universities, professors at their heads, adjourned in a body to the recruiting ground; Fichte and Schleiermacher drilled in the same company of the *Landsturm,* and the author of the *Vocation of Man,* when they would have made him an officer, refused with a simple, " Here, I am only fit for a private." To supply the exhausted state with funds for its military needs, voluntary gifts of every kind were made; it was a disgrace after this war to be found in possession of jewelry or of silver plate. One hundred and fifty thousand persons exchanged their wedding rings for rings of iron with the inscription, " Gold I gave for iron "; there were maidens who sold the very hair from their heads, others who marched off to battle in male attire.

The *Landwehr.*

The *Landwehr* especially — consisting of some one hundred and fifty thousand men, between the ages of seventeen and forty, each of whom wore the device, " With God for king and country " — did excellent service, the worst result of their want of proper training being shown in the terrible death-rate, in hard-fought battles, compared with the regiments of the line. General York, at first an opponent of the whole institution, lived to take off his hat to a battalion of the Silesian *Landwehr,* declaring that it had fought like a battalion of old grenadiers. Many of its members, from generals down to privates, won the iron cross, — that special mark of distinction, bestowed for the first time in this war, and intended to symbolize the bitter hardships of the time as well as the holiness of the uprising. Stein's suggestion for furnishing an incentive to great deeds, had been to abolish altogether the old nobility of birth and establish a new one founded on military achievement.

The *Landsturm*, as originally planned, was to offer a last desperate resistance, on the part of all who could brandish a weapon, against an invading enemy. Its members were to wear no uniform, but to arm themselves as they could, even with pikes, axes, scythes, and pitchforks. Should the enemy fall upon their towns, they were to destroy their flour, pour out their wine, burn their mills, choke their wells with rubbish, and shake the fruit from their trees. The unfortunate district that should fall into the hands of the enemy was to be under an interdict, as it were, — with deep mourning, no festivities, not even a marriage ceremony, without express permission. In the first enthusiasm, more was expected of the *Landsturm* than old age and unwarlike habits could possibly accomplish; its real province was eventually found to lie in police and guard duty that set free the *Landwehr*, and in furnishing reserves to the latter body. One indisputable benefit of the whole institution was the spreading broadcast of the sentiment, that this war was directly the affair of every person in the land. In Berlin, not only men, but even women of position, aided in building intrenchments. Never had Napoleon been more mistaken than when he spoke with scorn of this people, calling them the Gascons of Germany, and declaring that they would never fight. He had a plan all in readiness for dividing up the weak state; he was scathing in his denun-

The Landsturm.

ciations of its ungratefulness, and spoke of "the Tilsit Treaty which had *restored* the king to his throne," and the Paris Treaty which "*permitted* it [Prussia] to become a French ally."

Blücher.

Commander-in-chief of the allied forces was the old hero, Kutusoff; while the divisional commanders were the Russian Wittgenstein and the Prussian Blücher. The former, to whom Blücher voluntarily subordinated himself, was in no way a remarkable general; nor were the Russian contingents kept to their work by rigid discipline. Gneisenau writes, that he visited the Russian camp at Borna three separate times, once in the morning, once at noon, and once at night, and that each time he found the commanding generals in bed. As for Blücher, he was seventy years old and for decades at a time had lived the life of a private citizen; of late he had been very ill, even out of his mind. During the winter of 1810 and 1811 he had had all sorts of strange fancies, among them that he had a live beast in his body. But Scharnhorst had once said that he would prefer Blücher in a litter to any other able-bodied man; Blücher must command, Scharnhorst now declared, "even though he have inside of him a hundred elephants." Certain it is, that Blücher's soldiers idolized him, although on occasion he could be severe enough. Napoleon spoke of him as the *vieux renard*, and respected him more than any other of his antagonists.

Saxony the centre of operations.

The object of the French emperor was to unite all his forces, and, hurrying through Germany, to begin his campaign on the Vistula; that of the allies was to strike him as swiftly as possible, and, at the same time, to make the states of the Rhine confederation throw out their true colors to the wind. The natural meeting-point for the two hostile armies was Saxony, whose frightened king, accordingly, fled with the contents of his green vault, and

had the rarest pictures of the Dresden gallery transferred to the impregnable Königstein. With characteristic duplicity, his minister, Count Sennft, expressed friendship for Prussia, but at the same time negotiated secretly with Napoleon. It was, in fact, here in Saxony that the main battles of the campaign took place, — Lützen and Bautzen, Dresden and Leipzig, — while four separate attempts on the part of Napoleon to take the Prussian capital resulted in as many minor battles in that direction.

Lützen, or Gross Görschen, and Bautzen, were French victories, valuable in so far as they kept alive the traditions of Napoleon's invincibility. He made the most of them in his bulletins to Paris, comparing them to Austerlitz, Jena, Friedland, and Moscow. It was now that Saxony threw aside the veil, and declared openly for her old protector, her king severely punishing those who had been friendly to the Prussians. Yet never were victories bought more dearly. "What!" cried Napoleon himself, "no result, no trophies, no prisoners, and such a butchery!" Forty thousand men had fallen in the two engagements; and where were more to come from now that France was using up the last of her three million recruits called out since 1793? The issue of Lützen had long been exceedingly doubtful. "Do you think my star is sinking?" Napoleon had seriously asked General Berthier; and once he called out angrily, "These beasts have learnt something!" *Lützen and Bautzen.*

After Bautzen, Napoleon made what he himself later designated as the greatest mistake of his life, by entering into the armistice known as the truce of Poischwitz. He desired to strengthen his cavalry, which was relatively very small; but he thought, also, to break down the coalition by tempting offers to the Czar. He would give up Poland; he would renounce his European blockades. And against Austria, which was now demanding back the *The two months' truce.*

provinces wrested from her in 1809, and threatening to join the coalition, he would have time to call up an army from Italy. He despised this power that he had twice so thoroughly humbled. "If you want war you shall have it," he said to Metternich; "*au revoir* in Vienna!" By the Treaty of Reichenbach, Austria had agreed, should Napoleon refuse her terms, to join the allies with 150,000 men. England now promised to send subsidies; while Sweden, in return for freedom of action as regarded Norway, also joined in the war. Reënforcements arrived from Russia; while Prussia, in the course of these two precious months, was able to complete the training of her *Landwehr* and send them to the front. The grand total of the allied forces now amounted to 800,000 men, that of Napoleon's army to 500,000; but, owing to the necessity of defending many vulnerable points, the superiority of the coalition on the actual scene of war was not more than 52,000. Prussia, in this matter of raising troops, had made a splendid, almost unequalled, showing; with a population of but 4,500,000, and with resources wretchedly crippled since Tilsit, she furnished in all nearly 300,000 men.

Scharnhorst's death.

Scharnhorst, indeed, the indefatigable organizer, the only man of his time who can worthily be compared to the American Washington, did not live to see the fruits of his silent and self-sacrificing labors. Wounded at Lützen, he still continued to spare himself no fatigues; and a journey to Vienna and Prague, undertaken in order to hasten the new alliance, proved fatal to his shattered constitution. Not altogether appreciated even in his own day, those best able to judge regarded him almost as a deity. Ten years later Gneisenau wrote to Clausewitz, "You were his John, I only his Peter; yet I never played him false as the latter did his Master!"

At the end of the truce Napoleon's forces stood in the The distri-bution of forces. centre of a half-circle, on the circumference of which were Bernadotte's army near Berlin, Blücher's in Silesia, and that of the commander-in-chief, the Austrian Schwarzenberg, in Bohemia. In the latter camp were the three crowned heads, — the Czar, the emperor, and the Prussian king. Blücher, with the smallest of the three armies against the largest force of the enemy, had been told to avoid battle unless the chances should be all in his favor. Napoleon's plan was to burst through the barrier on the north and come in touch with the fortresses on the Vistula and the Oder, which still held French garrisons; that is why, apart from his natural predilection for taking the capitals of his enemies, he made such repeated attempts to occupy Berlin. He was thwarted by the necessity of remaining on the defensive against the Silesian and Bohemian armies, and of keeping them from uniting with Bernadotte's forces. That the allies from the first had followed the consistent plan of drawing the enemy into their net by concentrating around Leipzig, is a mistaken supposition; some such idea had influenced them in the beginning, but circumstances had greatly modified their proceedings.

By the terms of the armistice, a strip of neutral territory The battle on the Katzbach. had been left between Blücher's army and the French; this the latter had been the first to violate, and Blücher, in turn, pressed forward, the enemy retreating before him. Napoleon himself marched up with his guard to deal a decisive blow at this audacious pursuer, but hastily returned to Dresden on learning that Schwarzenberg was threatening that city. Blücher, with his hundred thousand men, unfolded an unheard-of activity, — now pursuing, now withdrawing, turning day into night and night into day, but always keeping close to the enemy. Each march and each countermarch cost him many lives; the *Landwehr* suffered terribly in the rain-sodden, shelterless camps; and, worst of all, some of those in the lesser commands lost faith in their superiors. General York, the hero of Tauroggen, burst into the room at Jauer, where Blücher and Gneisenau were dining with their officers, and cried out, "You are ruining the troops; you are marching them to no purpose!" In scathing terms York wrote and denounced to the king the whole plan of operations. But on the very day after this scene the French marshal, Macdonald, walked into the trap, and gave the longed-for opportunity for the great battle on the Katzbach, which, though fought in pouring rain and mainly with bayonets and the ends of muskets, inflicted on the French such a defeat as they had never yet suffered in any one engagement: — as Macdonald reported to his emperor, a whole army had ceased to exist. A noble woman wrote to Gneisenau that this one achievement had wiped out years of shame and sorrow, and, indeed, a very long time it was since the Prussians had come out of a battle with fifteen thousand prisoners.

Berna-
dotte's dis-
honesty.

In seven minor skirmishes, fought in the space of one week, Silesia was then cleared of the French; while an onslaught of the latter, in the direction of Berlin, had brought down upon them the defeat of Gross Beeren at the hands of General Bülow — a defeat which would have been still more severe but for the indecision and timidity, if not the masked treason, of the Swedish crown prince. Bernadotte had wished Bülow to evade the corps of the French marshal, Oudinot, by retreat; but the Prussian general had cried out to his soldiers, "Our bones shall bleach in front of, not behind, Berlin!" and, at the decisive moment, had directly disobeyed the orders of his superior commander. Yet Bernadotte, in his report of the battle, claimed the full credit for himself, and accepted the ovation of the Berlin magistrates! This former marshal of France, who had been elected successor to the Swedish throne, had strange and wonderful projects in his head ; and his reason in sparing the French is said to have been a desire to one day occupy their throne ! A fortnight later, at Dennewitz, in spite of continued friction, Bülow and Tauentzien routed the forces of Ney with vastly inferior numbers, the total loss of the enemy being little less than twenty-four thousand men. Bernadotte, as before, claimed the honors of this most important victory, gained in spite of his express commands.

For the last time in this campaign of 1813, fortune smiled upon the French emperor when, at Dresden, with one hundred thousand men, he put to flight the army of Schwarzenberg, with half again that number. The allies lost the battle through the incredible slowness and incompetency of their leaders, — Schwarzenberg having delayed his attack until Napoleon himself, who was miles away, could comfortably reach him. The disheartening news from Gross Beeren and from Silesia had alone prevented Napoleon from following up his advantage ; indeed, the allies had looked for the worst, and Gneisenau had taken the precaution of establishing a camp of possible refuge, far back in Silesia. The Austrians considered the campaign at a close, and began to talk of the invincibility of this enemy, who had until so recently been their own ally. *The battle of Dresden.*

But the moral effect of the victory was soon effaced by a brilliant achievement of the Prussian Kleist, who, while the Prussians engaged the enemy in the valley near Kulm, mounted the heights of Nollendorf, in the rear of Vandamme's corps, and descended upon it to such purpose that nine thousand French were made prisoner. Within the space of one single week Napoleon had lost *Kulm and Nollendorf* nearly eighty thousand men; while, in addition, his ally, Bavaria, trimming her sails to the wind, had gone over to the enemy. The Treaty of Ried, concluded with the allies, was all to the advantage of Bavaria, guaranteeing her practically all that she had gained by the grace of Napoleon, and, unfortunately, rendering impossible such a reconstruction of Germany as Stein, for instance, deemed indispensable.

The closing in on Leipzig.

These were ponderous blows that were falling upon the French emperor; this time his star was indeed sinking. And now, most fatal of all, Blücher had revived the old plan of closing in upon Leipzig, and had set to work with an energy that carried along even such dead weights as Schwarzenberg and Bernadotte,—neither of whom, for political reasons, particularly desired a decisive battle. Almost simultaneously, in the early days of October, Blücher crossed the Elbe at Wartenburg, and Bernadotte near Wittenberg; while Schwarzenberg, with the main army, descended from the Metal Mountains. At Wartenberg the resistance was very stubborn, and had it not been for the wonderful courage and perseverance of General York's corps, the attempt would have failed. This general, as usual, had demurred at his orders. "It is hard to bring the old grumbler York into action," Blücher said of him; "but once there, he is surpassed by no one." As for Napoleon, his first feeling on seeing the enemy assume the offensive was one of satisfaction; so little did he realize the desperateness of his position that he determined to prevent the capture of Dresden, and, for that purpose, left behind him thirty thousand men, which, as the event proved, he could ill afford to spare.

Between Blücher and Bernadotte the friction continued to the end; but old Marshal Forwards, as he had been called since the battle on the Katzbach,—whatever violent expressions he might have used in private, — showed the utmost self-restraint. When the Swedish crown prince objected to the danger of the position near Halle that Blücher would have had him take, the latter changed places with him; later, when still greater danger threatened him in his new position, Bernadotte had the assurance to demand to be put back in his original place. His evident desire to keep his precious Swedes out of action gave rise to one of the most remarkable protests that has ever been penned : on October 15, the headquarters of the Silesian army joined with the headquarters of Bernadotte's own army, and with the ministers or military representatives of England, Russia, Austria, and Prussia in a peremptory demand " to take part in an event which must decide the fate of Europe." It was, even then, too late to join in the first great day of the battle of the nations, though by doing so York's devoted corps might have been saved from terrible slaughter at Möckern. It must be said that when, on October 18, Bernadotte did at last fall into line, his army was of great service, completing the iron chain that was drawn so closely around Napoleon.

Blücher and Bernadotte.

All in all, the fighting on that first day of Leipzig, October 16, was far from decisive; there were skirmishes at Möckern, to the northwest, and at Connewitz and Wachau to the southeast. Neither in the totals of the forces engaged, nor in the separate skirmishes, was there a great numerical difference. At Wachau, Napoleon considered that he had won the day, and ordered that the bells of Leipzig should ring out a peal of triumph; he sent a message of congratulation to his ally, the king of Saxony, who was found skulking in his cellar for safety. But something more than a half-victory was needed to extricate the caged lion from his dangerous position; for, the next day, the allies were reënforced to the extent of nearly one hundred

The three days' battle of Leipzig.

thousand men. In vain Napoleon, on October 17, attempted
to open negotiations for peace; his messenger was not received. On October 18, fell the great decision. The allies
pressed closer and closer around Leipzig, the army of
Schwarzenberg passing over the field of Wachau, where
but two days before so many had fallen. The corpses lay
there unburied still, and the bones crunched as the heavy
carts and cannon passed along. In the midst of the battle
a number of Saxon soldiers went over to the side of the
allies, and, as the French at least maintained, decided the
fate of the day. They were received with no enthusiasm
and were relegated to the rear. That night and the next
day, Napoleon carried on his retreat, in the course of which,
prematurely, the bridge on the Elster was blown up, leaving some twenty thousand to become prisoners in the
hands of the allies. Of the French emperor's last half
million men only ninety thousand accompanied him across
the Rhine. Meanwhile, the Czar and the king of Prussia
rode proudly into Leipzig, passing without a greeting the
Saxon king, who had stationed himself bareheaded to receive them at his palace door. In the market-place, the
Czar was seen to embrace sturdy old Blücher, and was
heard to say, " You, my dear general, have done the most;
you are the liberator of Germany."

Horrors of   The battle of the nations had been fought and won, but
Leipzig.   at a cost to strike terror into the hearts of the victors.
Strong men to the number of nearly one hundred thou-
sand — enough to people a great city — lay dead or
wounded; so many corpses had fallen into the Elster
that the current was turned aside. The peasants had fled
the neighborhood in a panic, and could not help in bury-
ing the dead; the bodies were left in great naked piles to
be gnawed by dog and raven. We hear of 174 wounded
placed in a barn and then forgotten; of 20,000 more without

bed or covering of any kind; of corpses thrown from upper story windows on to the heaped-up carts below; of arms and legs seen to move amid the sickening mass; of their owners mercifully clubbed into quietude; of steady streams of filth and blood flowing down the steps of the improvised hospitals into the streets.

Yet, terrible as this all was, it would have been better in the end if the victory had been followed up with more emphasis; it would have been perfectly possible to have inflicted such ruin on this army that the campaign of 1814 could never have been fought. But disunion reigned in the camp of the allies. Schwarzenberg had taken but few precautions for cutting off his great enemy's retreat; Russia and Prussia wished to pursue Napoleon up to the walls of his own capital; England and Austria thought that already his punishment had been sufficient. Metternich, the new Austrian minister, was afraid the balance of power would be overthrown in Europe were Napoleon to be completely ruined; he mortally dreaded liberal principles, and was opposed to the Czar's Polish plans. It was only by Stein's urgent advice that the war was continued at all, and, even then, many months were lost in slow and purposeless evolutions, which gave Napoleon the needed time for rest. At the battle of La Rothière, Schwarzenberg, with two-thirds of the total forces, remained inactive while Blücher did the fighting. Yet, for the first time in centuries, a French army was beaten on French soil; for the first time, too, Napoleon and Blücher were directly pitted against each other. The former was so completely discouraged that he consented to the calling of the Congress of Châtillon.

Austrian negligence, if not actual Austrian treason, robbed Blücher of all his advantage. Schwarzenberg had arranged that Wittgenstein's corps should cover the

(margin note) The battle of La Rothière.

Blücher's
army
in great
danger.

country between the right bank of the Seine and the line
of march of the Silesian army, but then obeyed a secret
command of the Austrian emperor to remain on the left
bank of the river, lest a victory of the allies should disturb
the proposed negotiations for a peace.   Napoleon, in consequence, fell upon detached corps of Blücher's all-too
unsuspecting army, and at Montmirail and Chateau-Thierry
inflicted crushing blows.   In a skirmish near Vauchamps
the field-marshal himself, Gneisenau, Prince Augustus,
Kleist, and Grolmann were surprised, and on the point of
being captured, when they were saved by the presence of
mind of the last-named, who organized a successful rally
of the exhausted troops.   Old Marshal Forwards had
already sought death, determined never to be taken alive.
All that brave and desperate men could do these Prussians
had done : "even that dumb lean Englishman," writes
Treitschke, "who was wont to trot by Gneisenau's side,
always with the same tiresome, stiff expression of countenance, lashing the air with his stick — even Hudson
Lowe could hardly find words enough to praise the leonine
courage of these ragged, half-starved heroes."

Napoleon's
crest rises.

Blücher's army was reduced to such a level that Napoleon disdained to follow it.   To show what he had done,
he sent long trains of captives to Paris and had them
marched by the Vendôme Column.   These Prussians were
the most hated of all the allies ; it was they who were
supposed to have done the most in plundering and burning villages.   According to the popular Parisian gibe they
were *les plus chiens*, worse than the *rustres* and *les autre*
chiens.   The old national pride in Napoleon, so nearly extinguished, now flamed up anew.   The emperor himself,
humble enough but shortly before, had now recovered all his
assurance and spoke of returning to the Vistula.   He sent
word to his envoys at Châtillon to listen to no proposals of

the allies. He looked upon the latter as actually beaten :
" With my captives I am not in the habit of negotiating,"
he declared. And, indeed, at this very time the different
powers were quarrelling so fiercely, that Schwarzenberg
had entered into correspondence with the French, and
was already withdrawing his troops, when the king of
Prussia in person induced him to countermand the order.

As had happened before in Silesia and at Leipzig, it
was Blücher's energy that stemmed the ebbing tide. Bar-sur-
He grasped at a suggestion of Grolmann's, that an end Aube.
should be put to all this disorder by leaving the army
of Schwarzenberg to its own devices, marching north to
unite with the corps of Bülow and of Wintzingerode, —
which were advancing from Belgium, — and then descending in a straight line upon Paris. Even before the grudg-
ing consent of the allied sovereigns could reach him, his
army, rested and reënforced, was on the march, with
Napoleon in pursuit. After the latter's departure, Frederick William fairly forced Schwarzenberg, who had
fought no engagement since entering France, to take
part in a battle at Bar-sur-Aube ; at his father's side the
future emperor, William I., a boy of seventeen, rode into
the first military action of his life, and acquitted himself
with distinction, inaugurating his glorious record of victories untarnished by defeats.

When Blücher joined forces with Bülow, the latter was Blücher's
horrified at the wretched appearance of the much-tried march on
troops. But at Laon, where Napoleon at once attacked Paris.
them, and where the battle was fought in the darkness of
the night, a signal victory was gained. It is true, discords like those before the battle on the Katzbach prevented pursuit, and robbed the victory of much of its
importance. Blücher had fallen sick from over-exertion,
and sat in a dark room a prey to delusions; it was with

difficulty that he was prevented, in the very moment of his triumph, from laying down the command. York, Kleist, and Bülow refused to obey Gneisenau; and the first-named threatened to leave the army. Gneisenau himself was afraid that, after such constant fighting, by the time they reached Paris there would be no Prussian army left, and that the Austrians would be able to twist the terms of peace to suit their own needs.

But an unsatisfactory answer of Napoleon's to an Austrian ultimatum, infused new unity into the army of the allies; it was too apparent that nothing was to be gained by sparing this man, and the Congress of Châtillon was abruptly closed. The great army set out for Paris, while Napoleon tried the desperate manœuvre of frightening its leaders by cutting off their line of retreat. With eighteen thousand men he expected, thus, to paralyze the action of more than one hundred thousand. The Czar almost fell into his trap, consenting finally, however, to detach a small force of ten thousand to keep the French emperor in check, while, with the rest, the union was made with Blücher's army. A French division that stood in the way at La Fère Champenoise was cut to pieces with horrible butchery. One last struggle before Paris with Marmont's and Mortier's corps, where the combatants penetrated to the Bois de Vincennes, to Père la Chaise cemetery, and to the hill of Montmartre, ended the French resistance; Blücher had looked on, having donned a woman's hat and veil to protect his eyes, which were badly inflamed, and thus, to the very last, had remained the central figure in the campaign. The fall of Paris meant, that the one hundred and seventy thousand Frenchmen left in German fortresses must wait in vain for relief; and, indeed, in the course of the winter and spring, garrison after garrison surrendered.

In Paris itself, the spell of Napoleon's ascendency was

broken, and the day of reckoning had come for the millions The allies
of stout lives sacrificed to one man's ambition.   The crowd in Paris.
surged around the Vendôme Column, eager to tear down
the image of its fallen emperor.   Officers of the national
guard tied the star of the Legion of Honor to the tails of
their horses; and many displayed the white cockade of the
Bourbons.   The allies were greeted as deliverers, and
Madame de Staël relates, that Frederick William was astonished at finding what a pleasure it was to these people to
be conquered.   The handsome Czar was grossly flattered
by all kinds of persons : the head of a madhouse for
females one day told him that, since his entry into the city,
the number of those who had gone insane from unrequited
affection had greatly increased.   In consequence of all this
friendliness, the terms imposed by the allies were far too
lenient; and Prussia was looked upon as something of a marplot for demanding sterner measures.   When Louis XVIII.
came in, he took the attitude of rightful ruler, and in his
own palace, as the most august prince of Christendom, demanded precedence over the three monarchs who had just
regained him his throne.   France, on which no indemnity
was imposed, was given all of Alsace and a million more
inhabitants than she possessed in 1789.   Prussia, which had
borne the brunt of the war, could not even obtain payment
for the unjust contributions that had been imposed upon
her from 1808 to 1812 ; and it was with difficulty that she
regained possession of the sword of Frederick the Great,
and the figure of Victory, with her four great horses, that
had been taken from the Brandenburg gate.   The return of
the latter work of art, indeed, was a tangible proof of liberation, and the whole city of Berlin streamed out to meet
the great wooden chest as it was drawn by twenty horses
along the Charlottenburg Chaussée.
     But the worst act of folly on the part of the allies, was

to leave Napoleon sovereign prince of Elba, with the title of Emperor, with a retinue of officers, and with a standing army of four hundred men.

The calling of the Congress of Vienna.

In the moment of victory, a congress had been called to meet at Vienna for the sake of making changes in the map of Europe such as had not been known since the Peace of Westphalia; there was scarcely a country the boundaries of which were not to be fundamentally altered. The brilliancy of the assembly corresponded to the importance of the occasion; and the Turkish Sultan was the only European potentate who was not represented. Even France was allowed to send Talleyrand, the famous turncoat, who had sacrificed on the altar of liberty at the feast of brotherhood on the Champ de Mars, had served Napoleon in the days of his glory, had directed the compensation of the servile German princes, and who now came as envoy of the Bourbon king; wily and clever to the last degree, he took such advantage of the dissensions of other powers that at times his single voice was almost decisive.

The congress dances.

Since the Council of Constance there had been no such assembly as this great congress, where for a period of nine months the fate of nations was discussed. It was the policy of the Emperor Francis to play the part of genial host; and he expended in all some sixteen million guldens on his various entertainments. Balls and masquerades, card parties and exhibitions of *tableaux vivants*, followed each other in quick succession. Francis reaped his reward, for some of the most important business of the council was transacted on such occasions. " At a ball," writes a contemporary, "kingdoms were enlarged or sliced up, at a dinner an indemnity granted, a constitution sketched while hunting; occasionally a *bon mot* or a witty idea brought about an agreement where conferences and notes had failed." It was not quite true, therefore, that remark of witty old

Prince de Ligne : *"Le congrès dance, mais ne marche pas."*
It was said of Metternich that he understood most admirably how to entertain a foreign diplomat and show him most enchanting friendliness, when all the time he was preparing a fatal blow. Among the other attractions of Vienna in those days, was a concert given by Beethoven, for which the old blind king of composers sent personal invitations to all the great people. It is worthy of note, that questions of precedence at this congress played but a very little part; important acts were signed in alphabetical order, or else, to use a German term, *in bunter Reihe*, or by rotation.

In addition to general debates on international law, on the rules of navigation, on slavery, three cardinal matters— known as the Polish, Saxon, and German questions—occupied the time. The Czar wished to abrogate the former partitions of Poland and reëstablish that power with himself as king, and with liberal institutions. He considered that the Empress Catherine had committed a crime in dividing Poland; but, as Seeley remarks, the only crime for which Alexander really blamed her, was that of allowing others to share her booty. Stein, as well as other patriots, were much opposed to these Polish plans; but here Frederick William asserted himself and committed what has been rightly called the most independent and fortunate act of his whole reign. He told the Czar that he might have the greater part of Prussian Poland; he did not tell him that these vast tracts, peopled by an alien race, had always been to him more of a burden than a benefit. *The Polish question.*

In this way, one great dispute was ended, but at the same time an infinitely greater one begun. If Russia was to have the Polish provinces, where was Prussia to find indemnity? The most obvious answer was, in Saxony — an adjoining, Protestant, conquered country, whose king had acted in a despicable manner. Anticipating no oppo- *The Saxon question and Talleyrand's diplomacy.*

sition, Frederick William had the king sent off to Berlin and a Prussian administrator put in his place. But of all the mainsprings of action during these excited days, Austrian jealousy of Prussia was among the foremost ; by annexing Saxony, this dreaded rival would push her boundaries right up to the Bohemian frontier. There was no length to which the emperor would not go to prevent such a contingency — to which England also was opposed; and in the background was the tempter, Talleyrand, whose chief argument was, that Prussia was acting counter to the whole principle on which the war against Napoleon had been waged — the principle of legitimacy ; it was Napoleonic, not legitimistic, to depose the king of Saxony. It mattered little that Talleyrand's premises were utterly wrong ; that war had been waged against Napoleon for far other reasons than that he was not legitimate ruler ; that the king of Saxony, as king at least, was even less legitimate than his imperial creator. The wily Frenchman's absurd reasonings fell on willing ears; his influence grew from day to day, and on January 3, 1815, was formed the most preposterous of all alliances, that of England and Austria with the very power against which they had just been so bitterly warring. For six days, until the English Parliament repudiated the action of its minister, there was imminent danger of an outbreak. The Czar knew nothing of what had occurred until Napoleon, having returned from Elba, and finding the treaty of alliance in Louis XVIII.'s desk, sent it to him in order to disgust him with his allies.

After agitating Europe for four months, the Saxon question was settled by compromise ; Frederick Augustus was shorn of half his dominions, but left with the other half and with his royal title. In order to complete Prussia's indemnity, the Czar relinquished Thorn and Danzig; while

Aix, Cologne, Coblenz, and other territory on the left bank of the Rhine brought her boundaries up to almost their extent in 1806, and her population to half a million more. Throwing into the scale the wealth and industry of these provinces, her gain was infinite; while her proximity to France made her the natural guardian of German interests in that direction.

Talleyrand's triumph was one day to cost his country dear; but for the moment he had managed to interfere successfully in German affairs; and there is no knowing what he might still have accomplished, had it not been for Napoleon's return. The whole congress was thrown into confusion, and into a transport of excitement, by the news of that dramatic landing at Antibes, — of the Bourbon troops, which at sight of their old commander lost all control of themselves, and joined his standard; of the entry into Paris, the reinstatement in power, the expulsion of Louis XVIII., and the granting of a new constitution. The man for whom so many Frenchmen had already died was able to secure 200,000 new victims, and to organize them with a skill and rapidity that even he had never equalled. He ordered, besides, the *levée en masse;* which called out the whole male population of France. The congress stopped all business, and solemnly pronounced Napoleon an outlaw and an enemy of mankind. His envoys were not received. The powers agreed to furnish each 150,000 men; and four great armies, — under Wellington, Blücher, Schwarzenberg, and the Czar, — prepared to invade France; the two former by way of Belgium, the two latter by crossing the middle Rhine. *Napoleon's return from Elba.*

Blücher met the French at Ligny, and once more and for the last time an army of Napoleon conquered an enemy, and even one that was its superior in numbers. The Prussians lost some 12,000 in dead and wounded. At the same *Blücher at Waterloo.*

time, Wellington won the day at Quatrebras; and then
moved to the field near Brussels where was fought the
most famous battle of modern times. Blücher was not
far from right when he wrote from Waterloo, "Our victory is the most complete that has ever been gained;" or
Gneisenau when he declared that the enemy was annihilated as never an enemy before. If the brunt of the
fighting had been done by the English, the Prussians had
arrived at a moment so critical as to make it doubtful
what might have happened had they come an hour later.
Blücher's march from Ligny had been a wonderful achievement; when Wellington sent to ask him for a single
corps he had answered proudly that he would be present,
not with a corps, but with his whole army. On the day
after his defeat, without pausing for rest, and suffering
personally from the effects of a fall from his horse, he had
proceeded twelve miles to Wavre. On the day following,
the famous June 18, his half-fed troops had hurried for
eight hours through rain and mud before plunging into
the thick of battle. When the men despaired and declared
that they could go no further, the determined old man
had said to them: "Boys, we *must!* I have pledged my
word to my brother Wellington, and you would not have
me break it!" The brave English commander, in the
meantime, having withstood for hours the most murderous
fire of which history bears record, when approached by
Lord Hill, and asked his intentions, had answered simply:
"Hold fast to the last man!" Later, he was heard to
murmur to himself: "Blücher — or night!"

The question as to the relative merits of the achievements of these two commanders has much agitated posterity; it did not greatly trouble the persons most
concerned. Wellington, in his formal despatch, ascribed
the fortunate conclusion of the day to Blücher's advent;

while the Prussian general's own son wrote from the scene of battle, "Father Blücher embraced Wellington in such a hearty manner that everybody present said it was the most affecting scene imaginable."

For the first time in his career, Napoleon was personally forced to take to mad flight; as he sprang from his carriage, defending himself with his pistol, he left behind him his hat, sword, and field-glass, which fell into Blücher's hands. The carriage itself, which Blücher sent to his wife as a trophy, was found stuffed with valuables; diamonds the size of peas were thrown round among the soldiers, and sold for the immediate enjoyment of a few francs. Gneisenau carried off the fallen emperor's seal. The work of pursuit was left to the Prussians, who, wearied though they were, kept up the chase for five hours; after which a single drummer mounted on a horse managed to keep thousands in front of him in a state of panic.

The flight from Waterloo.

The carnage at Waterloo, if not equal to that at Leipzig, was yet a worthy holocaust even to the fallen greatness of a Napoleon. The losses of the allies were 21,400, those of the French, including prisoners, 25,000. Of heartrending scenes there was no end. An English resident of Brussels has recorded how a transport wagon stopped before his door, and how, when he went to carry nourishment, he found the wagon filled, exclusively, with men who had lost all four of their limbs.

With Napoleon once more defeated, forced to abdicate by his own Parliament, and sent off to eat his heart out on his desolate island near the equator, a second Peace of Paris was arranged with France which was not so favorable to that power as the first. It is true, in spite of the protests of Prussia, — which government would gladly have seen its enemy deprived of Alsace and Lorraine, — the boundaries of 1792 were left to the Bourbon dynasty; but this

The second Peace of Paris.

time an indemnity was required, the stolen works of art were to be restored to the various capitals, while the land was to support a force of one hundred and fifty thousand men until the terms of peace should have been carried out.

The settlement of the German question at the Congress of Vienna.

With the sudden storm-cloud thus dispersed, the Congress of Vienna was able to renew its deliberations and to embody in its protocol, or final act, some one hundred and eighty measures passed. The most important question of all, the reconstruction of Germany, was solved in the least satisfactory manner, and only after nine different schemes had been brought forward. One was, to make Stein president over kings and emperor; another, to have Austria nominal head, but Prussia to control the armies. Stein himself had desired an empire with Austria at its head, but the Emperor Francis had refused; moreover the minor states were unwilling to give up one jot or tittle of their sovereignty. The result was the passing of a mere Act of Confederation, with Austria as presiding power and with a Diet that was to meet at Frankfort-on-the-Main. The different states were left with much independence and might form their own alliances; they were all to send delegates to Frankfort; and it was one of the peculiarities of this political monstrosity, that a combination of the small states, representing one-sixth of the population of Germany, could nearly doubly outvote the seven larger states, with the remaining five-sixths.

Shortcomings of the "Act of Confederation."

Nor was this the worst: Saxony and Bavaria proved themselves far more dangerous as friends than they had ever been as enemies; the former managed to pass a motion that no change should be made in this most incomplete of all constitutions, save by unanimous vote; the old *liberum veto* of the Polish diets was revived for the benefit of the German princes. And Bavaria blocked all proceedings, until an act providing for a general federal council had been let fall. As a result there was no central authority with any real coercive power. The Diet of Frankfort had no army and no funds; and its only means of punishing a recalcitrant state was to vote federal execution, — which meant that individual states were to be deputed to exercise armed pressure. The net result of all these wars for the internal affairs of Germany, was a worse state of things than before; but the very weaknesses of this German confederation were to conduce to the aggrandizement of Prussia and lead to her final triumph.

CHAPTER VIII

THE STRUGGLE FOR CONSTITUTIONAL GOVERNMENT
AND THE REVOLUTION OF 1848

LITERATURE: Treitschke's work extends to 1847, but is too detailed
for the purposes of the ordinary student. Stern, *Geschichte Europa's*,
1815–71, is also incomplete, but promises to be a clear and forcible statement of facts. Constantin Bulle, *Geschichte der neuesten Zeit*, is excellent. Biedermann, who was in the thick of the constitutional struggle in
1848, has left two well-written and reliable works, 25 *Jahre deutscher
Geschichte*, 1815–40, and 30 *Jahre deutscher Geschichte*, 1840–70. Of
contemporary memoirs, those embodied in Seeley's *Life of Arndt* are
most interesting. See, also, the *Life of Bunsen*, edited by his widow,
and *Bunsen's* Correspondence with Frederick William, edited by Leopold von Ranke. The most complete history of the Revolution of 1848 is
that by Hans Blum. See, also, Fyffe's *Modern Europe*.

The
Metternich
policy.

THE three monarchs who at last, by the aid of England,
succeeded in overthrowing Napoleon were in reality men
of only mediocre ability. Francis of Austria was the incarnation of selfishness and narrow-mindedness. From
the first he had scented danger to himself in the popular
nature of the uprising in Prussia, for liberal ideas of
every kind were a bugbear to him. "*Omnes mundus stul-
tizat et vult habere novas constitutiones*," "The whole world
is foolish and wants new constitutions," he cried angrily,
in bad Latin, to a delegation of Hungarians. Hand in
hand with Metternich, a minister after his own heart, he
inaugurated a system of persistent political repression
that reminds one of the religious tyranny of his bigoted
ancestors. Under the remainder of his own reign, and
under that of his son, enlightenment was simply crushed
out in Austria. The votaries of literature and art went

324

elsewhere, and even the teachings of learned scientists were subjected to rigid censorship. A copy of Copernicus, *De revolutionibus orbium celestium*, was confiscated in 1848, because of the dangerous sound of its title.

The best and most intelligent of the trio was doubtless the Czar Alexander, in spite of his fickleness and vanity. He asserted himself on all occasions and posed everywhere as the real liberator of Germany, having come to consider himself an instrument chosen by Providence for the restoration of law and order. But his mind was no better balanced than in those early days, when he had sworn such loyalty to Prussia, only to desert her at Tilsit; or when, in reality autocrat of autocrats, he dreamed of becoming constitutional king of Poland. After the victories over Napoleon, he developed a religious enthusiasm, discussed dogmas and methods of doing penance with Frau von Krudener at Paris, and, at last, surprised his royal allies by laying before them the draft of a treaty, which provided nothing less than that the world should henceforward be ruled by the principles of common Christian brotherhood. A new alliance is to be formed, the writing declares, founded on the glorious truths of the religion of the Divine Saviour; the guiding threads of policy are to be the precepts of this same religion, — justice, love, and peace; the monarchs are to regard themselves as brothers, as fathers of their people, as "Plenipotentiaries of Providence," as rulers over three branches of one and the same people; the nations are exhorted to stand fast in the principles taught by the Saviour; and all powers that do so shall be worthy of reception into this Holy Alliance. Frederick William signed at once. Francis and Metternich, with scorn and mockery in their hearts, followed suit for fear of offending the Czar. Wellington refused, on the part of England, as did also the Pope, who sent

The Holy
Alliance.

word that "from time immemorial he had been in possession of Christian truth and needed no new interpretation of the same." The smaller powers of Europe all
handed in their allegiance; while the Sultan of Turkey,
who scented in this outburst of Christian sentiment the
preliminaries of a crusade against himself, had to be pacified by an express declaration to the contrary on the part
of Alexander. The chief trouble with the Holy Alliance
was, that it regarded the people as senseless flocks to be
driven by whatever measures the allied rulers might suggest. The treaty proved practically to be a dead letter;
nor was even the brotherly concord of long duration.
The Holy Alliance is responsible in a measure for the
unanimity of the powers in the repression of liberal ideas.

A con-
stitution
promised by
Frederick
William III.
But liberal ideas were in the air now, and the strivings
of the German people, for a generation to come, were to
be toward their realization. The first draft of an article
in the protocol of the Congress of Vienna had read: "In
every state of the German Confederation there shall be
a constitution in favor of the local estates"; but, by
Austrian influence, the "shall" had been changed to a
feeble "will," and no punishment placed on disregard of
the provision. While the Congress of Vienna was still
in session, — at a time when there was immediate need of
raising a new army on account of Napoleon's return, —
Frederick William had promised a constitution to his
Prussians. As a pledge of his confidence in the nation,
there was to be established a sort of parliament. Representatives appointed by the local assemblies of the estates
were to meet at Berlin; but they were to deliberate
and advise, not to vote. Small as these concessions were,
they were never fulfilled. Frederick William could not
trust his five and a half million new subjects, who had
belonged to as many as a hundred different states, to

exalt the Prussian monarchy : he was seized with the
same dread of an all-engulfing liberalism which filled his
companions of the Holy Alliance. It was two years
before the necessary commission was instructed to take
the matter in hand ; six years more before the preliminary
local assemblies were organized on a common basis. Not
until seven years after Frederick William's death, was a
united Diet to be called to Berlin ; and then it was to be
of no use, as the country was on the brink of revolution.
In other states of Germany, the course of events was
similar. In 1818, the only sovereigns who had granted
constitutions, were Bavaria, Baden, and the Grand Duke
of Weimar ; the latter the patron of Goethe and lord of
the famous Wartburg.

That the progress of liberal institutions was not more
rapid, is largely owing to the influence of the Austrian
chancellor who, for nearly a generation, stood over the
kings of Europe, and forced them into the narrow path
of his own policy. The name of Metternich has become
a synonym for reaction and conservatism. Not content
with surrounding Austria by a Chinese wall, he made it
his life-work to prevent Prussia and other German states
from introducing constitutional government ; well knowing
that, if the spirit of nationality should invade the many-
tongued Austrian dependencies, there would be an end of
the recently formed empire. Over the king of Prussia,
he not only exercised the ascendency of a stronger and
more determined mind — making use of every little popular disturbance, every outspoken paragraph of the news-
leaves, to terrify the timid ruler —, but he even threatened
to withdraw from the Holy Alliance, should Frederick
William refuse to take steps against the progress of
revolution.

On the brilliant period of the war of liberation, was

Metternich
opposed to
liberal in-
stitutions.

following one of petty suspicion and persecution. The days of absolute monarchy were counted, but the sovereigns could not and would not accept their doom.

Ingratitude of Frederick William III.

All the wonderful services rendered to him by his people, all the blood shed in war by men of peace, all the sacrifices made to raise the necessary funds, were now forgotten by the Prussian king; and he gave full credence to Metternich's devilish insinuations that the land was seething with sedition, concerned in which, were men like Arndt and Jahn. When Councillor Schmalz, the rector of the Berlin University, wrote an elaborate pamphlet to prove that the uprising of 1813 had not been the work of the people, but that the latter had simply streamed together at the king's summons as firemen obey an alarm bell: Frederick William saw fit to decorate him with an order, and to command his literary opponents to keep silent.

The founding of the *Burschenschaft*.

It is safe to say, that at no time in these earlier years was there any conspiracy which hazarded the king's safety or that of existing political institutions. But in one quarter there was a great deal of zeal for reform, a certain amount of incendiary eloquence, and two isolated cases of shocking crime, — enough, and more than enough, to focus Metternich's attention on the secret societies in the German universities. These *Burschenschaften*, as they were called, had been founded in 1815, with the noblest purposes, and in patriotic antagonism to the *Landschaften*, which represented the separatism of the various petty states. The originators of the association were eleven students of Jena, all of whom had learned the more serious side of life on bloody battle-fields, and had come home with a loathing for the shallow, vicious ideals of the ordinary student societies. Sobriety and chastity were conditions of entrance, and the silly twaddle of the *Commers* was condemned; while each member was admonished to attend his lectures regularly and to show industry in his work. The watchword of the *Burschenschaft* was "honor, liberty, fatherland"; and the academic, was to be a model of the larger national life, every moral and physical faculty being trained for the country's benefit. Fichte and Schleier-macher, Jahn and Arndt, were chosen as examples and leaders; and a song of the last-named, "*Sind wir vereint zur guten Stunde*," became the hymn, as it were, of the fraternity. Jahn, who had been given a degree from Jena, and who had established there one of his gymnastic training grounds, had been indirectly concerned in founding the *Burschen-schaft*. The glowing patriotism of this exalted and rather ill-balanced man—who seriously suggested allowing a strip of wilderness to grow up between France and Germany and peopling it with wild beasts—found a ready echo in these fiery young hearts.

From the beginning, it was designed to make the organization of the *Burschenschaft* as widespread as possible; and within two years it had found footing in sixteen different universities. A common flag had been adopted, made up of the red, black, and gold, which were erroneously supposed to have been the colors of the old Holy Roman Empire.   In 1817, it was determined to cement the union of all the chapters by holding a congress, or festival, which should, at the same time, be a memorial of great national events. The day chosen was the anniversary of the battle of Leipzig, and the *Landsturm* of Eisenach were to join in the celebration; while the place was to be the Wartburg, so memorable in the history of the Reformation, of which this was the three hundredth anniversary. There was a peculiar fitness, moreover, in this young band of patriots holding their assembly within the territory of the Grand Duke of Weimar; for, as was repeatedly emphasized during the proceedings, Charles Augustus was

The Wart-burg festival.

the only prince who up to that date — end of 1817 — had kept his promise and given his people a constitution.

The demonstrations on the Wartburg.
The Wartburg festival has become famous in history, not because of anything really remarkable in the rather harmless and boyish proceedings, but because of the effect that the report of those proceedings had upon Metternich and the sovereigns of Europe. In some of the speeches at the Wartburg it was, indeed, declared that the hopes of the war of liberation had not been realized; but, on the whole, the official program of the 18th and 19th of October was carried through with dignity and moderation. Addresses were made by professors of Jena; and, before parting, some two hundred delegates consecrated the closer union of their organizations, by partaking together of the Lord's Supper. But, on the evening of the 18th, some wilder spirits — in memory of Luther's burning of the Pope's bull — inaugurated an *auto-da-fe* on the little hill that faces the castle. Into the flames, with disquisitions on their demerits, were thrown a number of books; among them the writing in which Schmalz belittled the work of the patriots of 1813, a history of Germany by one Kotzebue, — who was hated as a Russian spy, — a Code Napoleon, and several writings against the new gymnastics. As emblems of the old military tyranny, there were also burned a corporal's staff, a pigtail, and one of the wonderful inventions by which officers prepared their figures for their faultlessly fitting uniforms.

Excitement at the different courts.
On receipt of greatly exaggerated accounts of what had taken place at the Wartburg, Prussia and Austria sent special envoys to the Grand Duke of Weimar; who, after investigation on the part of his ministry, failed to find that the students had committed any grave fault. But the Prussian minister of police denounced this "band of demoralized professors and corrupted students," and de-

clared that such " vandalism of demagogic intolerance "
had dishonored the classic Wartburg.   It was widely believed that, among the books burned, had been the act of
confederation of the German states.   Metternich saw in
the festival the beginning of a widespread conspiracy,
which, he declared, was not confined to students; and it
was reported that the members of the *Burschenschaft* had
sworn to die, if need be, for their organization.

At a meeting of sovereigns, which took place at Aix-
la-Chapelle, Metternich found an opportunity to work
directly on the feelings of Frederick William III., — who,
indeed, was already half beside himself with fear.   He
had investigated the case of every Prussian who had been
present at the festival, and had set a watch on the *Burschenschaften* as well as on all the *Turnvereine*, or gymnastic
associations in Prussia; and had threatened to suppress
any university where the spirit of disobedience should be
found.   Metternich persuaded him, that the granting of
a constitution would only increase the impending dangers.
Had not this very festival taken place in the dominions of
a too liberal-minded prince?   When, therefore, in these
days, a delegation from the Rhine provinces came to ask
for the carrying out of those former promises, the Prussian
king turned them ungraciously away.   He lent a willing
ear to Metternich's attacks on the freedom of the press
and on the want of supervision over the teachings of professors in the universities.   The Austrian recommended
the strictest kind of investigation into everything pertaining to student life.

Meanwhile, through this policy of repression, and through
the failure of the sovereigns of Germany to keep their
promise of granting constitutions, the *Burschenschaften*
really were becoming dangerous; not because of any
widely organized conspiracy, but because, in all such asso-

Repressive
measures of
Frederick
William
III.

ciations, there are sure to be extremists ready to draw the
full consequences from inflammatory talk.   Here and
there, it had actually been debated whether it was wrong
to kill a prince for the good of his people ; whether, indeed,
a political murder would not be the best way of stirring
men up to great deeds.   A party had been formed at Jena
called the *Unbedingten*, or unconditionals, which had in
mind a radical reform of the whole German system.   The
sovereigns were to be reduced to the condition of elected
officials responsible to the people.   The head of the
" unconditionals," Augustus Follen, was credited with the
design of calling a mass meeting on the battle-field of
Leipzig, for the purpose of proclaiming a German republic.

The murder
of Kotzebue
by Karl
Sand.

A special object of hatred was the publicist Kotzebue,
who furnished the Czar with political reports of what went
on in Germany, and who was looked upon by the students
as the " paid spy of despotism."   Jena was, finally, made too
unpleasant for him as a place of residence, and he removed
to Mannheim.

But in the heart of one exalted and not altogether
responsible student, Karl Sand by name, the conviction
had grown up, that the only way of saving the fatherland
was to rid it forever of such a traitor as Kotzebue.   Sand
was a gentle youth, who, according to his own confession,
had long thirsted to show his devotion to his country by
one decisive deed.   There was something fantastic in his
nature: he loved to go round in old Germanic costume, to
drink out of oak-crowned goblets ; while the place where he
met with his student friends he had named the " Rütli."   As
far as Kotzebue was concerned, Sand did him far too much
honor in regarding him as a dangerous enemy.   But all
the rulers of Europe were now thrown into inconceivable
excitement by the news of a crime, that seemed to them
but one demonstration of the whole *Burschenschaft* spirit:

how Sand had journeyed to Mannheim, and been admitted
to Kotzebue's house; how, as the old man walked unsus-
pectingly to meet him, the student had thrown himself upon
him and stabbed him to the heart.   Sand had then tried
to kill himself, but, his wound not proving fatal, he was
brought to trial, judged guilty of murder, and executed.
The trial took the form of an inquiry into a supposed
conspiracy, the belief in which was strengthened by the
enthusiasm shown for Sand.   Many of his fellow-students
looked upon him as a second Mutius Scævola, or William
Tell.   They had at one time contemplated marching upon
Mannheim for the purpose of setting him free.   As his
head fell upon the scaffold many stepped up and dipped
their handkerchiefs in his blood, as in the blood of a
martyr.   Even older men of good standing approved of
the motive, if not of the means, and wrote letters of con-
dolence to Sand's mother ; while, blasphemous as it may
sound, in the mouth of the people the spot where his head
had fallen came to be known as Ascension Meadow !

The rulers of the Holy Alliance looked, not unnaturally, Terror of
upon the murder of Kotzebue as a manifestation of the the rulers.
same spirit that had inaugurated the Wartburg festival.
This *Burschenschaft* seemed to them a revival of the old
Vehmgericht, the members of which had been told off by lot
to commit bloody deeds.   Its ultimate object was thought to
be the overthrow of all monarchical institutions : this murder was but one of a series, and others might presently be
expected.   And, sure enough, within a few weeks, an apoth-
ecary at Schwalbach, Löhnung, attempted to stab and shoot
the president of the government of Nassau ; and, on being
carried to prison, ended his life by eating broken glass.
An Austrian minister received a letter of warning.   These
were unhappy days for the Czar, whose own father had
been murdered ; for the autocrat in Vienna, but, most of

all, for the timid Frederick William.   The latter recalled
all Prussian students from Jena, and deprived them of
the chance of holding state offices.   Extraordinary powers
were given to the police, and students' letters were intercepted and opened.   Great excitement was aroused because one such missive was found to contain a quotation
from Goethe's *Egmont*, "Whenever I see beautiful, proud
necks, I think how fine it would be to run them through
with my sword."   Other expressions led to the conclusion
that an attempt was intended on Frederick William's life;
while, at the same time, an agent of the government reported from the University of Giessen, that a plot had been
detected to murder all the princes and to unite Germany.

Petty
oppression
in Prussia.

All this explains, if it does not justify, the severity of the
reaction that now set in.   In July, 1819, the gymnastic
establishments in Prussia were closed.   Father Jahn was
seized and dragged off to Spandau, and then to Küstrin.
A watch was set on the university professors ; while many
innocent persons were persecuted and their houses searched,
their papers read.   Even Gneisenau was surrounded by
spies, and Schleiermacher placed on parole.   Stein, who
had founded a society for German history, and was about
to start the great collection known as the *Monumenta
Rerum Germanicarum*, was suspected of a design to prove
that, in the Middle Ages, princes had no real supreme power

The perse-
cution of
Ernst
Moritz
Arndt.

over their subjects.   Perhaps the worst sufferer of all was
Ernst Moritz Arndt, the man who had been untiring in
helping to rid his country from French tyranny, and who
had been rewarded by a professorship at Bonn.   Early in
1819, he had been informed that "his Majesty could not
have any teachers in the Prussian universities who laid
down principles such as those contained in the fourth part
of the *Spirit of the Age* [which had just appeared]," and
that, on the next occasion of the kind, he would be removed

from his post. After the murder of Kotzebue and the attempt of Löhnung, Arndt's house was searched and his private papers were carted off in great sacks. In spite of his protest to Hardenberg that he "hated all secret intrigues like snakes of hell," he was treated as a suspect, and repeatedly examined by commissioners, who happened to be low, ignorant fellows. The charges against him were: secret conspiracy, corrupting of youth, and planning to form a republic. The investigation dragged on for years, and the inquiries extended to the pettiest conceivable matters. Chief Commissioner Pape once pointed out a passage in a letter, written twelve years before, in which Arndt had said that his head was full of so many things he could write no more : Just what things, asked Pape, was Arndt's head full of at that time? and witnesses were summoned to elucidate the point. For twenty years, so long as Frederick William III. lived, Arndt was refused permission to lecture ; although, on the accession of Frederick William IV., in 1840, he was made rector of the University of Bonn. He reopened his courses, at the age of seventy, amid demonstrations of the wildest enthusiasm.

This narrow-mindedness at the Prussian court was to no one more welcome than to Metternich. He kept his agents at Berlin, constantly egged Frederick William on, and finally, in the so-called "Teplitz Punctation," came to a secret agreement as to the policy to be pursued throughout Germany. Moreover he exacted a pledge that it should be carried out. Frederick William was to do nothing in the way of granting a constitution until the "inner and financial affairs of his state should have been brought into perfect order,"— which was equivalent to relegating the whole matter to the Greek Calends. Minister of Police Kamptz,— after publishing a definition of high treason, which made a crime of every expression of a desire *The Carlsbad decrees.*

for a constitution,—joined with Austria in calling a ministerial congress at Carlsbad to take further steps against
the spirit of revolution. The decrees there passed were
then made law by action of the Frankfort Diet; and Metternich's followers could boast that they had gained a
battle greater than that of Leipzig. If the *Burschenschaft*—which was now declared dissolved—could be
compared to the Vehmgericht, the new Central Investigation Commission, that was established at Mainz, was a
second Spanish inquisition. It was to be ever on the
scent for " revolutionary practices and demagogic associations," and, though without power to impose sentence,
could and did, as in the case of Arndt, make a man's life
miserable for years. Hundreds of innocent persons were
arrested, on no stronger ground than an incautious remark
or a passage in a private letter. As red, black, and gold
were the colors of the *Burschenschaft*, they might nowhere be displayed,—not even in the popular combination
of yellow straw hats, black coats, and red waistcoats.
Every writing under 320 pages in length was subject to
censorship; while government officials were to watch the
professors in the universities, and see that they taught no
evil. No wonder a man like Stein was unsparing in his
blame of Metternich and Hardenberg. To the former he
applied the adjectives "empty, ignorant, blatant, and con-
ceited "; to the latter, "frivolous, licentious, arrogant,
false, afraid-of-losing-his-place." In Prussia, there was a
ministerial crisis; and Humboldt, Boyen, and Beyme received their dismissal.

The Vienna
Final Act.

Yet Metternich went his way, called a conference to
Vienna, and, in the so-called Vienna Final Act, crystallized
all his reactionary measures. According to Article 57,
" the entire power in state affairs must rest unimpaired
with the head of the state." In certain matters no consti-

tution might bind him, in no parliament were the "lawful limits of free utterance to be exceeded." The federal Diet was to watch for dangerous expressions of opinion on the part of the state assemblies. On May 15, 1820, the "Final Act" was adopted by the Diet; — "worth more than the battle of Waterloo" was the verdict of Metternich's henchman, the Prussian Gentz.

The Mainz commission continued its activity for seven years. According to one of its own reports it endeavored to establish the degree of certainty, or of greater or less probability, not according to the rules prescribed by any special legislation, "but according to the principles of historic belief and its own subjective conviction!" Among those who are mentioned as having "caused, encouraged, and furthered revolutionary strivings, though possibly without intent," are mentioned Arndt, Stein, Gneisenau, Blücher, York, Schleiermacher, and Fichte! *The Central Commission at Mainz.*

The dissolution of the *Burschenschaft* took place, but with results directly opposite to those intended. Far and wide was sung the famous song of Augustus Binzer, "Wir hatten gebauet ein stattliches Haus,"—in which he tells of the happy, free, idyllic student life which has been crushed, like young green shoots of grass, by wicked men : — *The dissolution of the Burscherschaft.*

" *Das Band ist zerschnitten, war schwarz, roth und gold,*
  Und Gott hat es gelitten! wer weiss, was er gewollt?
  Das Haus mag zerfallen, was hat's denn für Not?
  Der Geist lebt in uns allen, und unsere Burg ist Gott."

On the ruins of the *Burschenschaft*, arose associations which really were political and revolutionary, and which were modelled on the Italian Carbonari and similar organizations in Spain, France, Russia, and Greece. The watchword of one of them was the seemingly innocent question : "Have you been on the Johannisberg to-day?"—with the answer, " Yes, I was there in May," or " I shall go there in May." The doings of another of these secret leagues were exposed in 1824, and some of the members were condemned to death, others to imprisonment; while Metternich, taking advantage of the general alarm, caused the Carlsbad decrees to be renewed, and a stricter watch to be kept on the different parliaments.

The Hambach festival.

The revolution of 1830 in France gave new stimulus to the discontented elements in Germany, and, in several states where crying evils existed, these were summarily swept away. Duke Charles of Brunswick, a bad character who nearly ruined his state by arbitrary taxes and inflation of the currency, was driven out. The same thing happened in Hesse, where the elector, William II., had been in the habit of using his cane, and even his knife, too freely, and was accused of combining with the bakers to raise the price of bread. In Saxony and in Hanover, concessions were demanded and obtained; while in Bavaria there took place a demonstration more serious than the much-decried Wartburg festival. In an immense gathering in the Palatine Castle of Hambach, inflammatory addresses were made, vengeance vowed against tyrants, and the sentiment uttered that " the best prince by the grace of God is a born traitor to the human race ! " Metternich brought forward a motion in the Diet, which was passed in an amended form, to the effect that all concessions won from a sovereign by violent means should be null and void; while another decree declared that, if a parliament should refuse taxes to the head of a state, it might be intimidated by troops of the Confederation.

But these repressive measures led to an exasperation on the part of the radical elements such as had not yet been known. The *Burschenschaft* awoke to new life, and two of the boldest projects were formed : one to march on Stuttgart and take prisoner the king of Würtemberg, who had revoked his constitution ; the other to raise in Frankfort a revolt which, it was believed, would spread all over South Germany ; and to capture the federal Diet. Both attempts proved ridiculous failures ;—in vain the great bell of the city of Frankfort tolled the signal for uprising ; in vain four hundred students marched in behind their black, red, and golden banners. They had miscalculated their own influence, and the citizens would not be roused. The whole extent of the damage was nine killed, twenty-four wounded, and thirty students taken prisoner. But, even had it been much greater, the authorities could scarcely have resorted to severer retaliatory measures. A commission like that of Mainz was once more established, and eighteen hundred cases were tried. A stricter censorship was introduced, and the system of passports carried to such an extent that no one could enter a hired carriage without producing such a paper. In Bavaria, those convicted of treasonable intents were forced to kneel before the picture of the king,—which was now set up in every court room,—and to sue for mercy. In Prussia, thirty-nine students were condemned to death, their sentences being afterward commuted to long imprisonment.

The attempt to raise a revolution in Frankfort.

On the whole, the revolutionary propaganda was confined to the students, and the dread and terror to the supreme rulers. The main body of the people were not discontented with their lot; and many agreed with Hegel that " whatever is is sensible and whatever is sensible is." Frederick William III., with all his faults, was much beloved. He had shared the darkest imaginable days with his subjects and was now sharing their peace and prosperity. It was recognized that his refusal to grant liberal institutions was not for the purpose of cloaking bad government, but rather from deep conviction. His

General commercial prosperity.

general policy with regard to trade and commerce was
wise, and the country was growing rich. Taxation was
moderate, justice was fairly administered, educational
reforms were introduced, and large sums were spent on
public works. The first railway was opened in Germany
in 1835, between Fürth and Nuremberg, and Prussia secured her full benefit from the change.

*The found-
ing of the
Zollverein.*
A peculiarly beneficent institution, and an important
step in developing Prussia's political as well as her mercantile ascendency, was the *Zollverein*, or Customs Union,
established in 1833. It showed what immense benefits
in every field could be expected from coöperation. When
Prussia reorganized her territory, in 1815, she had found
no less than sixty-seven different tariff schedules in operation in her various provinces; while, for one travers-
ing Germany at large, there were thirty-six different
boundaries, each with its own custom-house. Nor at
any single one of these frontiers, was the coin of the
neighboring state accepted, or were the postal arrangements the same. Prussia's first step, in 1818 A.D., was
to establish a single tariff for all her own lands; her next
to declare her willingness to accept neighboring principalities as partners in her new system. Her policy was
not to urge and not to use force. But the advantages
were so apparent, the profits so enormously increased, that,
by 1842, all the states of Germany, save Mecklenburg,
Hanover, and Austria, had been absorbed. Austria, indeed, was not desired, for the reason that no reliance could
be placed on all her heterogeneous dependencies. One
great result of the *Zollverein* was, that the smaller states
were now bound by strong ties of interest to Prussia.

The question of a constitution was allowed to slumber
during the last years of the reign of Frederick William III.;
but it was revived at the moment of his death, and Frederick

William IV., when he went to receive homage at Königsberg, was met by a petition that those earlier promises
might be fulfilled. The matter was assuming larger and
larger proportions; for the sentiment was gaining ground
that Prussia was the natural leader of Germany, and that,
in order to fulfil her mission, she must have liberal institutions. All depended on the character of the new Prussian
king : did he have the strength and the tact to hold the
loyalty of a united German people?

The reign opened well. In a series of brilliant speeches
the king let it be known that he meant to make great
changes, and he began by pardoning political prisoners.
Arndt was reinstated in all his university dignities. Jahn
was released from surveillance, and treated with respect
and consideration. The brothers Grimm, belonging to
the famous " Göttingen seven,"—who had given up their
professorships and gone into exile rather than submit to
an arbitrary abrogation of the Hanoverian constitution,—
were welcomed in Berlin and given chairs in the university. But, popular as these single measures were, a counter
current soon set in. Men began to perceive that the promises so abundantly offered by the new king were nothing
but glittering generalities. After listening to eloquent
speeches that seemed to portend a constitution, they found
that nothing of the kind was meant.

The people were very much in earnest if the king was
not. Their leading-strings had grown unbearable, and, as
year after year went by without their obtaining those
liberties which now seem a necessary adjunct of civilization, — political representation, freedom of the press, trial
by jury, — it was evident that a struggle must come which,
as likely as not, would be a bloody one. It is surprising,
indeed, to see how loyal the Prussians remained to the
House of Hohenzollern, even while they criticised its
momentary representative.

Brilliant as were some of his attainments, there is no
doubt but that from the first Frederick William IV. was
lacking in mental balance. He would shift at random
from one policy to the other, would one day pass a liberal
measure and the next go to the opposite extreme. He
would publicly profess to despise criticism and then try
to stop it by unjust means; even going so far as to suppress all the publications of a printing-house that had
displeased him. To a certain poet, Herwegh, who had
written against him, the king said affably, "I love a candid opposition"; but later proscribed and banished him,—
his ire having been aroused by a caricature in which his
love of a candid opposition was contrasted with the heap
of books and newspapers confiscated by his orders. Once
thoroughly gauged, his very wit and eloquence told
against him, and his every action was submitted to a fire
of criticism. It was taken ill that he set up his abode in
Sans Souci, the little castle at Potsdam so full of memories of Frederick the Great; and he was thought to wish
to copy him in other ways. A famous caricature of the
time represents him as following in Frederick's footsteps
in the snow, but always a little to one side. The great
Heinrich Heine wrote of him, with caustic severity:—

> "*Ein König soll nicht witzig sein,*
> *Ein König soll nicht hitzig sein,*
> *Er soll nicht Alten-Fritzig sein.*"

The tendency to be "*hitzig*," or vehement, is shown in
almost every letter that Frederick William wrote; there
being no end to the passionate interjections, the under-
scoring of words, the multiplication of exclamation points.

Even a Frederick William IV., overflowing as he was
with belief in the divine right of kings, could not close his

eyes to the discontent and want of confidence shown by his
people.   In 1842 he tried to stop the clamor for a general
Prussian parliament by calling together a committee from
the local assemblies.   Such a committee, consisting of
ninety-eight delegates, actually came together in Berlin,
only to find that on all matters of real interest to them the
king had already "made up his mind."   Five years later,
he took a great step in advance by summoning a *Verein-
igter Landtag*, or united Diet, including all the members
of all the local assemblies.   The issue of the royal patent
of February 3, 1847, caused great surprise and joy, until it
was found that the king's main object was to secure a loan
for a much-needed railroad between Berlin and Königsberg.
For his own part Frederick William meant to grant as
little as possible.   The Diet was there, he declared, to represent interests, not to offer opinions.   When the delegates
spoke of vested rights of the people he told them that the
assembly had no rights other than those granted by the
patent of February 3.   When the question of a constitution
came up he made one of his usual speeches and gave vent
to the famous peroration: " No written sheet of paper
shall ever thrust itself like a second providence between
the Lord God in heaven and this land."   Members of the
opposition were treated to petty slights, such as not being
invited to court festivities.

The summoning of the "united Diet."

The whole progress of the Diet was very unsatisfactory.
The delegates strove in vain to have their own position
defined, and the temper of the house was such that the
government's demand for a loan was rejected.   In itself
the demand was timely, just, and reasonable; but even the
delegates from East Prussia, which province would have
gained most by the proposed railroad, voted against it.
The "united Diet" was dismissed with apparently no
results; but in reality the gains were important.   In the

Results from the Diet.

first place, the differences between the crown and the people had come to a head. This king had been given a last opportunity, which he had failed to improve. No one doubted now that revolution alone would bring him to terms. Then, too, a hitherto unheard-of publicity had been given to all the proceedings; and the *London Times* had had a regular correspondent in the assembly, — so that the eyes of all Europe were on this state struggling for liberal institutions. Finally, this gathering had brought into prominence a number of men who were to be the leaders in the great national crises that were impending — among them Otto von Bismarck, as yet in the ban of narrow social prejudices, and therefore a violent conservative.

The outbreak of revolution.

It was an unfortunate time for Frederick William to fall out with his people; for Europe was on the eve of the most stirring events that had occurred since the fall of Napoleon. France was throwing over, not merely her old dynasty, but the very principle of monarchy as well; and her example reacted on every state of Germany as rapidly as a spark ignites tinder. The unwieldy Diet at Frankfort flew into a panic, and thought, when already too late, to regain its influence by revoking all the objectionable measures it had ever passed in the whole course of its existence. It declared for freedom of the press, voted to modernize its own organization, and asked for delegates from all the states to help it in its good work. The body that had once accepted the Carlsbad decrees now adopted the revolutionary colors of red, black and gold, and the revolutionary emblem of a gold eagle on a black ground. The new flag was soon floating over the hall of assembly in Frankfort. But reform in the government of Germany as a whole, was as much desired by the excited people as a reform in the government of each individual state. One of the common demands of all the revolutionary parties was for a really German parliament as opposed to the slack, inefficient Diet.

In almost all of the smaller German states the revolution was accomplished without bloodshed. The movement was so irresistible that the petitions for a constitution, for freedom of the press, for trial by jury, for the right of the people to bear arms, were almost immediately granted; while a body of fifty-one men, informally constituted, met at Heidelberg and nominated several hundred delegates to form a preliminary or ante-parliament, which should see to the calling of a really national assembly. The governments were preparing to call a separate assembly of their own for the purpose of revising the articles of confederation, when the radical course of the revolutions in the larger states put a stop to their endeavors.

In Bavaria, the disorders were complicated by the infatuation of King Louis I. for the famous dancer Lola Montez,—a woman who, to gain notoriety, had once taken off her shoe on the stage of the Paris opera house and thrown it at the men who would not applaud her. After dancing in the capitals of the Old and the New World, she had settled down in Munich, and induced the king to make her Countess of Lansfeld and give her a share in public affairs. She gained such ascendency in time, that ministries were dismissed to please her, and the university,— the better-minded students of which had attacked her infamous bodyguard, the "Alemannia,"—was declared closed. It was said that all Munich was divided into two parties· the ultramontanes, or clerical-conservatives, and the Lola montanes, or adherents of Lola. The immediate effect of the French Revolution was to give the ascendency to the reform party; and the university was declared reopened, the "Alemannia" dispersed, and Lola told to quit Munich at a day's notice. A story is recorded that shows, in an almost ridiculous way, how little of the true revolutionary spirit was present in the hearts of these Bavarians. After Lola's hasty departure, the crowd was engaged in sacking her villa when the king appeared, and in a loud voice said, "Spare my property!" Then all were silent, bared their heads, and joined in the song: "Hail to our king, all hail!" When, shortly after, Louis foolishly called out the military to protect him, the crowd surged before his palace and forced him into calling an assembly of the estates, and making great concessions, — the chief of which was ministerial responsibility to the people. The desire to be near Lola and the fear of an inquiry into his disposal of state funds, then forced him to the great step of abdicating the throne; and with sentimental, hypocritical assurances he took leave of his subjects.

The revolution in Austria.

By the rushing tide of revolution that spread so rapidly all the way from Paris to Warsaw, Austria and her dependencies were struck with peculiar violence. On the 3d of March, the Hungarian patriot, Kossuth, delivered a fiery speech in the Pressburg Diet, declaring that only a free constitution could ever bind together the scattered provinces of the monarchy. The present state of things, he cried, was unendurable; from the charnel house of the Vienna system was rising a pestilential vapor that paralyzed the nerves and banned the intellect; the future of the dynasty was being compromised, the foundations of the edifice were crumbling, and its fall imminent. In Vienna, police and censorship were openly defied, and Kossuth's speech was widely read. As the news came in of concession after concession granted by the smaller states, and of the complete change of front of the Frankfort Diet, the excitement grew to fever heat. Petitions poured in upon the Emperor Ferdinand, who, however, left all responsibility in the hands of the state conference, of which Metternich was the leading spirit. The estates of Lower Austria, called to meet in Vienna on March 13, drew up in the form of an address the moderate demands they intended to make; while the students of the university, who were destined to play a large part in this whole movement, followed suit, sending a deputation to the emperor himself.

The 13th of March, 1848, forms a sharply defined date in the annals of Austria, for it marks the fall of a system that had lasted a generation. On that day, the assembly of the Lower Austrian estates was declared opened; and an immense crowd of citizens and students thronged round the hall of meeting. A student read aloud Kossuth's speech. Wild with excitement, the multitude demanded admission to the hall, and six students and six citizens were allowed to enter. But soon came the rumor that these twelve had been arrested, and that the troops were approaching. The crowd burst into the assembly room, and compelled the members of the Diet to send a deputation to the emperor. In front of the chancery cries of " Down with Metternich! " were heard. As the report that the soldiers were advancing became a verity, the mob within the hall of assembly took to throwing down broken bits of furniture on the heads of their assailants, and even wounded one of the archdukes. Then two sharp volleys rang out, and many were killed and wounded; which gave the signal for a general arming. Everything depended on the attitude of the state conference, which had been in session in the castle for hours. Metternich tried to persuade the spokesmen of the people that the whole was merely a street riot, but was told proudly, " This is not riot, but revolution ! "   As a sop to the excited crowd, it was voted to revoke the censorship of the press, and Metternich withdrew to draw up the act.

The fall of Metternich.

But, from the adjoining room, he heard how one of the deputies demanded his resignation, and how no one spoke in his defence. With a certain dignity the apostle of repression bade farewell to his office, and to the scene of his labors. He declared that, from his own standpoint, he had always labored for the weal of the monarchy. If it was the general opinion that that monarchy would be endangered by his remaining, it was no sacrifice for him to go. " Your Highness, we have nothing against your person, but everything against your system," said a civic deputy, " and we must repeat, your abdication alone can save the throne and the monarchy." Metternich's house on the Rennweg was stormed, and he went off in exile to London; whither he had been preceded by Louis Philippe, and where he was to be followed in a few days by the brother and heir of the king of Prussia.

A constitution granted to the Austrians.

The state conference then granted all that the citizens demanded. A national guard and a student legion were established; and the Emperor Ferdinand,—who so hated the very word *constitution*, that he is said to have forbidden his physician to employ it, — was forced not only to grant one for his whole monarchy, but to stand at the window of his palace, waving a banner of black, red, and gold.

Frederick William IV. makes concessions.

Even more memorable than these happenings in Vienna were the events that were taking place almost simultaneously in Berlin. Never before nor since has a Hohenzollern played such a miserable rôle and been obliged to submit to such insults from his own people as Frederick William IV. in these tumultuous days. Cringing in his attitude and liberal with his promises when the mob seemed in the ascendant, he adopted the haughtiest tone when sure of his own safety.

Although perceiving, as did every other sovereign of Germany, the absolute need of making concessions, Frederick William lingered and affixed conditions. His grant of freedom of the press was so in the spirit of Metternich, that the latter had been in the act of transcribing it verbally, for the benefit of the clamoring Austrians, at the moment of his downfall. The Vienna revolution brought matters to a climax. Tumultuous assemblages of the people were held daily in that corner of the Thiergarten known as the "Zelten"; and, at last, the king promised everything that had been demanded, including a written constitution. The so-called "Patent of March 18th" called together the united Diet for April 2; and this and the other concessions were announced in the newspapers and by placards on the wall. The people thronged the streets and crowded into the square of the castle, raising cheers for the king, who appeared twice on his balcony and acknowledged them with thanks.

Just how much sincerity there was on both sides is hard to establish. The crowd took it ill that the castle was strongly garrisoned by troops from other places than Berlin, — there were cries of "Back with the military!" As for Frederick William, he tried in vain to get rid of his countless guests: it was announced that the king wished to work and desired quiet. One of the ministers and the governor of the castle appeared at the gate, and bade the people disperse. At last Frederick William gave the command of his troops to the determined General Von Prittwitz, and bade him put an end to this "scandal" in the courtyard. Assisted by Major Von Falkenstein, he had almost cleared the square, when the sound of two shots, — accidentally discharged as is now believed, — threw the people into a fever of excitement. With cries of "Treason!" "Vengeance!" "Barricades!", the varied elements of the Berlin population took to arms. The pavings were torn up and the streets rendered impassable; and, from the roofs

The shots in the castle yard and the barricade fights.

and windows, missiles, and even vitriol, were thrown down on the heads of the soldiers; while wires were drawn so as to trip them up, and glass strewn to wound them as they fell. For a day and a half, the reign of violence lasted. It was in vain that the king caused a white banner to be raised with the word "misunderstanding" in great letters; in vain that he issued a proclamation "to his dear Berliners," representing the revolution as the work of foreign agents. A wag placed the inscription "to his dear Berliners" under a piece of a bomb, fired by his own soldiers, that had struck into one of the public fountains. Nothing would satisfy the people but the withdrawal of the troops; and this at last the king ordered — intending them to return to the palace, but so wording his command that, at a moment when the tide was turning in their favor, they felt obliged to retire from the city.

The corpses in the castle yard.   The king was completely in the power of the populace. No attempt was made on his own person, but a spectacle was prepared for him in the courtyard of his own palace such as few civilized monarchs have been called upon to witness. Bedded in flowers and wreathed with laurel, but with their wounds laid bare to the utmost, the most mutilated corpses of those who had fallen in the barricade war were borne under his very window. As the litters were laid down in the presence of an immense crowd, the names and circumstances of the victims were called off: "Fifteen years old, shot at my side, my only son!"; or again, "a widow, mother of seven orphans!" The cry was raised, that the king must come and see his work; and as Frederick William delayed, the bearers started up the winding stairs with their ghastly burdens and threatened to enter his apartment. At last, half dead with fright, the king appeared on the balcony, at his side his invalid queen, — a nonentity in history save for this one trying experience.

" Take off your hat ! " was shouted from below; and as the Hohenzollern bared his head the corpses were thrust upward toward him.   Bidden to come down, he obeyed and bowed before the dead; while at last, content with their punishment, the crowd joined in the solemn strains of " Jesus, Lover of my Soul."

No further violence was attempted, save an attack on the palace of Prince William of Prussia, who was falsely supposed to have given the signal to fire.   In danger almost of his life, the object of general execration, the future idolized emperor of united Germany fled in disguise to England, and took up his abode with the Prussian ambassador, Bunsen.   The palace on Unter den Linden was only saved from destruction by the presence of mind of some one who wrote upon it: " property of the nation," and by a student who pointed out that the royal library would be in danger.

The last and most extraordinary act in this tragedy of humiliated royalty began with the posting of placards " To the German Nation," which announced that, for the salvation of Germany, Frederick William had placed himself at the head of the whole fatherland, and, on that very day, March 21, would appear on horseback in the midst of his people, bearing the " old revered colors of the nation."   It was the culminating triumph of the red, black, and gold. One of its banners waved from the castle top, another was borne before the king; who, as did also his princes and generals, wore a band of the same colors on his arm.   As he rode through the city, Frederick William stopped at various points and made enthusiastic addresses in favor of the national movement.   " I wish no crown, no sovereignty," he cried, alluding to the proposal to make him emperor of Germany; " I wish Germany's freedom, Germany's unity. I wish order, that I swear to God ! " and he solemnly raised his right hand.   A proclamation that same evening asked

The ride through Berlin.

for the confidence of the people, declaring that Prussia would henceforth be merged in Germany. Frederick William later described this ride through Berlin as "a comedy which he had been made to play," — one is tempted rather to regard it as a symptom of that want of balance which ended with insanity and death.

The burial of the corpses.

This first exciting period of the Prussian revolution closed on the 22d of March, with the burial of those who had fallen on the side of the people. The city was decked in mourning; while black flags waved from the city gates and from the roof of the castle. The two hundred or more bodies were borne in procession past the balcony on which stood the king with bared head. Bells were rung and anthems chanted; and, inasmuch as the bodies of the fallen soldiers were not included, the whole ceremony resolved itself into a triumph of the revolutionary party. It remained to be seen how the Prussian national assembly, called to meet on May 22, would acquit itself of the difficult task of drawing up a suitable and acceptable constitution.

The ante-parliament in Frankfort.

Meanwhile, a few days after the stirring scenes in Berlin, the preliminary Parliament had met in Frankfort, in the old church of St. Paul's, to settle the question of a constitution for all Germany. They were prepared to go very far, these five hundred delegates or appointees of the self-chosen committee of fifty-one, and to decide whether Germany should be a republic or an empire.

The ante-parliament was made up, for the most part, of men who had been before the public eye; and counted many members of local assemblies. Among them, were martyrs to the cause of liberty, like the Bavarian Eisenmann, who had spent fifteen years in undeserved imprisonment, and was now honored with a torchlight procession. As a body representative of all Germany, the Parliament was a failure; seeing that Austria furnished but two members, tiny Baden seventy-two, and Hesse-Darmstadt eighty-four. But more serious than this was the sharp antagonism that developed between the monarchical and the republican parties. Scarcely had the ante-parliament assembled in the venerable church of St. Paul's, in Frankfort, when a certain Hecker came forward with a number of articles, the fifteenth of which demanded abolition of hereditary monarchy and the formation of a confederation — after the model of the United States of America. Foiled in his radical plans on this arena, Hecker became a regular demagogue. He raised a revolt in Baden which cost several hundred persons their lives or their liberty.

The ante-parliament kept to its programme, declared for a national assembly to be formed by direct popular election, and appointed a committee to take the matter in hand. It did indeed make the important pronouncement that the decision regarding a constitution for Germany was to be the affair simply and solely of the national assembly. It would have been wiser, as the future showed, to pay some regard to the actual governing powers in the separate states. As yet there was no conflict. The governments showed no hostility to the national assembly, which met in Frankfort on May 18; while the Diet even sent it greeting. The members this time had been chosen from all Germany — theoretically one from every fifty-five thousand of the population. They considered themselves empowered to make great and permanent changes. They were, for the most part, men of ability, among them venerable figures like Arndt and Jahn, who were the objects of enthusiastic ovations. In the first session Arndt was called to the platform, and a motion passed that, in the light of recent events, he should be invited to write a stanza to his famous old song, "What is the German's Fatherland?" On the whole, the tone of the assembly was moderate, and, in a time of great

The national parliament in Frankfort.

ferment, much was hoped for from its action.   Its choice as first president of Heinrich von Gagern, a famous minister of Hesse-Darmstadt, was generally approved.

Initial errors of the Frankfort Parliament.

Unfortunately, no draft of a constitution had been prepared, and the assembly lost five valuable weeks before it could take the matter in hand at all, — the only important vote being one in favor of a national fleet, for which six million thalers were appropriated.   Then came the unfortunate choice of the Austrian Archduke John as provisional head of the nation.   There were legends of his great devotion to the cause of a common German fatherland.   He was quoted as having once proposed the toast : " No Prussia, no Austria — one united Germany ! "   He was believed, because he had married the daughter of a Styrian postmaster, to be democratic in his views.   As a matter of fact, in his insincerity, his intolerance, his one-sidedness, he was a true scion of the Hapsburgs ; and the mere fact that an Austrian had been chosen to the highest office, if only a temporary one, of the German nation, was a blow to the pride of Prussia, which might be pardoned but not forgotten.

But the greatest error of the Frankfort assembly was to begin its debates on the constitution with a discussion of the fundamental rights of the German man, a list of which had been drawn up in a hundred paragraphs.   Days passed into weeks and weeks into months, while the Parliament was still busy with underlying principles, and with disputed points of political economy ; and while enemies within and without were rising against it.   The iron that might once have been readily tempered was rapidly growing cold.   Moreover, various factors came in to distract attention from the matter in hand, — a war with Denmark, an uprising in Frankfort itself, increased rivalry between Austria and Prussia, and bloody happenings in both of those states.

It was now that the question of Schleswig-Holstein, which

was later to be so interwoven with the most fateful events of German history, first began to assume importance. These two provinces in the extreme northwest of Germany belonged, one to Denmark, the other to the German Confederation, and yet for centuries had been considered indivisible. Efforts on the part of successive kings to incorporate them in Denmark, in spite of the fact that the vast majority of the inhabitants were German, led to a revolution, in which Prussia, at the bidding of Archduke John, took the side of the insurgents. Her general, Wrangel, stormed the Danewerk, penetrated into Jutland, and could have brought the Danish king to terms but for a change in the policy of Frederick William IV., whose feelings had been worked upon by the Czar, as well as by England. The leading minister of the latter country, Lord Palmerston, had declared that, were he to meet the red-black-golden flag at sea, he would treat it as the flag of a pirate. Frederick William was fast receding from his recent liberal position. He was tired of this alliance with revolutionists; and he finally consented to the seven months' truce of Malmö, in which the advantages were overwhelmingly on the side of Denmark.

The Parliament of Frankfort felt outraged by this act, as well as by the fact that its envoy had not been admitted to the conferences; and only refrained from refusing to ratify the truce, from the consideration that, with Prussia as an enemy and Austria cool and indifferent, the Parliament would have no forces at its disposal at all, save the contingents of the minor states. The people of Frankfort were less philosophical. In the abandonment of the duchies they saw the holy cause of liberty betrayed. Representatives who had preached moderation, among them old Father Jahn, were chased, insulted, and even struck. One session of the Parliament was interrupted

The beginning of the Schleswig-Holstein difficulties.

Riot in Frankfort.

and barricades arose in the streets. Troops were called in, and the authorities remained masters of the situation ; though at the cost of many lives. Foul and dastardly was the murder, by citizens, of two men of eminence, — the Silesian representative, Prince Lichnowsky, and his friend and companion, General von Auerswald. Lichnowsky had been tied to a tree, and made the target for all sorts of missiles.

The problem of the Austrian dependencies.

It was under the gloomy shadow of these events that the Frankfort assembly, at last, proceeded to the actual task of debating upon a constitution. The very first articles, concerning the territory to be included in the new political creation, involved the assembly in a nest of difficulties : Should Austria be allowed to join the proposed empire with all her non-German dependencies ? Would Italians, Croatians, Hungarians, and Czechs be likely to obey, or even to understand, laws made for them in Frankfort by a German assembly ? Must the Diet interfere in every small Slavonic quarrel ? Austria's alternative was to abandon the idea of her own unity, and enter the new organization for a part only of her lands, — on the adoption of this alternative Prussia insisted.

Windisch-gratz retakes Vienna.

The fall of Metternich was far from ending the disturbances in Austria. The government was able in June, 1848, to put down the revolution in Prague, the imperial general, Prince Windischgratz, having bombarded the city. Against the Hungarians, Jellachich — a Croatian nobleman — was intrusted with the command ; while in Austrian Italy, Radetzky gained the victory of Custozza. Everywhere the star of the Hapsburgs seemed in the ascendent ; and, in the capital itself, the inexcusable violence of the rabble gave occasion for successful interference. The constitution promulgated almost immediately after Metternich's fall had not been satisfactory. During the month of May, riots and tumults occurred; the emperor fled from the city, and, for a time, the students of the university had practical control of the government. Early in October, Hungarian sympathizers murdered General Bredy and hung the minister of war, Baron Latour, to a lamp-post, after inflicting upon him forty wounds. The Emperor Ferdinand, who had taken refuge in Olmütz, endowed Prince Windischgratz with extraordinary powers, and sent him against Vienna, where the new constitutional Diet was in session. " I do not treat with rebels," Windischgratz declared, from the beginning, — and he gruffly repulsed two members of the Frankfort Parliament who came to mediate. Before the end of October, the city was taken by storm and treated as conquered territory. Countless arrests were made and a number of persons were executed, — among them Robert Blum, one of the envoys of the Frankfort Parliament, who had, indeed, done his best to further the opposition to the government. The Frankfort Assembly entered its protest against the act and demanded reparation, but with no result. It is believed, indeed, that the very fact of Blum's belonging to that body, had made Windischgratz the more bitter against him. The hey-day of the revolution was already past.

If the course of the Frankfort national assembly and the Austrian constitutional assembly had not been smooth, still less so had been that of the Prussian national Parliament, which met in Berlin two months after the barricade fights. The government treated the assembly with respect, and laid propositions before it as to the nature of the proposed constitution. The fact that the new head of the ministry, Camphausen, and the new minister of finance, Hansemann, were liberals, seemed to augur well for the success of the deliberations. But, if ever a move-

Radical measures of the Prussian Parliament.

ment failed through the folly of its own promoters, it was, from first to last, this revolution of 1848. What was the need of continually reopening the wounds caused by the barricade fights? Yet, in July, a motion that " those who had fought for liberty on the 18th and 19th of March de- served well of their country " aroused intense excitement, and only by a very narrow vote escaped being passed. A month later, it was decreed that the minister of war should be instructed to issue an order, forbidding officers to enter into conflicts of any kind with civilians, and com- manding them to show their sympathy for constitutional government or else leave the army. When the minister of war refused to pass such a decree, the whole ministry fell. The assembly grew more and more radical. In drafting the constitution, in the very first article, — which concerned the title of the king, — it was voted to leave out the old customary "by the grace of God." By a vote of 200 against 153, nobility was declared abrogated; titles and orders were no longer to be bestowed. Members who voted contrary to the radical element, were repeat- edly ill-treated by the mob that surrounded the place of meeting. Once, the crowd penetrated into the hall of meeting itself; once, they stormed the arsenal, and car- ried off the more valuable guns.

Over-
throw
of the
Prussian
Parliament.

One cannot blame Frederick William IV. for turning his eyes to the old safeguard of Hohenzollern prerogative, the Prussian army. The truce of Malmö had just been closed with Denmark, General Wrangel and his troops were free. They were ordered to draw closer to Berlin. The half-liberal ministry that had followed that of Camp- hausen was replaced by a conservative one, under Count Brandenburg, an illegitimate son of Frederick William II. A protest of the assembly against this nomination gave rise to a stormy scene. "We are here to give your

Majesty oral information about the true condition of the land; will your Majesty hear us?" cried one of the delegates sent to Potsdam. As Frederick William walked away, he cried after him, "That is just the misfortune of kings, that they will not hear the truth!" At last, on November 8, a royal decree prorogued the assembly, and ordered it to meet again in the town of Brandenburg. Berlin was declared in a state of siege. The assembly pronounced such acts unlawful; but, two days later, was expelled from its hall by Wrangel. To a deputation from the so-called citizen guard, which declared that it would yield only to force, the rough old general, sitting on a chair in the street, had merely answered: "Tell your citizen guard that force is now there." He had given the Parliament exactly fifteen minutes in which to vacate the premises. At a hasty meeting, held in another place, the ministers were forbidden to dispose of state funds or to levy taxes. But the king was determined now to carry the fight to the bitter end, even if it were to cost him his throne. Fortunately for him, the better elements of the population were now on his side. When, on the day appointed, the Parliament, in great minority, met in Brandenburg, it was declared dissolved; and the king announced that he would impose his own constitution upon the people.

This, to the joy of all moderate men, proved to be more liberal than any one had expected — so liberal, indeed, that Frederick William wrote characteristically to Bunsen, it made his own stomach ache. The separate clauses were to be revised by the representatives themselves; and not until January, 1850, was the work completed and the constitution as a whole adopted. The more radical elements had been kept in check by the so-called three-class system of voting at parliamentary elections: the small body of the large taxpayers could choose the same number of electors

Frederick William's new constitution.

as the larger body of moderately rich persons, or as the largest body of the lower classes. On the other hand, a number of personal liberties and checks to tyranny were assured. A reaction, indeed, soon set in, and, during the next few years, under one pretext or another, the king managed to pursue a most repressive policy. Nor was the Prussian court alone in this matter, Austria going so far as to entirely abrogate her newly granted constitution.

The Austrian question at Frankfort.

Meanwhile at Frankfort, in the matter of pairing German unity with liberal institutions, the hopes of the patriots had been sadly dashed; the blame for the failure of the long negotiations falling, mainly, upon Austria and Prussia.

It was, indeed, one of the most difficult of all political problems to which the formulation of the second article of the Frankfort constitution gave rise, — declaring, as it did, that a power might not enter the German empire save with its German provinces alone. This meant, for Austria, either national disruption, or total exclusion from the new organization. Yet the standpoint of the Frankfort assembly was more than comprehensible. It was the only rational one possible of adoption. Here was Austria, with a population, largely un-German, of thirty-eight millions, demanding entrance into an empire which, without her, would number but thirty-two millions. It meant an absolute Austrian majority in the parliaments ; it meant that the most vital questions of German policy must be voted upon by strange-tongued peoples on the banks of the Theiss, the Moldau, or the Po ; it meant the renunciation of every hope of real German unity.

Austria takes a high tone at Frankfort.

Austria, though vague in her utterances and dilatory in her tactics, and though offering no solution of the real problem, was very tenacious of her position. At Kremsier, in November, 1848, her ministers formulated the sentiment: " The continuance of Austria's national unity is a necessity for Germany as well as for Europe." In December came a threatening note from Olmütz declaring that: "Austria will know how to maintain her position in the projected German body politic." The Austrian delegates at Frankfort founded a party known as the *Grossdeutsche*, or advocates of a greater Germany; and allied themselves with those liberals who were opposed to any monarchical state at all. There is little doubt but that, in secret, the court of Vienna favored an Austrian empire, of which Germany should be merely an appendage.

The general sentiment of the least prejudiced minds at Frankfort was in favor of a narrower association, in which Austria should have no part; and, at the same time, of another, broader union which should assure her all possible safeguards and privileges. They were growing very tired, these reformers, of having their earnest work persistently ignored. "Waiting for Austria means death to German unity," declared one of the ministers, Beckerath. Gagern finally procured a vote, authorizing the ministry to treat with Austria, as with an extraneous power, by means of envoys.

The second important question: What, with or without Austria, should be the form of the new political creation, and what the nature of its head? gave rise to equally divergent views, and to equally violent opposition. Should there be an emperor, a directory, or a president? If an emperor, should his dignity be hereditary or for life, or for three or six or twelve years, or should it be shared in rotation by Austria and Prussia? The vote to confer the headship of the nation on one of the ruling German princes was finally passed, the vote to make the dignity hereditary, rejected. In February, 1849, a note from the Austrian government formally protested against the notion that an Austrian emperor and his government

Republic or empire?

should subordinate themselves to a central power wielded by any other German prince. Soon afterward, the feeble and yielding emperor, Ferdinand, — who had made promises he could neither keep nor well revoke, — resigned in favor of a youth of eighteen, that Francis Joseph who still, in ripe old age, holds the throne.

The crown of the empire to be offered to Frederick William.

Behind Francis Joseph was a government determined to fight the revolution to the very utmost. In March, 1849, a new constitution, which centralized the administration to the last degree, was imposed upon all Austrian lands. This was the crisis, this Austria's answer and final challenge to the Frankfort assembly: she would enter the Confederation with all of her provinces or not at all; and the new empire, if empire there was to be, must take its measures accordingly. Representative Welcker — up to this moment one of the heads of the Austrian or "greater German" party — now made a motion, that the constitution, as it stood, should be adopted by a single vote, and the hereditary imperial dignity be offered to the king of Prussia. The motion as offered was defeated by a slight majority; but by sacrificing the clause relating to the power of absolute veto, the rest of the section concerning the headship of the empire was passed. It was a solemn moment when the result was announced. "May the genius of Germany preside over this hour," was the invocation of the Parliament's president; and, when three cheers were given for the "German emperor," they were taken up by the dense crowds in the streets, and all the churches rang out their chimes.

Frederick William and the German question.

The deputation that left Frankfort for Berlin, on March 30, 1849, had a most important mission to perform. Could Frederick William be induced to subscribe to the Frankfort constitution and accept the imperial crown, the future of Germany was assured; though, possibly, at the cost of a war with Austria. Twenty-eight of the minor states had already promised their sanction to the new constitution. Others would be likely to follow Prussia's lead. And Frederick William had at various times so acted as to strengthen the hopes of the liberals. They could not know of his frequent changes of mind, of his weak susceptibility to new influences, of the incipient disease that was preying upon his brain.

In 1847, Frederick William had been ready to settle the German question " with Austria, without Austria, yes, if need be, against Austria." In March, 1848, he had proclaimed his intention of placing himself at the head of the movement for a united Germany, and had ridden around under the shadow of the revolutionary banners. But, soon afterward, he declared to a deputation from the Rhine provinces: " I am only the second in Germany;" and wrote to the historian Dahlmann, that none other than the "archhouse of Austria " could ever be at the head of the united fatherland. He meant to retain for himself, indeed, the command over the German military forces, — failing to see how impossible of acceptance such a proposition would be to Austria.

With the Parliament of Frankfort, his relations had been similarly undetermined. " Do not forget, gentlemen," he had cried to a deputation sent to assist at the opening of the Cologne cathedral, "do not forget that there are still princes in Germany, and that I am one of them ! " On the following day, however, he had drunk a toast to " the builders of the great work, the present and the absent members of the Frankfort national assembly." His enthusiasm had then received a rude shock through the September uprising and the murder of the deputies, Lichnowsky and Auerstadt ; and more and more there settled down upon him a horror of revolution, and of everything therewith connected.

Frederick William and the Frankfort Parliament.

Frederick
William's
views as to
the offer of
the im-
perial
crown.

He stood very much alone at this time, except for a faction of insignificant flatterers. His ministry, at the head of which was still Count Brandenburg, was in favor of conciliation, and received the Frankfort deputation with warmth. His friend and confidant, Bunsen, who was filling the post of ambassador to England, had urged him continually to accept the crown whenever it should be offered; and had prevailed upon him, in January, to send a note to Frankfort, which showed him in sympathy with the plans under consideration there. Three weeks later, Austrian influences had completely changed the king's mood; and a second note showed an entirely different standpoint. In one of his pessimistic attacks, Frederick William had written to Bunsen a letter which well shows the hysterical, extravagant side of his character, as well as his bitter hatred of everything republican. Bunsen had assured him that, although the offer of the crown might come originally from a popular assembly, the princes and governments of Germany would be sure to sanction its acceptance. But Frederick William wrote back, that he wanted neither the crown itself nor a subsequent consent of the princes. The kind of crown he would be willing to wear was not such a one as a revolutionary assembly could give, — not picked from the gutter like that of Louis Philippe, but carrying God's mark and making its bearer king by His grace: "The crown which the Ottos, the Hohenstaufens, the Hapsburgs have worn, a Hohen-zollern can naturally also wear; it does him unspeakable honor with its thousand-year halo. The one which you mean, alas, dishonors him unspeakably with its carrion odor of the revolution of 1848." With floods of invective, the king goes on to castigate this "imaginary crown, wrought of filth and mire." "I speak plainly," he writes: "if the thousand-year crown of the German nation, in abeyance now these forty-two years, is again to be given away, it is I and my likes who will give it."

His reception of the Frankfort deputation was cool in the extreme. An audience was granted, but no court carriages were sent to bring the members to the palace — an omission which the city of Berlin hastily supplied. The very lackeys in the anteroom were insolent, one of them refusing to bring a glass of water for the president, until ordered imperatively to do so. The king delivered his address very formally, standing, in uniform, surrounded by the princes, ministers, generals, and court functionaries. He had carried his conscience to the King of kings, he declared, and had decided that, not only must he await the consent of the princes, before accepting the crown, but, also, must determine with them whether the present form of the constitution was acceptable to one and all. With actual tears in their eyes, the deputation withdrew; these men knew well that, if thirty-six different autocratic governments might pick and tear at their work, not much of it would survive. Before taking their departure, they framed a writing which declared that, since his Majesty denied all right of existence or binding force to the national constitution, he must be considered as having refused the proffered election.

The reception of the Frankfort deputation.

Frederick William still dallied for a while with the national assembly, and summoned all the governments to send plenipotentiaries to Frankfort to discuss the matter — a summons which not one of them obeyed. Austria, meanwhile, had withdrawn her delegates; declaring that never would she bow to foreign legislation, never would her emperor subordinate himself to another prince. " For us, the national assembly no longer exists," — so wrote her ministers in an official note to Berlin. At this very time, the Prussian lower house voted to accept the constitution.

Austria and Prussia against the Frankfort Parliament.

Saxony and Würtemberg seemed wavering; while the national assembly sent out its demand for recognition almost in the form of an ultimatum. Frederick William came forward now with a categorical refusal of the imperial dignity. He had already sent an adjutant to the king of Saxony to harden the latter's heart against the adherents of the Parliament, and to offer armed assistance, should such be needed. He summoned a conference to Berlin of such governments as might care, in view of the mistaken steps that the national assembly had taken, and seemed inclined still to take, to deliberate concerning the needs of the nation. "The Prussian government," so ran the circular note, "cannot conceal the scantiness of the hope, that the national assembly will lend its hand to altering the constitution on which it has determined." The official *Staatsanzeiger* began openly to speak of the parliament as of a "revolutionary" assembly.

Rebellions in Saxony, Baden, and the Palatinate. All this reacted violently upon the Parliament itself, and gave rise to factions which were its final ruin. The "left" was in favor of encouraging an armed uprising among the people. The "right," determined on using a purely persuasive means, put through a vote to hold elections for a new constituent assembly, which should confer the crown upon the king of Prussia so soon as he should have recognized the constitution. Not unnaturally, the political agitation spread to the constituents of the members of Parliament. Addresses, words of advice, of encouragement, of blame, poured in upon the different rulers; and at last, in three states, — in Saxony, in the Rhine Palatinate, and in Baden, — the flames of discontent broke out into actual rebellion.

Saxony. In Dresden, where the dissolution of the chambers and a ministerial crisis had brought excitement to the highest pitch, the government, on the third of May, forbade a projected parade in honor of the national constitution. The crowd surrounded the arsenal and the palace, and the king fled to the impregnable Königstein. His ministers accompanied him; but returned, the same evening, to find a provisional government set up, the head of which was an extreme radical, Tzschirner. The advent of Prussian troops at once put a stop to the movement, and the ring-leaders were punished with long imprisonment.

In the Palatinate, and in Baden also, the existing governments were displaced. In Baden the military were drawn into the vortex, and the most republican designs were cherished; the neighborhood of two popularly governed states like France and Switzerland being of especial influence. Recognition of the imperial constitution was written on the banner of the insurgents, but "without the hereditary head." It was in this struggle that the then crown prince of Prussia, later Emperor William I., gained his spurs as a leader of armies. In response to a call for aid from Bavaria and Baden, Frederick William sent two army corps under William's command. The revolutionary forces, which combined against the Prussians and took numerous foreigners into their service, numbered between thirty and forty thousand men. Commander-in-chief was Mieroslawski, a famous Polish refugee. It needed many skirmishes, and a regular bombardment of the fortress of Rastadt, before this perfectly hopeless and meaningless rebellion could be put down. Many lost their lives on these petty battlefields; many were afterward sentenced to death or imprisonment. The poet Kinkel was given a life sentence; but was rescued from the fortress of Spandau by Carl Schurz, who afterward became a shining light in the political firmament of the United States of America.

If the cause of the Parliament of Frankfort had long

Prince William's campaign in Baden.

been losing ground, these revolts and their successful suppression gave it its *coup de grâce*. Prussia withdrew her delegates, after a vote had been passed that her interference in Saxony had been an unwarrantable breach of the peace. The conduct of affairs came more and more into the hands of the radicals. The feeling gained ground, among the more moderate elements, that they had no longer any positive policy to defend. On the 20th of May, 1849, sixty-five members, including in their number almost all whose names had given brilliancy to the assembly, seceded in a body — declaring their unwillingness to sunder the last legal ties between the governments and peoples of Germany, and to foster civil war. Among them, was old Ernst Moritz Arndt, who for nearly half a century, had sung of a united Germany which he was never to see.

Bereft of its sanest members, the parliament ran riot with its revolutionary ideas. The number necessary for a quorum was reduced from one hundred and fifty to a hundred. The place of meeting was moved from Frankfort to Stuttgart, for no other apparent purpose than to be nearer to the disaffected district. The "centre" party had already left because of the refusal to declare roundly, that the only object now aimed at was the furtherance of the constitution, and that all interference on the part of foreign countries was to be deprecated. It had come to be called the rump Parliament, — this survival of a once important body. It now elected a "regency for the empire"; and this "regency" proclaimed to the German people that, in the struggle against absolutism, they were to accept no commands save from itself and its plenipotentiaries. It called for a general arming, and for a credit of five million thalers.

But the "rump" had overestimated its strength. It was fain to obey the commands of the Würtemberg government, which first ordered it to vacate the assembly hall of the estates; then to hold the sessions of the "regency" beyond the state boundaries; and, finally, to move away altogether under pain of "suitable measures." It was given its quietus by being forced to disperse by soldiers with drawn swords. Thirteen months had the Parliament as a whole been in session, and its immediate results were absolutely nil; though it is safe to say that its deliberations, and even its mistakes, made it easier for the next generation to realize the dream of national unity.

CHAPTER IX

THE RECKONING WITH AUSTRIA

LITERATURE : In addition to the general treatments by Bulle, Biedermann, Pierson, and Fyffe, see the monumental work of Sybel, *Gründung
des deutschen Reiches*, and, almost more important still, Friedjung, *Kampf
um die Vorherrschaft in Deutschland*. Marcks's *Kaiser Wilhelm* is a
biography of the highest order. Bismarck's recently published memoirs
should be read as a whole ; they are made use of in a convenient compilation by Liman, *Bismarck's Denkwürdigkeiten*. The most comprehensive
biography of Bismarck is that by Hans Blum, with no charm of style.

The
Prussian
Union.

WHEN, at the beginning of the eighteenth century, the
Emperor Leopold would scarcely consent to the raising of
Prussia among the monarchies, it was because he feared
the rivalry of this new, wholly German state. That fear
was now to be realized, and the result was to be a deadly
war for supremacy. Austria's old prestige had carried her
safely through the trying time of the Congress of Vienna ;
while Metternich's ability had caused her still to retain the
leadership for more than a generation. But the revolution
of 1848 had been the beginning of the end. The Parliament
of Frankfort, representing the people of all Germany, had
had no room in its new political creation for the Croats,
Poles, Magyars, Czechs, and other strange nationalities
that went to make up five-sixths of Austria's population.

After the rupture with the Frankfort Diet, Prussia took
upon her own shoulders the task of uniting Germany, and,
on May 17, 1849, a conference to which all the German
powers had been invited was opened in Berlin. But only
Austria, Bavaria, Hanover, and Saxony responded to the

call, and the envoys of the two former powers withdrew
almost at once; while Saxony and Hanover joined in the
so-called League of the Three Kingdoms, merely to gain
time until Austria should have put down revolts in Hungary and in northern Italy.   On the other hand, the idea
of this union appealed to the former Prussian imperial
party of the Frankfort Diet.   One hundred and fifty of the
ex-members met at Gotha and voted to seize this new opportunity of healing the wounds of the fatherland.   They
urged their respective governments to join the cause, and
soon twenty-eight of the small states had handed in their
allegiance, Austria, Bavaria, and Würtemberg being the
only important powers to remain aloof.   It was determined
to adopt the Frankfort constitution, but to change the
mode of elections to the three-class system.   A Union Parliament was called to meet at Erfurt and came together in
March, 1850 ; by which time, indeed, Saxony and Hanover
had shown their true colors.   To the last these governments
had duped their own people with an apparent interest in
German unity.

The Prussian programme had been to form a greater and
a lesser union.   Into the former Austria was to be received,
the closest of alliances formed with her, her territory protected, agreements formed for the furtherance of trade and
intercourse.   With the latter, consisting of purely German
elements, she was to have nothing whatever to do.   But
this did not suit the views of the Vienna court ; and, as a
counter move, its ministers summoned an assembly to
Frankfort to debate on the question of reviving the old
Diet.   The princes belonging to the Union were willing to
send delegates, provided the matter could be discussed in
free conferences ; but denied that the convention itself
in any way represented the old Diet.

Had Frederick William IV. been possessed of a firmer

character, some good result might have come of the Prussian Union. But his heart was only half in the work With his own local Parliament he had been engaged in revising the recently granted Prussian constitution, and his success in that direction had turned his head. Everywhere he had caused offensive clauses to be modified: introducing the three-class system of voting, retaining for himself the right to pass decrees — if not contrary to the constitution — in the absence of the chambers, freeing the army from the obligation of swearing to the constitution, and restricting the Parliament's right of abolishing taxes. The upper house was to consist of hereditary and of life members, not of those elected by the people ; and a special court was to be established for political offences. No wonder the liberals were furious ; no wonder they called this Parliament a law-taking, not a law-giving assembly. The constitution, in its amended form, was finally promulgated on January 31, 1850 ; and the king, when taking oath to it, declared that it had come into being in a year which the loyalty of generations to come would wish with tears to see obliterated from Prussian history, and which still bore the broad stamp of its origin. But, under its amended form, it would at least be possible for him to continue to rule, though his people must beware and not use it as a cloak for their wickedness, or a substitute for divine Providence. This achievement reacted forcibly on the Erfurt Union Parliament ; and the Prussian ministers took the extraordinary step of demanding reactionary alterations in the very draft of a federal constitution which they themselves had shortly before presented, — a step which lost them the sympathy of all the national liberal elements in Germany.

Austria was growing more and more insistent that the old Diet should be restored, and that the whole Austrian-Hun

garian monarchy should be allowed to enter the Confederation. She proposed to alter the method of representation so
that all the minor states together, which were Prussia's
firmest allies, should have but one vote. " It is necessary
to *avilir*, or abase, Prussia," was a reported saying of the
Austrian minister, Schwarzenberg.

And abase Prussia Austria did, so completely, that the
journey of Frederick William's prime minister to Olmütz,
the temporary residence of the emperor, has often been
compared with the famous pilgrimage of Henry IV. to the
feet of Gregory VII. at Canossa.

The immediate occasion was a common claim to the
right of interfering in the affairs of a minor state. In
the electorate of Hesse, which belonged to the Prussian
Union, a fierce struggle was waging between a reactionary
minister, Hassenpflug, and a Parliament that refused him
taxes. Hassenpflug — whose enemies called him Hessen-
Fluch — appealed to the Diet of Frankfort, which was
finally declared reëstablished in September, 1850. Prussia
prepared to maintain the rights of the Union. Austria
held a meeting with the kings of Würtemberg and Bavaria, during which the former declared at a banquet that
a soldier must follow his emperor, wherever he might
lead. It was determined to raise an army of two hundred thousand men. Austrian and Prussian forces
entered Hesse. Frederick William in vain sought the
mediation of the Czar, while Schwarzenberg came out
roundly with demands, in the form of an ultimatum,
to the effect that the Prussian Union should be dissolved, that the federal Diet should be recognized, that
Hesse be evacuated, and that the Austrians be not interfered with in Schleswig Holstein, — where Prussia had
been pursuing a policy weak in itself and unpopular with
the rest of Germany. Austria desired that this matter,

as well as the Hessian dispute, should be handed over to the federal Diet.

There were not wanting indignant men, — like Crown Prince William, like Bunsen, like Pourtales, — who were ready for anything rather than lick the dust from the feet of a boastful enemy. But this was practically the course advocated by the band of intriguers who just then held the king's ear. Radowitz, in favor of resistance, resigned. Manteuffel, with no other thought than submission, took his place. He made, indeed, an outward show of mobilizing, but told the Austrian ambassador it was merely to calm the rabble, and ordered the troops to avoid real hostilities. This they did with such good effect that the only casualty in the one skirmish at Bronzell was the death of a white horse. At Olmütz, finally, Manteuffel laid Prussia prostrate at Austria's feet, as few unconquered states have ever been humiliated. The Union was abandoned, the Diet acknowledged, the troops, save one battalion, ordered from Hesse. Austria might even have entered the Confederation and formed her longed-for "seventy million" empire, had not England peremptorily interfered on the ground that the balance of power in Europe would be destroyed. The Schleswig-Holsteiners were ordered to submit to Denmark, and Prussian officials aided the Austrians in forcing these former allies to lay down their arms.

There were those who considered that Olmütz was unavoidable, that in her then condition Prussia could not possibly have taken up the struggle against Austria and her allies: among them was Otto von Bismarck-Schönhausen, the future imperial chancellor, at that time a strong conservative. His long term of devoted service to the royal house of Prussia had begun in 1847, as a member of the Prussian *Landtag*. When, in the following March, he

first heard of the bitter humiliations to which Frederick
William was subjected by the revolutionists, of the extraordinary scenes in the courtyard of the palace at
Berlin, of the flight of the heir apparent to England, he
had written to the king to offer his sympathy; and, shortly
after, had presented himself in person.   He was at this
time thirty-three years of age, had seen many sides of life,
had administered his father's estate of Kneiphof with
considerable success, and had served as a local magistrate.
He was strongly against liberal concessions and considered
that in making them the crown "had thrown earth upon
its own coffin."   Yet he soon reconciled himself to the
irrevocable, though seeking to save what could still be
saved of the royal prerogative.   In numerous assemblies
which he instigated he goaded on the nobles and the
country gentry.   He opposed the acceptance of the
Frankfort offer of the imperial crown, mainly because
the new emperor would have no veto power, — an objection
which he later let fall when it came to framing the present
constitution.   As a member of the Erfurt Parliament, he
often caused the liberals to writhe under his utterances.
His every action was bold and decided : when he first
entered the assembly he is reported to have torn from
the chairs of the Prussian conservatives the black, red,
and gold ribbons, and to have replaced them with black
and white.   But he could not save the dignity of the
Prussian crown when the man who wore it was a Frederick
William IV.

After Olmütz, Bismarck was sent to represent Prussia
in the restored Diet of Frankfort, — first as a subordinate of
Herr von Rochow, but soon as minister plenipotentiary in
his own person.   There were many who thought him too
inexperienced for the position ; but those who knew him
best argued strongly in his favor, knowing his coolness,

Bismarck
as envoy to
the restored
Diet of
Frankfort.

his cleverness, and his courage.   The Frankfort newspapers spread abroad the squib that, if asked to command
a frigate or to perform an operation in surgery, he would
doubtless declare that he had never done it, but that he
would gladly try.

Bismarck's first journey to Frankfort, as a member of
the Diet, has been likened to that pilgrimage of Martin
Luther to Rome which opened the eyes of the reformer to
the evils rampant in the church.   Hitherto he had been
more or less Austria's friend.   Now he found that her
settled policy was never to recognize Prussia as her equal.
The Austrian envoy, Count Thun, who presided over the
sessions of the Diet, treated the other states as subordinate powers.   His manners were lordly, his actions arbitrary.   In drawing up the protocols, he inserted or
omitted what pleased himself.   He required a unanimous
or a majority vote, according as Austrian interests demanded; and, in the same way, hurried through or postponed meetings.   It may seem a small matter, that at
formal committee meetings he would be the only one to
wear negligee costume and to indulge in a cigar; but it
marked a tacitly acknowledged superiority that galled
and irritated Bismarck.   The latter has related how, on
one such occasion, he himself astonished the count and the
assembly by coolly walking up and demanding a light.
So seriously was the matter taken that the envoys of the
smaller states wrote home to know if they might allow
themselves the same privilege ; and, as the answers came
in, one cigar after another was ostentatiously lighted.   It
was hard on the Würtemberg envoy, who disliked tobacco ; but for the honor of his state he was compelled to
smoke.

Bismarck's impressions as to a deep hostility to Prussia
found confirmation in a curious way.   Prokesch, who was

Austrian envoy in 1854, sold an old desk in Frankfort which eventually found its way to Berlin; in one of the drawers he had accidentally left a complete correspondence, — drafts of his own letters and originals of the answers, — in which members of the press were urged to foster an anti-Prussian sentiment in Germany. When this damning evidence was placed in his possession, Bismarck could readily have obtained the recall of Prokesch; but he refrained from doing so on the ground that he preferred an incautious to a cautious adversary. For their own parts, the Austrians hated the wary Prussian minister with a deadly hatred, and did not spare him actual insults. An archduke asked him sneeringly at a ball if certain medals, which were in reality tokens of valuable diplomatic services, had been won before the enemy. " All won before the enemy, all won right here in Frankfort," was the ready answer. The eight years spent at the Diet were mainly devoted to raising the sunken prestige of Prussia, to seeing that no slight should go unavenged; — that was the first step in the task of transferring the balance of power from Austria to his own state, and placing the latter at the head of Germany. By holding his own he paved the way for the final reckoning.

Bismarck upholds Prussia's dignity at Frankfort.

At the time of the Crimean War, Bismarck's advice maintained Frederick William in the path of neutrality, — even though the king's dearest friend, Bunsen, urged him to join with England and France; and though his brother, the Crown Prince William, was very zealous for war. Bismarck pointed out, that Prussia had everything to lose and nothing to gain, that there was no *casus belli* with Russia, that it was the height of political folly to provoke this " perpetual neighbor." In an interview with the Crown Prince, who strongly opposed him on this point, he protested against playing the rôle of an Indian vassal

Prussia and the Crimean War.

prince, and fighting England's wars under England's patronage. This policy toward Russia,—which prevailed in the end, and which was to be repeated at a later date, — stood Prussia, at the last, in good stead. Bismarck was the first of her statesmen to look far ahead on the political horizon and reckon with every possible disadvantageous element.

For a time, during the early stages of the Crimean War, Austria and Prussia had gone hand in hand. They had joined with the Western powers in presenting the famous four demands : abolition of the Russian protectorate over the Danube principalities, and of the Russian preponderance in the Black Sea; free passage of the Danube, and a general, not a particular, protectorate over the Christian subjects of the Porte. But, when these demands had been accepted by Russia as a basis for negotiation, and Austria joined with England and France in asking for still more, — then their ways parted. Prussia had nothing to do with the war and barely secured representation in the peace congress at Paris. Only on the ground that she had signed a former maritime treaty that had now to be abrogated was she finally admitted.

Prussia and the Franco-Austrian War.

When, in 1859, Austria's war with France and Sardinia broke out, the first-named power assumed, as a matter of course, that Prussia would stand by her, notwithstanding the fact that purely dynastic interests were at stake. Even in other parts of Germany, there was a great outcry that the Rhine must be defended on the Po; that in case of Austria's defeat this new Napoleon would turn upon Prussia, as his namesake had done in the days of Jena. But Prussia could not accept the conditions which Austria imposed. She was willing to aid her if treated as a great power, but not to subordinate the direction of her armies to commissioners from the federal Diet. Rather than yield the point, Austria preferred to lose the main part of her provinces in Italy. When signing the Peace of Villafranca the Emperor Francis Joseph declared, in a manifesto to the powers, that he did so because he had been deserted by his nearest and natural ally; and it was long before the wound ceased to rankle.

Frederick William IV., at this time, was passing into the entrance of the valley of the shadow of death. Early in 1857 his intellect gave signs of clouding, wild excitability alternating with mute despair. His brother William was named his vicegerent; and, after nine painful months of subserviency to the old policy and to the old advisers, was formally declared regent. Already sixty years of age, the prince, — whose one opportunity of distinguishing himself had been the insurrection in Baden, — had come to consider his career at an end. When answering the congratulations of the future Field-marshal Roon, on the occasion of his birthday, he declared that he had reached the age when men continued to live only in their children. He spoke of himself as an old man, little dreaming that he was merely on the threshold of a new era which was to bear his own name. Thirty years later the writer saw him strong and erect, the idol of enthusiastic crowds.

Prince William as regent of Prussia.

Yet in these earlier years popularity was the last tribute that was paid to this king. Frederick William died in 1861, and by that time there was culminating a struggle, in which William's opinions were so diametrically opposed to those of the majority of his subjects, so severe were the measures to which he lent his support, that, when he drove through the streets of Berlin, men passed him in stubborn silence, without raising their hats; and once, when a member of his family died, the most ordinary condolences were omitted.

King William's proposed army reform.

The levies which Prussia had made, against the possibility of becoming involved in the Italian war, had shown forth all the weakness of her military system, which, based on laws and regulations passed in 1814, when the population was very much smaller, no longer corresponded to the needs of the time. While, in theory, every sound man in the kingdom was bound to do military service, in practice there was only room in the existing regiments for two-thirds of the recruits. In time of war, in order to increase the army to the proper size, it would have been necessary to call out the *Landwehr*, which consisted largely of men burdened with the care of families; while some twenty-five thousand younger men remained idle. The essence of the reform that William proposed was to spare the *Landwehr* and to throw the burden of service on the regiments of the line, the numbers and efficiency of which he intended to increase.

Opposition to the proposed army reform.

It is not apparent, at first, why these propositions should have evoked such stubborn and unrelenting opposition on the part of the Prussian Parliament. As a matter of fact, as in most conflicts on special points, there were deeper principles involved than appeared on the surface. Prussia had become a constitutional monarchy; did this mean that, as in England or in Belgium, the sovereign had practically renounced all political power? It was the service of William I. to his country to answer this question in the negative. He admitted the legislative functions of the Parliament, he reserved the executive for himself; and he was ready to resign the office rather than not wield it as his fathers had done.

The change in the army presupposed an expense of only about nine million thalers. The country was prosperous, and the additional taxation was not likely to be felt. But the party of opposition, which possessed a clear majority in the House of Representatives, was determined to make its grant contingent on various concessions, — among them the shortening of the term of service from three to two years. They attacked the policy of the feeble Hohenzollern ministry, and asked, why should they place forty-nine new regiments at the service of a government too weak to use them? It was whispered that the chief object was to supply young nobles with positions as officers, and the whole movement was cried down as a reflection on the *Landwehr*, which had done such glorious service in 1813.

There is no doubt in the minds of men to-day but that there were serious errors on both sides. The government obtained its grant for the first year under something like false pretences, — the finance minister, Patow, explaining that the definite settlement of the army question would not be prejudiced by the provisional granting of the sum required, and hinting that the desired concessions might later be made. At all events, the regiments were formed, the officers appointed, the men enrolled, and the flags consecrated. *The refusal of the army grant.*

The weakness of the position of the liberal party rests on the fact, that it had authorized acts which could not well be undone, however much it might regard them as provisional. Indeed, in the following year, 1861, the parliament repeated its grant of nine millions, though placing it in the budget among the " once-recurring and temporary expenses." The trouble began in September, 1862 ; the elections to the new Diet had fallen out most disadvantageously for the government, there had been a ministerial crisis and a dissolution of the Parliament. In spite of pressure, fair and unfair, the opposition in the new house was stronger than ever. The majority had determined to take the last and decisive step. In the most abrupt and insulting manner every penny was refused for the support of the new regiments, notwithstanding the fact that money was due for the payment of officers' salaries. No greater blow had ever been struck at the prestige of the Prussian king. These were men whom he himself had appointed, who wore his uniform and carried his ensigns. They were dismissed against his will and without pay. In the most conservative state of civilized Europe, forty-five regiments were told to strike their colors at the voice of the democracy.

The interview at Babelsberg.
It was at this juncture that Bismarck first entered the stage as a leading character, not to leave it until, a generation later, a new, young impresario saw fit to dispense with his services. He was well known to William, who had often had interviews with him in Frankfort; but passed for too violent, too reactionary. The idea had often been broached of making him prime minister, but he had been appointed instead as ambassador to St. Petersburg — sent to cool on the banks of the Neva, as he himself expressed it, like champagne for future use. His name had always stood for a strong progressive policy; and to him William turned, at a moment when his people, and even his own wife and son, were against him, and when the very foundations of his throne were tottering.

Bismarck was summoned to Babelsberg, and held a private interview with the king in the park of the castle. He found William dejected and discouraged: between his desire not to break the constitution and his conviction of the need of a strong army, there seemed nothing left but abdication; and he had the document before him, already drawn up and signed. " To that let it never come," urged Bismarck; and then and there he undertook the task of ministerial government without a majority, without a budget, and without a programme — at the same time giving a promise that he would never renounce the army reform.

The main question, he declared, the one on which all others hinged, was whether in Prussia the crown should govern, or a majority of the House of Representatives.   And,
indeed, looking back, it is impossible to overrate the importance of the four years' struggle that now began.   Had
Bismarck been driven by the overwhelming majorities
against him to resign, had the king abdicated, had that
army which at the crucial moment proved strong enough
to defy the rest of Germany been reduced to its earlier
level: it is hard to see how German unity could ever have
been established.

It was an up-hill fight that had to be fought by the new
president of the ministry.   His first step was to withdraw altogether the budget the House had failed to approve, and to
carry on the business of governing — paying the regiments
as well — without giving an account of his expenditures.
He found a technical excuse in the wording of the constitution which declared, that " the amount of the budget shall
be fixed yearly by a law; " but which also provided, that "to
pass any law the consent of the king and of both Houses
of Parliament is needed."   That there was real danger in
the game they were playing both Bismarck and William
were aware: the latter once looked out upon the square
before his palace, and expressed his dread lest the minister's head might fall, and his own after it.   Bismarck
replied with words to the effect, that there were worse
deaths than those that had been inflicted on Strafford and
Charles I.

At all events the game was played with the greatest
boldness.   The press was gagged, unfriendly government
officials deprived of their places, political discussions forbidden at public meetings, and even freedom of speech in
the House itself interfered with by the police.   The climax
was reached, when the bayonets of the king's soldiers were

*Drastic
measures of
the govern-
ment.*

literally turned against the breasts of members of Parliament, who had accepted an invitation to the city of Cologne to a festival on the Rhine.

In the House, in spite of the harshest criticism, in spite of the remark of the presiding member, that "the country was tired of having a mountebank at its head," Bismarck held his ground unmoved. He thundered, he bullied, he threatened; he let loose the immensely powerful weapon of his wit. One day, in committee meeting, he drew forth a little twig from his pocket, and exclaimed to a progressionist member: "This olive branch I plucked in Avignon, to offer to the people's party as a token of peace: I see that the time has not yet come." "Prussia's kingship," he once exclaimed, "has not yet fulfilled its mission. It is not yet ripe enough to form a purely ornamental trimming of your constitutional structure, not yet ready to be inserted as a dead piece of machinery in the mechanism of parliamentary rule." And again, "Germany does not look to Prussia's liberalism, but to her power. . . . The great questions of the day are not decided by speeches and majority votes, — therein lay the weakness of 1848 and 1849, — but by blood and iron!" When Virchow accused him of "downright dishonesty," he rose to ask if political differences were to be settled after the manner of the Horatii and Curiatii, and sent a challenge to a duel. There were times when the personalities grew fairly Homeric. When the king was asked to restrain his ministers, he replied that he shared their views. A convention signed with Russia for putting down the Polish insurrection added fuel to the flames. The sending of soldiers to the boundary was likened to the selling of Hessians to England. Representative Twesten declared, "The honor of the present government is no longer the honor of the state and of the land!"

To add to his other difficulties, Bismarck was obliged to contend with adverse influences at court. The sympathies of the queen and of the crown prince were openly on the side of the House: "Two weeks of Baden-Baden and of Augusta," writes Bismarck in one of his letters, "had almost shaken the courage of the king." Bismarck was greatly hated at the court of London. Queen Victoria felt that her daughter's interests demanded her intervention in Prussian affairs, but could not but see that her advice was unwelcome. Once, indeed, she went so far as to hold an interview with the Emperor Francis Joseph, and to implore him not to ruin the prospects of her daughter's husband. The story is told of Princess Beatrice, that when asked what she would have for her birthday, she demanded the head of Bismarck on a charger. The crown prince himself, in a public speech, branded a measure of Bismarck's as "criminal"; and, on another occasion, formally asked to be allowed to give up his offices and dignities and retire into private life. He complained bitterly, as late as during the Franco-Prussian War, that he was being dragged against his will from one scene of carnage to another, and made to wade through blood to the throne of his fathers.

Into the conflict in the Prussian House, a new element was introduced by a revival of the Schleswig-Holstein difficulties, which gave Bismarck the opportunity he had been waiting for of testing the reorganized army, and which furthered his schemes for uniting Germany under Prussia's leadership. The turns and intricacies of this most involved of questions need not concern us here — Lord Palmerston once said that only three persons had ever understood the matter: one was dead, one crazy, and he himself, the third, had forgotten what it was all about. Prussia had fought first for, then against, the insurgents, —

Bismarck and the English influence at court.

Genesis of the Schleswig-Holstein troubles.

the Czar having upbraided Frederick William for joining hands with revolution. The last peace with Denmark, in 1850, had left the provinces to their own devices; but the London protocol of that year and the London Treaty of 1852, signed by all the great powers, had declared for the integrity of the Danish kingdom. It stipulated, however, that Schleswig-Holstein should retain its separate political organization, even though under the same ruler as Denmark; and that the rights of the Germans, who formed five-sixths of the population of the duchies, should be respected. In order to provide against future dangers, the protocol had further arranged that, — contrary to the rule of succession in Holstein at least, — the heir to the duchies should be a prince of the house of Glücksburg, who was also heir to the Danish crown. The Duke of Augustenburg, the nearest of the other claimants, had resigned his pretensions in return for a large sum of money.

The prince of Augustenburg.

The "protocol prince," Christian of Glücksburg, succeeded, in 1863, to the throne, and immediately crowned a decade of Danish oppression by publishing a constitution which treated Schleswig as an integral part of the monarchy, — disregarding its union with Holstein, which had lasted for five hundred years, and defying the very protocol to which he owed his own accession. In his defence it must be said, that the powerful, so-called Eider-Danish, party had driven him to this step, under threat of revolution. But the news of his act roused a flood of indignation in Germany. When the son of that Augustenburg who had sold his claims in 1852, came forward with the assertion that he had never consented to the act of renunciation, he was received with enthusiasm by the people of Germany as the rightful heir; and the various parliaments voted him their support.

But Prussia and Austria had signed the Treaty of London as independent European powers, not as members of
the German Confederation, — which organization, indeed,
had not even given its sanction. For a moment they forgot their own rivalries, which had become so bitter, of late,
that Austria had been categorically refused admission into
the *Zollverein*. William, ostensibly because of a slight
implied in the manner of the invitation, had not attended
a meeting of the princes held at Frankfort, under Austrian
auspices, for the sake of settling the German question.
Even now, in this matter of Schleswig-Holstein, although
the immediate interests of the two powers were the same,
their ultimate aims were very different. Francis Joseph
would have liked a return to the basis of the London protocol; while to Bismarck the whole incident was simply a
step to greater things — to the annexation of the duchies to
Prussia, to the assumption by Prussia of the supremacy in
Germany. Only a few months previously he had written:
" War alone can solve the Danish question in a sense favorable to us; provocation to such a war can be found at any
moment in which our relation to the great powers is favorable for military operations." He would go hand in hand
with Austria. He would uphold the London protocol, until
some open act of hostility on the part of Denmark should,
by the very principles of international law itself, render all
treaties null and void, and give him free play. Then, if
obtainable, he would achieve the annexation; if not, he
would be content to see the duchies under an independent
prince. From the very first, he had urged the appropriation
of the prize, — whereat, as he writes in his memoirs, " his
Majesty seemed to think I had spoken under the bacchana-
lian influences of a breakfast party," and the crown prince
had " raised his hands to heaven, as if he doubted the
soundness of my senses."

Bismarck's
plans with
regard to
Schleswig-
Holstein.

Austrian-
Prussian
ultimatum
to Den-
mark.

When the Diet, in its enthusiasm, voted federal execution
in Holstein, and sent an army of Saxons and Hanoverians
against Christian IX., Austria and Prussia, although they
had voted for the execution, held their armies aloof. It
vexed them that the young Augustenburg took the whole
demonstration as in favor of himself; that he formed a little
court at Kiel, chose a cabinet, and began to exercise influence in public affairs. Bismarck, especially, objected to
binding his hands by acknowledging this new candidate;
and the two powers at last determined to checkmate the
pretender by occupying Schleswig themselves. The Diet
was informed that Austria and Prussia, having seen their
wishes persistently thwarted, intended to act alone in the
matter by virtue of their position as European powers.
An ultimatum was sent to Denmark, and Prussia and Austria came to an agreement to determine the future of the
duchies not otherwise than by mutual arrangement and
common consent — as if mutual arrangement and common
consent were ever likely to be obtainable where one of the
parties had the preconceived idea of appropriating the
whole!

During all this time, in the Prussian House of Representatives the bitter contentions continued. Virchow declared
that, through Bismarck's policy, Prussia was becoming a
mere satellite of Austria; that the very existence of the
state was being threatened; that the president of the ministry had no conception of a national policy. The desired
loan of twelve million thalers was refused; and Bismarck
thundered out that he would make war with or without
the consent of the Diet, and would take the money wherever he could lay hands upon it.

Initial
events of
the Danish
War.

The great trio that were to lead Prussia through immeasurably greater wars were already beginning their
activity. It was Roon, then minister of war, who had

warmly recommended the calling of Bismarck to the ministry. It was Moltke who drew up the plan of campaign, which, however, was modified in practice by the commander-in-chief, Wrangel. The latter, already eighty years old, and lacking in vigor and decision, needlessly protracted the war.

As it was, the army, about sixty thousand strong, crossed the Eider, on the 1st of February, 1864 ; and, by the 20th of July, the final truce had been declared. The great events of the war were the capture of the Danewerk, the storming of the redoubts of Düppel, and the clearing of the Danish islands.

The Danewerk was a line of fortresses, extending for fifty miles or more, between the town of Schleswig and the source of the river Reide. All that nature and art could do had combined to strengthen this line of defence ; and the Emperor Napoleon III. was of the opinion that, by it, the advance of the Germans might be checked for a space of two years. Within five days, on the contrary, the Danish army had been dislodged, or, rather, had dislodged itself from its strong position. It was bitterly cold, and the marshes, which were otherwise a great protection, were frozen over. General de Meza, the commander-in-chief, dreaded a long bivouac in the snow. He might have taken the offensive, but feared to risk all on the result of a pitched battle — his orders being to avoid running Denmark's one available army into unnecessary danger. He preferred, instead, to retire to the heights of Düppel, facing the island of Alsen.

Great as was the triumph of the Germans, it would have been greater had Wrangel followed Moltke's plan and, in the beginning, cut off the retreat of the Danes by sending a part of his forces across the lower Schlei, and around the Danewerk. One of Wrangel's colonels wrote to Moltke :

The redoubts of Düppel.

" Few men are capable of carrying out a simple idea in an equally simple manner. . . . The Danes were cleverer on the 4th of February than we. We were two days late in surrounding them." The capture of the redoubts of Düppel, which was undertaken by Prince Frederick Charles of Prussia, was a longer affair, and required weeks of active preparation. The storm itself was the matter of half an hour, the Danes having taken refuge in improvised earthworks, a short distance away, from an incessant cannonading. At a given signal the cannon ceased, and the Prussian storming columns rushed upon the redoubts. A few hours more of fighting, and the Danish army had suffered a signal defeat, their guns being captured and many prisoners taken ; although the losses in dead and wounded were about equal on both sides. The whole of Schleswig now lay open to the conquerors ; and King William of Prussia came himself to the scene of war, to express his thanks to his brave army. The Danish forces withdrew to the islands of Fünen and Alsen, and the German troops proceeded to Jutland.

The London Conference.

The next link in the chain of events was a European congress, held at London, under the auspices of England and France. It was an assembly full of peaceful intents ; but, as Sybel has said, there was the wish among the powers concerned to take as little as possible from Denmark and to give as little as possible to Germany. Every plan imaginable was discussed : Schleswig-Holstein was to be politically independent, but joined by a personal union with Denmark ; Schleswig was to be divided between Prussia and Denmark — and any number of division lines were suggested ; the Prince of Augustenburg was one moment to be recognized, the next he was not. Russia thought of reviving an old claim of her own Czar, and of transferring it to the Duke of Oldenburg. Prussia was willing that the people of Schleswig should vote to what nation they should belong; but the conference refused to consider such a plan. Now that blood had flown, Bismarck considered himself no longer bound by the agreements of 1852. England and Russia, and even Denmark herself at the last, wished the maintenance of those treaties. After two months of negotiation, during which time hostilities had been suspended, the conference separated.

During the sessions of the London Conference, the king of Prussia received an address from the people of the duchies, with thirty thousand signatures, begging that Schleswig-Holstein might be freed from Denmark, and might become either an independent state, or, if need be, a part of the Prussian monarchy. The idea of Prussian annexation had by this time been freely discussed in more than one direction. Austria was naturally alarmed at such a possibility, and had tried at the conference to make propaganda for a personal union of the duchies with Denmark,—a proposition which Denmark herself had scornfully rejected. Austria had then turned to the oft-discarded idea of acknowledging the Prince of Augustenburg; but Prussia had felt bound to require certain assurances as to what policy that candidate would be likely to pursue as regarded herself. Bismarck had himself looked into the matter, had tried the prince in the balance, and had found him wanting. Augustenburg was too sure of his position, backed as he was by public opinion both in the duchies and in Germany. He was unwilling to submit to any trammels. " It would be better to try and win my heart," he said, " than to bind me fast with paragraphs." " We had hoped," Bismarck answered dryly, " by driving out the Danes, to have won your heart already."

Bismarck interviews Augustenburg.

Hostilities were reopened within three days after the closing of the conference. The outspoken goal of Austria and Prussia now was the definite separation of the duchies from Denmark; it was to depend on circumstances what should happen after that. Wrangel had resigned the chief command, and his mantle had descended on the shoulders of Prince Frederick Charles. The latter had intrusted General von Bittenfeld with the task of landing his army on the shores of Alsen, which was garrisoned by ten thousand Danes. The manœuvre was carried out with perfect success, batteries on the shore protecting the troops, as they crossed over, from the attacks of the Danish war-ships. Seven hundred of the Danes were killed and wounded; twenty-five hundred were taken prisoner; and the rest were driven to an extremity of the island, whence they were allowed to escape to their fleet. The blow was a final one for Denmark; and the German army pressed forward unopposed, in Jutland as well as on the islands.

It was the Eider-Danish party that had brought Denmark to such a pass by plunging her into this unhallowed war. In dismissing his cabinet, King Christian covered his departing prime minister with bitter but well-merited reproaches. The new ministry at once sent to Berlin and Vienna, to ask for a truce and for proposals as to the grounds of a final peace. According to the preliminaries drawn up in August, and definitely accepted in October, Denmark was to surrender unconditionally to her two enemies: Holstein, Lauenburg, and almost the whole of Schleswig, and was to accept any arrangement as to the future of the duchies that Austria and Prussia might make. The sundered provinces were to be saddled with their due proportion of the Danish national debt, and were also to bear the costs of the war. On this latter point, Denmark was inflexible. The country was on the verge of ruin, and, bereft of nearly half its territorial possessions, could never have borne a great financial burden. The Danish commissioner, Quade, refused to sign the peace rather than comply with such a demand.

The Danish War had been brought to a final, and, for Germany, happy conclusion. It was Bismarck whose policy had effected such brilliant results. He later declared repeatedly, that he considered the diplomatic moves of the year 1864 as the most difficult and the most successful of his life.

After the war, the court of Vienna did its utmost to come to a lasting understanding, and to form a lasting treaty, with Prussia. The old question of entering the *Zollverein* or Customs Union, was revived; and the Austrian minister, Rechberg, tried every means to induce Bismarck to relent in the matter. The latter considered that a treaty of close alliance between the two powers would answer all necessary purposes; that a unity of mercantile interests did not exist; and that the plan of entering the Union was simply a political move. The matter led to a ministerial crisis in Vienna; and Rechberg, reproached with the futility of his previous policy, and with having brought about the isolation of Austria in Europe, lost his place. Had he remained in office, it is probable that the Austrian-Prussian War would have been greatly delayed; for a close alliance was his constant goal. However, as Bismarck once said, " Sooner or later it had to come to war, and it is, perhaps, fortunate that it happened then, under comparatively favorable circumstances." Already, in the Frankfort days, he had written home, " I foresee that one day we shall have to fight for our very existence with Austria."

More and more the designs of the two powers showed

Irreconcilable designs of Austria and Prussia.

themselves absolutely irreconcilable. William made his recognition of Augustenburg contingent on conditions that would have reduced Schleswig-Holstein to a vassal state : her commerce was to be restricted, her strong places occupied, and even her armies placed under Prussian leadership. Austria, on the other hand, was willing to support Augustenburg, if the latter would engage to conclude no private treaty whatever with Prussia. Her ministers declared the formation of a half-sovereign state the most incomplete of all possible solutions of the difficulty. To the military suzerainty she never would and never could give her consent. On the receipt of this answer, Bismarck called upon Moltke to calculate just what forces Austria would be able to muster in case of war. From being indifferent to the person of Augustenburg, the king began to regard him with great aversion; while Austria came more and more to espouse his cause.

The Treaty of Gastein.   From now on, the breach between the two powers widened relentlessly. When King William issued an order transferring Prussia's marine station from Danzig to Kiel, a stern protest was sent to Berlin which was answered politely but equally firmly. In June, 1865, on the other hand, King William complained to the emperor of Augustenburg's conduct, declaring it to be a derogation to his own royal dignity. Pending the answer, which was evasive when it came, an inquiry was made into the military resources of Prussia; and the plan was discussed, in a ministerial conference, of carrying off the prince on a Prussian war-ship. Bismarck was already negotiating with Italy for an alliance which should gain Venice for the latter power, and should draw off to the southern frontier a larger portion of the Austrian forces. Steps had also been taken to render amicable the Emperor Napoleon, who desired a free Italy, and, beyond that, some little compen-

sation for his own kindness — some "trinkgeld," as his
enemies called it. The Treaty of Gastein, brought about
by Austria's internal troubles and King William's sincere
desire for peace, proved but a momentary obstacle to the
warlike current. It was agreed that Austria should
administer Holstein, and Prussia, Schleswig, until a
better arrangement could be made ; that Kiel should
be a federal harbor, Rendsburg a federal fortress. Lauenburg was sold outright to Prussia for two and a half
million thalers.

Again the brand of discord was the Prince of Augustenburg. His party continued to make propaganda in
Holstein, and Prussia considered that the Austrian governor, Gablenz, did too little to stop the public demonstrations. Newspapers spoke of "his Highness, the
Duke." In many of the churches prayers were made for
"Duke Frederick of Holstein" instead of for the emperor. The Princess of Augustenburg travelled from
Altona to Kiel as only royal personages are accustomed
to travel — past gayly decorated stations, and greeted
everywhere by deputations and by maidens in white garments bearing gifts of flowers. The climax was reached,
when Gablenz permitted the holding of a huge assembly
which gave cheers for the "lawful, beloved prince, Duke
Frederick." Bismarck at once told his ambassador to
demand redress in Vienna, and to inform that court that
"a negative or evasive answer to our request would con-
vince us that the imperial government has no longer the
desire to proceed with us along a common way." The
answer came, sharp and clear : "The emperor's minister
must decidedly disavow the claim of the royal Prussian
ambassador to receive a justification for an act of the
administration of Holstein."

Even this did not necessarily mean war, but the situa-

Annoying
demonstra-
tions in
Augusten-
burg's
favor.

tion had become so tense that the wildest rumors as to mobilization of forces were believed on both sides, and a mere playful remark of Bismarck's to a lady at a dinner party was magnified into a declaration of intended hostilities. " Is it true," asked the Countess Hohenlohe, " that you are going to fight Austria and conquer Saxony ? " " Of course," was the answer, " that has been my object since I first became minister." Strangely enough, the minister's laughing prophecy, that the Austrians would be defeated near the countess's own estates in Bohemia, was to prove almost literally true.

Austria threatens federal execution against Prussia.

Prussia struck a new blow at the party of Augustenburg by decreeing, that any attempt to undermine the provisional government in the duchies would be punishable by house of correction. Austria inquired officially if Prussia still considered herself bound by the Gastein Treaty; and informed the German courts that, should the answer prove unsatisfactory, she would submit the whole matter to the decision of the federal Diet, and move the mobilization of a federal army. This mere threat set Prussia to arming in furious haste, brought about the consummation of the Italian alliance, and caused Bismarck to make one of the master moves of his career by bringing into the discussion a plan for reorganizing the whole constitution of Germany. He was determined, should Austria find it possible to pass such a vote of federal execution, that Prussia should no longer belong to the German Confederation. He would found a confederation of his own, which the other states, should they not do so voluntarily, must be forced into joining. He, the ultraconservative of 1848, was willing now that the German people should have a general parliament chosen by popular election. If war was to come, posterity should not say that the cause was a trivial dispute regarding the ownership of a province. It was to be a fight rather for the holiest privileges of man — for nationality, for free government.

Early in June, Austria carried out her threat of bringing the Schleswig-Holstein matter before the Diet, and — what Prussia deemed a direct breach of the Gastein Treaty — ordered Gablenz to call together the Holstein estates, thus conjuring up the spirit of revolution. Manteuffel, the Prussian governor of Schleswig, announced that, since a return had been made to the condition of things before the Treaty of Gastein, he must once more place garrisons in Holstein. As his troops advanced, Gablenz retreated, complaining loudly, for his own part, of the breach of the treaty. The fateful vote in the Diet — the most fateful, doubtless, in all German history — took place on June 14, 1866. By a majority of three, the mobilization of the federal forces was decreed, — Austria's chief supporters being Bavaria, Hanover, Saxony, Würtemberg, Nassau, electoral Hesse, and the free city of Frankfort. The original form of the motion had had to be changed, as the kind of execution that Austria wanted was unknown to the Act of Confederation. It was this earlier form — betraying, as it did, Austria's real intent—that the Prussian envoy referred to when, rising from his chair, he declared that the law and the federal constitution had been broken. His Majesty, the king, he proceeded, should consider the treaties of confederation at an end ; but intended to hold fast to the principles of national unity. He then laid before the assembly the programme of a new confederation, which excluded Austria, divided the highest military command between Prussia and Bavaria, and arranged for a German parliament to be chosen by popular election. The German states were invited to join. Refusal meant war. When the president of the Diet inveighed against Prussia's conduct,

The voting of federal execution.

and declared the confederation indissoluble, the majority did refuse.

The whole machinery for starting the great war had been so perfected on the Prussian side that, before four days were over, King William could issue a stirring manifesto to his people : " The fatherland is in danger," it began ; " Austria and a great part of Germany stand in arms against it. . . . Austria will not forget that her princes once ruled Germany. In the younger but powerfully developing Prussia she will not acknowledge a natural ally, but merely a rival and an enemy." " The old unhallowed jealousy," the writing continued, " has flared up anew into blazing flames. Prussia must be weakened, annihilated, dishonored. . . . We are surrounded by enemies whose battle-cry is, down with Prussia !" " Should God lend us the victory," was the solemn and prophetic conclusion, " then shall we also have strength to renew, in a firmer and more hallowed form, the loose bond which, more in name than in deed, holds together the German lands, and which now is being torn asunder by those who dread the might and right of the national spirit. May God be with us ! "

In numbers the Prussian and Austrian armies were not unequal, the scale being rather in Austria's favor. But that was a mere fortuitous circumstance. In everything where human foresight was concerned, Prussia had immeasurably the advantage. A great part of the Austrian soldiers were enjoying leave of absence ; and, as a matter of principle, on account of conflicts of nationality, their regiments were quartered far from their homes. The Prussians, whose breech-loading needle-guns could fire three shots to one of the Austrian muzzle-loaders, had been trained in intricate evolutions ; the Austrians pinned their whole faith on weighty onslaughts. Prussia had **reserves** and a trained *Landwehr;* while Austria, for want of funds, had exempted hundreds of thousands of soldiers from their longer term of service in the line, and had no organized forces from which to draw.

Under capable leaders a little enthusiasm might have nullified these evils; but Benedek, the commander-in-chief on the northern scene of war, a man of tried and proven personal bravery, went into the struggle with a despondency and a dread of the worst that never left him. Against his own will he was withdrawn from Italy, where he knew every inch of the ground, to a field where — to use his own simile — he felt like an ass, and did not even know which way the Elbe flowed. He well knew the evils of the military system of Austria, and had often spoken of them with bitter mockery. He had long utterly refused to accept the command, and had urged the emperor to give it to another. Only after a remarkable interview with the Archduke Albrecht — who solemnly adjured him to accept the position as a sacrifice to the imperial house, which could not afford to have one of its own members suffer the odium that would come from defeat — had he at last relented. He knew, as he declared a few weeks later, that Austria was playing *va banque;* that he was staking his own civil and military honor. And to add to his misfortunes, he chose as military adviser a man whose reputation stood very high, Major General Krismanic, but whose counsels proved most faulty.

Benedek commands the Austrian army.

While Austria labored under the disadvantage of having a double line of boundary to protect, it must not be forgotten that Prussia had against her the greater part of Germany. By rapidity of movement, however, she proposed to prevent a union of the forces of the small states; and, with forty-eight thousand men — which was all she could spare from the main army — to hold one hundred

Overthrow of Saxony, Hesse, Hanover, and Nassau.

and nineteen thousand in check. The definite problems of the campaign were four in number : Saxony, Hesse, Hanover, and Nassau were first to be overcome ; then the same army was to be sent against Bavaria and the other South German states ; nearly a quarter of a million men were to oppose the main Austrian army in Bohemia ; while Italy, with some one hundred and sixty thousand more, was to invade Austria from the south.

Saxony and Hesse were disposed of immediately. Within a space of three days, King John and his son were exiles, and the elector was a prisoner in one of his own castles. The conquest of Hanover was marked by painful incidents. The land itself fell an easy prey, but the army of eighteen thousand men was allowed, through carelessness, to march away to the south. Moltke at Berlin, having ordered Falkenstein to cut off its retreat, supposed that he had done so, which was not the case. He informed King George accordingly, thus inducing him to capitulate. Injured in his feelings and considering himself betrayed, the king ordered an attack on Eisenach, which was countermanded by the Duke of Coburg and a Hanoverian major, under the impression that George had not received the latest despatches from Berlin. A skirmish at Langensalza ended favorably for the Hanoverians ; but the Prussian troops soon closed in on them, relentlessly, from all directions, and they were obliged to surrender. The king and his son were forbidden to enter the confines of Hanover. Falkenstein pressed forward almost unopposed, but had scarcely entered Frankfort in triumph, when, on account of his earlier disobedience, he was superseded by Manteuffel.

From Frankfort Manteuffel led his forces, which were greatly augmented, to one victorious field after another. At Bischofsheim, on the Tauber, the federal troops were

repulsed; and, after several successful encounters near
Würzburg, the Prussians drove an army nearly double the
size of their own across the river Maine. They remained
in this region until the truce of Nikolsburg put an end to
hostilities.

On the extreme southern field of war, in the meantime, The
the Italians had allowed themselves to be defeated by Italian field
forces vastly inferior in numbers to their own. Never was of war.
the science of dallying carried to such perfection, and never
was a commander torn by more conflicting interests than
the chief of the general staff, La Marmora. About two
hundred and thirty thousand regular soldiers had been
brought together, and Garibaldi had raised a troop of thirty-
five thousand volunteers; in addition to which one hundred
and fifty thousand men guarded the fortresses and stood in
reserve. Yet this immense force accomplished less than
nothing, although the Austrians only opposed it by one
hundred and forty thousand men,—nearly thirty thousand
of whom were stationed far apart from the rest in the Tyrol,
in Istria, and in Friaul. La Marmora was, unfortunately, a
politician as well as a leader of armies. He had learned
that Austria did not lay much stress on the possession of
Venice, and that Italy was likely to secure it whatever the
outcome of the struggle. Napoleon had hinted that Austria's honor required her to strike a few blows, but that the
Italians had better not make war too seriously. There is
scarcely a doubt but that La Marmora hoped and expected
to carry through the campaign without any serious encounters. He found it most inconvenient to treat with the
Prussian envoy, Bernhardi, who had been sent to discuss
with him the plan of campaign: Bernhardi's suggestion
that the Italian army should fight its way to the Danube
and effect a junction with the Prussians, was received as an
attempt at witticism; while the Prussian plan of sending

Garibaldi to raise a revolt in Hungary was most distasteful, the ruin of Austria being the last thing the Italian politicians desired.

The battle of Custozza.

When, on the 23d of June, La Marmora crossed the little river Mincio, which formed the western boundary of the Austro-Venetian territory, he did so in the belief that no Austrians would oppose him this side of the Adige. But he soon found that he was greatly mistaken. Early on the morning of June 24 the Italian army, the divisions of which were widely scattered, was forced into a desperate struggle with a large Austrian force, under the cautious and determined leader, Archduke Charles. The battle of Custozza was a long and hard-fought one, and individual Italian regiments did brave and brilliant service. By midday, the result was by no means decided, and the crown prince, Humbert, — who had thought of a manœuvre by which the enemy could be attacked in the flank, and its line of retreat cut off, — sent to submit his plan to La Marmora, and to ask his consent before executing it. Strange to say, the commander-in-chief was nowhere to be found. He had already given up the day for lost, had left the battlefield, and had hastened in person to the headquarters of General Cucchiari, who was miles away, asking him to come to the assistance of the oppressed army. Cucchiari informed him that it would be nightfall before the command could even reach his different brigades. La Marmora broke into a fit of weeping, and threatened to shoot himself. No wonder the day at Custozza proved disastrous. The Sardinian crown prince and the other generals waited in vain for their commands. Each brigade fought where it stood. There was no one to order a retreat, no one to summon the reënforcements, although regiments enough were at hand which had hardly engaged at all in the fray. For ten hours the brunt of

the attack had been borne by sixty thousand men; while as
many more had stood idle in the immediate neighborhood,
or, at all events, within a few hours' march.   It is surprising that the troops did as well as they did; surprising, too,
that the Austrian losses outnumbered, if anything, those
of their antagonists.

But all the military operations that had as yet taken **The**
place were small in comparison with what was occurring at **skirmish at**
this time in the hilly districts of northern Bohemia.   Here **Gitschin.**
it was that Benedek had decided to strike a blow with
his full and undivided forces — either against the army of
Prince Frederick Charles, which was advancing from the
north toward the Iser, or, as the case might be, against
that of the Prussian crown prince, which was moving
westward from Silesia over the Sudeten Mountains, and in
the direction of the Elbe.   The Prussian armies — that
of Frederick Charles had been joined by the troops with
which Herwarth von Bittenfeld had occupied Dresden —
had been ordered to unite in the neighborhood of Gitschin.
It remained to be seen whether or not the Austrians could
prevent this junction.

Gitschin forms the middle point of the irregular quadrangle formed by the bending Elbe, the Sudeten and the
Iser.   It was in this quadrangle that, in a quick succession
of conflicts, the fate of Germany was to be decided.   The
first fighting took place at Podol and Münchengrätz, —
points on the Iser which had been reached, separately, by
divisions of Frederick Charles's and of Herwarth's armies.
The Austrians were worsted in both skirmishes, their total
losses being about six times as great as those of their
antagonists.

At Gitschin itself a deadly struggle took place.   The
Prussians had been obliged to advance between towering
and wooded heights, which were crowned by the batteries of

some Austrian divisions. But the latter were hampered by orders from headquarters, which reached the troops after the fighting had already begun, but which instructed them to avoid a contest with forces numerically greater than their own. The result was a disastrous retreat, which ended in panic and confusion; and Frederick Charles's army was soon in possession of Gitschin. The Prussian losses amounted to fifteen hundred, the Saxon-Austrian to five thousand men.

The battle of Königgrätz.

The army of the crown prince, meanwhile, had crossed the Sudeten Mountains by three different passes, and had met with serious opposition. Near Trautenau, at the foot of the northernmost pass, the Prussians had been defeated, — with the unusual result, indeed, that the losses of the Austrians were three times as great as their own. At Nachod, Skalitz, Burkersdorf, and Schweinschädel, they had been successful. Their losses during the whole march had amounted to about five thousand men; those of the Austrians, to twenty-one thousand.

By the 30th of June a regiment of Frederick Charles's army was able to join the crown prince on the Elbe. The first great task of the Prussians, that of uniting all their armies, had been accomplished. It remained, with the combined forces, to deal a crushing blow to the enemy. That blow was struck between Sadowa and Königgrätz on the 3d of July. King William, Bismarck, Moltke, and Roon had left Berlin four days before, and were there to see the result of all their plannings, and the realization of all their hopes.

Königgrätz is one of the great battles of history, not only on account of its results, but also because of its actual operations. Seldom indeed have two such colossal armies stood over against each other. Two hundred and twenty-two thousand men, on the Austrian side, opposed two hundred and twenty-one thousand Prussians. The comparative discipline of the two armies, as well as the actual condition of the men after their week of fighting and of long marches, was very different. As late as the day but one before the battle, Benedek had telegraphed to the emperor at Vienna: "Most earnestly pray your Majesty to make peace at any price; catastrophe for army unavoidable." Francis Joseph had answered: "Impossible to close peace; I command, if only alternative, to begin an orderly retreat. *Has a battle taken place?*" On the afternoon of July 2 Benedek had telegraphed again: "The army remains to-morrow in its position near Königgrätz. Rest and care have accomplished much; hope that further retreat will not be necessary."

The Austrian army was utterly defeated — in spite of the facts that its position on the low hills, which it had crowned with its batteries, was an exceptionally strong one, and that the army of the Prussian crown prince, which had remained at Königinhof not knowing that the crisis was so near, had had to march from ten to fifteen miles on the very day of the battle. Benedek's plan of campaign had not been a bad one, but his generals — chief among them those scions of an effete nobility, the Counts of Thun and Festetics — had prevented its being carried out. They had imagined that they themselves knew more than their commander, and had disdained to obey his orders. The brunt of the attack had been turned against the army of Frederick Charles, while very insufficient forces had remained to cope with that of the crown prince. The divisions which Benedek had ordered to complete the chain that would have blocked the latter's way, engaged instead with Fransecky's division, the brave resistance of which formed the most heroic episode of the whole battle. Hour after hour, these fourteen thousand men resisted the attack of forty-three thousand.   Hour after hour with but twenty-four guns they resisted the fire of one hundred and twenty-eight.   By the time the long-looked-for crown prince arrived every seventh man had fallen.

Horrors at Königgrätz.

The crown prince's appearance decided not merely the fate of this one encounter, but also that of the whole day. Some sixty thousand Austrians were soon in wild flight — only to be overtaken by a worse fate than that which they were striving to escape.   The commandant of the fortress had closed its gates and opened the sluices of the Elbe. From the one narrow way that led to these inhospitable walls, thousands were crowded into the slimy marshes. War is never without its horrors; but there is something supremely awful in the idea of this human bridge over which, in a state of indescribable panic, passed the comrades of the fallen, followed by horses, cannon, and heavy wagons.   The total losses of the defeated army, including the prisoners that fell into Prussian hands, amounted to 44,393 men — a terrible chastening for any responsible people.   Yet the light-hearted Viennese seem scarcely to have felt the blow.   The theatres continued their performances, and Strauss's concerts were well attended.   A reliable witness relates how, on the very day on which the news of the battle arrived, some two thousand persons took part in a masked festival, a sort of Venetian Corso, and how, in the *cafés*, the public applauded and encored the little scenes and chansonettes.   "I asked myself," he writes, "if I had been only dreaming and if we had really received a bloody and signal defeat.   Will not fire and shame descend upon us?"

The intervention of Napoleon.

Two days after Königgrätz, on the 5th of July, the Paris *Moniteur* announced to the world that Austria had ceded Venice to the French emperor, and had asked him to mediate between the warring powers.   Napoleon had

taken upon himself a difficult office, — the more so as he had
to reckon with fundamental differences of opinion in his
own cabinet. The minister of foreign affairs, Drouyn de
Lhuys, was in favor of intimidating the Prussians, and preventing them from placing their demands too high, by
stationing an army of a hundred thousand men on the
eastern frontier. Marquis Lavalette, minister of the interior, declared that a mediator neither commands nor
threatens; and that, besides, France was in no condition to
go to war. Prussia accepted Napoleon's intervention, but
kept him on tenter-hooks before stating the terms on
which she would make peace.

Italy, on the contrary, hitherto a mere fledgling under
Napoleon's wing, refused the overtures of her former patron, who was ready, now, to buy her over at any moment
for the price of Venice. Italian pride rebelled at receiving, as a gift, what the country's weapons had failed to win.
"I will never," cried one of the ministers, "consent to
such a piece of 'piggery.'" Victor Emmanuel ordered
General Cialdini, whose army had remained inactive as yet,
to cross the Po into Venetian territory. He did so, and
Garibaldi broke into the Tyrol; while the forces of the
Italian fleet engaged with those of the Austrian admiral,
Tegethoff, on the heights above Lissa. But Lissa, on
a smaller scale, was a repetition of Custozza, Admiral
Persano proving a worthy disciple of La Marmora. The
second Italian campaign was as inglorious as the first
had been.

The delay of Prussia, meanwhile, in stating the conditions of a possible peace, began to make the French emperor ridiculous in the eyes of Europe. It seemed as
though Bismarck intended to dally with the would-be
arbiter until the Prussian army should have reached
Vienna. Napoleon could not even bring about a tempo-

rary truce; and, on June 16, a skirmish took place at Tobitschau, on June 22, another at Blumenau.

The credit of having prevented Napoleon from raising an army, and from breaking with Italy and Prussia, belongs to the Prussian ambassador in Paris, Count Goltz. Goltz held a discourse before the Empress Eugénie on the general state of things in Europe. He pointed out that the English government was momentarily friendly to Germany; that Russia still remembered the support furnished by Napoleon to Poland; and that Austria had never forgiven the emperor for aiding to free Italy. He ended by asking the empress if this were a time to mortally wound King William's just pride of victory, or to tamper with Italy. The ambassador's representations seem to have been effectual. Napoleon adopted a milder tone, and, when the Prussian proposals had finally arrived, and been formulated and laid before him by Goltz, he was graciously pleased to approve them, — adding for his own part this one paragraph: "Austria's integrity, save as regards Venice, shall be preserved." This coincided well with Bismarck's views. On the day of Königgrätz, as he rode over the battlefield with King William, who made light of the stray bullets that were falling about him, he had said to his sovereign: "The question at issue is decided; what now is at stake is to regain the old friendship with Austria."

Truce of Nikolsburg and Treaty of Prague.

The proposals submitted to Napoleon, and adopted as a basis of peace, ran that Austria should recognize the dissolution of the old German Confederation, and not oppose a reorganization of Germany in which she should have no part; that Prussia should form a North German Confederation, and not oppose a similar union of the South German states; that Austria and her allies should make good the costs — or, as Napoleon emended it, a part of the costs — of the war; that Schleswig-Holstein, with the possible exception of the northern districts of Schleswig, should be incorporated in Prussia. Goltz had omitted to mention one chief item, and Bismarck telegraphed to him on June 17: "The most important thing for us at the present moment is the annexation of from three to four million North German inhabitants." Fortunately for the cause of peace, Napoleon, who had his own ulterior motives, showed himself tractable as to this point also. He declared that the desired annexations were details, indifferent to him, of the inner German organization. He entered the lists, however, for the kingdom of Saxony, begging that it should be allowed to remain intact. The Saxons had been the chief allies of the Austrians, and it was a point of honor with the latter that the country should not be dismembered.

The preliminary Peace of Nikolsburg was concluded on June 26, on the basis of the proposals approved by Napoleon. The final one, in which Italy was included, was signed, two months later, at Prague. At Nikolsburg, a strong difference of opinion had shown itself between Bismarck and the king of Prussia. The latter wanted to make the most of his victory, and to annex at least two Saxon provinces. Bismarck's stern insistence on the necessity for moderation was, as even his enemies acknowledge, one of his greatest acts. He pointed out that the present moment was the time for peace; that clouds were rising on the political horizon; that the desire to gain a little more should not tempt Prussia to jeopardize the results already won. Bismarck tells himself, in his memoirs, how, during the interview with the king on the subject, the latter became so excited that it was necessary to drop the discussion; how, under the impression that his views had been rejected, he had asked permission to abandon a diplomatic career, and had retired to his own room; how

Bismarck
saves
Saxony.

the thought had come to him of ending all his troubles by falling from a fourth story-window, — when he heard the door open and a hand was laid upon his shoulder. It was the crown prince, who, knightly and frank in all his acts, had come to offer him his alliance. "You know that I have always been against the war," he said. "You have considered it necessary, and for it you bear the responsibility. If now you are convinced that the purpose has been achieved, and that peace ought to be concluded, I am ready to stand by you, and defend your opinion against my father." The old king eventually relented, but not without a final thrust at the minister who had deserted him before the enemy, and forced him to "bite into the sour apple" and sign this "disgraceful peace."

France wants compensation.

Bismarck had conquered. Saxony remained intact, and joined the North German Confederation. Austria's indemnity was reduced from fifty million thalers to less than half that amount. On the day on which the preliminaries of Nikolsburg were signed, the French ambassador, Benedetti, laid before Bismarck a despatch from Paris. France had desired not to disturb the negotiations; but, these being now ended, would like to have it known, that her consent to the Prussian annexations presupposed a moderate compensation for herself. What that compensation should comprise was to be the subject for future deliberations.

CHAPTER X

THE RECKONING WITH FRANCE AND THE ATTAINMENT OF GERMAN UNITY

LITERATURE : See under previous chapter. Of works dealing with the military events of the Franco-Prussian war that of Junck, *Der deutsch-französischer Krieg* is one of the best. Sybel gives only the genesis of the war. The letters of the *Times* correspondent, gathered into two volumes under the title of *International Relations before and during the War of 1870*, are extremely interesting reading. These *Times* correspondents were frequently furnished with their information by Bismarck himself. Count Frankenberg's *Kriegstageblätter* are exceptionally vivid war pictures written from day to day.

THE events that culminated in the battle of Königgrätz and the fall of the old German Confederation, had served also to clear the storm-laden atmosphere in other directions. King William and Bismarck were no longer the most unpopular men in the kingdom ; for, from the moment that war became imminent, the tide had begun to turn. An attempt on the minister's life by a fanatic, who thought thus to prevent the struggle, and who, on Unter den Linden, fired five shots at him, gave rise to an address signed by three hundred thousand names. Bismarck's coolness after the event, in entertaining invited guests as if nothing had happened, and in only casually informing his wife in an undertone of the danger he had escaped, excited general admiration. The return of the king from the battlefield — and especially his first appearance at a state performance in the opera house — was the occasion of such an ovation that, when William rose to make his acknowledgments, tears

Growing popularity of William and Bismarck.

choked his voice and he was forced to retire.   The *élite* of
Berlin gave a festival at Kroll's famous establishment in
the Thiergarten, in the course of which, the burgomaster
of the city drank a toast to: "Bismarck, who had taken
time by the forelock, and with unflinching resolution
realized the yearnings of his race for unity; Roon, who
had organized the army that shattered the enemy; and
Moltke, the unseen moving spring of all those splendid
operations."

The end of
the struggle
with the
Prussian
Parliament.
 It still remained to hold a final reckoning with the Prussian Parliament; but so bent was Bismarck on conciliation,
so completely did he throw aside every idea of humbling
his former adversaries, that the matter was soon arranged.
In his first speech from the throne to the two Houses of the
Prussian Parliament, the king confessed that the government had been obliged for some years to carry on the financial affairs of the state without the proper basis.   This had
been done, however, from a supreme sense of duty, and
William now demanded indemnification for his acts.   In its
reply, the House of Deputies was very outspoken, hoped that
henceforth there would always be a timely enactment of
the budget, and that moneys refused by the House would
not be expended under pretence of being required for the
public weal.   The king answered that he was ready to
admit that the case was unique of its kind.   Were a similar
emergency possible, he knew of no other expedient that
could well be adopted, but the like never could occur
again.   In his great speech of defence, Bismarck warned
against demanding a too specific acknowledgment of wrong-
doing, and declared that his party required peace, not
because it had been rendered unfit for combat, but because
the great task was not yet finished, and the fatherland
needed unity in word and deed.   The act of indemnity
was passed by 230 out of 305 votes; and, as a mark of

especial esteem, the sum of a million and a half thalers was set aside as a dotation for those who had most distinguished themselves in bringing about such great results. Bismarck received four hundred thousand, Roon three hundred thousand, and Moltke two hundred thousand thalers, with the recommendation that the money be expended in buying landed estates.

By the addition of Schleswig-Holstein, Hanover, Hesse-Cassel, Nassau, and Frankfort, Prussia received an increase of four and a half million population and of more than five thousand square miles of territory. The small states that were now received into the North German Confederation added a further four million inhabitants to that organization, and raised the numbers of the army at its disposal to some eight hundred thousand men. As a rule the annexations were accomplished without difficulty; but, in Hanover, the king carried away all the state funds he could lay hands on, and the nobility presented a pathetic address, asking that the dynasty which had ruled for so many centuries should not be driven out. William answered this address at great length, and the deputation departed in sorrow and sadness : "henceforward," it declared, "the most loyal and reasonable Hanoverian has no other resource but to endeavor to convert the bitterness and excitement, partly created by the intention of annexation, into a sentiment of hopeless resignation to the unavoidable decrees of Providence." As a matter of fact, far from showing "hopeless resignation," the Guelph king and his son proved such a thorn in the side of the Prussian government, and went so far in their hostility, that an indemnity originally granted them was withdrawn. For many years, their revenues went to make up the so-called "reptile fund" which was secretly used to suppress intrigues against the safety of the state.

Sorrow of the Hanoverians.

" We must follow these reptiles into their holes," Bismarck had said, in his virile way.

The constitution of the North German Confederation.

It remained to draw up a constitution for the North German Confederation; and this, as far as the essential points were concerned, Bismarck did with his own hand. It was he who invented the name *Bundesrath* for the federal council that was to represent the interests of the individual states: as opposed to the *Reichstag*, which was the organ for the whole confederation, and the members of which were chosen merely on a numerical basis — one for each hundred thousand of the population. The states retained the utmost freedom, save where the general good absolutely demanded a sacrifice. The president of the confederation was the king of Prussia, who, however, had no initiative in introducing laws, and no veto power. To the threat of some progressionist members of the first general Parliament, that the constitution must be made to conform to the less liberal one of Prussia, or that otherwise the Prussian Diet might refuse to accept it, Bismarck replied with overwhelming eloquence: "did the opposition really believe that the movement which had called men to arms from the Belt to the Sicilian Straits, from the Rhine to the Pruth and Dniester, was to have no result; and that the million German warriors who had fought and bled on distant battlefields could be deprived of the benefit of this national decision by the vote of a local Diet? What! he cried, would these gentlemen answer to a wounded soldier of Königgrätz, asking what he had achieved by all his sufferings? Oh, yes, — they would say, — again nothing has come of German unity, but we have saved the right of the Prussian Diet to render doubtful every year the existence of the Prussian army. "And herewith," he thundered in conclusion, "shall the wounded soldier console himself that he has lost his limbs,

herewith the widow that she has buried her husband?"
He constantly urged to haste. "Set Germany in the saddle," he cried; "she will soon know how to ride." After
less than two months of deliberation, the constitution was
finally adopted; and, already in the autumn of 1867, the
first regular Diet was held.

It was a grief to Bismarck, a grief to the states themselves, that Bavaria, Baden, and Würtemberg, and their
satellites, had been excluded from the Confederation. But
during all these years a strong factor to be reckoned with
was the possible enmity of Napoleon III. At the time of
the Peace of Prague, he had laid down his fiat that these
southern states should be allowed to form their own union.
So shaken was the emperor's own position by the fiasco in
Mexico, that he was considered ready to take up any
quarrel that might restore his lost prestige. He hoped to
exercise great influence over this second confederation, —
which, indeed, he was never able to bring to pass. He
had not counted on the strength of the commercial ties
that bound north and south together: with the Prussian
market closed to Bavarian beer, the wholesale price had
fallen to nearly one-half. The southern states were glad
enough to enter the *Zollverein*, and even to relinquish the
veto power in that organization, which each member had
formerly possessed. They were glad enough to enter into
secret treaties with Prussia, offensive as well as defensive,
the publishing of which, in 1867, completely checkmated
Napoleon.

The French emperor's efforts to gain compensation were
like the grasping at a straw of a drowning man. He
hinted, he threatened, he implored. Bismarck, when it
suited his purposes, would encourage him with a ray of
hope. In the summer of 1866 Napoleon made a specific
demand of the left bank of the Rhine, including Mainz:

Treaties o
Prussia
with the
southern
states.

Napoleon's
craving for
compensa-
tion.

his envoy, Benedetti, declared that could public opinion in France not be placated by such a concession the existence of the dynasty would be in danger. Part of the territory demanded belonged to Bavaria, and Bismarck used this circumstance to thoroughly embroil the emperor with the southern states. The chancellor's curt refusal to cede an inch of German territory, led to the fall of M. Drouyn de Lhuys, and to a disavowal of his policy, but not to a relinquishment of the hope of compensation. The emperor's star was waning fast. After his abandonment of the unfortunate Maximilian, the latter had been captured, court-martialled, and shot, — to the lasting disgrace of the French government. The rôle which Napoleon was playing in European politics was becoming farcical. The rapidity with which Prussia had crushed Austria had upset all his calculations. The French looked upon Königgrätz as a defeat, almost, of their own arms, and called loudly for revenge ; and no amount of stuffing the ballot could prevent the rise of a strong parliamentary opposition at home.

The Luxemburg question.

For a moment it seemed as though, by purchasing Luxemburg from Holland, Napoleon could throw a sop to his detractors. Luxemburg was practically German, although it had refused to enter the North German Confederation. The king of Holland was willing to sell. Bismarck, at first at least, seems not to have been averse to the transaction. But Russia and England interfered, and among the German people at large there arose a perfect storm of opposition. The member from Hanover, Bennigsen, denounced the project in the federal Parliament in most scathing terms. "Luxemburg," he declared, "is German, and has given emperors and margraves to the nation. It is a border country, the defence and preservation of which is a demand of honor. It is a fortress of extreme military importance, the loss of which would not a little impair our strength. . . . If France does not hesitate to insult us, the earlier that we say that we are all for war the better. It would be sullying our honor were we to act otherwise. It would be an indelible stain on the national escutcheon, were we to submit to arrogance and cupidity combined." And to war it all but came: there were moments when the mobilizing of the German forces hung on the turn of a hand. Bismarck, when asked later what had held him back, acknowledged that for a week the matter had occupied his whole attention. " It was not the possibility of defeat that concerned me," he declared, "for Moltke had assured me we should conquer. But it was a question whether we wish to begin war with France, even with the certainty or extreme probability of victory. This question we answered in the negative, and determined only to make war under absolute compulsion. We considered all the immense losses, all the grief and misery in thousands of families. Yes, gentlemen, stare at me if you will, do you think that I, too, have not a heart? Believe me, I have one that beats just like your own. War will always be war — the misery of the devastated lands, the wails of the widows and orphans — it is all so terrible that I for one would only grasp at this expedient under supreme necessity."

Although the Luxemburg matter was settled peaceably, its sting remained behind. " The Prussians need not be the most suspicious of men," wrote the correspondent of the *London Times*, " to regard this Luxemburg bargain as the shadow of coming events. If Napoleon III. deem it conducive to the interests of his dynasty to satisfy the inordinate ambition of the French, the rebuff he sustained in the present affair will only render it the more indispensable for him to engage in some similar venture as soon as he can." Numberless were the hostile acts com-

French jealousy of Prussia.

mitted by the French during the next two years. Unremittingly the press egged its readers on to war. The
official *Moniteur* once described the Prussian soldier as
the "pitiable slave of a despotic government," and said of
General Benedek and his defeat at Königgrätz, "This
proves him to have been even a worse ignoramus than the
Prussians, his adversaries." A pamphlet issued in May,
1868, speaks of war as sure to come, but expresses the
condescending hope that Prussia's conquerors would not
abuse their victory as they did after Jena, for "it is never
good to drive a courageous people to despair." Napoleon
III. was repeatedly saluted by his troops with shouts of
"*Au Rhin!*" and "*Vive la guerre!*" while the Hanoverian
Legion, with which King George hoped to recover his
lost dominions, was invited to France and allowed to
muster and drill on French soil.

Bismarck
and the
Spanish
candida-
ture.

But all these menaces were without a focus until, in the
autumn of 1869, it became known that the Spaniards had
offered their throne, rendered vacant by revolution, to
Prince Leopold, of the Sigmaringen branch of the House
of Hohenzollern — a very distant relative of the king of
Prussia, it is true ; indeed, an actually nearer one to Napoleon himself, and a Roman Catholic to boot — but he
bore the hated name, and the cry was raised to beware of
the new Charles V. on his double throne. Behind this
Spanish candidature there was suspected a wile of Bismarck's, as to some extent was the case. The minister,
in view of France's constant hostility, was glad to have a
friendly prince in her rear. He egged on the Hohenzollerns with the whole weight of his influence, knowing
that the choice would not be agreeable to the French government. He urged secrecy to the last moment, intending
to prepare a blow for Napoleon. But, with all this, he
never once placed himself formally in the wrong, and the

final renunciation of the throne of Spain by the Prince of Hohenzollern freed him from all responsibility. All the aggression, all the clumsy blundering, was done for him by the other side; and the French ministry must ever stand before the world's judgment-seat as having entered into a bloody struggle on grounds of the most unhallowed frivolity. The ultimate cause of the Franco-Prussian war was French jealousy of German unity. The immediate provocation was an insult to the Prussian king, at the news of which, as imparted in Bismarck's sharp, concise language, the whole of Germany, north as well as south, rose as a single man.

At a time when the political horizon seemed perfectly clear, and the high world of Germany had dispersed to the springs and the seashore for the summer, a perfect bomb exploded in the nature of a telegram from Ems, where the king was taking the waters. This was published in the North German *Allgemeine Zeitung*. It ran as follows: "After the news of the renunciation of the hereditary Prince of Hohenzollern had been officially announced by the royal Spanish to the imperial French government, the French ambassador made the further demand on his Majesty, the king, in Ems, that he should authorize him to telegraph to Paris that his Majesty, the king, would bind himself for all future time never again to give his consent should the Hohenzollerns revert to their candidature. His Majesty, the king, thereupon refused to receive the French ambassador again, and caused his aide-de-camp to say that his Majesty had nothing further to impart to the ambassador."

The famous telegram from Ems

There is little doubt but that, had this telegram been worded differently, the Franco-German struggle might have been postponed. It might, too, have turned out less advantageously for Prussia. It was all true what the tele-

gram stated, yet the impression given was a false one.
As it stood, it seemed to verify the report that Benedetti
had come with instructions to *brusquer le roi;* that he
had invaded the privacy of the promenade; that the king
had turned his back — "shown him the door," as the
French ministry figuratively put it.

What really
happened
at Ems.

As a matter of fact, there had been, not one, but three,
interviews, and all polite forms had been observed. Benedetti seems to have acquitted himself of his first instructions, — that he should demand of the king to order the
Hohenzollern prince to revoke his acceptance of the
crown, — with skill and moderation. William had dis-
claimed the right, as king of Prussia, to issue any such
order, having merely given his consent as head of the
family. He had told Benedetti, however, that he was expecting a despatch from Sigmaringen, and had made it
clear enough what he hoped that despatch would contain.
He would not abandon the standpoint that the Sigmaringen
branch of the family were acting on their own responsibility. Yet it was doubtless his doing that the renunciation was made, and that it was announced in Paris earlier
than in Ems. Nor did he hesitate to express his full and
frank approval of what had occurred. At the next interview, on the morning of July 13, Benedetti, — instructed
by wild, impatient telegrams from the French minister,
Gramont, who felt that his place depended on subserviency to the party of war, — had brought forward the demand, that the king should bind himself for all future
time. William had refused, but, far from turning his
back, still arranged with the French envoy that, when the
Sigmaringen letter arrived, he would communicate to him
its contents. This he had done in the course of a few hours,
— but through an adjutant, not personally, — declaring
that, as the prince had resigned, the affair was to be con-

sidered closed. Twice, after this, Benedetti had demanded an audience in the matter of the future guarantee, but had been told that his Majesty must refuse utterly to discuss this latter point. In the matter of personal relations there was no breach. Benedetti came to the station on the following day to pay his respects to the king, who was departing for Coblenz, and who received him politely. In the meantime there had come, through the Prussian minister in Paris, Werther, a demand of Gramont's that shows the whole madness and thirst for war of the French government. The ministers desired the king's signature to what amounted to a formal letter of apology for ever having sanctioned the candidature of Leopold : it was to be clearly stated that no offence had been intended to the French people. William was beside himself with anger. But already matters had gone over into other hands, for, in the course of the afternoon, he had caused an official of the Foreign Office, Abeken, to telegraph to Bismarck an account of the whole proceedings with Benedetti, with instructions to use the despatch as he saw fit. He saw fit, as we have seen, to reëdit Abeken's too benevolent and lengthy statement, shortening it, rendering it much more terse, and making out of it, according to Moltke's approving dictum, a *fanfare*, or signal for attack, rather than a *chamade*, or signal for parley.

Bismarck had been infuriated by the whole Benedetti episode. From the beginning he had found the king's attitude too yielding. This was a question for diplomatic intercourse, not for private and informal interviews. When the Prince of Hohenzollern renounced the throne, Bismarck considered it such a blow to Prussia that he spoke of handing in his own resignation. He purposely made the Ems telegram as decisive as he could, and took the further

Bismarck's sending of the telegram to resident envoys.

step of sending a copy of it to consuls and resident envoys at the different German capitals.

It was this last act, as misrepresented by the French government, that roused the excitement of the French Chamber to a white heat, and drove it into a formal declaration
of war. The Prussian king had refused to receive the
French ambassador, declared Olivier. If such refusal
were harmless and innocent, why did the Prussian government officially bring it to the knowledge of the European
cabinets by means of circular notes? "If ever a war was
necessary," he declared, "it is this war, to which Prussia
drives us. . . . Had they given us any satisfaction in
the matter we should have been contented, but the king
of Prussia persistently refuses to enter into a promise.
Have we in any way allowed ourselves to be carried away
by passion? Not in the least. We continued to negotiate
when they called us a ministry of cowardice and shame,
and in the meantime they announce to Europe that
they have shown our envoy the door!" The official war
manifesto, finally — issued on the 19th of July, 1870 —
set its seal on the weakness of the French cause by declaring that the emperor's government . was obliged to
perceive in the king's refusal to make the required promise an *arrière pensée*, dangerous alike to France and to
the balance of power in Europe. For an *arrière pensée*,
then, France went into this struggle, which was to cost
hundreds of thousands of lives and billions of money!
It was not the emperor, it was his ministers, Olivier and
Gramont, who were to blame. It was they who pretended to have in their hands insulting despatches from
the Prussian government, which they refused to show
and which did not exist. The declaration of war was
the first communication that passed through the ordinary diplomatic channels. There was no ultimatum, no

formal refusal. And the Empress Eugénie took the side of the excited ministers. "*Votre trône tombe dans la boue!*" she cried to her husband; and, when the die had been cast, "*C'est ma guerre à moi!*"

As for the German people at this crisis, their enthusiasm for the king of Prussia and his cause surpassed anything of the kind that has ever been chronicled in the nation's history. William's journey from Ems to Berlin was one hearty ovation. Everywhere the stations were decorated with garlands of oak, — the national tree, the symbol of German sturdiness. From the Potsdamer station to the palace, the streets were filled with an excited multitude in which all differences of rank were forgotten. " The king looked majestic as ever," writes the *Times* correspondent, "but with a melancholy shade overcasting his features. He had scarcely arrived when tables were brought out and placed *unter den Linden*, and loyal addresses, promising to lay down life and property for the country, signed *al fresco*." " As our fathers stood by the father of your royal Majesty from 1813 to 1815," — ran one of them, — " so will we all devote our lives and property to the support and security of your throne." Not only was the mobilization of a million soldiers carried on with feverish haste, but thousands of men, exempt for various reasons, pressed forward to share in the war. " Servants are running away," says the *Times*, " and tradespeople cannot trust their messengers to come back when sent out on errands. . . . One trade only flourishes at this moment. A universal change of costume has been made over night. The uniform has superseded the black garb of the judge, the merchant's overcoat, and the mason's apron. . . . In Bremen a merchant who dared to open his mouth against the king of Prussia has had his house demolished." And again, later : " If determination and resolve, if a longing

Patriotic enthusiasm of the Germans.

for the war that is unavoidable, coupled with a melancholy thought of the horrors it will bring in its train, may be said to constitute excitement, the country must be pronounced in a fever heat. . . . It is a sentiment which not only strengthens the will, but actually elevates the morals of the people. Never were the taverns emptier than now; never was the number of crimes and offences smaller than during the last agitated week. . . . The Greifswald and Marburg universities have had to be shut up because of the students volunteering in a body. . . . At least fifty gentlemen [the number rose later to nearly a thousand] have offered prizes to soldiers who may capture French flags and cannon. . . . The Germans at St. Louis telegraphed to Speaker Simson they would send him a million dollars as their contribution to the expenses."

North and South of one mind.

Not the least surprising feature of the preparations for war was the complete forgetfulness of all local differences. Napoleon tried to pose as the friend of the South German states and the liberator of those recently annexed lands, which he represented as groaning under the Prussian yoke. "Hanoverians, Hessians, inhabitants of Nassau and Frankfort!" wrote the Paris *Journal Officiel*, "it is not enough that you should be the victims of M. Bismarck's ambition; the Prussian minister desires that you should become his accomplices — you are worthy to fight in a better cause." Hostilities had been declared against Prussia alone, ignoring the newly formed North German Confederation. "By his mere declaration of war," writes the observant *Times* correspondent, "Napoleon has done more toward unifying Germany than in the ordinary course of things could have been accomplished in a generation or two." In Munich some fifteen thousand people went to the palace to thank the king for siding with the North; Iburg, a small town in Hanover, offered a hundred thalers to him who should seize the first French standard. The Saxon minister of war waited on King William to solicit for the Saxon army the honor of forming the van of the German forces.

On July 16, throughout the length and breadth of the land, the telegraph bore the message: "The army is to be mobilized according to plan;" and so completely had all details been arranged months beforehand that Moltke, as he said himself, needed but to announce the hour of departure of the trains to set the whole machinery in motion. Time and again, with his famous little tin soldiers, he had worked out the initial problems of the campaign. Roon, the minister of war, declared that the two weeks of mobilizing were the quietest of his official life : so clear had been the instructions that no questions remained to be asked or answered. There was no undue haste, no confusion. When the soldiers left the barracks they were all equipped, all ready for action. More than a million men were called out, about half of whom were actively engaged in the field.

Orderly mobilization of the Germans.

With the French it was all different. The minister of war, Le Bœuf, had, indeed, declared that the army was *archiprête*, that it was ready to the last button. The soldiers were huddled off to the neighborhood of Metz and Strassburg, but without the bare necessaries of existence. They had had the advantage of proximity, of convenient access by railroad, of so-called "standing camps," from which they were supposed to be all ready to march out. The army of the line was not so inferior in numbers to that of the Germans, though the reserves were weaker by several hundred thousand. The men were brave and devoted, but the central direction was altogether lacking in vigor and in forethought. The reports of the generals to the war office are monotonous

Confusion in the French camps.

in their similarity, in their constant tone of complaint:
"no money in the corps treasury," "no sugar, no coffee,
no rice, no brandy, no salt, very little ham and *Zwieback*;
send at once a million rations." Or, worse still: "we have
not a single map of the French frontier." One general
of artillery writes that five hundred out of eight hundred
harness collars are too tight for his horses, while another
sends word in utter despair: "not found my brigade, not
found my division general. What shall I do? Don't
know the whereabouts of my regiments!"

Ignorance
and conceit
of the
French.

Perhaps the worst fault of the French — the one that
caused them to commit the gravest errors — was their self-
sufficiency, their ignorance of what was happening in other
lands. Their original plan of campaign had been based
on the hope that the South German states could be separated from the North by thrusting an army in between.
They had fancied that foreign countries would feel a vast
sympathy for them. Their information about the Prussians — their character as well as their movements — was
ridiculously false. The rumor was believed that two
hundred persons had died in Berlin from dysentery
caused by fear of invasion. It was supremely typical
of the general ignorance, when, as late as September 5,
1870, the Paris *Figaro* announced that it now knew the
name of the Prussian general who had played France such
scurvy tricks and disclosed so many secrets: it was a
General Staff, who had been allowed to move in the very
best society of Paris. Well for them had their own
general staff been more efficient, and had it busied itself
more with gathering information with regard to the enemy.
But its members were chosen largely on the showing of
examinations for graduation from the military academy
of St. Cyr, passed years before; and it is not strange that
the organization itself was immeasurably behind the gen-

eral staff of the Germans, whose one idea was to employ the best talent the country could command.

With rare diplomatic skill Bismarck had almost elimi- nated the chance that foreign countries might prove inconveniently favorable to France. Well knowing that England would bitterly resent any attempt on Belgian independence,—which, indeed, it had formally guaranteed, —he had, two years before, lured Benedetti into committing to writing the most distasteful proposition that could well have come to the ears of a Briton: Germany was to aid France to acquire or conquer Belgium; France was not to hinder German unity, and to favor a Prussian increase of territory at the expense of North Germany. This draft Bismarck now published, sending the facsimile to the diplomatic corps, and showing the original to whom it might concern. "A predatory treaty," writes the *London Times*, "in the good old-fashioned style of the seventeenth century; . . . since the days of Napoleon I. the world has not seen the like of it." Benedetti's feeble defence, that the whole plan had originated with the Prussian minister, that he had written it down at Bismarck's dicta- tion, and that the idea had been repudiated by the French emperor, was refuted by the publication of a letter in which the ambassador spoke of receiving his original in- structions from Vichy, the temporary abode of Napoleon. Other disclosures followed, showing a greed of German territory which Bismarck had always refused to gratify. There arose a great wave of patriotism for this Prussia which had disdained to aggrandize itself with the help of a foreign dictator.

As to Austria and Italy, it was well known that a few French victories would have encouraged them to take part in the war; while Russia, bound by ties of gratitude for the neutrality observed in the Crimean War, and influ-

Exposure of French plans of aggrandize- ment.

enced by the blood relationship between the king of
Prussia and the Czar, declared her intention of remaining
aloof so long as Austria did the same.

German
zeal and
devotion.

The general plan of the Germans, as officially formulated, was simply "to seek the main force of the enemy
and attack it when found." Rapid successes were absolutely necessary in order to keep Austria and Italy at
bay, and to prevent France from calling out her *levée en
masse*. That is why, from the beginning, such desperate
chances were taken. The daring charges up steep heights
in the very teeth of batteries of *mitrailleuses* were very
costly of human life. In the case of almost every victory
the Germans lost more in killed and wounded than their
adversaries, but in the end it shortened the war. "Men,
it must be! Forward with God!" shouted brave Captain
von Oppen as he rushed his men up the fatal Red Mount
of Spicheren, and his was the spirit of the whole German
people.

The en-
gagement
at Saar-
brücken.

Moltke had divided his forces into three great armies:
the first and smallest, under Steinmetz, marched south-
ward from Treves, on the Mosel, and joined on the river
Saar with the second and largest, under Prince Frederick
Charles,—which had left Mainz, and passed down by way
of Kaiserslautern, Landstuhl, and Homburg. The third
army, consisting of South German troops, commanded by
the crown prince of Prussia, moved in a southwesterly
direction from Spires and Landau, arriving at the French
boundary near Weissenburg, on the river Lauter. In a
larger sense the German force formed one great army, of
which Prince Frederick Charles commanded the centre,
Steinmetz the right, and the crown prince the left wing.

The first skirmishing fell to the lot of the advance guard
of Prince Frederick Charles's army. For days, a small
force of fusiliers and Uhlans, under Lieutenant Colonel

Pestel, were able, at Saarbrücken, to hold in check some ten times their own number of the enemy. The French thought themselves opposed by a considerable force — French newspapers estimated it at two hundred thousand — an illusion which the Prussians kept up by riding one day in full uniform, another in white drill jackets, now with one kind of a cap, now with another. On August 2 Napoleon ordered Frossard to reconnoitre in force, and himself appeared on the field with his son and heir, who, to shouts of *vive le prince imperial*, turned the crank that discharged the first mitrailleuse. For the first ar almost the last time, victory smiled affably on the Frer n arms. The great invasion of Germany had begun aus ciously, and, after three hours of fighting, the Prussians ithdrew. Napoleon telegraphed home that " Louis " had sustained so well his baptism of fire as to move the soldiers to tears. The engagement, in which the total losses on each side had been about eighty-five men, was magnified into a great victory. The mitrailleuses and the chassepots were lauded to the skies, and newspapers declared that, with this second of August, a new era had begun. In the streets of Paris strangers fell upon each other's necks, weeping for joy. Singers from the opera were stopped in their carriages, and made to sing "The Marseillaise" in the open air, while fifty thousand voices joined in the chorus. Thick and fast came rumors of fresh triumphs. It was said, and believed, that the crown prince had been captured, with his whole army.

The first serious encounter occurred at Weissenburg, two days later, when the crown prince's army defeated a division of MacMahon's forces, under Douay. The two weeks that followed were crowded with more desperate engagements than had ever taken place within a period of the same length in the history of either nation. Weissen-

Weissen-
burg.

burg resulted in the capture of a thousand prisoners, and in a loss in dead and wounded, on the German side, of fifteen hundred, on the French, of twelve hundred. The feature of the day was the storming of the Geisberg, a steep little hill, crowned by a stone chateau, the garrison of which were finally taken prisoners.

Wörth.

Twelve miles to the southwest of Weissenburg, on the steep heights near Wörth, MacMahon drew up his army in line of battle, strongly fortifying his position by trenches and redoubts. Here, on the 6th of August, — while Frederick Charles was occupied with Frossard at Spicheren, — was fought a battle, in which the German losses were greater than at Königgrätz, but in which MacMahon was completely routed, losing nine thousand prisoners, thirty-three cannon, and even his own personal belongings. Under the necessity of reorganizing his forces, he marched off in the direction of Châlons.

Spicheren.

Meanwhile, at Spicheren, behind Saarbrücken, Frossard's corps had stood upon a hill a hundred feet high, and considered absolutely impregnable. Moreover, the French forces greatly exceeded in number the portions of the German first and second armies that could be employed against them. Yet Frossard was put to flight, and two thousand prisoners taken; while the important result was achieved, that the main French army, to which Frossard's division had belonged, now beat a retreat in the direction of the protecting walls of Metz. Not even yet were the boastful tones of the Parisian press reduced to silence, though a horrible faint-heartedness had seized upon the people at large. " General Frossard is retreating . . . " wrote the *Journal Officiel;* " it almost seems as if the enemy wished to offer us battle on our own ground. That would have for us great strategic advantages." Wörth was dubbed a "misfortune full of triumph," and the praises sung of the splendid retreat. When Edmond About, the writer of romances, spoke of what he had actually seen in the way of panic and disorder, he was cried down as a Prussian and a traitor. More in accordance with truth was the wail of a wounded officer as he saw the Germans clambering up the impregnable hill of Spicheren, "*La France est perdue!*"

One important consequence of these defeats was that Napoleon gave up the chief command to Bazaine, — whose problem now was how to unite most readily with the new army that MacMahon was organizing at Châlons. On Bazaine's track, endeavoring to drive him back into Metz, were the armies of Steinmetz and Frederick Charles; while the crown prince's army was making for Châlons, taking a number of small forts on the way. A division of Baden troops, in the meantime, — which was reënforced from Germany until it numbered fifty thousand men, and over which General Werder was given the command, — had begun the siege of the all-important Strassburg, which was heroically defended by the French general, Uhrich. *The battles around Metz*

Among the villages that lie among the hills around Metz are Colombey, Borny, Nouilly on the east; Vionville, Rezonville, and Mars-la-Tour on the southwest; and, on the west, Gravelotte and St. Privat — the latter controlling the northernmost road from Metz to the fortress of Verdun. At each of these groups of towns, with a view to preventing Bazaine's escape, there were furious and bloody battles on the respective days of August 14, 16, and 18. The Germans were victorious except at Vionville, — which was indecisive, and which cost each side sixteen thousand men. At Gravelotte, where the king of Prussia conducted operations in person, the Germans of the first army were needlessly ordered by Steinmetz into such a murderous hail that the latter, for this and other mistakes, was later dismissed from the command. The main part of his army was joined to that of Frederick Charles. During these two terrible weeks the Germans had lost some sixty thousand men, and their line of communication with Berlin was one continuous line of lazarettes.

Gravelotte.   Bazaine might have effected his retreat after Mars-la-Tour had he not been tempted into trying once more the ordeal of battle. But after Gravelotte the last avenue of escape was cut off, and, with his huge army of one hundred and seventy thousand men, he was forced to retire to Metz. This great fortress, strong by position and well built, was now hastily placed in order, a part of the neighborhood inundated, the moats filled with water, supplies and ammunition brought together — in short, every preparation made for withstanding a siege. To the regular 643 fortress cannon there were added as many more from the field army, not to speak of 72 of the deadly mitrailleuses. The main disadvantage was an overcrowded condition of the city that necessitated an enormous consumption of food: from having an ordinary population of but 47,000, Metz was now suddenly called upon to shelter and nourish some 260,000, among whom were 16,000 wounded soldiers. There was no chance of removing the feeble or the sick, for, within four days after Gravelotte, Metz was completely surrounded at a distance of seven thousand yards by the army of Frederick Charles. All supplies were cut off, and the terrible process of reducing by starvation begun in all form.

The battle of Sedan.   The Emperor Napoleon had left Bazaine's army and taken refuge with MacMahon. He would have returned to Paris had not the Empress Eugénie telegraphed that his life would not be safe from his own subjects in his own capital. The Parisians were determined that MacMahon should march to the relief of Bazaine, underestimating the danger from the crown prince's army, as well as from the seventy thousand men — the new fourth, or Maas army — that Frederick Charles had been able to spare from the siege of Metz. It was a wild hope, that of evading these vigilant forces and descending from the north on Metz; and Napoleon III. and his general both realized their danger. The French forces, already vastly inferior in discipline and *morale*, were actually outnumbered by two to one. On the last three days of August there were skirmishes, the results of which boded ill for the final engagement.

On September 1, 1870, was fought one of the decisive battles of the world — a battle that resulted in the surrender of the largest army ever known to have been taken in the field, a battle that dethroned a dynasty and changed the form of government in France. Aware at last of the impossibility of breaking through to Bazaine in Metz, and hoping for nothing more now than to save his own army, MacMahon took up a defensive position near Sedan. Here some protection at least was offered by the winding Maas on the west and south, and by the Givonne on the east. None the less it proved a death trap: the French called it *la souricière*. Fighting from early dawn to evening the Germans gradually surrounded them; drove them down from their positions at Bazeilles and la Moncelle, from Daigny, Haybes, and Givonne, from Floing, Illy, and St. Menges, and from the sheltering Bois de la Garonne; crowded them into such a narrow space that manœuvring became impossible, then, finally, after a significant pause to see if they were not ready to save further horrors by surrender, trained their heavy cannon on the worthless old fortress and on the chaotic mass of men, horses, cannon, and vehicles that overflowed the streets.

From the hill of Frénois, the king of Prussia, the crown

prince, Bismarck, and Moltke looked down on the most impressive spectacle that man could have well devised.   Just
below them, at Floing, took place a terrific conflict, at
closest quarters, between German sharpshooters and a
body of *chasseurs d'afrique*, who had remained hidden in a
little valley : the whole troop was half annihilated by the
relentless fire of the *Jägers*.   The horses plunged madly
down steep descents, or turned, riderless, and dashed into
the infantry behind them.   In Bazeilles, and in Sedan
itself, fire broke out, and blood-red columns of flame rose
in the air.

During the whole day none of the Germans had dreamt
that Napoleon himself was in the fortress.   He was known,
indeed, to have joined MacMahon's army, but was believed
to have slipped away — as his namesake had done in that
other disastrous retreat on the icy plains of Russia.   First
came rumors to the contrary; then, — when the situation in
Sedan had become too terrible for human beings to endure,
and the cry for mercy had gone forth, — an officer of the
general staff, Bronsart von Schellendorf, stepped up to the
king and said, " Your Royal Majesty, Sedan capitulates
with the whole army and with the emperor, who is in
their midst."   " For a moment," writes a distinguished
bystander, " the breath of every hearer stopped in his
breast ; but then broke forth a storm of rejoicing that for
a few minutes carried with it even the gravest men."   A
white flag rose over the fortress, and another waved in the
hand of the emperor's adjutant, Count Reille, who came
riding up with a letter for the king.   " My brother : " it
ran, " having failed in the attempt to die in the midst
of my troops, nothing is left me but to render my sword
into the hands of your Majesty."   For the last time the
wretched man addressed a crowned head as his equal.
It was ended, the struggle of a tottering despot for the

allegiance of his people.   Napoleon III. had had to contend, not only with the misfortunes of war, but with a
bodily sickness so great that he is said to have painted
his face to hide its pallor.   " My eyes chanced to wander
a little to the left," writes Count Frankenberg on the
day after the battle, "and I crossed glances with a faded,
bowed man who was sitting on a wooden stool in front of
a peasant's house.   It went through me like an electric
shock — this was Napoleon ! He feebly answered my
military greeting by lifting his fatigue cap."

The fallen emperor at the moment was waiting to be taken
to an interview with the Prussian king.   Bismarck had
already talked to Napoleon and had tried to settle the terms
of a peace; but the emperor had shifted responsibility by
declaring that, as a prisoner, he had no power to treat.
He hoped that the king would give him better terms for the
army than Bismarck was willing to grant; but the chancellor delayed the meeting until the capitulation had been
signed by the commanding generals.   When it did take
place, it was short but most affecting.   " We were both
deeply moved," wrote the king to his wife.   " I cannot
describe what I felt at this interview, having seen Napoleon only three years ago at the height of his power."
The prisoner was, indeed, bowed and broken.   " Your
army is sublime," he said to William, and, — speaking of
the superiority of the artillery, — " *that* touches me personally."   Napoleon was treated with great consideration.
Being offered several alternatives, he chose as a place of
banishment the castle of Wilhelmshöhe in Cassel, which
had been the residence of Jerome Bonaparte when king of
Westphalia.   He was allowed to take with him a suite of
forty persons, with their servants, besides some eighty-five
horses, and numerous carriages.   As the emperor would
have been an object of curiosity along the route, it was

Napoleon
sent into
exile.

arranged that his train should stop at none of the regular stations.

Meanwhile in Donchery the terms of the capitulation had been discussed by the military commanders until far into the night. General Wimpffen, who had taken over the command from the wounded MacMahon, had tried in vain to procure better terms than the unconditional surrender of fortress, men, and supplies, which Moltke and Bismarck demanded. Either this, he was told, or, at nine o'clock on the following day, the guns must recommence their deadly work, — and Moltke had drawn a ghastly, but true, picture of the helplessness of the French. After a council of war, held at six o'clock in the morning, and face to face with the fact that provisions and ammunition were at an end, Wimpffen sought out the king at Frénois, and in dignified terms acknowledged the necessity of complying with the German demands. He thanked for the one concession, that the officers might go free on parole, — a concession of which but few availed themselves. The rest were sent off to various towns of Germany, where at least they increased their geographical knowledge. Those banished to Breslau expressed their pleasure at finding that it was not, as they had supposed, a lonely village, but a city of two hundred thousand inhabitants.

For a moment it was believed that Sedan would bring about a truce to hostilities, — that an end would be put to this ghastly butchery for an *arrière pensée;* to these shallow graves where hundreds of shattered corpses were laid at a time only to be exposed by the next severe rain; to these forgotten wounded, who sighed their hearts out in dim forests and under hedges; to these improvised hospitals with the rough blood-red bench, and the slowly mounting heap of severed arms and legs and stiffening bodies in the corner; to the halt and maimed and blind, sent out to be a

forth, "You forget, count, that you are talking to a Frenchman!" He called Strassburg the key of the house — "of our house," corrected Bismarck — and refused to sanction the sacrifice of this heroic garrison, which had withstood a siege of six weeks, coupled with a fierce bombardment, but which now was at the end of its resources. It surrendered a week later. Toul fell on the very day of the interview with Favre.

All negotiations having failed, the siege of Paris was begun — the most elaborate single undertaking of which military history bears record. An immense area, that of the largest fortified city in the world, was to be surrounded by an army from which, at the moment, detachments were needed to conduct other important sieges, to guard innumerable prisoners, and to keep open a long line of communication. This army numbered, at first, but 150,000 men. The garrison of Paris, on the other hand, reached to the considerable total of 400,000, of whom less than a fourth, however, were regular soldiers of the line. Even these latter in the skirmishing that took place on September 19, the day of the closing of the iron ring, showed a deplorable want of bravery and discipline. The Germans trusted much to the effect of famine in an overcrowded town with a regular population of 2,000,000. They calculated that resistance could last, at the utmost, not more than ten weeks. But, in the few days of grace, Herculean efforts had been made to provision the city : from the neighboring towns, by ship, by rail, and by wagon, thousands of tons of supplies were brought in ; cattle in great numbers were let loose in the Bois de Boulogne ; chemists were set to work to invent nourishing compounds, and much that had been considered only fit for the manure heap was handed over to the sausage-maker. Whole stretches of vacant land were enclosed with glass, and florists devoted their energies

The beginning of the siege of Paris.

with great success to the growing of lettuce and cabbage.
On the forts which surrounded the city, work was pushed
with the utmost zeal. There was no lack of cannon, no
scarcity of ammunition — indeed, it was reckoned that
Mont Valerien, on one occasion, discharged some thousands of shots, at nearly 500 francs a shot, without hitting
a single German.

The pro-
visional
government
at Tours.

The hope of the besieged was that, now that its holy of
holies was in danger, the population of France would rise
as one man. And, indeed, new armies were at once started
at all four points of the compass; while a provisional government was established at Tours. Communication was kept
up, at first, by means of telegraph lines running under the
Seine, which were not immediately discovered; and, later,
by the aid of carrier pigeons — to the feathers of which
were attached messages reduced to the smallest possible
compass by the aid of the camera and microscope. A sheet
as large as the London *Times* could thus be brought within

Gambetta
at Tours.

the compass of four square inches. When it became evident that, for want of central direction, the efforts at relief
were not proceeding as fast as needful, the minister of war,
Gambetta, determined to leave Paris and to proceed himself
to Tours. To break through the German lines was an impossibility; but balloons had already been tried with some
success for reconnoitring, and for sending despatches.
To one of these, Gambetta committed himself. Though
discovered and shot at by German rifles, he reached his
destination safely, and soon, with the powers of a virtual
dictator, had the so-called army of the Loire well under
way. Early in November the *levée en masse* was decreed;
and only bodily infirmity could excuse a man between the
ages of twenty and forty from joining the standards, or
one under sixty from forming a reserve.

The German investment of Paris was a triumph of military art. Obliged, with a comparatively small force, to guard a line some fifty miles in length, and with few siege guns at their disposal, they set to work to remedy all defects by enormously strong fortifications. Thousands of men were put to digging trenches; to throwing up earthworks; to hewing down trees and piling them together, so as to form barricades of incredible thickness; to building blockhouses and subterranean refuges; to erecting posts of observation, from which, with the aid of the telescope, the whole field of operations could be surveyed; to damming up streams to render whole districts mpassable; to cutting roads so as to afford a continuous eans of communication for their own troops; and, finally, o drawing a network of telegraph lines in all directions. Iuch of the work had to be done by night in order to avoi the merciless hail from the enemy's forts. An elabora e system of pickets and out-posts, and of special and eneral reserves, provided for speedy massing of troops t points of danger.

Wonderful German intrenchments around Paris.

Victorious as the Germans had been, their position now — with armies forming on a l sides of them, and with French *francs tireurs* extremely active — was far from enviable. It was found necessary to detach troops in all directions to protect the newly drawn lines. Bismarck and Roon were in favor of hastening matters by proceeding to bombardment. But the bringing up of siege guns was a slow and laborious process, and, furthermore, a very strong sentiment, fostered particularly by the ladies of the royal family, against inflicting such injury on the most beautiful city in the world, had first to be combatted. Roon, especially, chafed against this delay in the "bombardment of Babylon." "The Parisians have too much to eat and too little to digest," he wrote in November — "iron pills, namely, of which too few have been employed. Though certain female intrigues stand in our way here, I hope that

The question of bombardment.

they — the pills — will take effect; it would be too great
a shame to let all the glory of the war go to the devil in
this way." The question was violently discussed, both in
the field and at home in Germany, and the majority were
on the side of Bismarck and Roon. Moltke, who, for a
time at least, was opposed to the bombardment, received
the following characteristic poem: —

> "*Lieber Moltke, gehst so stumm*
> *Immer um den Brei herum;*
> *Bester Moltke, nimms nicht krumm,*
> *Mach doch endlich, bumm, bumm, bumm!*
> *Theurer Moltke, schau Dich um —*
> *Deutschland will das bumm, bumm, bumm!*"

But the delays were to continue until Christmas time.
For the moment, the hope of the besiegers lay in drawing
more forces from Germany, and especially in the prospective fall of Metz, which would set free the two hundred
thousand men under Frederick Charles.

The fall of Metz.

By the middle of October, the situation of affairs in the
Lorraine fortress had become desperate. In the one great
sally which had taken place on the day before Sedan,
for the purpose of forming a junction with MacMahon's
army, and which had cost each side over three thousand
men, Bazaine had shown himself a poor commander.
From that time on he had played such a rôle as to
give ample color to the charges of treason that were
later brought against him. The besieging army was
scarcely greater than his own, and must have had points
at which a successful attack could have been made. But,
— whether from a constitutional lack of energy, or, as was
charged, from a desire to keep his army intact in order,
later, at its head, to play a more important political rôle, —
the commander had remained strangely inactive, attempt-

ing only operations on the smallest scale.   Early in
October, he entered into communication with Bismarck;
who would have allowed the army to go free, had it declared for the Empress Eugénie, and had she been willing
to accept the German terms of peace and call an assembly
to provide a new government.

Meanwhile, the sufferings within and without the fortress grew more and more severe.   One-fifth of the whole
German army was in the lazarettes from maladies caused
by the rains, by the pestilential vapors from the uncov-
ered bodies, by the unavoidable monotony of the fare and
the want of good drinking water.   The camps had become
great marshes, the improvised shelters proved small protection.   Frequently officers and men spent the long nights
on foot, shivering in the wet.   The condition of the
French, however, was growing desperate : the only meat
was horseflesh, and the horses themselves were starving.
They had eaten all the bark from the trees, and the Germans could see them in the barren fields tearing at each
other's manes and tails.   Finally, on the 27th of October,
after long attempting to gain better terms, Bazaine ran up
the flag of truce, and handed over the unprecedented number of 3 marshals, 6000 officers, 173,000 men, 1500 cannon,
72 mitrailleuses, and 260,000 rifles.   This immense army
was sent off to Germany, and French wits still had the
heart to remark that Bazaine and MacMahon had at last
effected their junction.

None too soon was the army of Frederick Charles left The Loire
free.   The Bavarian General von der Tann had taken Or- campaign.
léans, but, soon after, at Coulmiers, had fallen in with a
French force four times as large as his own, and had been
obliged to retire with a loss of fifteen hundred men.   Information of the victory, couched in such terms as to fill
the hearts of the people with joy and hope, was brought

by carrier pigeon to Paris. The fortune of war was turning, proclaimed Gambetta, and the brethren within and
without the walls would soon join hands and free the soil
of *la patrie*. But Coulmiers proved of no strategical advantage, and the army of Frederick Charles, after defeating the forces of Crouzat at Beaune-la-Rolande, and those
of Chanzy at Loigny and Bazoches, dislodged Aurelles
from Orléans.

The end of Bourbaki. Into the countless small engagements, with the different
armies that were attempting to relieve Paris, it is impos-
sible here to enter. France outdid herself in these months
in the raising of troops. Up to February, 1871, it was reckoned that she had armed and placed in the field 1,893,000
men. But, here, the German reserve and *Landwehr* system
showed its ' .nense superiority over these hasty musterings
of un⁺ .ied youths. Nowhere were the latter successful
sav at Orléans: not at Châteaudun, Étival, Ognon, or
Dijon in October; not at Amiens on November 27; not at
Beaugency in the early days of December, although they
possessed an overwhelming superiority of numbers; not on
the Hallue, December 23 and 24; not at Le Mans or St.
Quentin; not at Belfort or Villersexel. More than once,
the odds had been so enormous against the Germans that
Moltke, although he countenanced taking the risks, asked
the king not to blame his generals if they should fail.
The battle that took place at Montbéliard, in the middle of
January, between the French general, Bourbaki, and Prussian and Baden troops under Goltz and Werder, was one
of the most remarkable of the war; and William may be
pardoned for having compared it to the greatest feats of
arms of any age. Bourbaki had conceived the notion,
fairly astonishing at this stage of the conflict, of invading
Baden and inflicting all the injury he could. With only
forty-three thousand men, to oppose his one hundred and

thirty thousand, the Germans gave him battle on three successive days and forced him to retreat. Manteuffel's corps lay in his way, and Bourbaki was finally obliged to seek refuge near Pontarlier, on Swiss territory. At the news of his intention to do this, he was deposed from the command by telegraph, and wounded himself in an attempt to take his life. His successor, Clinchant, lost fifteen thousand men in a series of skirmishes. Twenty thousand more had escaped in small detachments, and the remaining ninety thousand were disbanded on Swiss territory.

By this time the crisis had occurred in Paris, though Favre, expecting great things from Bourbaki, had exempted this eastern army from the general capitulation. Late in October, Thiers, returning from his journey to the different courts, had made renewed efforts to effect a truce; but had failed, because the Germans refused to allow the re-provisioning of Paris, save in exchange for Mont Valerien, and also because disturbances within the city, where the radical element all but succeeded in gaining the upper hand, showed Thiers himself that the government was too unstable to make a lasting treaty. The situation of the besieged had grown appalling: horsemeat, even, was growing dear; while rats were selling at sixty centimes apiece. Almost all the infants had died for want of milk, and the whole death rate had trebled as compared with the same period of the previous year. The alternations of hope and fear were terrible. The frequent sallies, invariably unsuccessful, were costing great numbers of lives. In Christmas week there came on a bitter, unusual cold; while now, at last, the dissensions at the German headquarters with regard to the bombardment had been settled, and the first shells began to burst over the heads of the unhappy people, and to fall in the gardens of the Luxemburg and in the Rue St. Jacques. Mont Avron

Sufferings of the Parisians.

was the first fortress to fall, and proved a valuable acquisition for the Germans. Some fifty-six thousand shots were fired in all, and fort after fort was gradually silenced; though the damage in the city was comparatively slight. On the 19th of January took place the last sortie: one hundred thousand strong, under Ducrot, Bellemare, and Vinoy, the garrison issued forth. But many hours are needed for such large numbers to pass through a narrow space. They were driven back with a loss of seven thousand, and the doom of the city sealed. Its own factions began warring amongst themselves. Trochu was deposed from the governorship of Paris; the communists freed their comrades from prison; while, in the effort to put them down, blood was shed.

The Convention of Versailles.

And now a canvas of the city resulted in the dreadful certainty that the end had come, and that, by the first week of February, all supplies would have been consumed. Authorized by his government, Jules Favre issued forth on January 23, and was granted an interview with Bismarck at Versailles. He was none too soon. At the very same time agents of Napoleon III. were negotiating with the chancellor for a restoration of the empire, and with every chance of success. Better this than the commune, although the republic was preferable in German eyes to either. After three days of negotiating with Favre, the armistice was agreed to, which is known as the Convention of Versailles : for twenty-one days hostilities were to cease, and the forts were to be garrisoned by Germans. During this time, elections were to be held and an assembly to be called for the purpose of choosing a responsible head with whom the Germans could treat. The latter were to help in provisioning the starved city, but were not to enter it. The two armies were to keep within their own limits, at a distance from each other of about five miles. Although Gambetta bitterly opposed the truce and tried to spur the people on to fresh resistance, he was overruled. The Parliament came together within the allotted time; and, by the so-called Compact of Bordeaux, chose Thiers as executive head of the French Republic, regardless of the decision to which the nation might come with respect to its final form of government.

On February 21 began the formal negotiations for peace. The German demands were Alsace with Belfort, a portion of Lorraine with Metz, and a war indemnity of six billions of francs. Thiers, after days of discussion, in which the Frenchman more than once lost his temper and used abusive language, procured the remission of one billion francs, and saved Belfort by the counter concession that the German troops might make an entry into Paris. This agreement was reached on February 26, and the final treaty of peace was to be drawn up and signed at a conference to be held in Brussels. As a matter of fact it was signed in Frankfort on the 10th of May. On the 1st of March, thirty thousand Germans marched into Paris, and occupied the southwestern portion of the city; but withdrew after forty-eight hours, having completed the formal humiliation of the enemy. *The Treaty of Frankfort.*

Long before this the Germans had celebrated a still greater triumph over an enemy that had been besetting them since the days of the Hohenstaufens — over the wretched dissensions that had so long prevented them from acting as one nation. What Charlemagne, what the Ottos and the Fredericks, had found impossible,—the consolidating of their empire in such form that its crown could be handed down, without disturbance, from father to son, — was now to be achieved. The people had been educated to it by centuries of bitter experiences; the way had been prepared for it by unparalleled successes in the field, and by a broad statesmanship, the like of which had rarely been seen. *The question of German unity.*

After the very first victories in August and September, the question had been broached of admitting the South German states into the North German Confederation. Baden, bound by family ties to the court of Prussia, was a prime mover in the affair; but the real inspiration came from Bismarck. During the siege of Paris, there had been a busy coming and going of envoys at Versailles. There had been talk, indeed, of holding a federal Diet on French soil.

Conces-
sions to
Bavaria.

Baden and Hesse made the least difficulty and were the first to hand in their allegiance, Bavaria wished the federal constitution changed in no less than eighty points before she would subscribe to it, and Würtemberg held her in countenance. But Bismarck could afford to wait;—which was more than could be said of the Bavarian ministers, seeing that they had against them on the one hand their own king, on the other public opinion. Gradually the demands were pared down to a degree which made them acceptable, though not palatable, to the Parliament of the confederation. Indeed, but for Bismarck's threat of resigning the chancellorship at this the moment of his greatest glory, it is doubtful if the treaties would have been passed.

" Unity at any price " was now the watchword of Prussian diplomacy. For that reason Bavaria was allowed to have six votes in the new confederation—a number very much larger in proportion to the population than Prussia's seventeen. For that reason, although retaining her right to veto any modification of the military and naval arrangements, Prussia agreed never to make war without the sanction of the federal council. Bavaria retained the exclusive control of her army in time of peace, of her railroad, postal, and telegraph systems, of legislation regarding the remunerative industry of beer-brewing; and was also accorded some two dozen minor privileges.

Just when and where the idea of turning the German confederation into a German empire originated is not clear. The crown prince, in the diary that was surreptitiously published after his death, shows that much of the credit should be ascribed to himself; and certainly he did much in persuading his father to allow the time-honored title of "King of Prussia," to which he clung so passionately, to be overshadowed. But the kind of empire the crown prince wanted was somewhat different from that which was finally brought into being. His plan would have tended to reduce the minor sovereigns to peers in an upper house, and would have brought them to submission, eventually by force. The chancellor, with better foresight, was determined that the initiative should come from the states themselves, and it was he who prevailed on the king of Bavaria to personally suggest the change of title.

The question of an empire.

Bismarck argued that it was more consistent for a king of Bavaria to renounce rights to an emperor than to a king; and he actually drew up the draft of the letter that Louis, on December 4, addressed to William. On the latter, too, who cared not the least for the imperial title, and would gladly have remained merely president of the confederation, Bismarck brought to bear all his powers of persuasion: "Your Majesty will not always remain a neuter — *das Praesidium?*" he said to him on one occasion. To the very last the Prussian king made difficulties: at all events he would be "Emperor of Germany," not 'German Emperor," he declared — Emperor of Germany or nothing at all. To this, Bismarck objected that it would involve a claim to non-Prussian territory; that the king of Bavaria had expressly invited him to become "German Emperor"; that the federal council had used this designation in altering the old constitution to suit the new circumstances; and that the minor German sovereigns would

Bismarck wishes a " German Emperor."

be very likely to make difficulties. The discussion grew very stormy, and the old king lost his temper, and brought his hand down heavily upon the table.

The proclamation at Versailles.

With the matter still unsettled, the morning of the 18th of January dawned — the anniversary of the first coronation of a Prussian king, the day that had been set aside for proclaiming the empire. "How are you going to name the new emperor?" asked Bismarck, just before the ceremony, of the Grand Duke of Baden, who was to read the solemn announcement. "Emperor *of* Germany, according to his Majesty's command!" was the reply; but the chancellor, who relates the scene in his memoirs, prevailed upon him to return once more to the attack. At the last moment his Majesty gave in, but took the interference so ill that he publicly slighted his mentor as he entered the hall, and, walking past him, shook hands with the generals behind. The forts of Paris were belching forth their last defiant shots as the Hohenzollern raised the crown of a united fatherland and placed it upon his own head.

The coolness with the chancellor lasted but a moment. These two men — the strong, dignified, benevolent king, and the statesman endowed with wisdom and foresight — were born to supplement each other's work. It was a combination, an alliance that put an end, in Germany, to the anarchy of ages. Had William been an absolute autocrat like Frederick the Great, or had he, on the other hand, been merely a figure-head, it is difficult to see how German unity could have been accomplished. But fortunately he possessed the very qualities that made all Germans willing to accept his leadership, while Bismarck showed the strength of a Hercules in levelling the supervening obstacles.

CHAPTER XI

POLITICAL DEVELOPMENTS FROM 1871 TO 1914

LITERATURE: The most illuminating study of the period from 1871 to 1890 is Klein-Hattingen, *Bismarck und seine Welt*, 3 vols. A good short biography of Bismarck is that by Lenz. See also Egelhaaf, *Geschichte der Neuesten Zeit*. For the period from 1888 to 1913 we have the monumental composite work *Deutschland unter Kaiser Wilhelm II.*, of which Vol. I. deals with the political history. The new *Handbuch der Politik*, too, is useful for reference. A good narrative history of the reign of William II. is Felix Rachfahl, *Kaiser und Reich 1888–1913*.

"MAY the German imperial war which we have carried through with such renown be followed by a peace for the Empire no less glorious, and, from now on, may the German people confine their efforts to winning victories in the field of peaceful enjoyments. May God so ordain!" The first Reichstag opened.

With these words William I. concluded his speech from the throne at the opening of the first Reichstag on March 21, 1871. The scene was one of unwonted pomp and glitter, the formal reception of the members taking place in the famous White Hall of the royal castle at Berlin. The custom had been revived of having the great officials do homage by performing the duties attached to their posts, although no imperial, but only royal, insignia were available. Austria, so recently humbled, could not well be asked to hand out the crown, orb, sceptre and sword of the old Holy Roman Empire which were reposing in Vienna. So Count Moltke bore the sword of the old Kings of Prussia, Count Redern their crown, General von Peuker their orb, and Minister von Roon their sceptre, while old Count Wrangel followed with a banner.

The throne, it was said, had belonged to the old Saxon emperors of the eleventh and twelfth centuries and had been obtained from a collector in Goslar.

The
Reichstag
building.

The first regular session of the Reichstag took place in the old Zollverein building on the Dönhoffs-Platz, no provision as yet having been made for permanently housing the assemblage, which numbered nearly four hundred. The question of new quarters was immediately taken up and the result of the debates showed a modest, serious spirit. A member by the name of Smith had advocated an elaborate building to be set in a park on the bank of the Spree. The question of money, another member had declared, ought not to enter into the matter; to which a Progressive retorted that future ages would approve great decrees passed in plain halls; they should not, however, be in a position to say: "My God, the building is magnificent but the decrees leave something to be desired!" This remark doubtless contributed to the result that for twenty-three years the German imperial Reichstag was to sit in the old show-rooms of the royal porcelain manufactory on the Leipzigerstrasse. The transformation of the building was effected in one short summer, a task which the German architects had declared impossible. "All right," Bismarck had said angrily, "I shall send to London for builders!" The director of the porcelain works was induced to hasten his exit by the threat that whatever remained after three days would be thrown into the street.

Festivities
in Berlin.

Berlin was in a tumult of gayety and hopefulness. For the first, and last, time the Emperor invited the Reichstag in a body to dine in the palace, where, with other guests, they sat down to table six hundred strong. The court appeared, too, at a great function in the Rathaus, given in the Reichstag's honor, for which a thousand invitations had been issued. Eugene Richter, the great leader of the "Progressparty," has left us fascinating glimpses of Bismarck escaping

from the royal ladies, who held court until the guests were
half-starved, and being conducted by city-councillors to their
own particular assembly-room, where beer was on tap; and
of the Kaiser pausing at the head of the stairs that led to the
refreshment rooms and smiling back at the hungry, struggling
deputies who followed him.

There was every apparent reason for rejoicing. The five
billion francs which the French had been obliged to promise
as a war indemnity seemed to assure endless prosperity; the
National Liberals, placated by universal suffrage and hand
in glove with Bismarck, had double the number of representatives in the Reichstag of any other party, and though the
ultra-conservatives resented the merging of Prussia in Germany, that question was not likely to, and did not, become
a vital issue.

Causes for rejoicing.

All the same before many weeks had passed Prussia and
the empire were obliged to take up a struggle for supremacy
in a matter in which millions of their own subjects were solidly
arrayed against them. It is astonishing how like was this
Kulturkampf, or struggle for religious and educational ideals,
to that old bitter conflict of the eleventh and twelfth centuries when Gregory VII. and his successors claimed control
of episcopal elections in Germany. That conflict was in the
mind of every one now, and Bismarck scored one of the hits
of his career when he cried out in the Reichstag, "We won't
go to Canossa!" In those few words he conjured up the
image of a German emperor, barefoot and in penitent's
garb, humbly waiting in the snow, before the closed gates
that guarded an obdurate pope, for the absolution that his
own princes had required him to obtain. A marble monument on the Harzburg, whence Henry IV. started on his pilgrimage, has perpetuated Bismarck's utterance, though
many believe that the great chancellor was not true to his
promise and did go to Canossa after all!

"We wont go to Canossa."

The part of the rebellious Saxon prince of Henry IV.'s time was played in the new struggle by the Centre party, represented both in Prussian diet and the German Reichstag. It was made up of delegates from the Roman Catholic states and from the Prussian Rhenish, Westphalian, and Polish provinces. The cry had gone forth that the church was in peril and the party had secured next to the largest representation in the Reichstag — 57 seats as compared with 116 of the National Liberals. Its most noted members were Windhorst, von Mallinckrodt, and the two brothers Reichensperger. In the long run Windhorst was to cast all others in the shade, and he and Bismarck stand forth as the acknowledged protagonists of their respective sides. Windhorst's great assets were his coolness in debate, his quickness and readiness, his unfailing memory, and above all his power of drawing a laugh to the disadvantage of his opponent.

The details of the *Kulturkampf* can merely be summarized here. The whole episode is one of the most complicated in German history. Even the combatants in the struggle are changing all the time. Now it is the Pope, now the Jesuit order, now the German episcopacy, now the Centre party that represents the claims of the church; again it is the Reichstag, or again the Prussian Diet, or still again the government of Hesse or of Baden, that brings up counter claims. Bismarck is called upon to act at one moment as chancellor, the next in his capacity as presiding minister of the Prussian cabinet, which last position, again, he resigns for a time. We meet the German bishops themselves, first as opponents of the infallibility dogma, then as opponents of such of their own clergy as refuse to accept it. The very leader of the revolt later returns to the fold, hoping, as he declared, to leaven the lump. The questions at issue, too, change from time to time. Infallibility fades into the background. Episcopal elections, control of schools, jurisdiction over ecclesiastical offenders, civil marriage: these and other matters alternate in coming to the fore. Ever in the background is the matter of ultimate authority — the old, old conflict between rendering unto Cæsar the things that are Cæsar's, and unto God the things that are God's.

To appreciate the full bitterness of the struggle one must remember the church's plight at the time, with its temporal possessions taken away from it by Italy, with its most apostolic and most Christian allies, Austria and France, defeated in successive wars by a Protestant power, and with only a spiritual realm and the doctrine of infallibility to which to cling. The fight was entered into with great courage. Bismarck once wrote that the Pope's endeavor was "to control episcopal affairs in every single diocese and to substitute papal power for that of the state" and that the German bishops had been about to become "papal tools, officials of a monarch more absolute than any other in the world."

It was on July 18, 1870, that Pius IX., "servant of the servants of God," proclaimed his "dogmatic constitution concerning the church of Christ" as a result of the Vatican council's decrees. The Prussian representative in Rome, Count Arnim, had already uttered a warning as to what the council's deliberations portended. He had declared that, in consequence of the new dogmas, the new conception of the papal power, a church would result, different from the one protected by the Prussian constitution, and had prophesied that the episcopal sees would be vacant and that the schools would divorce themselves from religion. Nevertheless, in August an assemblage of German bishops issued a pastoral letter ordering their clergy and all the faithful to accept the Vatican decrees.

Then came revolt. Döllinger, the influential professor of theology at the University of Munich, organized a protest; and, in a document known as the Nuremberg declaration, **Döllinger's revolt.**

the decrees of the council were repudiated as ruinous to the Episcopacy and subversive of social order. "As a Christian, as a theologian, as a historian, and as a citizen," wrote Döllinger, "I am obliged to reject these teachings." He was promptly excommunicated, but his university showed its sympathy by electing him to be its head. Meanwhile, on September 20th, Italian troops occupied Rome and the last vestiges of the Pope's temporal power were swept away.

The Bonn faculty.

Many German Catholics considered it their duty to work for the restoration of that power, and, in an assembly at Fulda, called on the governments of Europe to interfere : "If they will not perceive their duty," the assembly proclaimed, "then their Catholic subjects must jog their minds !" The Archbishop of Cologne helped to fan the flame by ordering the Catholic professors in the theological faculty at Bonn to sign an acceptance of the dogma of infallibility. Whoever refused was forbidden to perform the sacred rites, and no Catholic student might attend his lectures. Such an interference with academic liberty was bitterly resented; the university appealed to the minister for education and the latter answered that professors were state officials and that episcopal dictation would not be tolerated.

Hostilities between church and state.

And so the cleft went on widening. The Döllinger party, or the "old Catholics" as they now called themselves, held a congress, set up their own ritual, and opened their own parishes. The partisans of infallibility, on the other hand, boldly thundered away at the government from their pulpits. The Reichstag then passed its famous "pulpit paragraph" making it a state-prison offence to endanger the public peace by agitation or discussion in the churches. There was no relenting on Bismarck's part. He saw to it that a stern, firm man, Adalbert Falk, was made Prussian *Kultusminister*, or minister of education and religion, and Falk's first act was to take the control of the schools from the hands of the clergy, a

measure that was opposed both by the Centrists and the Conservatives.   In order to pass it in the Prussian Upper House a
whole batch of new peers had to be created by the emperor.
Conspiracy, real or imagined, was laid at the door of the
Catholics; German unity was declared to be at stake.   Much
was made of the Pope's refusal to accept as Prussian envoy
to the Vatican one of his own cardinals, Hohenlohe, who,
however, was an opponent of infallibility.   Bismarck's boldest move, and the one that reminds one most of the Canossa
days, was to send a circular despatch to Germany's foreign
representatives telling them to sound the governments to
which they were accredited on the desirability of pledging
any new pope-elect to certain conditions and refusing to
recognize him otherwise.   Brought to the Pope's notice this
despatch did not help to mend matters.

As time went on blows more and more hammer-like were   The May
dealt, the conflict raging with the greatest intensity between   laws.
1872 and 1875.   Bismarck once declared that the *Kulturkampf* was but one in the series of struggles that had begun
when Agamemnon at Aulis, in conflict with his augurs, had
to make the sacrifice of his daughter, and that had lacerated
the German Empire during the Middle Ages.   The Prussian
state was in peril and had to fight for its existence threatened
by the greed of the church.   The Jesuit order, root and
branch, was expelled from German territory; the Prussian
constitution was amended so as to permit of severer measures.
The famous "May laws," finally, deprived the Prussian
bishops of much of their power over the clergy as well as
limiting their influence over the laity, gave new disciplinary
powers to the government, required young ecclesiastics to
have studied for three years at a German university before
being ordained priest, and directed that ecclesiastical
offenders should be tried in the ordinary secular courts.

One can imagine the bitter protests called forth by such

Retalia-
tion and
reprisals.

measures; the hatred, the fierce denunciations. The Prussian bishops flatly refused to carry out the May laws. It was a heathen principle, they declared, that the law of the state should be the last resort in matters of justice. Pius IX. spoke openly of the German "persecution." He even had an acrimonious exchange of letters with the emperor in which he declared that every baptized person was under his, the Pope's, authority. William I. answered him in kind. Candidates for bishoprics were now obliged to take a special oath that they would obey the state laws, while prosecutions on the one hand were answered by excommunication on the other. A measure most distasteful to the church was the introduction of civil marriage, — not even as optional but as obligatory; this was robbing the church of a sacrament. New Prussian laws concerning church property, too, cut very deep. In February, 1875, Pius retaliated with an encyclic, declaring such laws invalid and forbidding Catholics to obey them; nor might Catholics take part in religious celebrations conducted by priests who had taken the oath which the state required. And so matters went on with little slackening until the death of Pius in 1878.

The
attempt
to
assassinate
Bismarck.

Bismarck had drawn down upon himself an avalanche of personal hatred. That there were violent conflicts with the Centre both in the Reichstag and the Diet goes without saying. Then came an attempt to assassinate him in the street at Kissingen, where he was fired upon by a certain Kullmann, July, 1874. He made capital out of the affair and used it as a ground for greater and greater severity against the Catholics. The Centre took the attitude that Kullmann was an irresponsible person and protested against the exploitation of his act, but Bismarck, in the Reichstag, turned on the party like a tiger: the previous speaker, he declared, had called the murderer half-witted. Such was not the case, he begged to inform him. Not that he believed there was direct collusion between the speaker and the murderer: "Even in his inmost soul the former speaker will surely never have cherished the wish: 'if only something might happen to this Chancellor!' [*laughter*]. I am convinced that such a thought will never have crossed his mind [*laughter*]." And then fiercely: "But repudiate this murderer as you will, nevertheless he does cling to your coat-tails. He calls you *his party!*" Amid a storm of indignation Bismarck went on to declare that the man had said to him personally, "You have insulted my party!" The Centre jeered. "I asked, 'Which is your party?' Whereupon he said to me before witnesses: 'The Centre party in the Reichstag!'" Here there were wild cries of "Pfui!" from the Centre; but Bismarck continued: "'Pfui' is an expression of scorn and disgust. Do not think, Gentlemen, that I am immune from such feelings. But I am too polite to express them." And he repeated his charge that the murderer clung to the coat-tails of his party.

All the same, with the death of Pius IX. the *Kulturkampf* had spent its fury. The new Pope, Leo XIII., sent an amiably worded notification of his election to Emperor William. But just at this juncture events suddenly precipitated an equally fierce struggle of another kind. There came an attempt on the life of the emperor by an ex-member of the social democratic party, which proved unsuccessful. Bismarck brought in severe anti-socialist laws which, however, were not passed by the Reichstag. Then came a second attempt at assassination, more serious, for in full view of the passers by, on Unter den Linden, a charge of shot was lodged in the emperor's neck and arm. At once Bismarck dissolved the Reichstag, hastily summoned a new one, and passed the most drastic of laws.

The strength of social democracy lay less in the fact of its being a well-organized political party than in that of its tenets

Attempts to assassinate the emperor.

The rise of social democracy.

having become a veritable religion. As in the case of many another religion, persecution was to establish it all the more firmly. Social democracy had its prophet in Wilhelm Weitling, its Messiah in Karl Marx, its John the disciple in Friedrich Engels, its apostle Peter in Ferdinand Lassalle, and its gospel in Marx's treatise on "Capital." At the time of the anti-socialist laws, Marx and Engels were still alive, but were sojourning in foreign lands. Active in Germany, however, was August Bebel. Under arrest at the time in Saxony, he had been elected in 1871 as sole representative for the Socialist party in the Reichstag.

Weitling.

We must dwell for a moment on the general trend of the teachings of the Socialists in order to understand the bitter antagonism the German government has always shown towards them. Weitling, whose ideas created a considerable stir in his day, was the incarnation of the revolutionary spirit. He had belonged to the most radical secret society in Paris and once formulated it as his goal, "to accustom timid diplom.. ' magistrates, and petty tradesmen to the noise of the commun..'ic doctrine just as the sailor becomes accustomed to the washing of the waves." He was the kind of fanatic that we have met with among the leaders of the peasant uprising of the sixteenth century, with the same tendency to quote and pervert Scripture and the same belief that matters could only be remedied by the violent overthrow of existing conditions. Weitling carried on his propaganda on two continents and died in New York in 1871.

Marx and Engels.

Marx and Engels, too, were cosmopolites, though born on the Rhine. Both belonged to a communistic league in Paris and both assisted in drawing up the programme of the communistic congress held in London in 1847. In 1848 Marx was expelled from Prussia, from Paris, and from Brussels, and took up his permanent residence in London. From 1864 to his death in 1883 he was the virtual head of a great international labor organization. Marx had a well-trained mind, having studied in his youth at the universities of Berlin and Bonn. Social and economic questions had always interested him; and many of his theories, such as those relating to free schooling, progressive taxation and national industrial enterprises, have been put into practice with great succe... It is his attacks on such conceptions as fatherland, family, marriage, and religion to which the governments have chiefly objected and to his doctrine that relief from all the evils "can only be obtained by the violent overthrow of the whole existing social order." According to Marx's gospel, society falls apart into but two main categories the plunderers and the plundered. Landowners should be expropriated and all rents should flow into the state treasury; the state, too, should control all transportation and all credit, while the whole inheritance system should be abolished. This process will be simplified by an inevitable tendency of the rich to grow richer and the rest of mankind to grow poorer — a famous theory to which events have given the lie.

Ferdinand Lassalle was more of a practical agitator than Marx. To him the laboring class is "the rock on which the church of to-day is to be established." His "open answer," published in 1863, has been designated "the foundation charter of German social democracy"; and indeed his "general German working man's association" was later formally merged into the larger organization. Some of his ideas, too, have lived: universal suffrage, electoral reform, coöperative associations. Lassalle was so influential that Bismarck is said at one time to have sought his alliance, but the man was unbalanced and finally was killed in a duel after a sordid affair with a woman.   **Lassalle.**

At the time of the elections to the first Reichstag the Lassalle adherents and those of Marx were at daggers drawn, but in Gotha in 1875 the two factions composed their differences and the steady rise of social democracy began. In 1877 the party polled a vote of 493,000 and returned twelve members to the Reichstag. Trades-unionism was flourishing simultaneously, the majority of the trades-unionists being Social Democrats. Wider and wider was the appeal made by the party's programme, which included an eight-hour day, progressive taxes, the right of the people to decide on war or peace, and better labor conditions for women and children.

Bismarck maintained that his enmity to social democracy began on the day when he heard Bebel in the Reichstag defend the Paris communists of 1871 and declare that their battle-cry "war on palaces, peace to huts, death to misery and idleness" would soon be the battle-cry of the whole European proletariat. He tried to have it made a criminal offence to print attacks on such foundations of public order as the sanctity of family ties and the ownership of property, but failed to win the Reichstag for the measure, even though he eloquently prophesied the coming of the day when good citizens would long for such legislation "as the lonely pacer in a treadmill longs for a swallow of water." The draft of the law that he presented after the first attempt on the emperor's life took away freedom of the press and the right to hold assemblies. This proposition, as we know, was voted down. But after Nobiling had succeeded in actually wounding the emperor there were no bounds to the indignation against the Social Democrats, although Nobiling could in no way be identified with the latter.

Now began a time of ostracism and proscription. The police were authorized to suppress all "social democratic, socialistic, or communistic" gatherings and all publications that "tended to undermine the existing political and social order." The door was thus opened for a regular persecution. Berlin, in addition, was pronounced in a state of petty siege; and, literally, if three persons stopped to speak together in the street they were looked upon as technically assembling and could be ordered to disperse, as the historian knows by experience. This condition of things lasted for twelve years. A veritable White Terror had set in. The year 1878 alone saw the suppression of 189 associations and 258 publications, while it has been reckoned that in all 521 persons were condemned to a grand total of 1100 years for *Majestätsbeleidigung*, or high treason. For spreading the writings of John Most, the anarchist, nine Social Democrats were sentenced in a batch to the house of correction.

Yet Bismarck's policy of intimidation was to prove a failure in the end. At the first election after the dissolution of the Reichstag the Social Democrats had lost three members. These were regained, however, in 1881, and three years later the number of members had actually doubled — 24 instead of 12! The banishment of agitators from the large cities had proved an especially futile measure, for they quickly made new centres for themselves in the smaller towns. Repressive measures against the trades-unions, too, had embittered the whole laboring class. Minister von Puttkammer in a decree of April 11, 1886, went so far as to forbid strikes as revolutionary and to declare that they would be dealt with as coming under the anti-socialist laws! Futility of the measures.

Bebel in his memoirs has left a fascinating account of the way in which his party rose superior to persecution: of the clever subterfuges for outwitting the police; of the methods of tracking and trailing which the government employed, and the disguises and tricks by which they were evaded; of the secret meetings and the setting up of printing-presses under the very nose of the police. A newspaper which was started in Zurich — it was called the "Social Democrat" — was of course forbidden in Germany, and the wildest adventures were connected with its issue and circulation. Once a pulpit had to serve as a storage place and again bales of copies of the Subterfuges of the Social Democrats.

forbidden sheet that had been printed in England were transported on the very ship that carried the Kaiser. German spies followed the "comrades" even to foreign countries and tried to embroil them with their home governments. It is estimated that in all, in the twelve years in which the anti-socialist laws were in force, 1300 publications were suppressed, 332 workmen's organizations were broken up, and 900 persons suffered expulsion, not to speak of those imprisoned as described above. In the ot̲h̲e̲r̲ scale of the balance are to be placed 35 socialist members of the Reichstag elected in 1890, with a vote to their credit of 1,500,000!

Bismarck and the political parties.

Bismarck had begun his chancellorship upheld by a majority consisting mainly of liberals; in the elections of 1874, then, the National Liberal party had secured 155 seats in the Reichstag and already had 178 seats in the Prussian Lower House. But Bismarck was growing weary of the alliance, which was as one of fire and water; indeed, Roon had called it not an alliance but a *mésalliance*. The party was bitterly reproached, it is true, for being too friendly to Bismarck and for compromising with him on army bills, press laws, and judicial measures; but the fact remained that he could no longer be certain of having his policies indorsed. Also he had new and important policies in view that were likely to be of much more interest to conservatives, representing as the latter did the great industrialists and the agrarians. And with the conservatives and the Centrists the death of Pope Pius IX. seemed to pave the way for reconciliation.

The break with the National Liberals — 1879.

Two anecdotes are told in connection with Bismarck's growing coolness toward his former supporters. On hearing of the first attempt upon the emperor's life he brought his fist down on the table with "Now I have them!" "Your Highness means the Social Democrats?" "No, the National Liberals!" At the news of the second attempt he is said to have exclaimed, "Now I can dissolve the Reichstag," and then, as an afterthought, to have asked how badly the emperor was injured. In 1879 he gave the party a regular castigation in the Reichstag. His feelings toward them, he said, had grown "cool to the very heart"; he could no longer trust them, he found them lacking in modesty, he would remind them that the *Kulturkampf* (which made the Centre his enemies) would not last forever. He managed to pass his protective tariff practically without their aid and, soon after, the once powerful party fell a prey to inward dissension which culminated in a secession from its ranks. It never again recovered its old strength.

Bismarck approached nearer and nearer to Canossa. In July, 1878, he met the papal nuncio, Masella, as if by accident at Kissingen. A month later a papal letter betrayed the secret that Leo XIII. was desirous of a lasting peace. In May, 1879, Berlin learned that Windhorst, the great Centrist leader, for the first time in nine years, had appeared at a soirée in the Chancellor's palace. A cup of liquid had accidentally been upset over his clothes, but this had merely given a chance for added informality and heartiness. Two months later Falk, stern father of the May laws, resigned from the ministry and was succeeded by von Puttkammer. Some modifications were introduced in the schools. Evidently the tide had turned. Interviews and concessions alternated with each other until, in July, 1880, a so-called peace-law paved the way for the reinstatement of bishops and the resumption of ecclesiastical taxation. In 1882 and 1883 came further legislation and further modifications. The Pope and the emperor again began to correspond; the Pope filled the vacant sees of Cologne and Posen. In 1885 the Pope was made arbiter between Germany and Spain in the matter of the ownership of the Caroline Islands.

There is no need to follow all the intermediate steps, but when, in 1887, we find the Pope using his influence with the

Reconciliation with the church.

Centre to have it support the German government's army
bill, it is evident that the *Kulturkampf* as an issue was nearly
dead; in fact in May of that year the Pope in a public consistory declared the conflict ended. By no means all of the
laws had been abrogated. In the empire at large the so-
called pulpit paragraph and the laws against the Jesuits still
remained in force; while in Prussia laws concerning civil marriage, control of the schools, church property, the calling of
pastors, and religious orders were retained, though in a modified form.

Meanwhile the reform that, apart from the welding of the
nation into an empire, will be remembered by posterity as
the great achievement of William I.'s reign, was in full progress; for the year that saw the official conclusion of the
Kulturkampf saw also the announcement of a plan for invalidity and old age insurance that was to serve as a corner-
stone for social legislation in favor of the working-man. That
the introduction of compulsory insurance as a state enterprise
was mainly a political move intended to checkmate social
democracy cannot well be denied. As early as 1871 Bismarck
had written to Count Itzenplitz that the only way of calling a
halt to the Socialist movement was to realize what was just
and practicable in its demands. When bringing forward an
accident insurance law in 1881 he had spoken of "infernal
elements" with which the state was in conflict. It is well
known now that he intended the insurance to be a better
weapon in the state's hand than it eventually became. He
always maintained, indeed, that it would add to the dignity
of the working-man, but he had wished the state to contribute
much more largely to the fund and to keep it under its own
control. It would have been easy then to exclude the undeserving from its benefits. But here the Reichstag intervened. It was not charity, not a gift from the state, that was
wanted by the liberals. The original bill was so transformed

in debate that the government withdrew it, but it is noticeable that in the emperor's famous proclamation of November 17, 1881, the words occur : " the aid to which they (the people) *have a right.*" New drafts of laws concerning accident and sickness insurance were presented in 1882 ; in 1883 the sickness insurance and in 1884 the accident insurance went into effect, to be followed by the invalidity and old age insurance in 1889.

In one of its chief objects the insurance failed : it neither tamed the Social Democrats nor did it hinder their growth. It did not even earn their gratitude, for the taunt was often heard that cake was being offered with one hand while a whip was wielded in the other.   It was a sop, a palliative, and according to the Marxist creed there was to be no compromise : it was to be the " state of the future " or nothing at all.   Close students of Bismarck's policies think that they were all interwoven and that what he desired was advanced state-socialism or monopoly.   This he intended to put through with the aid of the adherents which the social insurance would win for the crown.   Commerce and agriculture were to be furthered by the new high tariff, and the state was to control the transportation rates by bringing all the railroads into its own hands.   This latter aim, at least, Bismarck achieved, though only for the Prussian state.

Partial failure of the insurance laws.

The scheme that he brought forward in 1875 was for the empire to buy up all the railroads and administer them as a unit.   Almost all the chambers of commerce in Germany were in favor of the plan and the Prussian Diet recorded a vote in its favor.   But the opposition from the smaller states, from private interests, and even from members of Bismarck's cabinet, was insurmountable.   The spirit of particularism was still so rampant that Saxony refused to have its railroad tickets of the same color as Prussia's because the government thought its people ought always to know whether

The Prussian state railroads.

they were travelling at home *or abroad!* A Württemberg minister declared frankly that his state would not sacrifice its railroads to this "Moloch of a German Empire."

Unable to carry out the larger plan, which some think he presented merely as a blind, Bismarck proceeded to consolidate the Prussian railroads and bring at least the principal ones under state ownership. There was nothing revolutionary in the policy, for Prussia, as well as other states, was already an investor in some of the lines. By the end of 1878 30 per cent of the Prussian railroads were in the government's hands and 20 per cent were actually run by it. The country meanwhile was being enlightened by debates, lectures, and publications as to the merits and disadvantages of public ownership. The more pronounced liberals, like Eugene Richter, were bitterly opposed. Richter declared in the Reichstag that the idea of such unnatural centralizatic. was unheard of in Europe, — that it would impose intolerable responsibilities; that it was an attempt to militarize commerce, transportation, and intercourse; that a state always conducted enterprises more extravagantly than did individuals; that there would be unutterable confusion in the budget. "In Prussia, in Germany, in the whole world," he said, "competition and private industry have produced the growth of the railroads." And he went on to predict dire calamity.

Acquisition of the lines.

In 1879, sure of a majority in the Prussian Diet, Bismarck brought forward a comprehensive plan involving the purchase and completion of nearly 2000 miles of trackage. At the same time he stated frankly that further purchases and practical monopoly were his ultimate aim. The project involved a doubling of the public debt, which already amounted to some 1,400,000,000 marks, and an increase in yearly interest of nearly 60,000,000 marks. The former shareholders were to be allowed to exchange their stock for government bonds. The whole measure was finally passed December 17, 1879. The further purchases were made as predicted, and by 1885 all the really important lines had been acquired.

Meanwhile slowly but surely the desire to mix in the larger affairs of the world was becoming apparent in Germany. Hitherto there had been no ambition to own colonies across the seas. Doubtless in 1871 France would have been only too delighted to cede islands or African tracts rather than Alsace-Lorraine, but the idea met with no response. Since then, indeed, the secrets of the jungles had been opened up by the English Stanley and Livingstone, and German explorers like Nachtigal and von Richthofen had penetrated in all directions.

The question of colonies.

One can trace the day and almost the minute when Germany determined to become a colonial power. On April 24, 1884, Bismarck cabled to the German consul at Cape Town: "According to information imparted by Mr. Lüderitz the (British) colonial authorities doubt if his acquisitions north of the Orange River can claim German protection. You are to declare officially that he and his settlements will be safeguarded by the Empire." Lüderitz was a Bremen trader who had conceived the idea of bartering with Southwest African chieftains for land grants and privileges which should enable him to start plantations, ostrich farms, and industrial enterprises. He had obtained from a Hottentot leader a grant of many square miles on the bay of Angra Pequena, and Bismarck had instructed his Cape Town consul to support Lüderitz in case there were no conflicting claims. England was approached in the matter and gave the oracular verdict that her own sovereignty extended only to Whale Bay and to some islands off the coast; but that any claim to territory between Cape Colony and the eighteenth degree of latitude was "an attack on Cape Colony's legitimate rights." De-

Southwest Africa.

signed to check Lüderitz's temerity this declaration had the opposite effect. Even before it arrived he had acquired by treaties the whole stretch of coast from the Orange River to the twenty-sixth degree of latitude; and England's acknowledgment that her sovereignty was restricted to Whale Bay and the islands was, of course, most welcome. She was now politely asked to give the basis for her other indefinite claims and in particular to state what arrangements had been made for protecting German subjects when engaged in legitimate undertakings.

Differences with England.

England was taken in a trap. Her Colonial Secretary, Lord Derby, was obliged to admit that, although ninety years previously troops had once landed on the Southwest African coast, England had never claimed it or attempted to set up a government. Cape Colony then tried to establish what Bismarck called a "Monroe Doctrine in Africa," but the prime minister, Lord Granville, finally offered excuses, and the Cabinet formally recognized the German protectorate over the whole territory. The whole matter had thus apparently been settled when, in July, 1884, Cape Colony suddenly declared that, with Lord Derby's sanction, she had annexed Southwest Africa. Without hesitation Bismarck then despatched three warships to the spot, and on August 7 the German flag was hoisted. England was not willing to go to war about those sandy wastes and her government explained that the annexation order referred only to such lands as were not actually occupied by the Germans and contented itself with Betschuanaland and Kalahari, well in from the coast.

Importance of German trade interests.

Bismarck had wished to leave the material side of the founding, management, and development of the colony entirely to Lüderitz. He had always been averse to having the empire assume such burdens. He had looked on with equanimity (except that he secured a coaling station in

Providence islands were declared within the sphere of influ- The Caro-
line and
Marshall
islands.
ence of Germany. Spain, indeed, flew into a rage at finding
that *her* Caroline Islands were thus to be disposed of, and the
populace attacked the German embassy in Madrid. But
Bismarck gave the dispute a graceful turn by leaving, as we
have seen, the whole decision to the Pope. It was a special
compliment to his Holiness, for Spain's original title to the
islands rested on the fact that a former Pope, Alexander VI.,
had drawn an imaginary line apportioning to her that part
of the ocean.

Germany's most valuable acquisition was made on the East
Africa.
east coast of Africa. Her pretexts for interference were somewhat artificial. The sister-in-law of the Sultan of Zanzibar,
who had become a German subject by marrying a Hamburg
merchant, was owed money by the sultan. The latter was
accused, too, of having disregarded German trading treaties.
Frau Ruete, the widow, was placed on a warship, while S.
Rohlfs, an explorer, was made consul to those parts; and Dr.
Karl Peters and two others, under the firm name of "German East African Society, Dr. Peters & Co.," were instructed
to find land for a German settlement. Herbert Bismarck had
meanwhile gained an admission from England's prime minister that the lands on the main coast facing Zanzibar were
under no recognized form of government.

But the sultan, prompted by English traders, claimed England
and
Zanzibar.
the lands in question, forbade any chieftain to cede rights
to the Germans, and sent troops to various points. However,
when, on Aug. 7, 1885, five German warships, including the
one which carried Frau Ruete, appeared off the Island the
sultan changed his tactics completely. So friendly indeed
did he prove that the Germans could not think of pressing
Frau Ruete's case for fear of hurting his feelings; and the
poor lady, although later she made a second journey to
Zanzibar for the purpose, never obtained satisfaction. Ger-

many acquired a large tract of land in the interior, but left
to the sultan a wide strip of coast.   There were the inevitable
rubs with England, where Dr. Peters and the German explorer Emin Pasha were suspected of planning further annexations on a grand scale.   But here, too, a treaty, concluded in
July, 1890, finally settled all difficulties.   In return for the
protectorate over Zanzibar itself, for Witu and Somaliland
and other districts, England used her good offices with the
sultan to make him abandon his strip of coast, allowed
Germany a clear title to a huge tract of land stretching west
to the Congo Free State, and, last but not least, surrendered
Helgoland   the Island of Helgoland in the North Sea, — one of the
supreme acts of folly in her diplomatic history.

Germany now had a colonial empire nearly five times its
own original size, and it had been gained without striking
a blow.   Bismarck's policy now was to keep the peace and
devote himself to internal affairs.

Foreign   After 1871 it was no secret that France would take the
policy.   first opportunity to endeavor to recover Alsace-Lorraine.
The statue of Strassburg in the Place de la Concorde was kept
draped with black against the day of liberation.   Bismarck's
efforts, accordingly, were directed to keeping France isolated
from other countries and especially to preventing her from
joining with Russia, a danger which seemed especially threatening in 1875 and in 1887.   In the former year the wily Russian
minister Gortschakoff did his best to embroil France and
Germany, while in the latter Boulanger seemed about to play
the part of a new Napoleon.   Bismarck's diplomacy was
masterly.   He used every artifice known to his trade :
bribery, threats and cajoleries, secret and underhanded agreements like his famous re-insurance treaty with Russia, above
all a frankness so amazing that it completely bluffed his
opponents.

Even before the surrender at Sedan Bismarck had sounded

the courts of St. Petersburg and Berlin as to a possible alliance.   He had earned the Czar's gratitude by helping him to obtain a modification of that clause in the Paris Treaty of 1856 which restricted the number of warships Russia might maintain in the Black Sea.   He was willing to some extent, too, to further her aims in the Balkan peninsula.   There was a close personal friendship between the Czar and Emperor William.   With Austria, on the other hand, Bismarck had purposely been lenient after the war of 1866 ; and as Austria's designs in the Balkans were sure to conflict with those of Russia, she could not refuse Germany's proffered friendship. The so-called three-emperor alliance was to remain in force until 1879.

The three-emperor alliance.

But it showed rifts before it broke.   Disturbances in the Balkans in 1876 caused the Czar, through the German military envoy, Count von Werder, to ask Bismarck whether Germany would remain neutral were Russia to attack Austria.   Bismarck answered what was doubtless the truth :   peace among the monarchies was Germany's prime need ;   should peace prove impossible between Austria and Russia, Germany might look on with equanimity while a few battles were won or lost, but she could not permit either of her friends to be crippled as a great power.   In consequence of this attitude Russia came to terms with Austria, secured her neutrality in the case of an eventual struggle with Turkey, and, as an earnest of her good will, abandoned to her in 1877 the old Turkish provinces of Bosnia and Herzegovina.

Bosnia and Herzegovina.

Not many months passed before the war between Russia and Turkey became an actuality.   We need not follow its details here.   What interests us chiefly is that Russia, though victorious, was prevented by Austria and England from imposing the terms she desired.   The Czar turned to Bismarck with the request that a congress of the great powers be held

The Congress of Berlin, 1878.

at Berlin; it was duly called and remained in session from June 13 to July 13, 1878.

The breach with Russia.

Bismarck had a difficult course to steer. If he were to offend Russia, she would naturally gravitate to France. Yet it soon became evident that he could not hope to retain the friendship both of Russia and of Austria, at least not as an open ally. The Congress of Berlin, as is well known, ended in a series of unsatisfactory compromises teeming with germs of future discord. There was discontent among the Balkan powers themselves, while the Russian press grew more and more bitter against Germany when it was found that Bismarck did not uphold Russia in her various contentions. Russian troops were massed near the frontier, while in August, 1879, the Czar intimated to the emperor very plainly that evil consequences must ensue should Russia's interpretation of the Berlin treaty be opposed. Bismarck, meanwhile, was conducting negotiations with the Austro-Hungarian minister of foreign affairs, Count Andrassy, with regard to a defensive alliance against Russia.

The Austrian-German alliance of 1879.

It was not easy to win Emperor William for the change of front. The friendship with Russia was traditional — was a fixed habit with him. The truth seems to be that he was personally fonder of Czar Alexander than he was of Emperor Franz Joseph. He insisted now on holding a personal interview with the Czar and in spite of Bismarck's remonstrances journeyed to Russia for the purpose. In the interview he actually wept and Bismarck speaks of his "inconsiderate sentimentality." The chancellor finally used his strongest weapon and threatened to resign, which brought the emperor to terms. Standing as he did on the edge of the grave, he had said, he did not wish to change his policies; but a change of chancellors was still more distasteful. The Austrian-German defensive alliance, still in force, was signed at Schönbrunn on September 24, 1879. Italy, alarmed by the French occupation of Tunis, joined the alliance in 1883. In 1884 Bismarck concluded his secret reinsurance-treaty with Russia, each agreeing to remain neutral should the other be attacked. It was a strange agreement to enter into behind the back of an ally, for Austria was the only enemy Russia feared.

In spite of the reinsurance treaty and in consequence of new Balkan wars (in 1885 Bulgaria joined East Roumelia in a revolt against Turkey, and defeated Servia which was on Turkey's side) the relations with Russia grew very strained. In the last important speech he ever held in the Reichstag (Feb. 6, 1888) Bismarck declared that Russian public opinion had shown the door to an old, influential, and reliable friend. "We won't thrust ourselves upon them," he cried; "we are not running after any one!"

With the death of Emperor William, March 17, 1888, the old order of things changed. The reign of the next emperor, Frederick III., was shrouded in gloom, for he came to the throne as a dying man. Had he lived he would have inaugurated a mild and liberal policy. His great desire, he said in a proclamation to his people, was to make Germany a sanctuary of peace. He was very open to English influences, and Bismarck hated those influences worse than poison. "We are a second-class race to them," he once declared, "fit only to serve them." The new emperor upheld Bismarck in his objection to a marriage between Prince Alexander of Battenberg, the ex-ruler of the Bulgarians, and Princess Victoria, Frederick's daughter: "Two empresses are fighting his and my views," Bismarck said to his friend Busch, "she of India and she of Germany; and daughter Victoria crushes him with her violence. She has and always has had a sharper tongue than he; and now that he is ill and cannot stand vexation he

Emperor Frederick III., 1888.

is less of a match for her than ever. . . . My pulse averages fifteen beats to the minute higher than under the previous reign." Frederick III. died on June 15, 1888.

Bismarck and William II.

Bismarck's pulse was to beat still quicker under the reign of Frederick's son. At first, indeed, no union could have been closer. After the speech from the throne at the opening of the first Reichstag, Bismarck had seized the young emperor's hand and pressed it to his lips. In public he praised the gifts and the powers of comprehension, the firmness of will, the administrative ability of the new ruler and declared that he had promised at the latter's urging to remain at his side, which promise he would keep so long as a breath was left in his body. "In his devotion to me he goes too far," the chancellor once said. "I believe at this moment that Prince Bismarck has completely captured the Kaiser,"

Stöcker.

wrote Court Preacher Stöcker in the famous "funeral-pyre" letter in which he conspired to down the chancellor's influence and break up the "cartell," or political combination in the Reichstag on which Bismarck placed his hopes. The wily preacher's secret advice to the influential editor of the *Kreuzzeitung* was "to light funeral-pyres and let them flame high" around the "cartell." The Kaiser must not notice the attempt to sow discord between him and Bismarck, but, went on this arch-conspirator, "by nourishing the points where he (the Kaiser) is instinctively on our side we build up his principles without personally irritating him."

William II.'s character.

The world at large expended much curiosity on William II.'s psychology. Many expected him, with his splendid army, at once to set out like Frederick the Great and conquer some new Silesia. Yet his first great interests proved to be reform in labor conditions and in education. What he did for the modernization of the school curriculum has never been sufficiently appreciated, and the same is true of the results of the great labor conference held in Berlin.

People at the time could only talk of the emperor's eccentricities: of his fondness for an American sportsman, of his speeches in public that were such as a mediæval crusading prince might have made; of his journeys in every direction. He was nicknamed *Wilhelm der Plötzliche* or William the Sudden; and again the *Reise Kaiser* or travelling emperor as opposed to the *Greise Kaiser* (William I.) or the *Weise Kaiser* (Frederick III.). His journeys in the first year took him to England, Russia, Italy, Turkey and Greece.

The emperor soon gave evidences of courage and determination. Stöcker, whose famous letter, indeed, had not yet been made public, was told to cease his political agitation or resign his position as court preacher; the official *Reichsanzeiger* declared the emperor's approval of the "cartell" and intimated that the emperor personally resented the attacks of the *Kreuzzeitung*. With Bismarck his relations continued of the best. After the completion of the insurance laws (May, 1889) and the passing of a bill for reorganizing the navy William wrote to his chancellor congratulating him on such achievements, and adding: "I pray God that in my difficult and responsible position as ruler He may preserve you to me as a faithful and tried adviser these many years to come." Less than three months later the news was flashed around the world that the greatest of statesmen had retired.

"It was a matter," said the Emperor to Prince Hohenlohe, "of whether the Hohenzollern or the Bismarck dynasty should rule." Several questions had been at issue. Russia wished a renewal of the "re-insurance treaty," as she planned to occupy Bulgaria and this would mean war with Austria. Bismarck, although he had declaimed against Russia, considered that a regular breach with her would be a fatal misfortune. His objection to the Battenberg alliance with the emperor's sister had been wholly on the ground that the

The Emperor's courage.

The fall of Bismarck.

ex-ruler of Bulgaria was hated at St. Petersburg. He was willing now to desert Austria. The Emperor wished to stand by Franz Josef even if it meant war with Russia and with France. Another sharp difference of opinion concerned the treatment of Social Democrats; Bismarck was for continuing the severity and renewing the anti-socialist laws, calling out the troops if need be, to repress violence. The emperor declared that he was not going to begin his reign by shooting down his subjects. In opposition to Bismarck he summoned a conference of ministers. Bismarck produced a cabinet order of 1852 directing that ministers might not confer with the crown independently of their chief. William acknowledged its validity but demanded its immediate cancellation. Bismarck acquiesced but took no steps in the matter. Relations became strained to the breaking point. After one stormy interview the emperor remarked: "He all but flung an inkstand at my head!" In public he declared his intention of continuing the social reforms of his grandfather; "and whoever opposes me in this work I shall crush!" He objected to Bismarck's conferring with parliamentary leaders behind his, the emperor's, back, and made a special issue of a visit of Windhorst to the Chancellor's palace. Bismarck is said to have told the emperor to his face that the latter's authority ceased at his own hall door. Windhorst had declared after quitting Bismarck, "I come from the political deathbed of a great man," and sure enough on March 17 came an official request from the emperor that the chancellor should lay down his office. When he delayed sending in his resignation the request was repeated. On March 20 the resignation was finally handed in and at once accepted.

Bismarck's version of the quarrel was that the Kaiser was upsetting policies it had taken him, the chancellor, a lifetime to build up and the success of which depended on

the order which the *Reichsanzeiger* published : "I add that his Majesty will take no notice of the wedding!" The Austrian emperor refused Bismarck an audience.

After Caprivi's fall the tension slackened for a time. Bismarck even visited Berlin and lodged in the royal palace; and the emperor returned the visit at Friedrichsruhe. All the same, in 1895 the Reichstag, by a majority vote, refused to congratulate Bismarck on his eightieth birthday, all his old political enemies having vented their spleen in debate. In vain a defender, von Kardoff, declared that such a vote would make the Reichstag "immortally ridiculous." In consequence of the vote the president of the Reichstag resigned and the emperor telegraphed to Bismarck his "deepest indignation."

Soon Bismarck committed an unpardonable indiscretion by publishing his old secret reinsurance treaty with Russia; he did it in order to flay the actual policy of the government. There was fierce denunciation in the Reichstag for this "betrayal of a state secret," and Eugene Richter declared that Bismarck looked on his dismissal as a dispossession and felt that under any other chancellor he was "living under a foreign yoke." The Emperor, too, was estranged once more and at the unveiling of a monument to William I., on which occasion Bismarck had been ignored, spoke of those who had "had the honor to carry out" the ideas of his grandfather and called them "tools of his exalted will." But William soon forgave the old Titan, who was already three-quarters in the grave, visited him once more, sent him messages and gifts, and, when death came in 1898, did full honor to the remains.

Publication of the "re-insurance" treaty.

Two main problems wound like the trail of the serpent through all the rest of the reign : Alsace-Lorraine and social democracy.

No effort has been spared to change the anti-German sentiment among certain classes in the conquered provinces. It is particularly fierce among the clergy. One of their papers, the *Avenir Lorrain*, writing in September, 1913, calls the Germans "disgusting birds that foul their own nests and leave nothing but a stench in the hand that nourishes them," and urges them to "get out as fast as you can; we'll pay the tickets and the cost of moving!" And a member of the legislative body in 1909 used the following language: "Germany is proud of her increase in population; she may be proud, too, of her increase in dogs!"

The clergy for one thing never can forgive the loss of their influence over the schools: "Compulsion in organization, compulsion in method, compulsion in text-books, — compulsion above, compulsion below, compulsion everywhere!" Such was the argument with which the introduction of the school law of 1873 was met. They wanted none of the strictness and thoroughness, none of the "corporal-staff discipline," none of the pagan methods of teaching history and natural science.

Opposition to the clergy and a closer study of the German school system have made good Germans out of the whole teaching class, although for the most part they are native-born. On the other hand, they have been made to suffer a regular martyrdom. They are attacked as spreaders of false religion and as a burden on long-suffering taxpayers. They were once branded as "bandits" by an Alsace-Lorraine deputy to the German Reichstag, although their pay is so low that life can scarcely be sustained upon it and about 70 per cent have to follow some side occupation. The maximum pay, only attained after many years of service, is 2700 marks or 675 dollars!

By the irony of fate the teachers are very dependent on the good will of the clergy. Not only have the latter, and their allies the "notables," a majority in the local diet that votes the school appropriations, but most of the side occupations in which teachers can engage have to do with the church. In connection with a pastor's requirement that his organist agree not to join the *German Lehrerverein*, or Teachers' Association, the *Pädagogische Zeitung* recently came out with the strongest denunciation of this "obliging of teachers to renounce liberty, independence, and manly dignity, in fact to sell themselves body and soul." The Teachers' Association has always been a thorn in the flesh to the Alsace-Lorraine clergy : "The teacher who joins the German *Lehrerverein*," wrote a clerical sheet in 1909, "will no longer be a Catholic teacher and will soon learn that the state neither can nor will continue him in office."

One reason for the prevalence of anti-German sentiment among the women is the fact that certain classes regularly send their girls to French convents and boarding schools, not necessarily for political motives, but largely because of the better accent they will acquire. Permeated with French ideas they return and marry in their home circles but, as a Strassburg woman writes : "There is a careful and well-considered undermining process carried on by the mother and sister and, later, by the wife. Aunts and cousins put in their little word, for in Alsace family feeling is still very strong. . . . The man wants peace in his household and, wearied by the guerilla warfare, at last gives in." *Influence of the women.*

Alsace-Lorraine is not in itself a state, but is administered by the empire as *Reichsland*, or imperial territory. Curiously enough the new constitution, granted to it in 1911, empowers it by a legal fiction to *pass as a state* in many regards. But it has nothing to do with military, railroad, or postal matters, may not even determine what language shall be used in its schools, and may not change its own constitution. It has no diplomatic corps, no consular *The status of Alsace-Lorraine.*

service, no flag, no colors. Its chief executive is the emperor, who deputes his duties to a *Statthalter*. The emperor appoints twenty-three out of the forty-six members of the Upper House in the Diet, while the sixty members in the Lower House are chosen by free election. The province has three votes in the Bundesrath, or Federal Council, and eleven members in the Reichstag.

The Statthalters.

The *Statthalters* have had no easy task, and they seem to have tried every kind of policy. There have been severe régimes and lax régimes, with no better results in the one case than in the other. Mannteufel, the first *Statthalter*, is said to have coddled the notables like babies, to have made visits which were never returned, and given entertainments to which no one came. Again there have been attempts at repression, where the use of the French language was forbidden not only in the schools but in public documents and even in street-naming. The carrying of banners, the writing of protests, the singing of songs, have all been forbidden at times, and freedom of the press has been greatly curtailed.

There are thoughtful Germans, even, who think that it was a great error to entrust the administration of this gay, happy-go-lucky land to stiff, warlike, bureaucratic Prussians. Bavarians or Badeners would have been more sympathetic. The Alsatian objects mightily to all the petty police regulations and to what is known as *Gesinnungsschnuffelei*, or poking one's nose into other people's private opinions. It has been suggested that the real solution of the difficulty would be to divide up the province between Prussia, Baden, and Bavaria, Württemberg being compensated with the principality of Hohenzollern. Prussia would have the portion including the great fortress of Metz, Baden the city of Strassburg and adjacent territory, while Bavaria would take the part adjoining the Bavarian palatinate. Obliged to fight their fights in three diets instead of in one, the solid wall of opposition now presented in the Alsace-Lorraine Diet would soon crumble away.

The emperor in his capacity as king of Prussia and his chancellors in their capacity as Prussian prime ministers (all except Caprivi, in whose case the two posts were temporarily separated) have had to face in the former Danish and Polish provinces very similar problems to that of the empire in Alsace-Lorraine. The long and short of the Danish problem is that an elaborate system of propaganda, not fully realized in Germany until 1914, has kept Danish sentiment alive in the province wrested from Denmark in the war of 1864. The Prussian Diet, in its last session before the present conflict broke out, occupied itself busily with the subject and considered a whole program of counter measures. *The Danish problem.*

The Danes, both within and without the province of North Schleswig, believe that they have a double grievance in that Prussia not only took their territory, but at the same time broke a solemn promise and agreement, viz. to let the question of reunion with Denmark be decided by popular vote. Into the rights or wrongs of the complicated question we need not enter. The result has been the formation all over Denmark of so-called South Jute associations — there are nearly sixty of them, with a central control — which raise the funds for a most systematic campaign. *Danish propaganda.*

Along the southern Danish boundary, like a belt of forts and earthworks, a chain of schools has been established. Schleswig children are induced to attend them by payment of their expenses when necessary, there being a regular fund for that purpose. The object of these schools has been well defined by a Danish agitator: "Entry into them will give you a national baptism that will retain its significance as long as you live!" A vow is said to be required of all children who receive financial aid that they will return to Schleswig and work for the cause. One of the studies on *The Danish schools.*

which most stress is laid is history, of course from the Danish point of view.

North Schleswig itself is covered with a network of secret patriotic associations: language clubs, gymnastic and social clubs, sick-nursing and abstinent societies; mortgage and loan associations which look after the economic interests of the Danish-minded; a real estate agency formed with the direct design to prevent land from falling into the hands of Germans. Even religion is pressed into the cause, and the so-called "Free Communities" preach that there is a true Christianity, the Danish, and a false Christianity, the German. The Danes began by establishing beer saloons as centres. When the government refused them licenses they established "non-alcoholic guest houses," which have become the very hotbeds of the agitation. The Danes have expressions for them such as "breakwaters against the German flood" and "shelters for Denmark," and there are now more than fifty of them.

When the Prussian Diet closed in July, 1914, it was at loggerheads with the Danish government with regard to the status of the children of the *optanten*, those, namely, who had been allowed to retain their Danish citizenship while still residing in Schleswig. These children had been admitted to Prussian citizenship in 1907 on condition that they should keep the peace. This they had not done, hence the reopening of the question with the Danish government.

Prussia's Polish problem has one feature that makes it different from either the Alsace-Lorraine or the Danish question. For years now — ever since 1886, when the so-called Settlement Commission was established — the government has been trying to make "islands of Germanism in the Polish sea" (the expression is Chancellor von Bülow's) by direct purchase of land. It has spent in all well over a billion marks. The general plan was to buy up large estates from impecunious Polish nobles and parcel them out among German settlers, offering inducements in the way of land improvements and building loans. Into Bismarck's calculations there had entered at the time the belief that the impecunious Polish nobles would squander the purchase money at Monte Carlo, and that the people, deprived of their natural leaders, could be dealt with easily.

Of all ambitious plans that a statesman ever laid few have turned out less in accordance with the expectations. Firstly, the impecunious Polish nobles did not squander their money at Monte Carlo, but stayed at home, founded great banks and fought the Prussian government with an energy and capacity that few would have credited to them. The Polish farmers, too, were driven by adversity to coöperate, and a new and totally unexpected strength developed. Their organ, the *Zwiasku spolek zarobkowych*, or Union bank, does an even greater business than the Ziemski bank, the organ of the nobles. The government's endeavors to weaken Polish nationalism have been the very salvation of the people; the banks have undertaken and carried through tasks that never before confronted institutions of the kind. They have educated their whole people to thrift and to foresight, entering into the private affairs of those to whom they loan money, teaching them to consolidate their debts, rescuing them from usurers, and enlightening them as to proper rates of interest.

The regeneration of Poland.

The banks have boldly faced the Settlement Commission, and it may be truly said that they have beaten it on its own ground. Prince Bülow showed in November, 1907, that Polish purchases of land for the purpose of parcelling it out among their own people exceeded the purchases of the Commission by nearly 250,000 acres. The tide level in the "Polish Sea" had not only not receded, but the waves had lapped over into Silesia and driven out thousands of Ger-

Polish methods.

mans. After the first few purchases the race of impecunious
Polish nobles with land to sell to Germans had died out, and
the estates for parcelling had had to be bought from Germans, with the result that prices had risen enormously, —
from an average of 216 marks an acre to one of 728 marks.
On the horizon had risen daring Polish speculators, working
on what they were pleased to call American methods, which
meant achieving wonderful results by fostering the spirit of

Sikorski.   speculation and blatantly advertising. In 1897 one Ignatius
Sikorski, with literally no capital, started a company and
attracted investors by guaranteeing dividends of 25 per
cent for six successive years, and offering interest on deposits
at $5\frac{1}{2}$ per cent. Through the medium of the *Catholic
Guide*, the *Word of God*, and other family sheets that
had never been used for such purposes before, he induced
countless Polish workers in the west to invest their earnings
in small farms at home and, for a wonder, not only built a
solid structure on his flimsy foundation, but incidentally
furthered the cause of Polish colonization immensely.

Bieder-   Much the same rôle was played in Silesia by Marcin Biedermann.   mann, a journalist who fostered the vanity of rich Poles by
acclaiming them as national heroes whenever they bought
land. He carried on a great business of lying in wait for
the Settlement Commission and buying in land on which it
had fixed its eye, often selling it finally at a greatly increased
price. Altogether Biedermann was a sort of Robin Hood,
taking from the Germans to help the Poles.

Legisla-   The legislators in Berlin left nothing undone in the way
tion   of drastic measures to stop the Polish land deals. They
against   required permits to found new settlements, and permits to
the Poles.   build in them ; no one might take an isolated tract and offer
lots for sale. But a loophole had been left ; and when a
Polish farmer brought suit the court in Berlin had to
decide against the Prussian government. It was still law-

ful to buy and build if the land was adjacent to some one else's house, and the peculiar custom of the old Polish nobles of settling their peasants as far away from themselves as possible on the fringe of their estates gave a superabundance of adjacent lots.

In 1907 the climax of government intimidation was reached. Bülow informed the Prussian Diet that the two great causes of the government's failure had been the system of adjacent parcelling and the fact that Polish nobles would not sell to the Settlement Commission. The Commission, he declared, must be empowered to expropriate Polish owners. In spite of a perfect storm of opposition he was able to put through a law to that effect. The owners were to be given full compensation.

The expropriation law.

The law was so unjust and so unpopular that it remained a dead letter until 1913; then four large estates were seized. The rage and excitement of the Poles knew no bounds. "Prussia is so hated on both sides of the boundary," writes the *Zukunft*, a noted Berlin periodical, "that any Pole who lives there will be ready to help the enemy. . . . How could one still venture, in a serious emergency, to employ Poles as soldiers!" We have an arraignment of the policy, in pamphlet form, from the pen of one who was formerly himself a Prussian official: "No insult could be greater than for a nation to say 'you are our fellow-citizens but of a different nationality and therefore we shall buy you out, substituting Germans for you in your old homes.'"

One result of all the severe measures has been to drive the Polish farmers into the small towns. Here they open shops frequented mainly by Poles, who have gradually invaded whole districts, as the German does not like the proximity. "The Pole stays, the German goes: that is the whole wretched Polish question in a nutshell," writes our chief authority, Ludwig Bernhard (*Die Polenfrage*).

In criticising the Prussian government for its Polish policy it must be admitted that the problem is difficult — more difficult than that of the American Indian or negro for the reason that the German Poles have solidly behind them the Russian and the Austrian Poles. The German's fear of being engulfed by Pan-Slavism is not altogether unwarranted. There was a time in the eighties when the influx of Russian Poles was so great that the Prussian government advocated banishing some thirty thousand of them as a burden on the state. It was as an alternative that the Settlement Commission was appointed in 1886 and was given 100,000,000 marks with which to begin operations.

The great majority of Poles are Catholics. During the *Kulturkampf* at least, members of the Catholic clergy in Posen and West Prussia tried to Polonize German children and thus win them for the church. The propaganda for having religious instruction given in the Polish language has twice led to serious strikes on the part of the children, who refused to answer questions put to them in German. Some of the participants in disturbances at Wreschen in 1901 connected with the school strike received prison sentences up to two and a half years. In 1906 more than 50,000 Polish school children were "on strike." The Poles have never tried to conceal the fact that their own nationalistic hopes are dearer to them than any interests of the German Empire; and when inclined to blame the Prussian government for its severity we must remember that, under Caprivi, it tried the opposite policy with no greater success.

The growth of social democracy.

The government's measures against social democracy have been no more successful than those against nationalistic tendencies. After Bismarck's quarrel with the emperor and the failure to renew the anti-socialist laws the party began to show great strength. In 1890 it had thirty-five members in the Reichstag; by 1903 the number had increased to eighty-three. There was a sudden fall, to be sure, in 1907, when the party lost no less than forty seats. By an unholy alliance with the Centre it had attempted to cut down the government's demands for men and means to suppress a rebellion in Southwest Africa. It was said that Bülow in dissolving the Reichstag had "aimed at the Centre but hit the Social Democrats," for the Centre lost comparatively few mandates.

In 1912 circumstances had completely altered. The other parties were disunited and demoralized and the Social Democrats scored the greatest triumph in their history, polling nearly four million votes and returning 110 members, later increased to 111, to the Reichstag. Even to the Prussian Diet, in spite of the severe restrictions of the three-class system of voting, the party returned eleven members.

All this does not mean that social democracy had become much more of a menace than before. The party is a house divided against itself. There is still the old faction of the extremists who wish the state of the future or nothing at all; Bebel was its leader up to the time of his death in 1913 and Liebknecht is probably its chief representative at present. But gradually there has grown up a very strong faction called the Revisionists headed by the much more moderate Bernstein. This faction, which has its own powerful organ, the *Sozialistische Monatshefte*, would subject Marx's dogmas to a revision and make them conform more with actual modern conditions. The theory, to take one example, that capital is thrusting the rest of mankind into greater and greater misery can be refuted by tax lists and savings banks accounts, which show that prosperity is spreading downwards as well as upwards. The Revisionists even go so far as to grant that capital is not always an unmixed evil. They are opportunists; they will take what they can get in this world and

The Revisionists.

Bebel

Liebknecht

Bernstein

not stake all on one throw. They are opposed to the idea of a general strike and have been influential in securing the dismissal of Rosa Luxemburg, the fierce woman agitator who is more of an anarchist than a socialist, from the party.

It is impossible to say which of these two factions holds the balance; the lines are too unevenly divided. The party as a whole is often forced into contradictions. After refusing for many years to join in voting appropriations, it helped in 1913 to pass the bill for raising revenues for the great army increase, against which the conservatives voted. The temptation had been too great, for the tax had been laid mainly on the property of the rich. In December, 1913, a still more curious contradiction arose. Angered at some action of the *Deutsche Bank* with regard to its officials, the party discussed the withdrawal of its funds, which are very considerable. But it was seriously argued that in that case the party itself would have to look after its funds, and would be playing the rôle of a capitalist.

Dislike of the government is still a mark of the good Social Democrat; and hatred of the present electoral system, especially the Prussian three-class system, is one of his tenets. As lately as June, 1914, at the closing session of the Reichstag, the party stolidly remained seated when the final cheers were demanded for the emperor. In 1913 the party at its yearly congress seriously discussed the advisability of going on a birth strike in order to frighten the government as to the future of the army.

In the Centre party there has been a schism very like that among the Social Democrats. On the one hand there has been the "Cologne direction," on the other the "Berlin direction"; and the conflicts between the two have been very bitter.

In March, 1906, an article in the *Historisch-politische Blätter*, by a prominent Centrist, Julius Bachem, created a great stir. It is known as the "tower article," for its refrain was "we must come out of our tower" — must cease looking at matters purely from a confessional point of view, and work for the good of the whole country. Pope Pius X. took a hand in the game, and in September, 1907, his encylic *de pascendi dominici gregis* classed the followers of Bachem with inter-confessionalists and modernists. A literary feud ensued that grew more and more intense as time went on.

On Easter-Tuesday, 1909, finally, Bachem's opponents organized a sort of *coup d'état*. In a conference at Cologne a number of members of the Centre set up a formula which included the statement that all the party's activities must be "in accordance with the Catholic viewpoint." According to this formula, as the Bachemites pointed out, the party would become involved in difficulties that were inextricable. It might not even vote on the Prussian budget, for this contained an appropriation for the state church, which was Protestant. Even the passing of the civil code would have been contrary to the spirit of the formula, since it permitted civil marriages. In short all future common action with other parties would be impossible and — matters were not minced — his holiness the Pope would have the final word in all military, naval, colonial, commercial, and industrial questions in Germany.

The Easter-Tuesday conference.

The fight raged on until 1912, when it was finally settled by the German voters, who defeated most of those candidates espousing the "Berlin" or extreme papal view. On February 8, 1912, the Centre unanimously defined itself as "a politically non-confessional party."

The Centre's goal has always been the repeal of the anti-Jesuit laws of 1872. One paragraph alone, that relating to the banishment of individual Jesuits, was repealed in 1904, but the opposition to the rest has continued. The argu-

The anti-Jesuit laws.

ments advanced are that the Jesuits demand unconditional subordination of the state to the church, that even prominent Catholics have condemned them as devils and pests, and that a pope, Clement XIV., had pronounced them an inveterate obstacle to peace. Utterances of particular Jesuits have been cited to show that they are as dangerous as ever and that they still advocate the burning of heretics. The *Osservatore Romano*, during the height of the *Kulturkampf*, to be sure, had claimed the Pope's right to depose a heretic emperor and order his subjects to expel him. As late as 1895, in a well-known periodical, a Jesuit extolled the Inquisition : "Oh, ye blessed flames kindled about the stakes ! Through you a few thoroughly corrupt persons perished, but thousands upon thousand were saved from the jaws of error and from eternal dan ation. . . . Oh blessed and revered memory of Thomas 'orquemada !"

The Conservative party.

The political party that has undergone tue least change of any is that of the German conservatives, who are also variously called *Junkers*, East Elbians, and agrarians, although the terms are not absolutely interchangeable. They are strongly represented in the Prussian Diet but have few members in the Reichstag — only 48 out of 397. In general they stand for kingship by the grace of God, for the maintenance of authority at any cost, for a great display of military force, for a high tariff on agricultural products, for Prussianism, and, in general, for what are known as reactionary measures. In 1913, at a meeting of the *Preussenbund*, or Prussian League, sentiments were expressed that raised a storm of protest all over Germany. The Berlin *Vossische Zeitung* declared that, judged by such standards, neither William I., Frederick III., nor even Blücher, the liberator of Germany, would have been eligible to the League. But the *Kreuzzeitung* defended the conservatives and declared that "the country must seek its salvation, not by merging Prussia in Germany, but by forcefully maintaining the firmly stamped Prussian individuality."

The strongest arraignment of the conservatives comes from no less a pen than that of the Imperial Chancellor Hohenlohe, himself a Bavarian. Two years before his resignation from office, on Dec. 28, 1898, he wrote in his indiscreet diary: "When I sit this way among the Prussian excellencies I see perfectly clearly the contrast between North and South Germany. South German liberalism has no chance against the *Junkers*. There are too many of them; they are too powerful and they have royalty and the army on their side. The Centre, too, goes their way. . . . All of these gentlemen snap their fingers at the empire and would prefer to abandon it to-day rather than to-morrow!"

This bitter arraignment was uttered nearly twenty years ago. Since then the Conservatives have lost some of their power. A new class of industrial princes has arisen with fortunes that overshadow those of the *Junkers*. The latter are handicapped for the reason that their lands are entailed and go to the one son, while the daughters and younger sons have to be provided for with ready money. So many estates are heavily mortgaged that a new form of insurance has been invented whereby the holder insures his life for a sum that will later lessen the debt. In the Reichstag the number of Conservative members has steadily decreased — from eighty in 1887 to only forty-eight in 1912. Even in the Prussian Diet there are far fewer *Junkers* than is popularly supposed. A recent count has shown that only about one fourth of the members of the Lower House have so much as the "*von*," the predicate of nobility, before their names. The rest are plain Herr Braun, Herr Müller, Herr Heinz, Dr. Levy, etc. Eighty-three of them are doctors of one kind or another. Germany is no feudal country. Only 22 per cent of the total territory is in estates of over two hun-

Decline of the Junkers.

dred and fifty acres, and this includes vast tracts of woodland and of unreclaimed land. A whole school of econo-
mists holds that large estates are far from being an evil
and that the highest results for agriculture can be obtained
by having large, medium-sized, and small holdings exist
side by side. And the small farmers are owners of the land
they till to a very unusual degree, only 10 per cent working
rented land.

Foreign affairs. A mere sketch must suffice for the German Empire's
foreign policies.

The Triple Alliance remained in force from 1883 to 1914.
During that time two great storm centres developed, the
one in the West and the other in the East. Disputes regarding Morocco led to trouble with France and England, while
the conflicting policies of Austria and Russia in the Balkans
still further endangered the peace.

Morocco. In 1880 an international treaty, signed at Madrid by
nearly all the powers, had settled the status of Morocco as
an independent sultanate. In 1890, after asking the consent
of the other signatories, Germany had concluded a commercial treaty with the sultan. In 1901 Germany's Moroccan trade had a value of five million marks and was increasing at a rate that was to treble it within ten years. Such
were the circumstances by which Germany justified her
interference when France and England attempted in 1905
to arrange the future of Morocco to suit their own interests.
For several years Morocco had been in a state of unrest, and
France, which already owned Algiers, had felt called upon
to interfere. Whether or not she was aiming wholly to
annex Morocco is a matter for conjecture. On the surface
it looks as though she had long been preparing the way for
such a step. A secret agreement with Spain, two treaties
with Italy, leaving the latter power free hand in Tripoli,

and a *rapprochement* with England that was the preliminary to the *Triple Entente* paved the way for such a step. On April 8, 1904, France signed an agreement giving England free hand in Egypt; a compliment which England returned to France by giving her a free hand in Morocco, while a secret clause gained the good will of Spain. This treaty was concluded without so much as a notification to Germany.

Germany's standpoint, as explained in the Reichstag by Chancellor Bülow, was the following: "We have no direct political aspirations there; we have not, like Spain, a centuries-old Moorish past, nor, like France, a M roccan boundary hundreds of 'kilometers' long; we ha e not, like those two powers, historical and moral claims won by many sacrifices. What we did have are economic interests in an independent country full of future promise. We took part in an international convention which approved the principle of the most favored nation; by treaty we possessed the rights of the most favored nation. It was a matter of German prestige not to have these disposed of without our consent, a matter affecting the honor of the German Empire in which we could not give way." "It is greatly to our interest," Bülow declared again, "that the free regions of the earth be not still further circumscribed; that the path be not closed in a commercially important and promising country to the activities of our industries and the spread of our commerce."

Bülow's standpoint on Morocco.

France, all the same, proceeded to "reform" Morocco and in such a way that the customs, the finances, and the police would be under her control as "mandatory of the European powers." The sultan of Morocco appealed to Germany and asked if the order really rested on a "European mandate." It was then that William II. made a most dramatic *coup*. On his good ship *Hamburg* he sailed to Tangiers and, being received with jubilation by the Moors,

France and Morocco.

declared that he came as a free and independent ruler who hoped that Morocco would always be open to the commerce of the world. He was met on the sultan's part by the latter's uncle, Abdel-Malek, and despatched an envoy of his own to Fez. Greeted as "Morocco's liberator and only friend," he induced the sultan to reject France's "reforms" and call a meeting of the signatories of the treaty of 1880. His whole visit lasted but three hours.

The Conference at Algeciras, 1906.

This meeting that had been called by the sultan gave place to a Conference of the European powers held at Algeciras. France had objected strenuously to its being called. Delcassé, the foreign minister, had wished, with England's aid, to administer a severe rebuff to Germany. We know now from Delcassé's own revelations that England in case of a German attack had promised to mobilize her fleet, occupy the Hamburg-Kiel canal, and land 100,000 men in Schleswig-Holstein. Germany was isolated at the conference, but the mere fact of its being held was a triumph for her. Moreover she secured the integrity of the sultan's possessions and the "open door" in Morocco.

War imminent.

But the matter was still far from settlement. In 1911 the French occupied Fez, and Spain the harbor of Larasch and the neighboring El-Ksar. Germany sent the cannon-boat *Panther* to Agadir, while Sir Edward Grey, British minister of foreign affairs, made pointed remarks in the hearing of the German ambassador as to what England would and would not permit. In fact nothing would she permit without her own participation. As Chancellor Lloyd-George expressed it, England was not going to abandon a position won by centuries of heroism and success and be treated as though she counted for nothing in the councils of the nations. There were circumstances under which peace at any price would mean humiliation too great to be borne. Germany formally notified the British government that "if it intended to confuse and involve the issue and effect a violent discharge," Lloyd-George was taking the best means to those ends by making such speeches, a communication which Sir Edward Grey found "extraordinarily stiff in tone." Altogether the danger of a European war was greater in those few days of 1911 than it had been in a generation. The turning of a hair would have made the difference.

The outcome of it all was that by a treaty (Nov. 4, 1911) Germany agreed not to interfere in Morocco and accepted compensation on the Congo, thus enlarging her colony of Cameroon. At home the German government was much blamed for having achieved such poor results, abroad the emperor's interference in the whole Morocco dispute was looked upon as uncalled for and aggressive. *The treaty of 1911.*

The Emperor's oft-cited remark about securing a "place in the sun" was originally uttered not as a programme, but as stating an accomplished fact. "We have conquered our place in the sun," he said in 1896, and added that he meant to maintain that place. That he was ever too modest in his utterances no one can maintain : "We are the salt of the earth," he said in 1895, "but we must show ourselves worthy . . . then we can stand hand on hilt, shield in ground, and cry *tamen!* Come what may !"

To characterize the emperor here would be superfluous. One episode, however, throws light simultaneously on his character and on foreign as well as internal relations. On October 28, 1907, in an interview published by the *Daily Telegraph*, the emperor pointed out how he, personally, had always been the friend of England, how he had refused the invitation of France and Russia to urge England to end the Boer war : "the English who to-day insult me, will see from it (*i.e.* from a letter he had written to the queen) how I acted in their moment of danger." He declared that he had worked out, with his general staff, the plan of campaign *The Daily Telegraph episode.*

that Lord Roberts successfully carried out. The English need not be disquieted at the increase in the German fleet; it was intended for use in the Pacific against the Japanese! All of which was very indiscreet and caused indescribable excitement in Berlin, the more so as the emperor was away at the time and the papers were full of the rather bizarre entertainments that were being provided for his pleasure by his host, Prince Egon Fürstenberg.

The emperor's surrender.

In the Reichstag Prince Bülow tried to deflect the storm on to his own head. The emperor had not a single defender. Even the leader of the Conservatives spoke of a "discontent that had been gathering for years." Bülow made a manly speech in which he promised to prevent a recurrence of the incautiousness. He pledged himself that measures to this end should be taken "without injustice but yet without any regard for the person." The interview between the Chancellor and his master lasted for several hours and the emperor made a complete surrender. The official *Reichsanzeiger* then published what amounted to a full apology to the people and a promise to do better in the future. For a time the emperor was like a Wotan with a broken spear; but the incident and its outcome in no way permanently impaired his popularity, which has steadily increased as his reign has proceeded.

Complications in the Balkans.

Regarding the difficulties of Austria with Russia and the Balkans, difficulties which were to prove so fateful for the German emperor and empire, but a few cardinal facts need to be kept in mind. Practical ownership of Bosnia and Herzegovina had been assured to Austria by Russia and by the Berlin Congress in 1878. In 1908, however, Turkey, with a reformed government, grew more assertive of her rights over those provinces. Austria decided on formal annexation. Russia and Servia put in their oars, demanding a European conference which, it was hoped, would compensate

Russia by giving her free passage through the Dardanelles and Servia in some other way. But Austria in 1909 came to a private agreement with Turkey and paid her in cash for the provinces. Germany showed her friendship for Austria by procuring from the signatories of the Berlin treaty their consent to Austria's move.

There remained the discontent of Russia and Servia. Russia, however, was still recuperating from her terrible war with Japan and was not eager for new ventures. Servia, on the other hand, took a very belligerent attitude. Many Servs inhabited the provinces in question; these provinces had entered into Servia's plans for future aggrandizement. Her aspirations were thus nipped in the bud. She tried to insist that Bosnia and Herzegovina at least be made autonomous and that she herself be compensated with other territory. She claimed that even Turkey's consent did not validate the new arrangement and harped on the idea of the European conference. She would arm day and night, she declared, and would know how to act if her interests were disregarded: Europe should see that only over a dead Servia could Bosnia become an Austrian province. Finally, however, on March 31, 1909, having made sure that Russia would not help her, she ceased her opposition. She signed a pledge to Austria "to abandon the attitude of protest assumed by her since the previous October with regard to the opposition;" and again: "to change the direction of her present policy towards Austria-Hungary and live with that power in future on a footing of friendly and neighborly relations."

Servia; 1909.

Bulgaria, Servia, and Greece had at first greeted the new "Young Turk" régime with enthusiasm. But the efforts of the new government to centralize and nationalize, and especially its endeavor to interfere with the hitherto practically independent position of the different religious bodies, began to estrange those powers. Soon the Turks came into direct

The Balkan war of 1912.

conflict with the free spirit of the almost primitive Albanians, who desired autonomy. The Albanian question was, then, one cause of the overthrow (early in 1912) of the Young Turkish government. The new government promised to fulfil the demand for autonomy.

Now Servia and Bulgaria desired neither an independent nor a powerful Albania. Already the Albanians had begun to spread out into Macedonia, which was looked upon as a field for Bulgarian expansion. There was a feeling, too, that Turkey was now too weak to offer successful resistance. With Russia's aid a close alliance was effected between Bulgaria and Servia, Greece and Montenegro, and in the autumn of 1912 the fierce drive towards Constantinople began. Kirkkilisse and Lule-Burgas fell before the Bulgarians and Kumanowo before the Servians, until finally at Tschataldscha the drive was checked. Then came a truce and a conference in London. The European powers determined to set up a free Albania under its own ruler, the Prince of Wied. In accordance with Austria's demand Servia was to have no territory and no port on the Adriatic, a provision that was to have great consequences. Foiled in her hopes of expansion in this direction, Servia turned her eyes on Macedonia, which she had agreed to leave to Bulgaria as a happy hunting-ground.

The Balkan war of 1913.

The memory of how the Balkan allies failed to agree on the distribution of their Turkish booty is still fresh. Roumania came in at the eleventh hour to secure her own compensation. Bulgaria, which had done the major part of the fighting against Turkey, was now forced at the sword's point to renounce the greater part of her booty — a considerable stretch of her territory went to Roumania, while Greece and Servia divided between them the greater part of Macedonia. Thrace had to be relinquished to the Turks, who were able to hold Adrianople and the Maritza region because

must be a mutual understanding in the interests of both countries. Good will, in this case the good will of peoples, will prove stronger than the folly of silly jingoes."

This unprecedented effort of the two parliaments to stave off the approaching war was supplemented by a visit of a British trade commission to Berlin, where they were fêted with enthusiasm and by a visit of the British fleet to the harbor of Kiel. One would have thought that an era of universal brotherhood was dawning when the murder of the heir to the throne of Austria cast the match into the powder heap and precipitated the greatest struggle in the whole history of man.

<!-- marginal note: Sarajevo. -->

CHAPTER XII

ECONOMIC PROGRESS BETWEEN 1871 AND 1914

LITERATURE: *The Handbuch der Politik,* 3 vols., has valuable articles by experts. *Deutschland unter Kaiser Wilhelm II.,* Vol II., is the most recent comprehensive treatment of the subject, containing many articles from different pens. Helfferich, *Deutschlands Volkswohlstand,* 1888–1913, gives useful tables and data which are superseded in some, though not in all, cases by the figures in the *Statistisches Jahrbuch,* 35th year, 1914. Wygodzinski, *Das Genossenschaftswesen in Deutschland* (1911) is an exhaustive and admirable treatment of the subject of coöperative societies. For agriculture see von Rümker, *Die deutsche Landwirtschaft* (Berlin, 1914).

The secrets of success.

WHAT the Elizabethan era was to literature in England, that the present generation has been to economic progress in Germany. The results surpass anything that the world has ever seen. A slow, heavy, contemplative people has been organized into efficiency much as water and steam power have been transformed into electric energy. The possibilities of coördination and coöperation have been probed and made available as never before.

Let us look at the advance in agriculture, in industry, and in commerce, and then examine the foundations on which the progress is based: government leadership, organization and coöperation, scientific investigation, and the thorough training of each individual worker. How much is due to the characteristics of the people, to their honesty, sincerity, devotion to duty, yes to their determination to win at any cost, must here be left out of account.

There was a time in the early nineties when Germany's agricultural prospects looked desperate. Russia with an

508

area forty times as great had unlimited grain for export; while on account of the fall in ocean freight rates (between 1868 and 1900 the freight charged on a hundred pounds between Chicago and Liverpool had been reduced from $3\frac{1}{2}$ shillings to only 1 shilling) it was almost more economical to buy grain from the United States or even from the Argentine Confederation than to grow it at home. The soil of Germany was unfavorable in comparison with those other countries, and many would not have been sorry to let the sandy plains in the North revert to pine forest and become, like England, an industrial country importing the greater part of its food-stuffs.

One must give the devil his due and acknowledge that it was the *Junkers* who saved Germany from this fatal course. Many ascribe all their acts to self-interest; but there are all grades even among *Junkers*, and there is among them as much concern for the good of the nation, as they see it, as is to be found in any other class of men. In answer to their clamors the tariff on grain, which had been lowered under Caprivi, was once more raised and everything was done to increase the yield of the crops. To-day Germany's agricultural products, counting the industries directly dependent on them, such as sugar refineries and distilleries, potato drying establishments, etc., have a yearly value approximating twelve billion marks. How new machinery has replaced the old, slow hand labor may be gathered from the fact that in 1882 less than 20,000 mowing machines were in use, in 1907 more than 300,000! Stated in other terms this is an increase of 1435 per cent! The population has risen from 40,000,000 in 1870 to 67,000,000 in 1913 and, besides, twice as much meat per head is consumed to-day: yet the country has succeeded in raising 95 per cent of the meat that it needs, whereas England imports about 45 per cent of all her meat. In the matter of what is known as intensive cattle

Agriculture in the nineties.

The Junkers save Germany.

The showing to-day.

raising Germany has been surpassed only by the little states of Holland, Belgium, and Denmark. The last animal census, in 1913, showed twenty-two million pigs. Curiously enough poultry seems to have been neglected. Duties are paid on eggs entering the country to the extent of some 200,000,000 marks a year, while from Russia alone 7,387,454 geese were imported in 1913. Horse and dog meat are both sold publicly, but have to pass inspection. More than 150,000 horses and 7000 dogs are on the records for 1913.

Germany's grain and potato crops.

A weakness of Germany lies in the fact that she has had to import so much of her grain — about two million tons of wheat, three million tons of barley, and one million tons of corn. She grows wheat and she grows barley, but not in sufficient quantities; while corn does not seem adapted to her soil and climate. Rye grows well, on the other hand, and is exported to the extent of nearly a million tons; while potatoes are grown in quantities that no other country can even approximately equal. Year by year the huge crops have increased, with only an occasional set-back due to natural conditions: 43 million tons in 1903, fifty million tons in 1912, sixty-four million tons in 1915. The average harvests are now at least 80 per cent greater than they were in 1887, for not only has the area cultivated increased, but the yield to the acre has made phenomenal strides. It is a commentary on the relative excellence of the methods of agriculture in the two countries when we find that in 1912, with three million more acres under cultivation with the crop than Germany, Russia's actual yield was nineteen million tons less! But in yield to the acre Germany excels every country on the globe, not only as regards potatoes, but also as regards wheat, rye, barley, and oats. In the past ten years her own average yield of grain per acre has increased by 150 pounds. It needs only an increase of another hundredweight per acre to make her self-supporting, entirely independent of foreign countries; and that estimate is made on the basis of the area now under cultivation, whereas there are millions of acres of swamp land that can be reclaimed.

A crop that coins money for Germany is the sugar beet. In 1910, 354 sugar factories extracted the sugar from more than 15½ million tons of beets; and the value of the output, about one third of which was exported to England, amounted to some 625 million marks. In 1912 more than ten million acres were planted to sugar beets as opposed to only six and a half million in 1887.

The few instances we have studied will suffice as illustrations of Germany's agricultural progress. But perhaps the best products from the farms are the men and women who work on them. The statistics from the country are in the most marked contrast to those from the cities. The birth rate is higher, as is also the proportion of those fit for military service who present themselves at the regular yearly muster. Latterly there has been a great increase in the number of women employed on the farms : two and a half million according to the agricultural census of 1882; four and a half million according to the census of 1907. They are for the most part, of course, members of the family of the owners of the farm. The increase is mainly due to the fact that the men migrate to the industrial centres and it is a blessing that the women are willing to step into the breach. The rough work on the farms has of late more and more been done by so-called seasonal workmen — a rather low grade of foreigners, for the most part Russian Poles, who wander about in bands and break up the land or gather in the harvests. Even women go round in such bands. The German has felt humiliated at having to employ these foreigners, about half of whom turn to industry, half to agriculture. They are obliged to take out cards of legitimation and to quit the country by a given day. Not far from a million such cards

The sugar beet.

The workers or the farms.

were issued in 1913. The Polish women are immensely powerful; the author has seen them excavating for an artificial lake and throwing the earth far above their heads into cars that waited on the rails.

Industrial development.

If we turn now to industry its achievements since the founding of the empire have been still more remarkable than those of agriculture. After 1871 the spirit of enterprise ran high, and there was enormous expansion due largely to the fact that France's indemnity of five billion francs found its way indirectly into hundreds of undertakings. There was wild speculation, finally; company after company was formed, building after building erected. But it was too great a discounting of the future. In 1873 came a crash from which the country did not recover for fully ten years. Many wished that the indemnity had never been exacted, and a French authority asserts that Germany would willingly have returned the sum to France but that France would have refused to accept it. One is reminded of the ring of the Nibelungen that brought such ill luck to all of its possessors. What Germany had gained, however, was valuable experience; and the growth during the eighties, if slow, was based on firm foundations. There were fluctuations, of course, as in 1907, when the panic that had such severe consequences in America affected the whole world. But the year 1912 may be looked upon as the high tide of prosperity in the history of the German Empire, and it is doubtful if for decades to come the same magnificent showing will be made again. It is a significant fact that in that year the emigration figures fell to 18,545, a vast contrast to 1881, when they reached 220,902. England's emigration figures for 1912 were 467,762; and Italy's, 711,446!

Output of coal.

In determining the extent of a country's economic progress the output of such basic products as coal and iron will always be an important factor. From iron, of course, all the machinery of industry is made, while coal still supplies the greater part of the motive power. Germany's finest coal regions are in Westphalia and in Silesia. Near Essen, Werden, Dahlhausen, and in a few other places it crops to the surface, but as a rule the coal is very far down in the bowels of the earth. In the Ruhr valley, where are some of the richest mines, the veins or strata are shallow and are separated from each other by layers of limestone and slate, a condition of things which makes mining especially difficult. A single shaft may run through sixty or seventy such layers, and more accidents occur from the falling slate and stone than from explosions. The total German coal supply is roughly estimated at a hundred billion tons, though it is believed that, could certain difficulties of mining be overcome, double that amount could eventually be extracted. In 1912 Germany mined no less than 240 million tons, besides importing 17 million tons. This is less by 36 million tons than England and far less than the United States of America; but the interesting fact to note is that Germany has trebled her output since 1886. In the Ruhr valley alone there are nearly 350 shafts and more than 300,000 miners are employed.

Of iron ore Germany produces more and of a better quality than any other country in Europe; yet so great are her requirements for her manufactures that she is at the same time the largest importer, having purchased in 1913 alone more than fourteen million tons. In 1902 she was turning out the same quantity of pig iron as England, which was less than nine million tons, while by 1912 she had almost doubled England's output. Between 1887 and 1911 the one country increased her production by 387 per cent, the other by only 30 per cent. For steel the showing is still more amazing. Germany's output increased between 1886 and 1910 from 954,600 tons to 13,698,600 or 1335 per cent as opposed to England's 154.1 per cent. Characteristic of German

Iron output.

methods is the extent to which old iron is utilized. Nearly 210,000 tons of it were imported from France, Belgium, and Holland in 1913, while the Saxon railroads alone furnished 17,000 tons. Yearly the conversion of scrap and of old iron plays a more and more considerable rôle, and it is estimated that by 1940 as much pig iron will be made in this way as from the fresh ore.

Iron manu-factures. There is no end to the variety of Germany's iron manufactures. One firm alone, the M. A. N. (Machine Works Augsburg-Nuremburg), turns out iron-ribbed festival halls, bridges, viaducts, ship-landings for dangerous coasts like the one at Duala, dry-docks, Zeppelin sheds, and even huge roller dams to stem but not stop the tide of rivers. Such products, even the roller dams, it exports to all parts of the world. Yet the M. A. N. is by no means the largest iron foundry in Germany. Machinery headed the list of the country's exports in 1912, with a total value of well over six hundred million marks, while the value of the other iron-products came to almost as much more. The value of the machinery exported has increased more than tenfold since 1887, for it amounted in that year to only 52,800,000 marks.

Increase in the use of elec-tricity. The increase in the use of electricity both for lighting and for industrial purposes is almost as good a gauge of the country's prosperity as is her output of coal or iron. The 4000 public electric plants now in use represent a capital of more than three billion marks, while some of the private plants rival the public ones. It has been reckoned that 50,000 men have been employed each year in erecting new plants or enlarging old ones. No less than 17,500 communities had current at their disposal in 1913, seven thousand more than in 1911! Motors have been installed in even the smallest shops, and the work of many a sempstress has been lightened by an electric attachment to her machine. High tension lines bring current to at least two-thirds of the population; the power is obtained wherever it can be had most cheaply, often near the mouth of a mine or occasionally in the midst of a peat-bog.   Many square miles of such bogs are now being reclaimed for agricultural and for settlement purposes, and the bogs themselves supply the power for their regeneration.   In Bavaria the state has practically made electric power from watercourses a monopoly, and the current is to be distributed in the manner that will best promote the welfare of the inhabitants.   In consequence of the spread of the use of electricity Germany has worked up a flourishing industry in electric appliances, her exports, not including cars, vans, and cycles, having attained a value of 300,000,000 marks.

It would be monotonous to give an account in detail of the progress made in all the different industries.   Some idea of that progress as a whole may be gained in other ways. For one thing, by observing the growth of a new form of business enterprise, the limited liability company.   First permitted and legalized in 1892, there were, by 1909, no less than 16,500 such companies.   Again the fact that between 1885 and 1911 the tonnage of German ocean-going ships has trebled is illuminating.   During the same period the total tonnage of American and of French ships has scarcely increased at all.   Germany in 1913 had a total foreign trade of twenty-two and a half billion marks, outstripping the for-eign trade of the United States of America by four billion marks.   Yet the United States has a much greater popu-lation and a territory sixteen times as large.   Germany's trade still lags behind Great Britain's, but has grown since 1887 by 214 per cent as opposed to England's growth of only 113 per cent.   Already in 1887 it had overhauled France's trade; in 1913 it surpassed that trade by as much as ten billion marks!

Nor does foreign trade by any means tell the whole story:

Other indications of progress.

Inland
traffic.

the increase in inland traffic is equally phenomenal. The German railways more than doubled their trackage between 1895 and 1911, and the same is true of the rolling stock and of the number of employees. The amount of freight carried on the railroads has increased from approximately four hundred million tons in 1903 to seven hundred million tons in 1912, the number of passengers from 950 million to 1750 million. The number of boats plying the rivers, lakes, and canals has risen from 20,000 to 30,000 since 1887, and 4000 of them are now propelled by their own power. The secret of all this, as I have intimated, lies in government initiative, example, and control; in organization on the part of the people themselves; in scientific investigation that gives a sound basis for progress; and in the training of the individual.

The
Prussian
state
railways.

As an example of what government initiative and control can accomplish one need only point to the Prussian state railroads, the consolidation of which we have described in the previous chapter. What private railroads still exist in Prussia are there because the state encourages them; it even subsidizes small lines, having, alone in that way, expended 109 million marks up to April, 1912. The small lines serve as feeders to the large ones, and nearly all end at the main railroad stations. The gross capital-investment of the Prussian state was reckoned in 1911 at more than eleven billion marks. For 1912 the net profit was 539,954,000 marks. The state is assured of a regular yearly revenue by the establishment of a huge fund or *Ausgleichfonds* designed to insure against chance fluctuations in earnings. The financial showing is altogether of the most brilliant, although there are many other benefits besides the earning of revenue. In time of war there is a vast difference between owning the means of transportation and having to hire them. Or, again, the most delicate adjustments are possible when it is a matter of encouraging trade or dampening foreign competition. Since 1888 the Prussian railways have issued approximately 100 important special or exceptional rate-tables. There are even so-called "regular exceptional rate-tables" — one for wood, one for goods forwarded in a mass, such as earth, ore, potatoes, sugar beets, etc. There is a special rate-table for potash in the rough, another for agricultural lime, another for road-making materials. When Germany needs meat from Holland the rates are made low, when Holland is likely to import from Germany the reverse is the case.

There are few countries in the world that can point to a steady average decrease of rates in the last twenty-five years, yet that is Prussia's happy position. Between 1888 and 1911 the average charge per ton has decreased from 4.27 marks to four marks; while the average kilometer-ton has sunk from 3.71 pfennige to 3.51 pfennige. The general passenger rates in force in 1914 had been established in 1907 with a loss of income to the railroads of 15,600,000 marks, — a loss made up only to the extent of nine million marks by withdrawing the privilege of free baggage. Comparison with the rates of other countries is rendered impossible by the fact that bulkier freight like coal and iron is transported by water wherever possible, by all the rebates, by the extra payment for certain trains, by the many classes for passengers, by the above-mentioned restriction as to baggage, and by the frequent special reductions for excursions and on holidays. *Railroad rates.*

The benefits of the Prussian railway system are by no means purely local. There is now such close coöperation between the states that the utmost unity prevails. By an agreement made in 1909, if you hire a freight car and load it with your goods it can go from end to end of the empire without annoying formalities, and the empty car need not even be returned to the state from which it started. In *Unity of the whole German system.*

the same way you can purchase a direct passenger ticket to any destination.

Water-ways.

Although canals and natural waterways are the chief rivals of the railways, the Prussian government has spent enormous sums on their development. One can travel for weeks on the water in central Germany; it is a favorite sport with school crews. By canals scheduled for completion in 1914 one can travel from the Rhine to the Ems and Weser, each of which rivers is in the centre of a new system of harbors and canals. A project had been started for a deep, broad canal to leave the Rhine at Wesel and divert all its traffic to the sea at Emden, thus altogether avoiding Holland. Much has already been done in the way of deepening river channels, much more was in prospect. On her own portion of the Rhine alone Prussia has already expended twenty million marks, while Bavaria, Baden, and Alsace-Lorraine are at work deepening the river to an average depth of seven feet between Mannheim and Strassburg. A further plan to make the river navigable, or build canals, all the way to the Lake of Constance is under discussion, and a special international association exists with that end in view; while Württemberg had already determined to regulate the depth of the Neckar. Bavaria was seriously discussing a most ambitious plan to run a wide canal from the River Main to the Danube and on to Munich and Augsburg, at a cost of hundreds of millions of marks.

Canals.

As our only object is to show in broad outline in what ways the German governments seek to further commerce there is no need to enumerate all the canals built or to mention all the projects on hand. Roughly speaking two and a half billion marks have been expended on inland waterways during the present reign, and the spending of as much more was in nearer or more distant prospect. Some of the canals are no inconsiderable feats of engineering. Not to speak of the broad Kiel-Hamburg canal, built at an expense of 379 millions, the new Berlin-Stettin canal, opened in June 1914, has very interesting features. The water passes over a deep valley on an earthen arch or bridge, and one can stand and watch the strange sight of ships sailing above and trains passing through below. Again, the water which escapes from one part of the canal is made to generate the electricity that pumps water back into another part.

One of the noteworthy developments of the last quarter century is the inland harbor, the building of which is usually the concern of the city governments. There are harbors which are strictly commercial and there are also so-called industrial harbors where factories and warehouses are built, each with direct access to the water. The cities along the great rivers buy large tracts of low-lying land and then cut canals and cross canals just as though they were laying out streets. The walls of these blind canals are of stone or reinforced concrete, are built very solidly, and have every facility for landing the boats and for lifting the cargoes. Frankfort has great travelling cranes that seem endowed with almost human intelligence as they run and turn and twist and pull.

Duisburg, the largest of the many Rhine harbors, has an area of a thousand acres of which only about one-half is water. Lying in the heart of the great iron and coal districts and with the broad Dortmund-Ems canal running from it, it had a traffic of more than forty-one million tons in 1910, and is comparable only to Hamburg. Other important harbors are those of Berlin, Mannheim, Düsseldorf and Cologne. The Mannheim harbor, at the junction of the Neckar and the Rhine, covers about 700 acres and represents an enormous amount of planning and of labor. It is said of it that where now there is land there was formerly water, and where now there is water there was formerly land. Through this development of its facilities for traffic Mannheim has become

Duisburg.

Mann-
heim.

the granary of Germany and also the centre for the distribution of the American Standard Oil Company's products. It is the destination for cargoes from all over the world that are transshipped in Holland. The railroad tracks run to the very point where the Neckar and Rhine meet, and here are the great oil vats from which the tank cars are filled by means of great tubes.

Ludwigs-
hafen.

Directly across the Rhine from Mannheim and almost a part of the same harbor system is Ludwigshafen, the site of the world-renowned Baden Aniline and Soda factory, which turns out a great proportion of the dyes used in industry. The traffic of the greater Mannheim harbor, if we may so call it, has risen from less than a million tons in 1875 to nearly ten million in 1912. Düsseldorf's harbor was not completed until 1896, since which time her population has risen from 180,000 to 397,000 and her water traffic from four hundred thousand tons to a million and a half tons, — an eloquent argument for inland harbors. Canals have their harbors, too. Along the new Duisburg-Hanover-Minden canal provision has been made for no less than sixty-five of them at a cost of 47,000,000 marks.

Düssel-
dorf.

Govern-
mental
solicitude.

Providing cheap transportation facilities is but one way in which German state and municipal governments aid industry and commerce. They aid them also by favorable taxation and by protective legislation. These are subjects too deep for us to enter into here, but with regard to the first point one could instance the separate special tax that is laid upon the large department stores so as to handicap them, as it were, and prevent their crowding out the smaller tradespeople. As to protective legislation nothing could be more drastic than the laws of 1909 against unfair competition.

These laws affect not merely the petty tradesmen but even the great enterprises and concern themselves with the following evils: unjustifiable assertions in advertising, fake clear-

ance and bankrupt sales, spreading calumnies about competitors, betraying trade secrets, misusing labels, bribing
employees, and making misrepresentations either as to
quantity or quality. The design of the laws is not so much
to protect the individual as it is to raise the whole tone of
German trade. It is part of a campaign for world-conquest;
and for fear that the laws are not sufficiently comprehensive
there is a general blanket clause condemning any act that is
contrary to *gute Sitten*, or trade morality, and intended to
apply to professional men as well as to tradesmen.

"Unfair competition laws."

A few clauses from the "unfair competition" laws will
show their extreme severity, and laws in Germany are not
allowed to remain a dead letter. One of them runs: "whoever, after announcing a clearance sale, offers at it goods
specially procured for the purpose is punishable with imprisonment up to one year and with a fine up to 5000 marks or
with either one of these penalties." The same penalties
are to strike "whoever in business intercourse, from motives
of rivalry, offers, promises, or hands gifts or advantages to an
employee or commissioner of a business firm, with a view
through such person's improper conduct to securing prefer-
ential treatment for himself or another in the purchase of
goods or the performance of services in the line of trade."

Severity of the "unfair competition" laws.

The German government stands like a protecting wall
behind commerce and industry; likewise behind agriculture.
Just as there is a *Bundesrat*, or Federal Council, for political
matters, so there is a *Landwirtschaftsrat*, or agricultural
council to which all the different states send delegates and the
sessions of which are often attended by the emperor. Each
individual state has, in addition, its own agricultural department.

The government and agriculture.

Governmental leadership alone could never have brought
either agriculture or industry to the pitch of prosperity
to which they had attained just before the outbreak of the

war. A second main factor of success has been what we may call internal organization, which does not, however, mean that the government has had nothing to do with the process. Even in the case of syndicates and coöperative societies it has had its hand in the game. At intervals it takes a census both for agriculture and for industry. It counts the produce and the livestock down to the individual hen, yes, where it is a question of proportional production, down to three-eighths of a goat! Its statistics are the most thoroughly digested and the most practical of those of any country in the world.

Chambers of agriculture.

Apart from the *Landwirtschaftsrat* and the *Landesökonomiekollegien*, or state agricultural departments, there is a great "German Agricultural Society" founded in 1885 on the model of the famous British institution as a centre for scientific investigation and practical experimentation. In addition there are innumerable local agricultural societies. Since 1894 regular "chambers of agriculture" have been established in the great majority of states — one for each province. The Prussian law provides that the "chambers" shall look after the agricultural and forestry interests of their districts, aid the local administrative boards with information, have experts draw up reports, further the technical progress of agriculture, and investigate prices on the produce exchanges and in the markets. The "chambers" again, since 1898, have a "Centre for the performance of common tasks of the chambers of agriculture," which now forms one department of the *Landesökonomiekollegium*.

Coöperative societies.

Extremely characteristic of German organization methods is this close knitting together of associations by means of centres or *Zentralstellen*. We see it in the labor bureaus, of which we shall speak in the next chapter; we see it in the trades-unions; and we see it in the *Genossenschaften* or coöperative societies that have been developed to a higher degree in Germany than in any other country. The Anglo-Saxon thinks of the coöperative mainly as an institution that enables the purchasing of goods more cheaply than in the common market. To the German farmer his society is a guide, philosopher, and friend. It helps him not only to purchase all his supplies, the quality of which it guarantees, but it secures him credit at as favorable rates as the greatest capitalist could procure; it disposes of his products for him, and even undertakes to work his raw materials into forms in which they will be more remunerative. There are no less than seventeen forms of coöperative societies, classed according to the services which they render. There were 31,757 societies in 1912, with 5,555,803 members, and if we reflect that only one member from a family is apt to join, it is evident that about one-third of the German population benefit directly from the institution.

The coöperative movement is essentially German. It began in 1850, when the shoemakers of Delitzsch were induced by one Schulze to borrow 960 thalers on their collective responsibility and buy their leather in a lump at the Leipzig fair. About the same time Raiffeisen, a burgomaster in the Westerwald, began organizing societies of farmers along much the same lines. Both were active in the matter for years, Schulze-Delitzsch dying in 1883, Raiffeisen in 1888. Between 1890 and 1911 more than fifteen thousand new societies were founded, while even between 1907 and 1912 the number was increased by six thousand. The law requires that for purposes of supervision each society shall belong to some recognized league, or *Verband* as it is called. Chief among these is the "Imperial League of German Agricultural Societies," known for short as the *Reichsverband,* and to it belong nearly half of all the societies. Next in size comes the "Central League of German Consumers' Associations," while the Schulze-Delitzsch and the

Progress of the coöperative movement.

Raiffeisen leagues are to-day relatively unimportant. The leagues do much more than supervise; they encourage the organization of new societies and help in every way to set them on their feet. While the vast majority of the societies (26,026 out of the 31,715) are agricultural, those in the towns have a proportionately larger membership, being popular with the Social Democrats. Between the leagues and the thousands of societies are 120 central and main societies. They are called central societies when they do merely a credit and loan business, main societies when they have other objects in view. Back of the leagues and of the central societies is the most interesting institution of all — the heart of the system, so to speak — the Prussian Central Coöperative Society Exchequer, known as the *Preussenkasse*. Founded in 1895 and aided by the Prussian government to the extent of 75,000,000 marks, a sum which would be increased if needed, it is an inexhaustible reservoir of credit and does a business of about a billion marks a year. The rate of interest charged is extremely low, only $3\frac{1}{2}$ per cent, and the loans are made, not to individuals save in rare cases, but to the leagues and central societies, to communal savings banks, and occasionally to large single coöperative societies. An interesting feature, a much debated novelty when the bank started in 1895, is that the bank loans not merely on tangible securities but on the general credit of the societies and of the members who compose them, and that, for the purpose of estimating the amount of credit to be allowed, the state permits access even to the secret data collected by the tax assessors.

Central coöperative societies.

Distinct from the coöperative societies and almost equally important are the organizations known as *Vereine*, or associations for the purpose of furthering the interests of some particular trade or branch of trade, or of trade in some particular region or locality. British consular reports from

Vereine, or associations.

all parts of the world are unanimous in asserting that these *Vereine* are a highly important factor in German success. Their number is countless, their activities are limitless; they set in motion every bit of machinery that can further their ends.   For instance the Stettin *Verein* for the development of oversea relations establishes classes for foreign languages and commercial geography, has a library of works on foreign commerce, and also a fund from which the travelling expenses of those sent to look over the ground are paid. An English writer calis this "disseminating spies throughout the world"; but it is this aristocratic way of looking at things on the part of England that has cost her a large part of her trade.   "We receive by each boat," writes the governor of the Bahamas, "English wares absolutely unsalable, quite unsuited to the climate and the needs of the consuming public."   "In China," writes the consul at Shanghai, "tea and silk are the aristocratic trades; our compatriots therefore deign to take an interest in them.   But to touch any of the other articles would be considered altogether *infra dignitatem*.   These other articles, therefore, go to our competitors."   The German treats this matter of trade psychologically.   He knows the language and can read the mind of his customer.   In his Verein he has profited by the experiences of his predecessors.   He knows that the catalogues must be printed in the language of the country, that his prices must be given in the local currency.   "The English manufacturer," writes the British consul at Hamburg, "always lives in the belief that his customers ought to take what he likes, not that he should supply them with what they desire."   In Stettin, on the other hand, the Verein maintains a museum of dolls and models showing the costumes of every country so that the tailors and clothiers can study them.   They make the national or habitual dress for all the people under the sun, and of exactly the color and material desired. In 1897 Stettin exported no less than 70,000 tons of ready-made clothing!

A Frenchman, Bérard, has extolled the German character to the skies in connection with the *Vereine*: "The small immediate profit of the individual is almost always subordinate to the more distant but greater advantage to the nation. . . . The German *Vereine* have shown the maximum of mutual moderation and liberality."

That in such a land of collectivism as Germany labor also should combine for mutual advantage is not surprising.

Trades-unions.

Trades-unions are organized somewhat similarly to the coöperative societies. They have a larger membership than in any other country, but, on the whole, are less aggressive than elsewhere. Between 1910 and 1912 England, with a much smaller population, had a million more persons on strike. The figures for 1912, too, show that a much smaller proportion of strikes are successful in Germany, a fact doubtless due to the better organization of the employers among themselves. In the United States of America 73 per cent of the strikes were successful in 1899, compared to only 26 per cent in Germany, a ratio, however, that has been modified since then. Germany had more than four million trades-unionists in 1912, besides nearly 800,000 belonging to confessional associations designed to further trade interests. This is an enormous increase over 1871, when organized labor had a following of but 6000.

The "Free unions."

By far the majority of the German trades-unionists belong to the *Freie Gewerkschaften*, or free unions, which are mainly social democratic. Their membership was 2,530,390 in 1912, including 216,462 women. Strange to say, the unions represent the moderate element in the social democratic party, having frowned on the general strike propaganda as well as on the repeated attempts to celebrate the first of May as a protest against the long working hours. They have been accused by the more radical socialists of holding a "petty tradesman's point of view" and there have been violent scenes at party gatherings. In 1906 the scale was all but turned the other way.

There are "Hirsch-Duncker" unions, which are too mild to be popular; also "Christian unions" that have been attacked with success by the church, which "suffered" Catholics to belong to them for a while, but only "so long as on account of unforeseen circumstances this suffrance does not cease to be advisable or permissible." The Pope has latterly made good his claim to have the bishops supervise the Christian unions, although they have many protestant members, and this on the ground that "whatever a Christian does, even in managing earthly affairs he must not disregard supernatural benefits. . . . All his actions, in respect to their agreement with natural and divine law are subject to the judgment and sentence of the church." The latest unions are the *Wirtschaftsfriedliche*, commonly known as the "yellows," which consider that they have the same interests as their employers, and do not even maintain a strike fund. They have a membership of approximately 250,000, which is doing well for an organization not founded until 1906.

Other "unions."

One of the strong tendencies in the industrial world has been that towards greater and greater concentration. The homely little article known as the "Kohinoor," a press button used on women's skirts, is practically a monopoly of one firm with branches in Dresden, Prague, and Wrschowitz, and agencies in Vienna, London, Paris, New York, and Montreal. To go to the other extreme of the scale, almost the whole steel production is in the hands of the *Stahlwerksverband*, a league of thirty-one firms entered into for the purpose of regulating supply and demand. The Rhenish-Westphalian Coal Syndicate controls 54 per cent of the whole German output, and all but 2 or 3 per cent of the production of the richest mines,

Tendency toward concentration.

those of the Ruhr district. The mines deliver to the syndicate and the syndicate does the selling. The same process is going on in the banking world, the four D. banks (Deutsche, Dresdener, Darmstadter, and Diskonto) having absorbed hundreds of smaller institutions. A concentration process of a different kind and one that helps to neutralize the other is going on simultaneously. In order not to have to pay the coal syndicate's prices the Krupp iron works at Essen have acquired their own coal mines. This company, which already in 1912 employed nearly 70,000 persons, also owns its own wharves and its own line of steamers.

"Concerns." Akin to syndicates and also to the form of organization just described are the so-called "concerns." The great Siemens electric "concern," that deals in almost everything into which electricity enters, disposes of a capital of hundreds of millions of marks and has 169 agencies in different parts of the world. Another "concern," the "Allgemeine Elektrizität-Gesellschaft," is organized on an equally grand scale, while single companies with high tension lines count whole cities among their customers.

Science and progress. We have spoken of government leadership and of organization as factors in Germany's economic progress. We must not forget the credit due to her scientists. But for their long, patient devotion to the cause, their years of theorizing before the practical applications could be made, their constant watchfulness in keeping abreast of the needs, the country would never have attained such a lead in the race. This applies to agriculture as well as to industry.

Schulz-Lupitz. The discovery made by Schulz-Lupitz that clovers and similar plants grown on the ground and ploughed into it would be as beneficial to the soil as some of the expensive fertilizers has revolutionized the farming of poor lands. Rimpau-Kunau, on the other hand, found that the excess of nitrogen in swampy soils could be neutralized with the help

Rimpau-Kunau.

of potash, which, in Germany, is obtainable in quantities that are inexhaustible. At the same time von Lochow, Beseler, Heine, Paulsen and others have, by cross-breeding and by cross-fertilization, greatly improved the strains of cattle and the varieties of plants. Not only, for instance, has the yield of sugar beets to the acre been improved, but as much sugar can now be extracted from three beets as formerly from four. Another notable achievement that has proved of inestimable value is the discovery of a process for drying potatoes and reducing them to a meal which can be used like flour. It is reckoned that formerly one-tenth of the crop went to waste through rotting or freezing; this loss can be almost entirely eliminated by the new discovery, and there are now a number of coöperative potato-drying plants. A way has been found, too, of so drying the leaves both of beets and of potatoes that they can be fed to cattle like hay. Since the outbreak of the war scientists have discovered many substitutes for the kinds of food that have grown scarce, but this knowledge is kept secret in great part.

Von Lochow, Beseler, etc.

The share of science in the growth of industry is incalculable. The fact, for instance, that to-day Germany's steel and iron output nearly doubles that of England is largely due to new processes of smelting, the English having clung to the plain Bessemer method. Siemens and Martini evolved a process by which each smelting oven becomes a sort of Bunsen burner, giving out the hottest kind of flame. The air is first heated in tall towers and then blown by means of huge bellows into the ovens. The great chimney-like structures that one sees when passing through the German iron district are often not chimneys at all but hot-air towers. In the ovens, as is well known, a gas is generated, known as carbon dioxide, which is essential to the process of smelting. It remained for German thrift and for German science to find that in the new type of ovens

Science and industry.

Utilizing oven gas.

much more gas is generated than is actually required in the smelting and to invent an engine that can transmute this fuel into electric power.   The first gas engine of the kind was put in use in 1895, and the Augsburg-Nuremburg Machine Factory, which holds the patent, has since turned them out in considerable numbers.   Individual iron-works obtain sufficient power in this way to run all their rolling mills and other machinery, while often there still remains a sufficient surplus of current to light small towns and villages.   By various inventions the ovens themselves have been so improved that one of them can now turn out from 65 to 70,000 tons a year when formerly the capacity was only 19,000.

New inventions in coal-mining. In coal-mining, new inventions and appliances have achieved results almost as important.   Quicksands, formerly a serious interruption when sinking shafts, can now be frozen stiff and kept in that condition until the force is prepared to cope with them.   Shafts can be sunk, too, without the usual costly lining by driving a circle of deep artesian wells and pouring in concrete.   The concrete spreads among the rifts in the rock and, as it hardens, prevents the danger of caving in.   Science, too, has devised methods by which millions of tons of coal which formerly could not be extracted because of danger from falling slate can now be mined.   Great quantities of rubble from the surface are pumped into the cavities, and the great pillars of coal that were formerly left as supports can now be utilized.

Coal-tar products. But it is in the utilization of by-products that German science has achieved its most remarkable results.   One has only to think of the many valuable substances that have been extracted from coal tar, of the great dye industry that had put the whole world into vassalage.   To the very Orient, which once supplied the markets with indigo, Germany has been exporting an artificial product that has almost put an end to the growing of the natural plant.

The daily production of artificial indigo was reckoned before the war at no less than twenty tons. Some of the most valued drugs in medicine, too, are derived from coal tar: aspirin, antipyrine, phenacetine, sulfonal, trional, veronal. Salvarsan, too, a specific for a horrible and hitherto almost incurable disease, is a product of German science.

To what extent chemical science has become transmuted into practical benefits can be gathered from the fact that, in 1894, employees in chemical factories drew salaries totalling 99 million marks, whereas in 1912 the sum was 325 million! The chemical exports in the latter year rose to the great total of 825 million marks, though the necessary imports of raw materials greatly reduce the clear gain to the country. *Exports of chemicals.*

The hope of the future is placed not in fluctuating markets but in still further improvement of the products. The great chemical plants have splendidly equipped laboratories and libraries and employ hundreds of scientists (the Baden Aniline and Soda works alone some two hundred and fifty) whose chief work is to keep abreast of discoveries or to make inventions of their own. Some 20,000 patents already attest their achievements.

If the battle of Waterloo was won on the playgrounds of Eton, Germany's industrial battles have been won in her institutes of technology, her trade schools and her industrial continuation schools. The rise and development of these scientific and technical institutions are a distinguishing mark of German civilization during the period since 1871. *Industrial training.*

To begin with the *Technische Hochschulen,* or, as we should call them, the polytechnic schools and institutes of technology. Previously to 1870 they were of small importance and not until 1900 when, largely through the present Emperor's initiative, it became possible to obtain the degree of " Doctor *Institutes of technology.*

of Engineering" (Dr. Ing.) were they considered as in any way on a plane with the universities. Even then, Prussia's universities, like dames jealous of their social position, obtained the reservation that the doctor diploma of the scientific schools must be written in German as opposed to Latin. About an average of one hundred students a year have taken their doctor's degree in the new institutions since the old restrictions were removed.

There are now eleven *Technische Hochschulen,* one each in Berlin, Munich, Aix-la-Chapelle, Brunswick, Darmstadt, Dresden, Hanover, Carlsruhe, Stuttgart, Danzic and Breslau. They are all organized on the same general principle, with academic freedom, power to choose their own rectors or heads, and with recognition by the state of their diplomas for those entering its service. The state railways especially offer a broad field for scientifically trained men, but so do a number of other state and city-run enterprises. For these, then, the *Hochschulen* are regular recruiting grounds, — one more example of how in Germany all elements are made to serve each other and conduce to the same end.

Curricu-
lum of the
*Hoch-
schulen.*

The model on which the *Hochschulen* were based was the French *école polytechnique* and, as is the case in that institution, the interests of higher science are always kept in the foreground. To be sure there have been conflicts between those favoring this direction and those who wish more practical training; and concessions to both sides have so increased the requirements that the German scientific student is apt to enter very late upon his life work. The demands of the government service, too, have tended to crowd the curriculum. Officials were needed who were not only experts but who also knew something of economic and legal questions, and some of the schools have introduced courses on those subjects. The new practical uses of electricity, on the other hand, the changes in motors and machinery caused by the advances in ship-building and in aëroplane construction, the wide application of chemistry to industry have necessitated such additions to the plants of the *Hochschulen* that they bear little resemblance to the old type of school with its one physical and its one chemical laboratory.

The merchant class has its own special commercial institutes, the *Handelshochschulen,* which are supported by the city governments or by the chambers of commerce. The first school of this new type was opened at Leipzig in 1898. There is now one at Aix-la-Chapelle, one at Cologne, one at Frankfort, one at Berlin, one at Mannheim, one at Munich, and one at Königsberg. They are institutions for scientific investigation in the field of production and consumption in the markets of the world. They are of university grade, with academic freedom, and in Berlin, in June, 1914, there was a student strike because the removal of a professor was effected by the commercial body that financed the school, in a way that was considered arbitrary. But on the whole there is not the same uniformity of organization or of goal as in the technological institutes. The period of study covers four semesters or terms — five for those who wish to take a diploma as "teachers of commerce." The curricula, too, show general uniformity and include political economy, commercial law, history and theory of commerce, geography, the study of materials, physics, chemistry and languages.

One great achievement of the *Handelshochschulen* is the raising of the social level of the merchant class, inasmuch as the demands on the intelligence, in the upper circles at least, are now as strenuous as in many of the higher professions. More and more men so trained will be called, too, to take leading places in the service of the state.

Trade schools are now to be found in great numbers all over Germany and often they are housed in splendid buildings. They are financed either by the state, the com-

Commercial institutes.

Trade schools.

munity or by industrial or commercial corporations, such as boards of trade. They are called *Fachschulen,* the word *Fach* in this case meaning occupation or calling. Different branches of industry like building, machine-making, metal work, and weaving have their own schools. There are also a great number of industrial art schools for decorators, furniture designers, jewellers, engravers, lithographers, and the like. These schools have their regular students through the day and often, in addition, give Sunday and evening classes for the benefit of those who already have to work for their living. These schools have broken away from old traditions and, since early in the nineties, encourage origi-nality of design instead of slavishly following old models. The work has become more and more practical and has so increased in popularity that in the winter of 1912–13 in the Prussian schools alone there were 3525 day scholars and 11,738 evening scholars. The other states, following the example of Prussia, have taken over the direction of the schools for the building trade. Since 1899 there is a normal curriculum for these building-trade schools for the whole empire and, since 1908, this curriculum has been broadened so as to cover five semesters. There are always two divi-sions, one for above-ground work or *Hochbau* and the other for below-ground or *Tiefbau*. All the students work together for the first three terms, after which the nature of the tasks becomes different.

Schools for metal workers.

Similar to the organization of the building-trades schools is that of the schools for metal workers, also in the hands of the states and with a unified and common curriculum drawn up in 1910. Included in the category are schools for machine-makers and schools, in Kiel and in Hamburg, for ship-building and ship machinery. The states also con-tribute to the support of schools for textile industries, but have not sought to control them. There is in Germany no

Other trade schools.

trade that has to be learned by haphazard methods. As a help to the dwellers on the North Sea and on the Baltic the Prussian state has even organized navigation schools and special schools for the machinists of steamers. Both Prussia and Saxony have schools for training workers in mines. There are schools, too, for training women for special occupations like glove making, lace making, and embroidery. The schools for housekeeping are especially numerous. There are four institutions run by the Prussian state which give courses extending over the whole year and including cooking, baking, preserving, washing and ironing, the use of the sewing-machine, hygiene and the care of children and of sick people. The course can be extended to include millinery, fancy work, drawing, and painting. Such courses are attended not so much by amateurs as by persons intending to earn their livelihood.

But Germany's distinct contribution to the cause of industrial training, the greatest educational contribution to the present generation, is the *Fortbildungschule*, or continuation school. Here 96 per cent of the youth of Germany are cared for. In Prussia alone, in 1912, there were 2637 of these schools with a total of 455,478 scholars. The schools are not all of one type — some are compulsory, a few are voluntary. Some require a few hours out of the week, others require many. Some have evening classes. The general aim is to get hold of the children after they have left the elementary school and train them as men and women, as citizens and as workers. In one locality more stress is laid on the one function of the school than on the other, but the government, through ministerial decrees, tries to achieve as much uniformity as possible. Gradually, too, a class of teachers is growing up, all trained in the same traditions. In September, 1912, the Prussian ministry of commerce and industry opened a seminar course for continuation school-

The continuation schools.

teachers in the industrial art school of Charlottenburg, when no less than 299 candidates, four-fifths of them artisans, presented themselves for the entrance examination. As only ninety teachers were likely to be needed, the rest were at once disposed of by severe processes of elimination.

Features of the continuation schools.

Common to all the schools are two features: the making of the pupil's calling or occupation the pivot of all instruction, and the importance attached to mechanical and artistic drawing.

In the large cities there are separate classes for every trade and there is an entirely separate curriculum for each class. The reading, the mathematics, the correspondence, all have to do with the pupil's immediate needs. He learns about his materials, his tools, about new methods of manufacture and accounting. He learns many a secret regarding the treatment of customers that may one day make the difference between failure or success. In fact his horizon is broadened in every direction, he is taught to be business-like and fair in all his dealings, and is warned at every turn of the special dangers that lurk in his path. Young barbers, for instance, who may one day hope to start their own shops, are taught to weigh the advantages and disadvantages of different localities and to note all the special points that must be regarded in signing a lease or effecting a purchase; also the intricacies of loans, mortgages, and interest.

The importance attached to drawing.

Drawing is considered the one subject of vital importance in all continuation schools. "It is the speech of the workshop," writes an authority; "he who does not understand it is useless as a journeyman and still more useless as a master. Daily the artisan experiences this and has experienced it for a century." It is not the mere elements of drawing, however, that are taught, for these have already been taught in the primary school. It is exclusively drawing as applied to the actual needs of the trade. "The instruction in drawing," says a ministerial decree of 1907, "shall bring the pupil to a point where he can thoroughly understand working plans and if possible draw plans himself for the ordinary tasks of his calling." If you go into the class rooms of the continuation schools you will find the little shoemakers drawing soles and uppers, the saddlers drawing straps and buckles, the plumbers drawing pipe joints or even plans for water systems, the carpenters drawing cornices, roofs, windows and the like, the barbers drawing heads and *frisures*, and even the chimney sweeps drawing chimneys. Painters, decorators, engravers, goldsmiths, lithographers, and even confectioners go quite deeply into artistic designing.

It must be remembered that the majority of continuation school pupils are apprentices and that apprenticeship plays a very different rôle in Germany from what it does in our own land of factories. In Germany some 800,000 youths are working, practically without pay, for masters who are bound by contract to give them an all-round training in their trade. At the end of the period the boy passes an examination before regularly constituted examiners and qualifies as a "journeyman." The whole matter is regulated by the *Gewerbeordnung* or imperial industrial ordinance and, since 1897, there are "chambers of industry," one main object of which is to look after the welfare of apprentices. These "chambers," of which there were sixty-three in 1900, insist that the contract with the masters be drawn up in due form, determine the qualifications of a master, the number of apprentices he may keep, and the length of time he may keep them, make uniform requirements for technical training, and see that the examinations are properly conducted. The "chambers" keep a register of all the masters and all the apprentices and provide inspectors who appeal to the police if the regulations are not properly observed. The "chambers" go so far as to advise boys personally about the con-

Appren-
ticeship.

tracts they are about to sign.   Altogether the dignity of apprenticeship has been so upheld that the average apprentice, though he be earning much less than the mere factory hand, feels himself higher in the social scale than the untaught, and there is the greatest pride in the *Gesellenstück*, or finished piece of work that is always required for the examination. These *Gesellenstücke* are usually placed on exhibition and prizes are awarded for the best piece of work. The German public takes the greatest interest in such matters, as will be seen from the fact that an exhibition of *Gesellenstücke* in Freiburg in 1908 was attended by 11,000 persons.   Yet the *Gesellenstück* may be of the most prosaic nature, — for an upholsterer, for instance, the stuffing of a chair or of a lounge or of a spring mattress.

Methods of the continuation schools.

The continuation schools differ greatly in the amount of actual technical work they require in connection with the studies. The Frankfort schools, indeed, have laid down the principle that practically all work of this kind should be done by the apprentice in his master's workshop, believing it possible to bring about in this way a much-to-be desired coöperation between the masters and the schools. Düsseldorf goes on a different principle. The schools try not to duplicate, but to supplement, the workshops. The young tailors, for instance, are given bits of finer material than they would be apt to be intrusted with by their masters and are practised in the more difficult processes of their trade, such as buttonhole and lapel making. Incidentally in all the classes the difference between good and bad materials is insisted upon, and it is shown that a reputation for integrity will outweigh any slight momentary increase of profits. The pupils are taught very carefully to compute the cost of each item, including every minute of their own labor, and then to add only a reasonable and normal profit. Such ideas, thus spread throughout the empire, have very quickly raised the whole level of industry and paved the way for world conquest.

It is in Munich that the combination of continuation school and school workshops is seen in its full glory. The expenditure for industrial training purposes has been so lavish that the cost per head is about double that of other cities. In all about 21,000 persons are yearly being trained in the city's schools, if we include the trade schools and all the special classes, some of which are designed even for masters. Seven thousand girls are trained in housekeeping. At the continuation schools attendance is compulsory for a number of hours equalling one whole working day out of the six and for a period of three years. The masters and journeymen are in full sympathy with the whole movement and helped, in 1907, to draw up the curriculum as it now stands. How thoroughly the matter was thought out may be judged from the fact that no less than 92 conferences were held, of which 46 were in conjunction with masters and journeymen. Indeed a standing committee of employers aids in supervising the practical instruction. Its members attend the examinations and, in general, serve as a connecting link between the trades and their new recruits. The city government itself is, of course, deeply interested. It gives the use of the city slaughter-house and cattle yard for the instruction of the butchers and has also set apart a special tract of land for the use of the gardeners. The city of Düsseldorf goes even further in this regard. There is a continuation school class for the training of delivery wagon drivers; and the city, in connection with a teamsters' association, provides a driving park as well as the carts and horses.

The Munich continuation schools.

The practical work in the Munich continuation schools is highly amusing and interesting to watch. The barbers, for instance, sit like little Robespierres with rows of wax heads before them on a table, cutting and parting, brushing

Practical work in the Munich schools.

and curling, crimping and burning; now making and fitting a wig, now trimming the whiskers and beard. They are made to practise handling capes and towels, sharpening razors and soaping with the brush and with the hand. They must know how to apply the moustache guard that is a specialty with German officers. They are taught to meet and greet their customer, how to take his hat and cane. In the same way, young innkeepers and waiters are placed before an actual table and made to cover it with the cloth; to place the napkins, plates, glasses, and cutlery; to pour the wine and water; to hand the dishes; and to carve. They must know how to arrange for dinner and supper parties, how to draw up a menu, how to keep and serve wines at the temperature suitable to each. They are instructed in cleanly habits, in the tone of voice they are to employ, yes in the very words they are to use when accepting *trinkgeld*. These are trivial details, but they show the new note of realism that has gone through German education and helped the nation to forge ahead. Just so in army practice the soldiers have been trained to rush at real obstacles almost as formidable as any they will be called upon to encounter in the field.

Butcher boys.

There is an increased dignity attached to every calling taught in this way. The butcher boys in the cattle yards learn to judge the good points of a beast and to appreciate the effect upon the quality of meat of the different kinds of feeding. They can detect the signs of disease. Just so the coachman is made to study the geography of his town and find the quickest way from point to point; he learns the sights and monuments and everything connected with them so as to be able, if need be, to entertain his fare. Better still, he learns the anatomy of the horse from actual stuffed animals, and is taught how to give his animal the best care. Gardeners learn botany and designing.

Not even the chimney-sweep is neglected in Munich. The chimney is his sphere, and he must learn all that can possibly be known about it : the mathematical relations of height and draft, the correct dimensions for proper functioning, the chemical properties of soot, the different reasons for the formation of gases. But even there the young man's responsibilities do not end. He must have at his fingers' tips all the insurance laws that concern his trade.

Chimney-sweeps.

Surely here is a system of education that helps to sharpen every weapon that can be used in the great economic struggle. These standards of thoroughness have permeated the whole German race.

Conclusions.

The industrial schools stand in close relation with the public labor bureaus, many of which have special departments for would-be apprentices. But these bureaus have a social betterment side that is even more important than their economic side.

CHAPTER XIII

SOCIAL PROGRESS BETWEEN 1871 AND 1914

LITERATURE: *Deutschland unter Kaiser Wilhelm II. Handbuch der Politik.* Martin Wenck, *Die Geschichte und Ziele der deutschen Sozialpolitik,* is good as far as it goes. The lectures of the Cologne *Hochschule für Kommunale und soziale Verwaltung* are on a very high level. Two volumes have as yet appeared: *Die soziale Fürsorge der kommunalen Verwaltung in Stadt und Land,* and *Die neuen Aufgaben der Sozialversicherung in der Praxis,* both published in 1913. Kleeman, *Die Sozialpolitik der Reichs-Post und Telegraphenverwaltung,* shows what the post office does for its employees. Thissen-Trimborn, *Soziale Tätigkeit der Stadtgemeinden,* treats of all varieties of topics and is excellent. The city reports give the different social betterment activities in detail. But the literature of this, as well as of the preceding topic, is inexhaustible.

Design of the chapter.

IT has been said of the Roman Catholic church that, with its sacraments and its required duties, it watches over men from the cradle to the grave. The same is true of the German Empire. The design of this chapter is to follow human life and see what is done, according to modern German methods, to make it more safe and pleasant. Social science is almost wholly a product of the present generation, and while Germany has not always been a pioneer, it is safe to say that nowhere have the new ideas been more systematically carried out.

Illegitimate children.

The registering of births is most thorough, and the penalties for want of promptness are most severe. It must always be stated whether the child is legitimate or illegitimate, in which latter case it is put in the care of a professional guardian, one of whose chief concerns is to see that the father contributes to its support. This *Berufsvormundschaft,* or

542

professional guardianship, is a new institution but has been
so successful that, according to Dawson, a society of fathers
of illegitimate children has been formed to resist excessive
or unjust demands. There is a special guardianship court
to which appeal can be made. The guardian is usually a
state or municipal official or may be the head of a children's
asylum. His place is no sinecure, for the number of illegitimate births is very large — in Munich, about one-third of
the total number. The guardian, who is assisted in Munich
by eighty-eight nurses, looks to it that the child is well
treated and, where necessary and practicable, finds foster-
parents for it. One result has been that the hideous baby-
farming and wholesale murders of which we occasionally
hear in America are unknown in the Germany of to-day,
for the guardians exercise the greatest care and the foster-
parents are kept under inspection. In Berlin the foster-
mothers are licensed.

Everything is done to check infant mortality. The birth
rate has been falling very steadily of late years — even more
rapidly than in other countries, and the government has been
making great efforts to reduce the death rate. That it has
had some success is shown by statistics. Between 1886 and
1906, the Munich death rate for infants had fallen from
33 per cent to 20 per cent, and even more striking figures
could be adduced for other cities. The elaborate statistics
kept by German cities have proved of great use in pointing
the way to betterment. It has been found that illegitimate
children furnish the largest quota of deaths as well as of
degenerates, paupers, and criminals. It was found, too, that
the percentage of deaths for children nursed at the breast
was very much less than that for children brought up on the
bottle. Many German towns, accordingly, offer prizes
to mothers nursing their infants; and Charlottenburg, one
of the most progressive of all the cities, makes regular weekly

Infant mortality.

payments, the limit being six marks a week. In the first year of this experiment the mortality of the children thus cared for in Charlottenburg fell to 6 per cent, as opposed to a general infant mortality for the city of 14 per cent. Magdeburg, which also gives prizes for nursing, has organized regular consultations between the mothers and physicians, while

Mother-advice stations.

so-called "mother-advice stations" are now very common; there were more than 20 such in Munich alone in 1911, the stations at the same time distributing pure milk. In Cassel, which city in 1903 started the first milk kitchen in Germany, about 300,000 bottlefuls are distributed yearly at a moderate price or entirely free as the case may be. The experiment has not pauperized the women, for the deficit to the town is only 1000 marks a year. Day nurseries where mothers can place their infants while they themselves are at work are very common, while one of the finest institu-

Widowers' lodging-houses.

tions, which originated in Glasgow, is the widowers' lodging or apartment house where the children are cared for *en masse* and, even at night, crying babies are prevented from tormenting their breadwinners.

The public schools.

In all but a very few states the age for entering school is six years. There are three types of elementary schools: the *Volksschulen*, or free public schools, attended by 94 per cent of the children; the *Mittelschulen*, at which a small tuition fee is charged; and the *Progymnasia*, or preparatory schools for the gymnasia, where the tuition fee is quite large from a German point of view. The *Volksschule* course is eight years, and the subjects taught are religion, history, geography, natural science, free-hand drawing, singing, gymnastics, and, of course, the German language.

Aid schools.

A comparatively new development is the aid school, or *Hilfsschule*, that now has separate buildings and takes care of those children who, after repeated attempts, fail to keep up with their classes in the public schools. The number of such children is not small; in Breslau alone in 1911 there were 1036 of them. The aid schools have been defined as intellectual hospitals. Occasionally they can bring a child so far that he can resume his place in the regular school; more often the children are given special courses adapted to their needs. The way in which the least gleam of intelligence is hunted down and fanned into life is truly admirable. A few years ago such children would simply have been committed to asylums. Now there are even preparatory classes for the aid school. Charlottenburg has eight kindergartens for such children, where not only their mental needs are looked after, but where they are fed and nursed back to bodily strength. These schools have gardens where the feebler ones spend a part of the day lying out in extension chairs. There are also forest schools for the tuberculous. Frankfort has a farm where the very worst cases from the aid schools are kept under observation with a view to developing some one ability that may later help to make the child self supporting. At first little more is attempted than the building up of the children's physical strength and the training of their motor impulses. Gradually they become accustomed to regular work and even aid in erecting the farm buildings. The station keeps in touch with farmers and industrial workers with a view to finding eventual employment, and an investigation extending over the period from 1903 to 1909 showed that 54 per cent of the boys and girls had turned out satisfactorily.

Public kindergartens.

Observation stations.

There is wide general interest in the aid schools. A congress of federated schools held in Bonn in 1913 was attended by 775 people, and the results reported to the congress were most encouraging. Indeed, it was asserted, doubtless with some exaggeration, that, out of 4000 aid-school children investigated, 70 per cent had become self-supporting. There are charitable organizations that make

Aid school congresses.

it their chief task to follow up the aid-school children and help them in later life.

The *Mittelschule* is a new form of school that only received its present organization in 1910. It was designed to meet the needs of parents who desired something better than the "poor man's school" and yet could not afford the gymnasia. Attention had been called to the problem because so many parents had been obliged to withdraw their children from the gymnasia either from lack of ability to pay or from the failure of the boys to keep up with their work. Such children were practically shipwrecked, so rigidly are the lines drawn in Germany between the different occupations. That there was an urgent call for such an institution is shown by the fact that the *Mittelschulen* now have over 240,000 pupils, girls and boys, — a number greater than that of the three higher types of schools combined. The training is very practical.

The gymnasia are the aristocratic schools and the strongholds of the classics — in the Württemberg gymnasia ten hours a week for five years are devoted to Latin — but there are now so-called real-gymnasia, where only one dead language is taught and there are so-called *Ober-realschulen* where the curriculum is entirely modern. The worst feature of the system has been that, once embarked on a given course, there was no turning back, no shifting over. This has been remedied, however, in many towns by adopting the "Frankfort plan," which postpones the beginning of Latin until the fourth school year, and substitutes French for the younger classes. The plan is proving popular, but there is still a clamor for greater unification. "As there is one emperor and one empire," said Dr. Kerschensteiner to 8000 teachers assembled in Kiel shortly before the war broke out, "so there should be one school and one body of teachers." But the clericals and conservatives are much opposed; they like to see the apartness of the gymnasia preserved. As matters stand to-day a man of the aristocracy who has not passed his final examination at a gymnasium finds almost every career closed to him.

Two tendencies in modern German education are of interest: the one is to make the schools more practical, to have the pupils "do" rather than "learn," the other, which has made much more headway, is to make the instruction as realistic as possible by the aid of every kind of illustrative material. With regard to the first-mentioned tendency the great "German Teachers' Association" has gone on record as favoring a reform such as would "bring the intellectual powers more into accord with the organs of the senses" and "take heed of the child's delight in actual creative work." As a careful student of the question puts it, personalities are more needed than heads stuffed with knowledge. The schools have been training the ear at the expense of the hand. Go out and measure a real field rather than work out a problem regarding a supposed one; learn to count from a three-leafed clover, a four-wheeled cart, a five-pointed maple leaf, a six-legged butterfly; make a visit to the factory or the mine the starting point for your technical knowledge; get your geometry from arches, windows and roofs, your zoölogy and botany from the fields and woods, your physics from electric plants, pumps, and water supplies in general. Actual mountains, lakes, rivers, trees, thermometers and barometers, stereopticons, watches, clocks, telephones, machinery of all kinds; these should be the real text-books.

The "do" school.

That there is truth in all this no one can doubt, but there are insuperable difficulties in the way of turning it into a fixed programme and discarding the old approved school curriculum. It is to be regarded as a compromise that so much outside aid to visualization is being brought into the schools. One is amazed when visiting a modern school

Aids to visualization.

museum to see the innumerable devices of this kind. For religious instruction one can buy Solomon's temples, altars for burnt offerings, manna, myrrh, aloe, and hyssop, water from the Jordan, salt from the Dead Sea, crowns of thorns, golden calves, David's slings, parchment indulgences, and other such objects; one firm in Berlin has between 60,000 and 70,000 stereopticon slides representing different phases of ancient art; the number of pictures and of illustrated books on all subjects is legion. Some of the schools have their own moving-picture apparatus and there is a "Central office for scientific and school cinematography." Graphophones grind out the pronunciations of words; calculating apparatuses represent fruit gardens; false heads and throats show the actions of the vocal cords; in some schools fresh hearts, stomachs, lungs, eyes, etc., are procured from the butcher for the classes in biology, while firms make a specialty of pickled or embalmed organs. There are skeletons with attachments for hanging the organs in their proper places. For fifty or sixty marks one can even purchase the arm of a human embryo, while in some of the industrial art schools the young pupils, girls as well as boys, sit and draw details from actual human corpses.

School hygiene.
In the matter of school hygiene Germany is very far advanced. The new school buildings are strikingly handsome and airy. They now have their regular physicians and some have instituted very thorough examinations of every pupil. Frankfort gives a regular certificate of health while Wiesbaden has its pupils reëxamined in the third, fifth and eighth, or final year. Often the physician confers with the teacher and parents as to the child's future vocation. The trouble hitherto has been that too many children are assigned to one physician, — in Berlin about 5000, in Barmen almost 12,000! Of course under such circumstances the examinations are perfunctory. On the other hand the

physician is not expected to treat the actual cases himself.
Charlottenburg has Sisters of Mercy whose duty it is to see
that the physicians' recommendations are carried out.

The dental work, too, is admirable. Düsseldorf, since
1912, has a school clinic consisting of nine well-lighted rooms,
besides operating and sterilizing rooms, a library, a laboratory, and facilities for photographing. Parents who can
afford it pay one mark yearly, but the charge is remitted
to those with an income of less than 1200 marks. In that
case, too, even the car fares of the children are paid. The
proportion of those with defective teeth is found to be
very large indeed. Out of 21,119 children examined in
1912–13 in Düsseldorf, 17,230 had to be treated, on an
average, three or four times. In Munich out of 17,384, no
less than 16,196 had their teeth classed as "defective or
bad." The clinics furnish tooth brushes either at cost
price or free. Indirectly the clinics are doing educational
work; for the parents, seeing the importance attached
to the matter, are more anxious to have their own teeth
attended to.

School dental work.

The schools have latterly awakened to an appreciation of
the benefit of baths and every modern schoolhouse is now
equipped with them. They are considered such an innovation, however, that the consent of the parents must first
be asked before making their use compulsory. Pforzheim
sends out a little yearly pamphlet drawing attention to the
shower baths and asking for the coöperation of the parents.

School baths.

One evil in the schools, the existence of which will seem
incredible to many, must be mentioned here: the use of alcohol by the pupils. The children themselves, of course,
are not so much to blame as are their ignorant parents, many
of whom think that beer is wholesome and strengthening.
But the nation of late has been thoroughly aroused to the
extent of the evil. Various comprehensive investigations

The use of alcohol in the schools.

have been made.　An examination of 30,000 pupils in Saxony showed that 197 drank brandy daily and that 2282 drank it at least once a week.　An inquiry by a teachers' temperance society, conducted in different parts of the Empire, showed that out of 7338 children examined only 2 per cent had never tasted alcohol and that 11 per cent indulged in it daily in one or another form.　Many schools have now opened a regular campaign against the evil.　In the "Workman's Museum" in Munich there are wax models showing the ravages of alcoholism on the human organs; and the "beer liver," swollen to many times its normal size and honeycombed by disease, is a sight to frighten the boldest child. It may not be entirely due to that beer liver, but the consumption of beer in Munich between 1912 and 1913 fell off by 20,000 hectolitres.

Playgrounds.　There have been great advances of late in the matter of playgrounds, both school and public.　Breslau now devotes ninety million square metres to the purpose, and Berlin has seemingly endless tracts stretching along the bank of the Spree in the direction of Treptow.　Here thousands of children can be seen of a summer afternoon engaged in football and other games.　Once a year the city organizes a regular holiday of sports and feeds the children throughout the day at a cost to the city treasury of some 30,000 marks. An interesting experiment is being tried in Königsberg. In certain new parts of the city the regulations regarding frontage lines are suspended and the houses may be built well forward on condition that the back yards be all thrown into one.　Here the children can play together and yet remain under closer supervision than in the public parks.

The degeneration of youth.　At the age of fourteen the average German boy ends his elementary school course, is confirmed in the faith of his fathers, and goes out as an apprentice or as an unskilled worker.　In either case he is bound to attend the continuation schools for a number of hours a week until his seventeenth or eighteenth year. A few years ago some startling evidence in the way of statistics waked Germans up to the fact that all was not well with these youths. In the large cities nearly two-thirds of those who presented themselves for military service were found not up to the physical standards, while at the same time the police records showed a great increase in the matter of juvenile crime. The generally accepted explanation was that the evolution of industry had drawn more than a million and a half boys and girls away from the farms and the small towns and freed them from the old restraints of church, school, and family. The high cost of lodging had crowded them together; their only relaxations were cheap shows and amusements that were often harmful.

The work of reclaiming youth was taken up with a zeal and a unity that are intensely interesting to follow. Not private individuals alone, but still more the cities and the state took up the task. In 1908 the Prussian minister for trade and commerce, whose department controls the industrial continuation schools, issued a liberal and suggestive decree concerning the activities to be encouraged in those institutions: the different sports are enumerated that can best be carried on in the different seasons; it is urged that comfortable quarters be secured where apprentices can spend their free hours in the society of those of their own age, and that books, lectures, music, and other means of entertainment be provided for them. *The work of redemption.*

Associations for the furtherance of the interests of youths have long existed in Germany as in every other country. In the Roman Catholic church alone there are no less than 2615 sodalities or congregations with 266,000 members, and 921 *Gesellenvereine*, or journeymen's associations, with 61,000 members. The Protestant church, too, has its *Catholic associations.*

Protestant associations.

"Young Men's Christian Associations," introduced after the American model in 1883; its "White Cross League," borrowed from England; its "International Christian Waiters' Association," with homes in Frankfort, Düsseldorf, Berlin, Breslau, Hamburg, Leipzig, and Cologne.

Secular associations.

There are associations for social democratic youths, too, under the auspices of which some 3500 lectures are given a year, while one of the news journals alone has a circulation of 80,000. More important still are the German gymnastic associations with more than a million members, the German Football League with 161,613 members, the German athletic associations with 131,137 members, as well as special "German" associations for almost every conceivable form of sport: skating, fencing, golf, tennis, hockey, cycling, rowing, etc. There are innumerable walking clubs, too, like

The Wander-vögel.

the "League of German *Wandervögel*," or "migratory birds," the "national league for young wanderers, etc." The *Wandervögel* as a body have been through so many revolutions, schisms, and dramatic experiences that a three-volume work has been published about them.

The "Central Committee."

No nation but Germany with its amazing genius for organization could have brought such order and unity into all these separate endeavors and focussed them all on the single purpose of bettering the race. Since 1891 there is a "Central Committee for the care of the people and of youth," which in reality is not a committee but a huge association. As members we find state governments (Prussia pays 7000 marks a year), no less than 328 communities with Berlin at the head, and nineteen associations of which one alone, young Germany, has 750,000 members. The main object of the "Central Committee," as it says in its programme, is to "make exercise in the open air and especially games for the people and for the young the general custom in Germany." Congresses are held, each year in a different part

of the empire. A comprehensive year-book is also published and the committee issues a periodical, *Körper und
Geist.* It has sub-committees for every kind of activity,
one even for the "strengthening of the female sex." To
the "Committee" the various sport associations turn for
decisions as to the rules of games, and during its existence
it has trained well over 20,000 persons in special courses as
teachers of sport. More comprehensive in its objects is a
similar organization founded in 1906, and called the "Centre
for the whole field of popular welfare." To it, also, belong
state authorities, leagues of cities, chambers of commerce,
all sorts of associations, big firms, and private individuals.
Its special fields are investigation and propaganda; and it,
too, publishes a large amount of literature.

Meanwhile closer touch between many of the different "Young
associations, like "boy scouts" (*Pfadfinder*), some forms of Germany."
the *Wandervögel*, and the different sport clubs, as well as
hitherto unorganized elements, has been achieved by "Young
Germany," founded by General von der Goltz. According
to the latter there is no intention of "militarizing." Young
Germany aims merely "to supply the army with recruits
sound in body and soul, whose native capacities have been
brought out by the 'young German' leaders." These leaders
are usually officers of the army, and the experience is as useful for them as it is for their young charges. On the whole
the officers have devoted themselves to the task with enthusiasm. They lead squads of boys on long tramps, during which they camp in the open or spend nights in the
barracks. A regular part of the programme is to teach boys
"to brave wind and weather, night and cold." There is no
limit to the variety of useful, manly activities; the eye is
trained to sight objects at a distance or in the air; the ear
to detect the nature of sounds. From the hoof-beats, for
instance, it can be told whether a horse has a rider or is run-

ning free. Tracks and trails are followed, trees are climbed for the sake of taking observations, maps are read and followed. Games are played, among them the elaborate *Kriegsspiel*, or war game. First aid to the injured is practised, and the boys learn to bandage, to tie knots, and to construct impromptu litters.

Resources of "Young Germany."

"Young Germany" has funds at its disposal from various sources: among them a lottery which brings in an income of 150,000 marks a year. There have been handed over to the organization, too, the royalties from a book written by the Crown Prince and entitled *Germany in Arms*. By a special arrangement and at a cost of only 10 Pfennige or $2\frac{1}{2}$ cents apiece, all the 750,000 members are insured against accidents.

By a regular sort of treaty between "Young Germany" and the Roman Catholic church authorities young Catholics may join the organization which, in turn, pledges itself that "in general," in Catholic neighborhoods, the tramps, sports, etc., shall not interfere with the regular hours for divine service.

Ministerial decree of 1911.

A decree of the Prussian *Kultusminister*, in whose hands are all educational and religious matters, shows better than anything else how the government feels it to be its function to take an active part in all such endeavors as have been described above — to give the impetus, to unify and consolidate, in short to assume the ultimate direction. The decree in question is of January 18, 1911. It begins by describing the evil effects of the modern struggle for existence on the health and morals of the young, tells what a wide field of usefulness is here opened up to city administrations and school boards, and recommends the establishment of city and rural special committees. Not compulsory training, not reformatory work in the criminal sense is needed, but preventive work, work that shall be voluntary for all

been collected and victory had been organized with the usual German thoroughness. The *Kultusminister* had called upon the schools, and the war minister on the army to hold athletic meets all over the empire; and all promising material was to be handed over to the "Imperial Committee" for special training. Five hundred meets in the army and two thousand in the schools had either already been held or were about to be held when the war broke out. A special committee had been sent to America to see wherein lay the acknowledged superiority of that people and had published a glowing report stating the features worthy of imitation. English trainers had been engaged at high salaries. To conquer in those games was the dominant passion of the whole German youth. A victory in football, won over Paris in the Berlin stadium in June, 1914, had aroused the greatest enthusiasm; and army contests held in the same place at the end of the month had filled the great arena for three successive days, the emperor himself awarding the prizes. The memory of those thousands of splendid young soldiers who only a few weeks later were called to the deadliest kind of real warfare is one that will always remain with the historian. The nature of the sports was significant of the thorough training in the army. In one of the events some fifty soldiers started at the farther end of a long pool, dashed into the water, then out over every sort of obstacle, including a perpendicular wall higher than themselves, until they came tearing down the home stretch. Not one of them remained behind. Another race, for officers, was over rough country for a distance of four miles. It was won by a prince of the royal house. Instead of parade-grounds the German army now has what we may call obstacle-fields.

The Berlin-Paris football match.

Army contests.

Enough has been said to show that all along the line the struggle for the bodily and moral redemption of the young — the two go together — has been taken up in Germany

Juvenile delinquents.

with the utmost energy. The courts, too, have recently changed all their methods of dealing with juvenile delinquents. The hand of the law no longer merely cuffs and beats; it leads along the path to better things. In 1908, after considerable agitation on the subject, the first juvenile court was established in Frankfort, and the judge became the guardian rather than the condemner of the youths. There is now such a combination of judge and guardian in no less than 556 localities. It was a great advance in Berlin when it was determined no longer to try cases against juveniles in the criminal court-house in Moabit, where the boys were apt to come into contact with the really bad and depraved, but rather in the civil court building. The Berlin judges now extend their guardianship not merely to the delinquent himself, but to his brothers and sisters as well, for they look carefully into the environment that may have disposed the youth to crime. They are assisted by a "Central Association for the reformation of youth," which conducts the actual investigations and which not only looks into the boy's home affairs, but into his school record. Each delinquent boy, moreover, is asked, though not compelled, to submit to a complete physical examination. On the ground of all the information thus obtained the judge makes up his mind whether or not the boy was sufficiently intelligent to realize the seriousness of the act that he has committed, and if the conclusion be favorable he is not sentenced, but is handed over to the care of the proper organizations. In any case the proceedings are divested of their old-time terrifying formality. The boy is not placed on the prisoner's bench, nor does the judge even sit in his usual seat. While awaiting trial the boys are not placed in cells, but are given shelter and occupation in special homes for the purpose.

The whole subject has been receiving much attention, and new laws, to apply to the whole state of Prussia, occupied

the Prussian Diet on the eve of the war. Cities have made
studies with regard to every phase of the problem, and
Düsseldorf even made an investigation among 20,000 school
children in order to find how many of them might have been
affected by the habit of attending moving-picture shows.
It was found that 18,000 of them had been at least once to
such entertainments and that quite a large number attended
them *every day.* Many cities forbid the admission of children under sixteen years of age. Not only films but the
books on news stands and the pictures in shop windows are
censored to a degree that has provoked some opposition, for
ignorant police authorities have condemned some of the
finest classic productions. The work, however, has not been
purely negative. Much has been done to spread good literature through cheap editions that can be purchased on the
penny-in-the-slot plan, and some cities have even started
their own moving-picture shows. The "Urania" in Berlin gives representations of real scientific value, and the whole
building is a sort of practical physical laboratory where the
visitors can turn cranks and set the exhibits in motion.

General interest in the boy problem.

At eighteen the ordinary German youth is emancipated
from apprenticeship and from the continuation school and
seeks to establish himself in life. A system of free public
labor exchanges or employment offices (*öffentliche Arbeits-
nachweise* they are called) has made this task much less
formidable than it was only a few years ago. These *Arbeits-
nachweise* found employment for a million persons in 1901,
for 1,600,000 in 1913, and for 2,100,000 in 1914. They are
organized much as are the coöperative societies or the associations for the betterment of youth, with hundreds of
associations grouped into leagues or central associations, and
with an "imperial central association" and a central information bureau at Berlin. The war has given the whole
institution a great impetus; new associations were formed

The labor bureaus or public employment offices.

in all directions and even new leagues. The associations are usually administered by committees representing the more important local organizations both of employers and employed, this method having proved much more satisfactory than that of having the municipal authorities appoint the directors. The manager is a business man, not a politician, and on his tact and ability hangs the success of the enterprise.

Importance of the labor bureau.

This institution of the labor-bureau is a much more important one, much more far-reaching in its influence, than the casual observer would imagine. It saves the workers millions of marks and much waste of time formerly spent in running from employer to employer or in inserting and answering advertisements. Four cities, Berlin, Cologne, Elberfeld and Munich, now have handsome buildings in which to house the bureaus and have thus become the centres for a whole new range of activities. The institution does much to raise the self-respect of the jobless man. The buildings are like club-houses, with comfortable, well-heated and well-lighted waiting-rooms where refreshments can be purchased at a low price. There are tailor shops for making the applicants more presentable; writing rooms where clerks out of employment can obtain temporary work at

Efficiency of the bureaus.

copying and folding; free legal advisers to whom they can bring their troubles. The bureaus are conducted with the utmost efficiency. The system of control is admirable, every applicant with his demands and his qualifications being carefully card-catalogued and indexed. There is a breadth of view, a generosity that is only obtainable through long experience. It is now considered safe to supply men sent to distant points with their railway tickets and trust to the honesty of their employers for reimbursement. This is frequently done and the results have been satisfactory. The telephone is used lavishly and as a rule cases are dis-

posed of within the twenty-four hours. It is interesting
to note that in the German bureaus it is no longer merely
the unskilled laborer who comes to seek employment. About
half of the places filled in Cologne are of men trained to
some special occupation and there is a marked tendency to
go higher and higher in the social scale. Teachers and
engineers are now among the applicants.

Many of the bureaus make it their special care to find work
for persons of diminished earning power who would otherwise be a charge on the charity institutions of their city.
Moral and physical wrecks, discharged prisoners and con-
sumptives, the maim, the halt, and the blind, are given
part-time work if it be anywhere obtainable. A capable manager establishes personal relations with employers. Doubtless the best results in this regard have been obtained in
Düsseldorf where, according to a regular expert's computa-
tion, enough money has thus been saved the city's institutions to pay the whole expense of the bureau itself.

Placing the handi- capped.

One feature of the modern German labor exchange, although sometimes seen independently of it, is the free city
real estate agency. The object is to suit the laborer with a
house or apartment with the least possible trouble and loss
of time. Landlords with apartments to rent must send in
full descriptions of the rooms with drawings to show the
positions of the windows, the plumbing arrangements, etc.
Often, as in Cologne, the agency sends its own men to make
the drawings. The applicant can see at a glance whether
the rooms are suitable for his needs and is sure of not being
cheated. People of not inconsiderable means are beginning to make use of these *Wohnungsnachweise* or free real
estate agencies.

Free real estate agencies.

Once embarked in industry or even, now, in domestic
service, the German worker begins to feel the burdens of
the national compulsory insurance. He must pay his share

The national compulsory insurance. of the sickness insurance and also of the invalidity and survivor insurance, while the accident insurance is altogether paid by the employers. But the benefits far outweigh the burdens. It is possible for a young man of twenty-one who has worked since he was sixteen and has paid in only forty marks to receive an invalidity pension of 141 marks for the rest of his life. Between 1885 and 1910 indemnities were paid or services rendered to no less than 100 million persons; and since 1911 sweeping extensions have been made both as regards the number of persons insured and the amount of the benefits accorded to the individual.

A French verdict on the insurance. This national or social insurance is Germany's great contribution to modern civilization and almost every great nation has copied the institution either in whole or in part. In the words of the well-known Frenchman, Edouard Fuster: "The money spent in carrying out the insurance laws in Germany reappears in a thousand forms. It is transmuted into family happiness, health and dignity, and creates a strong, vital Germany that will last forever." The main feature of the institution is, that the element of charity is altogether lacking. To the sickness insurance the worker himself contributes two-thirds, the employer one-third; while to the invalidity insurance both contribute equally, the state adding a fixed amount, fifty marks, in the case of each pension. Bismarck's idea had been to have the state bear the whole expense of the insurance and thus make the workers dependent on its bounty: a project which had been defeated after violent debates in the Reichstag. The majority of the members had felt, and rightly, that here was a cardinal point.

The "Ordinance of 1911." The *Reichsversicherungsordnung*, or Imperial Insurance Ordinance of 1911, codified all the previous legislation on the subject in no less than 1805 paragraphs. It is a wonderful monument to human ingenuity, and no constitution of a realm was ever drawn up with more patience and care. Here, too, we meet the thoroughness of organization so often noted. There is a *Versicherungsamt*, or upper insurance board, for each *Kreis* or province, and a *Reichsversicherungsamt*, or imperial insurance board, to which all disagreements are referred from one or the other of the lower instances. The contributions to the sickness insurance are paid into so-called *Krankenkassen* or sickness exchequers of which, previously to 1911, there were 21,000, the number then being reduced to 10,000. To these exchequers, too, word is sent in case of sickness, and thus they become busy daily centres. They have each their own staff of physicians and usually make contracts with large city hospitals to keep a number of beds at their disposal. The Imperial Ordinance specifies for all exchequers a minimum amount of benefits that they must accord and a maximum that they may accord should their finances permit. It is an admirably elastic system. Some of the *Krankenkassen* have many members and are rich, while others are situated in poorer or less thickly settled districts. Formerly one was allowed to choose one's exchequer but now one is assigned according to fixed rules. The exchequers, like the labor bureaus, are administered on the principle of self-government, the employers electing one-third, the workers two-thirds of the members of the governing board — a proportion, one sees, that is based on the relative amounts of the contributions to the fund.

"Sickness exchequers."

It is inadvisable to go into all the intricacies of the payments and the benefits. Both are reckoned on the basis of the wages received and there are five wage-classes. The normal or minimum benefits accorded are medical care for a period up to 26 weeks (after which one is either cured or considered invalid), all the medicines prescribed, small appliances such as eye glasses, trusses, and bandages, and a money payment up to the half of the wages earned. In case

The benefits accorded by the *Krankenkassen*.

of death a fixed sum is allowed for funeral expenses, a sum equivalent to twenty times an ordinary day's wages.

The accident insurance.

The mechanism of the accident insurance is quite different from that of the sickness insurance. Instead of the *Krankenkassen* there are special associations of employers called *Berufsgenossenschaften*, which are more in the nature of banks. By an arrangement with the *Krankenkassen* the latter take care of the patient for the first thirteen weeks after the accident and are then reimbursed. By that time it is expected that the full extent of the injury will have been ascertained and the pensions can be estimated accordingly. The *Berufsgenossenschaften* have branch offices, 544 in all, through which the actual business can be transacted and the tendency is more and more to take charge of the patient from the beginning. There is no arbitrary scale of indemnities, but custom is gradually forming one — so much for an arm, so much for an index finger, so much for a big toe. It reminds one of the old Salic or Bavarian laws where fines for acts of violence were computed according to the length of the wound and to the amount of blood that spurted from it. A workman who loses his right arm would be awarded a yearly sum equal to about two-thirds of his former wages. A woman is usually awarded 10 per cent more for the loss of a right arm than would be the case with a man, for it is realized what a privation it is to her not to be able to sew and to move about her pots and kettles. Disfigurements, even where the earning power is not directly affected, are well paid for, on the ground that it will be more difficult to find employment. Altogether psychology has more to do with the matter than one would expect, and here it is that the German schooling and general bent of mind show to the best advantage.

The invalidity and survivor insurance is organized on still another plan. With the aid of only forty-one organs called *Versicherungsanstalten* and *Sonderanstalten* (thirty-one of the former and ten of the latter), the imperial government controls the funds. More initiative is required of the workman, who must affix a stamp representing his contribution to a card that is given him and must also see that his employer does the same. Only after 200 stamps have been affixed does one become eligible for an invalidity pension, and only after 1200 have been affixed for an old-age pension. The age limit has been reduced during the war from 70 to 65. Many of these pensions lapse because of the carelessness or the poverty of the insured. The pensions are small but may be increased by a system of extra voluntary contributions.

Invalidity and survivor insurance.

The *Krankenkassen*, with all the daily calls upon them, have little capital to invest, but some of them do build their own hospitals and convalescent homes. They are often very liberal to their patients, actually paying them not to return to work too soon or sending them to watering places to recuperate, and also conducting an extensive campaign against ignorance, prejudice, and superstition in the matter of hygiene. Their property in 1912 was estimated to be worth 362,399,600 marks. The property of the *Versicherungsanstalten*, on the other hand, was estimated in the same year at more than five times that amount. The reason is that the demands, though large, come only once in a lifetime for each client and that great reserves have to be accumulated.

Investment of funds.

The *Versicherungsanstalten*, then, subject to the oversight of the *Reichversicherungsamt* or highest instance for the Empire, are able to make enormous yearly investments, and the beauty of the system here becomes apparent. The huge capital is kept working for humanitarian objects. It is loaned, usually to city governments and responsible associations, for specified purposes. Up to 1912 more than three hundred million marks had gone for the improvement of

The Versicherungsanstalten.

workmen's dwellings, more than five hundred millions for hospitals, homes, and allied purposes.   More than 100 million marks had been loaned for the benefit of farmers.   Large direct expenditures, too, are made for the purpose of staving off invalidity, — the most striking item in 1912 being the purchase of false teeth for forty thousand clients at a cost of more than a million marks!

The
Berufsge-
nossen-
schaften.

The *Berufsgenossenschaften*, too, spend large sums for the prevention of accidents.   They keep inspectors with a payroll totalling two million marks, whose duty is to travel about and see that the safety regulations in factories and workshops are observed.   These are trained and educated men, and their reports are often made the basis of new legislation, although they work independently of the state inspectors. The number of accidents has steadily decreased, although there were more than 70,000 of them, with 5800 deaths, in 1911.   The insurance has joined hands with the Red Cross in giving courses of instruction in first aid to the injured.

Objections
to com-
pulsory
insurance.

The charges are made against the compulsory insurance that it takes away personal initiative, induces simulation of ills, and is unduly burdensome on the employers.   All three objections have some foundation, but as yet the moth has not eaten very far into the garment.   The institution is so colossal that the defects are scarcely noticeable.   The employers, after all, were more prosperous in 1912 than ever in the country's history, though the insurance had been in force for more than a quarter of a century.   One can give many instances of simulation and not have them affect the general perspective.   It is perfectly true that a champion wrestler and an aërial gymnast, giving regular performances, were found to be drawing pensions, the one for a stiff elbow, the other for pain in old wounds.   But what does that prove?   There is some leakage in every water system, and physicians are becoming more and more astute.   By the wiliest inventions they make the deaf hear, the dumb speak, the blind see, and the lame walk.   There is another great controlling agency, too : the average German will protest vehemently if he discovers that another is cheating the treasury on which he himself may one day hope to call. Also if the *Berufsgenossenschaften* have the least suspicion that a client is not playing fair they can keep him under observation and prosecute him for obtaining money under false pretences.

The social insurance is not compulsory for those who can prove that their future is provided for in some other way. Thus postal and railroad as well as municipal officials are exempt.   Their wages are paid even in case of illness, or else they draw the equivalent from special insurance funds. Like the *Versicherungsanstalten* the pension exchequer of the Prussian state railroads has considerable sums to invest. Up to 1911 it had advanced to building associations for the improvement of dwellings for its employees no less than 24 million marks.   Workmen who have not attained the rank of officials must still insure with the national insurance ; but in 1904 the railroad organized a sickness exchequer so designed that the combined benefits from both sources will equal the regular wages.   In many small ways, too, the railroad contributes directly to the welfare of its people — so much for day nurseries, so much for sport and gymnastics among the apprentices, so much to individuals for long and faithful service, so much as extra aid to needy workmen. This last item alone amounted in 1911 to more than two million marks.   There are items, too, of 20,000 marks for bees, and 16,500 marks for goats and rabbits, that show the spirit that guides the whole.   The keeping of bees, goats, and rabbits helps the workers to eke out their wages, which are very moderate.   But as a result of all the benefits and of the certainty that their families will be provided for in case of

Social work of the railroads.

accident, the service in the Prussian railroads is exceedingly popular.

Post-office social work.

The imperial post-office treats its employees in exactly the same way. There are items in the budget for 1914 of 30,700,-000 marks for pensions, of 4,444,500 marks for aid and assistance of various kinds, of 690,000 marks for extra gifts to pensioners or their survivors. Ten million marks have already been spent in improving housing conditions for employees; special care is taken in providing boarding places for the younger men, where they will be kept away from evil influences, and especially for the young women who are employed as telephone operators. One instance must suffice of the liberal spirit which animates the post-office: since 1909 officials who have fallen into the drink habit but are not considered incurable are placed in some institution, given a year's leave of absence with full salary, and a substitute is provided for them. In the buildings and workrooms everything is done to make the surroundings safe and hygienic, and every precaution is taken against accidents on trains and other conveyances. Curiously enough a postal official is more exposed to accidents on the Prussian railroads than are ordinary passengers. There is a regulation that the car next to the locomotive shall carry no travellers, but that "railroad and postal officials on duty as well as persons accompanying corpses and animals shall not be rated as travellers."

City officials.

The German cities treat their officials and their workmen much as do the post-office and the railroads, but there is of course much less unity in the matter. The wages and salaries differ greatly in amount according to the local customs. Crefeld raises the pay as the family increases; Düsseldorf after a certain number of years of service allows a yearly vacation without loss of pay, and also gives "honorary gifts" for 25 and again for 40 years of service. Cities frequently

build houses for their officials.   Since the entry of the cities
into the industrial field a whole new class of technically
trained employees has come in and, relatively speaking, they
are highly paid, as skill and regularity are absolutely essential. Indeed it is so common to have employees make
valuable discoveries and inventions that the question as to
whom the patents belong has become a burning one.   Düsseldorf and Königsberg go to the extreme of claiming the full
ownership of all patents taken out for inventions of men
working in their service.

These city industries are of the most varied kind.   Almost City-run
every German city of any size owns its waterworks and industries.
many make them pay a good rate of interest, Hamburg and
Cologne between 9 and 10 per cent.   Very many communities own their electric plants, Berlin having acquired hers
since the war broke out; and the profits, as is the case with
Frankfort, sometimes rise into the millions.   The ownership
of gas-works is less common on account of long-term con- Gas-
tracts that have still to expire.   In 1910–11 out of 407 gas- works.
works only 64 per cent were municipally owned.   But with
the new processes and the new uses of gas municipal ownership of that product, too, is extending rapidly.   Berlin's clear
profit from its gas-works in 1911 was 13,633,572 marks.
The city has introduced automatic metres on the penny-in-
the-slot principle for the poorer classes.   Gas is in very
common use, too, for cooking.   Some of the cities have made
a regular propaganda for *Koche mit gas*, while new inventions
in the way of burners have made gas a successful rival even
of electricity in the matter of street lighting.   The utilization of by-products, too, like coke, tar, ammonia, etc., has
helped to make the gas-plants profitable.

Municipal tramways have on the whole not proved Municipal
profitable enterprises in Germany, as nearly half the cities tramways.
have to assist in making up deficits.   But one would fail to

appreciate the German conception of municipal ownership were one to attach much significance to this showing. The moment there is a surplus in tramway earnings there is a clamor to have the fares cut down. The service is excellent and yet the fares are absurdly low; in almost any town one can travel a considerable distance for ten *Pfennige*, or two and a half cents. There are still further reductions for workmen and school children.

The purpose of municipal industries.

It is safe to say that the purpose behind German municipal industrial enterprise is never profit pure and simple, and that the cities are ready to pocket the loss if there are other advantages to compensate. Thus Düsseldorf runs a great concert hall combined with a municipal wine business and there is always a yearly deficit. But the people get their wine of guaranteed quality; concerts of the best music are given at frequent intervals, not to speak of innumerable lectures; and the city has splendid facilities for honoring guests or holding other functions. Almost every city with a municipal theatre or opera house has to subsidize liberally, — Frankfort up to 400,000 marks a year; but the purpose is considered an educational one and there is little murmuring on the part of any one. The actual staging of the performances is usually handed over to an impresario who risks his own funds in the undertaking; but the cities, in return for their aid, make their own stipulations. Düsseldorf, for instance, requires that no new chorus girl more than thirty-five years of age shall be engaged, and also reserves the right to enter an objection to any special singer, actor or ballet dancer.

Various city-run industries.

The benefit of the people as a whole — that is the purpose behind every German municipal industrial enterprise. A city that does nothing in this way is not considered progressive. No less than 425 towns now have their own slaughterhouses and cattle yards, the main object of which is to make thorough inspection possible. The city of Munich has its asphalt factory that utilizes all the waste from torn-up streets. There are small communities that exploit their communal forests to such good effect that their people are subject to little or no taxation. One town, Langenaubach in Baden, which owns valuable chalk-pits in addition to its forests, not only demands neither taxes nor water-rates, but lays by money every year. This town sells peat, another sand or gravel. More than 100 towns have their own inns or restaurants, twenty-three their own grain-mills, forty-five their own brick-yards. Düsseldorf does its own banking, Mannheim has lately gone into the milk business. Munich, for the benefit of its taxpayers, has for years conducted experiments with the divining-rod in the effort to locate leaks in the water-pipes and save the tearing up of the streets.

Doubtless the most profitable and at the same time the most utilitarian of all the enterprises is the real estate business that cities carry on. Frankfort sold land in 1912 to the value of $3\frac{1}{2}$ million marks, not to speak of several profitable exchanges. Aix-la-Chapelle, between 1898 and 1908, bought 275 acres at two marks a square yard and sold sixty-eight acres at 17 marks a square yard, making a profit of more than two million and being left with 200 acres besides. The general procedure is to buy great tracts of unimproved land, reserve all that could possibly be needed for public purposes, and sell the rest at an advance. The most interesting municipal land experiment is that of Ulm. A consistent policy of purchasing has been pursued until now the city owns five-sixths of all its area. It builds houses for persons of moderate means and allows them to pay on the amortization plan. The yearly payments are little if any in excess of the customary rental for less desirable quarters. The scheme is very popular, and the houses, which are of good architecture and well built, are in great demand. There are other systems

City real estate dealings.

where, as in the English leasehold, the land reverts to the town after a long term of years. The constant aim is to prevent speculation and consequent inflation of land prices. The city helps its poorer purchasers by making the terms of payment as convenient as possible; also by charging cheap rates for water and gas.

Increase of area.

The lucrativeness of land deals is one of the considerations that have led German cities, by amalgamation with surrounding villages, to increase their territory enormously. Mülheim in 1905 incorporated six times as much land as that contained within its former limits; Gelsenkirchen in 1903 increased its territory by 1076 per cent! Frankfort between 1910 and 1914 was the largest city, in area, in Germany, being more like a small kingdom; but Berlin, since a recent large purchase of woodland from the state, probably surpasses her. All the large towns are following suit in thus increasing their holdings. Cities owning their own tramways are in the fortunate position of being able to contribute to the development of the new districts by extending the lines; and, of course, the municipal gas and electric works are glad to find new customers.

Improved housing conditions.

A general movement for improving housing conditions has been going on of late in German cities. Many, like Cologne, are cutting great boulevards through their most congested districts so as to let in light and air. Investigations have been made into the living conditions of families, the most elaborate one being that of Munich, which was undertaken at a cost of 130,000 marks. Many cities now have regular inspectors of housing conditions; and in Frankfort even the houses of the rich are inspected to see if suitable provision is made for the servants. A very enlightened, unbureaucratic spirit is at work, for it is realized that legislation and the strict enforcement of laws alone will not do everything to remedy matters. Families choose

narrow unhygienic quarters mainly because they can find
nothing else for their money ; and simply ejecting them without providing something better does not solve the problem.
Frequently the inspectors can improve matters by inducing
the landlords to make alterations or the families to take in
fewer lodgers. There are now city-owned interim lodging-
houses for families that have been ordered to move. The
cities keep close watch on the real estate market and when
there is a dearth of small dwellings or apartments step in
with their whole influence. Munich, between 1909 and 1913,
herself expended ten million marks in the cause. The cities
have regular loan departments, the transactions of which
often assume enormous dimensions. These departments
often make a practice of loaning on second mortgages that
would not be easy to float among private investors.

In order to provide for the young men who make a large Bachelors'
proportion of those lodgers that help to overcrowd tenements, homes.
cities have opened *Ledigenheime*, or bachelors' homes. Charlottenburg has a fine large building erected by a stock company, but with financial aid and guarantee from the city
which has also given the land on a long lease. There are
three hundred and forty rooms with a large general gathering
room. Housed in the same building are a public bath establishment, a restaurant, a branch of the public library
with its own reading room, and a roof-garden where in
summer food is served. The rent of a room, including
heating, lighting, and breakfast, ranges from ten to fifteen
marks a month!

Cities encourage thrift by maintaining municipal savings Municipal
banks, the activities of which are extended in all directions. savings
Even the schools act as feeders, the children contributing banks.
not inconsiderable sums. The total deposits in public savings
banks at the beginning of 1912 amounted to seventeen
billion marks, as opposed to only one billion 300 million in

private institutions. It has long been the custom, too, for German cities to run pawnshops, which very properly go by the name of "loan establishments" and are run on the same strict principles as banks, but without expectation of profit. The intention is to keep the people out of the hands of usurers and relieve distress by affording a convenient means of raising money. And the institution is made use of to the fullest extent. Munich, for instance, in 1912 lent money on 545,697 objects, besides continuing in pawn 172,643 objects from the previous year. This makes an average of one article pawned for each man, woman, and child in the city! Payments are made almost to the full value of the objects; and if an appraiser make a mistake in valuation he has to pay the difference. The number of articles redeemed is large, — 434,407 in Munich in 1912 — while in many cases the pawnshop is used merely as the grave of objects no longer desired. The loans vary from a mark or two to many thousands, and there is scarcely a conceivable article that is refused.

The pawnshops are but one homely illustration of the way in which the cities try to promote the well-being and happiness of their inhabitants. We have already in this chapter treated of many other ways in which the same endeavor is shown. The subject is inexhaustible. One would gladly dwell on the means that are taken to insure good, honest and faithful government, on the spirit of devotion that inspires the citizens; to show how mistaken is the view that all the paternalism destroys private initiative. In Frankfort alone there are four hundred different private funds or organizations for charitable work, functioning, however, in the strictest coöperation with the city. One central charity organization holds together the whole fabric; the city is mapped into districts and young men have to do charity work in their district just as they have to do jury duty, with a penalty for refusal or neglect.   This is in keeping with the whole manner of looking upon civic duties.   Even the men highest in the city's service, the Ratsherren, or Councillors, are punished by the trebling of their taxes if they refuse to serve when elected.   One would like to dwell, too, on what the German cities do to improve the public taste through the museums and the expositions.   In the matter of art this theme needs no elaboration.   In the matter of industry it is not so familiar. A report of one of our own teachers' colleges declares that the industrial museum at Stuttgart is worth a journey half round the world to see.   Here, in addition to countless objects to be admired, one finds a whole suite of rooms full of deterrent examples, — of articles made as they should not be made.   The *Deutsches Museum* at Munich already holds within its four walls more objects of interest for practical and scientific men than any other single building in the world, and a magnificent new building enabling the museum greatly to enlarge its scope was nearing completion when the war broke out.   Another form of museum is the *Arbeiter-Museum*, which shows safety appliances and illustrates the dangers of carelessness and of unhygienic living in a realistic way by the aid of wax models.   There are hygienic congresses, too, that spread broadcast the knowledge of sanitation.   Expositions along special lines have latterly become popular : one at Düsseldorf dealing with "Woman," one at Breslau dealing with "the Child," one at Leipzig dealing with "the Book"; while the *Werkbundaustellung* in Cologne, in progress when the war broke out, aimed at beautifying all manufactured products, and making them better adapted to their purpose.

Industrial museums.

Workmen's museums.

The improvement in German city hospitals is another subject on which one would gladly dwell.   The poorest sufferers to-day may have comforts of which the richest king never dreamt a century or two ago.   These great

City hospitals.

clean palaces, in which the very air is washed before it passes through the rooms, and where the soft-footed attendants are summoned by flash-lights instead of by bells, fill the visitor with wonder.

Care of the insane.

More and more the German cities are taking care of their own insane. The capital invested in Berlin's asylums amounts to almost 50 million marks. The fourth great building was to have been completed in 1915, and it was expected that henceforth very few patients would be sent to private institutions. In 1869 the city took care of but 500 cases; the yearly average is now 8500. The population has trebled, to be sure, but the number of patients has increased manyfold; a result partly due to the fact that many more cases were formerly treated at home. Since 1911 Berlin runs an advisory bureau, or *Beiratstelle*, for keeping in touch with discharged patients and, if possible, preventing relapses.

Cities in the undertaking business.

We have touched, often lightly enough, on almost every field in which a German city is of use to its people, — safeguarding them in infancy, training them in youth, lightening the burdens of married life, alleviating pain and sickness, making the world a better place in which to live. Cities will now perform even the last sad services that are apt to be needed. They own their own graveyards and crematories and act as their own undertakers. In Frankfort 95 per cent of the funerals start from the city's receiving vaults. The whole undertaking business is a city monopoly, and it is against the law for any other corporation or for any person to transport a corpse through the streets, or to lower it into the grave. The city will attend to every detail at a fixed tariff: will send a *Leichenfrau* or corpse-woman to make the body presentable; will furnish the coffin and see that the body is laid in it; will arrange for the religious ceremonies and see that the announcement is inserted in the newspapers.

Possibly nothing better illustrates the benevolent des- Funeral
potism of German municipal governments than the way in fees.
which these Frankfort funeral charges are estimated. The
fees are graded according to the income of the head of the
family. With an income under 1500 marks the funeral
charges, including the coffin, will amount to thirty marks;
and even this will be reduced by one-half if the head of the
family have no capital or property and have three people to
support. The prices ascend by classes until, with an income of 7500 marks or over, one pays 150 marks. Again,
the age of the deceased is the basis of another scale. All
charges for a still-birth come to two marks, for a child a
few weeks old, to five marks; for a child up to four years old,
from twelve to seventy marks; for one between five and
fifteen from 20 to 100 marks. Single graves are cheap but in
a row and must be vacated after twelve years; but in 1912
no less than 313 so-called family graves were sold, for 200
marks apiece. A family grave may contain two persons
imposed one upon the other and will be safe from disturbance
for thirty years. The 200 marks includes a monument unless one be desired of a special size.

The idea beneath all this is to spare bereaved families The
care and expense at a moment when they are apt to be off thought
their guard and incur indebtedness that may seriously hamper under-
them later. For that reason it is felt that the schedules must neath the
be made as clear and definite as possible. And where all Frankfort
are treated alike there need be no concessions to fashion or system.
custom. All honor to the Frankfort burial system!

Cremation is making great strides in Germany, after Crema-
having been kept back for years by the insensate opposition tion.
of the clergy. Until recently, in Prussia, no ceremony
might be performed over a corpse that was to be cremated.
All legislation on the subject was opposed, and even that
which finally went through had to be in the nature of a com-

promise. No one can be cremated who has not during his lifetime, in his will or in a document sworn to before a notary, given notice of his desire and intention. Even then, unless the exact formula has been observed, the declaration is invalid. It is said that a boy under sixteen may not be cremated in any case, as he is not old enough to draw up a will or take an oath. The opposition has seen to it, too, that the charges for cremation are higher than those for burial. All the same, between forty and fifty German cities now have their crematories; some of them, like the one at Dresden, of great architectural beauty. Dresden has a tariff of eighteen different classes, the charges varying according to the character and placing of the urn. In Frankfort the expense of cremation averages 22 marks more than that for burial.

A powerful society now makes propaganda for the cremation cause, and its strongest arguments are the ever increasing area that cities require for cemetery purposes and the frequency with which graveyards must be disturbed in order to make room for improvements. The showing is indeed appalling and helps to strengthen the feeling that the future of the cities should be for the living and not for the dead. Germany has taught us this truth as well as many other truths of social progress.

CHRONOLOGICAL TABLE[1]

A.D.
1658–1705 *Leopold I.:* The rise of the Prussian monarchy, — early margraves; acceptance of the
Reformation in Brandenburg; the Cleves heritage (1614); John Sigismund becomes a Calvinist (1612); the Thirty Years' War; the
accession of the Great Elector (1640–1688);
Prussia and Brandenburg united (1618); the
Great Elector takes part in Swedish-Polish war
(1655–1660); the battle of Warsaw (1656); the
Peace of Oliva (1660); subjugation of the
Prussian estates (1660–1662): the Great Elector
and Louis XIV. — the Diet of Ratisbon becomes
perpetual (1663); wars of the empire with the
Turks (1663–1699); battle of St. Gothard (1664);
devolution war of Louis XIV. (1667–1668);
second war of Louis XIV. against Holland
(1672–1679); the Great Elector conquers the
Swedes at Fehrbellin (1675); rebellion in Hungary under Emmerich Tököly (1678–1687);
Peace of Nymwegen (1679); Peace of St. Ger-
main-en-Laye, by which the Great Elector gives
back Hither Pomerania to Sweden (1679);
Maximilian II., Emmanuel, elector of Bavaria
(1679–1726), exiled (1705–1715); the "Re-
unions" of Louis XIV. (1680); Louis XIV.
takes Strassburg (1681); siege of Vienna by
the Turks (1683); revocation of the Edict of
Nantes (1685); William of Orange becomes
King of England (1688); Frederick III., elector

---

[1] This table contains some facts that are not in the text.

[1] A list of the kings and queens of Prussia : —

Deputation (1803); Napoleon becomes emperor (1804); Francis II. assumes the hereditary title of Emperor of Austria (1804); murder of the Duke of Enghien (1804); the third coalition war against France (1805–1807): surrender of Mack at Ulm (1805); battle of Austerlitz (1805); Peace of Pressburg (1805); the Rhine Confederation (1806); end of the Holy Roman Empire (1806).   232–257

1804–1835   *Francis II.* as emperor of Austria: battles of Jena and Auerstadt (1806); battles of Eylau and Friedland (1807); Peace of Tilsit (1807); Westphalia under King Jerome (1807–1813); reforms of Stein, Scharnhorst, and Gneisenau in Prussia (1807–1808); Fichte's addresses to the German nation (1807–1808); Austria's war against Napoleon (1809); uprising in the Tyrol under Andreas Hofer (1809); battles of Aspern and Wagram (1809); Peace of Vienna (1809); attempted uprising in Prussia under Dörnberg, Schill, and Frederick William, Duke of Brunswick (1809); Metternich, Austrian minister (1809–1848); founding of the University of Berlin (1810); Hardenberg, Prussian Chancellor (1810–1822); Napoleon's Russian campaign (1812); Convention of Tauroggen between Russia and Prussia (1812).   257–298

1813–1814   *War of Liberation:* Treaty of Kalisch between Russia and Prussia (Feb. 28, 1813); proclamation of Frederick William III. to his people (March 17); battle of Lützen or Gross Görschen (May 2); battle of Bautzen (May 20 and 21); Truce of Poischwitz (June 4th to August 10th); Austria's declaration of war against Napoleon (Aug. 12); battle of Gross Beeren (Aug. 23); battle of Dresden (Aug. 26 and 27); battle on the Katzbach (Aug. 26); battle of Culm (Aug. 30); battle of Dennewitz (Sept. 6); battle of Leipzig (Oct. 16–19); battle at La Rothière (Feb. 1, 1814); battle of Bar-sur-Aube (Feb. 27);

1864); provisional government for Schleswig-
Holstein (March 23, 1848); Frankfort Ante-Parliament (March 31); defeat of Hecker's volunteers at Kandern (April 20); General Wrangel
conquers at Schleswig (April 23); flight of Emperor Ferdinand from Vienna (May 15); opening of
German national parliament in Frankfort (May
18); storming of the Zeughaus in Berlin (June
15); election of Archduke John as temporary
head of the nation (June 29); opening of parliament in Vienna (July 22); Truce of Malmö
(Aug. 26); uprising in Frankfort (Sept. 17 and
18); Pfuel ministry in Prussia (Sept. 21); new
uprising in Vienna (Oct. 6); Vienna surrenders
(Oct. 31) — Prince Felix Schwarzenberg at the
head of affairs — Diet transferred to Kremsier
(Oct. 31); ministry of Count Brandenburg in
Prussia (Nov. 8); Emperor Ferdinand abdicates
(Dec. 2); Emperor Francis Joseph (1848 ——);
dissolution of the Prussian national assembly
(Dec. 5); promulgation of a constitution for Prussia (Dec. 5); dissolution of the Austrian national
parliament and promulgation of a constitution
(March 4, 1849); vote in Frankfort to offer the
imperial crown to the king of Prussia (March
28, 1849); refusal of the crown by Frederick
William IV. (April 3, 1849); suppression of uprising in Dresden (May 5–9, 1849); dissolution
of remnant of national assembly (June 18,
1849); suppression of revolt in Baden and the
Palatinate (June, 1849); Prussia signs truce
with Denmark (July 10, 1849); withdrawal of
Archduke John from head of affairs (Dec. 20,
1849); publication of revised Prussian constitution (Jan. 31, 1850); Union parliament in Erfurt
(March and April, 1850); peace between Prussia
and Denmark (July 2, 1850); battle at Idstedt
(July 25, 1850); constitutional troubles in
Hesse and journey of Manteuffel to Olmütz
(1850).   344–374

of Sadowa, or Königgrätz (July 3, 1866); truce
of Nikolsburg (July 26); Treaty of Prague
(Aug. 23); secret treaties of the Southern
States with Prussia (1866); demand of France
for Rhenish territory (July 25–Aug. 7, 1866);
the Belgian project (Aug. 16–Aug. 30).   374–409

1866–1871 *The North German Confederation:* The Luxemburg Question (February to May, 1867); publication of the South German treaties (March,
1867); acceptance of the Spanish crown by
Leopold of Hohenzollern (July 3, 1870); French
declaration (July 6); Benedetti and King William at Ems (July 9–14); Leopold withdraws
his candidature (July 12); war decided upon at
Paris (July 14); delivery of the declaration of
war (July 19); opening of the North German
Reichstag (July 29); the skirmish at Saarbrücken
(Aug. 2); battle of Weissenburg (Aug. 4); battle of Wörth (Aug. 6); battle of Spicheren
(Aug. 6); battles of Colombey, Nouilly (Aug. 14);
battles of Vionville, Mars-la-Tour (Aug. 16);
battles of Gravelotte, St. Privat, Resonville
(Aug. 18); siege of Metz (Aug. 19–Oct. 27);
siege of Strassburg (Aug. 14–Sept. 27); battle
of Sedan (Sept. 1); capitulation of Sedan
(Sept. 2); republic in France (Sept. 4); siege of
Paris (Sept. 19, 1870–Jan. 28, 1871); abolition
of the temporal power of the Pope by entry of
Italian army into Rome (Sept. 20, 1870); capture of Toul by the Germans (Sept. 23); Gambetta in Tours (Oct. 9); Tann takes Orléans
(Oct. 12); Tann driven from Orléans (Nov. 9);
defeat of French army of the Loire by Prince
Frederick Charles at Beaune la Rolande
(Nov. 28); battles of Orléans (Nov. 28–Dec. 2);
battle of Amiens (Nov. 27); occupation of
Rouen (Dec. 6); battle of Bapaume (Jan. 3,
1871); battle of Le Mans (Jan. 12); battle
of Montbéliard (Jan. 15–17); proclamation
of the German Empire in the Hall of Mirrors

in Versailles (Jan. 18, 1871); last great sortie
from Paris (Jan. 19); battle of St. Quentin
(Jan. 19); capitulation of Paris by the Convention of Versailles (Jan. 28); the eastern
army (formerly Bourbaki's) crosses the Swiss
frontier (Feb. 1); preliminaries of peace at Versailles (Feb. 26); entry of 30,000 German troops
into Paris (March 1); evacuation of Paris
(March 3); Peace of Frankfort-on-the-Main
(May 10, 1871); first German imperial parliament (March 21–June 15, 1871).　　　　　409–450

1871–1914　　The three-emperor alliance (1871–1879); the
Kulturkampf (1871–1887); expulsion of the
Jesuits (1872); Kullmann's attempt on Bismarck's life (1874); attempts on the life of
Emperor William I. (1878); anti-socialist laws
in force (1878–1890); dual alliance (Austria
and Germany) (1879); International Moroccan
treaty (1880); compulsory sickness-insurance
in effect (1883); triple alliance (Germany, Austria, Italy) (1883–1915); compulsory accident-
insurance in effect (1884); "reinsurance" treaty
with Russia (1884); colonies acquired (Southwest Africa, Togo, Cameroon, Kaiser-Wilhelms-
land, Bismarck Archipelago, Brown, Providence and Marshall Islands, part of Solomon
Islands, East Africa) (1884–1890); death of
Emperor William I. (March 17, 1888); death
of Emperor Frederick III. (June 15) and accession of Emperor William II. (1888); fall of
Bismarck (1890); Caprivi chancellor (1890–
1894); Hohenlohe chancellor (1894–1900);
adoption of civil code (*bürgerliches Gesetzbuch*)
(1896); death of Bismarck (1898); Kiaouts-
chau acquired (1898); Caroline and Marian
Islands, Samoan Islands (Sawaii and Upolo)
acquired (1899); Bülow chancellor (1900–
1909); repeal of Paragraph II. of the Jesuit
laws (1904); conference of Algeciras (1906);
Polish expropriation law (1907); Bethmann-

INDEX

Abdel Malek, 500.
Abeken, sends telegram from Ems, 421.
Abensberg, 286.
About, Edmond, 431.
Academy of Sciences, 42.
Adrianople, 504.
Agamemnon, 507.
Aix-la-Chapelle, Congress of, 1748 A.D., 146; land deals, 571.
Albania, 504.
Albert of Hohenzollern, dissolves the Teutonic Order, 11–12.
Albert II., of Prussia, 13.
Alexander, Czar of Russia, forms third coalition, 251; at Tilsit, 268; at Erfurt, 274; breach with Napoleon I., 291, 319; forms the Holy Alliance, 325.
Alexander III., Czar of Russia, 475–476.
Alexander VI., pope, 473.
Algeciras, conference at, 500.
Algiers, 498.
Alsace, claimed by Louis XIV., 55.
Alsace-Lorraine, 469, 474; problem of, 483–485; status of, 485–487.
Alsen, Prussian landing on, 392.
Altenstein, 276; Prussian minister, 285.
Alt-Ranstadt, Peace of, 78.
Ambas Bay, 472.
Amiens, battle at, 444.
Andrassy, Count, 476.
Angra Pequena, Bay of, 469.
Ante-parliament, the, 345.
Arndt, Ernst Moritz, 276, 282; in St. Petersburg, 294, 329; petty persecution of, 334–335, 337, 353, 368.
Arnim, Count, 455.
Arnold, miller, case of, 196.
Aspern, battle of, 288.
Auerstadt, battle of, 262.

Auerswald, General von, murder of, 356.
Augsburg, League of, 58.
Augustenburg, Duke of, 386; interview with Bismarck, 391; as a brand of discord, 394–395.
Augustus the Strong, of Saxony, 50, 51; king of Poland, 77.
Augustus III., of Saxony (II. of Poland), 121, 154.
Augustus William, brother of Frederick the Great, 160.
Aulis, 457.
Aurelles, French general, 444.
Austerlitz, battle of, 254.
Austria, deserted at Utrecht, 83; allies of, 131; shares in the partition of Poland, 209; becomes an empire, 250; at odds with Frankfort parliament, 360; at war with France, 1859 A.D., 378; at odds with Prussia on Schleswig-Holstein question, 394; threatens federal execution against Prussia, 396; breach with Prussia, 1866 A.D., 397; at war with Prussia, 1866 A.D., 398 ff.; alliance with Germany, 475–476; and the Balkans, 475, 502–504, 507.
Austrians, constitution granted to, 348.

Babelsberg, interview at, 382.
Bachem, Julius, 494–495.
Baden, Margrave of, 73.
Baden, Treaty of, 1715 A.D., 85; grants constitution, 327; rebellion in, 1848 A.D., 366; campaign of Prince William in, 367; for a united Germany, 448; and the Kulturkampf, 454.
Balkans, wars in the, 475, 477, 502–505.

591